Illustrated Enable/OA

Peter Kent

Wordware Publishing, Inc.

Library of Congress Cataloging-in-Publication Data
Kent, Peter.
Illustrated Enable/OA / by Peter Kent.
p. cm.
ISBN 1-55622-163-0
1. Enable/OA (Computer program) 2. Business—Data processing.
I. Title.
HF5548.4.E56K46 1990
005.369—dc20 89-29613
CIP

1506 Capital Avenue
Plano, Texas 75074

Printed in the United States of America

ISBN 1-55622-163-0

10 9 8 7 6 5 4 3 2 1
9005

All inquiries for volume purchases of this book should be addressed to Wordware Publishing, Inc., at the above address. Telephone inquiries may be made by calling:

(214) 423-0090

Contents

Contents (Cont.)

Contents (Cont.)

Recommended Learning Sequence Sequence

Recommended Learning Sequence Sequence (Cont.)

Recommended Learning Sequence Sequence (Cont.)

Module 1
ABOUT THIS BOOK

DESCRIPTION

This book describes how to use Enable Software's program, Enable/OA, an advanced, integrated-applications program. There have been several versions of Enable—Version 1.0, Version 1.1, Version 2.0, and Enable/OA. This book describes features in Enable/OA, although many of those features also appear in earlier versions. There have also been several releases of Enable/OA, but Enable Software does not disclose release numbers. The first release did not include the 3D spreadsheet, but purchasers of that release could mail in a voucher to get a free copy of the new spreadsheet software. Later releases include the 3D spreadsheet, as well as more and improved printer drivers and a number of minor changes in other parts of the program. The text in this book describes the few differences between releases.

The information in this book describes the many Enable commands, in all the different applications, and suggests ways that Enable's features may be used in your business or personal work. The text is designed for a broad range of users. It is a self-teaching text for beginners, a quick reference for intermediate and advanced users, and a textbook for use by instructors in the classroom.

ORGANIZATION

This book is organized in easy-to-read modules. Most of the modules are short, although in some cases the extensive capabilities of Enable require a longer format. Each module covers one command or a few related commands. The modules explain what the commands do, describe exactly how to use the commands, suggest uses for the commands, and provide an easy-to-follow example in simple steps.

The book is divided into seven parts: this Introduction, Section 1—Word Processing, Section 2—Database, Section 3—Spreadsheet, Section 4—Graphics, Section 5—Telecommunications, and Section 6—System-wide Features. Each of the Sections 1 through 5 begin with a Sample Session and an Overview and then contain modules in alphabetical order.

The book also has a recommended learning (or teaching) sequence that guides you through the Enable commands in a logical order. This sequence begins with Word Processing, but you can also pick up the learning sequence at the start of Sections 2, 3, 4, and 5 if you want to begin using those applications first. The sequence can be easily modified to fit any curriculum, and teachers may want to use it as an aid in curriculum design.

At the end of the book are several appendixes:

- Appendix A is a useful list of terms and definitions.
- Appendix B describes how to customize Enable using your Profile.
- Appendixes C to G describe function keys and Expert Commands for each application.

- Appendix H describes advanced Telecommunications features.
- Appendix I discusses the system print queue.
- Appendix J lists Enable's start-up parameters.
- Appendix K describes 3D Spreadsheets.
- Appendix L contains a chart that lists the ASCII codes and characters.
- Appendix M contains exercises related to each module. If you are a classroom instructor you may want to use these exercises as part of your student assignments. If you are learning Enable on your own, you can use the exercises to check on your progress. If you can answer the questions, you are ready to begin the next module in the learning sequence.

HARDWARE AND SOFTWARE REQUIREMENTS

Enable runs on any IBM PC or true IBM-compatible PC operating under DOS 2.x or higher, or OS/2. You need at least two floppy disk drives or one floppy disk drive and a hard disk drive. However, Enable is a big program, and ideally you should be using a hard disk drive.

You need at least 512K RAM (Random Access Memory), although 640K or more is recommended. To use Enable's graphics you need some kind of graphics card—an inexpensive monochrome card is sufficient. To print the graphics you also need a graphics printer of some kind. To use Enable's telecommunications application you need an internal modem or an asynchronous communications card with an external modem.

WHAT YOU SHOULD KNOW

You should be familiar with your computer and its keyboard layout. You should know enough about your operating system to start programs and format disks. If you are using a floppy drive system you should make backup copies of the disks. If you have a hard disk system, you should have installed the program (refer to the Enable manual for the procedure). With these tasks completed you are ready to learn Enable. Proceed to Module 2, Enable Overview.

Module 2
ENABLE/OA OVERVIEW

INTRODUCTION

Enable is an integrated applications program. Unlike most programs, which do just one job, Enable does several. It contains a word processor, a spreadsheet, a database, a telecommunications program, and a graphics program, all rolled into one. The OA in Enable/OA means "Office Automation," and Enable/OA contains all the most important office applications.

Enable is not the only integrated program available, but the difference between Enable and most other such programs is one of sophistication—while, for example, Microsoft Works contains all the same applications as Enable, they are very simple versions, without the advanced features you expect from full-blown word processors, spreadsheets, and so on. Enable, on the other hand, has the features it needs to compete with the single-application programs. As *PC Magazine* put it, Enable's word processor "could easily stand by itself, offering such features as expert commands, a table of contents function, mail-merge, a spell checker based on an 80,000-word dictionary, and a sophisticated calculator....but when the spreadsheet, graphics, database, and telecommunications modules are included, Enable becomes an outstanding overall package." *PC Magazine* rated Enable/OA as its Editor's Choice.

(All this sophistication comes with a price; *PC Magazine* went on to say that "Because of its many advanced functions and commands, Enable's learning curve is steep." That's where this book comes in, of course.)

But integration is more than just having a few programs wrapped up in one. Enable can also run several applications at the same time, has a similar user-interface in all the applications, so each one has a similar "feel" and can share information between applications, to use word processing lists in databases, for example, or swap numbers between the spreadsheet and database.

MAIN MENU

The Main Menu is Enable's control panel. This is where you begin your work once you have logged onto Enable, and you return to it when you want to begin another task or leave Enable. The following screen shows an example of the Main Menu. When the menu is first displayed, only the first line of options is shown (Use System, Help, MCM, and Return to DOS). Additional lines appear as you select options.

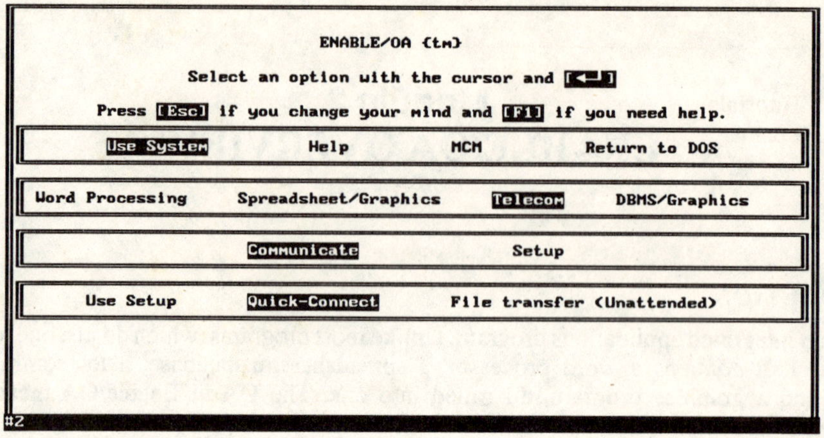

```
                    ENABLE/OA (tm)

       Select an option with the cursor and [←┘]

 Press [Esc] if you change your mind and [F1] if you need help.

   Use System        Help        MCM        Return to DOS

 Word Processing   Spreadsheet/Graphics   Telecom   DBMS/Graphics

              Communicate              Setup

   Use Setup      Quick-Connect     File transfer (Unattended)

#2
```

The following table shows the options available from the Main Menu. As you can see, the options are "nested." If you select an option, Enable displays several more options from which to choose. For example, you can select Use System, followed by Telecom, followed by Communicate, followed by Quick-Connect, as shown in the previous screen. The table also directs you to the modules that describe the functions of each menu option.

Menu Option	*Function*	*Module*
Use System		
Word Processing		
Create	Create a WP document	32
Revise	Revise a WP document	32
Print	Print a WP document	35
Dictionary	Edit the dictionaries	43
Mail Merge	Create form letters	30
Spreadsheet/Graphics		
Create	Create a Spreadsheet	78
Revise	Revise a Spreadsheet	78
Print	Print a Spreadsheet	79
Telecom		
Communicate		
Use Setup	Call using a Setup	104
Quick-Connect	Call without a Setup	103
File Transfer (Unattended)	Call and send automatically	112
Setup	Build a Telecom Setup	111
DBMS/Graphics		
Design		
Database-Definition	Design a Database	50
Input-Form	Design an Input-form	59
Report-Form	Design a Report	62
Build	Enter Data	48
Interact	View and use the commands	60
Report	Produce a Report	62

Menu Option	*Function*	*Module*
Help		
Tutorials	Use the Tutorials	This Module
Customer Service	Customer-Service Phone #s	"
MCM		
Windows		
Return to last window	Display previous window	46
Display window summary	List open windows	46
Files		
Word Processing	Display WP files	114
Spreadsheet	Display Spreadsheet files	114
Telecom	Display Telecom files	114
DBMS	Display Database files	114
All	Display All files	114
Macros		
Create	Build macro scripts	115
Revise	Revise macro scripts	115
List	List macro files	115
Profile	Change your user profile	App B
Screen		
Mono	Set screen to Mono	This Module
Co80	Set screen to Co80	"
Bw80	Set screen to Bw80	"
Graphics	Set screen to Graphics	"
Tools		
Menus		
Create	Build menus	116
Revise	Revise menus	116
Test	Test menus	116
Telecom		
Transmit/Receive Map		
Create	Build Filter Maps	App H
Revise	Revise Filter Maps	App H
Unattended Transfer Form		
Create	Build Transfer Forms	112
Revise	Revise Transfer Forms	112
Keyboard Mapping		
Create	Build Telecom macros	App H
Revise	Revise Telecom macros	App H
Quit	Return to top of Main Menu	81
DOS	Open the DOS Window	113
Return to DOS	Close Enable	3

THE TOP LINE MENU

Each application uses a Top Line Menu to provide you with options. To use the Top Line Menu after selecting an application you press F10, then type a series of letters or numbers associated with the desired option. In this book instructions using the Top Line Menu use this format: "Press **F10** and type **EA1** (EditOpts;Screen displays;Headers)." The bold keys and characters are the ones you actually type; the words in parentheses are the options you are selecting.

THE STATUS LINE

Each application has a status line to provide information about your work. The status line varies from application to application, but there are some common features. The window number is on the left side of the line, and the current filename and the disk the file is saved on always appear. The status line also displays error messages and prompts when necessary. The other features of the status lines are explained in the applicable sections.

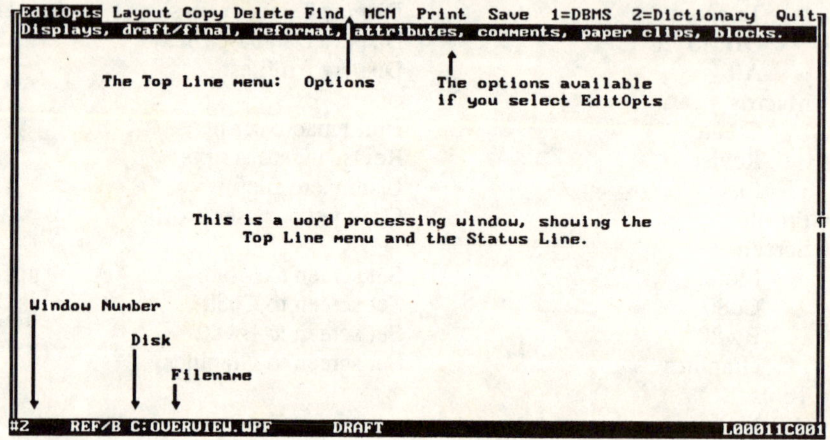

HELP

Enable has several types of Help available. Press F1 at any time to access a series of Help windows. Or press Ctrl-F1 (in any application except Graphics) to view Hypertext, much more extensive help messages (you must use the Start-Up parameter \H to use Hypertext — see Appendix J). You can also use the Tutorials by typing HT (Help;Tutorials) at the Main Menu, or view Customer Service telephone numbers by typing HC (Help;Customer Service).

In addition you can press Alt-F1 in word processing, database, or spreadsheet to see a function key chart listing the available function keys for that application.

WINDOWS

Enable's windows provide one of the most important capabilities of this program—the ability to have more than one window open at any time, up to eight, in fact. This lets you refer to other files or carry out telecommunications sessions while your original window is open. You can also copy data from another window, view a list of files, or even perform DOS commands. The window options on the Main Menu (Return to last window and Display window summary) display either the last window you were in, or a list of all the open windows. The other window commands are explained later in the book. (You won't use the "Return to last window" option much, because pressing Esc has the same effect.)

SHARING DATA

Enable's integration lets you swap data between applications. You can use spreadsheet data in a word processing document, for example, or database information in a spreadsheet. These operations are described in the applicable modules, as shown in this table.

Transfer From	*To*	*Module*
Word Processing	Spreadsheet	75
Word Processing	Database	57
Word Processing	Word Processing	31
Spreadsheet	Database	57
Spreadsheet	Word Processing	46
Database	Spreadsheet	75
Database	Word Processing	56
Graphics	Word Processing	93

GRAPHICS SCREEN DISPLAY

Enable lets you change your word processing screen to graphics mode. You do this if you want to see the special text attributes (italics, superscript, etc.) as they appear on the screen, or view a chart you have imported into the file. (Displaying a graph automatically turns the screen to graphics mode; but closing the file changes back to non-graphics mode, so if you want to see the graph again you have to select graphics mode.)

There are four screen options: Mono, Bw80 (80 columns x 25 lines), Co80 (80 columns x 25 lines), and Graphics. Select Graphics if you want to see a graph. If you want to see your text attributes select either Co80 (if you have a color graphics screen or a black and white monitor with multiple shades), or Bw80 if you have a black and white graphics screen. Select Graphics to display graphs, and Mono to return to non-graphics mode. Play with these settings to find the one that is most suitable for your monitor.

Select graphics mode from the Top Line Menu by pressing F10 and typing M3 (MCM;Screen) and one of the following commands: 2 (Co80, color text mode), 3 (Bw80, Black and white text mode) or 4 (Graphics).

EXPERT COMMANDS You don't always need to use the menus to access commands. You can also use expert commands, short sequences of keystrokes intended to speed things up. We have only used a few expert commands in this book, for several reasons. First, expert commands are only useful for features you use often; if you don't use them frequently you forget them. Also, if you learn the program using the Top Line Menu, you will know how to find features and commands and how to find your way around the system. Expert commands can be very confusing, because they have no basis in the perceived structure of the program—you can't see them, whereas you can see the menu options. If you know the expert command for splitting your screen horizontally, you don't necessarily know how to do it vertically. However, if you know where to find the horizontal-split command in the menus, you also know how to find the vertical-split command. Finally, some of the expert commands use the same number of keystrokes as the Top Line Menu commands, providing few advantages.

This is not to say that you shouldn't use expert commands—you should. When you are using an operation so often that you use the Top Line Menu without even looking at it, just typing the letters of the options from memory, then you should turn to the appendixes at the back of this book and find the related expert command. If you find it saves you time and you can remember it, keep using it. Don't try to learn too many expert commands at once. Add them one by one, as you progress.

Enable has several groups of keyboard commands: function keys, cursor commands, expert commands, and keystroke commands. In the appendixes the expert and keystroke commands are grouped together, as there is usually no significant difference. You will also notice that the groups overlap in places; you can often do the same thing with two different keyboard commands.

MULTITASKING

Enable is *multitasking,* it has the ability to do two or more things at once. For example, you could print a document and then open and work in another window while the document is printing. However, multitasking depends on memory. If you don't have much RAM, and if you have a lot of windows open (especially Database windows), you will occasionally find that Enable cannot carry out a procedure. Enable will ask you to close one of the other windows. Also, as long as Enable displays BUSY in the right side of the status line you cannot do anything else—just wait until it is finished.

Multitasking while printing is automatic. Once Enable has built a temporary print file, you are free to continue while Enable prints your document or holds it in a queue waiting for other documents to finish.

With other processes, however, you must ask Enable to begin multitasking. If Enable is in the middle of a lengthy database sort, for example, press Alt-Tab and Enable displays the Task Switch Options screen, a list of the open windows. You can then open one of the other windows, or press Alt-Home or Enter to open another window. In order to use multitasking from a window that has displayed a graph, press Spacebar and then Alt-Tab.

CUSTOMIZING ENABLE

Enable provides several ways for you to customize the program to suit your specific needs. The first of these is the *user profile,* the description of how you want Enable to operate. This is described in Appendix B and tells Enable what hardware to use, how to print a page of text, what you want the text to look like on the screen, whether or not to use a print queue, and so on. When you finish learning about an application, scan through the relevant section in Appendix B to see if there are any changes you want to make. (All the modules in this book either assume you are using the default profile, or explain the changes you can make in the profile.)

Another way to customize Enable is to build macros. Module 115 explains how to program keys to perform long sequences of commands that you use frequently. Module 116 explains how to take macros a step further by building your own menu system. These menus let you use many different macros, without having to remember all the macro keys—you just select the option off your new menu. You can use these macros and menus to bypass Enable's standard menus and even to run other programs while Enable remains open.

To continue the learning sequence turn to Module 3.

Module 3
OPENING AND CLOSING ENABLE

OPENING ENABLE

This module describes how to begin working with Enable, once you have installed it on your hard disk or made your backup copies of the floppy disks. Hard disk users should build an AUTOEXEC.BAT file and a start-up batch file according to Enable's instructions. This module's hard disk instructions presume your start-up batch file is called EN.BAT.

HARD-DISK STARTUP Access the directory that contains the Enable program, type EN, and press Enter. (EN300 is the name Enable uses if you do not specify another one.) For example:

1. At the DOS C prompt, type **CD EN300** and press **Enter**.
2. Type **EN** and press **Enter**. Enable displays the Sign-On screen.

FLOPPY-DISK STARTUP Insert the Utility Disk in drive A and a formatted data disk in drive B.

1. At the DOS prompt type **A:** and press **Enter**. This gives you the A> prompt.
2. Type **ENABLE** and press **Enter**. Your computer displays the Enable Sign-On screen.

THE SIGN-ON SCREEN The following screen is an example of the Enable Sign-On screen.

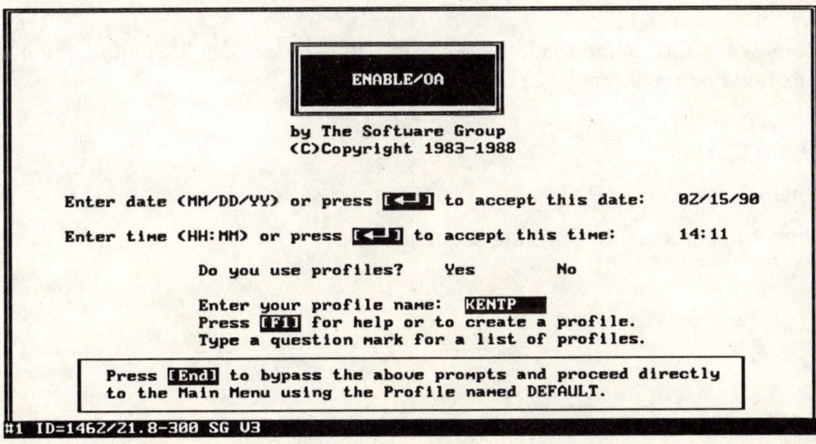

If you have previously entered the time and date in DOS, or if your computer has an internal clock, this information should be correct. If not, type the date (mm/dd/yy), press Enter, type the time (hh:mm), and press Enter.

USING A PROFILE

Enable has a way that you can customize the program, fine-tuning it to suit your particular needs. You use *profiles* to do this, but for the moment this is not necessary, because if you do not select a profile Enable automatically uses one called DEFAULT; this book presumes that you are using the DEFAULT profile. To accept DEFAULT press End at the Time prompt (or even when Enable first displays the Sign-On screen if the date and time are correct) to bypass the profile prompts and display the Main Menu.

However, if you share your computer with other users (in an office, for example) you may have been assigned a profile. If so, press Enter at the Time prompt, and type Y at the "Do you use profiles?" prompt. When Enable asks for the profile name, type the name you were assigned and press Enter. Enable displays the Main Menu, as shown in the following screen.

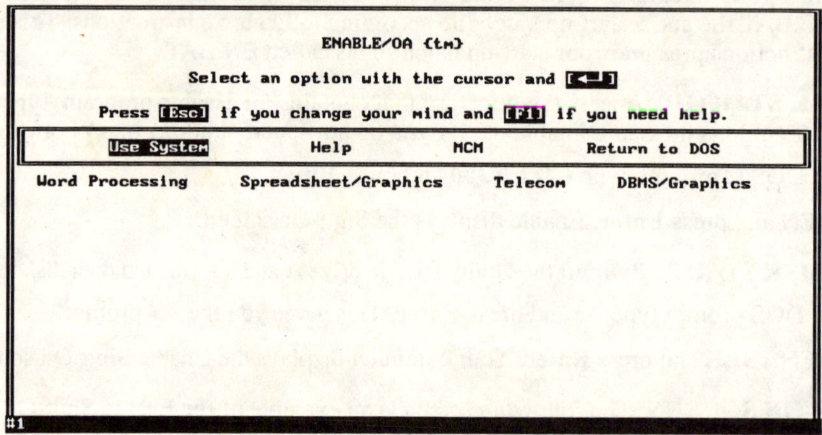

The Main Menu is the fork in the road, the place where you decide which application to use. All sections in this book begin at this point.

CLOSING ENABLE

To end the Enable session type R (Return to DOS) at the Main Menu.

Turn to Module 4 to continue the learning sequence.

Module 4
A SAMPLE SESSION WITH ENABLE WORD PROCESSING

GETTING READY

In this module you create a word processing file and type, edit, print, and save the letter.

This session begins at Enable's Main Menu. Before beginning this module you should read the introductory modules, in particular Module 3, Opening and Closing Enable.

CREATING THE FILE

1. At the Main Menu, type **UWC**. (Pressing the first letter of an option selects that option. Thus, typing U selects Use System, typing W selects Word Processing, and typing C selects Create.) You see the following screen:

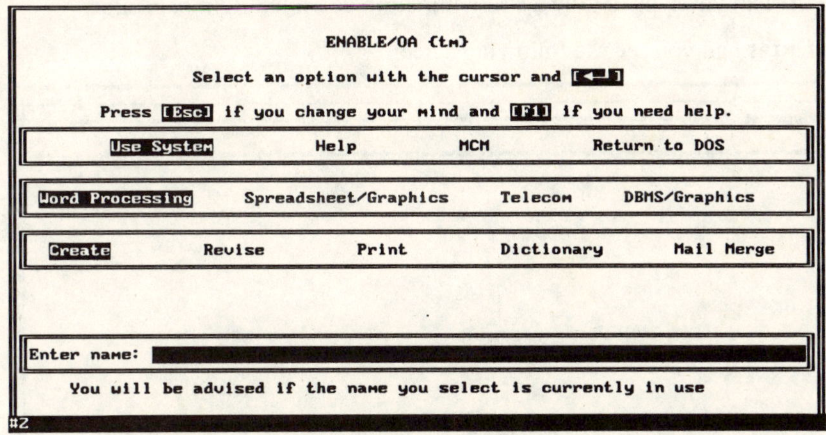

2. Type **LETTER** and press **Enter**. You see the following:

```
L-------T-------T-------T-------T------+T---------------------------------R

         To accept the margins and tabs on the ruler above,
                          press Enter ↵

             To change the margins and tabs on the ruler,
             use the arrow keys to move the cursor and
                       type L for left margin
                       type T for tabs
                       type R or J for right margin

                       Then press Enter ↵

#2   REF/B C:LETTER.WPF          DRAFT                          L00000C001
```

3. Press **Right Arrow** to move the cursor five spaces to the right of the margin, and press **L** to place the left margin. Use **Right Arrow** to move the cursor to the second T on the line, and press **Spacebar** to delete the tab.

4. Repeat step 3 for the third and fourth Ts. Then move the cursor to five spaces before the right margin and press **J**. This sets a *justified* right margin at that point, meaning Enable will space the text you type to give a straight margin down the right hand side.

5. Press **Enter** and you see the following screen:

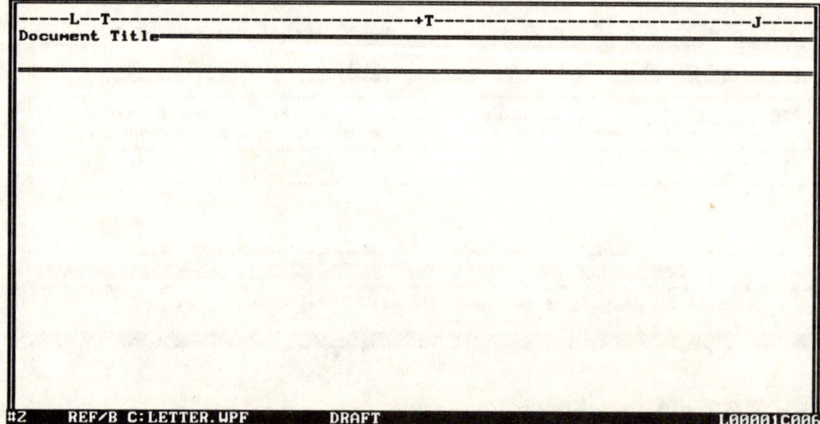

The document title will print on a title page when you print your document. The title also appears in the File Summary screen and on the Extended Functions screen, which is explained later. (The document title will not appear if you turned this feature off in your user profile.)

6. Press **Up Arrow** twice to move the cursor into the title. Then type **This is the letter to Mr. Anderson about the EnableOA training course.** Press **Down Arrow** to move the cursor out of the title, and press **Enter** to put the cursor on the left margin.

TYPE THE LETTER

7. Type the letter shown in the following screen. Make sure you type **to** twice as shown in the illustration. This mistake will be corrected when you do a spell check.

```
-----L--T------------------------------+T-------------------------------J-----
     ▪  ▪                                Andrew Andrews                        ¶
     ▪  ▪                                Corporate Structures, Inc.            ¶
     ▪  ▪                                2099 Carpenter Rd.                    ¶
     ▪  ▪                                Dallas, TX 75007                      ¶
     Mr. John Anderson                                                         ¶
     Computer Training Courses, Inc.                                           ¶
     3343 Juniper Drive                                                        ¶
     Dallas, TX 72005▪                   December 1, 1989                      ¶
                                                                               ¶
     Dear Mr. Anderson                                                         ¶
                                                                               ¶
     ▪  Thank you for visiting us last week.  Your visit really helped me
     clarify  the type of training we will need during the next year.  As
     you  know,  our operations  are expanding very  quickly and we would
     like all the new people to get up to speed as fast as possible.           ¶
                                                                               ¶
     Thanks  again for your help.  We will  look forward to to seeing you
     and your training staff soon.                                             ¶
                                                                               ¶
     ▪  ▪                                Sincerely Yours,                      ¶
                                                                               ¶
     ▪  ▪                                Andrew Andrews                        ¶
#1   REF/B C:LETTER.WPF        DRAFT                                  L00022C055
```

8. Press **Tab** to move the cursor across the page to the first address. (Use Delete and Backspace to make corrections if necessary.) Press **Enter** to end each paragraph and after typing the last word (otherwise Enable will try to justify the last two words by putting too many spaces between them).

CHECK THE SPELLING

9. You now check your spelling. Press **F10** and the Top Line Menu is displayed, as shown below.

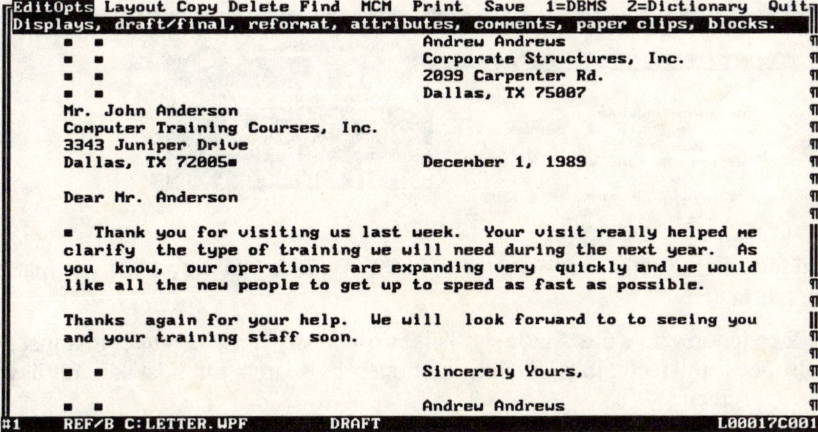

```
EditOpts Layout Copy Delete Find  MCM  Print  Save  1=DBMS  2=Dictionary  Quit
Displays, draft/final, reformat, attributes, comments, paper clips, blocks.
     ▪  ▪                                Andrew Andrews                        ¶
     ▪  ▪                                Corporate Structures, Inc.            ¶
     ▪  ▪                                2099 Carpenter Rd.                    ¶
     ▪  ▪                                Dallas, TX 75007                      ¶
     Mr. John Anderson                                                         ¶
     Computer Training Courses, Inc.                                           ¶
     3343 Juniper Drive                                                        ¶
     Dallas, TX 72005▪                   December 1, 1989                      ¶
                                                                               ¶
     Dear Mr. Anderson                                                         ¶
                                                                               ¶
     ▪  Thank you for visiting us last week.  Your visit really helped me
     clarify  the type of training we will need during the next year.  As
     you  know,  our operations  are expanding very  quickly and we would
     like all the new people to get up to speed as fast as possible.           ¶
                                                                               ¶
     Thanks  again for your help.  We will  look forward to to seeing you
     and your training staff soon.                                             ¶
                                                                               ¶
     ▪  ▪                                Sincerely Yours,                      ¶
                                                                               ¶
     ▪  ▪                                Andrew Andrews                        ¶
#1   REF/B C:LETTER.WPF        DRAFT                                  L00017C001
```

10. Type **2** to select Dictionary, and the Dictionary Options Menu, shown below, is displayed.

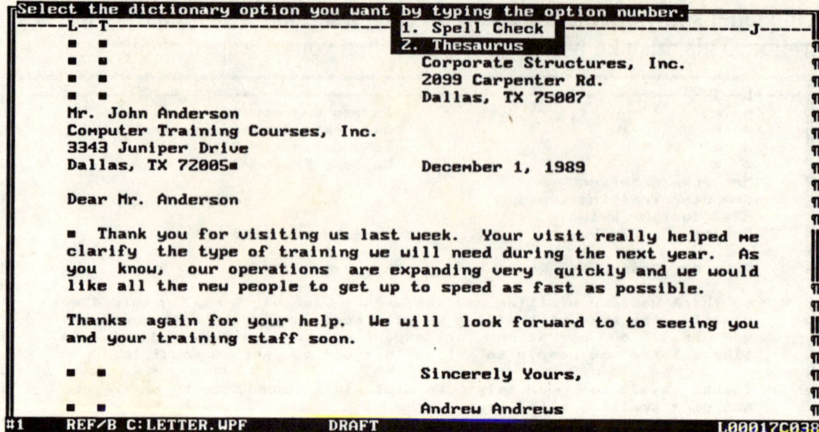

11. Type **1** to select the Spell Check and you see the following screen:

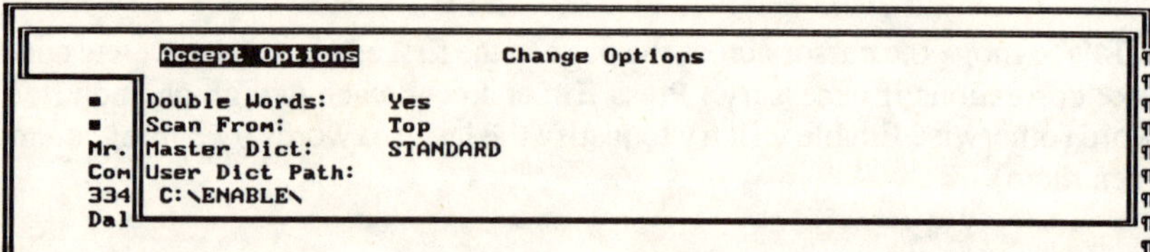

12. Press **Enter** to begin the spell check using the standard options. You see the following screen when the spell check finds a word it does not recognize:

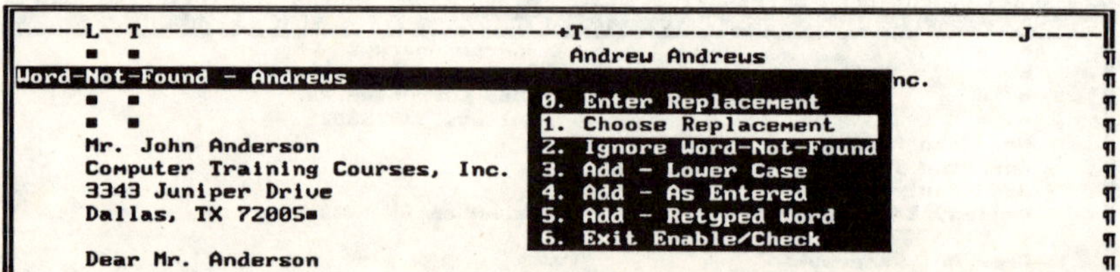

If you typed the letter exactly as shown, the unknown word is "Andrews." If you made a mistake it may find that first.

13. Type **2** to ignore the word Andrews. This is obviously not a mistake, it is just a name that Enable does not recognize. Enable continues its search for mistakes until you see the following screen:

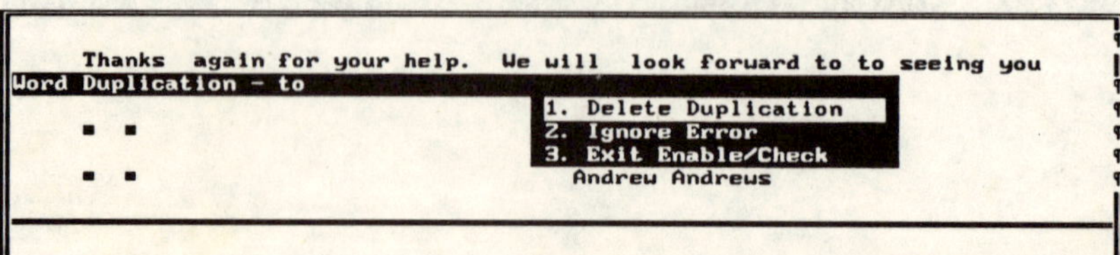

14. Enable found the duplicate "to." Press **Enter** and Enable deletes one of the words and continues. When the spell check is complete you see this summary screen:

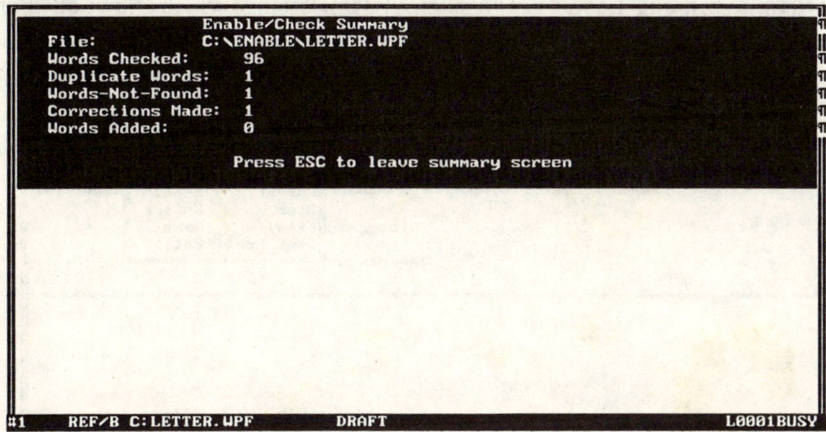

```
                Enable/Check Summary
File:           C:\ENABLE\LETTER.WPF
Words Checked:      96
Duplicate Words:    1
Words-Not-Found:    1
Corrections Made:   1
Words Added:        0

        Press ESC to leave summary screen

#1   REF/B C:LETTER.WPF         DRAFT              L0001BUSY
```

Read the information on this screen, and when you have finished press **Esc** to continue.

PRINT THE LETTER

You are now ready to print the letter.

15. Press **F10** to display the Top Line Menu and type **P** to display the first page of the Print Form. (It may take three or four seconds to appear.)

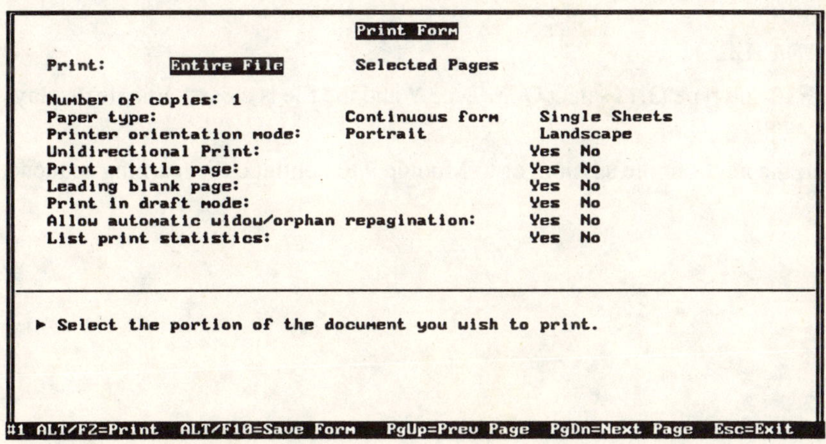

```
                                 Print Form

Print:         Entire File        Selected Pages

Number of copies: 1
Paper type:                     Continuous form    Single Sheets
Printer orientation mode:       Portrait           Landscape
Unidirectional Print:                             Yes  No
Print a title page:                               Yes  No
Leading blank page:                               Yes  No
Print in draft mode:                              Yes  No
Allow automatic widow/orphan repagination:        Yes  No
List print statistics:                            Yes  No

 ▸ Select the portion of the document you wish to print.

#1 ALT/F2=Print  ALT/F10=Save Form  PgUp=Prev Page  PgDn=Next Page  Esc=Exit
```

16. Press **PgDn** four times to see the different print options that can be changed. These will be explained later in the book. The fourth time you press PgDn you see the first page again. Press **Alt-F2** to print the letter.

SAVE THE LETTER

You can now save the file (the letter will be used again in other modules). You do not need to wait for the letter to finish printing. Enable has "background processing" which allows other operations to continue, even while information is being sent to the printer.

17. Press **F10** to display the Top Line Menu, and type **S** to select the Save Options Menu, displayed below.

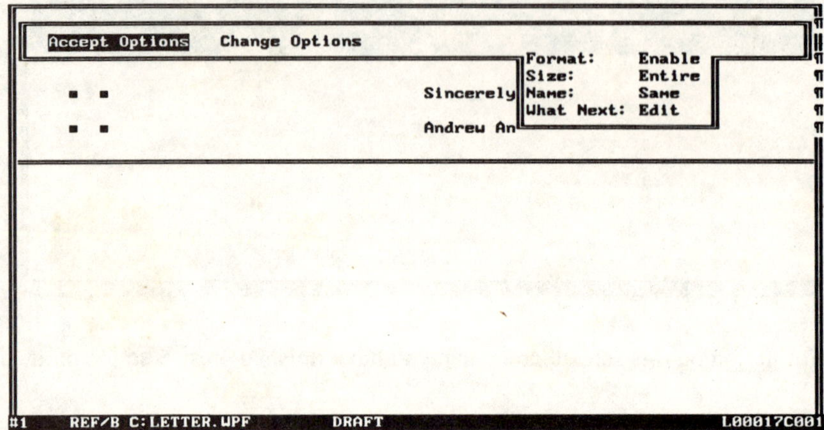

18. Press **Enter** to save the file without changing any options—the entire file is saved in Enable format, with the name you used when you created it, and you can continue editing. (Other save options are explained later.)

CLOSE THE FILE

19. Press **F10** and type **Q**, to select Quit. Type **Y** and the file is closed. Enable displays the Main Menu again.

20. Turn to the next sample session, or to Module 9 to continue the learning sequence.

Module 5
A SAMPLE SESSION WITH ENABLE DATABASE (DBMS)

GETTING READY

In this module you use Enable's DBMS (Database Management System). You add information to a record, edit a record, and print a report. Before using DBMS you make a copy of the file SUPPLY, so that you can use it in this and later examples. This sample database file is on one of the Enable tutorial disks, which you may have loaded when you installed Enable. If you did not load the tutorial files, do so before beginning this module. (You can use Enable's setup procedure to do this, or use DOS commands to copy the files named SUPPLY.$BF and SUPPLY.DBF into the same directory as Enable's program files.)

This session begins at Enable's Main Menu. Before beginning this module you should read the introductory modules, in particular Module 3, Opening and Closing Enable.

COPYING THE SUPPLY DATABASE

1. At the Main Menu, type **MFA** (MCM;Files;All). A directory similar to the following is displayed.

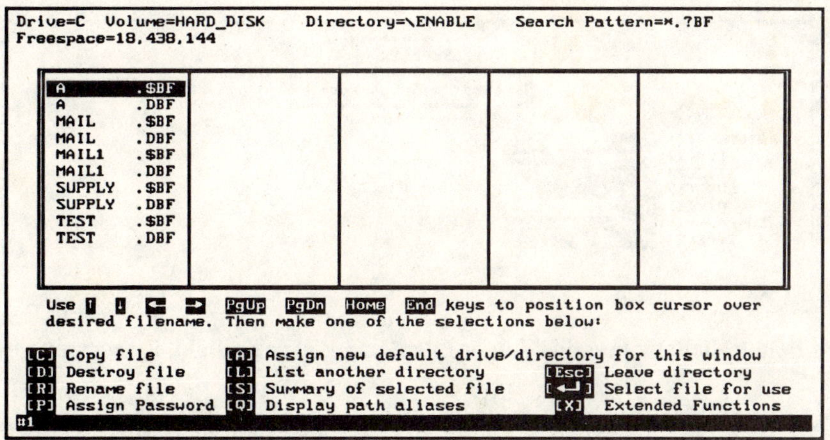

2. Press **Down Arrow** to put the cursor on **SUPPLY.DBF**. Type **C** (Copy) and Enable prompts for the drive name. Press **Enter** to accept the same drive, and press **Enter** again when Enable prompts for the directory name. When Enable prompts for the filename, type **SUPPLYX.DBF** and press **Enter**. When Enable has finished copying the file, press **Esc** to return to the Main Menu.

ADDING TO THE DATABASE The next step is to add data to the database.

3. At the Main Menu, type **UDI** to display the Interact screen. Type **A** to select Add. You see the Add command screen.

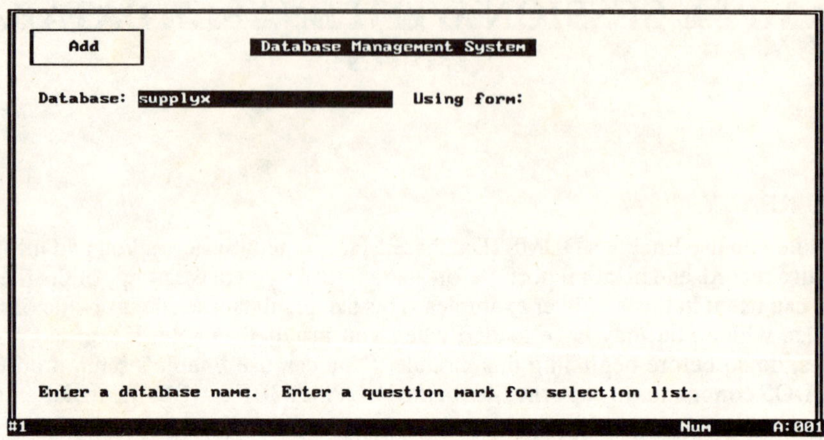

4. Type **SUPPLYX**, as shown in the screen. Press **Enter**, and Enable replaces SUPPLYX with the drive, directory name, and filename, and displays the Using Form prompt. This prompt is blank because there is no customized input form for the new database. Press **Enter** and Enable uses the standard input form. (Enable may ask if you want to build a new form. Just press Enter again.) Type the information into the input form, as shown in the following screen (press **Enter** after each line):

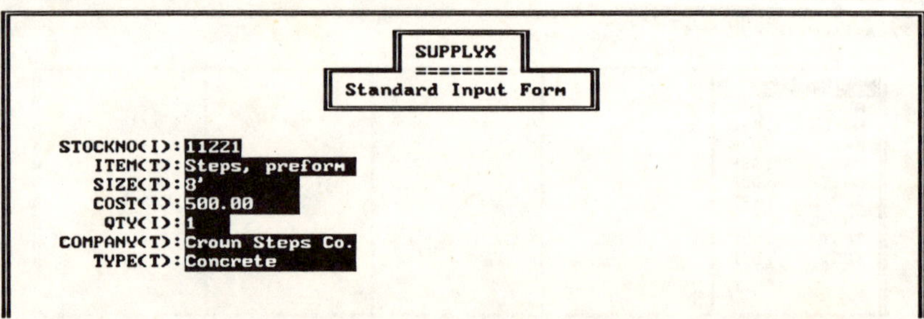

Move from field to field by pressing Tab or Enter, and go back a field, if necessary, by pressing Shift-Tab.

5. When you have filled in all the information, press **F10**. Enable displays a Top Line Menu. Type **N** (Next), and Enable saves the information and displays a blank form. Type the following information into the form. Stock number: **11879**; item: **ladder**; size: **8'**; cost: **48**; company: **Jones**; and type: **wood**.
6. Press **F10**, and type **S** to save the information. Press **F10** and type **Q** to quit, and press **Esc**. The Interact screen is displayed.

7. Type **D** and the Display command screen is displayed. The database you have just been using is displayed at the database prompt. Press **End**, and you see the Display screen.

```
SYS:RECORD DELETED STOCKNO ITEM........... SIZE..... ......COST .QTY COMPANY
         1 No        10001 Nails           3in.            4.20   84 Osmose
         2 No        10002 Nails           4in.            4.74   51 Osmose
         3 No        40144 Suppt. Lumber   2x4x8           2.35  805 Pine Cr
         4 No        40149 Suppt. Lumber   2x4x12          4.02  401 Pine Cr
         5 No        61844 Plywood         4x8x.5         11.22  953 Gerrity
         6 No        60012 Plywood         4x8x.75        13.24  662 Gerrity
         7 No        11227 Nails           2in.            3.33   67 Hauthor
         8 No        11239 Nails           1in.            2.49   99 Hauthor
         9 No        11234 Nails           2in.            3.49   43 Osmose
        10 No        91432 Door            32x80         119.00   35 ThermSa
        11 No        93356 Door            36x80         121.00   40 ThermSa
        12 No        84432 Window          6x3           202.01   17 Malta
        13 No        84435 Window          6x5           262.78   23 Malta
        14 No        82333 Window          5x8           213.44   19 Malta
        15 No        41222 Suppt. Lumber   2x4x16          6.07  555 Arlingt
        16 No        67745 Plywood         4x8x.25         8.29  322 Gerrity
        17 No        12222 Nails           5in.            6.66   77 Osmose
        18 No        50001 Sheetrock       4x8x.5          4.79  300 Lufkin
        19 No        53344 Sheetrock       4x8x1           5.33  233 Lufkin
        20 No        55501 Sheetrock       4x10x.5         7.49  130 Lufkin

 Use cursor keys to page through display.  Press ESC when done.
#2.        SUPPLYX        Records ....27 Rd ....20 Sel ....20 Cur .....1  D:000
```

You can move through the screen by pressing the arrow and Tab keys.

8. Press the arrow keys until the STOCKNO column is next to the left border of the screen, and the cursor (the thin line or the highlighted line) is under the last record. Press **F4** and Enable displays a prompt in the lower left corner of the screen asking for the stockno. Type **22344** and press **Enter**. Notice that the new number is added to the last record.

9. Press **Esc** twice to return to the Interact screen, and type **9** to select Report. Enable displays the Report command screen.

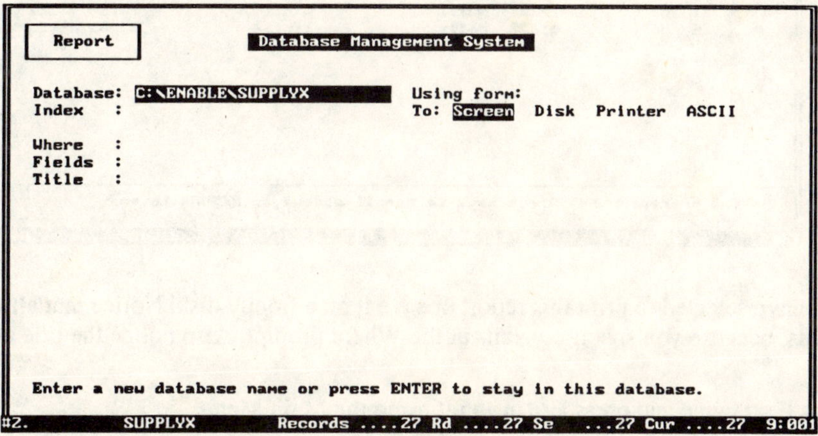

10. Press **Enter** three times to accept the SUPPLYX database, to bypass the "Using form" prompt (thereby selecting a columnar report), and to bypass the Index prompt. Press **Enter** to select Screen. The cursor moves to the Where prompt. Press **PgDn** to move the cursor into the list of fields, and move the cursor to ITEM with the arrow keys.

11. Press = (the equal key) and ITEM= is displayed at the Where prompt. Type **"Nails"** and press **Enter** twice. At the Title prompt type **This is a sample report**.

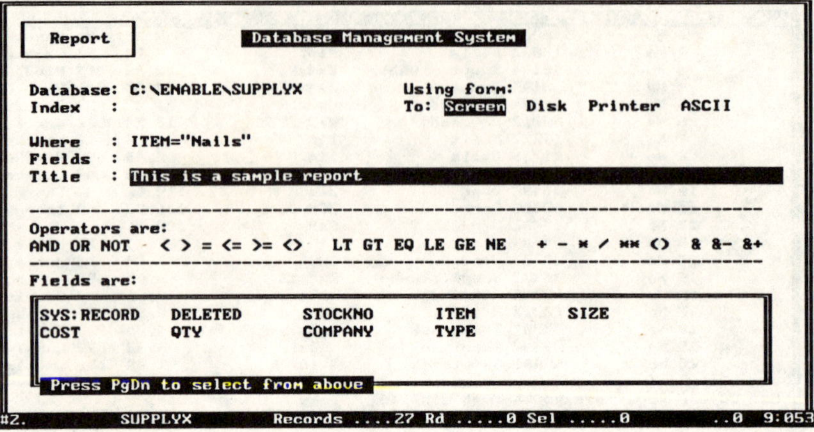

12. Press **Enter** and Enable displays the following screen.

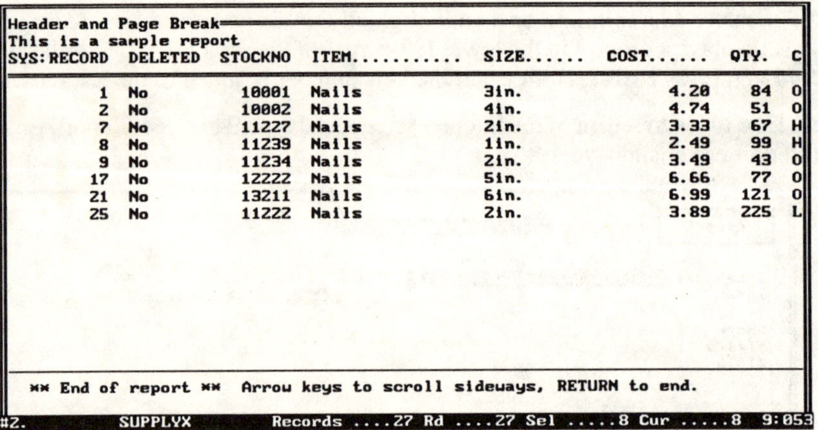

You could have selected to print this report or save it on a floppy disk. Notice that all the records are for Nails, because you specified Nails at the Where prompt. Also notice the title at the top of the page.

13. Press **Esc** twice and press **Enter** to return to the Main Menu.

14. Turn to Module 47 to continue the learning sequence.

Module 6
A SAMPLE SESSION WITH ENABLE SPREADSHEET

GETTING READY

In this module you create a spreadsheet called EXPENSES, enter data, make a simple calculation, and print the spreadsheet. You then save the spreadsheet so that it can be used in later modules.

This session begins at the Main Menu. Before beginning this module you should read the introductory modules, in particular Module 3, Opening and Closing Enable.

CREATING THE SPREADSHEET

1. At the Main Menu, type **USC** (Use System;Spreadsheet;Create). When Enable prompts you for a filename type **EXPENSES** and press **Enter**. Enable displays a blank spreadsheet, with a highlighted block in the top left corner.

2. Type **Business Expenses, 1990** and press **Enter**. Your spreadsheet looks like this:

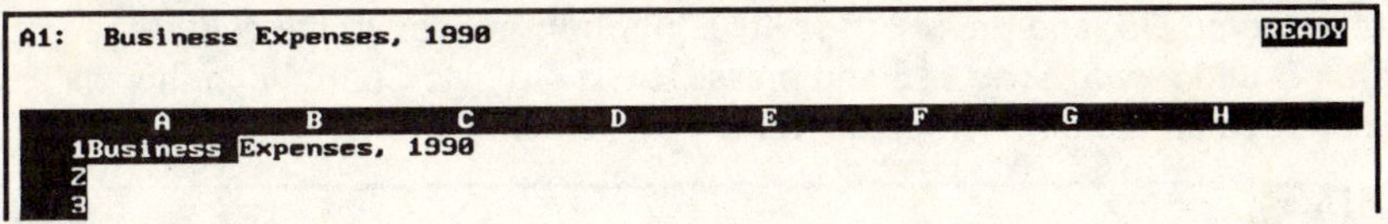

3. Press **Down Arrow** and type \=. Press **Enter**. Press **F10**, type **WC** (Worksheet;Copy) and press **Enter**. Press **Right Arrow**, type **.** (period), press **Right Arrow**, and press **Enter**. Notice that you have copied ===== into the first three "cells" in the second row.

4. Press **Down Arrow** three times, type **Advertising**, and press **Down Arrow** again. Type **Bank Service Charges**, and press **Down Arrow**. Continue in this way until you have entered all the labels shown in this screen:

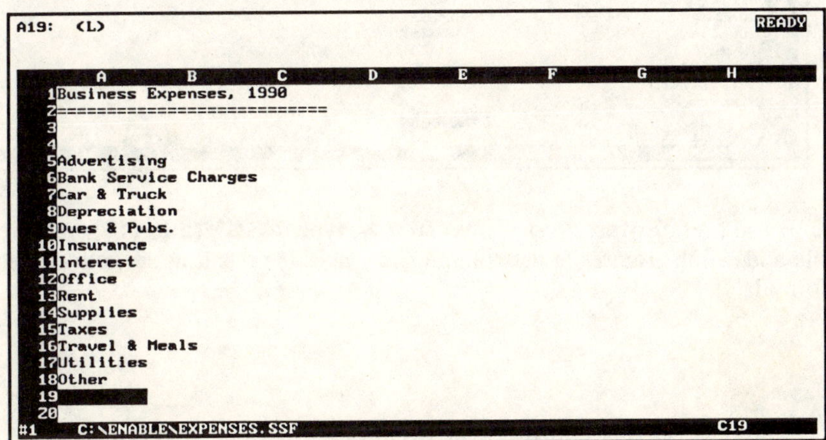

5. Press **Home**. The "pointer" (the highlight) moves to the top left corner of the spreadsheet. Press **Right Arrow** three times and **Down Arrow** two times. Type **JAN** and press **Right Arrow**; type **FEB** and press **Right Arrow**. Continue in this manner to enter **MAR, APR, MAY, JUN, JUL, AUG, SEP, OCT, NOV, DEC**. DEC is in column O (look at the letter in the bar above DEC. Press **Home**. Your spreadsheet looks like this:

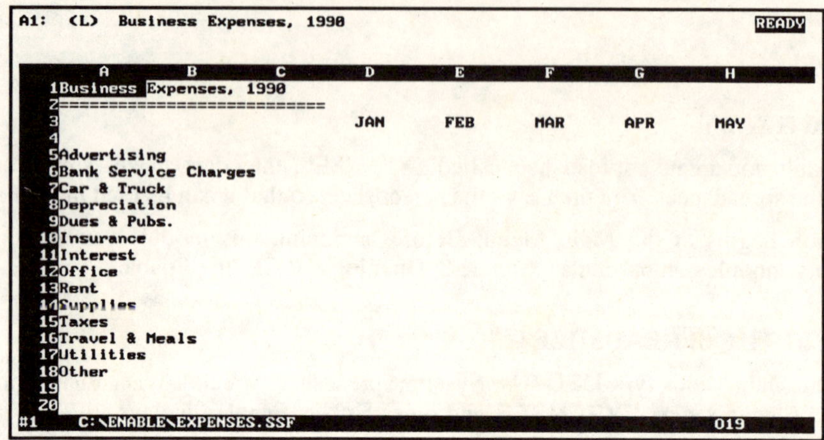

ENTERING AND USING THE DATA

6. Press **F2**, type **D5**, and press **Enter**. The highlight moves to the cell at the intersection of column D and row 5. Type **115** and press **Down Arrow**. Continue in this manner until you have entered all the numbers in the following screen:

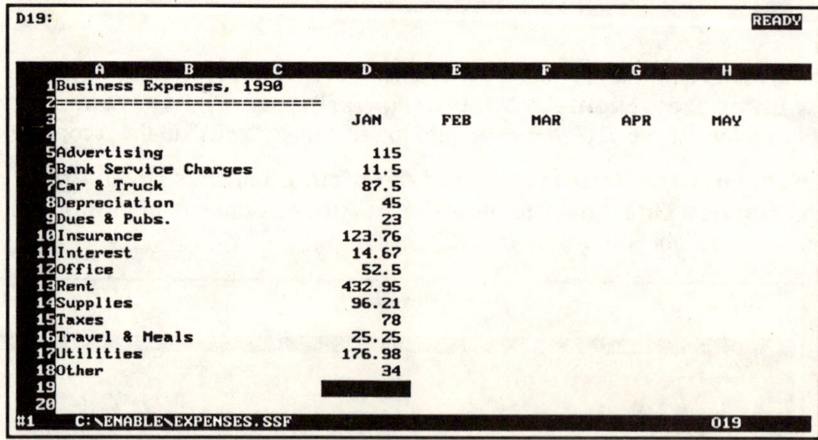

7. Press \= and press **Enter**. Press **Down Arrow**, type **@SUM(d5..d19)**, and press **Enter**. Enable adds all the figures in the column and places the result in the cell where you typed the formula.

PRINTING AND SAVING

8. Press **F10** and type **PR** (Print;Range). Press **Home**, type **.** (period), and press **Down Arrow** 19 times (or hold Down Arrow down until the highlighted area reaches row 20). Press **Right Arrow** four times. Press **Enter**. Your screen looks like this.

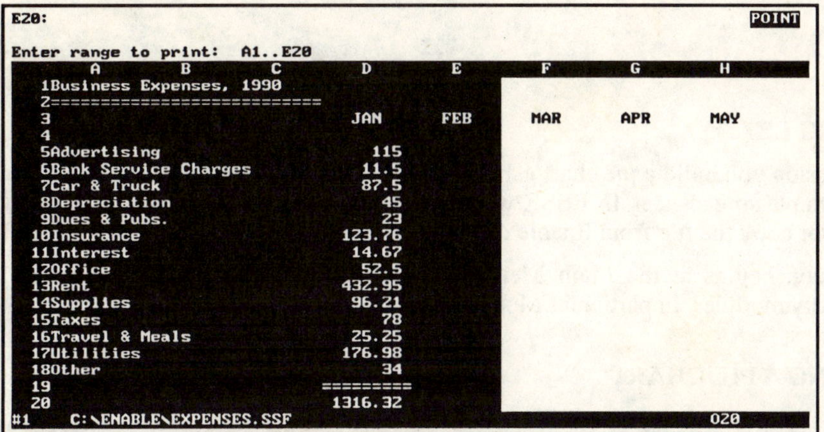

```
E20:                                                              POINT

Enter range to print:   A1..E20
        A         B         C         D         E         F         G         H
   1Business Expenses, 1990
   2===========================
   3                                 JAN       FEB       MAR       APR       MAY
   4
   5Advertising                      115
   6Bank Service Charges            11.5
   7Car & Truck                     87.5
   8Depreciation                      45
   9Dues & Pubs.                      23
  10Insurance                     123.76
  11Interest                       14.67
  12Office                          52.5
  13Rent                          432.95
  14Supplies                       96.21
  15Taxes                             78
  16Travel & Meals                 25.25
  17Utilities                     176.98
  18Other                             34
  19                           =========
  20                             1316.32
#1    C:\ENABLE\EXPENSES.SSF                                          020
```

9. Type **EP** (Execute;Print) and Enable prints the spreadsheet. When Enable has finished, press **Alt-F10**, press **Enter**, and when Enable prompts you to confirm the save operation type **R** (Replace). Enable saves the file.
10. Press **F10** and type **QY** to close the file and return to the Main Menu.
11. Turn to Module 65 to continue the learning sequence.

Module 7
A SAMPLE SESSION WITH ENABLE GRAPHICS

GETTING READY

In this session you build a pie chart using Enable graphics. The data for the chart comes from an Enable sample spreadsheet, INT.SSF, which is usually copied to your hard disk when you install Enable. (Or copy the file from Enable disk 12 [the Tutorial B disk] to your data disk.)

This session begins at the Main Menu. Before beginning this module you should read the introductory modules, in particular Module 3, Opening and Closing Enable.

BUILDING A PIE CHART

1. At the Main Menu type **USR** (Use;Spreadsheet;Revise). When Enable prompts for the filename type **INT** and press **Enter**. Enable displays the spreadsheet.
2. Press **F10** and type **G** (Graph) to see the following screen.

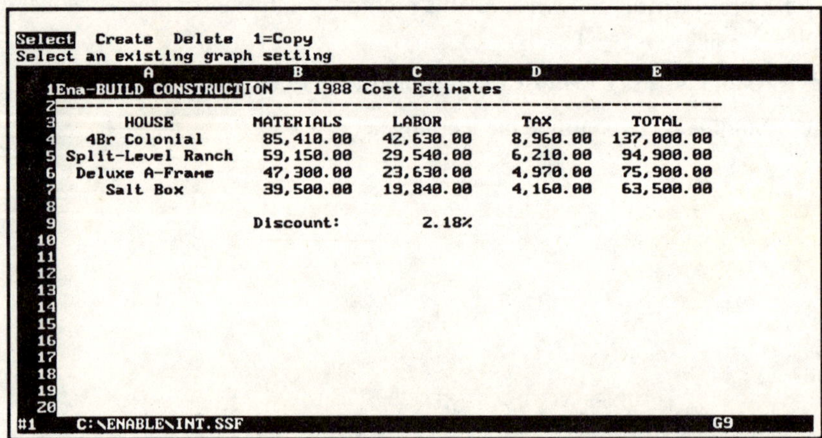

3. Type **C** (Create) and Enable prompts for a graph settings name. Type **Build**.

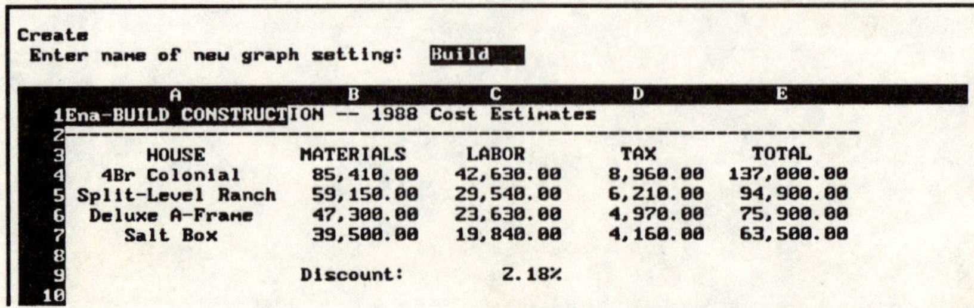

4. Press **Enter** to see the Task Options Menu.

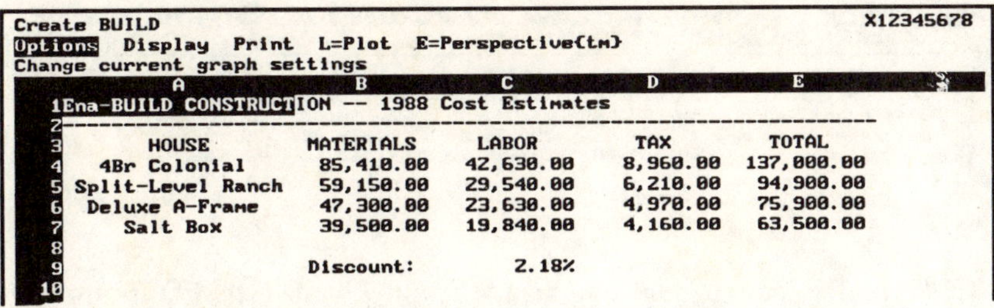

5. Type **O** (Options) to see the next menu level.

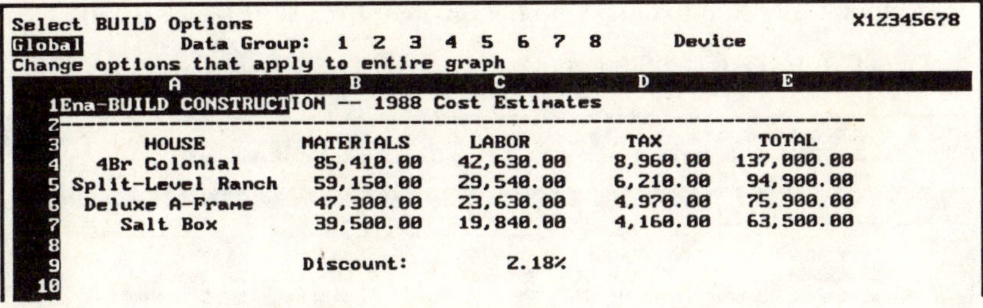

6. Type **G** (Global) to see the next level.

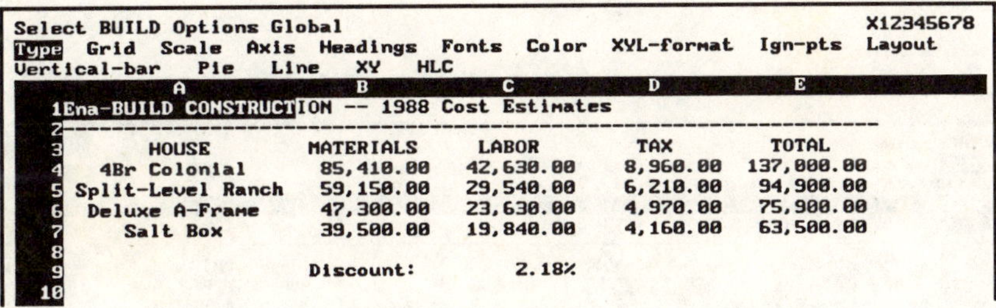

7. Type **T** (Type) to see the next level.

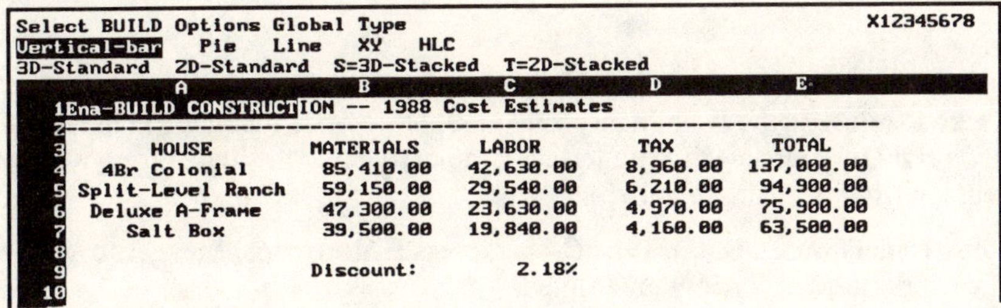

8. Type **P** (Pie) to select a pie graph.

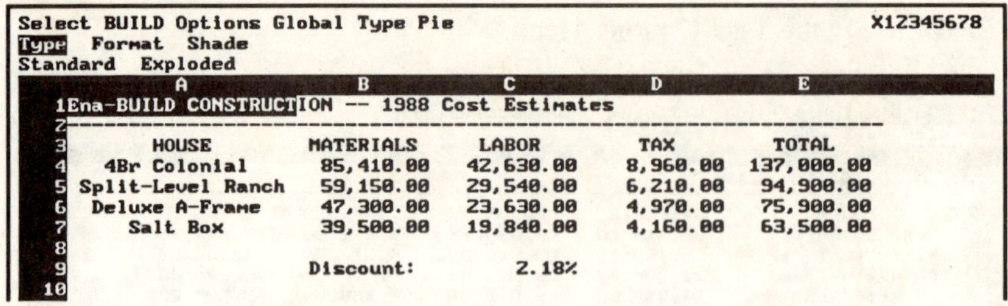

```
Select BUILD Options Global Type Pie                                  X12345678
Type  Format  Shade
Standard  Exploded
        A                B              C              D              E
 1Ena-BUILD CONSTRUCTION -- 1988 Cost Estimates
 2-------------------------------------------------------------------------
 3      HOUSE         MATERIALS        LABOR          TAX          TOTAL
 4   4Br Colonial     85,410.00      42,630.00      8,960.00    137,000.00
 5 Split-Level Ranch  59,150.00      29,540.00      6,210.00     94,900.00
 6  Deluxe A-Frame    47,300.00      23,630.00      4,970.00     75,900.00
 7     Salt Box       39,500.00      19,840.00      4,160.00     63,500.00
 8
 9                    Discount:          2.18%
10
```

9. Type **TE** (Type;Explode) to select an exploding pie graph. Type **FD** (Format;Data-labels) to select the type of label used to indicate what each of the graph's elements represent. Type **SU** (Shade;User) to use the individual data group's shades.
10. Press **Esc** three times to move back up the menu to the list of Data Groups.
11. Type **1** (Data Group:1) to see the next level.

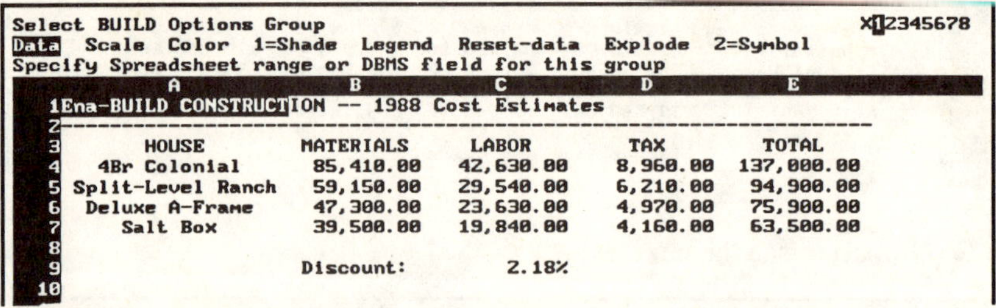

```
Select BUILD Options Group                                            X12345678
Data  Scale  Color  1=Shade  Legend  Reset-data  Explode  2=Symbol
Specify Spreadsheet range or DBMS field for this group
        A                B              C              D              E
 1Ena-BUILD CONSTRUCTION -- 1988 Cost Estimates
 2-------------------------------------------------------------------------
 3      HOUSE         MATERIALS        LABOR          TAX          TOTAL
 4   4Br Colonial     85,410.00      42,630.00      8,960.00    137,000.00
 5 Split-Level Ranch  59,150.00      29,540.00      6,210.00     94,900.00
 6  Deluxe A-Frame    47,300.00      23,630.00      4,970.00     75,900.00
 7     Salt Box       39,500.00      19,840.00      4,160.00     63,500.00
 8
 9                    Discount:          2.18%
10
```

12. Type **D** (Data). Use the arrow keys to move the pointer to B4.

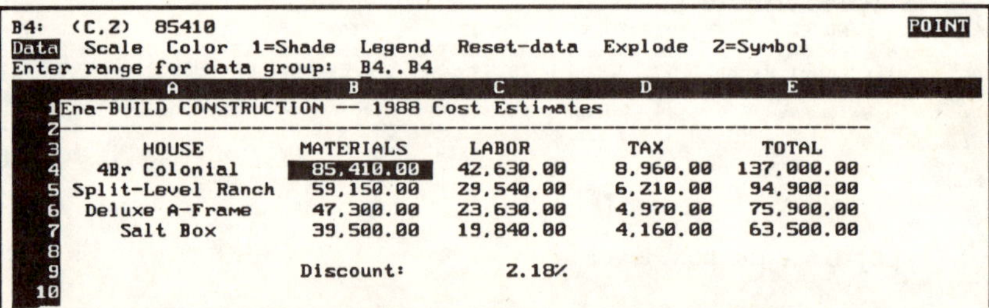

```
B4:  (C,2)  85410                                                      POINT
Data  Scale  Color  1=Shade  Legend  Reset-data  Explode  2=Symbol
Enter range for data group:  B4..B4
        A                B              C              D              E
 1Ena-BUILD CONSTRUCTION -- 1988 Cost Estimates
 2-------------------------------------------------------------------------
 3      HOUSE         MATERIALS        LABOR          TAX          TOTAL
 4   4Br Colonial     85,410.00      42,630.00      8,960.00    137,000.00
 5 Split-Level Ranch  59,150.00      29,540.00      6,210.00     94,900.00
 6  Deluxe A-Frame    47,300.00      23,630.00      4,970.00     75,900.00
 7     Salt Box       39,500.00      19,840.00      4,160.00     63,500.00
 8
 9                    Discount:          2.18%
10
```

13. Press **Enter** to select B4 as the data cell.
14. Press **Esc** to return to the list of data group numbers. Notice that the 1 in the list of numbers at the top right of your screen is underlined, indicating that this data group will be included in the graph (that is, it has been defined).
15. Type **2D** (Data Group:2;Data). Type **C4** and press **Enter** twice. Press **Esc**. Notice that the 2 in the list of numbers is now underlined.
16. Type **3D** (Data Group:3;Data). Type **D4** and press **Enter** twice.
17. Type **EY** (Explode;Yes) to tell Enable to "explode" this data group. Press **Esc**. Notice that the 3 in the list of numbers is now underlined.

18. Type **GA1** (Global;Axis;1=X-axis-data). Type **B3..D3** and press **Enter**. The labels in the cell range you defined will be used to label the pie graph slices.
19. Press **Esc** three times to return to the Task Options Menu. Type **D** (Display), and Enable displays the graph on your screen.

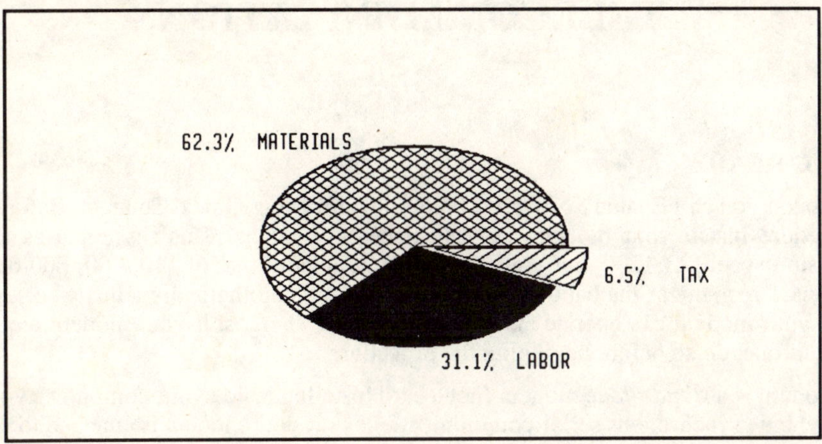

20. Press **Esc** three times to return to the spreadsheet. Press **Alt-F10**, press **Enter**, and type **R** to save the graph settings with the spreadsheet.
21. Press **F10** and type **QY** to close the spreadsheet.
22. Turn to Module 77 to continue the learning sequence.

Module 8
A SAMPLE SESSION WITH ENABLE TELECOMMUNICATIONS

GETTING READY

In this session you call Enable Software's bulletin board using Quick-Connect. Before beginning this procedure install your modem and any necessary cables. This session uses a *baud rate* (transmission speed) of 1200, but you can substitute a baud rate of 110, 300, 600 or 2400. The bulletin board recognizes the baud rate you are using and automatically adjusts—uses the fastest baud rate your modem can operate at, to save telephone charges. If your modem requires you to set the baud rate, do so before beginning the procedure.

If your modem is a *stand-alone* modem (not a card installed inside your computer), you also need to know which asynchronous serial-communications port your modem is attached to. If you don't have a serial communications port, you either need to use an internal modem or install a card with a serial port on it. You may have the modem attached to port COMM1, COMM2, or to a Zenith Z404 or Z304 board. If you are using an internal modem, check your documentation for the COMM number to use.

You also need to know if your telephone line is tone or pulse. If your telephones have buttons that "beep" when you press them, you have tone (Touch-tone or DTMF). If your phones have rotary dials, or if they have buttons that "click-click-click" when you press them, you have pulse. (Many lines support both types of phone at the same time, so if some of your phones are tone and some pulse, use tone. If you only have pulse phones, use pulse.)

CALLING ENABLE

Remember to turn your modem on before you begin.

1. At the Main Menu type **UTCQ** (Use System;Telecom;Communicate;Quick-Connect).

```
                              ENABLE/OA (tm)
               Select an option with the cursor and [<-┘]
      Press [Esc] if you change your mind and [F1] if you need help.

      Use System          Help            MCM           Return to DOS

 Word Processing    Spreadsheet/Graphics    Telecom      DBMS/Graphics

                 Communicate                    Setup

      Use Setup        Quick-Connect        File transfer (Unattended)

#1
```

2. At the Quick Connection Form type **4** to select a baud rate of 1200. The cursor jumps to the next line.
3. Type **3** to select protocol option 3. The cursor jumps to the next line.
4. Type **F** to select Full Duplex. The cursor jumps to the next line.
5. Use the arrow keys to move the cursor to the correct communications port. Your screen looks like this:

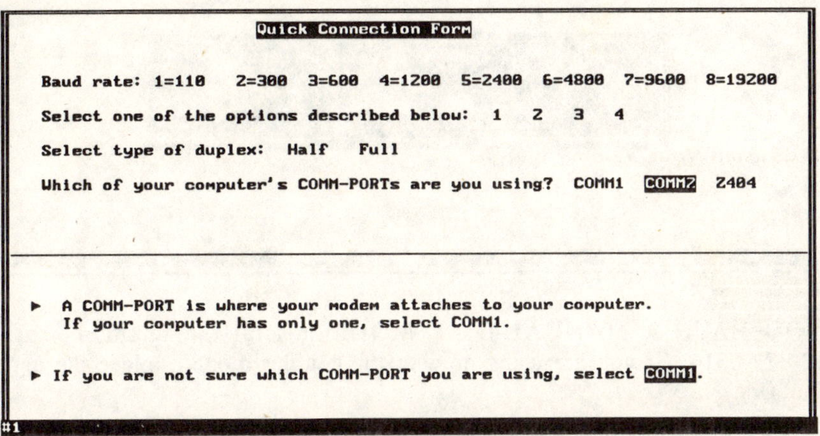

6. Press **Enter** and Enable displays the next screen. Type **TENABLE**.

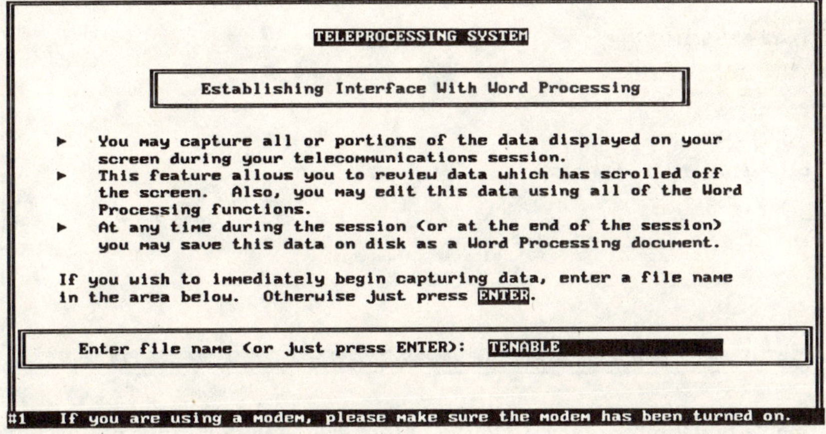

7. Press **Enter**. Enable displays a message telling you that it is initializing the communications port and the modem, and then displays the blank Telecom screen.
8. Press **F10** and type **TC** (Tele;Call).
9. IF YOU HAVE AN AUTO-DIAL MODEM: Type the telephone number, preceded by the letter T (Tone) or P (Pulse). If you are in an office where you need to dial an outside number first, include that with two commas after it. So, if you need to dial 9 for an outside line and

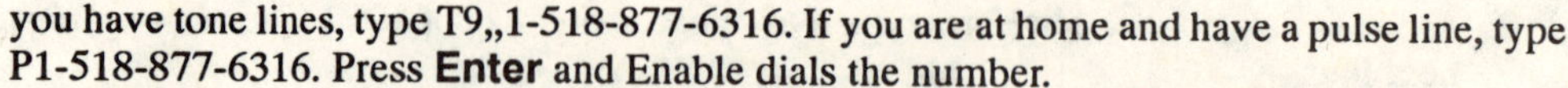

you have tone lines, type T9,,1-518-877-6316. If you are at home and have a pulse line, type P1-518-877-6316. Press **Enter** and Enable dials the number.

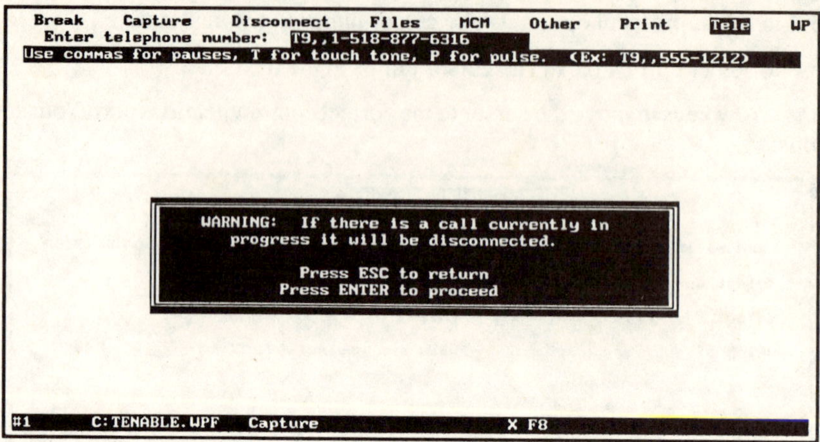

IF YOU HAVE A MANUAL-DIAL MODEM: Dial the telephone number. Call 1-518-877-6316. (If you are using an acoustic-coupler modem, place the handset in the modem first).

When the bulletin board answers it transmits the following screen.

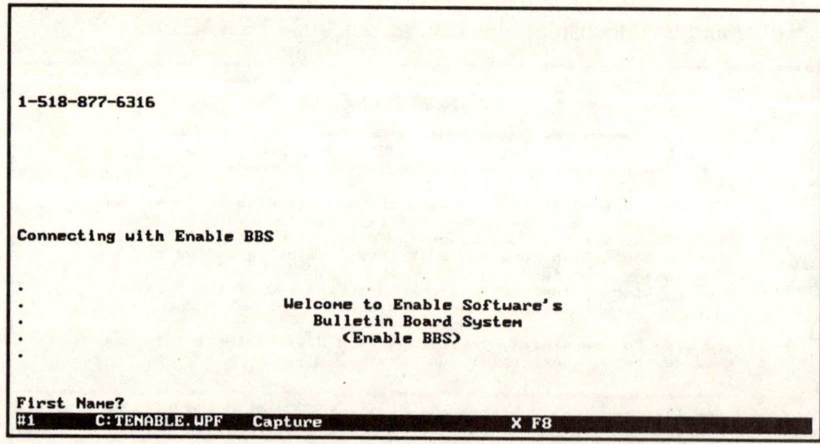

11. The Enable bulletin board system (BBS) prompts you with a series of questions. Answer each question very carefully. Make sure you don't type the wrong character. After each response press **Enter** and the BBS goes on to the next prompt. Enter your first name, last name, city, and state. After you enter these, the BBS displays what you entered and asks if it has the correct information.

12. Type **Y** if the information is correct (otherwise type **N** and the BBS asks the same questions again).

13. The BBS prompts for the width of your screen. Type the number of characters wide and press **Enter**.
14. The BBS prompts for the type of terminal you are using. Type **A** for the IBM PC and compatibles.
15. The BBS then asks if you want to change the terminal profile. Type **N**. Your screen looks like this:

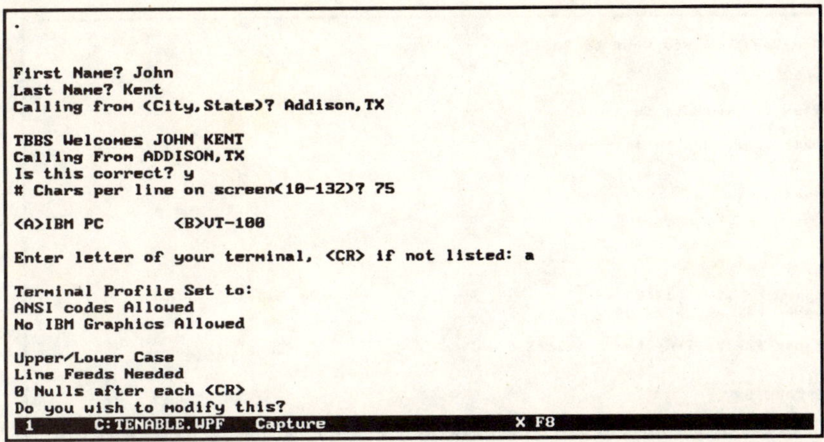

```
First Name? John
Last Name? Kent
Calling from (City,State)? Addison,TX

TBBS Welcomes JOHN KENT
Calling From ADDISON,TX
Is this correct? y
# Chars per line on screen(10-132)? 75

<A>IBM PC        <B>VT-100

Enter letter of your terminal, <CR> if not listed: a

Terminal Profile Set to:
ANSI codes Allowed
No IBM Graphics Allowed

Upper/Lower Case
Line Feeds Needed
0 Nulls after each <CR>
Do you wish to modify this?
 1        C:TENABLE.WPF    Capture                        X F8
```

16. The BBS asks if you want to pause after each display page. Type **Y**, and the BBS asks how many lines your screen has. Type the number and press **Enter**.
17. The BBS next prompts you for a password that lets you onto the bulletin board next time. Type your password (no more than eight letters) and press **Enter**.
18. The BBS then asks a number of survey questions. Answer the questions, pressing **Enter** if the BBS doesn't automatically continue after your response. Bypass questions you don't want to answer by pressing **Enter**.
19. After the questions you see the Main Menu.

```
-Press Any Key-
♀
♀Enable BBS - Main Menu
-------------------------
<G>oodbye, <X>pert Level

*Line 1*

<N>ew user info

<E>nable Message Boards  (All Message Bases are here)

<M>essage to the Sysop    (Not for Tech Support Questions)

<U>tilites                (Change Password, Terminal Options, System
Stats)

<F>ile Transfer section   (Upload and Download Files)

<H>ow to Upload Problem Files

-More-
 1        C:TENABLE.WPF    Capture                        X F8
```

20. Continue with the telecommunications session as you wish. Type the letter associated with the choice you want (type **N** to see the New User information, for example). Follow the BBS's instructions.
21. When you have finished, return to the Main Menu (usually by pressing **Enter**).
22. At the Main Menu type **G** (Goodbye) and the BBS asks you to confirm. Type **Y** and the BBS hangs up.

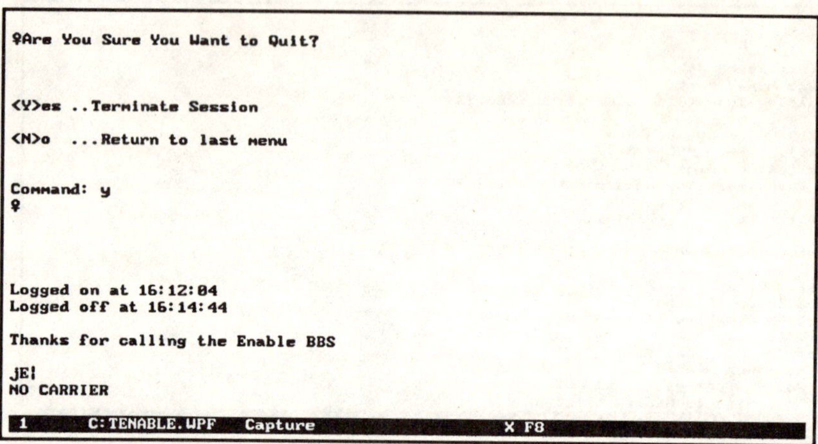

23. Press **F10** and type **DY** to terminate the telecom session. Enable asks if you want to save data. Type **Y** and Enable displays the word processing screen with the data in it, and the Save options are displayed on the screen.

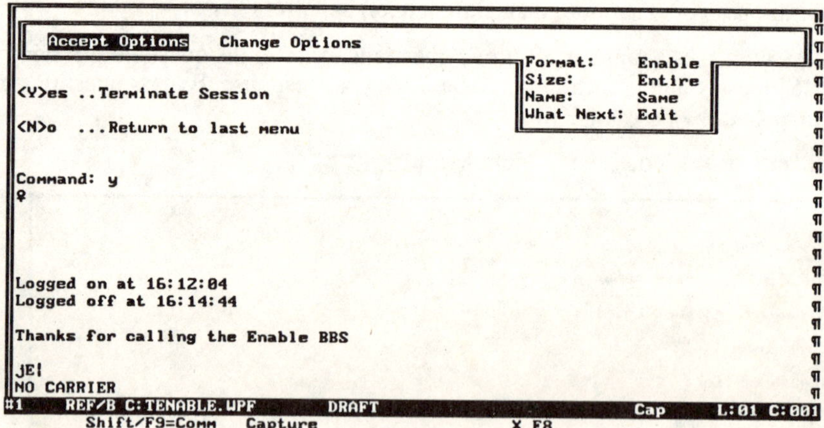

24. Press **Enter** to save the data. Press **F10** and type **QY** to close the file.
25. Turn to Module 102 to continue the learning sequence.

Module 9
WORD PROCESSING OVERVIEW

INTRODUCTION

Enable's word processing application is a full-featured, WYSIWYG (*what you see is what you get*) program—or at least close to it—with most of the capabilities of a stand-alone word processing package such as WordStar or WordPerfect. Its features include a spelling check and thesaurus, indexing, table of contents creation, landscape or portrait printing, footnote and reference table creation, multiple columns, and automatic file saving. In addition, as part of a five-application system, Enable's word processing package benefits from the ability to quickly and easily import graphs, spreadsheets, and database information, and the ability to transmit files, all without ever leaving the Enable program. You can even import documents from other word processing programs and use them in Enable.

TOP LINE MENU

You press F10 to access the Top Line Menu, shown in the following screen:

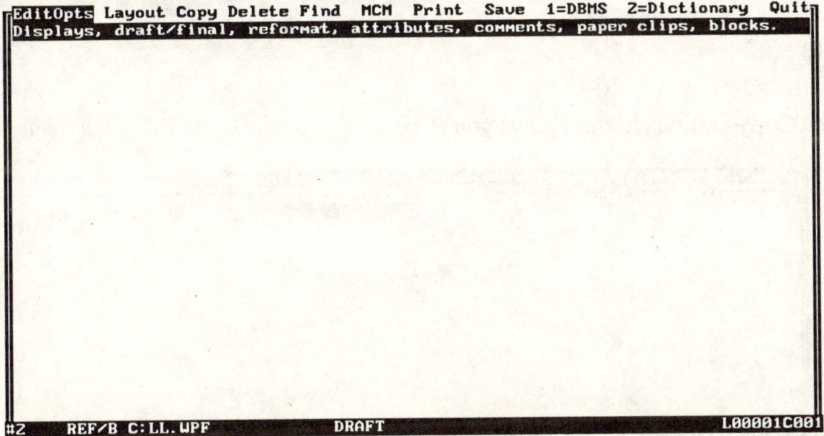

As you can see, there are eleven options. You select an option by typing its first letter or number, or by moving the cursor to the option (with the arrow keys or the Spacebar) and pressing Enter. The associated second-level menu or option will appear. You can clear the menu for the selected option by pressing Esc.

EditOpts: The Editing Options Menu allows you to turn on or off the screen display of features such as headers, footers, index entries, paper clips, and page breaks; to view your document in draft or final form; to turn on or off automatic reformatting of paragraphs; to reformat a paragraph; to display the Attribute Help Screen (which assists you in using text attributes);

to insert a comment or a paper clip; to move blocks of text; and to retain blank spaces when reformatting a paragraph.

```
Select the editing option you want by typing the option number.
L-------T-------T-------T-------T---  a. Screen displays  ------------R
                                      b. Draft/final
                                      c. Reformat on/off
                                      d. Reformat paragraph
                                      e. Attribute help on/off
                                      f. Insert a comment
                                      g. Insert a paper clip
                                      h. Block options
                                      i. Keep blanks on/off
```

Layout: The Layout Options Menu allows you to insert and format a ruler, to insert a default ruler (formatted in your Profile), to set line spacing, to insert a page break, to insert a header or footer, to use special characters, to create a footnote, to create or modify a table of contents, to create or modify an index, to create or use shorthand, to sort lines or paragraphs, to modify footnotes, or to create a table of authorities (a references table).

```
Select the layout option you want by typing the option number.
L-------T-------T-------T-------T---  1. Insert a ruler  -----------R
                                      2. Insert default ruler
                                      3. Set line spacing
                                      4. Insert a page break
                                      5. Insert a header
                                      6. Insert a footer
                                      7. Use special characters
                                      8. Create a footnote
                                      9. Table of contents options
                                      0. Index options
                                      A. Shorthand
                                      B. Sort
                                      C. Modify footnote layout
                                      D. Table of authorities
```

Copy: The Copy Options Menu allows you to copy or move text within or between documents.

```
Select the copy option you want by typing the option number.
L-------T-------T-------T-------T---  1. Copy  -----------------------R
                                      2. Move
```

Delete: The Delete Options Menu allows you to delete lines, blocks, sentences, paragraphs, pages, blanks between words, and paragraph markers. It also allows you to delete from the cursor to the end or to the beginning of the file or to "undo" the last deletion.

```
Select the text you want deleted by typing the number of the desired option.
L-------T-------T-------T-------T---  1. Line at the cursor  ------R
                                      2. The block that is marked
                                      3. To the end of the sentence
                                      4. To the end of the paragraph
                                      5. To the end of the page
                                      6. To the beginning of the file
                                      7. To the end of the file
                                      8. White space between words
                                      9. Paragraph marker
                                      0. Undo
```

Find: The Find Options Menu allows you to find specified characters, words, phrases, numbers, or symbols. You can also replace or mark the found text.

```
Select the find option you want by typing the option number.
L-------T-------T-------T-------T---- 1. Find only         ------------R
                                      2. Find and replace
                                      3. Find and mark
```

MCM: The MCM (Master Control Module) Menu allows you to go to another window, to change window sizes, to display a window directory, or to close a window; to view a file summary or file directory; and to set display options.

```
Select the Master Control Module option you want by typing the option number.
L-------T-------T-------T-------T---- 1. Windows        ---------------R
                                      2. Files
                                      3. Screen
```

Print: The Print Form allows you to change the format of the printout. The following screen shows the first of the four Print Form pages.

```
                                  Print Form

   Print:          Entire File         Selected Pages

   Number of copies: 1
   Paper type:                        Continuous form    Single Sheets
   Printer orientation mode:          Portrait           Landscape
   Unidirectional Print:                                Yes  No
   Print a title page:                                  Yes  No
   Leading blank page:                                  Yes  No
   Print in draft mode:                                 Yes  No
   Allow automatic widow/orphan repagination:           Yes  No
   List print statistics:                               Yes  No

 ► Select the portion of the document you wish to print.

#2 ALT/F2=Print   ALT/F10=Save Form   PgUp=Prev Page   PgDn=Next Page   Esc=Exit
```

Save: The Save Options Menu allows you to save a file without changing any options; to save an entire file or only a block of text or marked text; to select a different format or a new name; and to choose what to do next—resume editing, revise or create another document, close the window, or return to DOS.

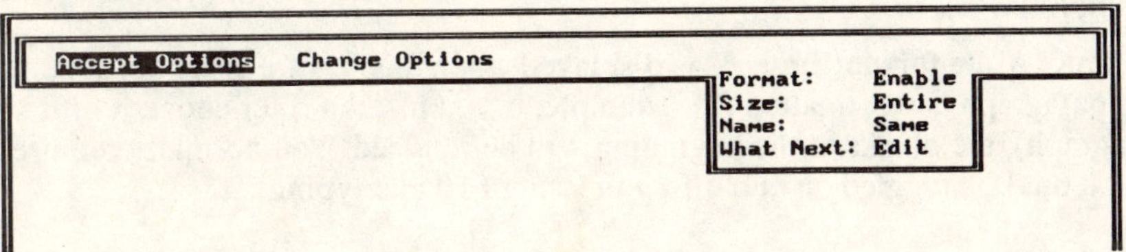

1=DBMS: The DBMS Option allows you to view a list of the field names in a specified database. You can then select a name to insert into your text or mailmerge document.

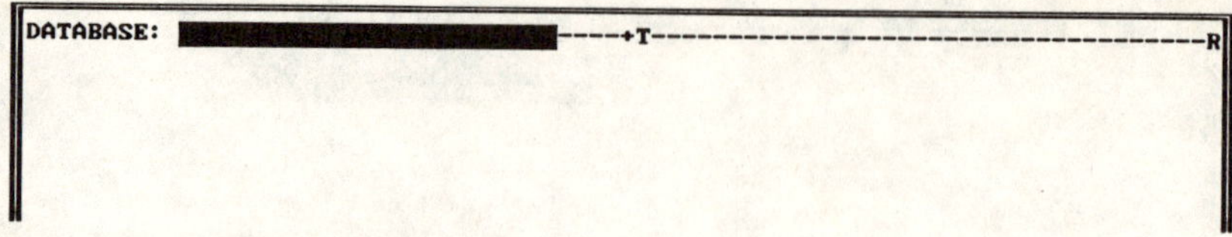

2=Dictionary: The Dictionary Options Menu allows you to check your document's spelling or to look up a word in the thesaurus.

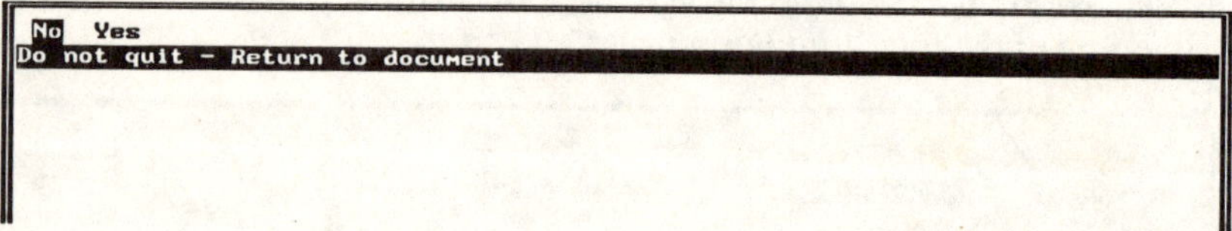

Quit: The Quit option allows you to leave the file without saving it.

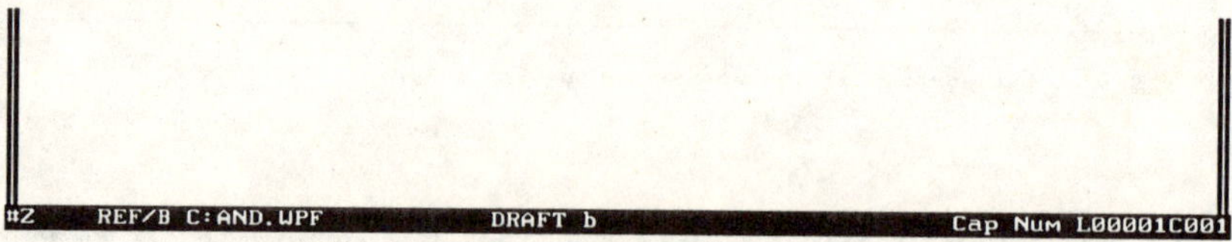

STATUS LINE

Enable's status line provides valuable information about your word processing file. The following conditions are shown on the status line, from left to right:

```
#2    REF/B C:AND.WPF              DRAFT b                         Cap Num L00001C001
```

Window Number: The window number is shown in the left corner.

Automatic Reformat: REF is displayed if automatic reformat is turned on. This feature automatically "wraps" text onto the next line, and adjusts spacing when you delete text. You normally need automatic reformat turned on. It is toggled on and off by pressing F10 and typing EC.

Retain Blanks while formatting: /B is displayed when this feature is set on. When the first line of a paragraph is reformatted (for example, if you insert a ruler above it or if you copy the paragraph), the blanks at the beginning will be retained. You normally require this feature turned on. It is toggled on and off by pressing F10 and typing E1.

Disk Name: The disk drive that your file is saved on is displayed next.

File Name: The name of file is displayed immediately after the drive name—the status line does not display the directory name.

Draft or Final Mode: If DRAFT is displayed, the file is in Draft mode—this is the most convenient mode for creation and editing of text. If the file is in Final mode, Enable displays "Page" followed by the page number. Final mode displays the document more as it will appear when printed, with page breaks, headers and footers, and numbers correctly placed. You can change from Draft to Final (or vice versa) by pressing F10 and typing EB.

Text Attributes: If you are applying a text attribute, you will see a letter to the right of DRAFT or FINAL, indicating which attribute (bold, italics, etc.) you are applying.

Caps Lock: If the Caps Lock key is on, Cap appears on the status line. When this key is on, any letters pressed will automatically be uppercase. You must still press Shift if you want to type the Shift characters on the number or punctuation keys.

Num Lock: If the Num Lock key is on, Num appears on the status line. Num Lock disables the arrow keys on your keyboard's numeric keypad and allows you to use the keypad to type numbers.

Line/Column: The final display on the status line is the Line and Column counter. For example, L00203C030 means the cursor is on line 203, column 30.

BUSY: The last five numbers in the Line and Column counter are replaced with the word BUSY when Enable is carrying out an operation that stops you from using the program; for example, while it is saving your document.

Turn to Module 32 to continue the learning sequence.

Module 10
ALIGN TEXT

DESCRIPTION

The following types of text-alignment and positioning features are available:

Ruler: Left and Right Margins
Right Justified Margin
Tabs
Numeric Tabs
Alphanumeric Tabs
Character Alignment Tabs
Centering-Column Tabs
Outline Tabs

Center a Line
Move a Line to the Right or Left
Hanging Indents
Proportional Spacing
Multiple Columns
Block Alignment
Release Margin
%TAB Command

RULERS The Ruler Line shows the left and right margins and various types of tabs. The margins and tabs work in a way similar to a typewriter. Text cannot be typed outside the margins, and tabs are used by pressing the Tab key to move the cursor across the page to a set position. However, Enable's ruler has several features that make it more than a simple way to limit cursor movement. Justified margins and four different types of tabs make professional-looking documents simple to produce. The screen display of rulers can be turned on and off. Press F10 and type EA3 (EditOpts;Screen Displays;Rulers) to toggle the display on and off.

The Default Ruler Enable has a default ruler. When you create a document the first screen you see is the ruler screen. You have the opportunity to modify or accept the default ruler. (See Module 32, Open a Document.) Even if you decide to accept the default you still have a chance to change the settings later.

Inserting or Selecting a Ruler If you decide to change the ruler after you have begun typing, you have several options:

- To insert a new ruler line, position the cursor on the first line you want to conform to the new ruler, press F10, type L1 (Layout;Insert a ruler), and press Enter. A copy of the current ruler is inserted above the cursor line. Make your changes to the ruler and press Enter. (Modifying the ruler line is described further on in this module.)

- To insert a default ruler, position the cursor on the first line you want to conform to the new ruler, press F10, type L2 (Layout;Insert default ruler), and press Enter. A copy of the default ruler is inserted above the cursor line. Make your changes and press Enter.
- To select an existing ruler, position the cursor on the ruler, press F10, type L1 (Layout;Insert a ruler), and press Enter. (Or use the keyboard command, Alt-F6.) Make the modifications, and press Enter.

When you insert or change a ruler, all the text from the new ruler down to the next ruler will be modified to conform to the new ruler.

Modifying the Ruler To modify the ruler, insert or select a ruler (as described in the previous section), use the Tab or arrow keys to move the cursor to the position you want to set a margin or tab, and press one or more of the characters described in the following table:

Type..	*To set..*	*Description*
L	The left margin	Defines the left-most position of the text.
R	The right margin	Defines the right-most position of the text.
J	A justified right margin	Defines the right-most limit of the text and also *justifies* the text. Enable inserts extra spaces to spread the words out across the page, producing a straight right margin instead of a ragged one.
T	Tabs	Defines an indent position. After you set tabs on the ruler, pressing the Tab key moves the cursor to the next tab position. Pressing Shift-Tab moves the cursor backwards, to the last tab position. If you have Display Tab Character set in your profile, you will see a block displayed on the line each time you press Tab. (This is only displayed in draft mode, not in final mode.)
N	Numeric tabs	Aligns columns of numbers. See text following this table.
X	Alphanumeric tabs	Aligns columns that have both numbers and letters, such as columns with serial or part numbers. See text following this table.
. ; : | / \ ) }]	Character alignment tabs	Alignment characters in numeric or alpha-numeric tabs. See text following this table.
^	Centering tabs	Used to center text within a column. See text following this table.

If you want to delete a tab or margin, move the cursor to the character on the ruler and press the hyphen (-) or Spacebar. If you delete a margin, you are not able to leave the ruler line until you place the margin somewhere else on the line. However, there is no real need to delete a margin—just move the cursor to where you want to move the margin, type the letter, and the margin automatically moves to the new position.

Once the ruler is set as you want it, press Enter and you can continue typing the document.

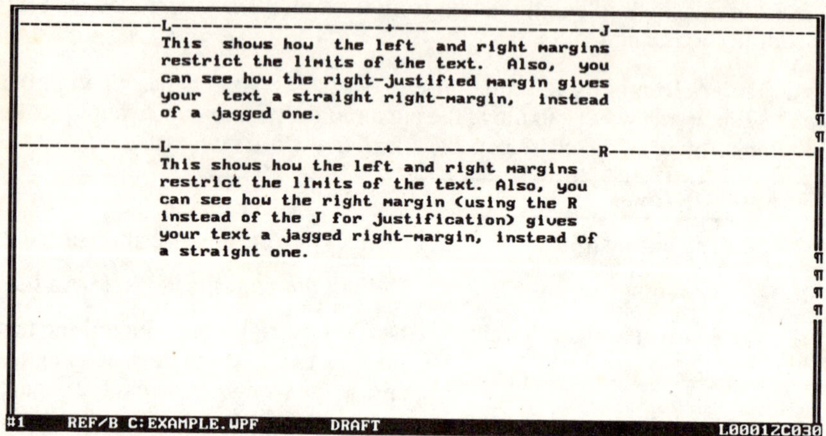

Quick Margin Settings The following is a quick way to change the left or right margins, without inserting a ruler first. Place the cursor where you want the new margin and press Alt-L (to place the left margin), Alt-R (to place the right margin), or Alt-J (to place a right-justified margin). Enable inserts a new ruler above the cursor (or modifies the ruler if the cursor is on a ruler line). Of course, this method can only be used if you want to bring the margins in, not if you want to expand them.

Numeric Tabs To set numeric tabs, type Ns on the ruler in the desired position of the column. Type as many Ns as digits in the column, plus one (that is, for a five-digit column, type six Ns). If the numbers will contain decimals, count the decimal point as the extra N, but do not add Ns for the numbers to the right of the decimal point. For example, if the largest number will be 9999.99, place five Ns on the ruler line. The last N will be the decimal position.

When you press Tab and Enable encounters a numeric tab set on the ruler, the cursor moves to the last N in group. Start typing and the numbers are inserted to the left of the cursor position. As each new digit is typed, the previous ones are moved to the left. If you type more than the column width, the extra characters are inserted to the right of the column. And, if you type any character other than the following, the subsequent characters are inserted to the right of the column:

1 2 3 4 5 6 7 8 9 0 ([{ + $, # ' "

So, typing a period (decimal point) will put the next numbers to the right of the last N. If you do not add an extra N or an N for a decimal place, the columns will not line up correctly.

When you have finished with the first column, press Tab to move to the next one. When you come back to edit a column, pressing Tab puts the cursor on the first N, not the last.

Alphanumeric Tabs To set alphanumeric tabs, (used to align columns that have both numbers and letters, such as columns with serial or part numbers) type Xs on the ruler in the desired position of the column. Type as many Xs as characters in the column, plus one (that is, for a five-digit column, type six Xs).

When you press Tab and Enable encounters an alphanumeric tab set on the ruler, the cursor moves to the last X in the group. Start typing and the characters are inserted to the left of the cursor position. As each new character is typed, the previous ones are moved to the left. If you type more than the column width, the characters are inserted to the right of the column.

When you have finished the first column, press Tab to move the cursor to the next column. The following screen shows numeric and alphanumeric tabs used together.

```
                                                                              ¶
---L------------T--------------+-----T--------------------R---------------------||
   ■            Part Number■         Cost                                      ¶
---L------------XXXXXXXX-----------NNNNNN-----------------R---------------------||
   ■               S342T■             34.56                                    ¶
   ■               423TR■            123.87                                    ¶
   ■                 R45■             12.90                                    ¶
   ■              S343T1■             38.98
```

Character Alignment Tab You can incorporate any of the following alignment characters into your numeric or alphanumeric tabs:

. ; : | / \ ) }]

Then, when you are using the columns, you can type the same character as a point of right-alignment. For example, if you type NN/NN/NNN in the ruler line, the first time you press tab the cursor moves under the first slash. You can type one or two digits, and then type /. The cursor moves to the second slash. Type one or two digits, and /. The cursor moves to the last N. Type one or two digits, and you have typed in a date, aligned correctly in the column.

Centering-Column Tabs To set centering tabs, type carets (^) the width of the column. For example, typing ^^^^^^^ will give you a column seven characters wide. When you press Tab, the cursor moves under the middle caret—in this example under the 4th caret. As you type, Enable centers the text under the middle caret. When you exceed the column width, Enable continues inserting text in the normal manner. If you want a blank space at the beginning of the column, insert a *hard space*. This is done by pressing Alt-= (Alt-Equals). See Module 24, Hard Spaces.

The following screen shows centering-column tabs and character alignment tabs.

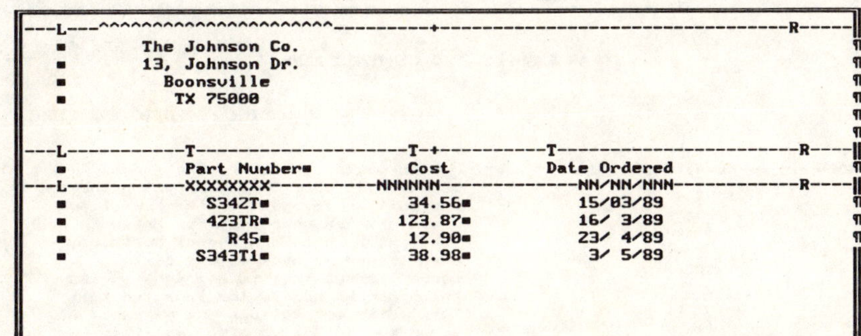

```
---L---^^^^^^^^^^^^^^^^^^^^^^^----------+-------------------------------R-----||
   ■       The Johnson Co.                                                     ¶
   ■       13, Johnson Dr.                                                     ¶
   ■         Boonsville                                                        ¶
   ■          TX 75000                                                         ¶
                                                                               ¶
                                                                               ¶
---L-----------T-------------------T-+----------T-----------------------R----||
   ■           Part Number■        Cost         Date Ordered                   ¶
---L-----------XXXXXXXX-----------NNNNNN-----------NN/NN/NNN------------R----||
   ■              S342T■           34.56■         15/03/89                     ¶
   ■              423TR■          123.87■         16/ 3/89                     ¶
   ■                R45■           12.90■         23/ 4/89                     ¶
   ■             S343T1■           38.98■          3/ 5/89
```

Outline Tabs Enable has special tabs used to create an outline-style document. These tabs are fully explained in Module 33.

Deleting a Ruler If you want to delete a ruler, place the cursor on it and press Alt-F3.

CENTER A LINE A line of text can also be centered between the left and right margins, without changing the ruler. Center the text by positioning the cursor anywhere on the line and pressing Alt-F4. You must type the text before using this command—you cannot use the command and then type the text.

The text is actually centered on the plus sign on the ruler. Enable automatically places the plus sign in the middle of the page between the margins. Whenever you insert a ruler, or whenever you adjust the right or left margin, Enable moves the plus sign into the middle. However, once you have set the margins you can move the plus sign to any position you want. Then, when you center text by pressing Alt-F4, the text is centered below the plus sign, not the actual center of the page. Uncenter text by positioning the cursor on the line and pressing Ctrl-[.

MOVE A LINE TO THE RIGHT OR LEFT You can move a line flush with the right margin by putting the cursor on the line of text and pressing Ctrl-]. Move the line back to the left (or un-center text) by pressing Ctrl-[.

HANGING INDENTS Use a hanging indent to indent short sections of text. Move the cursor to the place you want the text to begin and press Alt-H. Now type the text. When the text comes to the end of the line and wraps to the next line, it begins at the hanging indent position, not the left margin.

PROPORTIONAL SPACING Proportional spacing adjusts your text to use only the amount of space necessary for each character. Instead of each character having exactly the same amount of space as every other, the I, for example, will use up less space than the W. This gives your documents a professional, typeset look. You can set the entire document to proportional spacing by selecting this option in the Page Form. (See Module 35.)

You can also set specific sections of text to proportional spacing by putting the cursor at the beginning of the text, pressing Alt-P, moving the cursor to the end of the text, and pressing Alt-P again. Enable displays a diamond character and a letter P (◆P) at the beginning and the end of the text. The text does not appear to change on your screen, but when it is printed it is proportionally spaced. (Not all printers support this feature — see Enable's Getting Started booklet for a list of printers.)

The following screen shows a centered line, a line that has been moved to the right margin, and indented text set for proportional spacing.

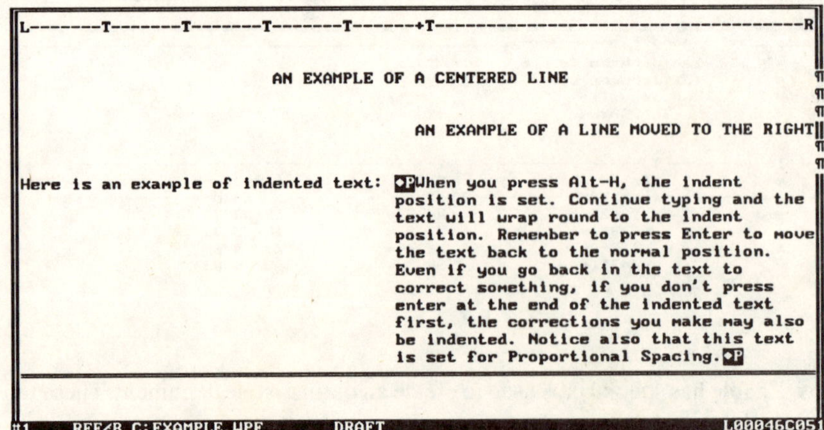

MULTIPLE COLUMNS Enable also has a multiple-column feature. The ruler can be adjusted to allow you to print up to five columns of text on one page. See Module 13 for more information.

BLOCK ALIGNMENT You can use block commands to align blocks of text. These commands are discussed in Module 11.

RELEASE THE MARGINS Press Ctrl-M to release the margin settings. If the right margin is set at column 80 or less, the left margin is released to column 1 and the right margin is released to column 80. If the right margin is set at column 81 or more, the margins are released to columns 1 and 160. Ctrl-M only affects one line; the next line reverts to the ruler's margins, even if the text wraps from the line with the released margins down onto the next line. Each line that has released margins has a small arrow displayed in the window's left border. To change a line back to the original margins, press Ctrl-M again.

%TAB COMMANDS If you have used text attributes that change the size of the text, you can use these commands to align text correctly. Enable adjusts the width of the tabs to the width of the characters. These commands are only necessary when you use tabs with text attributes. (See Module 45 for information about Text Attributes.) If your printer doesn't work very well with combinations of different attributes, refer to the embedded control codes in your printer's manual.

%TABS ON and %TABS OFF Command Type %TABS ON on the line before you begin proportional spacing and press Enter. The % must be in column one; don't type anything else on the same line. After the proportional spacing is finished, type %TABS OFF and press Enter; again, the % must be in column one, and the command must be on its own line.

%TABS ATTRIBUTE Command When you apply any other attribute that affects the size of the text, type %TABS followed by the attribute you are using: COMP (Compressed), ELCOMPE (Elite Compressed), PICA, ELITE, DOUBLE (Double-Strike), or QUAL (Quality). The % must be in column one, and the command must be on its own line. If you are using proportional spacing *and* one of the other attributes, use both commands, each on its own line.

APPLICATIONS

You align text for a number of reasons. The left and right margins are used to set the limits of text on the page, and the justified right margin also provides a straight right margin, instead of "ragged" text. The tabs are useful for moving to the beginning of paragraphs with indented first lines, and to set up simple columns. The numeric and alphanumeric tabs let you build more complex columns, such as date or serial number columns. Character alignment tabs are an enhancement of numeric and alphanumeric tabs, allowing you to incorporate slashes or brackets, for example, into your columns of numbers.

The centering-column tabs let you set up columns of text that are centered within the column. You may want to put an address in a column and have it centered within the column, for example. You can also center a line across the page—this allows you to center headings, warnings, and notes.

The "move a line to the left or right" features allow you to un-center text, and to adjust the location of a specific line without setting up a new ruler. The hanging indent also lets you set up a special indented format without changing the ruler.

TYPICAL OPERATION

In this activity you create a file, set up rulers, and build a simple form. Begin at the Main Menu.

1. Create a new file called RULERS. (Type **UWC**, type **RULERS**, and press **Enter**.)
2. When the default ruler appears, press **Right Arrow** once to move the cursor off the left margin, and then **Spacebar** four times. Type **T** to set a tab. Press the **Spacebar** 12 times, and type **T**. Press the **Spacebar** another 12 times, type **T**, and press **Enter**.
3. Delete the Document Title by pressing Alt-F3. Type **APARTMENTS SOLD IN 1988** and press **Alt-F4**. This title is centered, as shown in the following screen.

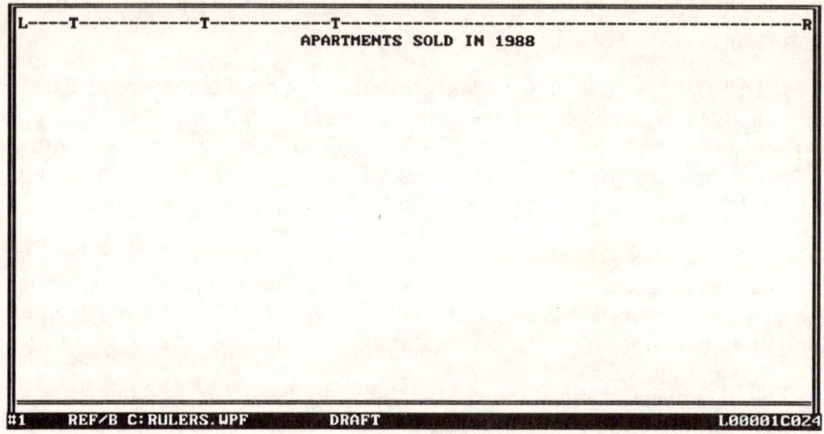

4. Press **Enter** twice. Press **Tab** to move to the first tab position, and type **APT#**. Press **Tab** and type **PRICE**. Press **Tab** and type **DATE SOLD**. Press **Enter**.
5. Press **F10** and type **L1**. Press **Enter**. The cursor moves to the next line, and a copy of the last ruler is displayed. Use **Right Arrow** to move the cursor to the first T, and type **XXXXXX**. Move to the next T and type **NNNNNNNN**. Move to the next T and type **NN/NN/NNN**. Press **Enter** and your screen looks like this:

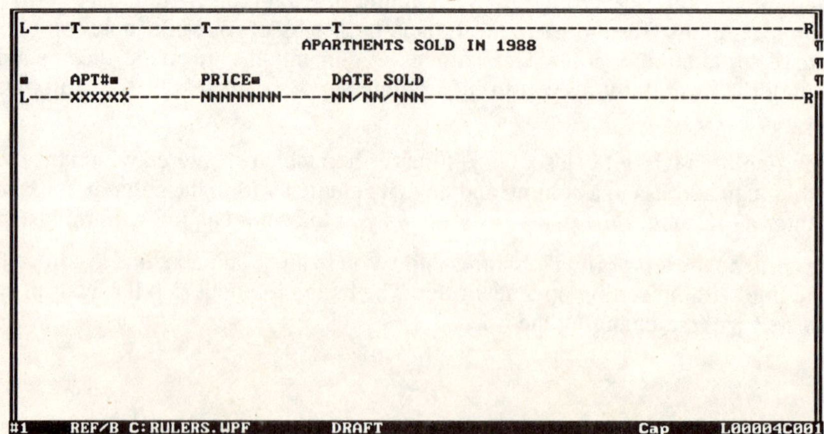

6. Press **Tab** and type **113B**. Press **Tab** and type **$55,050**. Press **Tab** and type **4/13/88**. Press **Enter**.
7. Press **Tab** and type **2001C**. Press **Tab** and type **$48,010.99**. Press **Tab** and type **04/18/88**. Your screen looks like this.

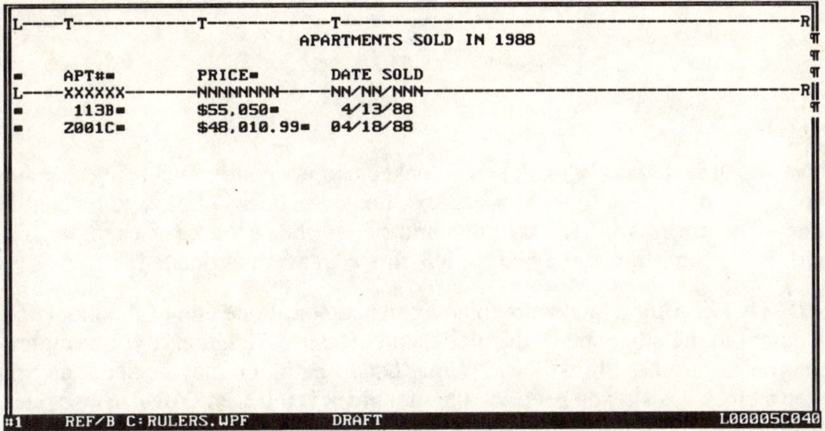

8. Press **Enter** twice. Press **F10** to display the Top Line Menu, and type **L2**. Press **Enter** twice. The default ruler displays and you are ready to continue typing. Press **Tab** and type **These apartments were sold through our special Spring Into Savings plan that we ran from March to May of 1988**.
9. Press **Enter** twice, press **Tab**, and press **Alt-H**. Now retype the same line. Notice that this time the second line of the text is indented, as shown below.

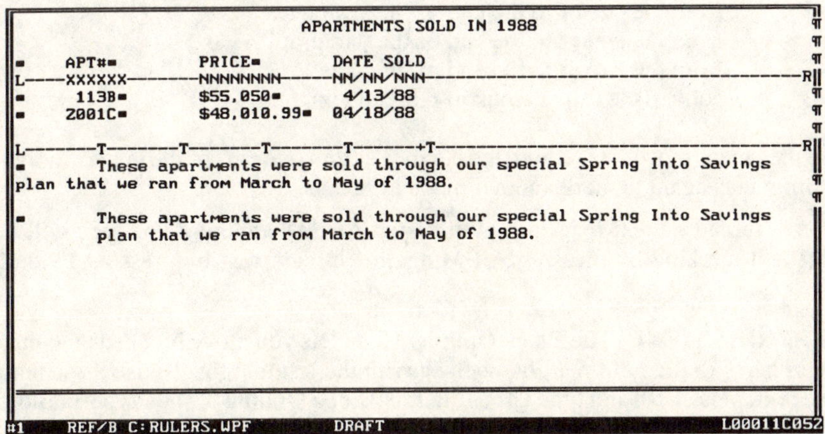

10. Press **Alt-F10** followed by **Enter** to save the file, and press **F10** and type **QY** to exit the file.
11. Turn to Module 38 to continue the learning sequence.

Module 11
BLOCKING/MARKING TEXT

DESCRIPTION

Enable allows you to set blocks or mark text. Blocked text is a continuous string or column of text; only one block may be set at a time. Marked text, however, does not have to be continuous. You can mark one sentence in the first paragraph and one in the second, for example. The text you block or mark is highlighted and may be copied, moved, saved, or deleted.

SETTING BLOCKS Blocks are set by placing the cursor at one end of the block, pressing F7, moving the cursor to the other end of the block, and pressing F7 again. If you want to set a block on a column you must press Shift-F7 each time. Only one block may be set at any time. If you press F7 when a block has already been set, the first block is released. You can also release a block by pressing Alt-F7.

MARKING TEXT Text is marked by pressing Alt-M, moving the cursor to the start of the text you wish to mark, and using one of the following segment commands (the same segment commands that are used with uppercase and lowercase conversion and applying text attributes).

Press...	*To Mark...*
Ctrl-C	the character at the cursor.
Ctrl-W	from the cursor to the end of the word.
Ctrl-L	from the cursor to the end of the line.
Ctrl-S	from the cursor to the end of the sentence.
Ctrl-P	from the cursor to the end of the paragraph.
Ctrl-G	from the cursor to the end of the page.
Ctrl-B	converts text in a block to marked text.

You can use the cursor movement commands to move from one part of the text to another and then use these commands again to mark another piece of text.

Once you have turned on text-marking (by pressing Alt-M), anything you type will be marked. You turn off text-marking by pressing Alt-M again. Unmark text by pressing F9 and Del, and typing MT.

BLOCK OPTIONS MENU The Block Options Menu lets you move blocked text into the center of the page, flush with the right margin, or flush with the left margin. To use these features, set a block on the text, press F10, and type EH (EditOpts;Block Options). Then type 1 (Block Center), 2 (Block Flush Right), or 3 (Block Flush Left). Press Alt-F7 to release the block.

When you center the block, the text is centered below the plus sign on the ruler line. For more information on centering text, see Module 10, Align Text.

APPLICATIONS

Blocked and marked text makes certain commands easier. Rather than retyping text, you can set a block on it and move or copy it. Rather than deleting a section word by word, you can block or mark it and delete it all at once. And, blocked or marked text may be saved in separate files. For more information on using the blocks, see Module 31 (Move or Copy Text), Module 39 (Save), and Module 17 (Delete Text).

TYPICAL OPERATION

In this activity you set blocks in the document named RULERS, created in Module 10. Begin at the Main Menu.

1. Open the document named RULERS.
2. Move the cursor to the beginning of the second "These." Press **F7**. Press **Down Arrow** twice and press **F7** again. Notice that the area between the two positions is now highlighted.

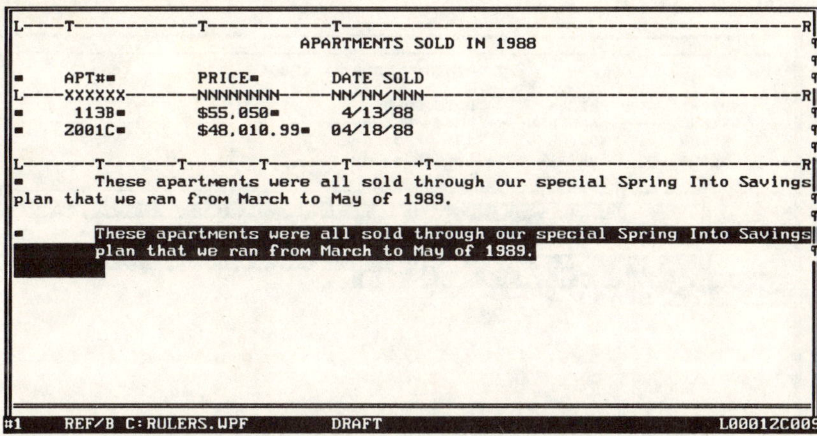

3. Press **F10** and **Enter** and type **H** to select the Block Options Menu.

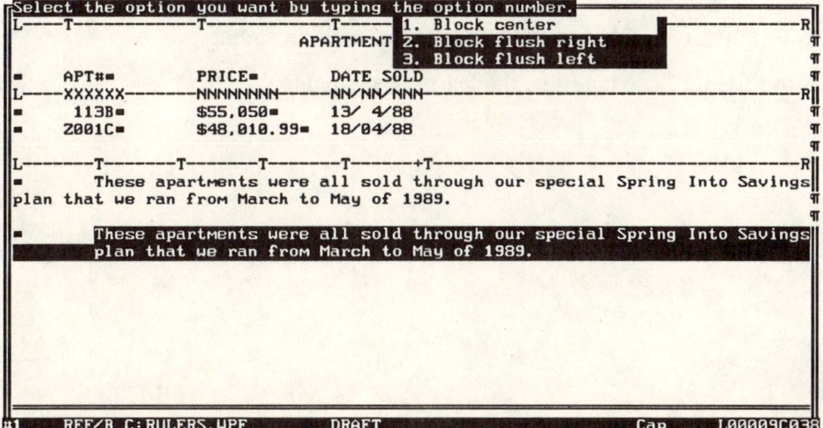

4. Type **1**. Notice that Enable centers the highlighted text.
5. Press **F10** and **Enter** and type **H3**. Notice that the text moves back to the left, and it is no longer centered. Press **Alt-F7**. The text is no longer highlighted.
6. Move the cursor to the A in "APT#." Press **Shift-F7**. Move the cursor to the second 9 in "$48,010.99" and press **Shift-F7**. Notice that a column of text is now highlighted but the ruler between the headings and numbers is not. Press **Alt-F7** and the text is no longer highlighted.
7. Move the cursor to the beginning of the first "These." Press **Alt-M**. Press **Ctrl-P** and notice that all the words to the end of the paragraph are highlighted. Press **Ctrl-W** six times. The cursor moves to the beginning of the next paragraph and then individually highlights five words. Press Ctrl-P and Enable highlights the rest of the paragraph. Type **This is a test.** Notice that the new text is also marked.
8. Press **Alt-M** to turn text marking off, and type **This is a test**. Notice that the new text is not marked.

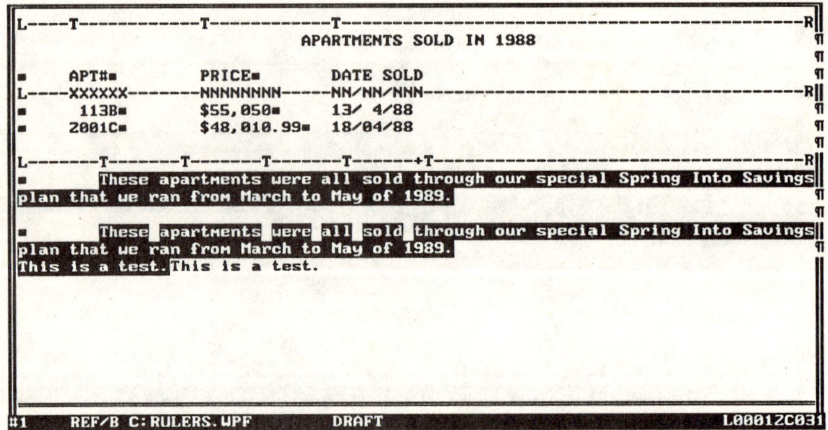

9. Press **F9** followed by **Del**, and type **MT**. The marked text is no longer highlighted.
10. Press **F10** and type **QY** to exit the document without saving.
11. Turn to Module 31 to continue the learning sequence.

Module 12
CALCULATOR

DESCRIPTION

Enable's calculator is a very flexible tool. It can sum columns of numbers, make simple calculations, or calculate complex equations using Enable's spreadsheet functions.

EQUATIONS You can use Enable's calculator function by typing a calculation, pressing F9, and typing +. (The cursor must be immediately after the equation before using the command.) The equation you typed is replaced by the result, rounded to two decimal places. You can use the number keys on the main keyboard or on the numeric keypad (press Num Lock to use the numeric keypad). If there are any blanks or $ signs, only the part of the equation to the right of the blank or $ is calculated.

COLUMNS To sum columns of numbers, mark the column as a block (place the cursor at the top left and press Shift-F7, move to the lower right and press Shift-F7 again), place the cursor in the first space after the last digit in the column, press F9, and type M+.

MATHEMATICAL OPERATORS AND FUNCTIONS The calculator uses almost all of the spreadsheet functions, such as @SIN, @AVG, @ASIN, and @EXP. These functions are described in Part 3: Spreadsheet. The following is a list of mathematical operators used by Enable's calculator.

Symbol	*Meaning*	*Example*
+	Add	1+2
–	Subtract	1–2
–	Negative Number	–1
*	Multiply	1*2
/	Divide	1/2
=	Equals	1+2=3
**	Exponent	10**5=100,000
<	Less Than	4<5
<=	Less Than or Equal To	4<=8
>	Greater Than	9>5
>=	Greater Than or Equal To	9>=5
<>	Not Equal To	1+6<>10
( )	Indicates the Order	(5+5)/4 means add 5 and 5 and divide the result by 4.

APPLICATIONS

Enable's calculator can be used in two ways. You can use it to calculate something, and then delete the calculation. For example, you want to add the prices on an invoice and don't have a calculator available; use Enable's calculator and delete the result when you have finished.

Or you can use the calculator when you are inputting the results of a calculation into the text. Type the equation, make the calculation, and continue typing.

TYPICAL OPERATION

In this activity you create a file, type a block of figures and an equation, and make the calculations. Begin at the Main Menu.

1. Create a file named MATHS. Press **Enter** when Enable prompts you to change or accept the ruler.
2. Type each of the following figures, followed by Enter, to build a column of figures: **15, 22, 33, 91, 105**. Move the cursor back onto the last 5, and press **Shift-F7**. Move the cursor to the first 1, and press **Shift-F7**. Enable marks the block.
3. Move the cursor to the first space after the last 5, press **F9** and type **M+**. Enable sums the numbers in the column and places the result, 266, immediately after the block.
4. Press **Enter** twice and type **$(133+91)*(10x2)**. Press **F9** and type **+**. Enable displays "Error in formula" in the status line. Press **Enter**, move the cursor back to the x between 10 and 2, and type * over it. Move the cursor to the first space after the equation, press **F9**, and type **+**. Enable makes the calculation and replaces the equation with the result, $4,480.
5. Press **F10** and type **QY** to exit without saving.
6. Turn to Module 33 to continue the learning sequence.

Module 13
COLUMNS (MULTIPLE)

DESCRIPTION

Enable lets you put up to five columns of text across a page. Setting up multiple columns is a simple matter of placing margins in the ruler.

SETTING UP THE RULER You can set up the ruler displayed when you create the document, or (if only part of the document is going to be in multiple-column format), you can insert and modify a ruler later on. Start by placing an L where you want to put the left column's left margin. Then put an R or J for the left column's right margin. And finally, put a C on the ruler for the left margin of each subsequent column. There is no need to put right-margin markers for these subsequent columns, because each column will be the same size as the first. Enable will not let you type a C on the ruler if it is within the previous column, so you cannot accidentally overlap a column. And you cannot put a C on the ruler if it means the column will extend over the 160th column.

You can return to non-columnar format, or change the margins of the columns, by changing the ruler again.

ENTERING TEXT Type text as normal. All the text will be placed in the first column. When you have finished with the multiple-column format, insert a default ruler by pressing F10 and typing L2 (Layout;Insert default ruler).

DISPLAYING MULTIPLE-COLUMNS Change the document to final mode (F9 OD) to see the text displayed as it will print. The text is spread equally across the columns; i.e., if you have three columns and you typed 60 lines, each column will have 20 lines of text. When you change back to draft mode Enable changes the text back to single-column format, but it displays column markers, as shown in the last screen in this module.

NOTE

You can only edit the text in draft mode.

APPLICATIONS

This feature is useful for producing documents in newsletter or newspaper format. Whenever you change the text, Enable automatically readjusts the columns to put the text in its correct position.

TYPICAL OPERATION

In this activity you create a document called COLUMN, set up the ruler for two columns, type some text, and view the text in columnar format. Begin at the Main Menu.

1. Create a file called **COLUMN**.

2. When Enable displays the default ruler, put the **L** (left margin) in column 1, **J** (justified right text) in column 22, and **C** (second text column) in column 28. (Look at the right corner of the status line for the column number). Press **Enter** to accept the changes to the ruler.

3. Delete the Document Title. Type: **This is an experiment with multiple columns of text. When you type the text, in draft mode, all the text is displayed in one column; but when you change to final mode, Enable divides the text between the columns.**

4. At the end of the text, press **Enter**, press **F10**, type **L2**, and press **Enter** to insert a default ruler. Press **Enter**. Then press **F10**, press **Enter**, and type **B** to change to final mode. Your screen should look like the following screen:

```
L-------T--+----T----J-----C-----------------------------------------
Page Break═     1 ═══════════════════════════════════════════════════
                                                                    x
                                                                    x
                                                                    x
                                                                    x
This   is an experiment      column;    but when you                x
with  multiple columns       change  to final mode,
of text. When you type       Enable  divides     the
the  text,    in  draft      text    between     the                x
mode,  all the text is       columns.                               x
displayed    in     one                                             x
L-------T-------T-------T-------T------+T---------------------------R
```

5. Press **F10**, press **Enter**, and type **B** again to change back to draft mode. Your screen will look like the following screen:

```
Page Break═     1 ═══════════════════════════════════════════════════
Column # 1═══════════════════════════════════════════════════════════
This   is an experiment
with  multiple columns
of text. When you type
the  text,    in  draft
mode,  all the text is
displayed    in     one
Column # 2═══════════════════════════════════════════════════════════
column;    but when you
change to final  mode,
Enable   divides    the
text     between    the
columns.                                                            ¶
L-------T-------T-------T-------T------+T---------------------------R




#1    REF/B C:COLUMN.WPF         DRAFT                     L00011C001
```

Although the text is in one column again, notice the column-number markers below each column's text.

6. Press **F10** and type **QY** to exit the file without saving.

7. Turn to Module 30 to continue the learning sequence.

Module 14
COMMENT LINES/PAPER CLIPS

DESCRIPTION

Enable has two special tools to make documents easier to manage. Comment lines are like messages written on a piece of paper and taped to a document; they do not print, but you can see them on your screen in draft mode. Paper clips act just like the real thing. They mark a place in your text, just as you might use a paper clip to mark a page in a book. You can use a command to move the cursor to a specified paper clip.

You can make Enable display or hide comment lines and paper clips using the Screen Display command. Press F10 and type EA4 (EditOpts;Screen displays;Comments) or press F10 and type EA9 (EditOpts;Screen displays;Paper clips) to toggle the display of comments and paper clips on and off.

COMMENT LINES To place a comment line in your text, press F10, type EF (EditOpts;Insert a comment), and press Enter. Enable places the comment entry space below the cursor line and puts the cursor inside it. Type your message or comment (as long as you want, the space adds lines if you need them), and then move the cursor out of the entry space with the arrow keys. You can see the comment in draft or final mode, but Enable will not print it.

To remove a comment, place the cursor on the double line at the top of the comment and press Alt-F3.

PAPER CLIPS To place a paper clip, press F10, type EG (EditOpts;Insert a paper clip), and press Enter. Enable prompts you for a number. Type the number and press Enter and Enable places the paper clip below the cursor line and puts the cursor below the paper clip. You can place as many paper clips as you want.

> **NOTE**
>
> Enable does not check for duplicate numbers, so make sure you don't give a paper clip the wrong number.

You can see paper clips in draft or final mode, but Enable will not print them. To delete a paper clip, place the cursor on it and press Alt-F3.

Using Paper Clips To find a paper clip in a document, press F2 and type *n*MC, where *n* is the number of the paper clip. Enable places the cursor on the paper clip. If you know you only have one paper clip in the document, or if you know that you want the first one after the cursor, just press F2 and type MC.

APPLICATIONS

Comment lines are useful for leaving reminders or useful information in a file, just as you might place a note inside a book. You might leave a message to another person that will be working on the document, for example, explaining what you have done or what still remains to be done.

Paper clips help you find a section of text without remembering exactly where it is. For example, you may have left some information out of the text, meaning to find the information and add it later. Place a paper clip, and when you return to the file press F2 and type MC, and Enable will place the cursor on the paper clip.

TYPICAL OPERATION

In this activity you place a comment and a paper clip in the LETTER file created in Module 4. Begin at the Main Menu.

1. Open the file named LETTER.
2. Move the cursor to the space after the word "possible" at the end of the first paragraph. Press **F10**, type **EF**, and press **Enter**. Enable places a comment line with the cursor inside it. Type **Remember to send them the numbers.**
3. Move the cursor to the line above the name "Andrew Andrews" at the bottom of the letter. Press **F10** and type **EG**. Press **Enter**. Enable prompts you for a number. Type **1** and press **Enter** and Enable places a paper clip after the cursor line. Your screen should look like this:

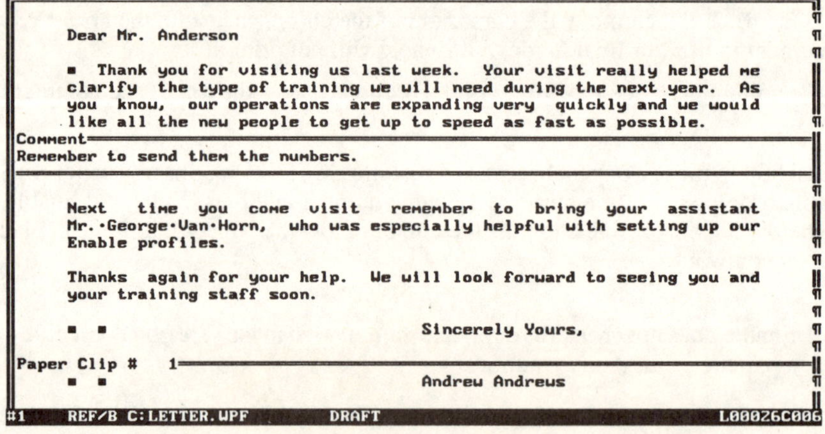

```
      Dear Mr. Anderson                                              ¶
                                                                     ¶
      ▪ Thank you for visiting us last week.  Your visit really helped me
      clarify  the type of training we will need during the next year.  As
      you  know,  our operations  are expanding very  quickly and we would
      like all the new people to get up to speed as fast as possible.  ¶
Comment══════════════════════════════════════════════════════════════
Remember to send them the numbers.
═════════════════════════════════════════════════════════════════════
                                                                     ¶
      Next   time  you  come  visit   remember  to  bring  your  assistant
      Mr.·George·Van·Horn,  who was especially helpful with setting up our
      Enable profiles.                                               ¶
                                                                     ¶
      Thanks  again for your help.  We will look forward to seeing you and
      your training staff soon.                                      ¶
                                                                     ¶
      ▪ ▪                            Sincerely Yours,                ¶
                                                                     ¶
Paper Clip #   1═════════════════════════════════════════════════════
      ▪ ▪                            Andrew Andrews                  ¶
#1    REF/B C:LETTER.WPF         DRAFT                      L00026C006
```

4. Press **Ctrl-Home** to move to the top of the file. Press **F2** and type **MC** and Enable places the cursor on the paper clip.
5. Press **F10** and type **QY** to abandon the file without saving it.
6. Turn to Module 16 to continue the learning sequence.

Module 15
CURSOR CONTROL

DESCRIPTION

Once you have opened a document you can begin word processing. First, however, you must know how to control movement of the cursor, the flashing bar that sits at the place on the screen at which text entry occurs. The following tables list the methods of moving the cursor, in order of importance.

CAUTION

Do not press Enter to move the cursor through the document. Doing so puts paragraph markers on each line, which will stop Enable reformatting the text correctly. Only use Enter at the end of a paragraph or when you need to start a new line.

SIMPLE CURSOR MOVEMENT

To Move...	*Press...*
One character left	Left Arrow
One character right	Right Arrow
One line up	Up Arrow
One line down	Down Arrow
To beginning of line	F2 Left Arrow
To end of line	F2 Right Arrow
Up half a screen	PgUp
Up a full screen	Ctrl-PgUp
Down half a screen	PgDn
Down a full screen	Ctrl-PgDn
To bottom left of screen	End
To top left of screen	Home
One word left	Ctrl-Left Arrow
One word right	Ctrl-Right Arrow
To previous page preak	F2 PgUp
To next page break	F2 PgDn
To first line of page	F2 Home
To last line of page	F2 End
To document beginning	Ctrl-Home
To document end	Ctrl-End

NOTE

Replace *n* in the folloing commands with a number. For example, F2 5 MC moves the cursor to paper clip number 5.

MORE ADVANCED CURSOR CONTROL

To Move To...	*Press...*
Beginning of sentence	F2 Up Arrow S
End of sentence	F2 S
Beginning of paragraph	F2 Up Arrow P
End of paragraph	F2 P
Margin on other side of page	F2 Tab
Next tab	Tab
Previous tab	Shift-Tab
Column number *n*	F2 *n* Spacebar
Beginning of block	F2 Up Arrow B
End of block	F2 B
Next ruler	F2 R
Previous ruler	F2 Up Arrow R
Next paper clip	F2 M C
Paper clip number *n*	F2 *n* M C
Previous paper clip	F2 Up Arrow M C

SPECIAL CURSOR MOVEMENT

To Move To...	*Press...*
Page number *n* (final mode)	F2 G *n* Enter (Replace *n* with page number)
Next comment	F2 N C
Previous comment	F2 Up Arrow N C
Next footer (draft mode)	F2 F
Previous footer (draft mode)	F2 Up Arrow F
Next footnote (draft mode)	F2 N F
Previous footnote (draft mode)	F2 Up Arrow N F
Next header (draft mode)	F2 H
Previous header (draft mode)	F2 Up Arrow H
Next index	F2 I
Previous index	F2 Up Arrow I
Next table of authorites entry	F2 M A
Previous TOA entry	F2 Up Arrow M A
Next table of contents entry	F2 T
Previous TOC entry	F2 Up Arrow T

AUTO-SCROLLING

You can use the following commands to begin the cursor moving in the chosen direction. The cursor will continue to move until it reaches the beginning or the end of the file, or until you press Ctrl-Break.

To Scroll...	*Press...*
Forward each line	Alt-F9 Down Arrow
Backward each line	Alt-F9 Up Arrow
Forward each page	Alt-F9 PgDn
Backward each page	Alt-F9 PgUp
Right each character	Alt-F9 Right Arrow
Left each character	Alt-F9 Left Arrow
To momentarily stop scrolling	Pause
To begin scrolling again	any key
To stop scrolling	Ctrl-Break

APPLICATIONS

The ability to move the cursor in any direction is vital to word processing efficiency. This separates word processors, sometimes referred to as full screen editors, from line editors. Line editors restrict cursor movement to one line at a time. An example of a line editor is the DOS EDLIN utility. To move to a different line you must type the line number and press Enter. Inserting and deleting text is difficult with a line editor.

TYPICAL OPERATION

In this activity you open the file named LETTER (created in Module 4), and practice cursor movements.

1. At the Main Menu type **UWR**. When Enable prompts you for a filename type **LETTER** and press **Enter**.
2. Press **PgDn** and notice that Enable moves the screen up so that what was the middle of the screen is now at the top of the screen, with the cursor on it. Press **Ctrl-Right Arrow**. The cursor moves to the beginning of the next word. Repeat **Ctrl-Right Arrow** until the cursor is on the first word of the second paragraph, as shown in the following screen.

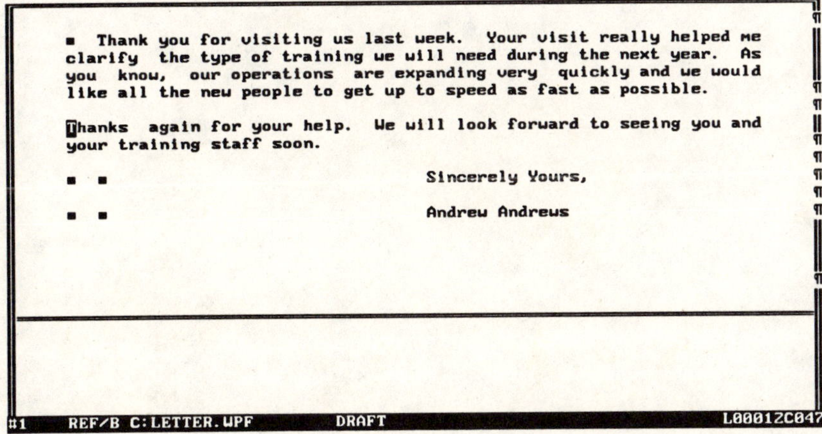

3. Press **Down Arrow**. The cursor moves down to the next line. Press **Right Arrow** five times. The cursor moves five characters to the right. Press **F2 Left Arrow** and notice the cursor move to the left side of the line. Press **F2 Right Arrow** and the cursor moves to the opposite end.
4. Experiment with the various cursor-movement commands. Start with the simple commands first. (Many of the cursor movements are not possible because the document is too small, but you will be able to try the most important ones). Notice where the cursor moves each time. Practice until you are comfortable with all the simple commands.
5. Press **F10** and type **QY** to abandon the document without saving.
6. Turn to Module 19 to continue the learning sequence.

Module 16
DATE INSERTION, AUTOMATIC

DESCRIPTION

Enable can automatically enter the date into a document. Type %DATE where you want the date to appear, and when you print the document or change to final mode, %DATE is replaced by the date you entered in the Sign On screen, or the date provided by DOS if your computer has an internal clock. Enable reformats the paragraph to fit the date in. In final mode, diamonds are used instead of spaces in the date to show that the automatic date function is being used, though the diamonds are not printed.

You can use the automatic date function in text, headers, footers, footnotes, and document titles. It cannot be used in a comment entry space. You can use this function as many times as you want in text, but only once in each header, footer, footnote, or title. You can apply text attributes to the %DATE command, and Enable will apply those attributes to the date.

The format used for the date is the one chosen in the Page Form (see Module 35, Print). The different date formats are as follows:

Standard	January 19, 1990
Military	19 January 1990
Numerical	5/19/90
European Numerical	19/5/90
Picture	Your own format, defined in the Page Form.

APPLICATIONS

The automatic date function is useful in any document, with a life of more than one day, that requires a date. For example, you can put %DATE in a form letter. Every time you print the letter the date will be correct, without any action on your part.

TYPICAL OPERATION

In this activity you use the automatic date in the document named LETTER, created in Module 4. Begin at the Main Menu.

1. Open the file named LETTER.
2. Move the cursor to the first letter of the date. Type **%DATE** over the date, and then delete the rest of the date.
3. Press **F9** and type **OD** to change to final mode. Notice that the date is replaced with today's date. The format used for the date is the one set in the Page Form.
4. Press **Alt-F10** and **Enter** to save the file. Press **F10** and **QY** to exit the file.
5. Turn to Module 12 to continue the learning sequence.

Module 17
DELETE TEXT

DESCRIPTION

Enable has a number of ways to delete text, depending on whether you want to delete characters, words, lines, or blocks of text. Text is deleted using the Delete, Backspace, Spacebar, F3, and F4 keys, and the Delete Options Menu.

DELETING WITH KEYS The following list defines the delete operations using keys:

Press...	*To Delete...*
Delete	The character at the cursor. Moves the characters from the right of the deleted character to fill the space.
Spacebar	The character at the cursor. Replaces the character with a space.
Backspace	The character at the cursor. Moves the cursor to the left. Replaces the character with a space. (The manner in which Backspace operates can be modified in your user profile. See Appendix B.)
Ctrl-Backspace	From the cursor to the beginning of the line.
F4	From the cursor to the end of the word the cursor is on, or (if the cursor is on a space) to the end of the next word.
Alt-F3	The line at the cursor position.

DELETING WITH THE DELETE OPTIONS MENU The Delete Options Menu gives more flexibility in deleting text. To display the Delete Options Menu press F10 and type D (Delete).

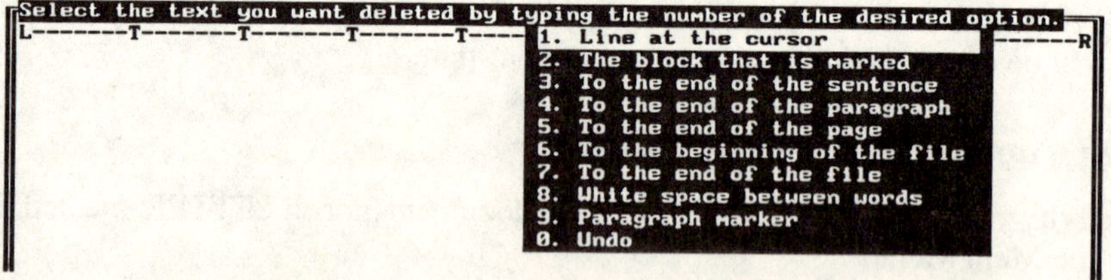

The following list explains the options:

Type...	*To Delete...*
1	The cursor line, whether it is ordinary text, a ruler, paper clip, user-defined page break, footnote, header, or footer.
2	The block that is marked. For information on setting blocks, see Module 11.
3	From the cursor to the end of the sentence (the next period, question mark, or exclamation mark that is followed by a space, quote, or right parenthesis).

4	From the cursor to the end of the next paragraph marker.
5	From the cursor to the end of the next header or page break, or to the end of the file if no page break or header is found.
6	From the cursor to the beginning of the file.
7	From the cursor to the end of the file.
8	White space between words, i.e., any spaces in excess of one space between words. You may need to use this when deleting paragraph markers if the text in the second paragraph is not moved into the correct position.
9	A paragraph marker. Combines two paragraphs into one.
0	Restores the last piece of deleted text. The text is restored at the cursor, even if that is not the original text position. This feature does not restore deleted paper clips, paragraph markers, or footnotes.

RESTORING DELETED TEXT You can restore most kinds of deleted text using option 0 in the Delete Options Menu. Also, pressing Esc will restore lines you deleted by pressing Alt-F3. The last line deleted with Alt-F3 is restored wherever the cursor is. However, you must press Esc before you delete anything else, using any other deletion method.

TIP: This feature can be used as a quick way to move a line of text. Delete the line by pressing Alt-F3, move the cursor to the destination, and press Esc. The line moves to the new location.

APPLICATIONS

The delete function is used to delete text while creating or editing documents. Deletions are most useful for correcting or removing mistakes. But you may also wish to delete a paragraph marker to combine two paragraphs (remove the blank lines and then delete the paragraph marker), or to delete excess white space after deleting text with the backspace key.

TYPICAL OPERATION

In this activity you delete text in the document named LEARN, created in Module 32. Begin at the Main Menu.

1. Open the document named LEARN. (Type **UWR**, type **LEARN**, and press **Enter**.)
2. Press **F4**. Notice that the first word is deleted.
3. Press **F10**, type **D1**, and press **Enter**. The first line is deleted.
4. Use **Down Arrow** to move the cursor to the line between the first and second paragraphs. Press **Esc** and the deleted line moves to the cursor line.
5. Move the cursor around the text and practice deleting. Press **Alt-F3** to delete a line. Press **Spacebar** to replace text with spaces. Press **Delete** to delete the character at the cursor. Press **F10**, type **D3**, press **Enter**, and type **Y** to delete from the cursor to the end of the line.
6. When you have finished practicing, press **F10** and type **QY** to exit the file without saving.
7. Turn to Module 10 to continue the learning sequence.

Module 18
DOCUMENT MODE (DRAFT/FINAL)

DESCRIPTION

Enable lets you view your document in two different ways, draft mode or final mode. Most of the time you will use draft mode, because it is easier to work in this mode. But when you want to see what your document will look like when it is printed you can change to final mode.

In draft mode the word DRAFT is displayed in the status line. Headers, footers, and footnotes are not shown in the position they actually occupy on the printed page. Enable will not show you when your text runs off the bottom of one page and onto the top of another. Top and bottom margins are not shown. Page numbers are not shown in the status line; only the line number is shown.

When you change to final mode, Enable calculates the positions of each page break and displays the page as it will appear in the printed document. Each line that cannot be typed on (such as top and bottom margins or footnote lines) has an x on the right edge of the screen. Headers, footers, and footnotes are shown in their correct positions. Also, if you have a graphics monitor and graphics mode is switched on, attributes such as italics or wide text are displayed. (Press F10 and type M34 [MCM;Screen;Graphics] to turn on Graphics mode. See Module 2 for more information.) Comments and paper clips are still shown in final form, although these features do not print. The page number is shown in the middle of the status line. The line number is also shown, but it is different from the line number in draft mode, because it includes headers and footers.

When you change back to draft mode, the page breaks that Enable inserted in the final mode are still shown.

EDITING Don't try to do much typing or editing in final mode. It is possible, but because Enable calculates the position of page breaks each time one becomes necessary, it can be very slow.

CHANGING MODES Two methods are used to change between draft and final modes. You can press F10 and type EB (EditOpts;Draft/Final) to toggle between draft and final. Or, you can use the expert command—press F9 and type OD.

APPLICATIONS

Draft mode is the most convenient mode for text input and editing, because you are not slowed down each time Enable has to calculate page breaks. Final mode is useful to check the page format before printing, to ensure it looks right, and that the page breaks all fall in the right position. For example, you may find, in final mode, that a table is broken between two pages, or that a paragraph with three lines on one page and ten on the next would look better if the page break occurred before the beginning of the paragraph. (For more information on page breaks, see Module 34.)

TYPICAL OPERATION

In this activity you change the document named LETTER, created in Module 4, to final mode. Begin at the Main Menu.

1. Open the file LETTER.
2. Press **F10** and type **E**. Enable displays the EditOpts Menu.

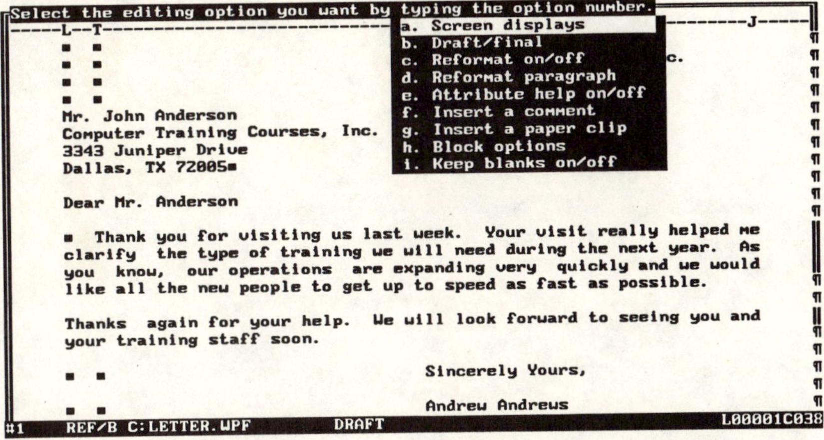

3. Type **B** (Draft/final). Press **PgUp**. Your screen should look like this:

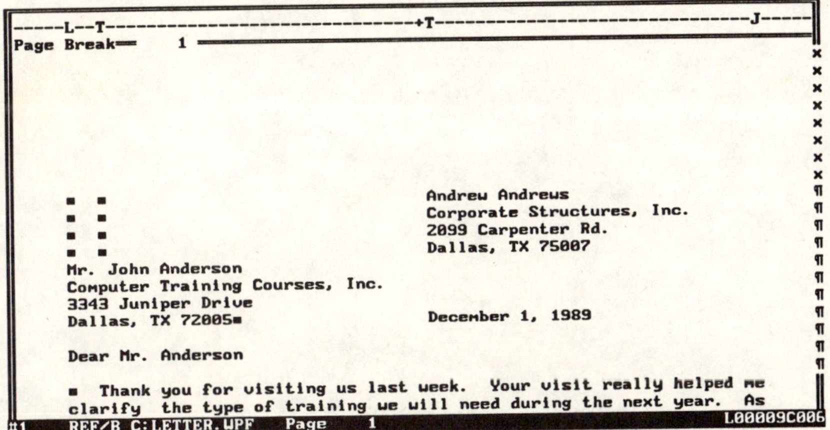

Notice that a page marker indicates the beginning of the first page. Below that, an x is shown on the right margin of the screen for each line in the header—these lines cannot be typed on. (If you move the cursor into the header and start typing, your computer beeps, and no text is entered.) Notice also that the page number is shown in the status line, and that the line number of the first line in your letter is now line 9, because Enable is now counting lines in the header. (Look at the right hand side of the status line. You will see L00009, which means line 9.)

4. Press **F9** and type **OD**. Enable changes the document back to draft mode. Notice that DRAFT is now displayed in the status line, that the page break is still shown at the top of the page, and that the first line of the address is once again line 1.
5. Press **F10** and type **QY** to exit the file without saving it.
6. Turn to Module 35 to continue the learning sequence.

Module 19
EDIT TEXT

DESCRIPTION

When you have typed a document you may need to edit it. This module describes Enable's editing features. You may overtype or insert text, insert blank lines or paragraph markers, correct transpositions, or change text from uppercase to lowercase (or vice versa). (You may also delete text—see Module 17, Delete Text.)

OVERTYPE TEXT Placing the cursor at a character and typing another character replaces the original character with the new one, unless Enable is in insert mode. The cursor is in overtype mode when you open a document file.

INSERT TEXT MODE When you press the Insert (Ins) key the cursor becomes a highlighted, flashing block. Anything you type is now inserted to the left of the cursor, moving the existing text to the right to make room. Press Ins again, and you are no longer in insert mode.

INSERT BLANK LINES If you want to adjust your document layout by moving a block of text down or adding a sentence or whole paragraph, you can insert a line. Press F3 and the text on the line below the cursor line is moved down one line, leaving a blank line below the cursor. Pressing Alt-F3 deletes a blank line.

INSERT PARAGRAPH MARKERS If you want to break a paragraph into two separate paragraphs, position the cursor at the end of the text that will be the first paragraph and press Ctrl-Enter. The text after the cursor is moved to the next line.

CORRECT TRANSPOSITIONS A common transposition is the typing of "teh" instead of "the." To correct mistakes like this, move the cursor to the character or space immediately after the mistake (in this case, put the cursor after the h). Press Ctrl-T and Enable corrects the transposition.

CHANGE TEXT FROM UPPERCASE TO LOWERCASE (AND VICE VERSA) If you want to change existing text from uppercase to lowercase, position the cursor on the first character that you want to change, and press Alt-K. If you want to convert from lowercase to uppercase, press Alt-F. A small k or f appears near the middle of the status line at the bottom of the screen. Now use one of the following segment commands to convert the desired amount of text.

Segment Commands

Ctrl-C	converts a character.
Ctrl-W	converts a word.
Ctrl-L	converts a line.
Ctrl-S	converts a sentence.
Ctrl-P	converts all text from the cursor to the next paragraph marker.
Ctrl-G	converts all text from the cursor to the end of the page.
Ctrl-B	converts all text set as a block (see Module 11).

The text you wish to convert does not have to be continuous. For example, you can use a segment command to convert a line, move the cursor down to another paragraph, and use a segment command to convert a word. When you have finished converting text, press Alt-K or Alt-F again to turn off the conversion mode. The small k or f in the status line disappears.

APPLICATIONS

Believe it or not, now and again you will make mistakes in your typing that require correcting. In addition, the ability to edit lets you change your mind about how you said something—just go in and change the words. The ability to edit is what makes even the simplest of word processing programs so superior to typewriters.

TYPICAL OPERATION

In this activity you edit the document named LEARN, created in Module 32.

1. At the Main Menu type **UWR**, type **LEARN**, and press **Enter** to open the LEARN document.
2. Press **F2** and type **S** to move the cursor to the end of the first sentence. Do it again to move to the end of the next sentence. Press **Right Arrow** to move the cursor to the space after the period.
3. Press **Ctrl-Enter** three times to add three paragraph markers. The sentence after the cursor moves down. Press **Enter** twice, and type the paragraph in the following screen, exactly as shown.

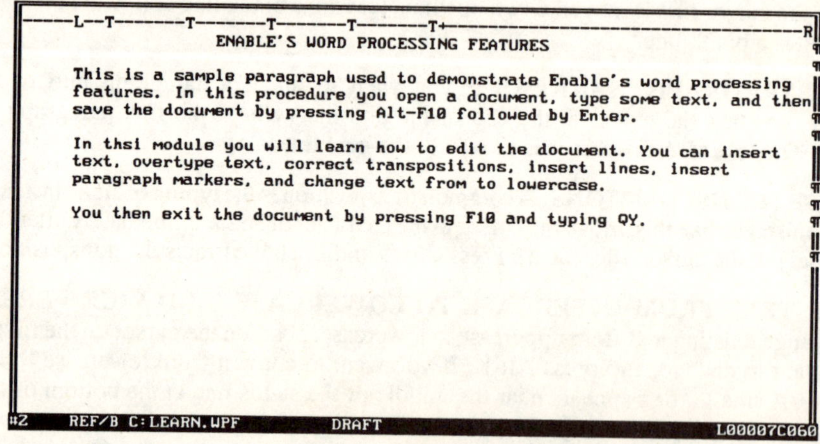

4. Press **Up Arrow** three times to move the cursor to the line above the second paragraph. Press **Ctrl-Right Arrow**, followed by **Left Arrow**, to move the cursor to the space after "thsi." Press **Ctrl-T** to correct the transposition.
5. Press **F2**, type **P**, and press **Ctrl-Left Arrow** to move the cursor to the beginning of the word "to" near the end of the second paragraph.
6. Press **Ins**. The cursor becomes a flashing, highlighted block. Type **upper**, followed by a space. This text is inserted. Press **Ins** and the cursor returns to overtype mode.

7. Move the cursor to the beginning of "upper" and type **lower**. Then move the cursor to the beginning of the original "lower" and type **upper**.

8. Press **F2**, then press **Up Arrow** and type **P**. The cursor is now at the start of the paragraph. Press **Alt-F**. Notice the small f in the status bar. Press **Ctrl-W**, **Ctrl-L**, and **Ctrl-P**. Notice that a word, then the rest of the line, and then the rest of the paragraph, converts to uppercase.

9. Move the cursor to the start of the paragraph again and press **Alt-K**. The small f in the status bar is replaced by a k. Press **Ctrl-P** and all the paragraph changes back to lowercase. Move the cursor back to the first character in the first word and overtype an uppercase I. Change the first character in the second sentence to an uppercase Y. Your text should look like the following screen.

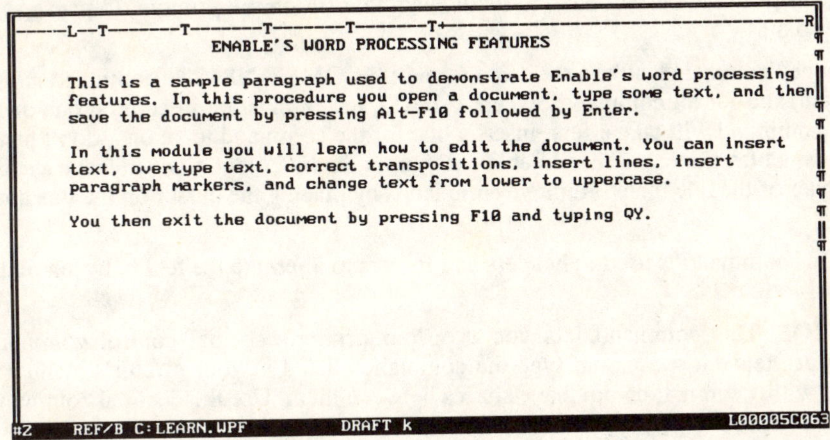

```
-----L--T-------T-------T-------T-------T+---------------------------------R
                ENABLE'S WORD PROCESSING FEATURES                          ¶
                                                                           ¶
     This is a sample paragraph used to demonstrate Enable's word processing
     features. In this procedure you open a document, type some text, and then
     save the document by pressing Alt-F10 followed by Enter.              ¶
                                                                           ¶
     In this module you will learn how to edit the document. You can insert
     text, overtype text, correct transpositions, insert lines, insert
     paragraph markers, and change text from lower to uppercase.           ¶
                                                                           ¶
     You then exit the document by pressing F10 and typing QY.             ¶
                                                                           ¶

#Z    REF/B C:LEARN.WPF            DRAFT k                        L00005C063
```

10. Press **Alt-F10** and **Enter** to save the file. Press **F10** and type **QY** to exit the file.

11. Turn to Module 17 to continue the learning sequence.

Module 20
EMBEDDED PRINT COMANDS

DESCRIPTION

Embedded print commands provide special features that operate when you print a file. You can tell Enable to print the current date, to include another file in the printout, to pause at a specific point, and so on.

The embedded commands all use the same format: %COMMAND. The command name must be in uppercase, and for all commands except %DATE the % must be in column one of the line in which the command will take effect. Insert a line for the command to sit on—don't just place the command on a blank line, because Enable will ignore the line; it won't even leave a space. Leave the remainder of the line blank. Remove commands by placing the cursor on the line and pressing Alt-F3.

%ALT This command is used in headers and footers to alternate the text between odd and even pages. See Module 25.

%CONTROL This command lets you use your printer's special control commands. Type %CONTROL, leave a space, and type the commands listed in your printer's manual. Separate commands with a comma; do not leave spaces between them. Use the decimal command, not the hexadecimal. For example, if you have an Epson LX810, typing %CONTROL 71,78 will select double strike mode and set skip-over-perforation mode.

%DATE This command inserts the current date in the text. See Module 16, Date Insertion, Automatic.

%FNUM This command resets the footnote sequence. See Module 23, Footnotes.

%INCLUDE This tells Enable to print another file at the command point, and to then continue printing the original file. This feature is explained in the modules on Indexing and Table of Contents.

After the command, leave a space and type the filename and extension; for example, "%INCLUDE Letter.wpf". If the included file has a %INCLUDE command that command is ignored. Enable will keep table of contents and index entries from the included file, so a new table of contents or index can be compiled. If the %INCLUDE command is placed in a footer, header, or footnote, the included file's footers, headers, and footnotes take precedence over those of the original file.

NOTE

> The last ruler in the included file has an effect on the original file when printing continues. If necessary, place a new ruler immediately after the %INCLUDE command.

%LANDSCAPE and %PORTRAIT These commands control the way text is printed on a page. Portrait is the standard format, with the page placed so that it is taller than it is wide (11" high and 8.5" wide, for example). Landscape mode is the other way around (8.5" high and 11" wide).

This feature may also be controlled by the Printer Orientation Mode in the Print Form, but the % command overrides it. Not all printers can print in landscape mode.

%LINES This command adjusts the number of lines per inch. See Module 29, Line Spacing.

%PAGES and %PAGEE These provide a conditional page break. See Module 34, Page Break.

%PAUSE This tells Enable to stop printing. You can then adjust the printer (change the daisy wheel or print format, for example). You can add a comment to the %PAUSE command. Leave a space and type the comment (no more than one line); before the printer stops, Enable prints the comment. To begin printing again, press Enter.

%TABS Commands These commands allow you to correctly align text when using special attributes that change the size of the text. See Module 10, Align Text.

%UNI ON and %UNI OFF These commands turn unidirectional printing on and off. In unidirectional printing, the printhead only prints from left to right, providing better alignment of vertical lines and graphics printing. Bidirectional printing, the normal method, is quicker. The Print Form's Unidirectional Printing option also controls this, but the % command overrides it.

GRAPH COMMANDS

Enable has several commands used for printing graphs that have been imported into a word processing document (see Module 93).

%DENSITY *n* This command sets the density with which your printer will print a graph, where *n* is the density you want; 1 is single, 2 is double, 3 is triple, and 4 is quadruple density. To reset graphs to the density used when the graph was originally created, type %DENSITY 0. If you set a density that your printer does not support, the graph will print in the next lower density.

%GR COLOR *n* This command sets the color with which your graph will be printed, where *n* is 0 (black and white), 1 (color), 2 (shades), 3 (positive photo image), or 4 (negative image). You can combine commands by using %GR COLOR 0, 1, or 2 on one line and %GR COLOR 3 or 4 on the next line.

%GR LANDSCAPE or %GR PORTRAIT These commands set the graph orientation; landscape makes the graph print "sideways," with the horizontal axis along the longest side of the paper, and portrait makes the graph print the normal way, with the horizontal axis printed across the narrowest side of the paper.

APPLICATIONS

The embedded commands, especially the %CONTROL command, provide a host of printer features. The Epson LX810 mentioned previously, for example, has almost 75 features that can be used with the %CONTROL command. Read your printer manual for information on its commands.

TYPICAL OPERATION

For examples of typical operations, see Modules 16 and 25.

Turn to Module 5 to continue the learning sequence.

Module 21
FILE SUMMARY/FILE DIRECTORY

DESCRIPTION

The Word Processing Top Line Menu provides access to a file summary screen and a file directory.

FILE SUMMARY SCREEN The file summary screen provides information about a file. To display this screen, press F10 and type M21 (MCM;Files;File Summary). The summary shows the name of the file and which disk directory it is filed in, the document title you typed at the top of the file, the date the file was created and the date it was last saved (Date Revised), the approximate number of words in the file, the total number of lines in the file, and the total number of pages in the file.

The file summary screen only shows you information from the last time you saved the file, so if you have been editing the file for a few minutes without saving, and if the automatic save feature has not automatically saved the file, some of the information in the file will not be correct (the word count and number of lines, for example). The pages are only counted when you change from draft to final mode, so if you haven't done that, even if you have printed the document, the Total pages field will show 0.

The file summary can also be printed, on a separate sheet of paper, when you print the document (see Module 35 for more information).

FILE DIRECTORY Press F10 and type M22 (MCM;Files;File Directory) to display the file directory. You can do a number of things with the files, such as copying, marking, sorting, and renaming. See Module 114 for information on using the file directory.

APPLICATIONS

The file summary offers a quick way to view information about a document, or to provide information with a printout. It is particularly useful when you are writing a document that has size constraints. For example, you need a five-page sales letter, or are writing a 2000-word magazine article. If you want to check how many pages you have written so far, change to final mode and then back to draft mode (press F9 OD twice) and then look at the file summary screen. If you want to check the word-count, save the document (press Alt-F10 and press Enter) and then look at the file summary screen.

TYPICAL OPERATION

In this activity you view the file summary screen of the file named LETTER, created in Module 4. Begin at the Main Menu.

1. Open the document named LETTER.
2. Press **F10** and type **M21** to view the file summary screen.

```
                File Summary
File:            C:\ENABLE\LETTER.WPF
Document Title:  This is the letter to Mr. Anderson about the EnableOA traini
Date Created:    12/01/89
Date Revised:    12/15/89
Approx. Words:   134
Total Lines:     27
Total Pages:     0
              Press ESC to leave summary screen

    Dear Mr. Anderson

    ■ Thank you for visiting us last week.  Your visit really helped me
    clarify  the type of training we will need during the next year.  As
    you  know,  our operations  are expanding very  quickly and we would
    like all the new people to get up to speed as fast as possible.

    Thanks  again for your help.  We will look forward to seeing you and
    your training staff soon.

                                    Sincerely Yours,
    ■ ■

                                    Andrew Andrews
    ■ ■
#1   REF/B C:LETTER.WPF      DRAFT                         L00001C006
```

3. Press **Esc** to remove the file summary.
4. Press **F10** and type **QY** to abandon the file without saving.
5. Turn to Module 22 to continue the learning sequence.

Module 22
FIND/REPLACE/MARK TEXT

DESCRIPTION

Enable lets you search a document for a specified word, letter, number, symbol, or string of characters. When it finds the text it places the cursor on the first character. You can also make Enable mark the text when it finds it, or even automatically replace the text. The Find options are selected through the Find Options Menu.

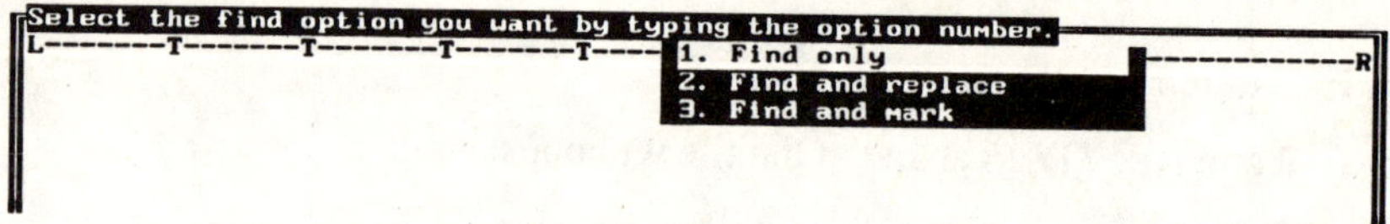

FIND ONLY Pressing F10 and typing F1 (Find;Find only) selects Find Only. Enable prompts you for the text you want to search for. Type the text and press Enter. Enable then gives you the option of accepting or changing several options. Press Enter to begin the search without changing options. Type C to change the options. Enable displays a series of choices and prompts. To select an option, type the first character of the option, or move the highlight with the arrow keys and press Enter.

Case: Ignore If you accept the options, Enable will search for the text without regard to its case. For example, if you type "car" and Enable finds "CAR," it will stop. If you decide to change the options, you could select "As entered;" Enable would then ignore "CAR."

From: Current Accepting the options starts the search from the current cursor location. The alternatives are "Top" and "Bottom." In other words, you could start searching from the top or the bottom of the document.

To: Bottom If you accept the options, Enable will search till it reaches the bottom of the document. This works in conjunction with the "From" option. You could choose to search from the cursor position to the top of the document, from the top to the cursor position, or from the bottom to the cursor position, for example.

Col: All If your document has multiple columns (see Module 13), you can choose to search all or just selected columns. Enable prompts you for the From and To column numbers (the columns are numbered 1 to 5, from the left to right). Type in the column numbers or press Enter to select All.

When you have finished selecting your options, Enable searches for the first occurrence of the specified text. If Enable finds the text, it places the cursor on the first character. If Enable is unable to find the specified text, your computer beeps.

Continue the Search If you want Enable to continue searching for the same text after it has found an occurrence, press F5.

Wild Cards You can use wild card characters when searching for a word that you are not quite sure of, or if you are searching for several similar words. The question mark (?) can be used to replace a single character. For example, if you are searching for two serial numbers in your text, "19645023" and "19645024," you can search for both at the same time by typing "1964502?" when Enable prompts you for the search-string.

Use the dollar sign ($) to replace several characters. For example, typing "1964$" will find 19645023, 19645024, 19648, 19648702, and so on. Typing "$nish$" will find "finish," "garnished," and "finished." The dollar sign can be used to replace up to nine characters.

You can specify how many characters have been replaced by the dollar sign. For example, typing "2$nish$2" tells Enable that the first two and the last two characters are missing, so Enable would ignore "garnished" and "Finnish." (Punctuation is not included in the character-count, so "finish," is still found, because Enable doesn't count the comma as one of the 2 dollar-characters. Quotation marks are also ignored.)

TIP: When you are using Find, turn the insert mode on (press Ins). This makes the cursor easier to see when Enable finds the text you are searching for.

FIND AND REPLACE This option lets you replace the text once you have found it. Select this option by pressing F10 and typing F2 (Find Options;Find and replace). Most of the procedure is the same as Find Only. After you have typed in the text you want to search for, Enable prompts you to Enter Replace String. Type in the new text, and then continue as described before. The options already described remain the same, but another option is available.

Occurrences If you accept the options, Enable will search for and replace the first occurrence of the specified string. You may change the number of occurrences, so that, for example, Enable replaces the first five or ten occurrences. After Enable has replaced the number of occurrences you specified, you can press F5 to replace the next set of occurrences.

Verify Replacement If you want to see the text to confirm that it should be replaced, type 0 in the occurrences field. Enable will find the word and place the cursor on it. Press F5 if you want to continue searching without changing the text. Press F6 if you want to replace it; the text is changed and the cursor placed at the end of the text. To continue, press F5 or F6.

FIND AND MARK You can find and mark text using this procedure (see Module 11 for more information on marked text). Press F10 and type F3 (Find Options;Find and mark). The procedure is exactly the same as Find and Replace, except that instead of being replaced, the text is marked.

APPLICATIONS

These features are useful in many situations. If you discover that you have been using the wrong spelling of a word or name, you can quickly replace the mistake with the correct version. You could use Find and Replace to quickly personalize a letter without using mail merge, by replacing one name with another. You can search through a long document for a particular passage that you want to edit or print. Or you can mark text that you want to move. The possible applications for this feature are almost unlimited.

TYPICAL OPERATION

In this activity you find, mark, and replace text in the document named LEARN, created in Module 32. Begin at the Main Menu.

1. Open the file called LEARN.
2. Press **PgDn**. Press **F10** and type **F2** to select Find and replace. Enable prompts you to Enter String to Find. Type **procedure**.

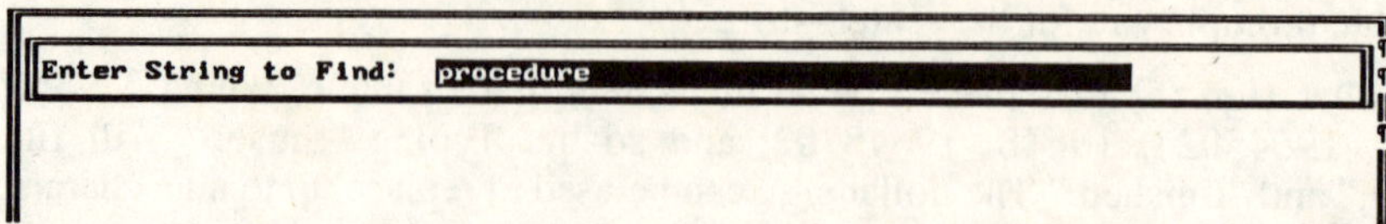

3. Press **Enter**. Enable prompts you to Enter Replace String. Type **operation** and press **Enter**. Enable displays the options.

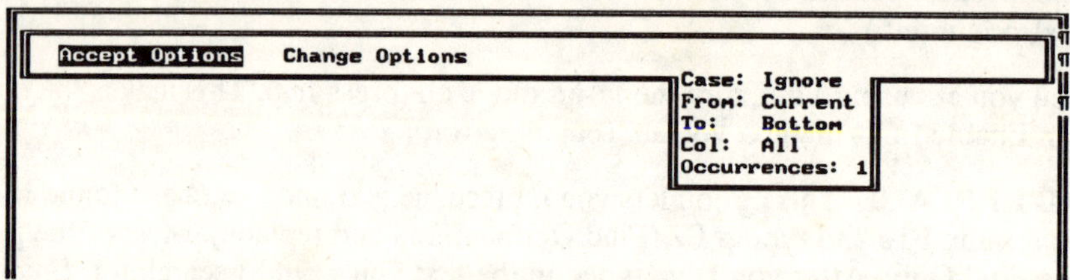

4. Type **C** to select Change Options. Enable displays "Case: Ignore As Entered." Press **Enter** to select Ignore. Enable displays "Find From: Top Current Bottom." Type **T** to select Top. Enable displays "To: Top Current Bottom."
5. Press **Enter** to select Bottom. Enable displays the "Find From Column" field. Press **Enter** to select all columns, and Enable displays "To Column:" Press **Enter** again. Enable now prompts you for the Number of Occurrences. Type **0** and press **Enter**.
6. Enable finds the word and puts the cursor on the first letter. Press **F6** and Enable replaces the word procedure with operation. Press **F5** to continue, and your computer beeps because the word does not occur anywhere else.
7. Press **F10**, and type **F3** to select Find and Mark. When Enable prompts you to Enter String to Find, type **this** and press **Enter.** Type **C** to select Change Options. When Enable displays the Case: options, press **Right Arrow** to select As Entered.
8. Press **Enter**. Enable displays the Find From: options. Type **T** to select Top. Enable displays the To: options. Press **Enter** to select Bottom. Press **Enter** twice to ignore the Column options. When Enable prompts you for the Number of Occurrences, type **10** and press **Enter**.
9. Enable searches the file and marks two occurrences of the word, this. Notice that the first occurrence of the word is not marked, because it is spelled with a capital T.
10. Press **F10** and type **QY** to abandon the document without saving.
11. Turn to Module 29 to continue the learning sequence.

Module 23
FOOTNOTES

DESCRIPTION

Enable has an excellent footnote capability. Footnotes are notes relating to your text that appear at the bottom of each page or at the end of the file. Enable has a very flexible system that allows you to design exactly the type of footnotes you need. There are two stages in creating footnotes; inserting footnotes in your text, and modifying the footnote layout.

> **NOTE: REFERENCE NUMBERS VS. FOOTNOTE SYMBOLS**
> You must understand the difference between *footnote reference numbers* and *footnote symbols*. Reference numbers are placed in the text when you insert a footnote; they are not printed in your document. Footnote symbols may be numbers or characters, and appear in your text and at the beginning of a footnote when you print the document, replacing the reference number.

INSERTING FOOTNOTES When you reach a place in your text that needs a footnote, press F10, type L8 (Layout;Create a footnote), and press Enter. Enable inserts a footnote reference number at the cursor position and a footnote marker below the cursor line, and places the cursor in the marker.The marker looks similar to an index marker or header. The reference number is inserted between diamond characters; see the following screen.

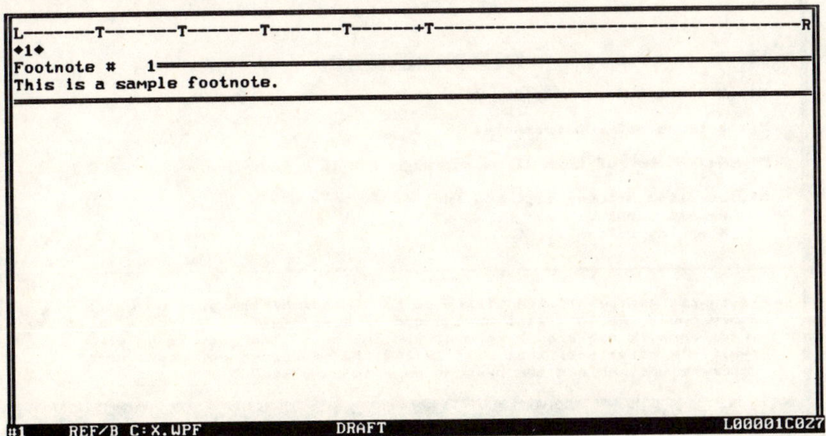

NOTE
You cannot insert a footnote while in final mode.

The footnotes are numbered from 1 to 1000, in the order in which you create them. This means that they may not be numbered in the order in which they appear in your text; however, you are given the opportunity to make Enable resequence the numbers when you print or go to final mode, so that the footnote reference numbers appear in numerical order in your text. (This is explained later in this module.)

Entering Footnote Text Begin typing the footnote text at the left margin, or, if you want to be sure that there will be a space between the footnote symbol and the text, leave a space first. Type until you've finished; the footnote marker will add extra lines if you need them. When you have finished, use the arrow keys to move the cursor out of the footnote.

Rulers in Footnotes You can insert multiple rulers in footnotes, and (unlike headers and footers) each footnote's rulers are independent of all other footnotes. It is important to remember though, that the first line of a footnote is always controlled by the document's default ruler. If you insert a ruler at the top of the footnote it affects the second and subsequent lines, not the first one.

COPYING FOOTNOTES To copy a footnote, place the cursor on the first diamond of the reference, press F7, move the cursor to the second diamond, and press F7 again. Then place the cursor in the position that you want the copy to appear, press F10 and type C (Copy), and press Enter twice, or use the Expert command, F9 BC. Enable will assign the new footnote the correct reference number.

DELETING FOOTNOTES To delete a footnote, place the cursor on the double line at the top of the footnote marker and press Alt-F3. Then delete the footnote reference number, and the diamond symbols on either side by using any word processing deletion tool (Del, backspace, spacebar, etc.) or just type new text over it.

MODIFYING THE FOOTNOTE LAYOUT The footnote layout is specified in your user profile (see Appendix B), but you can also modify it for a particluar file while you are creating or editing it. Press F10 and type LC (Layout;Modify footnote layout). Enable displays the following screen, the first of three:

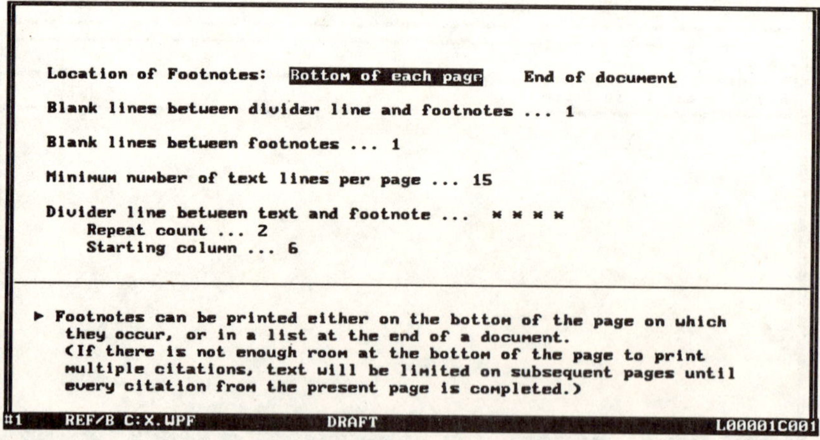

You can modify the layout by pressing Down Arrow to move to each option and typing in a value. You can exit this screen without saving by pressing Esc (the cursor backs-up to the beginning of the screen and then exits, so you may have to press Esc several times), but if you want to save your changes you must press Down Arrow until you have moved all the way through all three screens. Select each option by the first letter of the option, or by moving the cursor to the option and pressing Down Arrow. The following is a list of the options in the first footnote modification page.

Location of Footnotes: Bottom of each page/End of Document You have your choice of positioning footnotes at the bottom of the page or the end of the document.

Blank lines between divider line and footnotes Enable places a dividing line between the main text and the footnotes. The value you input here determines how many blank lines appear after that dividing line.

Blank lines between footnotes Input the number of blank lines to appear between each footnote.

Minimum Number of text lines per page Some long footnotes may be continued on the next page. You can set the minimum number of lines of main text that should appear on the next page if this happens. However, if the footnote is very long, and another footnote is inserted after it on the same page, Enable overrides this minimum number of lines and uses the entire page for the footnote. (This option is not applicable if you chose to put the footnotes at the end of the document.)

If you set the minimum to too large a number you may cancel footnotes entirely, so if you have problems try reducing the lines per page. Of course if the number you enter is too low (one or two lines), Enable's "widow and orphan control" feature will not work correctly.

Divider line between text and footnotes You can tell Enable with which character to draw a dividing line between the main text and the footnotes. For example, you could use + signs or a hard hyphen (Alt-hyphen, -). Type in a string of up to 30 characters.

Repeat Count You can tell Enable how many times to repeat the string of characters in the divider line. For example, if you typed a string of five characters and you input a repeat count of 3, Enable will print a line 20 characters long; the first string of five, plus three repetitions.

Starting Column Tell Enable which column to begin printing the dividing line.

The following screen shows the second modify-footnote page.

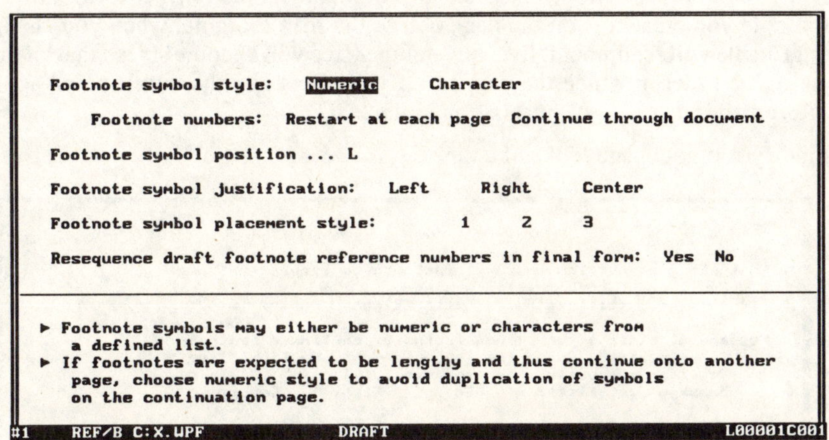
```
Footnote symbol style:    Numeric    Character

   Footnote numbers:  Restart at each page  Continue through document

Footnote symbol position ... L

Footnote symbol justification:   Left    Right    Center

Footnote symbol placement style:      1    2    3

Resequence draft footnote reference numbers in final form:  Yes  No

► Footnote symbols may either be numeric or characters from
   a defined list.
► If footnotes are expected to be lengthy and thus continue onto another
   page, choose numeric style to avoid duplication of symbols
   on the continuation page.
#1   REF/B C:X.WPF        DRAFT                        L00001C001
```

Footnote Symbol Style: Numeric/Character If you want to number your footnotes, select Numeric. If you want to use characters, select Character.

Footnote numbers: Restart at each page/Continue through document This prompt only appears if you select Numeric in the preceding prompt. You may want to use the Restart option if your document has only a few, short footnotes; but if not the Continue option will be better.

List of footnote symbols This prompt only appears if you select Character in the first prompt on this page. Type the characters you want to use as footnote symbols. For example, you might type a b c d etc., or i ii iii iv etc. (Separate symbols with spaces.) Character symbols only work well if you don't have many footnotes. A symbol may be up to five characters long.

Footnote symbol position Type L to place the symbol at the left margin of the default ruler, L+*n* to begin at the margin plus *n* spaces, or L–*n* to begin at the margin minus *n* characters (where *n* is a number of spaces). Make sure you get your calculations right, or Enable may put the symbol inside the footnote itself. For example, L+10 means place the symbol in column 11.

Footnote symbol justification: Left/Right/Center This option positions the symbol on the five-character space allowed for it in the footnote. For example, if you have a one-character symbol and choose Right justify, the symbol will be preceded by four spaces; choose Left justify and the spaces are placed after the symbol; choose Center and the symbol is preceded by two spaces and followed by two. This string of five characters and spaces always starts in the first column of the footnote symbol position.

Footnote symbol placement style These options only work if you are using numeric symbols. Type 1, 2, or 3 to select one of the following styles.

1	Superscript symbols in the text and the footnote.
2	Legal style (underscored and followed by a slash), in the text and in the footnote.
3	Superscript in the text, but level with the footnote text and followed by a period.

Character footnote symbols are always superscript in both the text and the footnote.

Resequence draft footnote reference numbers in final form: Yes/No Select Yes to make Enable resequence the footnote reference numbers and footnote symbols in final form. For example, if the sixth footnote you created is on the page before the fifth footnote, when you change to final form or print Enable will renumber it five, and number five will become six, so that all the footnote numbers are in the order in which they appear. If you select No, the number first applied to the footnote will remain regardless of its position in the text.

The next modify-footnote page looks like this:

```
Footnote continuation message: footnote continues next pag
    Position of continuation message ... 1
    Message justification:    Left    Right    Center

Message at start of continued footnote: continued footnote
    Place message: Above the footnote        On first line
    Position of continuation message ... 1
    Message justification:    Left      Right      Center

► The message will appear on the last available footnote line.
  Only the first 80 characters entered will be retained.

#1    REF/B C:X.WPF              DRAFT                    L00001C001
```

The options on this page only have an effect if your footnotes are going to be positioned at the bottom of the page.

Footnote continuation message Type the message, up to 80 characters long, that Enable will print at the end of the first page of a footnote when the footnote is continued on the next page. If you want a blank line between the footnote and the message, type a tilde (~) in the first space of the message. For example, you could type "~Turn to the next page for the rest of the footnote...." Not all 80 characters appear in the space allowed for this message on the modify-footnote page, but the message scrolls to the left as you type it.

Position of continuation message Type L to start the message at the left margin of the default ruler, L+*n* to start at the left margin plus *n* spaces, L–*n* to begin at the left margin minus *n* spaces (*n* represents a number of spaces). For example, if the left margin is in column one, L+10 means place the first character in column 11 (1 + 10). You can also type R, R+*n*, or R–*n* to place the message in relation to the right margin, but make sure you get your calculations correct or you may lose some of the message.

Message justification: Left/Right/Center Select where on the previously set position the message should be placed. For example, if you selected L+20, select Center for Message justification, and have a 12-character message, the message is centered on column 20, and begins on column 15. (L+20 is column 21, minus the first half of the message, six characters, equals column 15). Selecting Right will end the message at the continuation-message position, and selecting Left will begin the message at that point.

Message at start of continued footnote Type the message you want to appear before the continued footnote. The same rules apply as for the first message (described earlier in this module), except that you can insert a blank line between the message and the footnote by typing a tilde (~) after the message instead of before.

Place message: Above the footnote/On first line Select where the message appears. Selecting On first line places the message on the same line as the first line of the continued footnote, followed by a space and the beginning of the footnote. If you select this option, a tilde placed at the end of the message has no effect.

Position of continuation message This operates the same as the previous position of continuation, explained earlier. Type L, L+*n*, L–*n*, R, R+*n*, or R–*n*, where *n* is a number of spaces. Remember, however, that if the message is on the same line as the footnote the message position also affects the position of the beginning of the continuation.

Message justification: Left/Right/Center These choices work the same as for the previous message justification, explained earlier.

NOTE

After changing the footnote layout you must save the file, or the footnote changes are not saved.

DISPLAYING FOOTNOTES IN FINAL MODE When you change to final mode Enable places the footnotes in the correct position; either at the bottom of each page or the end of the document. Both the footnote reference number and the footnote symbol precede the footnote. The footnote reference number is on the first line after the divider line (or after the blank line if you have specified one). The reference numbers start at 1 and go up to 1000. (If you chose Yes at the "Resequence draft footnote reference numbers in final form" the numbers will be in the order in which the footnotes appear in the text, but if you chose No, the numbers are in the order in which you inserted the foonotes.) Even if you told Enable to restart numbering on each page, the reference numbers will continue through the document (Enable will make the footnote symbols restart though). The reference number also appears in the text where you inserted the footnote.

On the next line, before the footnote, is the footnote symbol. This is the actual symbol that will appear when you print the document. It is either a number or a character (see "Footnote symbol style: Numeric/Character" earlier in this module). If it is a number and you have chosen to continue footnote numbers throughout the document, it will be the same number as the footnote reference number, but if you chose to restart numbering on each page, after the first page of footnotes the reference number and the symbol will be different.

When you switch back to draft mode, or print the document (which will automatically change the file back to draft mode), Enable places all the footnotes at the top of the file, in the order in which they were created, not in the order in which they appear in the text. Footnote display can be toggled on and off by pressing F10 and typing EA5 (EditOpts;Screen displays;Footnotes).

PRINTING FOOTNOTES When you print the file Enable places the footnotes in the correct position. The reference number is not printed; only the footnote symbol appears. The reference number in the text at the footnote insertion point is not printed either, being replaced by the footnote symbol.

RESETTING THE FOOTNOTE SYMBOL SEQUENCE You can reset the sequence of the footnote symbols by using an embedded print command. Type "%FNUM *n*" immediately after a user-defined page break, where *n* is the number of the first footnote symbol on the page, and press Enter. The % must be in column one, and the command must be on its own line. If you don't specify *n*, Enable starts with 1. %FNUM only works on one page. If the next page doesn't have a %FNUM command, the symbol sequence continues without resetting, using the footnote numbers setting. This feature only works if you are using Numeric footnote symbols. For more information on embedded commands, see Module 20.

APPLICATIONS

Footnotes are used in documents that require extra explanatory text. Rather than clutter the text with detailed book references or explanations, such information can be put in footnotes at the end of the document or at the bottom of the page. Enable's footnote feature makes this easy to do. Even if you modify the document later, Enable can readjust the footnote positions and keep everything in its correct sequence.

TYPICAL OPERATION

In this activity you insert footnotes in the file named LEARN, created in Module 32. Begin at the Main Menu.

1. Open the file named LEARN.
2. Move the cursor to the space after "F10" in the last line. Press **F10**, type **L8**, and press **Enter** to insert a footnote. Enable puts a reference number (1) with two diamonds in the cursor space, and inserts a footnote marker. Press the **Spacebar** and type **See Module 9 for information about the Top Line Menu.**
3. Using the arrow keys, move the cursor to the space after "Alt-F10" in the third line of the first paragraph. Press **F9** and **Ins**, and type **NF** (the expert command) to insert a footnote. Press the **Spacebar** and type **See the appendices for information on expert commands.**

4. Press **F10** and type **LC** to display the first modify-footnote page. On the first line type **E** to select End of Document. On the second line type **1** to put one line between the text and the footnote.

5. Press **Down Arrow**. Type **3** on the next line, to put three lines between the footnotes, and press **Down Arrow** twice. Type **++++++++++** for the divider line between text and footnotes, and press **Down Arrow**. Type **2** on the next line, to repeat the divider line twice.

6. Press **Down Arrow** and type **5** to start the divider in the fifth column. Press **Down Arrow** and Enable displays the next page.

7. Type **N** to select Numeric footnote symbols. Press **Down Arrow** once to move the cursor to the Footnote-symbol-position line. Type **L** to put the symbol in the left column, and press **Down Arrow**.

8. Type **L** to select left justification and type **1** to select superscript footnote symbols. Type **Y** to select the resequencing of footnote reference numbers; Enable displays the next page. Press **Down Arrow** seven times to move through this page; Enable displays your document again.

9. Press **F9** and type **OD** to change to final mode, and press **Ctrl-End** to move to the end of the document. Your screen should look like this:

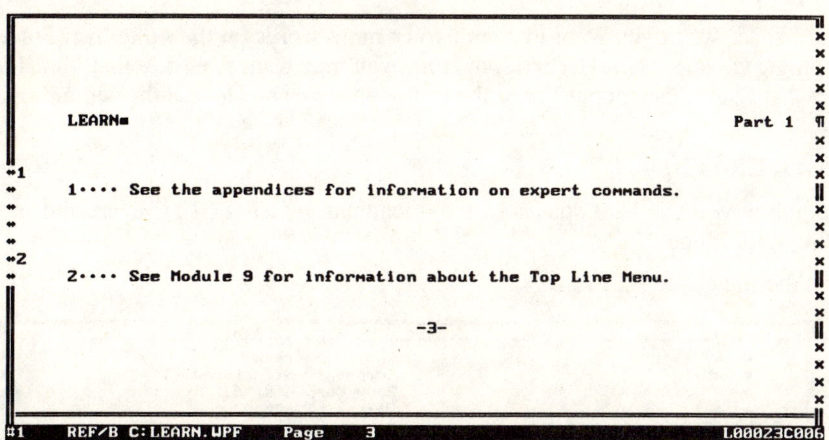

10. Notice that Enable has reordered the footnote reference numbers, that the reference numbers are followed by four diamonds (i.e., they are left justified in a 5-character field), and that there are three spaces between the bottom of the first footnote and the reference number of the next.

11. Press **Alt-F2** to print the file. Notice that the reference numbers are not printed; they are replaced by the footnote symbols (superscript numbers).

12. Press **F10** and type **QY** to exit without saving.

13. Turn to Module 14 to continue the learning sequence.

Module 24
HARD SPACES

DESCRIPTION

You can use a hard space to make sure that a series of words remains on the same line. In some ways Enable regards the hard space as an alphanumeric character, although it will not hyphenate a phrase with hard spaces. Instead of pressing the Spacebar after typing the first word, press Alt-= (Alt-Equal key) and then type the second word. If the phrase extends past the right margin, Enable keeps the two words together by pushing them both onto the next line. If the phrase is not at the end of a line, but is moved to the end of a line later on, when you reformat the document, Enable moves it to the next line to keep it all together. Enable displays a small diamond instead of leaving a space, but when you print the document Enable leaves a space; it doesn't print the diamond.

APPLICATIONS

Use the hard space when you want to keep two or more words on the same line. For example, if you are typing a name, such as Herbert Van Horn, you may want to ensure that Van Horn remains together, so that Enable cannot put Van at the end of one line and Horn at the beginning of the next.

TYPICAL OPERATION

In this prodedure you use hard spaces in the document named LETTER, created in Module 4. Begin at the Main Menu.

1. Open the file called LETTER.

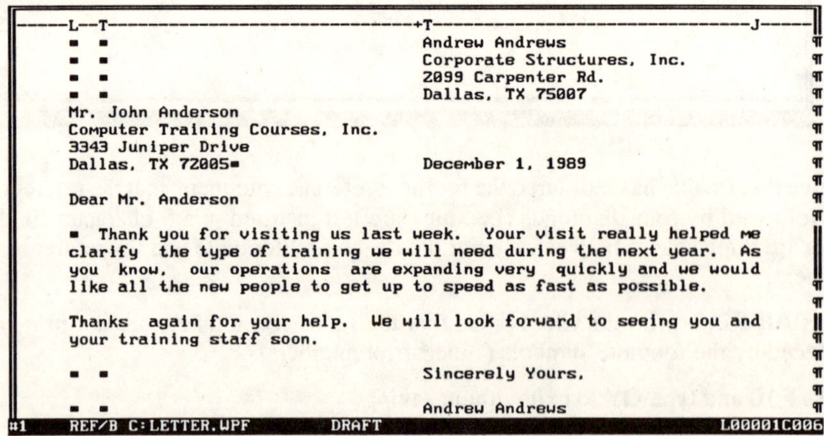

2. Move the cursor to the space after the word "possible," and press **Ctrl-Enter** twice, to insert two paragraph markers, and then press **Enter** twice. Type **Next time you come visit remember to bring your assistant Mr.** Press **Alt-=**, type **George**, press **Alt-=**, type **Van**, press **Alt-=**, and type **Horn, who was especially helpful with setting up our Enable profiles.**

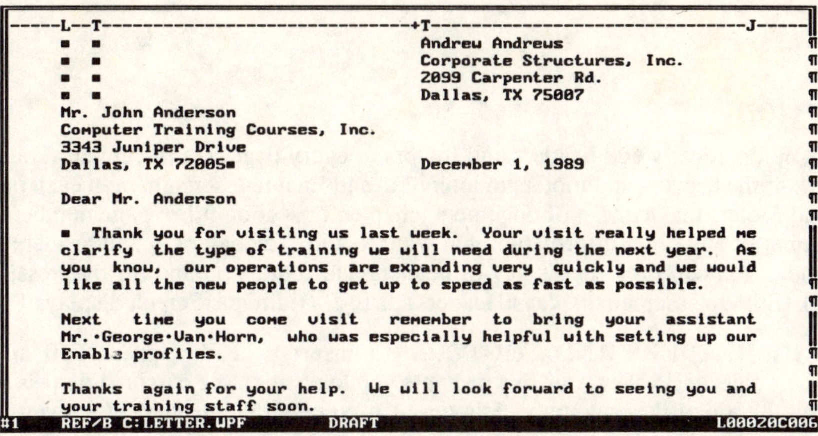

Notice that Enable moved the entire name onto the next line.

3. Press **Alt-F10** and press **Enter** to save the file. Press **F10** and type **QY** to exit the file.
4. Turn to Module 43 to continue the learning sequence.

Module 25
HEADERS AND FOOTERS

DESCRIPTION

Enable can automatically add headers and footers to every page in a document. You tell Enable what you want the headers and footers to look like, and Enable inserts them in each page for you. Headers and footers may consist of document, chapter, or section titles; page numbers; dates; the author's name; or any other information you want to add. You can only add headers and footers in draft mode. You can turn the display of headers and footers on and off by pressing F10 and typing EA1 (EditOpts;Screen displays;Headers) or EA2 (EditOpts;Screen displays;Footers).

INSERTING HEADERS AND FOOTERS To insert a header, press F10 and type L5 (Layout;Insert a header). The status line prompts you to position the cursor and press Enter. Place the cursor at the top of the page on which you want to begin the header. When you press Enter, Enable inserts a Header-and-Page-Break symbol below the cursor position and places the cursor inside it. Type the text you want printed in the header, and then use the arrow keys to move the cursor out of the header. When you change to final mode or print the document, this text will appear at the top of every page after the new page break, until another header is inserted.

To insert a footer, place the cursor under the header, or near the bottom of the first page on which you want to begin the footer. Press F10, type L6 (Layout;Insert a footer), and press Enter. Enable displays a footer below the cursor position and places the cursor inside it (Enable does not put a page break with the footer). Type the text you want printed in the footer, and then use the arrow keys to move the cursor out of the footer. When you change to final mode or print the document, all subsequent pages will contain the footer text at the bottom of the page.

The following screen shows a header and a footer together at the top of a file.

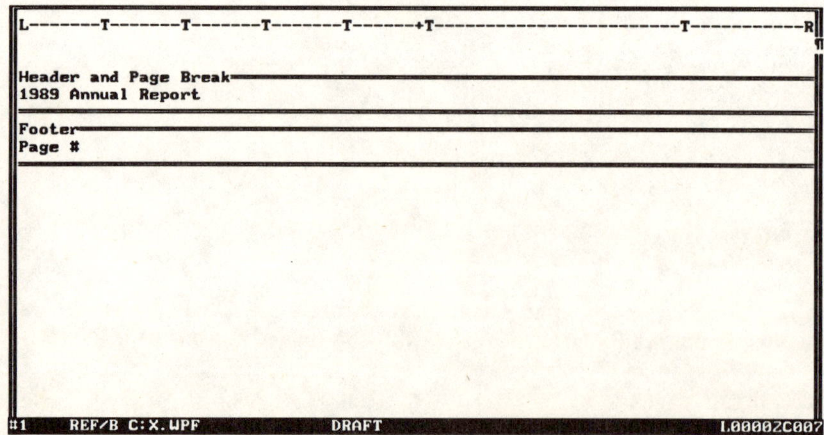

NOTE

You can place a footer anywhere on the page if you wish—when you change to final mode or print the document Enable will place the footer at the bottom of the page. However, you may find it less confusing to put the footer with the header or at the bottom of the page.

EDITING HEADERS AND FOOTERS You can edit text in the headers and footers by moving the cursor into the entry space and using any of Enable's editing tools.

RULERS IN HEADERS AND FOOTERS You can apply a ruler to the top line of a header or footer. Place the cursor on the double line at the top of the header or footer and press Alt-F6. The text and double line disappear and are replaced by a ruler line. Set up the ruler as usual (see Module 12). Press Enter and the ruler disappears and is replaced by the text and double line.

A ruler applied to a header applies to every header in the document, both before and after the header you set it up in. The same goes for footers; all footers are controlled by the same ruler.

PAGE NUMBERS Enable has several different types of page numbers you can insert in a header or footer. Typing # will make Enable insert the page number in that position. You can precede that symbol with "Page" or a section number. For example, if you type "2 - #" Enable will print "2 - 8" in that position on page 8.

If you want to start page numbering with any number other than one, type "*#=n*" where *n* is the page number you want to start with. For example, if you type "2 - #=10," Enable will print "2 - 18" on page 8.

If you want to make the next page number begin several pages ahead of the current page, type "*#+n*" where *n* is the page number. For example, you are on page 18 and you want to leave 5 pages for illustrations or tables that will be added to the document after printing. Instead of leaving 5 blank pages you can type "2 - #+5." The next page number will be 23.

You can also surround page numbers by symbols of your choice. Type the symbol you want to use, type up to three characters of page number specification (#, #=n, or #+n) plus a space, and type the symbol again. The following list shows some examples, assuming the page is the first page in the document:

Typing	-# -	produces	-1-
Typing	Page *# *	produces	Page *1*
Typing	Page *#=9 *	produces	Page *9*
Typing	S1, P-#+3 -	produces	S1, P-4-

You must have a total of four characters and/or spaces between the two symbols.

NOTE

Page numbers inserted in headers or footers override the page numbering feature in the Page Form. See Module 35, Print.

AUTOMATIC DATE An "automatic" date can be added anywhere in the header or footer. When you print the document Enable inserts the date you entered (or entered from the DOS date) at the Sign On screen. Type %DATE where you want the date to appear. For more information on the date see Module 16.

ALTERNATING ODD AND EVEN PAGES You can set up your headers and footers so that when you print the file the odd and even pages are different. For example, you may want the page numbers in a book to be on the outside of the document; the right side of odd pages and the left side of even pages.

When you set up your header or footer, type in the text as you want it to appear on the page you have placed the header or footer and on every other page after that. For example, if you have placed a footer on page 8, type the text you want to see on page 8, 10, 12, 14, etc. Then press Enter and type %ALT. Press Enter again and type the text you want to see on the opposite pages (in this case on pages 9, 11, 13, 15, etc.). When you have finished, press an arrow key to move the cursor out of the header or footer and continue creating or editing your text. In the document in the Typical Operation at the end of this module the headers will show the chapter number on the left side of odd pages and on the right side of even pages.

DELETING HEADERS AND FOOTERS To delete a header or footer, place the cursor on the double line at the top and press Alt-F3.

APPLICATIONS

Headers and footers are commonly used in book- and magazine-length documents. You can get Enable to automatically insert page and section numbers at the top of each page. To do this manually would be extremely difficult and time-consuming, because each time the format of your document changed you would have to change all your headers and footers; one line pushed down onto the next page at the start of a document could mean all the headers and footers would have to be changed. The automatic page and date features are also extremely useful, allowing you to quickly add page numbers and the current date to each page.

TYPICAL OPERATION

In this activity you set up headers and footers in the file named LEARN, created in Module 32. Begin at the Main Menu.

1. Open the file named LEARN.
2. Press **Up Arrow**. Press **F10**, type **L5**, and press **Enter** to insert a header. Press **Up Arrow** and press **Alt-F6**. When Enable displays the ruler line use **Tab** and **Spacebar** to delete all the Ts. Move the cursor to the R and press **Left Arrow** six times. Type **T** and press **Enter**.
3. Press **Down Arrow** and type **LEARN.** Press **Tab** and type **Part 1**. Press **Enter,** and type **%ALT**. Press **Enter,** type **Part 1**, press **Tab** and type **LEARN**. Press **Down Arrow** to move the cursor out of the header.
4. Press **F10**, type **L6**, and press **Enter** to insert a footer. Type **-#   -** (put three spaces between # and -), and press **Alt-F4** to center the text. Press **Down Arrow** several times to move the cursor out of the footer and down to the space between the first and second paragraphs in the text. Press **F9** and **Ins** and type **MP** to insert a page break. Your screen looks like this:

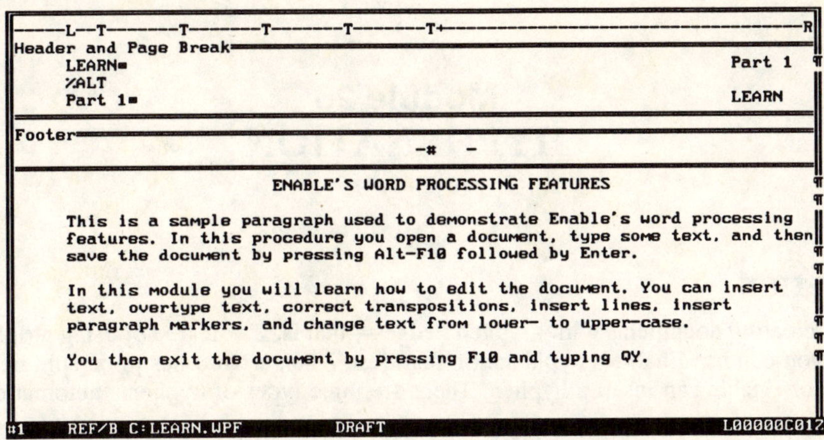
```
-----L--T--------T--------T--------T--------T+----------------------------R
Header and Page Break
     LEARN                                                        Part 1
     %ALT
     Part 1                                                        LEARN
Footer
                                    -#  -
                     ENABLE'S WORD PROCESSING FEATURES

     This is a sample paragraph used to demonstrate Enable's word processing
     features. In this procedure you open a document, type some text, and then
     save the document by pressing Alt-F10 followed by Enter.

     In this module you will learn how to edit the document. You can insert
     text, overtype text, correct transpositions, insert lines, insert
     paragraph markers, and change text from lower- to upper-case.

     You then exit the document by pressing F10 and typing QY.

#1    REF/B C:LEARN.WPF          DRAFT                              L00000C017
```

5. Press **F9** and type **OD** to change to final mode. Use **PgUp** and **PgDn** to move through the file. Look at the headers and footers. Notice the page number in each footer, and that LEARN and Part 1 are in different places on each header.
6. Press **Alt-F6** to print the file. Press **Alt-F10** to save the file, and then press **F10** and type **QY** to exit the file.
7. Turn to Module 44 to continue the learning sequence.

Module 26
HYPHENATION

DESCRIPTION

If you are creating documents with "ragged" edges—that is, if you are *not* using a right-justified margin—you can use Enable's hyphenation features. When a word has to be split between two lines, you or Enable can insert a hyphen. There are three types of hyphens: automatic, soft, and hard.

AUTOMATIC HYPHENATION The easiest type of hyphenation is automatic hyphenation. You can set up a hyphenation zone that begins a few spaces from the right margin. Words that begin to the left of the zone and are too long to fit on the line are hyphenated, but words that begin within the zone and cannot fit on the line are moved to the next line. Enable uses the Proximity/Merriam-Webster Linguibase to decide where to place each hyphen. Set up the hyphenation zone after you have finished typing your document and are ready to print.

TIP: Enable's spelling checker has trouble recognizing hyphenated words, so set up the zone after you have done the spell check. If you ever have to modify the document and redo a spell check, you may want to delete the hyphenation zone, do the spell check, and set up the zone again.

Position the cursor on the line below a ruler and press Alt-F6. A new ruler is inserted for modification. Press Tab to move the cursor to the right margin, and then use Left Arrow to move the cursor about five spaces to the left of the right margin. Type a lowercase letter z and press Enter. The margin is modified and Enable reformats the document from that ruler to the next ruler, or to the end of the document if there are no more rulers set.

Words that begin to the left of the z (that is, to the left of the hyphenation zone) and are too long to fit on the line will be hyphenated. Words that begin to the right of the z (that is, inside the hyphenation zone) and are too long to fit are moved to the next line.

SEMI-AUTOMATIC HYPHENATION If you set up a hyphenation zone using an uppercase Z instead of the lowercase z described previously, Enable may occasionally ask for your assistance in hyphenating words. Enable displays the word it is having trouble with in the status line and puts brackets [ ] around the part of the word that extends beyond the right margin. Enable may show a hyphen in a suggested position in the word, or before the word (which means Enable will move the word to the next line). You have these options:

- Press Enter to accept Enable's suggested hyphen position.
- Press Del to move the word to the next line.
- Press the arrow keys to move the hyphen to a different position, and press Enter.

MANUAL INSERTION OF HYPHENS You can also insert hyphens manually while you are typing. You can insert a soft hyphen or a hard hyphen.

Soft Hyphens If you are typing a long word when you reach the end of a line, press the Hyphen key and then press Right Arrow to move to the next line. Later, if your document is reformatted and the word is no longer at the end of the line, Enable will remove the hyphen.

Hard Hyphens If you are typing a word that is always hyphenated, you want to insert a hyphen that will remain in the word, even if a reformat moves the word to the middle of the line. For example, you are typing the word "self-educated" near the end of the line. Press Alt-Hyphen to specify a hard hyphen between the f and the e. Even if the word is later moved to a different position, the hyphen will always remain.

Hyphen Duplication If you set up a semi-automatic hyphenation zone before typing, and type your own soft and hard hyphens, Enable may sometimes duplicate the hyphens that you typed. In this case two of the status-line choices will operate differently, as follows:

- Press Enter to break the word at the user-defined hyphen.
- Press Del to push the entire hyphenated word to the next line, retaining the pre-existing hyphen.
- Press the arrow keys to move the hyphen to a different position and press Enter.

HYPHENATED WORDS If you type a hyphenated word in a position other than the end of a line, don't worry about soft and hard hyphenation. Just press the Hyphen key. The hyphen is treated like a hard hyphen and always displayed, regardless of reformatting.

APPLICATIONS

Hyphenation is only a problem if you don't right-justify your text. Unjustified text has a ragged right margin. If you want to reduce the indentations in the margin caused by long words, you have to hyphenate the words. If you don't hyphenate these long words, Enable moves the entire word onto the next line. (This is called *word wrap.*)

TYPICAL OPERATION

In this activity you create a file called HYPHEN, type some text and reformat it using a hyphenation zone, and use soft and hard hyphens. Begin at the Main Menu.

1. Create a new document called HYPHEN.
2. When Enable displays the ruler line, move the cursor to column 34 and type **R**. (Look at the column number on the far right side of the status line [C034]; move the cursor with the Tab and arrow keys.) Then press **Enter**.
3. Type the text shown in the following screen:

```
L-------T-------T+------T---------R--------------------------------------------
This is an experiment in
hyphenation. If a word begins
before the hyphenation zone and
extends past the right margin it
will be hyphenated, but if it
begins inside the the zone, it is
wrapped onto the next line, as it
would be if no hyphenation zone
existed.

#1    REF/B C:HYPHEN.WPF          DRAFT                         L00009C009
```

4. Move the cursor to the ruler line and press **Alt-F6**. The ruler line will flash once, and the cursor moves to the left edge. Press **Tab** to move the cursor to the R, and then press **Left Arrow** to move to column 29. Type **z**, and press **Enter**. Notice that the text is reformatted. The right edge is straighter, and two words are hyphenated.

5. Press **Ctrl-End** to move the cursor to the end of the file, and press **Enter** twice. Press **Alt-F6**. When Enable displays the ruler line, move the cursor to the z and press **Spacebar** to remove it. Then move the cursor to column 25, type **R**, and press **Enter** five times, to accept the ruler and move the end-of-file marker down.

6. Move the cursor to just below the ruler and type **This is a test with hyph-** and press **Right Arrow**. The cursor moves to the next line. Type **enation**. Press **Enter** and type **This is a test with self**, press **Alt-Hyphen**, and type **educated**. The word self-educated is moved to the next line.

```
L-------T-------T+------T---z----R---------------------------------------------
This is an experiment in hyphen-
ation. If a word begins before the
hyphenation zone and extends past
the right margin it will be hy-
phenated, but if it begins inside
the the zone, it is wrapped onto
the next line, as it would be if
no hyphenation zone existed.

L-------T---+---T-------R------------------------------------------------------
This is a test with hyph-
enation.
This is a test with
self-educated.

#1    REF/B C:HYPHEN.WPF          DRAFT                         L00013C015
```

7. Move the cursor to the first "This is a test" line and press **Alt-F6**. When Enable displays the ruler line, move the cursor to column 40, type **R**, and press **Enter**. Then move the cursor to the first T in "This is a test" and press **F7**. Press **Down Arrow** several times to move the cursor to the space under the four lines of text, and press **F7** again. You have now set a block.
8. Press **F9** and type **OAP** to reformat the text. (Reformatting is described in more detail in Module 38.) The text is adjusted to fit inside the new right margin. Notice that the word "hyphenation" no longer has a hyphen, because you gave it a soft hyphen. "Self-educated" still has a hyphen, because you gave it a hard hyphen.
9. Press **F10** and type **QY** to abandon the file without saving.
10. Turn to Module 24 to continue the learning sequence.

Module 27
IMPORTING NON-ENABLE DOCUMENTS

DESCRIPTION

Enable lets you import files produced in other word processing programs. At the Main Menu, type UWR (Use;Word Processing;Revise). Type the name of the file you want to import into Enable, and press Enter. (If the file is not in the default directory, include the pathname.) Enable searches for the file and then displays a line of options: ASCII, Volks (Volkswriter), Easy (EasyWriter), Wstar (WordStar), Mmate (Multimate), Peach (PeachText), DCA (Document Content Architecture), 1=DIF, 2=Wperf (WordPerfect), and Samna. Type the first character of, or move the highlight to, the desired option and press Enter. This tells Enable which program the file comes from, so Enable knows how to convert the file.

Enable may not perfectly convert the file. Some characters and formats are not available. See Enable's Word Processing manual for a list of the ones that Enable can convert. In some cases Enable may substitute a character for one that is not available.

Enable files can also be saved in other formats (exported). See Module 39 for information. Enable cannot save in Samna format, though, and some early releases could not save in WordPerfect format. Note also that the word processing DIF format is not the same as the spreadsheet DIF format, so DIF spreadsheets cannot be imported into word processing.

APPLICATIONS

Athough this feature may not import other files perfectly, it is still very useful for bringing in long blocks of text typed in other programs. Perhaps you typed them before you started using Enable, or maybe someone else produced them on another system. Rather than retyping text, import it and do any minor formatting that may be necessary.

TYPICAL OPERATION

In this procedure you save the file named LETTER, created in Module 4, in WordStar format, and then import it into Enable. Begin at the Main Menu.

1. Open the file named LETTER. Press **F10**, type **SCW**, and press **Enter** to save the entire file in WordStar format. When Enable asks if you want to use the same name or a new name, type **N**. Type **Wstar** and press **Enter**. Enable saves the file and asks what you want to do next. Type **W** to close the window.
2. Enable displays the Main Menu again. Type **UWR** to revise a file. Type the name **Wstar**. Enable displays a list of options. Type **W**, and Enable displays your file again.
3. Press **F10** and type **QY** to exit the file without saving.
4. Turn to Module 20 to continue the learning sequence.

Module 28
INDEXING

DESCRIPTION

Enable has a feature that helps you build an index. You can insert markers (the same way you do for the table of contents), or you can use a special indexing text attribute to mark the text itself. You can make Enable automatically compile the index for you, and print the table, either on its own or with the document.

MARKING TEXT When you come to a place in your text that you want to be included in the index, you mark the text in one of two ways: using the text attribute, or using the index marker.

Index Text-Attribute You can select the words you want to put in your index in two ways. First, before typing the text, press Alt-X. Then, type the text. All the text is marked (it will be shown as highlighted text). Press Alt-X again when you have finished typing the index terms.

The second way is to apply the attribute to existing text. Press Alt-X, move the cursor to the beginning of the text you want to mark, and use one of the following text segment commands to apply the attribute.

Ctrl-C	marks a character.
Ctrl-W	marks a word.
Ctrl-L	marks from the cursor to the end of the line.
Ctrl-S	marks from the cursor to the end of the sentence.

The text you wish to convert does not have to be continuous—for example, you could use a segment command to mark a word, move the cursor down to another paragraph, and mark another word.

Remember to press Alt-X again when you have finished.

NOTE

> Text that is bold, italic, underline, superscript, or subscript, and text in headers, footers, and footnotes, cannot be marked with Alt-X.
>
> Also, if you mark text that is divided by a paragraph marker, Enable will treat it as two separate index entries.

If you mark a word that appears with different case in different places in the text, Enable makes one entry in the index, and uses the case of the first entry in the document. For example, if "automobiles" appears first in the text, but you have also marked "Automobiles" later on, Enable will use a lowercase a in the index.

Index Markers Index markers look much like table of contents markers, and are set by pressing F10 and typing L01 (Layout;Index options;Create an entry). The following screen shows you the Index options.

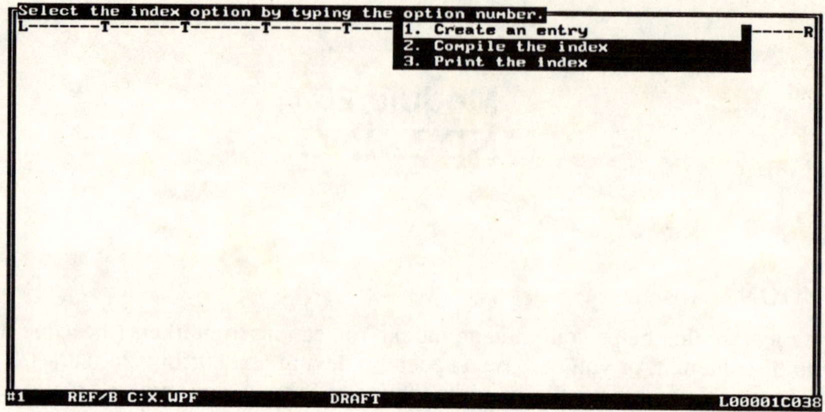

The status line prompts you to place the cursor above the place you want the index marker put and press Enter. When you press Enter Enable places the Index marker below the cursor line and places the cursor in the marker. Type a one-line entry; if you type more than one line, Enable will make each line a separate entry in the index. Then use the arrow keys to move the cursor out of the marker.

Subheadings You can use subheadings in your index. Up to five subheadings may be added to a marker. Type the main heading, type a semicolon, type the subheading, type another semicolon, type the second subheading, and so on. The following screen shows you an example of an index marker with subheadings.

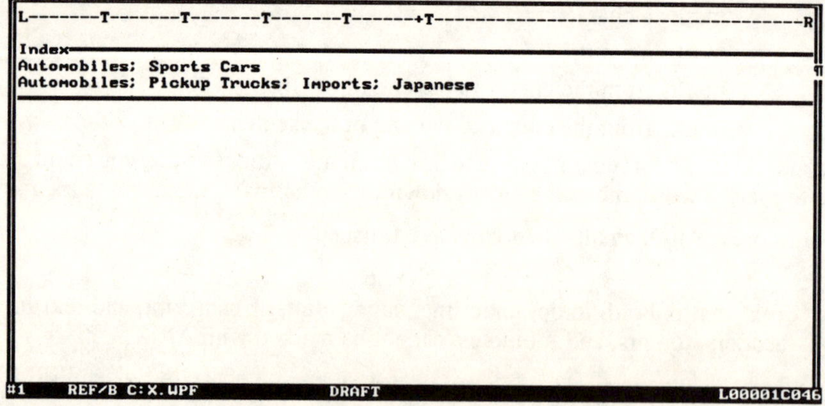

Editing and Deleting Index Markers You can use the standard word processing tools to edit the markers. If you marked text using the Alt-X text attribute, you can use the Alt-N command to delete the marking. Use it just as if you are applying an attribute (press Alt-N, move to the text, and use the text segment commands). If you want to delete an inserted marker, just place the cursor on the double line at the top of the marker and press Alt-F3.

NOTE

Remember to re-compile your index after editing or deleting entries. See the following section on compiling.

COMPILING THE INDEX When you have inserted or marked all the index entries, and the document is formatted as you want it to appear in the index, you are ready to compile the table. Press F10 and type L02 (Layout;Index options;Compile the index); Enable displays the following prompt.

Do you want periods between the entry and the page number: Yes/No. If you select Yes, the index will have dots joining each entry and its page number. After you have made your choice, Enable displays a default ruler line, along with the following prompt.

Change margins or tabs and/or accept this ruler by pressing Enter. Adjust the margins and rulers as you want them to appear in the index. The tabs are used to indent subheadings. When Enable builds the index, the main heading will be placed on the left margin, the first subheading will be placed at the first tab, the second subheading at the second tab, and so on. The page numbers are placed to the right of each heading. If you used a justified right margin (J), Enable puts the page numbers on the right side of the page; otherwise, Enable places each page number a few spaces after its entry.

When you press Enter, Enable builds the index and saves it in a separate file. The file has the same name as your original document, but has the extension .WPI.

PRINTING THE INDEX To print the index, press F10 and type L03 (Layout;Index options;Print the index).

You can also print the index at any point inside the document itself. For example, place the cursor at the bottom of the file, type %INCLUDE, skip a space and then type the name of the file with a .WPI extension. The %INCLUDE must start in column one, and must be in uppercase. For example, "%INCLUDE Cars.wpi" prints the index belonging to a file named Cars. If you want the index to appear on a separate sheet of paper you must insert your own page breaks.

PAGE NUMBERS If you have not specified page numbers in the document, Enable uses "absolute" page numbers. For example, if an entry has been inserted on the third page of the document, Enable puts 3 in the index. However, if you specified in the Page Form that the document begins at page 50 Enable will put 53 in the index. (See Module 35, Print, for information about the Page Form.) Also, if you have created headers or footers with page numbers in them, Enable uses those page numbers to define the index page numbers. (See Module 25 for information about Headers and Footers.) The numbers in the headers or footers take precedence over the number in the Page Form.

EDITING .WPI FILES You can edit the index (.WPI) files in the same way as any other word processing file. You could combine files to build an index for a large document, for example, or change the attributes of some of the entries. Remember, though, that editing the .WPI file does not change the index entries in the text file.

APPLICATIONS

An index is essential for any long document. Putting one together manually is very time-consuming, and has to be redone each time the document is reformatted and the page numbers change. Using Enable's automatic indexing you can begin the index effortlessly as you type the document, and compile a new index in just a few seconds.

TYPICAL OPERATION

In the following activity you build an index for the file named LEARN, created in Module 32. Begin at the Main Menu.

1. Open the file named LEARN.
2. Move the cursor to the word "Word" in the title line. Press **Alt-X** to turn on the indexing attribute, and then press **Ctrl-W** to apply the attribute to the words "Word Processing Features." Enable highlights the words. Press **Alt-X** to turn off the indexing attribute.
3. Move the cursor to the word "features" in the second line of text. Press **F10** and type **L01** and press **Enter** to insert an index marker. Type **Save the Document; Alt-F10** in the marker, and then press **Down Arrow** to move the cursor out of the marker. Place the cursor on the page break.
4. Press **F10** and type **L01**. Type **Editing; Inserting; text** on the first line of the marker, and press **Enter**. Type **Editing; Inserting; lines** on the second line, and press **Enter**. Type **Editing; Inserting; paragraph markers** on the third line. Press **Down Arrow** to move the cursor out of the marker.
5. Move the cursor to the word "exit" in the last line. Press **Alt-X**, and press **Ctrl-W** three times, to mark "exit the document." Press **Alt-X** again. Press **F10** and type **L02** to compile the index. Enable asks you if you want periods between the entries in the table and the page numbers.
6. Type **Y** to select Yes, and Enable asks if you want to change the ruler. Press **Enter** to accept the ruler, and Enable compiles your index. Press **Enter** twice, and then press **F10**, type **L4**, and press **Enter** to insert a page break.
7. Type **%INCLUDE learn.wpi**. This tells Enable to include the index file when you print LEARN. Your file looks like this:

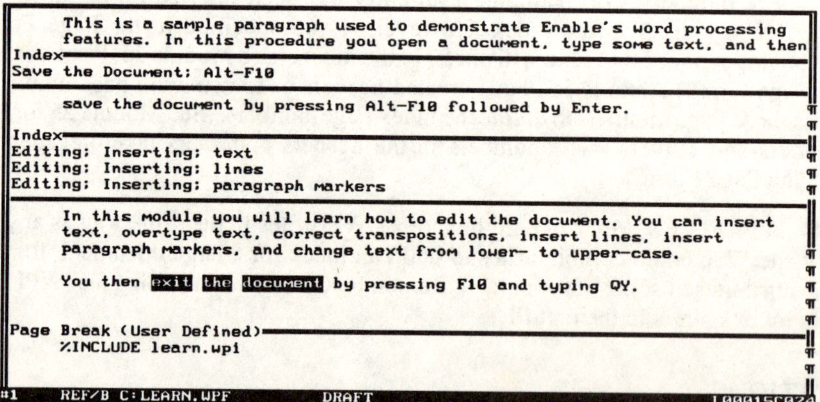

```
        This is a sample paragraph used to demonstrate Enable's word processing
        features. In this procedure you open a document, type some text, and then
Index
Save the Document; Alt-F10

        save the document by pressing Alt-F10 followed by Enter.
Index
Editing; Inserting; text
Editing; Inserting; lines
Editing; Inserting; paragraph markers

        In this module you will learn how to edit the document. You can insert
        text, overtype text, correct transpositions, insert lines, insert
        paragraph markers, and change text from lower- to upper-case.

        You then exit the document by pressing F10 and typing QY.

Page Break (User Defined)
        %INCLUDE learn.wpi

#1      REF/B C:LEARN.WPF          DRAFT                              L00015C024
```

8. Press **Alt-F2** to print the file. The last page is the index. Notice that the entries have been arranged in alphabetical order, and that the the subheadings are indented. Also notice that some entries are uppercase and some are lowercase, depending on how you entered them or marked them.
9. Press **F10** and type **QY** to exit the file without saving.
10. Turn to Module 23 to continue the learning sequence.

Module 29
LINE SPACING

DESCRIPTION

Enable lets you adjust the spacing between lines of text. You can adjust the entire document's line spacing, or adjust it for a particular part. There are three ways to adjust line spacing. You can set line spacing for the entire document in the Page Form (see Module 35); you can set line spacing (measured in lines) with a Top-Line-Menu command; and you can set line spacing measured in lines per inch with the %LINES command. The Page Form setting is overridden by both the Top-Line-Menu command and the %LINES command, and these two commands override each other; the text is always controlled by the preceding command.

TOP-LINE-MENU COMMAND Press F10 and type L3 (Layout;Set line spacing). Enable displays a prompt on the status line telling you to position the cursor and press Enter. Put the cursor on the line above the beginning of the new line spacing, and press Enter. Enable then prompts you to "Enter number." Type 1 if you want single spacing, 2 for double spacing, 3 for triple spacing, and so on (if you type 3, Enable leaves two blank lines between lines of text). Press Enter and Enable displays a Line-Spacing marker at the beginning of the new setting. You can turn the display of the Line-Spacing marker on and off by pressing F10 and typing EA8 (EditOpts;Screen displays;Line spacing). When you change to final mode or print the file, Enable inserts the extra spaces.

This method can be used to set line spacing before you type the text, and to adjust text after you have typed it. All the text after the Line-Spacing marker will have that line spacing, until another spacing is set.

%LINES COMMAND This command sets the number of lines per inch. Type the command, with the % in column one, leave a space, and type the number of lines per inch. For example, type %LINES 1 to specify one line per inch. The command must be typed in uppercase, and must be on its own line.

DELETING A LINE-SPACING SETTING Place the cursor on the Line-Spacing marker or the %LINES command and press Alt-F3 to delete the setting. All the text below that point will have the spacing of the setting immediately before the one you deleted, or the Print Form setting if you haven't set spacing.

APPLICATIONS

Line spacing is another way to adjust how your document looks when you print it. You may want to change the line spacing for a particular quotation, for example, or you may be required to submit documents with particular spacing. For instance, magazine articles are usually submitted with double-space printing.

TYPICAL OPERATION

In this activity you change the spacing of the document called LETTER, created in Module 4. Begin at the Main Menu.

1. Open the document called LETTER.
2. Press **F10** and type **L3** to select Set line spacing. Enable beeps and displays a prompt in the status line telling you to position the cursor and press Enter.
3. Put the cursor on the line below the salutation (Dear Mr. Anderson) and press **Enter**. When Enable prompts for you to "Enter number," type **3**.

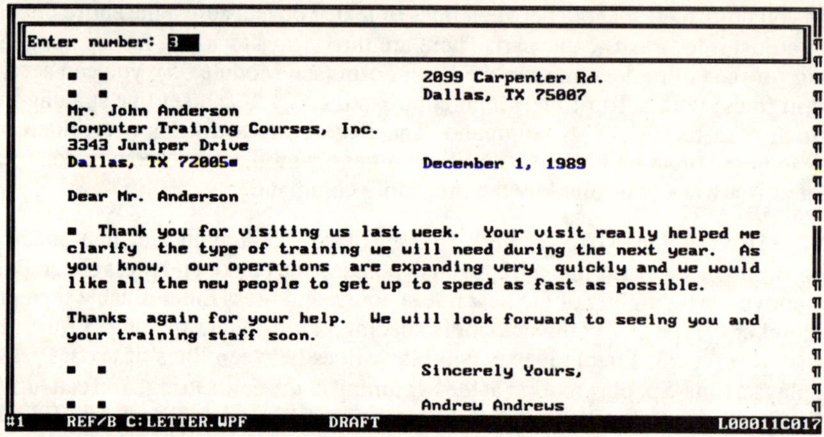

3. Press **Enter**. Notice that a Line-spacing marker has been inserted below the cursor line. Press **F9** and type **OD** to change to final mode.

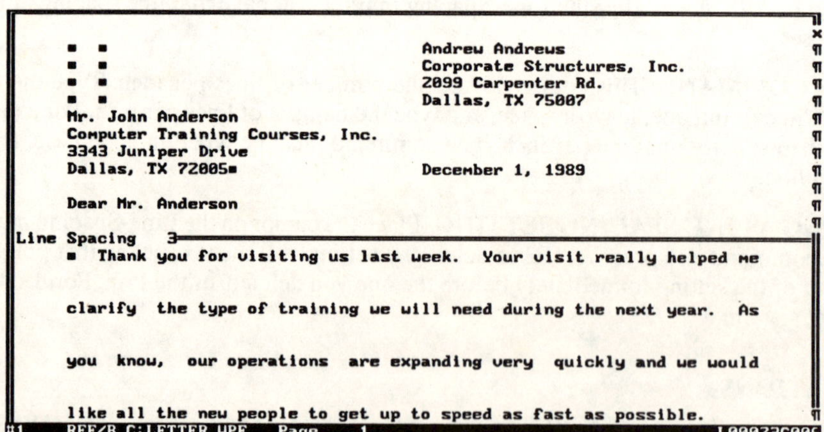

Notice that, in final mode, the text below the marker is triple-spaced.

4. Move the cursor to the marker and press **Alt-F3**. The marker disappears and the text moves up again, to its single-spaced position.
5. Press **F10** and type **QY** to abandon the document without saving.
6. Turn to Module 26 to continue the learning sequence.

Module 30
MAIL MERGE

DESCRIPTION

Enable has a feature that allows you to combine word processsing files with database files to produce form letters or labels. You will learn more about building mailing lists in the section on Enable's DBMS application, but you don't have to learn about the database to use mail merge; Enable has a built-in, generic mail-merge letter, a mail-merge database, and a mailing label form. These files (MAIL.$BF, MAIL.DBF, MAILIN.$IF, LETTER.TSG, and LABEL.TSG) are on the Install disk 10, and are normally copied to the default data directory.

Producing a mail-merge document consists of three steps: creating a mailing list (the names and addresses of the people receiving the letter); creating a form letter or form label (the document that the names and addresses will be added to); and merging the two documents (so that each letter contains the main text merged with one name and address, or each label contains one name and address). But you can take a short cut by copying the generic files, and modifying them by adding your information.

NOTE

> Later, when you understand how to use the database, you may want to bypass mail merge. It is more efficient to mark the records you want to use in DISPLAY, and use REPORT to print your letters.

COPYING THE GENERIC FILES At the Main Menu, type UMFA (Use System;MCM; Files;All). When the directory is displayed, use the PgDn, PgUp, and arrow keys to find the first file you want to copy and put the highlight on it. Type C (Copy) and Enable prompts for the drive name. Press Enter to accept the same drive, and press Enter again when Enable prompts for the directory name. When Enable prompts for the filename, type a new filename and press Enter.

Copy the following files:

MAIL.DBF	Mailing-list database
LETTER.TSG	Sample mail-merge letter
LABEL.TSG	Sample mailing label form

Copy a separate mailing list database for each mailing list.

THE MAIL MERGE SCREEN Once you have copied the generic files, go to the Mail Merge screen. Begin at the Main Menu and type UWM (Use System;Word Processing;Mail Merge). Enable displays the following screen.

```
MAIL MERGE

The mail merge feature lets you produce form letters, labels and
other printed output by combining word processing documents with
address lists stored in DBMS files.  Enable provides a model DBMS
file, called MAIL, on the Tutorial Disk.   You may use this file
or create your own.   Consult your DBMS guide for more information on
the options available to you, including database design and various
sorting and data extraction commands.

Your choice:   Build List    Letter  1=Label Layout  Merge/Print  Quit



▶   Build a mailing list database.


#3
```

Build List:	Select this when you want to build the mailing list, the list of names and addresses.
Letter:	Select this when you want to produce the form letter.
1=Label Layout:	Select this when you want to build the form label.
Merge/Print:	Once you have finished building the mailing list and the form letter or label, use this option to merge the two together to produce the final documents.
Quit:	Select this option to return to the Main Menu.

BUILDING THE MAILING LIST Type B to select Build List. Enable will prompt you for the "mail list name," that is, the name of the mailing-list database. Type the name you gave the copy of MAIL.DBF, and press Enter. Enable then prompts you for the mailing list input form. Press Enter to accept the generic input form, MAILIN. Enable displays the generic Mail List Input Form, shown later in this module. You will add the names and addresses to your mailing list using this form. Most of the fields are self-explanatory (LAST NAME, FIRST NAME, MI, etc.). SALUTATION means the way you will "greet" this person. For example, you type Garfield for the LAST NAME and John for the FIRST NAME; if you want to say "Dear Mr. Garfield" at the beginning of your letter, write Mr. Garfield in the SALUTATION field. However, if you want to say "Dear John," just type John in the field. The STATE must be the U.S. Postal Service two-letter code (Enable won't accept anything else), PHONE is a 10-digit number, and EXT is up to four digits.

You can move from field to field by pressing Tab or Enter, and you can return to a previous field by pressing Shift-Tab. When you type to the end of a field the cursor automatically moves to the next field. When you have filled in the information for one person, press F10 to display the Top Line Menu. This is shown in the following screen.

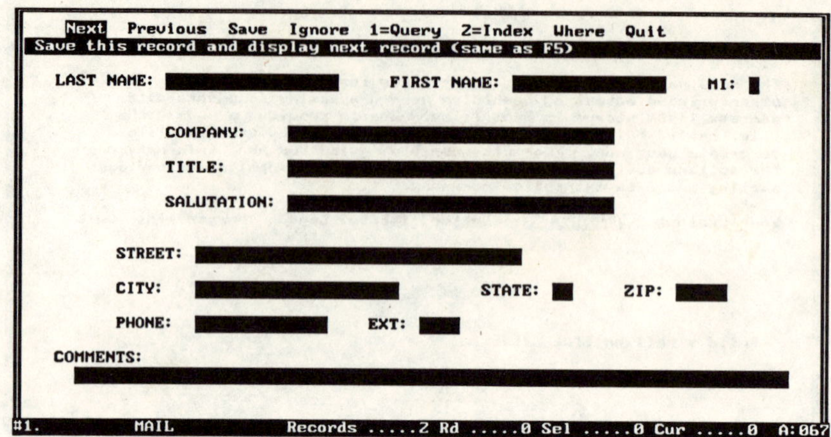

Select a command by typing the first letter or number, or by using the keys shown in parentheses in the following list.

Next (F5) — This saves the information you have typed in, and displays the next record (a blank input form if you are at the end of the file).

Previous (F6) — This displays the previous record, allowing you to edit it if necessary.

Save (Alt-F10) — This saves the information you have typed, but continues showing the same record.

Ignore (Alt-F6) — This deletes all the information you have typed into the current input form, letting you start again.

1=Query (Shift-F1) — This lets you find and edit other addresses by entering a "query."

2=Index (Shift-F5) — This lets you find and edit other addresses by entering an "index" clause.

Where — These commands are described in more detail in the section on Enable's database.

Quit — This displays the Mail Merge Menu again. Remember to save the last record you typed, before quitting.

When you have typed all the names and addresses, select Quit to return to the Mail Merge Menu. You can edit and delete records later using these simple tools, but if the mailing list is a long one you may want to use the Edit and Delete database commands, explained in the section on Enable's database.

BUILDING A FORM LETTER OR LABEL A form letter or label is like a template. You are showing Enable what the final product will look like, with the only difference being that instead of typing the actual names and addresses you will type the field names corresponding to those in your mailing-list input form. For example, instead of typing the name of a company you type [COMPANY]. When the files are merged and printed, Enable will substitute the actual name of a company.

To modify Enable's generic letter or label file, start at the Mail Merge Menu. Type L (Letter) or 1 (Label). Enable asks whether you want to create or revise the document. If you have copied one of the generic files, type R to revise. Enable prompts for the name of the file. Type the name and press Enter.

The form letter or form label uses dot commands (Procedural Language commands) and database field names. The form tells Enable where to put the database fields ([FIRSTNAME], [COMPANY], etc.) from each database record. For a full explanation of how to use dot commands see the section on Enable's database. The first part of the generic form letter works in the following manner (see the generic form letter in Typical Operation at the end of this module): .body—tells Enable where the letter starts; .reformat on—turns on the automatic reformat feature; .if[initial=" "] [FIRSTNAME] [LASTNAME]—means that if there is no initial, Enable should print the firstname followed by the lastname; .else [FIRSTNAME] [INITIAL]. [LASTNAME]—means that if there is an initial, Enable should print the firstname followed by the initial, followed by a period, followed by the last name; .endif—means that the "if" condition has ended.

The next part of the form letter (.if[title=" "] .else [TITLE] .endif) tells Enable to see if a title is included in the database record. If it isn't, Enable continues to the next command, but if there is a title, Enable prints it before continuing.

You can modify the generic form letter. The generic form has no tab settings, so you should insert a new ruler at the top of the file (don't use a justified right margin). Six lines are left at the top of the file (after ".body") for your address. Simply move the cursor to that space and type your return address. Then move the cursor to below the [SALUTATION] line and type your letter. If you need to insert a name inside the letter, just type the database field name in place of the actual name ("just let me know, [FIRSTNAME], if I can be of any help"). When Enable prints the letter, the actual first names are printed in place of the database field name. Both the generic letter and label contain instructions in boxes. Delete the instructions before saving the file.

NOTE

If your letter is over one page long, put a page break at the end of the letter.

Checking Database Field Names While you are typing a form letter, you may need to confirm the database field names. For example, is the first name field called [FNAME] or [FIRSTNAME]? Press F10, type 1 (DBMS), press Enter, and Enable prompts for the name of the database you want to refer to. Type the name, press Enter, and Enable displays a list of the field names. You can move the cursor to one of the names and press Enter (to insert the name in your text at the cursor), or press Esc to return to your text.

PRINTING THE LETTER OR LABEL Once you have built your mailing list and the form letter or label, you can merge the files. At the Mail Merge screen, type M (Merge/Print). Enable prompts for the names of the database and form letter or label. After you input these, Enable displays the Database Management System (DBMS) screen. (The Index and Where fields on this screen allow you to select the particular records you want to use—you may not want to mail to everyone on the list. These fields are explained in the DBMS section; in this module we will assume that you want to use all the database records.) Press Enter to remove the Index field, and Enable displays "To" options: Screen, Disk, Printer, and ASCII.

Screen This displays the merged form on the screen, allowing you to confirm that it works correctly before actually printing it. Press the PgDn or Enter keys to move through the merged documents, screen by screen, or press Esc to return to the DBMS screen.

Disk This allows you to store the merged forms on a disk, for later use. Enable prompts for a filename, and then displays the Print Form, letting you change the print format.

Printer This allows you to print the merged documents. Enable displays the Print Form, letting you change the print format.

ASCII This also stores the merged files on a disk, but in ASCII format. In this case, Enable doesn't display the Print Form.

When you select one of these options, Enable displays the "Where" field. Press Enter and Enable displays the print form (for Print and Disk) or immediately merges the documents (for Screen or ASCII). If Enable displays the Print Form you can modify the format and then press Alt-F2 to print the document.

If you selected Print, when Enable has finished printing the documents it displays the Main Menu. Type MWR (MCM;Windows;Return to the last window) to return to the DBMS screen. Enable automatically displays the DBMS screen if you selected any of the other options. To leave the DBMS screen, press Esc, and Enable displays the Mail Merge screen.

APPLICATIONS

Mail merge lets you personalize large numbers of letters, in a very short time. By typing in a mailing list and one letter, you can produce hundreds of letters, all with different names and addresses. Or you can use mail merge to print labels for you. Instead of typing each label individually, Enable can go to the same mailing list you used for the letter, and quickly print hundreds of mailing labels. But mail merge can be used for more than names and addresses. For example, you could have fields in the mailing list database called [DATE] and [TIME], for the date and time of an appointment. In the form letter all you need to type is "your appointment is on [DATE] at [TIME]," and Enable automatically inserts the correct date and time.

TYPICAL OPERATION

This activity is divided into four parts. When you copy the files, follow the instructions exactly; if you copy the files to a different directory Enable will not be able to use the default input form (MAILIN) in step 4, because that input form must be in the same directory as the database (MAIL1.DBF).

COPYING THE GENERIC FILES The easiest way to build form letters is to use Enable's generic files. The first step is to copy the files.

1. At the Main Menu, type **MFA**. The following directory is displayed.

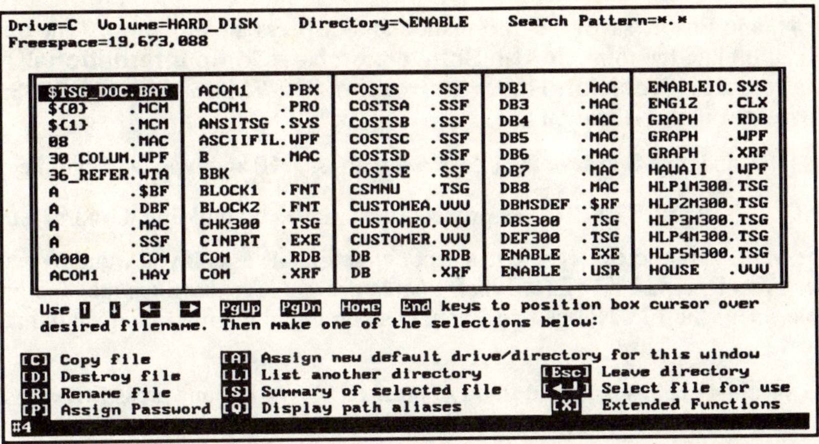

2. Using the PgDn, PgUp, and arrow keys, find the file named **LETTER.TSG** and put the highlight on it. Type **C** (Copy) and Enable prompts for the drive name. Press **Enter** to accept the same drive, and press **Enter** again when Enable prompts for the directory name. When Enable prompts for the filename, type **LETTER1.WPF** and press **Enter**.

3. Find and highlight the file named **MAIL.DBF**. Using the method described in step 2, copy it to a file named **MAIL1.DBF**.

BUILDING THE MAILING LIST The next step is to build the mailing list. In this procedure you will put two names and addresses into the mailing list.

4. At the Main Menu, type **UWM** to display the Mail Merge screen. Type **B** to select Build List. When Enable prompts you for the name of the Mail List Name, type **MAIL1** and press **Enter**. Enable prompts you for the name of the Mail List Input Form. Press **Enter** to accept the generic form, MAILIN.

5. When Enable displays the input form, type in the information shown in the following screen. Move from field to field by pressing Tab or Enter, and go back a field by pressing Shift-Tab. When you have filled in all the information, press **F10**. Enable displays a Top Line Menu, as shown in the following screen.

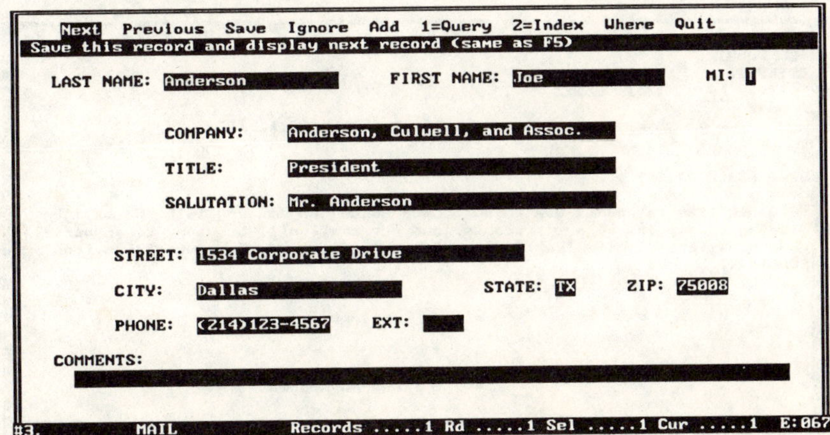

6. Type **N**, and Enable saves the information and displays a blank form. Type the following information into the form. **JoAnn Schweitzer; NewComp International; Marketing Manager; 331 Precision Road; Carrollton; TX; 75006; 214-111-3333**. Type **Ms. Schweitzer** in the salutation line.
7. Press **F10**, and type **S** to save the information. Press **F10** and type **Q** to exit the mailing list.

CREATING A FORM LETTER The procedure continues by building the form letter.

8. At the Mail Merge screen, type **L** to select Letter. Enable asks if you want to create or revise a file. Type **R**, type **LETTER1** when Enable prompts for the filename, and press **Enter**. Enable opens the file. Notice that Enable has provided the mail merge commands for the address.
9. Place the cursor below the word ".body," press **F10**, type **L2**, and press **Enter** twice to insert a default ruler. Then type the address, as shown in the following screen.

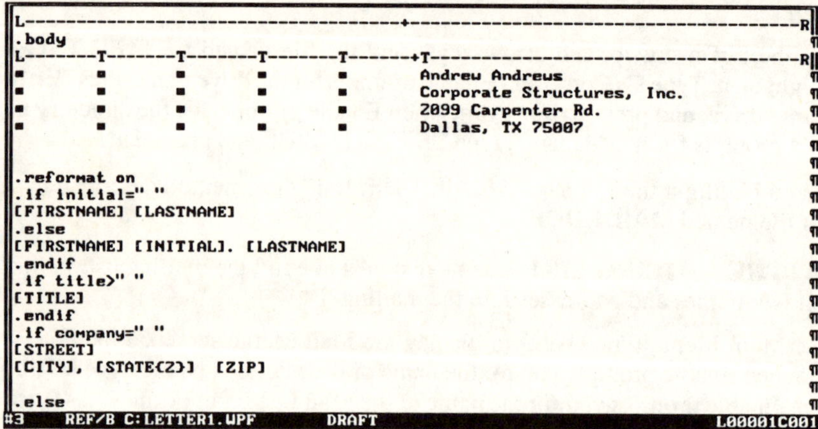

```
L-----------------------------------+--------------------------------------R
.body
L--------T-------T-------T-------T------+T---------------------------------R
■        ■       ■       ■       ■       Andrew Andrews
■        ■       ■       ■       ■       Corporate Structures, Inc.
■        ■       ■       ■       ■       2099 Carpenter Rd.
■        ■       ■       ■       ■       Dallas, TX 75007


.reformat on
.if initial=" "
[FIRSTNAME] [LASTNAME]
.else
[FIRSTNAME] [INITIAL]. [LASTNAME]
.endif
.if title>" "
[TITLE]
.endif
.if company=" "
[STREET]
[CITY], [STATE(2)]  [ZIP]

.else
#3    REF/B C:LETTER1.WPF          DRAFT                          L00001C001
```

10. Use PgDn and the arrow keys to move the cursor to the line above the [SALUTATION] line. Type the date and the body of the letter, as shown in the following screen.
11. Move the cursor to the first line of boxed text and press **Alt-F3** eight times to delete the box. Your screen looks like this:

```
.else
[COMPANY]
[STREET]
[CITY], [STATE(2)]  [ZIP]
.endif
■        ■       ■       ■       ■       December 29th, 1989



Dear [SALUTATION]:

We would like to invite you to our "Open House" on January 15th. We will be
displaying samples of our products, and our staff will be happy to answer all
your questions. I will look forward to seeing you and your associates from
[COMPANY].



■        ■       ■       ■       ■       Regards,




■        ■       ■       ■       ■       Andrew Andrews.

Page Break (User Defined)==================================================
#3    REF/B C:LETTER1.WPF          DRAFT                          L00021C001
```

12. Press **Alt-F10** and **Enter**, to save the document, and then press **F10** and type **QY** to return to the Mail Merge screen.

MERGING THE DOCUMENTS Once you have built your database and your letter, you are ready to merge and print your form letters.

13. At the Mail Merge screen, type **M** (Merge/Print). When Enable prompts for the "mail list name you wish to merge," type **MAIL1** and press **Enter**. When Enable prompts for the "existing letter/label layout," type **LETTER1** and press **Enter**. Enable displays the Database Management System screen. Notice that the database name is shown on the left, the form letter name is shown on the right, and the cursor is on the INDEX field.

14. Press **Enter** and the INDEX field disappears. Your screen looks like this:

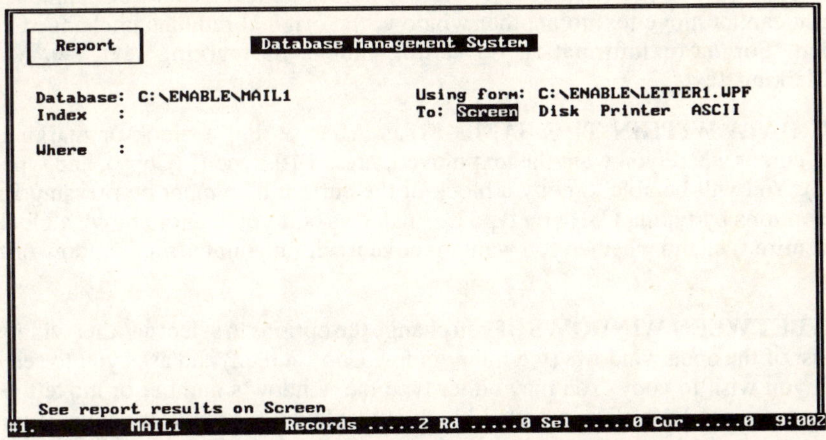

15. Type **P** to select Print. Enable displays the WHERE field. Press **Enter** and Enable displays the Print Form. Press **Alt-F2**, and Enable prints your form letters, one with Joe Anderson's name and address, and one with JoAnn Schweitzer's. Notice also that the company names have replaced [COMPANY] in the last line of the letter.

16. Enable displays the Main Menu. Type **MWR** to return to the DBMS screen, press **Esc** to return to the Mail Merge screen, and type **Q** to quit mail merge.

17. Turn to Module 46 to continue the learning sequence.

Module 31
MOVE OR COPY TEXT

DESCRIPTION

Enable lets you move or copy text. You can move or copy blocks of text or marked text to other parts of the document and you can also copy blocks, marked text, or the entire document to another window. You cannot move text to another window; the original remains unchanged after it has been copied. For more information on setting blocks or marking text, see Module 11, Blocking/Marking Text.

COPYING DATA WITHIN THE SAME FILE After setting a block or marking the text, position the cursor where you want the text moved, press F10, type C (Copy), and type 1 (Copy) or 2 (Move). You will be able to copy a block in the current document by pressing Enter, or to change the options by typing C. If you type C, Enable asks if you want to move a block, marked text, or the entire file, and whether you want to move it within your current window or to another window.

COPYING BETWEEN WINDOWS If you change the options to select another window, Enable displays a list of the open windows (the Interwindow Copy screen) and asks you to select the one from which you wish to copy. You may either type the window's number or move the cursor to the window and press Enter. The selected block is displayed (or mark one now, if you haven't already done so), and when you press Alt-F5 the text is copied to the other file.

You can also bypass the menu when copying from another window. When you are ready to copy just press Alt-F5 and Enable displays the Interwindow Copy screen. Continue from there as already described.

COPYING AN ENTIRE FILE INTO ANOTHER You can also copy an entire file into the current file. Press F10 and type C1CF (Copy;Copy;Change Options;File) and Enable prompts for the filename. Type the name (or type ? and press Enter to select from a list of files) and press Enter to insert the file. Or, use the expert command, F9 Ins D to make Enable prompt for the filename.

APPLICATIONS

The ability to move or copy text makes word processing extremely efficient. A first draft document can be reviewed and entire blocks of text moved around very easily if you decide to change the flow or emphasis of the document. And if text must be repeated in the document, you don't need to retype it, you can simply copy it. When the same text appears in more than one document, you can copy it from one document to another.

TYPICAL OPERATION

In this activity you move text in the document named LETTER, created in Module 4. Begin at the Main Menu.

1. Open the document named LETTER.
2. Move the cursor to the first letter of the first paragraph and press **F7**. Move to the last letter of the second sentence and press **F7** again. The first two sentences are now highlighted.
3. Move the cursor to the end of the paragraph, press **F10** and type **C** to select the Copy Menu, and type **2** to select Move.

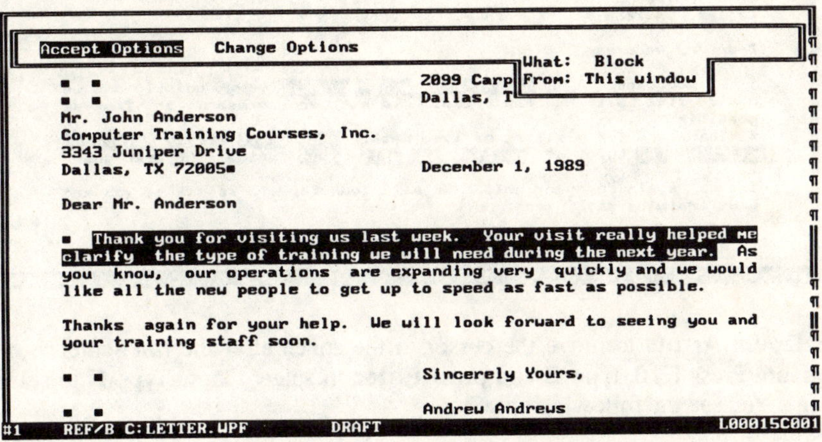

4. Press **Enter** to Accept the Options, and Enable moves the block. Notice that it is placed on the line after the cursor, because the cursor line has a paragraph marker at the end of it. Press **Alt-F7** to release the block.

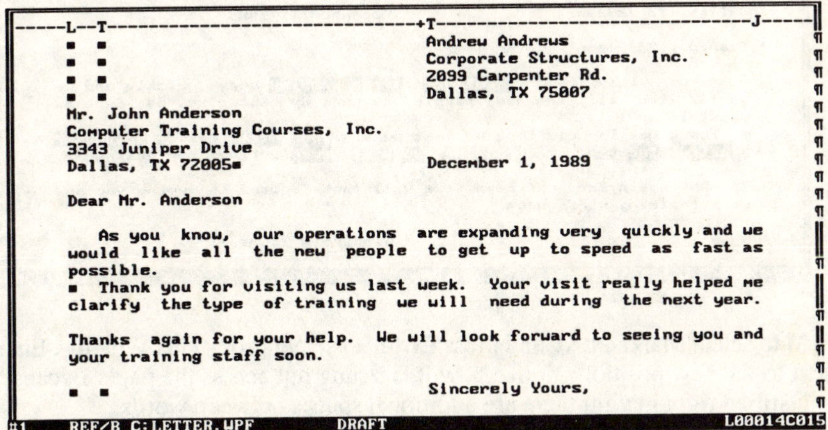

5. Move the cursor to the word "our" in the first sentence. Press **Alt-M** to set text-marking on. Then press **Ctrl-W** four times to mark the words "our operations are expanding." Press **Ctrl-Right Arrow** to move to "Your," and press **Ctrl-W** twice to mark "Your visit." Continue in this way until you have also marked "helped me clarify the" and "training we will need." Press **Alt-M** to turn off text-marking. Your screen looks like this:

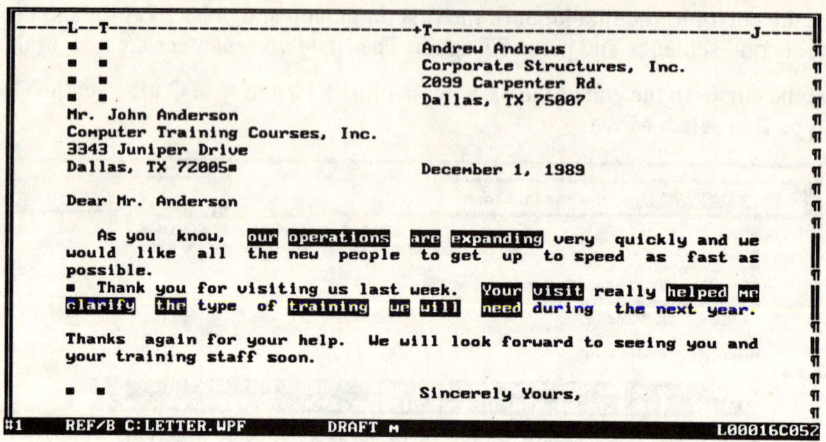

```
-----L--T-----------------------------+T------------------------------J-----
                                        Andrew Andrews
                                        Corporate Structures, Inc.
                                        2099 Carpenter Rd.
                                        Dallas, TX 75007
Mr. John Anderson
Computer Training Courses, Inc.
3343 Juniper Drive
Dallas, TX 72005                        December 1, 1989

Dear Mr. Anderson

   As you know, our operations are expanding very quickly and we
would like all the new people to get up to speed as fast as
possible.
Thank you for visiting us last week. Your visit really helped me
clarify the type of training we will need during the next year.

Thanks again for your help. We will look forward to seeing you and
your training staff soon.

                                        Sincerely Yours,
#1   REF/B C:LETTER.WPF        DRAFT M                        L00016C052
```

6. Press **Down Arrow** to move the cursor to the space after the last sentence of the third paragraph. Press **F10**, type **C** and press **Enter** to select Copy. Type **C** to select Change Options. You see the following options:

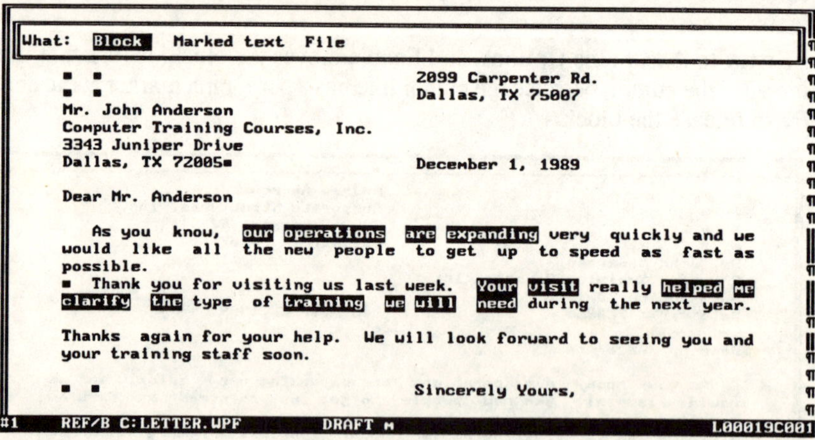

```
What: Block  Marked text  File

                                        2099 Carpenter Rd.
                                        Dallas, TX 75007
Mr. John Anderson
Computer Training Courses, Inc.
3343 Juniper Drive
Dallas, TX 72005                        December 1, 1989

Dear Mr. Anderson

   As you know, our operations are expanding very quickly and we
would like all the new people to get up to speed as fast as
possible.
Thank you for visiting us last week. Your visit really helped me
clarify the type of training we will need during the next year.

Thanks again for your help. We will look forward to seeing you and
your training staff soon.

                                        Sincerely Yours,
#1   REF/B C:LETTER.WPF        DRAFT M                        L00019C001
```

7. Press **M** to select Marked text, and press **Enter** to select From This Window. Enable copies the text to the new position. Notice how it is strung out across the page. Because the letter has a justified right margin there are additional spaces between words.

8. Move the cursor to the space immediately after the word "need" and press **Ctrl-Enter** to insert a paragraph marker. Notice how the last line is no longer spread out across the page.

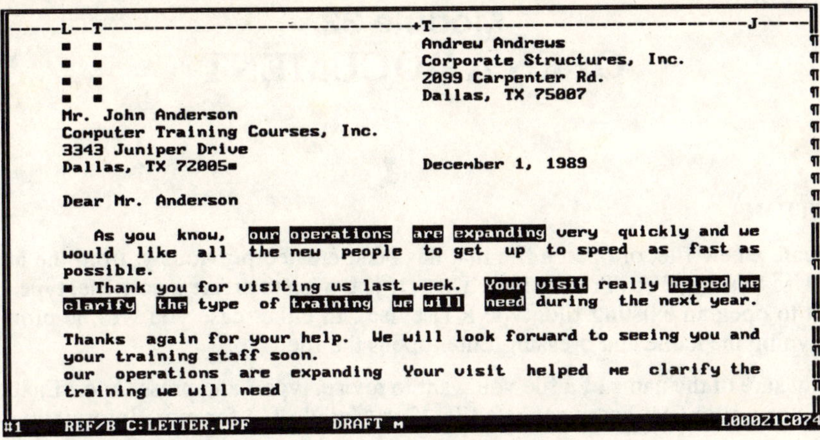

```
-----L--T-----------------------------+T-------------------------J-----
■ ■                                    Andrew Andrews
■ ■                                    Corporate Structures, Inc.
■ ■                                    2099 Carpenter Rd.
■ ■                                    Dallas, TX 75007
Mr. John Anderson
Computer Training Courses, Inc.
3343 Juniper Drive
Dallas, TX 72005■                      December 1, 1989

Dear Mr. Anderson

     As you know, our operations are expanding very quickly and we
would like all the new people to get up to speed as fast as
possible.
■ Thank you for visiting us last week. Your visit really helped me
clarify the type of training we will need during the next year.

Thanks again for your help. We will look forward to seeing you and
your training staff soon.
our operations are expanding Your visit helped me clarify the
training we will need
#1   REF/B C:LETTER.WPF        DRAFT M                    L00021C074
```

9. Press **F10** and type **QY** to exit the document without saving.
10. Turn to Module 45 to continue the learning sequence.

Module 32
OPEN A DOCUMENT

DESCRIPTION

You can create a new file, or open a file that has been created previously, from the Main Menu. Type UW (Use System;Word Processing). Then, if you wish to create a new file, type C (Create). If you want to open an existing file, type R (Revise). In either case you will be prompted for a filename. Typing the name and pressing Enter opens the file.

If you are not sure of the name of a file you want to revise, type ? and press Enter; Enable displays the file directory, allowing you to select a file. (See Module 114 for more information on the file directory.)

If you open a new file, Enable asks if you wish to accept the margins and tabs. (The defaults are set in your user profile. See Appendix B.) You will usually press Enter to accept them, but if you want to change them you can do so by using the arrow keys to move the cursor and typing L (Left Margin), T (Tab), R (Right Margin), or J (Justified Right Margin). When you have finished, press Enter. For more information on rulers, see Module 10.

After pressing Enter you see a Document Title bar at the top of the document. You can type a title, and even set up a separate ruler for the title if you need to. Or you can move the cursor to the top of the Document Title entry spaces and press Alt-F3 to delete the title bar.

APPLICATIONS

Opening a document file allows you to create a new file, revise an existing file, or display a file for examination. You may also open an existing file, modify it, and then save it with a different name, thereby creating a modified version of the existing file.

TYPICAL OPERATION

In this activity you create a new file, type a paragraph, and save the file. You then open the file again and abandon it without saving.

1. At the Main Menu, type **UWC**. When Enable prompts for the name of the file you want to create, type **LEARN**.

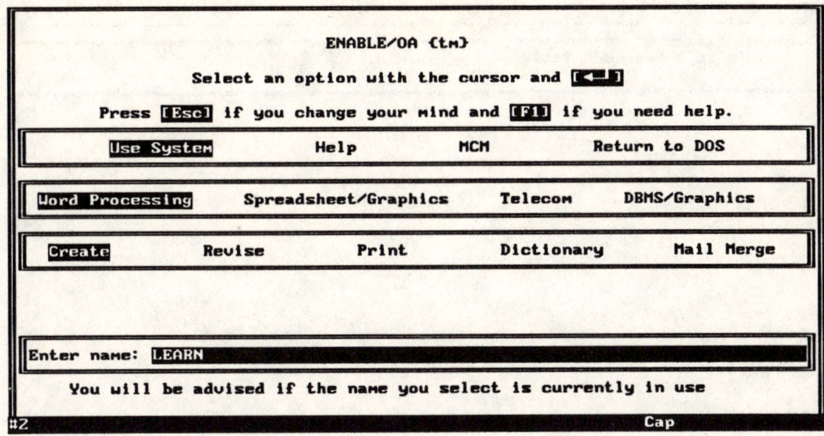

Enable prompts you to name the file you want to create.

2. Press **Enter**.

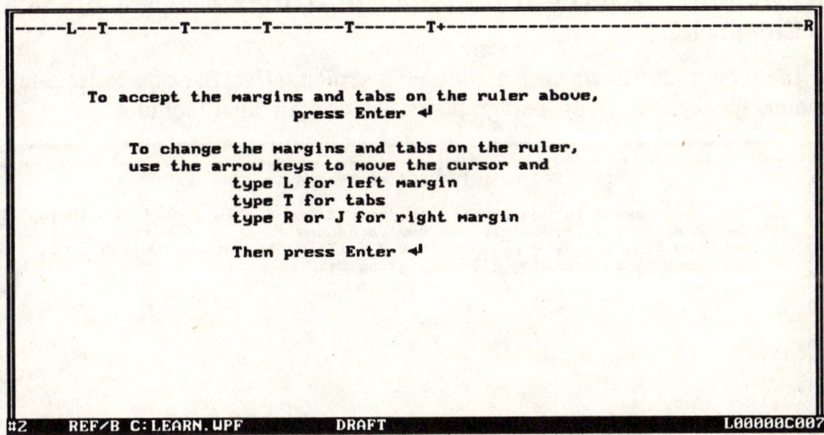

Enable asks if you want to change the document's margins and rulers.

3. Press **Right Arrow** until the cursor is five spaces from the left side of the screen. Type **L** and press **Enter**.
4. The Document Title bar is displayed on the screen. Use **Up Arrow** to move the cursor into the bar, and type **This is a Document Title**. Then press **Enter**. The title bar expands to two lines, as in the following screen.

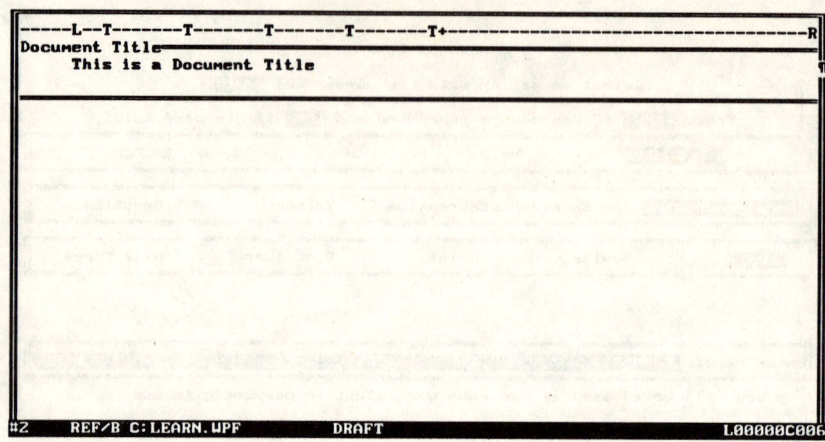

5. Use **Up Arrow** to move the cursor to the top of the Document Title bar. Press **Alt-F3** to delete the Document Title.

6. Type **ENABLE'S WORD PROCESSING FEATURES** and press **Alt-F4** to center it. Press **Enter** twice.

7. Type the paragraph shown in the following screen. (Use Backspace to delete mistyped characters if necessary.) This paragraph will be used in other modules.

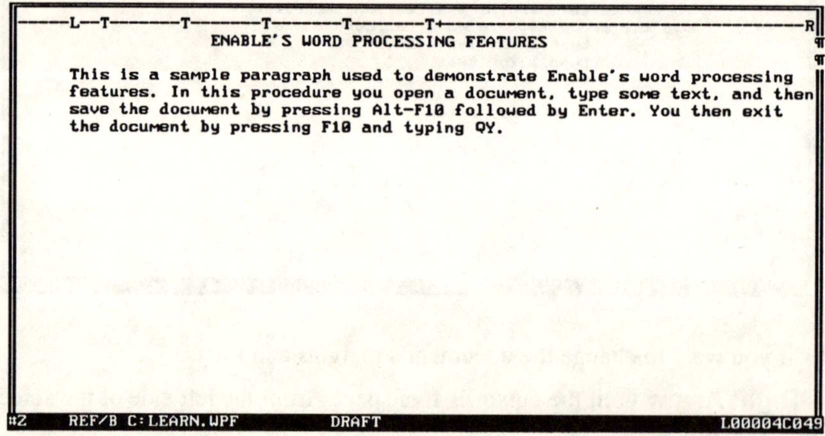

8. Press **Alt-F10** and **Enter** to save the file. Then press **F10** and type **QY** to exit the file. The Main Menu is displayed again.

9. Type **UWR**. Enable asks you for the name of a document to revise. Type **?** and press **Enter**.

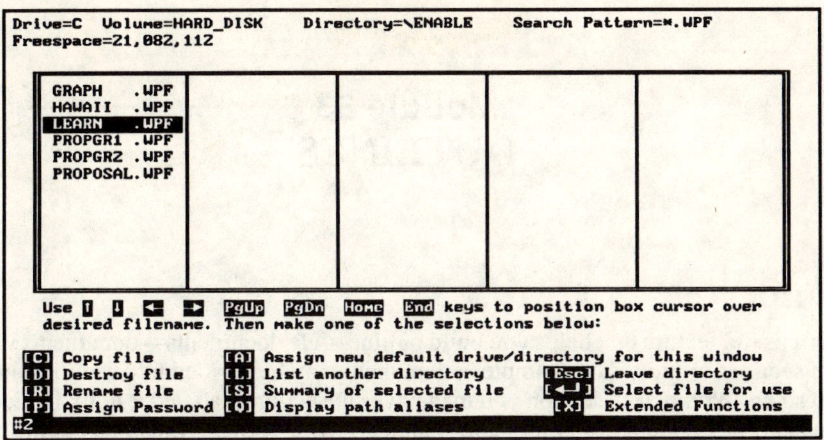

10. Press **Down Arrow** to move the cursor to the document called LEARN.WPF, and press **Enter**. Your recently saved document is displayed.
11. Press **F10** and type **QY** to exit the file without saving (since you made no revisions).
12. Turn to Module 39 to continue the learning sequence.

Module 33
OUTLINES

DESCRIPTION

Enable has a useful feature that helps you build outline-style documents—documents with several "layers" of sections or units. For example, a document may be divided into sections, labeled I, II, III, IV, and so on. Within each section you may have subsections, labeled i, ii, iii, iv. Each of these subsections may be divided further into units labeled 1, 2, 3, 4. Using Enable's outline feature you can set up a special ruler that will postion the labels where you want them (a certain amount of indentation is unavoidable, you cannot make them all start in the same column). When you type the text, you type a # sign at the start of each new section or subsection. You don't need to keep track of the section's numbers, because when you change to final mode or print the document Enable automatically assigns the correct labels to each part of the document.

NOTE

> Unfortunately, using the outline tabs limits your use of other types of tabs, depending on how much of the ruler you use for the outline.

SETTING UP THE RULER (For detailed instructions on setting up rulers see Module 10.) You can set up an outline ruler when you first open the document or in an already created document. Look at the screen in the Typical Operation; it shows an example of a numbering sequence in a ruler.

In the document controlled by this outline ruler, the first level will be labeled with uppercase Roman numerals, the second with lowercase Roman numerals, and the third with uppercase letters. The full list of options is shown below:

I	Uppercase Roman numerals
i	Lowercase Roman numerals
A	Uppercase letters (AA follows Z)
a	Lowercase letters (aa follows z)
1	Arabic numerals

Type as many of these characters as the longest label will have; for example, if you have no more than ten first-level sections labeled with Roman numerals, you can type II on the ruler, because the widest number is only two characters, IX. If you have 50 sections labeled with uppercase letters, type AA; when Enable reaches Z it starts over again with AA, AB, AC, etc.

You can also include these characters with each label; ., [ ], { }, ( ), < >. For example, in the screen in the Typical Operation, {iii} means that each of the second-level labels will be enclosed in {}.

USING THE OUTLINE At the beginning of each section or subsection, press Tab to move the cursor into the correct column and press #. Leave a space, type Alt-H if you want to use the hanging indent (i.e., if you don't want the next line of text to wrap back to the left margin), and begin typing your text.

NOTE

If you type this # sign in final mode, Enable does not display the correct label until you leave final mode and return to it.

When you change to final mode or print the document, Enable changes the # signs to the correct section labels. The labels are right justified on the rightmost character in that section's ruler-column. If you haven't typed a large enough column in the ruler (for example, you typed "1" and there are more than 9 sections in that level), the leftmost characters are truncated to fit the label in the section. Just go back to the ruler and add another column, leave final mode (if you are in it) and return to final mode, and Enable will correctly format the labels. The outline format is maintained until you insert another ruler.

CAUTION

Don't type over sequence numbers in final mode, or you may cause numbering problems later.

APPLICATIONS

The outline feature is especially useful in long documents with several section levels. If you insert new sections, you do not need to change all the subsequent section numbers—Enable will automatically do this for you when you go to final mode or print the document.

TYPICAL OPERATION

In this activity you create a file with an outline format. Begin at the Main Menu.

1. Open a file named OUTLINE. When Enable displays the ruler, set it up as in the following screen, then press **Enter**.

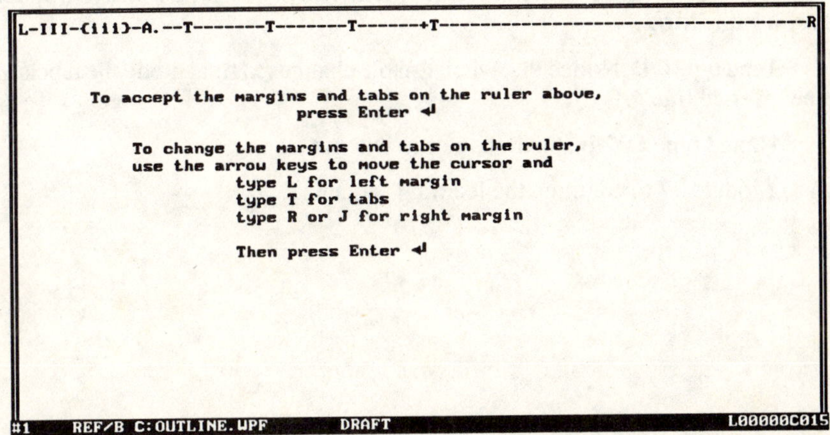

2. Press **Tab**, type **#**, press **Spacebar**, and type **This is a first-level heading**. Press **Enter**, press **Tab** twice, type **#**, press **Spacebar**, and type **This is a second-level heading**.

3. Press **Enter**, press **Tab** three times, type **#**, press **Spacebar**, and type **This is a third level heading.** Press **Enter**, press **Tab** three times, type **#**, press **Spacebar**, and type **This is the second third-level heading.**

4. Press **Enter**, press **Tab** three times, type **#**, press **Spacebar**, and type **And again**. Press **Enter**, press **Tab** twice, type **#**, press **Spacebar**, and type **Another second-level**.

```
L-III-{iii}-A.--T-------T-------T-----+T------------------------------------R
Document Title
■   # This is a first-level heading                                          ¶
■   ■      # This is a second-level heading                                  ¶
■   ■      ■  # This is a third-level heading                                ¶
■   ■      ■  # This is the second third-level heading                       ¶
■   ■      ■  # And Again                                                    ¶
■   ■      # Another second-level                                            ¶

#1    REF/B C:OUTLINE.WPF        DRAFT                              L00007C001
```

5. Press **F9** and type **OD** to change to final mode. Enable changes the headings, inserting the correct outline labels. Press **F9** and type **OD** to change back to draft mode.

6. Move the cursor to the end of the first line. Press **Ctrl-Enter** to insert a paragraph marker, and press **Enter** to move to the new line. Press **Tab** twice, type **#**, leave a space, and type **Insert a heading.**

7. Press **F9** and type **OD**. Notice that when Enable changes to final mode the labels are adjusted for the inserted line.

8. Press **F10** and type **QY** to abandon the file without saving.

9. Turn to Module 37 to continue the learning sequence.

Module 34
PAGE BREAK

DESCRIPTION

There are two types of page breaks: system-generated and user-defined. System-generated page breaks are inserted automatically when you change to final mode or print a document; Enable decides where to put them, depending on page size, page margins, and line size. Enable does not put page breaks in positions that leave one or two of a paragraph's lines above or below the page break.

You can tell Enable where to put a page break, by inserting a user-defined page break. Position the cursor on the line above where you want the page break, press F10, type L4 (Layout;Insert a page break), and press Enter. Enable inserts the page break below the cursor line, and the cursor is moved to the line below the page break.

DISPLAYING PAGE BREAKS The system-generated page breaks are not displayed until you enter final mode. (For more information on draft and final modes, see Module 18.) Entering final mode causes Enable to calculate the page break positions. When you return to draft mode the system-generated page breaks are shown. User-defined page breaks are always shown. In draft mode they look like this:

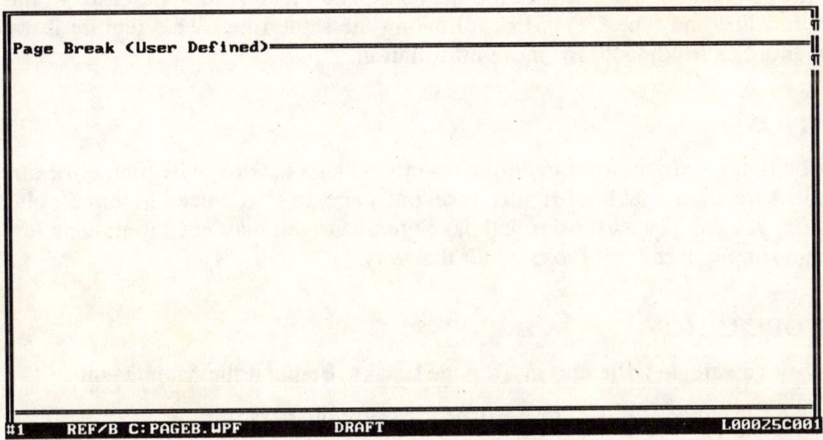

In final mode both types of page breaks look the same and are all consecutively numbered, as shown in the following screen. (This is also what the system-generated page break looks like in draft mode.)

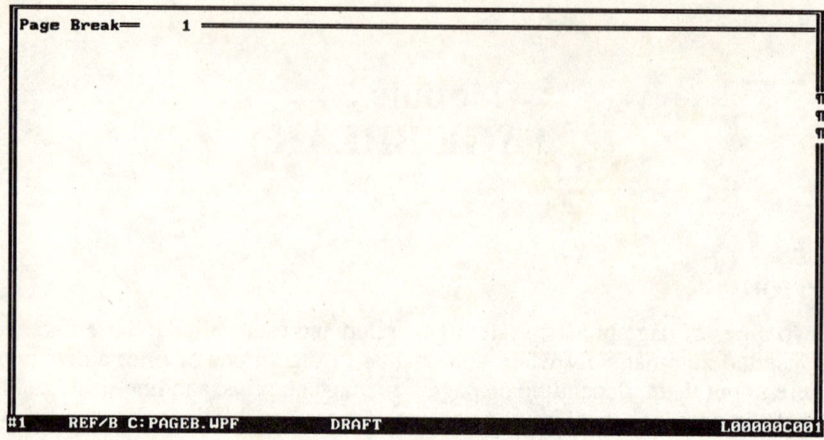

You can turn the display of user-generated page breaks on and off in draft mode by pressing F10 and typing EA0 (EditpOpts;Screen displays;Page breaks). This has no effect on system-generated page breaks, or on user-generated page breaks in final mode.

DELETING A USER-DEFINED PAGE BREAK To delete a page break, move the cursor onto it and press Alt-F3.

CONDITIONAL PAGE BREAKS You can use the Conditional Page Break feature to ensure that a section of text is held together in a document. Insert a line above the section you want to hold together, and type %PAGES. The command must be on its own line with no other text on the same line, the % must be in column 1, and the command must be in uppercase. At the end of the section insert a line and type %PAGEE, following the same rules. This feature is an embedded print command. See Module 20 for more information.

APPLICATIONS

There may be times that you want to define exactly when a new page begins. For example, if you want to make sure all of a table of figures is on one page, or if you need to leave a blank page for an illustration, you can use a user-defined page break. Or you may need to move a few lines onto the next page simply because it looks better that way.

TYPICAL OPERATION

In this activity you create a file and insert page breaks. Begin at the Main Menu.

1. Create a file called PAGE. Press **Enter** to accept the default ruler.
2. Press **F10**, type **L4**, and press **Enter** to insert a page break.

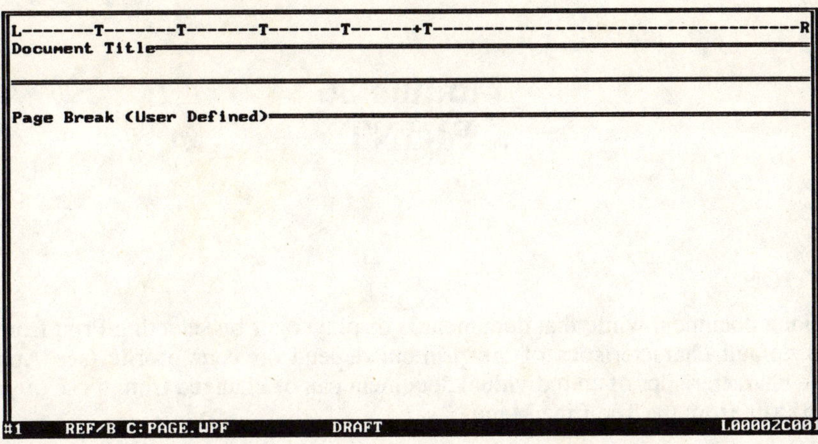

3. Press **F9** and type **OD** to change to final mode. After a few seconds you see "Page 2" in the status line. Press **PgUp** several times until you come to Page Break 2. This is the page break you inserted.
4. Press **PgUp** again until you see Page Break 1. Enable inserted this page break after the Document Title.
5. Press **F10** and type **QY** to abandon the file.
6. Turn to Module 11 to continue the learning sequence.

Module 35
PRINT

DESCRIPTION

You can print a document while that document is displayed, or by selecting Print from the Main Menu. The default characteristics of the printout depend on your profile (see Appendix B), although the characteristics of an individual document can be changed from those of your profile by selecting Print from the Top Line Menu.

NOTE

A system print queue is available. You must set it in your profile if you want to use it. See Appendixes I and B for details.

QUICK PRINT—FROM THE MAIN MENU To print a document from the Main Menu, type UWP (Use System;Word Processing;Print). Enable prompts you for the name of a file. You can type the name and press Enter, or type ? and press Enter to select a file from the directory. (Move the cursor to the file and press Enter.)

QUICK PRINT—FROM WITHIN A DOCUMENT While a document is displayed on your screen you can press Alt-F2 to print it. It will be printed using the format in your profile.

CANCELING A PRINTOUT You can cancel a printout by pressing Ctrl-F2.

CHANGING THE PRINT SPECIFICATIONS The form in which your document is printed usually depends on the profile you used when you created the document. However, that profile can be changed for an individual document, by modifying the Print Form and the Page Form.

Press F10 and type P (Print) to display the first page of the Print Form, as shown below. (It may take a few seconds for the Print Form to appear.)

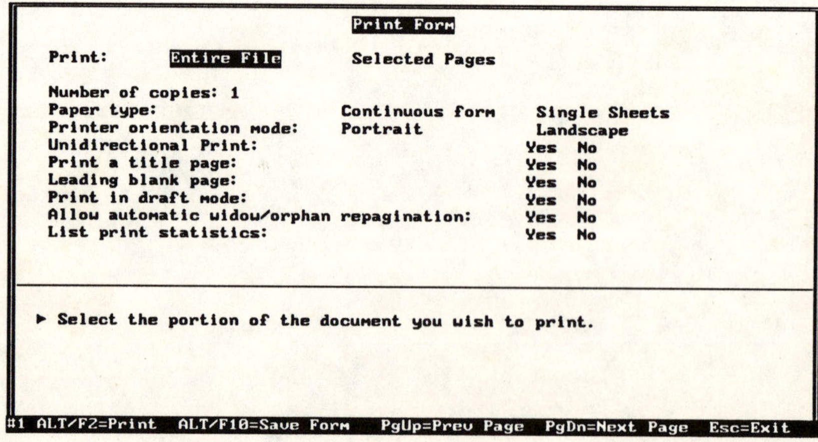

There are two Print Form pages followed by two Page Form pages. You can move through the pages using the PgUp and PgDn keys. If you go past the fourth page, the first one is displayed again. At the bottom of each page is a description of the field the cursor is on; as you move the cursor, the text changes to describe the field you moved to.

You can press Alt-F2 to begin printing at any time, but if you make changes to the Print or Page Forms you must press Alt-F10 to save those changes, or the printout will not use your changes.

To change specifications on the Print or Page Forms first move the cursor to the line with the item you want to change; then either type the first letter of the option you are choosing, or move the cursor onto the option and press Down Arrow or Enter. In some fields you have to type in a value. For example, use the Right Arrow key to move the cursor to Selected Pages. Two new lines appear below. Move the cursor down into the "Pages selected" field and type the pages you want to print. Press Alt-F10 to save the changes.

NOTE

> After you change a specification, you must press Down Arrow, or the change will not be saved. Do not press PgDn until you have pressed Down Arrow. Remember to press Alt-F10 before pressing Esc or Alt-F2 unless you do not want to save your changes.

The following sections describe print specifications in more detail.

Print: Entire Document/Selected Pages You can elect to print the entire document or specified pages. When you choose Selected Pages the screen changes, as shown in the following screen:

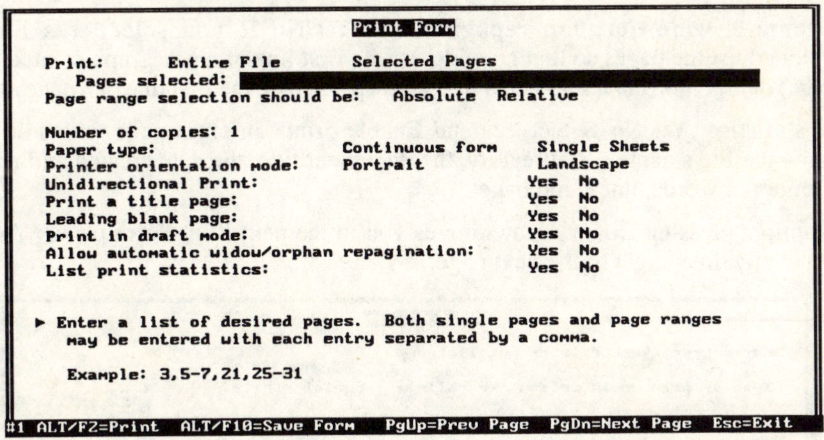

Pages Selected: Type the numbers of the pages you want to print. To print a series of pages type the beginning and ending pages separated by a hyphen (for example: 14-23). To print individual, noncontiguous pages, type the pages separated by a comma (for example: 3,6,8,27). If you want to mix several series and individual pages, separate each entry with a comma (for example: 3,6,8,14-23,27,29-34).

Page range selection should be: Absolute/Relative. Assume you have selected page 10 to print. If you have numbered the pages in your document, selecting Absolute prints the page that has page number 10 (even though you may have begun the document at page 8, so page 10 is actually the third page in the file). If you have not numbered the pages, the tenth page in the file is printed. In this case selecting Relative prints the tenth page in the file, regardless of its actual number.

Number of copies You can tell Enable how many copies of the document you want to print.

Paper type: Continous form/Single sheets If you are using continuous-form paper or a sheet feeder, select Continuous form. If you select Single sheets, Enable stops printing after each page and prompts you to insert another sheet.

Printer orientation mode: Portrait/Landscape Portrait is the standard method of printing across the paper so that the width is less than the length of the paper. Landscape mode means the paper is inserted in the printer so that the longest edge lies horizontally across the printer. Not all printers support this option.

Unidirectional Print: Yes/No Some printers have a mode in which the print head only prints when it moves one way across the page, and not when it returns. This is slower than bidirectional printing but gives better quality printouts. Check your printer manual to see if your printer has this option.

Print a title page: Yes/No If you select Yes, Enable prints the Document Title (on a separate page). If you deleted the Document Title when you created the file, a blank page is fed through the printer.

Leading blank page: Yes/No Selecting Yes gives you a blank page before the document to use as a cover sheet or divider.

Print in draft mode: Yes/No Selecting Yes prints the document in draft mode instead of final mode. The printout looks the same as the draft mode you use when you are editing the document.

Allow automatic widow/orphan repagination: Yes/No If you select Yes Enable will automatically adjust the pages so that no widows (the first line of a paragraph printed on the last line of a page) or orphans (the last line of a paragraph printed on the first line of a page) are printed.

List print statistics: Yes/No Select Yes and Enable prints an extra page with File Summary information—the file's name and directory, the document title, the date created and revised, and the total number of words, lines, and pages.

After this option, pressing Down Arrow moves you to the next Print Form page. (You can also press PgDn at any time to get to the next page.)

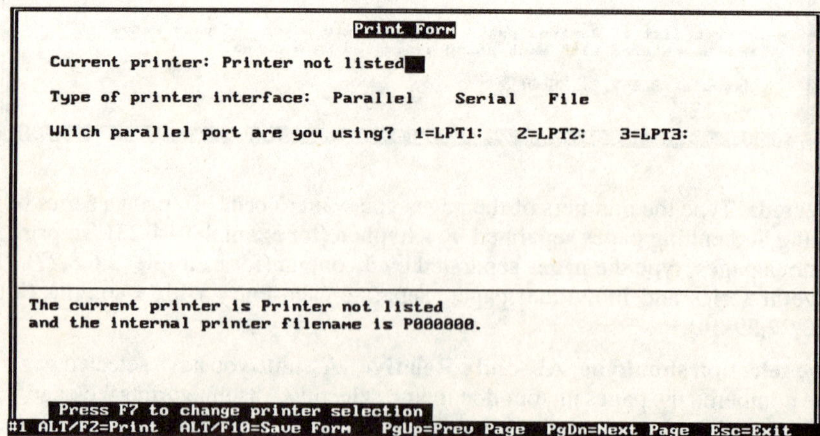

Current printer: If you have more than one printer available, you can select which one to use for this document. (In your profile you tell Enable which printer you expect to use most of the time.) If you only have one printer available, this field will either have the name of that printer displayed, or "Printer not listed." Press F7, and the following screen is displayed.

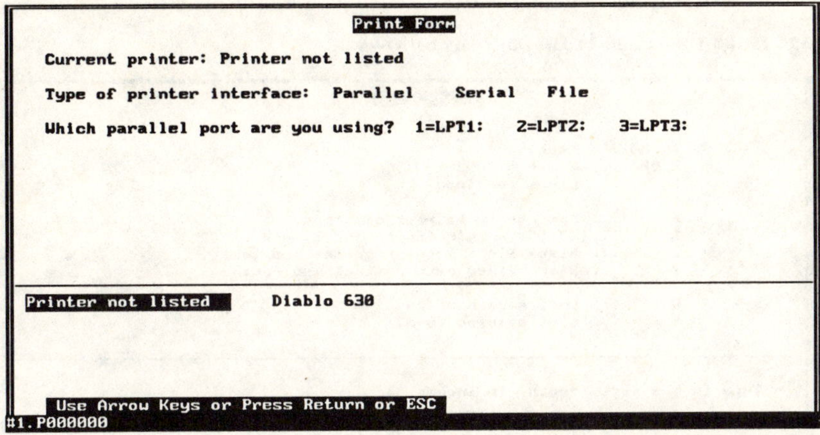

Move the cursor to the printer you want to use, and press Enter. The name of the selected printer is displayed in the Current Printer field.

NOTE

If you are unsure of any of the following printer information, refer to your printer's manual.

Type of printer interface: Parallel/Serial/File If you selected a different printer at the previous prompt, select the interface type. If you select Parallel, Enable prompts you for the parallel port.

Which parallel port are you using? 1=LPT1/2=LPT2/3=LPT3 Type 1, 2, or 3 to select the parallel port. If you select a serial printer interface, Enable prompts for a number of other items, as shown below. (Some of these prompts are not displayed until you move the cursor to the fifth line on the page, and to number 4 on that line.)

```
                              Print Form

 Current printer: Printer not listed

 Type of printer interface:  Parallel    Serial    File

 Which serial port are you using?  1=COMM1:    2=COMM2:

 Baud rate:  1=110   2=300   3=600   4=1200   5=2400   6=4800   7=9600

 Select one of the options described below:   1    2    3    4
 Select the parity:   Even    Odd    None
 Select word size:    5    6    7    8
 Select number of stop bits:    1    2    X=½

1 = Parity even,   Word size = 7 bits,   Stop bits = 1.
2 = Parity odd,    Word size = 7 bits,   Stop bits = 1.
3 = Parity none,   Word size = 8 bits,   Stop bits = 1.
4 = You will be prompted for parity, word size, and stop bits.

#1 ALT/F2=Print   ALT/F10=Save Form    PgUp=Prev Page  PgDn=Next Page   Esc=Exit
```

If you select File, Enable will produce a DOS print file. It will be given the name of the document, with the extension ".WPD." You can print the file later, using the DOS PRINT command. (You can also edit the file later. Enter the file name with the .WPD extension. Enable will give you a choice of formats at the bottom of the screen. Select ASCII and press Enter. Once you have finished, editing save it in ASCII format again.)

The next page is the first Page Form page, as follows:

```
                         Page Form

     11.00 ... Length
     8.00  ... Width
     6     ... Lines per inch

     6     ... Top margin (number of lines)
     6     ... Bottom margin (number of lines)
     2     ... Blank lines between header and text
     2     ... Blank lines between text and footer

     0     ... Left margin offset
     0     ... Line spacing (0-9)

 ► Type in the page length, in inches.

#1 ALT/F2=Print  ALT/F10=Save Form  PgUp=Prev Page  PgDn=Next Page  Esc=Exit
```

Length This is the length of the paper, in inches, to one decimal place.

Width This is the width of the paper, in inches, to one decimal place.

Lines per inch This is normally six lines per inch, and will rarely be changed.

Top Margin (number of lines) This is the number of blank lines to leave at the top of the paper. Headers (see Module 25) come after the top margin and are not part of the margin. The actual space from the top of the paper to the beginning of the text body comprises the top margin, the header, and the blank lines between header and text.

Bottom Margin (number of lines) This is the number of blank lines to leave at the bottom of the paper. Footers come before the margin.

Blank lines between header and text This is the space between the header and the text. The header, if there is one, comes immediately after the top margin, and is followed by these blank lines. For example, if the top margin is three lines, the header is one line, and the value typed here is two lines, the total space from the top of the paper to the beginning of the text is six lines. If you have not set up a header, the total is five lines.

Blank lines between text and footer This is the space between the footer and the text. (Don't confuse footers, explained in Module 25, with footnotes, which are explained in Module 23. Footnotes are regarded as part of the text.)

Left margin offset This is an offset in addition to the left margin set in your document's ruler. If your document's ruler is set at column one, at the far left of the screen, it can still be given a margin by offsetting the print margin. The offset is measured in tenths of an inch. Make sure you don't use an offset so large that the right hand side of the text is forced off the paper.

Line spacing (0-9) Up to nine blank lines can be inserted between lines of text. If you have changed line spacing in your document by using the Layout Options Menu or the %LINES command, changing line spacing here has no effect.

CAUTION

Using this Line Spacing option at the same time that you use the Page Numbering (at Bottom of Page) option can cause Enable to print the first page's number on the top of the second page. Use one of the other Line Spacing options instead. See Module 29 for information.

The second page of the Page Form looks like this:

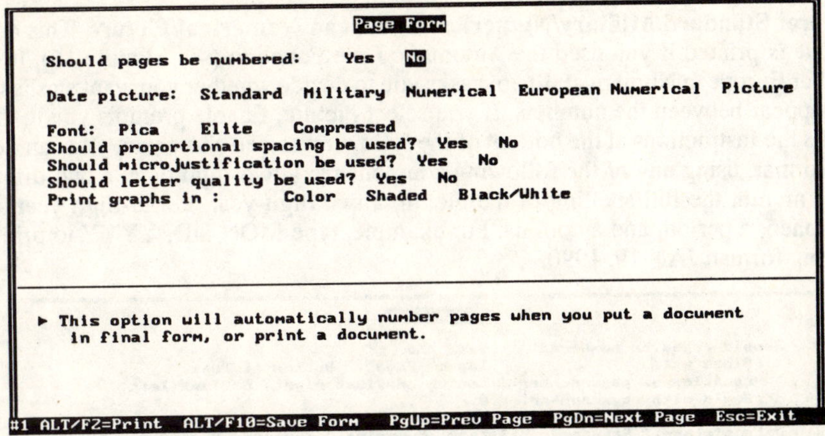

Should pages be numbered Yes/No If you select Yes, Enable displays the following screen.

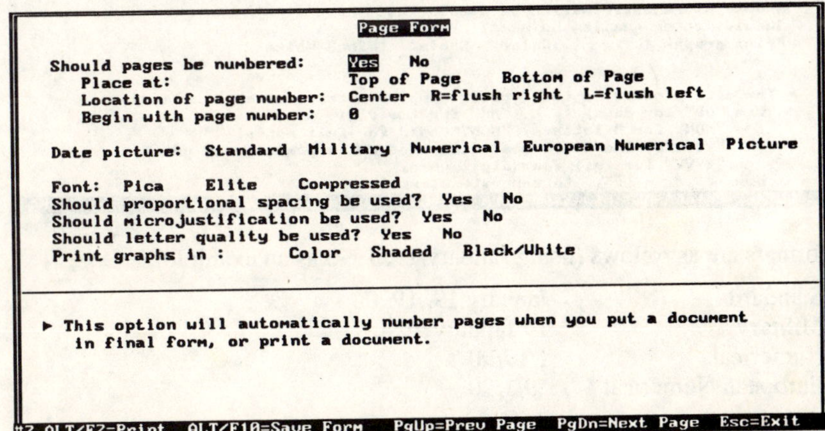

NOTE

If you used headers in your document this page numbering feature does not work. You must insert the page number in the header. See Module 25.

Place at: Top of page/Bottom of page Selecting Top puts the number in the first line after the top margin. Selecting Bottom puts it in the first line above the bottom margin.

NOTE

See the Caution earlier in this module about using page numbering with line spacing.

Location of page number: Center/R=flush right/L=flush left The page number can be printed in the center of the page or flush with the right or left margin.

Begin with page number You may want to begin printing with a different page number if this file is a continuation of another document.

Date Picture: Standard/Military/Numerical/European Numerical/Picture This controls the way the date is printed if you used the Automatic Date Function (see Module 16). If you select Numerical or European Numerical, Enable asks you to decide whether you want slashes, hyphens, or dots to appear between the numbers. If you select Picture, Enable prompts you to "Enter date picture." As the instructions at the bottom of the following screen show you, you can design your own date format, using any of the following components: a two-digit date, a two-digit month, a three-letter month, the full spelling of the month, a two-digit year, a four-digit year, a colon, a slash, a hyphen, a period, and a comma. For example, type MON DD, YYYY to print a date in the following format: JAN 19, 1990.

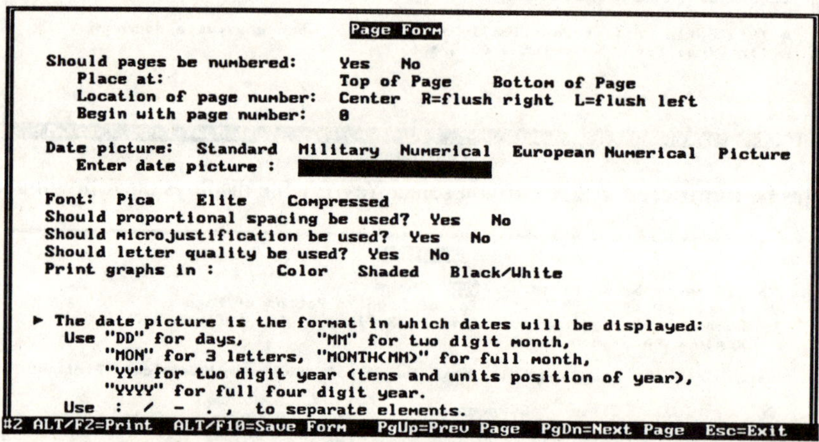

The other formats are as follows (using January 19, 1990 as an example):

Standard	January 19, 1990
Military	19 January 1990
Numerical	1/19/90
European Numerical	19/1/90

Font: Pica/Elite/Compressed The font affects the horizontal size of the type, which is also dependent on the type of printer you have. Pica is 10 characters per inch, Elite is 12 characters per inch, and Compressed is 15 or 17 characters per inch. If you have a daisy-wheel printer make sure you have inserted the correct print wheel.

Should proportional spacing be used? Yes/No If you select Yes, Enable prints each character in the actual space required for it, so, for example, the w will take up more space than the i. This gives your documents a more professional look, but cannot be used on all printers. If you use proportional printing with tabs you should use the %TAB commands; see Module 10.

Should microjustification be used? Yes/No Selecting Yes will make Enable use the spaces between letters to justify text. By slightly compressing or expanding the space between letters, the text can be spread across the page without large spaces between words. Some printers cannot use this feature, and some of the ones that can, print very slowly when using it. If you choose No, Enable has to rely on the spaces between words, and the end result doesn't look quite as good. Justification only occurs if you have set a justified right margin in your document's rulers.

Should letter quality be used? Yes/No If you have a dot-matrix printer, selecting Yes instructs the printer to use Near-Letter Quality printing. This is much slower than ordinary Draft printing, but it is a much darker, clearer print. This will not work on all printers.

Print graphs in: Color/Shaded/Black&White Graphs can be printed in color if you have a color printer. If you choose color and print on a non-color printer, Enable will use Shaded mode. If you choose Black&White, the graph will be printed in outline only, with no shading or coloring of the components.

SAVING THE PRINT SPECIFICATIONS AND PRINTING When you come to the end of the last page, pressing PgDn or Down Arrow moves you back to the first page. At any time you are in the Print and Page Forms, you can press Alt-F10 to save the changes you have made or Esc to return to your document without making any changes. You can also press Alt-F2 to begin printing, but remember that any changes you have made will not affect the printing until you press Alt-F10. Then, Enable displays your document, and you can press Alt-F2 to begin printing.

APPLICATIONS

The Print and Page Forms give you great flexibility in printing. You may choose to print a page of a document you have just edited, or the entire document. You can print extra copies, select a different printer, change the left margin set in your document's ruler, or choose letter quality printing. These options allow you to quickly and easily choose the printout that most suits your needs.

TYPICAL OPERATION

In this session you print the document named LEARN, created in Module 32. Begin at the Main Menu. (Make sure your printer is turned on and has paper.)

1. Open the file LEARN.
2. Press **F10** and type **P**. Enable displays the first Print Form.
3. Press **Down Arrow** until the cursor gets to "Print in draft mode." Notice that when you move the cursor the description in the bottom half of the page changes.
4. Press **Left Arrow** to move the cursor to "Yes," and then press **Down Arrow** until the cursor reaches "List print statistics." Press **Left Arrow** to move the cursor to "Yes." Your screen looks like the following illustration:

```
                                Print Form

Print:         Entire File          Selected Pages

Number of copies: 1
Paper type:                         Continuous form    Single Sheets
Printer orientation mode:           Portrait           Landscape
Unidirectional Print:                                  Yes  No
Print a title page:                                    Yes  No
Leading blank page:                                    Yes  No
Print in draft mode:                                   Yes  No
Allow automatic widow/orphan repagination:             Yes  No
List print statistics:                                 Yes  No

► This option produces a printed summary of information about your
  document.  It includes number of words, pages, and other information
  and is printed as a separate page at the end of your document.

#1 ALT/F2=Print   ALT/F10=Save Form   PgUp=Prev Page   PgDn=Next Page   Esc=Exit
```

5. Press **Down Arrow**. Enable displays the second Print Form page. Press **PgDn**, and Enable displays the first Page Form page. Press **PgDn** again, to display the second Page Form page. Press **Down Arrow** to move the cursor to "Should pages be numbered?" Select "Yes."

6. Enable inserts three new lines. Press **Down Arrow** to move the cursor to "Place at," and select "Bottom of page." Press **Down Arrow** again, and select "R=flush right." Press **Down Arrow** again, to move into the "Begin with page number" field, and type **15**. Your screen will look like this:

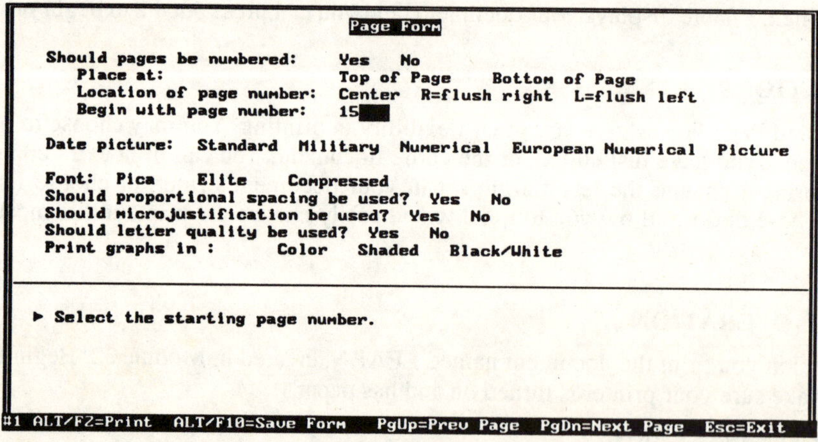

```
                                Page Form

Should pages be numbered:     Yes   No
   Place at:                  Top of Page    Bottom of Page
   Location of page number:   Center  R=flush right   L=flush left
   Begin with page number:    15

Date picture:  Standard  Military  Numerical  European Numerical  Picture

Font:  Pica    Elite    Compressed
Should proportional spacing be used?  Yes   No
Should microjustification be used?  Yes   No
Should letter quality be used?  Yes    No
Print graphs in :      Color   Shaded    Black/White

► Select the starting page number.

#1 ALT/F2=Print   ALT/F10=Save Form   PgUp=Prev Page   PgDn=Next Page   Esc=Exit
```

7. Press **Alt-F10** to save the changes. Enable displays the letter again. Press **Alt-F2** and Enable prints the letter. Notice that, because it is printed in draft mode, the ruler and Document Title are printed. Number 15 is printed in the lower right hand corner, and a file summary is printed on the next page.

8. Press **F10** and type **QY** to abandon the file without saving.

9. Turn to Module 21 to continue the learning sequence.

Module 36
QUIT (EXIT A FILE)

DESCRIPTION

This feature allows you to exit a word processing file. It doesn't save your file, so if you want to keep the work you have done you must save the file before using Quit.

To use Quit, press F10 and type Q (or press Alt-End). Enable then gives two options: typing Y closes the file without saving your document, and returns you to the Main Menu without saving the document; typing N returns you to the document.

APPLICATIONS

You must use Quit after you have finished working with a file. You do not need to quit, though, if you just want to find some information in another wordprocessing file, a spreadsheet, or a database, or if you want to return to the file in a few minutes. Instead of quitting you may open another window using the Windows command, and keep the original window open. See Module 46.

CAUTION

If you want to save your file you must remember to do so before quitting. Enable does not warn you that you will lose data if you quit without saving.

TYPICAL OPERATION

In this activity you open the file named LEARN (created in Module 32), and immediately exit without saving it. (No data is lost, since no changes are made to the file as previously saved.)

1. At the Main Menu type **UWR**. When Enable prompts you for a name, type **LEARN** and press **Enter**. The file is displayed.
2. Press **F10** and type **Q**. Enable displays the Quit prompt, as shown below.

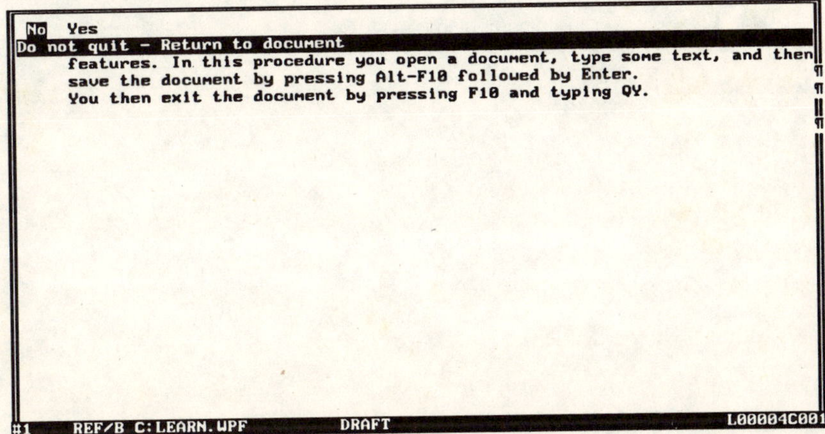

3. Type **N** and the Top Line Menu disappears, allowing you to edit your file. Do not make any changes at this time.
4. Press **F10** and type **QY**. The file is abandoned and Enable displays the Main Menu.
5. Turn to Module 15 to continue the learning sequence.

Module 37
REFERENCES TABLE (TABLE OF AUTHORITIES)

DESCRIPTION

Enable has a useful feature for building bibliographies and reference tables (or Tables of Authorities, as Enable calls them). When you reach a point in your text that should be supported by a reference, or if you want to list the name of the book or magazine that a piece of information comes from, you can mark the text, tell Enable which section in your reference table you want to put the information, and give Enable the name of the reference source. Later you can build a format file, telling Enable what you want your reference list to look like, and then you can ask Enable to build the table. Enable builds an alphabetical list of your references, and each listing gives the page number of the text related to the reference.

INSERTING REFERENCES When you type something that you want referred to in your references table, place the cursor in the space immediately before the text. Press F10 and type LD1 (Layout;Table of authorities;Create an entry). Enable prompts you to position the cursor and press Enter. When you press Enter, Enable prompts you to "Enter the short name for this Table of Authority entry."

The Short Name Type up to five characters. This short name can be used later in the text when you want to refer to the same publication or source. For example, if you are referring to the *New England Journal of Medicine*, you might type NEJM for the short name. The next time you want to refer to the Journal you can type the NEJM when Enable asks you for the short name, and Enable will not ask you for the reference itself; it will assume that the information is the same. Of course, if your text refers to more than one issue of the Journal you will have two different references and, therefore, two different short names. After typing the short name press Enter.

NOTE

> One weakness of Enable's references feature is that a reference can only have one section number; when you use a short name from a different section, the section number first given to the reference is replaced with the new one you enter. This means that if you want a document to appear in the reference table under, for example, both Chapter 1 and Chapter 5, you must create two different references. When you get to Chapter 5 you cannot use the same short name you used in Chapter 1.

Section Number When you have entered the short name Enable asks you to "Enter the section number (1-256)." This could be a section, chapter, or unit number. For example, if you are in Chapter Eight, type 8. Later, when you build your Format file, you can break the table down into references from individual chapters. If you want all the references together, not in individual sections, type 1. (You will tell Enable, in the Format file, that only section 1 is valid.) After typing the section number press Enter.

The Reference When you have entered the section number Enable displays a spade character in the cursor position, places a Table of Authorities entry space below the cursor line, and places the cursor in the entry space. You can now type the reference. You might want to type the name of a book, a magazine, or a journal. You can include dates, volume numbers, and page or section numbers if you want. If the reference is longer than a line, just keep typing; Enable will add as many lines as you need. When you have finished typing the reference, move the cursor out of the entry space by pressing the arrow keys. If you have actually named the reference in the text, you could mark the text and use the copy command to copy the name into the Table of Authorities entry space.

Repeating References When you reach text that relates to a reference or citation that has already been added to the references table, follow the same procedure. When Enable prompts you for the Short name, type the short name that you used the first time you added the reference or citation. Enable prompts you for the section number, but it won't display the Table of Authorities entry space; it will just use the information you typed earlier.

Viewing the Entry Space and Spade When you change to final mode the entry spaces disappear, but the spades remain. Changing back to draft mode makes the entry spaces reappear, but you can turn them off again by pressing F9 and typing OAT. If you save and quit the document, the entry spaces will not be visible when you open the file again, but you can use the F9 OAT command to turn them on and off. All references are automatically displayed when you insert a new one. You can also do a quick check of citations by pressing Alt-S, and moving the cursor to one of the spades; the status line will display the short name you input when you inserted the reference. Neither the entry space nor the spade will be printed.

References in Footnotes You can insert a reference inside a footnote; when you first insert the reference it is placed after the footnote. After the file is printed or changed to final mode, Enable moves the footnote entry spaces to the top of the file, and leaves the reference entry space where the footnote was originally inserted into the text. The spade symbol remains in the footnote entry space.

Deleting References If you want to delete a reference, place the cursor on the spade and press Del; then place the cursor on the double line at the top of the entry space and press Alt-F3.

THE FORMAT FILE At some point before compiling your references table (it doesn't matter whether it is before or after inserting references), you have to build a format file. The format file tells Enable what the references table should look like. You can insert headers and footers, titles, and section names. You also tell Enable where and how to place the references.

Open a word processing file, and give it a .WPA extension. For example, you might want to give it the same name as the text file, (but with the .WPA extension), or call it something like REFS.WPA. Then type the headings and titles you want. You could break it down by chapter number, for example.

Then type format commands where you want Enable to insert the references. Each format command tells Enable which section's references should be inserted at that point, and what layout to use. The format commands are in the following format: [SEC: *n/switches*]. (Leave a space after the colon.) *n* represents the section number or numbers. For example,

1	means section 1
1-5	means sections 1 to 5
1,5	means sections 1 and 5
1,5-8	means sections 1, and 5 to 8

The *switches* have the following meanings:

/S	Put the next entry on the next line (single-spacing).
/D	Leave a blank line between entries (double-spacing).
/I=*n*	Indent the second line of a multiple-line entry *n* spaces.
/.	Put periods between the entry and its page number.
/M=*n*	Put the page numbers in column number *n*.

If you don't want to use the switches, leave out the slash (e.g., [SEC: 1]). If you don't use any of the switches, Enable leaves a line between entries, doesn't indent the second line, doesn't put periods before the page number, and puts the page number 12 spaces from the right margin.

In the following format file, the references will appear below headings. The first references will all be from section 100; in other words, when you insert references in your text in the Introduction, you will tell Enable that the section number is 100. (Using 100 is less confusing than picking 1 and then using section 2 for chapter 1, section 3 for chapter 2, and so on.) You can see that under the heading CHAPTER 1 all the references will be from section 1, and under CHAPTER 2 all the references are from section 2. In all cases the entries will be single spaces (/S), and there will be periods before the page numbers (/.).

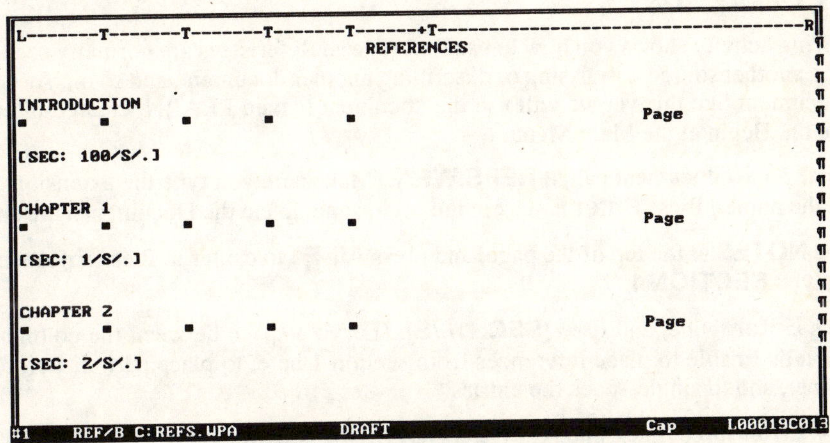

COMPILING THE REFERENCES TABLE Once you have built a format file and have inserted all the references into the text, you can compile the table. Press F10 and type LD2 (Layout;Table of Authorities;Compile the table). Enable prompts you for the name of the format file. Type the name, including the .WPA extension, and press Enter.

NOTE

If Enable beeps at you at this point, either it is unable to find a format file with that name, or the format file is open. The file must be closed.

Enable then asks if you want to save the file. If you have not done so since making changes, including inserting references, type Y, because Enable is going to close the file; you will lose your changes if you type N. Press Enter and Enable changes the document to final mode (to check the page numbers) and then closes the file and opens the new references (or Table of Authorities) file. The file has the same name as the text file, but with a .WTA extension. The references are listed alphabetically.

NOTE

If the references you inserted in the text file do not have the section numbers specified in the format file they are not included in the table. If a format command has been typed incorrectly, Enable displays an error message immediately below the bad command.

You can edit this file like any other word processing file. However, a copy of this file is automatically saved when Enable first compiles it, so if you don't make any changes to it you don't need to save it.

APPLICATIONS

Many documents have lists of references at the end of chapters or the end of the document itself. Enable provides an easy method for building these lists. And because you can compile new tables as many times as you want, even major changes to the document are no trouble; page numbers may change, and references may be inserted, but within a few seconds Enable can build a new and accurate references table.

TYPICAL OPERATION

The following activity shows you how to use References. References are normally used when you are quoting another source, discussing or describing another document, and so on. As you haven't typed a document like this yet we will use the document named LEARN, created in Module 32, to practice on. Begin at the Main Menu.

1. Create a new document called **REFS.WPA**. (Make sure you type the extension .WPA, not just the name.) Press **Enter** to accept the rulers, and delete the Document Title entry space.
2. Type **NOTES** at the top of the page, and press **Alt-F4** to center it. Press **Enter** three times, and type **SECTION 1**.
3. Press **Enter** twice, and type **[SEC: 1/./S]**. (Leave a space between the colon and the 1.) This tells Enable to place references from section 1 here, to place periods before the page number, and to single-space the entries.
4. Press **Enter** three times, and type **SECTION 2**. Press **Enter** twice and type **[SEC: 2]**. This tells Enable to place references from section 2 here, not to put periods before the numbers, and to double-space the entries.

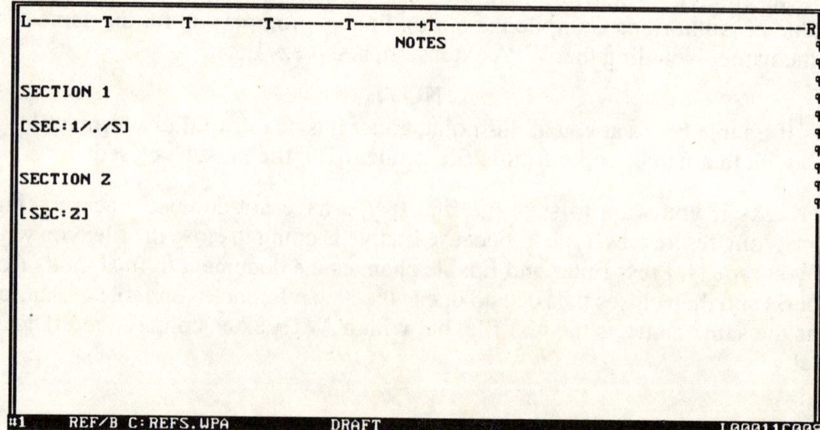

5. Press **Alt-F10** and **Enter** to save the file, then press **F10** and type **QY** to exit.
6. Open the file named **LEARN**. Move the cursor to the T in the first word of the text, "This". Press **F10**, type **LD1**, and press **Enter**.
7. When Enable prompts you to enter the short name, type **BOOK1** and press **Enter**. Enable then asks for the section number; type **1** and press **Enter**. Enable displays a spade in front of the T, and a Table of Authorities entry space below it.
8. Type **Illustrated EnableOA, Wordware Publishing, #1**. Press **Down Arrow** to move the cursor out of the entry space, and then move it to the t in "type," in the second line.
9. Press **F10**, type **LD1**, and press **Enter**. When Enable prompts for the short name, type **BOOK2** and press **Enter**. When Enable prompts for the section number, press **Enter** to accept 1.
10. In the entry space, type **Illustrated EnableOA, Wordware Publishing, #2**. (Normally you would use the same short name, so you wouldn't need to type the reference again, but this example is to show you how section 2 can "rob" section 1 of a reference.) Use the arrow keys to move to the i in "insert," in the first line of the second paragraph.
11. Use the expert command to insert a reference: press **F9**, press **Ins**, and type **A**. When Enable prompts for the short name, type **BOOK3** and press **Enter**.
12. When Enable prompts for the section number, type **2** and press **Enter**. In the entry space, type **Word Processing, The Software Group**. Using the arrow keys move the cursor to the letter F in "F10," in the last line.

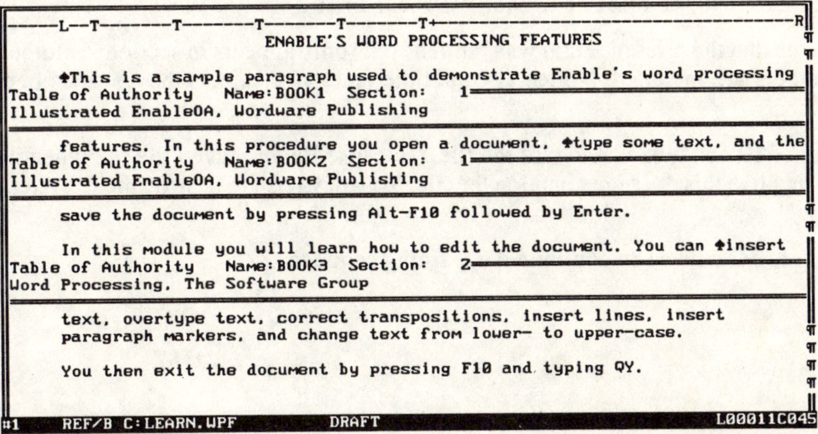

13. Press **F9**, press **Ins**, and type **A**. When Enable prompts for the short name, type **BOOK1**, the first short name you used. Press **Enter**, and notice that when Enable prompts for the section number it also displays the section number you used when you created BOOK1.
14. Type **2** and press **Enter**. Notice that the section number in the original Table of Authorities entry space has now changed from 1 to 2; section 2 has now taken this reference from section 1. Your file looks like this:

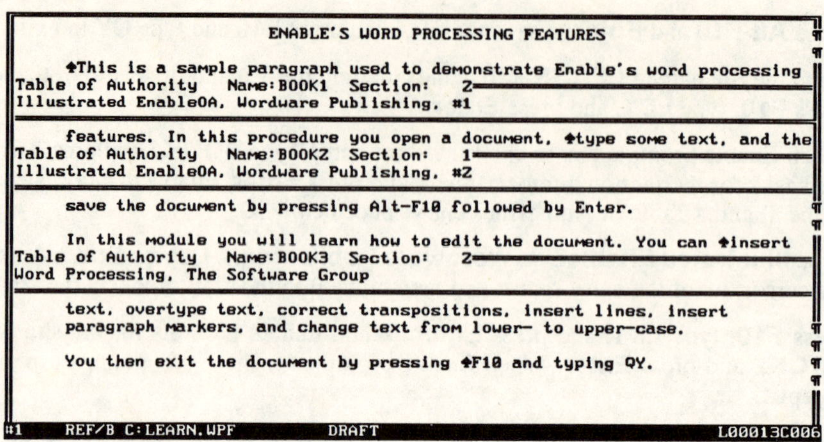
ENABLE'S WORD PROCESSING FEATURES

This is a sample paragraph used to demonstrate Enable's word processing
Table of Authority Name:BOOK1 Section: 2
Illustrated EnableOA, Wordware Publishing, #1

features. In this procedure you open a document, type some text, and the
Table of Authority Name:BOOK2 Section: 1
Illustrated EnableOA, Wordware Publishing, #2

save the document by pressing Alt-F10 followed by Enter.

In this module you will learn how to edit the document. You can insert
Table of Authority Name:BOOK3 Section: 2
Word Processing, The Software Group

text, overtype text, correct transpositions, insert lines, insert
paragraph markers, and change text from lower- to upper-case.

You then exit the document by pressing F10 and typing QY.

#1 REF/B C:LEARN.WPF DRAFT L00013C006

15. Press **F9** and type **OAT**. The Table of Authorities entry spaces are turned off. Press **F9** and type **OAT** again, and they reappear.

16. Press **F10** and type **LD2** to select "Compile the table." When Enable prompts you to enter the "form" filename, type **REFS.WPA** and press **Enter**. Enable then asks if you want to save your file. You will normally save the file; if you don't, Enable can build a references table this time, but the references will not be saved so Enable will not be able to build another table. In this lesson you should type **N** so that the references are not saved. Enable begins compiling the table; your file is changed to final mode and then closed. Enable then displays the references, or Table of Authorities file, named LEARN.WTA.

17. Notice that the reference that was "stolen" (#1) only appears in section 2, although both page numbers are included. Notice also that the entry in section 1 has periods before the page number.

18. Press **F10** and type **QY** to exit the file. (Because Enable saved the file when it compiled it, exiting like this does not abandon the file. You may wish to destroy the file later. See Module 114.)

19. Turn to Module 41 to continue the learning sequence.

Module 38
REFORMATTING

DESCRIPTION

Enable has two reformatting features: Automatic Reformat, and Reformat a Paragraph. Automatic Reformat should be turned on almost all of the time, because it allows text to wrap to the next line automatically as you type a document. When you delete or insert words, Automatic Reformat automatically adjusts your text, pulling text back from the next line, or moving text down to the next line. With Automatic Reformat off, the cursor stops at the right margin; Enable won't allow you to keep typing, and it won't wrap text down onto the next line. When Automatic Reformat is on, the word REF appears in the status line, to the right of the window number. You won't turn Automatic Reformat off very often. You may want to delete words from a line without the next line's text being moved up, but this will probably be rare, and you can always use the Spacebar to replace the text with spaces.

To set Automatic Reformat off, press F10 and type EC (EditOpts;Reformat On/Off). This function is a toggle, so do the same to turn it back on.

You will want to use the "Reformat a Paragraph" feature occasionally. This allows you to reformat a block of text into a paragraph. And if you have "accidental" hanging indents, you can use reformat a paragraph to delete them. An accidental hanging indent occurs when you have set a hanging indent on a paragraph, typed some text in that paragraph, and then moved to another paragraph to insert some text. If you didn't press Enter after typing your intentional hanging indents, Enable continues indenting all your text, regardless of where you type. The solution is to set the paragraph with the accidental hanging indent as a block, and use Reformat a Paragraph.

To use Reformat a Paragraph, use F7 to set a block on the paragraph you want to reformat, then press F10 and type ED (EditOpts;Reformat Paragraph). Press Alt-F7 to release the block. (Blocks are discussed in Module 11.)

RESUME HANGING INDENTS Hanging indents often get interrupted. For example, you are typing a paragraph with a hanging indent and you go to another place in the text to edit. You press Enter at some point, return to your hanging-indent paragraph, and resume typing. Because you pressed Enter the hanging indents have been turned off, and your text wraps round to the left margin. Also, if you reformat two paragraphs to put them together, and one of them has a hanging indent, the hanging indentation is turned off.

To fix this, go back to the first character in the paragraph and press Alt-H, to set hanging indents on again. Then go to the last word of the line just before the text begins wrapping back to the left margin. Begin typing, and when the text wraps onto the next line, it will move back to the hanging indent position. Delete the extra characters you typed in, and continue.

This method can also be used to apply a hanging indent to an existing paragraph.

RETAIN BLANKS AT THE BEGINNING OF A LINE If you want to retain the blank spaces at the beginning of a line during Reformat a Paragraph, you can set Keep blanks on. Press F10 and type EI (EditOpts;Keep blanks on/off) to toggle on or off. When it is on you will see /B in the status line.

For example, if you typed a few blank spaces at the beginning of a paragraph, reformatting the paragraph with Keep Blanks turned off removes those spaces, but if Keep blanks is on they are kept.

APPLICATIONS

Word processing programs let you change your text at any point. You can delete or insert text, move sections or bring sections in from other documents. The Automatic Reformat feature lets you do this with the minimum of trouble, but there will be times when you need to reformat entire sections or paragraphs.

TYPICAL OPERATION

In this activity you reformat the file named LEARN, created in Module 32 and modified in Module 19. Begin at the Main Menu.

1. Open the file named LEARN.
2. Place the cursor on the first letter of the first paragraph. Press **Ins** to turn insert mode on. (The cursor turns into a flashing block.) Press **Tab**, and press **Spacebar** three times. Then press **Alt-H** to turn the hanging indents on. Press **Ins**, and move the cursor to the end of the first line, after the word "word."
3. Type **processing**. The word wraps onto the next line, causing the text to reformat. Press **Spacebar** and press **F4**, to delete the duplicate word, processing. Now move the cursor to the line above the first paragraph, and press **F7**.
4. Move the cursor to the end of the second paragraph, and press **F7**. Enable sets a block on the two paragraphs. Press **F10**, press **Enter**, type **D**, and Enable reformats the two paragraphs. Notice that the hanging indents have been removed. Your screen looks like this:

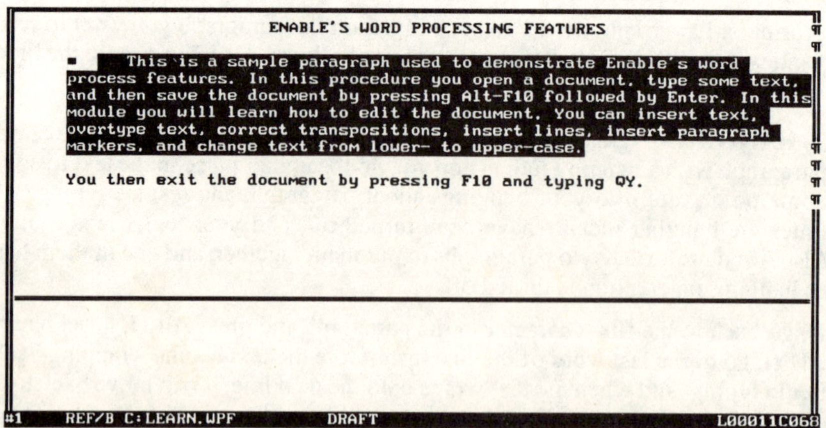

5. Press **Alt-F7** to turn off the block. Press **F10** and type **QY** to abandon the file without saving.
6. Turn to Module 34 to continue the learning sequence.

Module 39
SAVE

DESCRIPTION

Once you have created a document, you can save it. You have a number of options: you can save it in one of eleven word processing formats; you can save all or a portion of the document; you can use the name you opened the document with, or a new name (which creates a new file, leaving the original file unchanged); and you can decide what to do next (continue editing, revise a document, create a document, close a window, or go to the DOS screen).

OPTIONS To save, press F10 and type S (Save). You see the following:

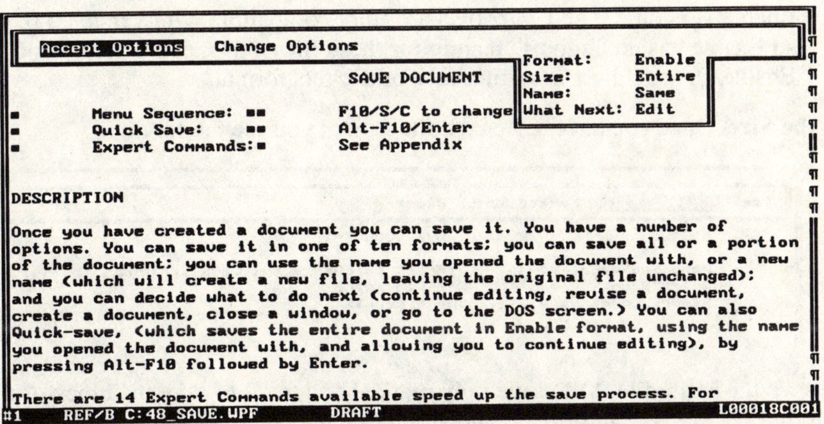

If you press Enter or type A (Accept Options), Enable uses the default options: the entire file is saved in Enable format, the name remains the same, and you are able to continue editing the document. (For a shortcut to accomplish this kind of save, press Alt-F10 and Enter.)

Selecting a Format If you type C (Change Options) you see the following:

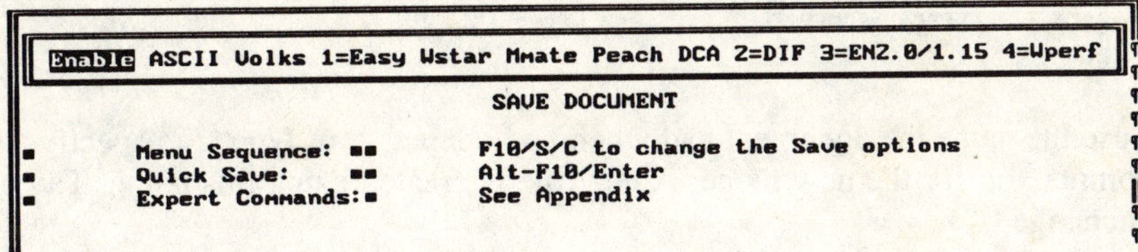

These are the different formats in which the file can be saved. The file can then be used by the corresponding word processing program, although some attributes may not be perfectly "translated" into the new format. The following table shows the character you type and the name of each format.

E or Enter	Enable
A	ASCII
V	Volkswriter
1	EasyWriter
W	WordStar
M	MultiMate
P	PeachText
D	DCA
2	DIF
3	Enable version 2.0/1.15
4	WordPerfect

NOTE

Enable version 2.0 and 1.15 files are fully compatible with version 3.0, so Enable has no "import" feature for these files. Also, early releases of Enable/OA could not save files in WordPerfect format.

Selecting the Size Once you have selected a file format you see the following:

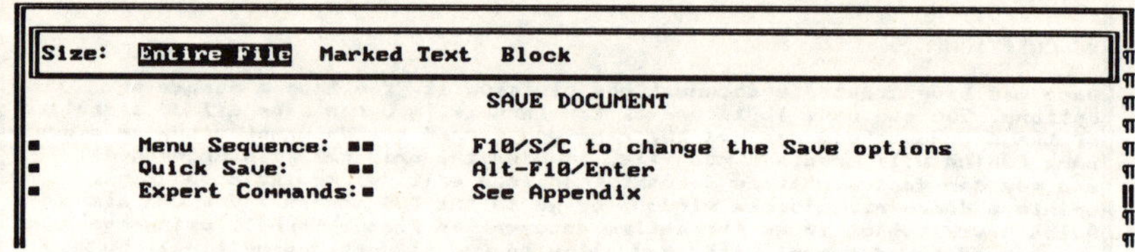

Type E to save the entire file, M to save only marked text, or B to save the block of text already set. See Module 11 for more information about blocks and marked text.

Choosing the Filename Once you have selected the text to be saved you see the following:

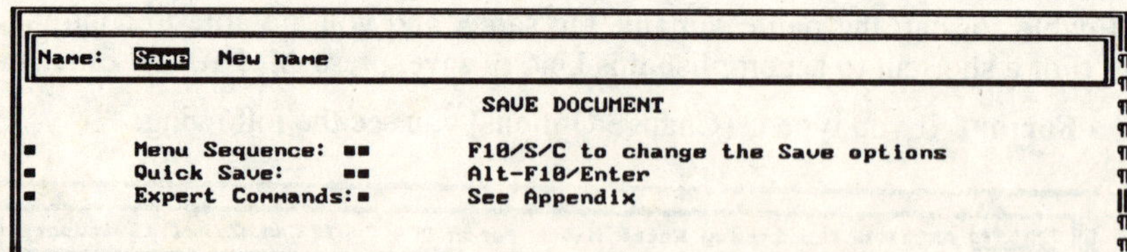

Type S to use the name the document had when you opened it, or type N to specify a new name. Enable prompts you for the new name. A new file is created using this name. The original file remains unchanged.

TIP: You can also select New name if you want to save the file on a different disk or in a different directory. For example, when prompted for a new name you could type A:*FILENAME* to save the file on the disk in drive A, or C:\DATA*FILENAME* to save the file in directory DATA on the hard disk. You may even use the same filename.

Choosing What To Do Next Once you have chosen the filename, the file is saved and you can choose from the following options for what to do next (type the first character or highlight the option and press Enter):

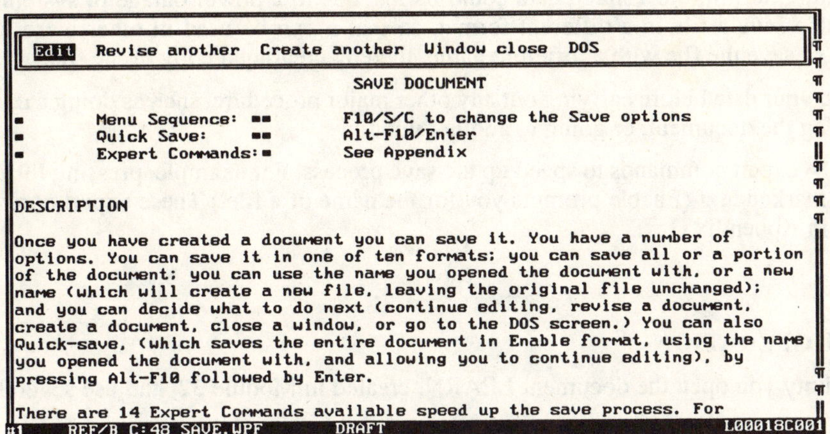

Edit Revise another Create another Window close DOS

SAVE DOCUMENT

Menu Sequence: F10/S/C to change the Save options
Quick Save: Alt-F10/Enter
Expert Commands: See Appendix

DESCRIPTION

Once you have created a document you can save it. You have a number of options. You can save it in one of ten formats; you can save all or a portion of the document; you can use the name you opened the document with, or a new name (which will create a new file, leaving the original file unchanged); and you can decide what to do next (continue editing, revise a document, create a document, close a window, or go to the DOS screen.) You can also Quick-save, (which saves the entire document in Enable format, using the name you opened the document with, and allowing you to continue editing), by pressing Alt-F10 followed by Enter.

There are 14 Expert Commands available speed up the save process. For

#1 REF/B C:48_SAVE.WPF DRAFT L00018C001

Edit The same file is displayed again. You may continue editing. You may press Enter instead of typing E.

Revise Another Enable asks you for the name of another file. That file is displayed, and you can revise it.

Create Another Enable asks you for the name of a new file, which is created. You can then begin typing.

Window Close Enable closes the window you are working in. You return to the Main Menu if no other windows are open, or to the previous open window.

DOS Enable displays the DOS window. You cannot select this option if you have other windows open.

BACKUP FILE Each time (other than the first time) you save a file, Enable copies the new data over the original file. By modifying your user profile you can make Enable automatically back up the original file each time. Enable will then save the data in a file with the same name as the original, but with the extension .WP@. Each time you save a file Enable replaces the .WP@ file with the latest backup. To use this feature you must turn it on in your user profile. See Appendix B for more information.

AUTOMATIC SAVE You can also make Enable automatically save your document after a predetermined number of keystrokes. You define the number of keystrokes in your user profile. After you have typed the specified number of keystrokes Enable saves your work in a file named TMPWPOO*n*.WP@, (*n* is the window number).

CAUTION

Enable does not update the original file. If your system "crashes" due to power loss or a hardware or software problem, you should rename the TMPWPOOn.WP@ file and delete the original file. Open TMPWPOOn. WP@ to make sure it is the right file first.

APPLICATIONS

You save files after you have finished working with them. You may want to save long documents during editing, to limit how much data could be lost due to a power outage or system problem. You can also save a file in a different format, so that it can be used in other word processing programs, or save the file with a different name, thereby creating a copy of the file.

TIP: Save your data before carrying out any other major procedure, such as doing a complicated sort, printing the document, or going to another window.

There are 14 expert commands to speed up the save process. For example, pressing F9 and typing SM saves marked text (Enable prompts you for the name of a file.) These expert commands are explained in Appendix G.

TYPICAL OPERATION

In this activity you open the document LEARN, created in Module 32, and use several methods to save it.

1. At the Main Menu type **UWR**, type **LEARN**, and press **Enter**. Enable displays LEARN.
2. Press **Alt-F10** and **Enter**. Notice that the file is saved. It is still displayed, so you could continue editing.
3. Press **F10** and type **SC**. Notice the list of format options.
4. Type **A** for ASCII. (The ASCII format saves the file as pure text, without Enable's formatting codes for margins, text attributes, and so on. This format can then be used by almost any kind of text software.) Press **Enter**, and type **N** (New Name). Notice the prompt for a new name. Type **ASCIIFIL**.

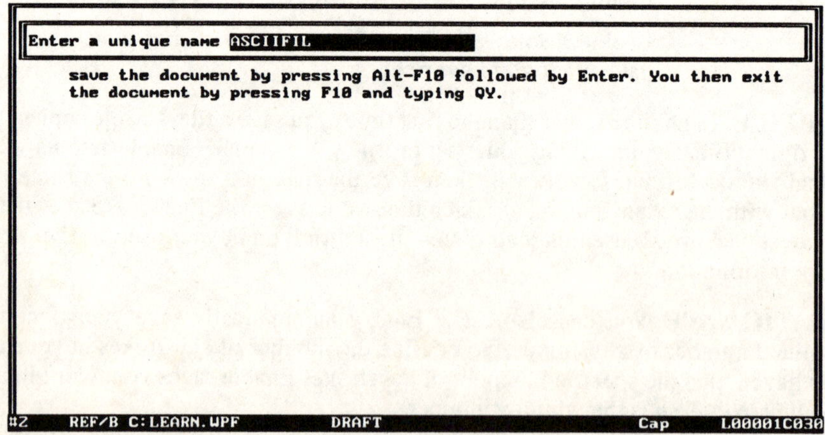

5. Press **Enter**. Enable saves the file and displays the list of subsequent operations.

6. Type **C** (Create another document). When you are prompted for a new name type **LEARN2** and press **Enter**.
7. The ruler page of a new document is displayed. Press **Enter**, **F10**, and type **QY** to abandon the file without saving.
8. Turn to Module 36 to continue the learning sequence.

Module 40
SHORTHAND

DESCRIPTION

Enable has a shorthand feature that lets you use abbreviations in your text to represent long strings of text, numbers, or special characters. When you "compile" the abbreviations later, Enable replaces the abbreviations with the full string. There are three stages to using shorthand: defining the abbreviations and associated string, typing the abbreviation in your text, and compiling the abbreviations.

DEFINING THE ABBREVIATIONS Press F10, type LA1 (Layout;Shorthand;Create an entry), and press Enter, and Enable displays a Shorthand entry space. Type ?, the abbreviation you want to use, a space, and the full string, as shown in the screen in the Typical Operation of this module. The abbreviation may be up to 8 letters or numbers, in addition to the question mark. If the full string is longer than one line just keep typing and the entry space will expand. You can put more than one abbreviation and string in an entry space; put them on different lines or just leave a space before each abbreviation.

TYPING THE ABBREVIATION When you want to use the shorthand in your text, type the abbreviation, including the question mark. You can apply text attributes to the abbreviations if necessary. You can type abbreviations into the text and define them later.

COMPILING THE ABBREVIATIONS When you have finished the document, press F10 and type LA2 (Layout;Shorthand;Compile the abbreviations). Enable replaces the abbreviations with the associated strings, and moves all the entry spaces to the top of the file.

APPLICATIONS

This feature is useful when you have to type the same text many times. Simply type the abbreviation and let Enable do the hard work for you. The feature is especially useful if the string contains special characters; it is much quicker to use the abbreviation than the special character sets.

TYPICAL OPERATION

In this activity you use abbreviations in the file named LETTER, created in Module 34. Begin at the Main Menu.

1. Open the file named LETTER. Move the cursor to the space below the final line in the letter, press **F10**, type **LA1**, and press **Enter** to insert a Shorthand entry space.
2. Type **?newaddrs We have recently moved our offices. Please note our new address at the top of the page.**

3. Press **Down Arrow** to move the cursor out of the entry space. Type **P.S. ?newaddrs**. Your screen looks like this:

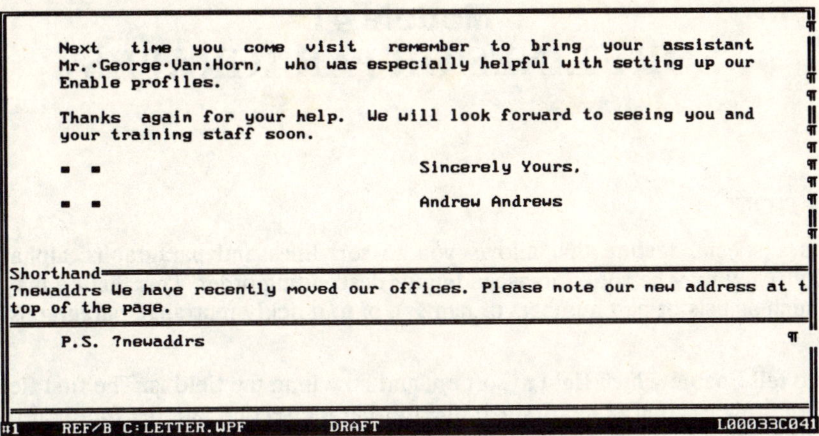

```
Next  time  you  come  visit  remember  to  bring  your  assistant
Mr.·George·Van·Horn,  who was especially helpful with setting up our
Enable profiles.

Thanks  again for your help.  We will look forward to seeing you and
your training staff soon.

■ ■                                  Sincerely Yours,

■ ■                                  Andrew Andrews

Shorthand
?newaddrs We have recently moved our offices. Please note our new address at t
top of the page.

P.S. ?newaddrs

#1    REF/B C:LETTER.WPF          DRAFT                           L00033C041
```

4. Press **F10** and type **LA2** to compile the abbreviations. Enable moves the entry space to the top of the file, and replaces the abbreviation with the text. Notice that the last line of text has been spread across the page, because the file has a justified right margin.

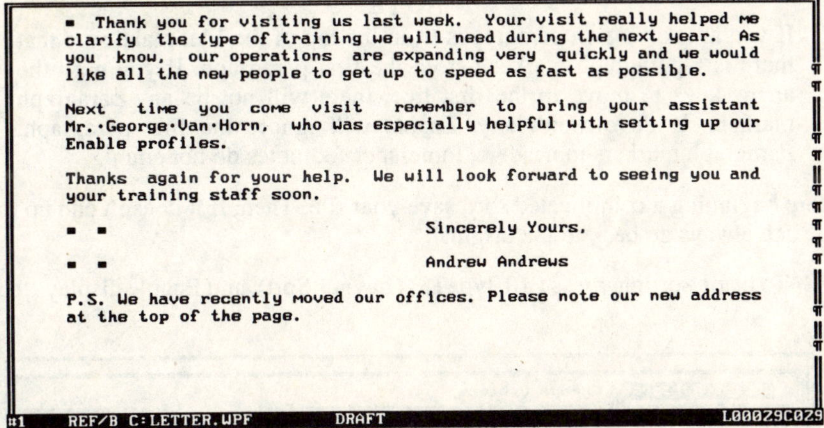

```
■  Thank you for visiting us last week.  Your visit really helped me
clarify  the type of training we will need during the next year.  As
you  know,  our operations  are expanding very  quickly and we would
like all the new people to get up to speed as fast as possible.

Next  time  you  come  visit  remember  to  bring  your  assistant
Mr.·George·Van·Horn,  who was especially helpful with setting up our
Enable profiles.

Thanks  again for your help.  We will look forward to seeing you and
your training staff soon.

■ ■                                  Sincerely Yours,

■ ■                                  Andrew Andrews

P.S. We have recently moved our offices. Please note our new address
at the top of the page.

#1    REF/B C:LETTER.WPF          DRAFT                           L00029C029
```

5. Move the cursor to the last line of the P.S. and press **Enter**. The last line is no longer justified.

6. Press **F10** and type **QY** to exit the file without saving.

7. Turn to Module 27 to continue the learning sequence.

Module 41
SORT LINES OR PARAGRAPHS

DESCRIPTION

Enable has a special feature that allows you to sort lines and paragraphs, alphabetically or numerically. They may be sorted in ascending or descending order. This feature may be used to sort lists (such as lists of part numbers or names), or to quickly rearrange paragraphs of text into a better order.

You have to tell Enable which field to sort on, and how long the field is. The first field begins at the left margin, the second at the first tab, the third at the second tab, the fourth at the third tab, and so on. So, if you tell Enable to sort on the second field, and that the field length is three characters, it sorts the lines and paragraphs according to the three characters beginning at the first tab. The text on each line remains in the same order, regardless of which field you chose to sort. Enable sorts until it reaches a ruler or a blank line, so when you are sorting paragaraphs you usually have to delete the blank lines first.

NOTE

> If you are sorting on paragraphs from the top of the file, make sure that there is a paragraph marker before the first paragraph. If you used the arrow keys to move to the first line, there will not be any paragraph markers. If there aren't any, Enable will ignore the first paragraph. Paragraph markers in headers, footers, or footnotes do not count.

TIP: Before beginning a complicated sort, save your file. Then, if it doesn't end up the way you want it you can always go back to the original.

SORTING To begin sorting, press F10, type LB (Layout;Sort), and Enable displays the following screen:

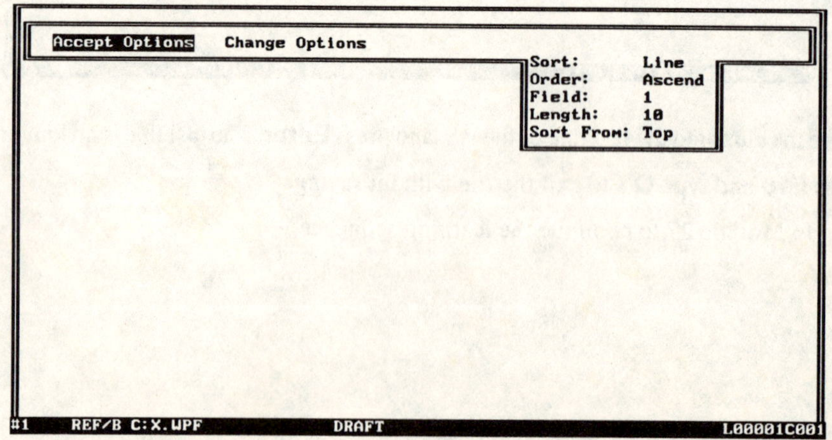

If you press Enter at this point, Enable sorts lines in ascending order; it sorts according to the first ten characters beginning at the left margin, and begins sorting from the beginning of the file.

You can change or accept the following options (the defaults, i.e., the ones that are used if you press Enter at this point, are shown first):

Sort: Line/Paragraph You can sort by line or paragraph. A paragraph is a block of text between paragraph markers, and may include blank lines. Before sorting, delete the blank lines between paragraphs. If you want to sort paragraphs you will probably be sorting numerically; see "Sorting on Numbers," later in this module.

Order: Ascending/Descending Enable sorts in ascending (a to z or 0 to 9) or descending (z to a or 9 to 0) order. Uppercase letters are sorted before lowercase letters when doing an ascending sort.

Field: 1 Put the number of the field you want to sort on. One is the field beginning at the left margin, two begins at the first tab, etc.

Length: 10 Put the number of characters Enable should look at when sorting. For example, if you are sorting names in a column 12 characters wide, type 12.

Sort From: Top/Current You can make Enable sort all the lines or paragraphs from the top of the file, or from the current cursor position. In either case, Enable will continue sorting until it reaches a ruler or a blank line. (A blank line inside a paragraph, i.e., with no paragraph marker inside it, is ignored; Enable keeps sorting.)

When you accept the options, or once you have finished changing the options, Enable highlights the fields it intends to sort. The status line then displays "Keyword fields identified correctly (Y/N)?" Typing Y makes Enable complete sorting, N aborts the sort.

SORTING ON NUMBERS You may want to sort lines with fields that have numbers (such as serial or part numbers), or paragraphs that begin with numbers. However, you may need to reorder text in an order other than alphabetical or numerical. In such a case you can insert a number in the first column (in the order in which you want to see the text), delete blank lines between the lines or paragraphs, sort the text, and then delete the numbers. For example, if you have written a magazine article or a company memo, you may want to change the order of the paragraphs to change the emphasis or the flow of the writing. As you edit the document you can insert a number at the beginning of each paragraph, and then sort on these numbers.

TIP: If you are sorting numbers over 9 but less than 100, place a zero before each one-digit number (01, 02, 03). If the numbers exceed 100, each one-digit number must have two zeros, and two-digit numbers must have one zero, and so on.

APPLICATIONS

This feature is especially useful for sorting columns of numbers or text, such as names, dates, serial numbers, or employee numbers. And, as described already, it is a quick way to reorder paragraphs in a document; you will find it easier to do it this way than setting blocks and using the Copy function, unless you are only moving one or two items.

TYPICAL OPERATION

In this activity you sort paragraphs and a column in the file named LEARN, created in Module 32. Begin at the Main Menu.

1. Open the file named LEARN.
2. Move the cursor to the first letter in the first paragraph. Press **Ins** and type **2**. Move the cursor to the blank line after the first paragraph. Press **Alt-F3** to delete the line.
3. Move to the first letter in the first word in the next paragraph and type **1**. Go to the blank line after the paragraph and delete the line. Go to the first letter in the next paragraph and type **3**. Move the cursor to the line above the first paragraph.
4. Press **F10** and type **LB**. When Enable asks if you want to accept the options, type **C** to change them. Enable prompts you for the Sort Type. Type **P** for paragraph. Enable then prompts for the Order; press **Enter** to accept Ascending.
5. When Enable prompts for the Field, type **1** and press **Enter**. When it prompts for the field length, type **1** and press **Enter**. When Enable prompts for the Sort From position, type **C** (Current).
6. Enable highlights the numbers you typed in, and the status line asks if the keyword fields are identified correctly. Your screen looks like the following:

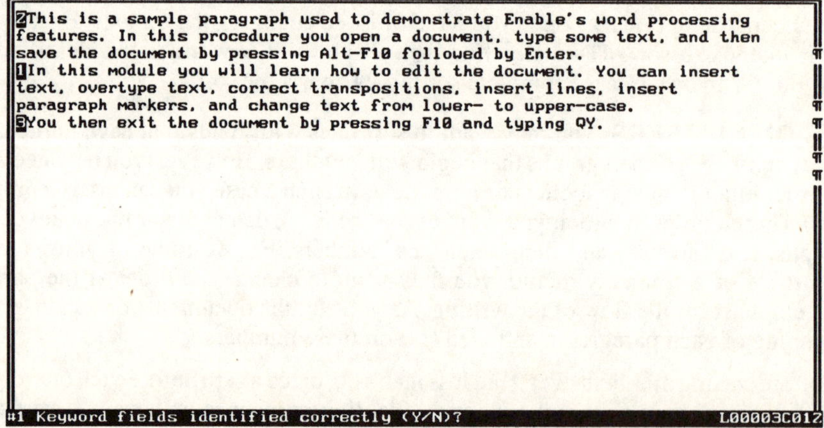

7. Type **Y**, and Enable sorts the paragraphs.
8. Press **End** to move the cursor to the bottom left of the screen. Press **Alt-F6** and delete the second tab mark on the ruler. Press **Enter**, and type the names and employee numbers, as shown in the following screen.

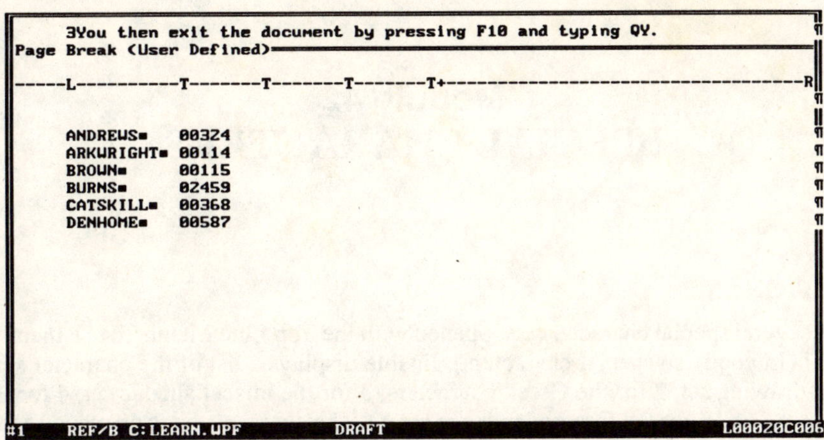
3You then exit the document by pressing F10 and typing QY.
Page Break (User Defined)
-----L----------T-------T-------T-------T+-----------------------------------R
ANDREWS 00324
ARKWRIGHT 00114
BROWN 00115
BURNS 02459
CATSKILL 00368
DENHOME 00587
#1 REF/B C:LEARN.WPF DRAFT L00020C006

9. Place the cursor above the column and press **F10**. Type **LB** and type **C** to change the options. Press **Enter**, type **D2**, and press **Enter**; type **5** and press **Enter**; type **C**. Enable highlights the numbers, and the status line asks if the fields are correctly identified.
10. Type **Y**, and Enable sorts the lines. Notice that although the lines were originally in alphabetical order by name, they are now in employee-number order.
11. Press **F10** and type **QY** to exit without saving.
12. Turn to Module 42 to continue the learning sequence.

Module 42
SPECIAL CHARACTERS

DESCRIPTION

Enable has several special character sets, opened with the Top Line Menu. To use them, press F10 and type L7 (Layout;Use special characters). Enable displays a list of the character sets; press 1 for the box-drawing set, 2 for the Greek characters, 3 for the miscellaneous set, 4 for the foreign language set #1, and 5 for the foreign language set #2. The character set is displayed at the bottom of the screen until it is turned off.

NOTE

> Only systems with graphics boards (a monochrome graphics board or better) can display the special characters.

Once you have turned on a special character set, whenever you press any of the number or hyphen keys, or any of the shift-number or shift-hyphen keys, a special character is displayed in your text. If you want to type a number in your text while a special character set is turned on, press Num Lock, use the numeric keypad to type your numbers, and press Num Lock again. If you want to type any of the hyphen or shift-number characters (such as * or %), you will have to turn off the special characters first.

NOTE

> Not all printers can print the special characters. Refer to your printer's documentation for more information.

BOX-DRAWING CHARACTERS The box-drawing character set, shown in the following screen, allows you to draw boxes around text. By turning on this character set, positioning the cursor, and pressing the number keys, you can draw corners or straight line sections.

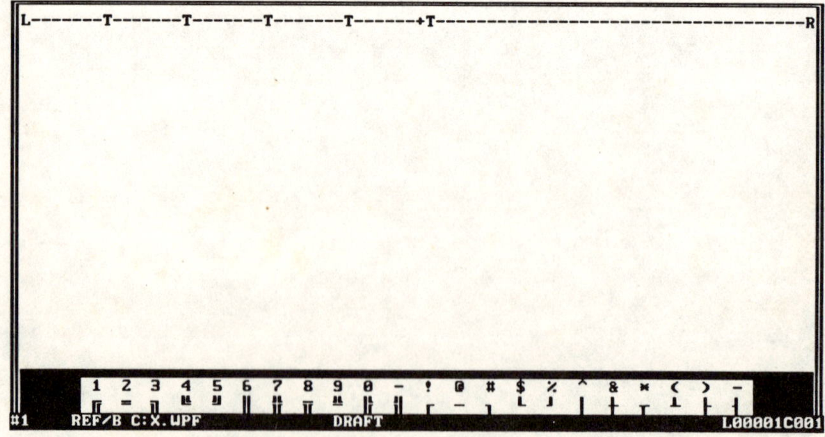

GREEK CHARACTERS The Greek characters are shown in the following screen.

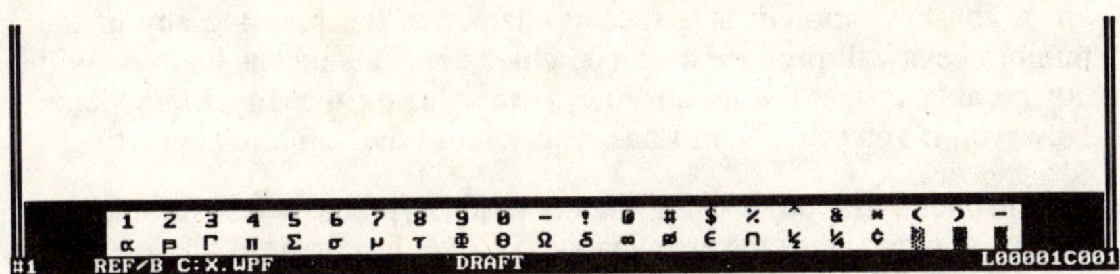

MISCELLANEOUS CHARACTERS The miscellaneous characters are shown in the following screen.

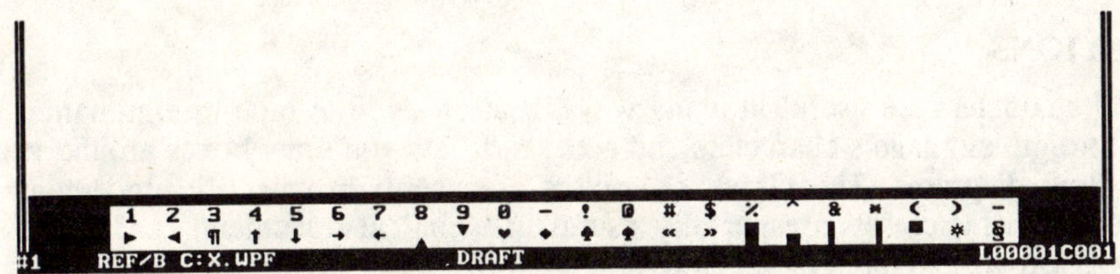

FOREIGN LANGUAGE CHARACTERS The foreign language characters, sets #1 and #2, are shown in the following screens.

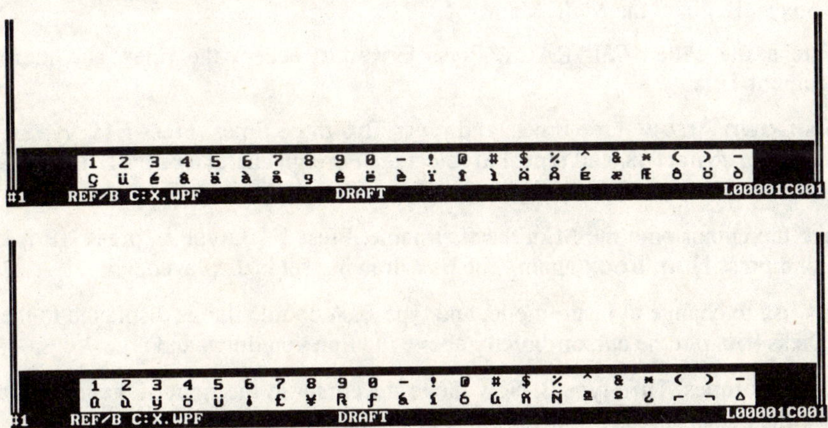

TURNING OFF THE SPECIAL CHARACTERS The easiest way to turn off the special characters is to use the expert command—press F9 and type OCO. If you can't remember this command you can use the Top Line Menu: press F10, type L (Layout), press Num Lock to allow you to use the numerical keypad, and type 76 on the numerical keypad (Use special characters;Turn character set off).

NOTE

Once you have turned on a special characters set, pressing any of the number keys will produce a special character. This means that you will not be able to use the number keys when using the Top Line Menu. However, if you press Num Lock, you can use the numeric keypad.

Alternatively, instead of using the numeric keypad to select lines in the menus, you can press the arrow keys to move the cursor to the line, and press Enter.

THE EM DASH To create an em dash (—), press Alt-hyphen twice. (On some printers this may show as -!-).

APPLICATIONS

The special characters are useful in many ways. It allows you to type foreign names correctly, using the foreign language's characters and accents. It lets you draw boxes around text, in such things as flow diagrams. The Greek characters are useful in scientific documents, and the miscellaneous character set is especially useful in technical documents, because it has such characters as arrows and paragraph markers.

TYPICAL OPERATION

In this activity you create a file called CHARACT, type some text using the special characters, and draw boxes. Begin at the Main Menu.

1. Create a file called CHARACT. Press **Enter** to accept the ruler, and then delete the Document Title.
2. Press **Down Arrow** three times, and press **Tab** three times. Press **F10**, type **L7** to select Use special characters, and type **4** to select the Foreign character set #1. Type **M2ller**. Press **Enter** three times, and press **Tab** twice. Type **B3ranger**. Press **Tab** twice, and type **L3on**.
3. Move the cursor onto the M in the first name. Press **F10**, type **L**, press **Num Lock**, type **71**, and press **Num Lock** again. The box-drawing set is displayed.
4. Press **Ins** to change to insert mode, and type **6**. A double line is displayed to the left of the M. Press **Ins**, put the cursor directly above the line you drew, and type **1**.
5. Type **2** six times. Then type **3**. Now move the cursor to the right of the letter r, and type **6**. Move the cursor directly under the line to the left of the B, and type **4**.
6. Type **2** six times, and type **5**. You have now drawn a box around the name Müller. Use the same method to draw boxes around the other two names, and your screen looks like this:

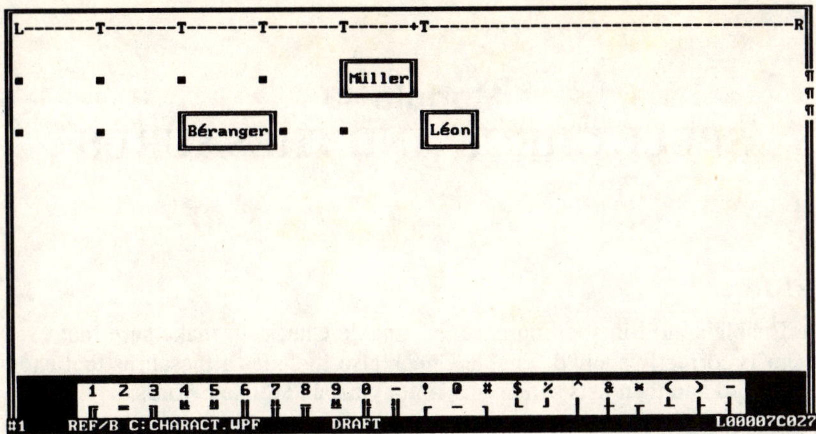

7. Press **F10** and type **QY** to abandon the file.
8. Turn to Module 13 to continue the learning sequence.

Module 43
SPELL CHECK AND THESAURUS

DESCRIPTION

You can use Enable's built-in spelling checker, Enable/Check, to make sure that every word in your document is correctly spelled. Enable/Check also includes a thesaurus that shows you the definition of a word and then lists synonyms, antonyms, and related words.

Enable has several dictionaries. The Standard dictionary, the one you will use to check most documents, is the Proximity/Merriam-Webster Linguibase which has 80,000 words. Enable also has a User dictionary. When Enable/Check finds words that are not included in its Standard dictionary but are still correctly spelled, you can add them to the User dictionary. If your document uses a lot of medical or legal terms, you can use Enable's Legal or Medical dictionary.

TIP: Do a spell check before using automatic hyphenation. Enable/Check does not handle hyphenation very well. See Module 26 for more information.

USING ENABLE/CHECK SPELLING CHECKER To check a document's spelling, press F10 and type 21 (Dictionary;Spell Check). (Dual floppy-disk users will be prompted to insert the Enable/Check disk.) The Enable/Check options are displayed, as on the following screen:

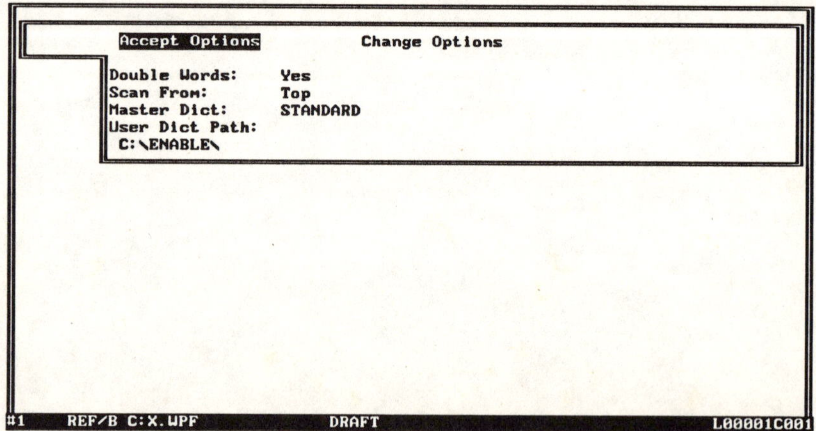

Type A or press Enter to accept Enable's default options for the spell check, or type C and Enable displays a series of prompts that let you change the spell check options, as described in the following paragraphs.

Double Words Enable stops whenever it finds two identical, consecutive words (such as "in in"). Enable lets you remove one of the words or continue without changing them.

Scan From Enable usually starts the spell check from the beginning of the document, but you can tell it to start from the cursor position if you want.

Master Dictionary Enable normally uses its Standard dictionary, but you can tell it to use the Legal or Medical dictionary instead.

User Dictionary Path Enable has a User dictionary in the default data directory (or on the data disk for dual floppy systems). However, if more than one person uses your computer, each person can have his or her own User dictionary. Each one must be in a different directory, so Enable gives you the option of choosing which dictionary to use.

UNRECOGNIZED WORDS Once you have finished changing the options, or if you pressed Enter to accept the options when they were first displayed, Enable begins checking the document. Enable checks any group of recognized characters between a space and an unrecognized character, two spaces, or two unrecognized characters. Recognized characters are letters, numbers, apostrophes, hyphens, and the following characters: Ä ö Ü É ü ü â ä à ç è ë ê ï î ì ô ò ö û ù β

When Enable finds a word that isn't in the Master dictionary you selected, it looks in the User dictionary. If the word is there Enable continues looking for errors, but if it isn't, Enable stops and displays a list of "Word-Not-Found" choices. If you select any of these choices (except number 6), and then change your mind, press the Esc key.

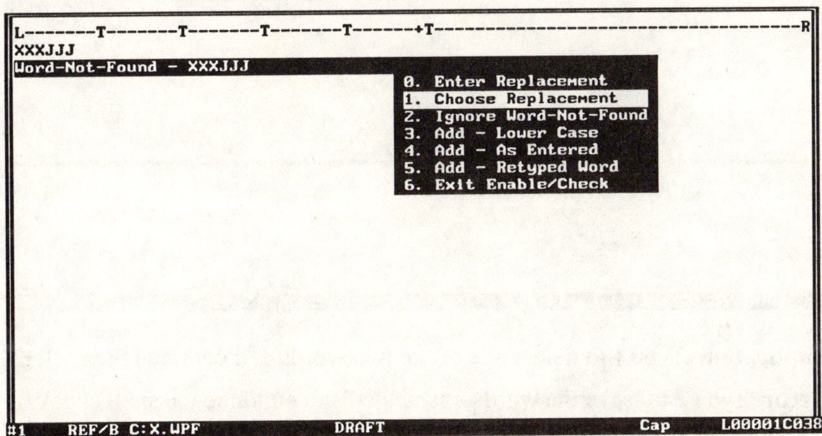

0 Enter Replacement Type 0 (zero) to enter a replacement word. Enable prompts you for the word. Type the word and press Enter, and Enable replaces the incorrect word and continues with the spell check. Enable does not check the word you have typed though, until the next time you do a spell check.

1 Choose Replacement Type 1 if you want Enable to suggest the correct word. Enable searches its dictionaries and lists up to four words. Type the number corresponding to the word you want to replace the error with, or type 0 (zero) to enter a replacement. If Enable cannot find a similar word, it displays the "Enter Replacement Word" prompt instead.

2 Ignore Word-Not-Found Type 2 to continue the spell check without changing the word or adding it to your dictionary. Enable will ignore the word if it sees it again during the current spell check, but will stop when it sees it in any subsequent spell check. You may want to use this when you used a word in a particular document, but rarely use that word at any other time.

3 Add - Lower Case Type 3 to add the word to your User dictionary. Enable adds the word in lowercase and continues the spell check. Words in lowercase in the dictionary are ignored by Enable even if spelled in uppercase.

4 Add - As Entered Type 4 to add the word to your User dictionary exactly as typed. Acronyms and proper names should be added in this way. When Enable sees the word correctly spelled but with different case (such as an acronym in lowercase, or a proper name with the first letter in lowercase) it assumes it is a mistake. For example, if you wish to add the name Aland to your dictionary you should type 4 (to Add as entered). Then, if Enable ever sees the word "aland," it will stop and treat it as a word-not-found.

5 Add - Retyped Word Type 5 and Enable will prompt you to retype the word. When you type the word and press Enter Enable corrects the text and adds the word to the User dictionary.

6 Exit Enable/Check Type 6 to end the spell check.

DUPLICATE WORDS If Enable finds two words spelled exactly the same next to each other, it stops and displays the Word Duplication options.

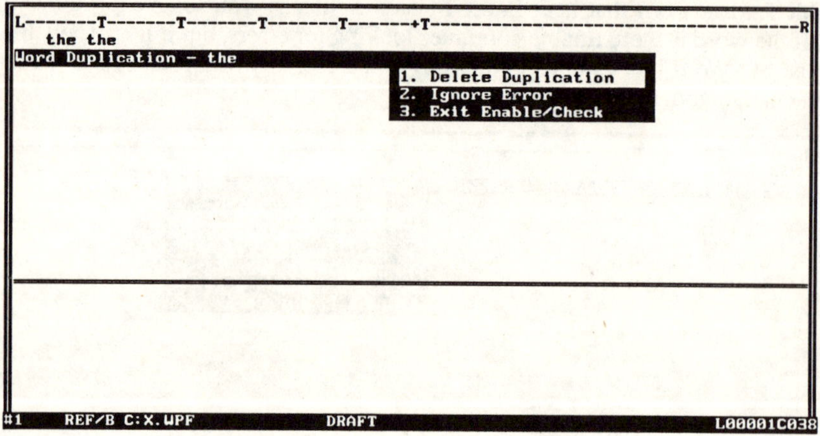

1 Delete Duplication Type 1 to delete one of the two words and continue the spell check.

2 Ignore Error Type 2 to leave the words unchanged and continue the spell check.

3 Exit Enable/Check Type 3 to end the spell check.

PROBLEMS WITH SPELL CHECKS All spell check programs have limitations, and Enable/Check is no exception. Enable/Check only finds words it doesn't recognize. It doesn't know if you are using a word incorrectly. For example, if you type "to" when you really mean "two" Enable will not stop. Also, if you have two correctly spelled words incorrectly linked by an unrecognized character, Enable will not stop; it recognizes the two words as correct. "As&correct" will be ignored by Enable. So don't think Enable/Check is an alternative to proofreading. It isn't; it just speeds up the proofreading process and acts as a double-check on spelling, which is just one part of editing a document.

ENABLE/CHECK SUMMARY Enable displays a summary screen at the end of the spell check. The summary gives the name of the file, the number of words in the file, the number of duplicates found, the number of unrecognized words found, the number of corrections made, and the number of words added to the User dictionary.

Press Esc to clear the summary. Enable places the cursor on the last unrecognized word.

CAUTION

> Enable has not saved any modifications to your document. If you want to save the changes made, you must save your document before exiting. (If you are using a floppy disk system remember to replace the System or Operation disk first.)

MAINTAINING THE USER DICTIONARY Enable allows you to open the User dictionary like a word processing file. This allows you to add words without waiting for Enable to find them first, and to delete incorrect words accidentally added to the dictionary.

Opening the User Dictionary To open the User dictionary from the Main Menu type UWD (Use System;Word Processing;Dictionary). Enable prompts you for the name of the directory in which the dictionary is filed. Normally you will only have one dictionary in the default data directory (or the data disk for dual floppy systems), in which case you just press Enter.

If you have more than one User dictionary you must specify the directory in which the one you want to open is stored. You do not have to specify the User dictionary name, as all User dictionaries are called USERDICT.TSG.

When Enable opens the User dictionary you will see a list of words, one per line. They may not be in alphabetical order — it doesn't matter to Enable, but if you would like to see them in order to help you search the list, use Enable's text-sorting feature to put them in order (see Module 41).

Editing the User Dictionary You can edit the dictionary using normal word processing procedures. Automatic reformat is turned off. Only put one word on a line; begin at the left margin and press Enter each time you finish a word. Words may be up to 30 characters long. Words with unrecognized characters (such as "Bed&Breakfast") must be added as two separate words ("Bed" and "Breakfast"). To delete a word, press Alt-F3, which deletes the entire line. You can also copy a list of words from another file using the Copy feature (see Module 31).

You can use the Find feature (Module 22) to search for a word, and you can use the Paper-Clip feature (Module 14) to mark words you may want to return to and revise.

NOTE

> You cannot use Enable/Check in another window while the User dictionary is open.

Saving the User Dictionary The dictionary is saved like any other word processing document. However, Enable only saves characters that Enable/Check recognizes.

Printing the User Dictionary The dictionary can be printed when it is displayed on screen by pressing Alt-F2.

USING THE THESAURUS Enable also has a thesaurus. To use it, place the cursor on the word you want to look up, press F10, and type 22 (Dictionary;Thesaurus). Enable takes a few seconds to look up the word, and then displays a table that gives one or more definitions of the word, as shown in the following screen:

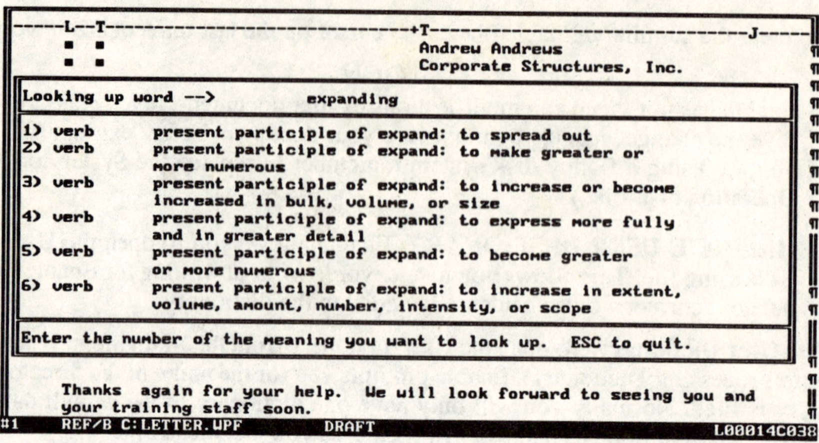

You can press Esc to return to the document, or type the number of the definition in which you are interested. For example, if you press 4 when the previous screen is displayed, Enable displays the following screen.

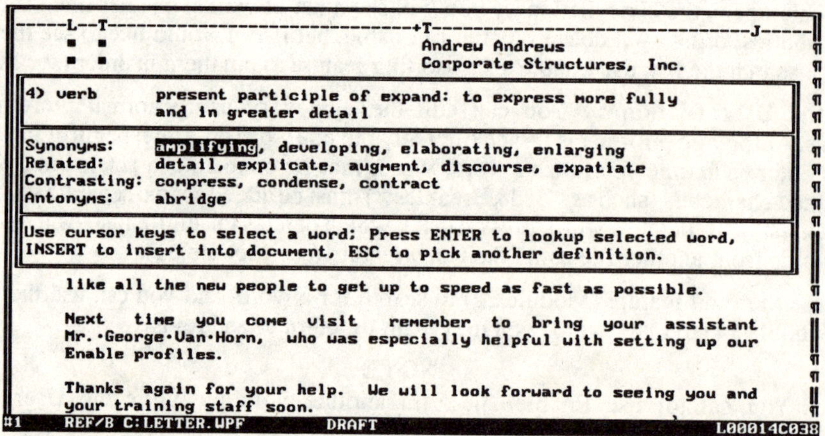

In this screen Enable is showing you synonyms (words similar to the selected definition); antonyms (words that are the opposite); words related to the definition; and words contrasting with the definition. You can now press Esc to return to the previous list of definitions, or select one of the words by moving the cursor. If you want to replace the word you looked up, put the cursor on one of the words in the thesaurus and press Ins. If you want to look up the definition of one of the words, place the cursor on the word and press Enter. And if you want to return to editing the document, press Esc twice.

APPLICATIONS

Enable's spell checker and thesaurus are important tools that make writing easier. Although it is not an alternative to careful editing, Enable/Check is a good way to speed up the process. Editing is quicker and more effective when obvious spelling mistakes are cleared up first. And Enable/Check will often find errors that you miss when editing.

The thesaurus is a great tool you can use to improve your writing. It helps you find clearer and more effective words and lets you check the meanings of words about which you are unsure.

TYPICAL OPERATION

In this activity you use the thesaurus in the file named LETTER, created in Module 4 and last modified in Module 24 (for a sample spell check, see Module 4). Begin at the Main Menu.

1. Open the file named LETTER.
2. Move the cursor to the word "clarify" in the second line of the body of the letter. Press **F10** and type **22** to select the thesaurus. Enable displays the following screen.

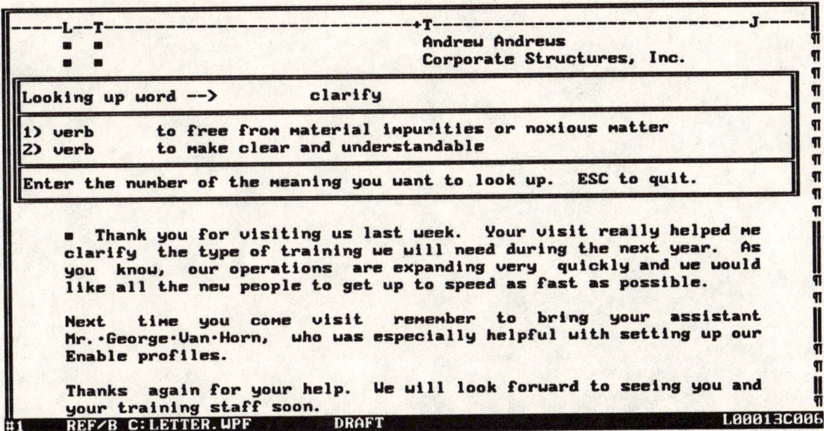

Notice that Enable is showing you two different definitions for the word, clarify.

3. Type **2** to select the second defintion. Enable shows you a list of words. Press **Down Arrow** three times, and **Right Arrow** once, to move the cursor to "straighten out." Your screen looks like the following.

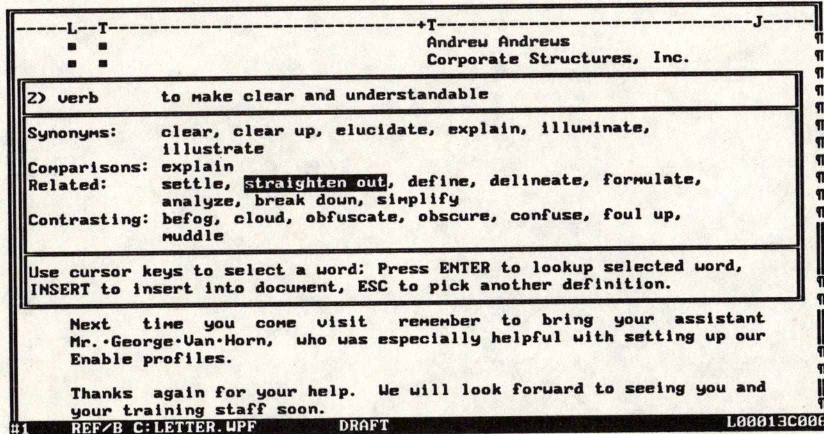

4. Press **Ins** and Enable removes the list of words from the screen and shows you your letter again. Enable then removes the word clarify and replaces it with "straighten out."
5. Press **Alt-End** and type **Y** to quit the file without saving it.
6. Turn to Module 25 to continue the learning sequence.

Module 44
TABLE OF CONTENTS

DESCRIPTION

Enable has a feature that helps you build a table of contents. You insert markers in the text you want to appear in the contents, and then get Enable to automatically compile the table. You can then print the table, either on its own or with the document. And Enable lets you choose from several table of contents formats. Table of contents entries are not printed, but you can have Enable insert the entry into the text if you want. You can then use the table of contents entries in your text instead of titles. For example, if you use table of contents entries instead of chapter titles, you can make Enable insert the entry into your text when it compiles the table, along with the chapter number.

You can toggle the display of table of contents markers on and off by pressing F10 and typing EA6 (EditOpts;Screen displays;Table of contents entries).

There are three stages in building a table of contents. First you create the entries. You place a table of contents entry (which looks similar to a header or a footer) on the page of text you want to reference. This step can be done while you create the text, or after you have finished the document. In the second stage you decide if you want sequence numbers and what they will look like; whether the table should be inserted into the document, and where; and whether you want to use "outline" style. In the third stage you compile the table.

TABLE OF CONTENTS ENTRIES When you come to a place in your text that you want to be referenced in the table of contents, place the cursor on that line, press F10, and type L91 (Layout;Table of contents;Create an entry). The status line prompts you to position the cursor and press Enter. When you press Enter, Enable puts a table of contents marker (similar to a header) below the cursor line, and moves the cursor into the marker.

Omitting Sequence or Page Numbers If you don't want each entry in the table to be preceded by a sequence number, type N#. If you don't want page numbers included in the table, type NP. If you don't want sequence or page numbers, type N# NP. (Leave one space between the N# and NP.) Then press Enter, and begin the entry.

First Space: Outline Format The first character of the entry determines whether you are using an outline format, and, if so, in what position the entry appears. In an outline format you can have subheadings that are indented below the previous headings, as shown in the following screen.

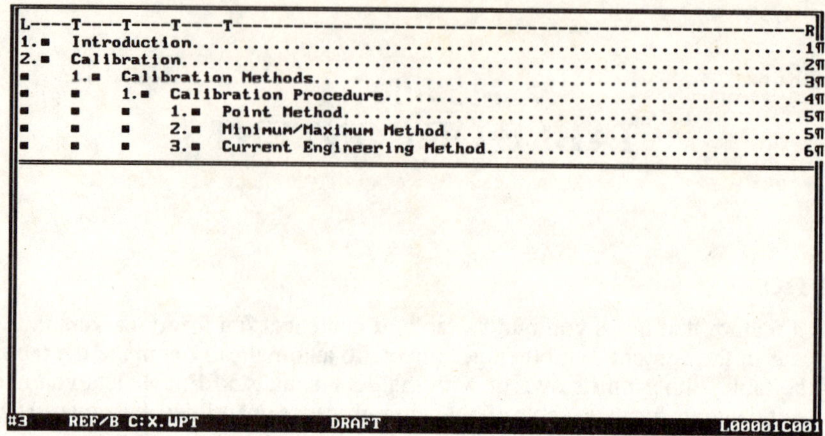

If you do not want to use an outline format, leave a space. If you do want to use an outline format, type one of the following characters:

U	First Level ("Unit")
C	Second Level ("Chapter")
S	Third Level ("Section")
M	Fourth Level ("Minor")

Then type a space, and begin typing the entry.

NOTE

If you begin typing the entry without leaving a space, Enable presumes you want to use the outline format and uses the first character of the entry to determine the entry position.

The Entry The entry is the title that appears in the table of contents. You may want to type a title that already appears in your text. Or you can leave the title out of your text; when you compile the table you can have Enable insert the table of contents entries into the text, so that the titles and sequence numbers (if any) are displayed and printed in the text.

In some earlier releases of Enable/OA each entry was limited to only one line. If you type two or more lines into a table of contents entry marker in one of the earlier releases, Enable treats each line as a separate entry. However, later releases allow you to type multiple line entries, as long as the lines are not separated by paragraph markers or blank lines.

If you want a blank line between each entry in the table, press F3 after you type the entry, press Enter, and move the cursor out of the marker using the arrow keys. The following screen shows several different types of table of contents entries.

```
L-------T-------T-------T-------T------+T-----------------------------------R
Table of Contents
 N# NP
 Calibration

This is a table of contents entry without sequence or page numbers

Table of Contents
 Calibration

This is a table of contents entry with both sequence and page numbers

Table of Contents
U Calibration

This is a first level (Units) entry in an outline-format table of contents.

#1    REF/B C:X.WPF            DRAFT                          L00008C076
```

Editing Entries You can come back at any time and edit your entries. Move the cursor into the marker and use the word processing tools to change the entry. If you want to add the "N# NP" line, place the cursor on the double line at the top of the marker and press F3 to insert a blank line; then type in NP or N# NP.

Deleting Entries You can delete entries by placing the cursor on the double line at the top of the marker and pressing Alt-F3.

NOTE

Remember to re-compile your table of contents after editing or deleting entries. See the description of compiling, later in this module.

MODIFYING THE TABLE OF CONTENTS OPTIONS Press F10 and type L94 (Layout; Table of contents options;Modify table of contents options). Enable displays the following screen:

```
Should Table of Contents entries be copied into text:       Yes  No
Should Table of Contents entries have sequence numbers:      Yes  No

Select style of Unit numbers:              1  2=A  3=a  4=I  5=i
Select style of Chapter numbers:           1  2=A  3=a  4=I  5=i
Select style of Section numbers:           1  2=A  3=a  4=I  5=i
Select style of Minor Section numbers:     1  2=A  3=a  4=I  5=i

Optional outline style: end-mark only:     Yes     No

 ▸ This option copies Table of Contents entries into a document
   when you place it in Final Form, or print it.  This option eliminates
   the need for manually copying Table of Contents entries into the text.

#1    REF/B C:X.WPF            DRAFT                          L00008C076
```

Should Table of Contents entries be copied into text? No/Yes If you selectYes, Enable places a copy of the entry into the text at the marker position when you print the file or change to final mode. This appears as a header or title.

You can determine the position of this header in the text; if you want the header to start in column

10, for example, begin it in column 10 in the table of contents marker. Insert blank lines between the marker and the text if you want lines between the header and the text, but make sure that the text is within three lines of the marker; if it is, Enable will not allow a page break to separate the header from the text.

Should Table of Contents entries have sequence numbers? No/Yes This prompt only appears if you answered Yes to the last one. If you select Yes at this prompt Enable will include the sequence number when it places a copy of the entry in the body of the text.

Select style of Unit numbers:
Select style of Chapter numbers:
Select style of Section numbers:
Select style of Minor Section numbers: 1 2=A 3=a 4=I 5=i These four prompts allow you to specify the type of sequence numbers Enable uses in the table of contents. Select 1 for Arabic numbers, 2 for uppercase letters, 3 for lowercase letters, 4 for uppercase Roman numerals, and 5 for lowercase Roman numerals.

Optional outline style; end-mark only: No/Yes If you select No, all the sequence numbers in the second, third, and fourth levels are displayed in the table of contents, as shown below.

```
L----T----T----T----T------------------------------------------------------R
1.■  Introduction...........................................................2¶
2.■  Printer................................................................3¶
■    2.1.■Print Intervals.....................................................4¶
■    ■    2.1.1.■   Alarm Status................................................5¶
■    ■    ■    2.1.1.1.■Alarm 1.................................................6¶
■    ■    ■    2.1.1.2.■Alarm 2.................................................7¶
■    ■    ■    2.1.1.3.■Alarm 3.................................................8¶

#5    REF/B C:X1.WPT               DRAFT                              L00001C001
```

If you select Yes, the numbers are shown as in the screen below; only the last number is displayed (3. Alarm 3, instead of 2.1.1.3 Alarm 3.)

```
L----T----T----T----T------------------------------------------------------R
1.■  Introduction...........................................................2¶
2.■  Printer................................................................3¶
■    1.■  Print Intervals...................................................4¶
■    ■    1.■  Alarm Status.................................................5¶
■    ■    ■    1.■  Alarm 1.................................................6¶
■    ■    ■    2.■  Alarm 2.................................................7¶
■    ■    ■    3.■  Alarm 3.................................................8¶

#4    REF/B C:X1.WPT               DRAFT                              L00001C001
```

When you have completed selecting the options, use the Down Arrow to move the cursor out of the options page. Enable displays your document again.

COMPILING THE TABLE OF CONTENTS Once you have inserted all the entries, and the document is formatted as you want it to appear in the table of contents, you are ready to compile the table. Press F10 and type L92 (Layout;Table of Contents options;Compile the table); Enable displays the following prompt.

Do you want periods between the entry and the page number: Yes/No. If you select Yes, the table of contents will have dots joining each entry and its page number. After you have made your choice, Enable displays a default ruler line, along with the following prompt.

Change margins or tabs and/or accept this ruler by pressing Enter. Adjust the margins and rulers as you want them to appear in the table of contents. The tabs are used to indent outline format entries, as follows (assuming you are using sequence numbers): the first number is placed on the left margin; the first entry and any second level numbers begin on the first tab; the second level entry and any third level numbers begin on the second tab; the third level entry and any fourth level numbers begin on the third tab; the fourth level entry begins on the fourth tab; the page numbers are placed on the right margin. You must use a justified right margin (J) if you want the page numbers on the right side of the page; otherwise Enable places each page number a few spaces after its entry.

When you press Enter, Enable builds a table of contents and saves it in a separate file. The file has the same name as your original document, but has the file extension .WPT.

PRINTING THE TABLE OF CONTENTS To print the table of contents press F10 and type L93 (Layout;Table of contents options;Print table of contents).

You can also print the table at any point inside the document itself. For example, place the cursor at the top of the file, type %INCLUDE, skip a space and then type the name of the file with a .WPT extension. For example, type "%INCLUDE Calibrat.wpt" to print the table of contents built for the file named Calibrat. The %INCLUDE must start in column one, must be in uppercase, and must be on its own line. The line is omitted in a printout, so insert a line for the command, don't just put the command on a blank line. If you want the table of contents to appear on a separate sheet of paper you must insert your own page breaks.

PAGE NUMBERS If you have not specified page numbers in the document Enable uses "absolute" page numbers. For example, if an entry has been inserted on the third page of the document, Enable puts 3 in the table of contents. However, if you specified in the Page Form that the document begins at page 50, Enable puts page 53 in the table of contents. (See Module 35, Print, for information about the Page Form.) Also, if you have created headers or footers with page numbers in them, Enable will use those page numbers to define the table of contents page numbers (see Module 25 for information about Headers and Footers.) The numbers in the headers or footers take precedence over the number in the Page Form.

EDITING .WPT FILES You can edit the table of contents (.WPT) files in the same way as any other word processing file. You could combine files to build a table of contents for a large document, for example, or change the attributes of some of the entries. Remember, though, that editing the .WPT file does not change the table of contents entries in the text file.

APPLICATIONS

A table of contents is essential for any long document. Putting one together manually is very time-consuming, and has to be redone each time the document is reformatted and the page numbers change. Using Enable's automatic table of contents you can begin building a table effortlessly as you type the document, and compile new tables in just a few seconds.

TYPICAL OPERATION

In this activity you build a table of contents for the file named LEARN, created in Module 32. Begin at the Main Menu.

1. Open the file named LEARN.
2. Move the cursor to the line immediately above the title. Press **F3** three times to insert three lines, then press **F10**, type **L91**, and press **Enter**. When Enable displays a table of contents marker type **C Word Processing**.
3. Move the cursor to the blank line above "This is a sample." Use the expert command (press **F9** and **Ins**, and type **T**) to place a table of contents marker.
4. Type **C Sample Paragraph** in the marker. Move the cursor down and place it on the page break. Press **F9** and **Ins**, and type **T**. Then type **C Editing the Document** in the marker.
5. Move the cursor to the blank line above the last line of text. Press **F9** and **Ins**, and type **T**. Type **S Exiting the Document** in the marker. Your screen should look like the following:

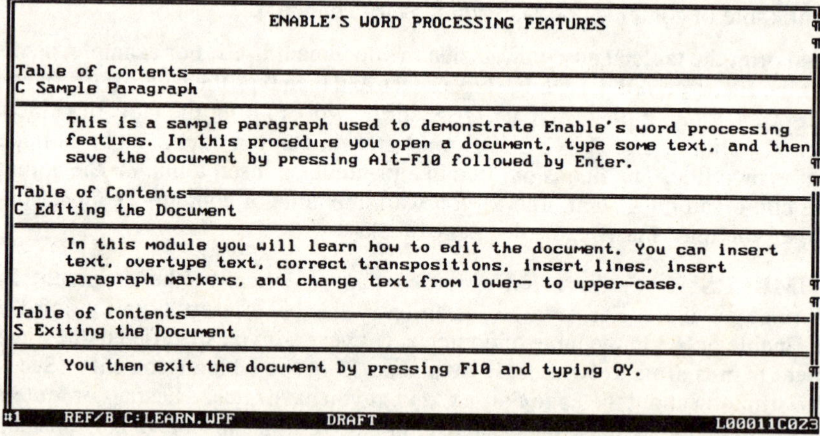

```
                 ENABLE'S WORD PROCESSING FEATURES

Table of Contents
C Sample Paragraph

     This is a sample paragraph used to demonstrate Enable's word processing
     features. In this procedure you open a document, type some text, and then
     save the document by pressing Alt-F10 followed by Enter.

Table of Contents
C Editing the Document

     In this module you will learn how to edit the document. You can insert
     text, overtype text, correct transpositions, insert lines, insert
     paragraph markers, and change text from lower- to upper-case.

Table of Contents
S Exiting the Document

     You then exit the document by pressing F10 and typing QY.

#1    REF/B C:LEARN.WPF         DRAFT                          L00011C023
```

6. Press **F10** and type **L94**. After a few seconds Enable displays the Modify Options screen. Use the cursor to select **Yes** at the "Should Table of Contents entries be copied into text," and then press **Down Arrow**. The "Should Table of Contents have sequence numbers" prompt is displayed. Select **Yes** and press the **Down Arrow**.
7. For each of the four "Select style of numbers:" prompts select **2=A** to choose uppercase letters. Press the **Down Arrow** to move to the "Optional outline style; endmark only:" prompt, and select **Yes**. Press the **Down Arrow** and Enable displays your file again.

8. Press **F10**, type **L92**, and Enable asks if you want periods between the entries in the table and the page numbers. Type **Y** to select Yes, and Enable asks if you want to change the ruler.
9. Press **Enter** to accept the ruler, and Enable compiles your table of contents. Press **Ctrl-End** to move the cursor to the top of the file; move it down to the first blank line after the footer.
10. Type **%INCLUDE learn.wpt** and press **Enter**. This tells Enable to include the table of contents file when you print LEARN. Press **F10**, type **L4** and press **Enter** to insert a page break.
11. Press **Alt-F2** to print the file. Notice that the sequence numbers in the table of contents are uppercase letters, and only show the endmark (A. Exiting the Document instead of A.B.A Exiting the Document). Notice also that Enable has inserted the entries and their sequence numbers into the text.
12. Press **F10** and type **QY** to exit the file without saving.
13. Turn to Module 28 to continue the learning sequence.

Module 45
TEXT ATTRIBUTES

DESCRIPTION

Enable's text attributes let you change the size and style of characters in your documents. You can make text bold, underlined, or italic; use superscripts or subscripts; and use compressed, wide, or quality text. These override the fonts in Page Form (Module 35).

CAUTION

> Some of the text attributes affect the size of the printed characters. While this is not usually a problem, it can cause misalignment if you are trying to line text up with tabs. If so, you may have to use the %TABS commands. See Module 10 for more information.

APPEARANCE ON SCREEN If you don't have a graphics monitor, some of these attributes will not be shown on your screen, but they will still be printed correctly if you have a compatible printer. (See the Enable "Getting Started" booklet for information about printers.) You may also change the screen appearance by changing your profile (see Appendix B). If you do have a graphics monitor you must change to text-graphics mode to see all of the attributes (press F10, type M3, and type 2, 3, or 4, depending on your screen type. See Module 2 for more information.)

ATTRIBUTE HELP SCREEN Enable has a help screen that lists the attributes and their corresponding commands. Press F10 and type EE (EditOpts;Attribute Help Screen). You see the following:

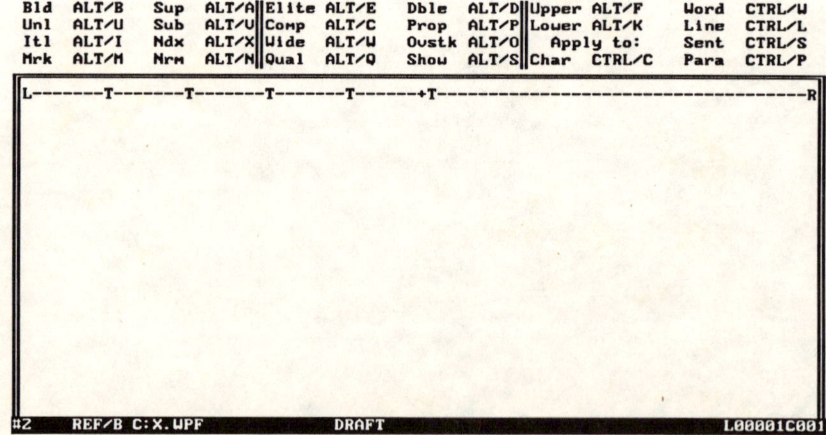

This screen is displayed until you use the same command to remove it. The help screen lists the attributes (commands preceded by Alt/) and some of the text segment commands (preceded by Ctrl/).

The attributes are of two main types: those that are shown on the screen, and those that are indicated by a highlighted diamond and letter. The attributes that are shown on the screen also have a lowercase letter that is shown on the status line. These attributes are described next.

STATUS-LINE ATTRIBUTES If you have a graphics monitor you see all of these attributes on your screen. Italics, for example, are actually italicized. If you don't have a graphics monitor the attributes are shown in a different way. Color monitors use different colors to indicate different attributes, and the colors can be defined in your profile (see Appendix B). Monochrome monitors can show attributes such as boldface and underline, but cannot indicate all of the attributes—italic, for example, appears as boldface. These are "status line" attributes because when you turn on the attribute a lowercase character is displayed in the status line to the right of DRAFT or FINAL. These characters are shown in parentheses next to each attribute in the following table:

Attribute	Command	Description
Boldface (b)	Alt-B	Text is converted to boldface.
Italic (i)	Alt-I	Text is converted to italic.
Normal Text	Alt-N	The command Alt-N is used to remove other attributes.
Subscript (v)	Alt-V	Text is lowered half a line below the normal position.
Superscript (a)	Alt-A	Text is raised half a line above the normal position.
Underline (u)	Alt-U	Text is underlined.
Index (x)	Alt-X	See Module 28.
Marked Text (m)	Alt-M	See Module 11.
Lowercase Text (l)	Alt-L	See Module 19.
Uppercase Text (u)	Alt-U	See Module 19.

Applying Status-Line Attributes You can apply status-line attributes in two ways. The first way is to turn on the attribute before typing the text, (using the command in the preceding table). For example, press Alt-U (underline), then type the text. All the text is underlined. Press Alt-U again when you no longer need underlined text.

The second way is to apply the attribute to existing text. Position the cursor at the beginning of the text you want to modify, use a command from the preceding table, and use one of the following text segment commands to apply the attribute.

Text Segment Commands

Command	Description
Ctrl-C	converts a character.
Ctrl-W	converts from the cursor to the end of a word.
Ctrl-L	converts from the cursor to the end of a line.
Ctrl-S	converts from the cursor to the end of a sentence.
Ctrl-P	converts from the cursor to the next paragraph marker.
Ctrl-G	converts from the cursor to the end of the page.
Ctrl-B	converts text set as a block (see Module 11).

The text you wish to convert does not have to be continuous. For example, you could use a segment command to convert a line, move the cursor down to another paragraph, and use a segment command to convert a word. Remember to turn off the attribute when you have finished, by repeating the attribute command.

Removing Status-Line Attributes You can use the Alt-N command to remove attributes. Use it just as if you are applying an attribute (press Alt-N, move to the text, and use the text segment commands). All the attributes that have been applied to the text are removed.

Showing Attributes If you have a graphics monitor and you want to see the attributes, you must first change Enable to graphics mode. Press F10 and type M34 (MCM;Screen;Graphics). If you do not have a graphics monitor use the Show command; press Alt-S and move the cursor through the file. When the cursor lands on a character with an attribute other than normal (or the diamond-attributes described below) the corresponding status line character is displayed in uppercase on the status line to the right of DRAFT/FINAL.

Searching for Text Attributes To find a character that has had a text attribute set, place the cursor at the top of the text you want to search, turn on the text attributes you want to search for, press F2 and type A. The cursor moves to the first occurrence. To continue, press F2 twice. If you search for two attributes, Enable only shows you text that has both of them set.

DIAMOND ATTRIBUTES Diamond attributes are indicated by a diamond and a letter, both preceding and following the text. For example, even if you have a graphics monitor, wide text is not shown on the screen any differently from normal text. Instead a highlighted diamond and a letter W (◆W) are shown immediately before and immediately after the text. No indication is shown in the status line.

The indicators are shown in parentheses next to each attribute in the following table.

Attribute	Command	Description
Elite (◆E)	Alt-E	This overrides pica or compressed type and prints the text at 12 characters per inch instead of 10.
Compressed (◆C)	Alt-C	This overrides pica or elite to print the text closer together, 15 to 17 characters per inch, but the same height.
Wide (◆W)	Alt-W	These characters are wider and further apart (5 characters per inch) although they remain the same height. This modifies pica, elite, and compressed text. Some of the text may be forced onto the next line when it prints.
Quality (◆Q)	Alt-Q	This prints the text in Near Letter Quality.
Double-Strike (◆D)	Alt-D	Sometimes called "enhanced" or "shadow print," and similar to boldface, this is produced by printing the same character twice, slightly offset.
Proportional Text (◆P)	Alt-P	Text is adjusted for the letter size, for example, a w takes up more room than an i.
Overstrike (◆O)	Alt-O	A selected character is printed on top of the text. Press Alt-O and type the overstrike character (a hyphen or backslash, for example). Then type the text. At the end of the text press Alt-O and type the overstrike character again.

Applying Diamond Attributes Again, there are two ways to apply attributes; before and after typing the text. To apply before, use the command, type the text, and use the command again to turn the attribute off. Each time you use the command the diamond/letter indicator appears on the screen. All text between the indicators has the attribute.

To apply the attributes to existing text, place the cursor at the beginning of the text, use the command, move the cursor to the end of the text, and use the command again.

Overriding the Page Form Some of the diamond-attributes override the Page Form. The Page Form defines how your document is printed (see Module 35, Print). Using elite, compressed, proportional, or quality overrides the Page Form. So, if the Page Form has pica set, applying elite will change the print to elite. If, however, elite is set in the Page Form, applying the elite attribute will turn elite off—so pica will be printed.

Removing Diamond Attributes Remove diamond attributes by deleting the diamond/character in the same way you would delete any kind of text.

MULTIPLE ATTRIBUTES More than one attribute may be applied to text at the same time. For example, you may wish to have text that is both boldface and underlined. Press Alt-B, press Alt-U, and use the text segment commands. Both attributes are applied at the same time, and the status line shows both b and u. The following combinations of attributes are not possible: superscript/subscript, subscript/underline, superscript/underline/index, and subscript/index.

CORRECTING TAB ALIGNMENT If you apply some of these attributes to text that contains tabs, the text may print with incorrect alignment. This can be solved by using an embedded print command, %TABS. For more information see Module 10.

PRINTER CONTROL CODES Embedded control codes may be available to your printer, allowing you to use attributes that Enable is unable to send to your printer. See your printer manual for more information.

APPLICATIONS

Text attributes make your document appear more professional. Headings can be boldface and underlined. Italics can be used to stress words. Superscripts can be used for exponential values and fractions, while subscripts may be used for fractions and scientific notation. And the type of print used can be changed for different documents or parts of the text within a document. For example, you can change the size and type of print for a long quotation.

TYPICAL OPERATION

In this activity you apply attributes to the file named LETTER. Begin at the Main Menu.

1. Open the file LETTER.
2. Move the cursor to the M in Mr. Anderson. Press **Alt-B**. Notice the small b that appears in the status line. Press **Ctrl-W** three times. The next three words change to boldface.
3. Press **Alt-U**. Notice that a u appears in the status line next to the b. Press **Ctrl-S**. The next sentence is changed to boldface and underlined.
4. Press **Alt-B** and **Alt-U**. The bu in the status line disappears. Press **Alt-I** and an i appears in the status line. Press **Ctrl-P** and the rest of the paragraph is changed to italic text. If you have a non-graphics monitor the text looks like boldface.

5. Press **Alt-C**. ◆C displays on the screen, but no indication of the attribute appears in the status line. Move the cursor to the space after the word "soon." Press **Alt-C** again. ◆C is displayed again.
6. Type **I am now typing in italic**. Because you have not yet turned off italic text, anything you type is in italic. Press **Alt-I** to turn off italic text. Your screen looks like this (this is from a monographics monitor—other screens may look slightly different):

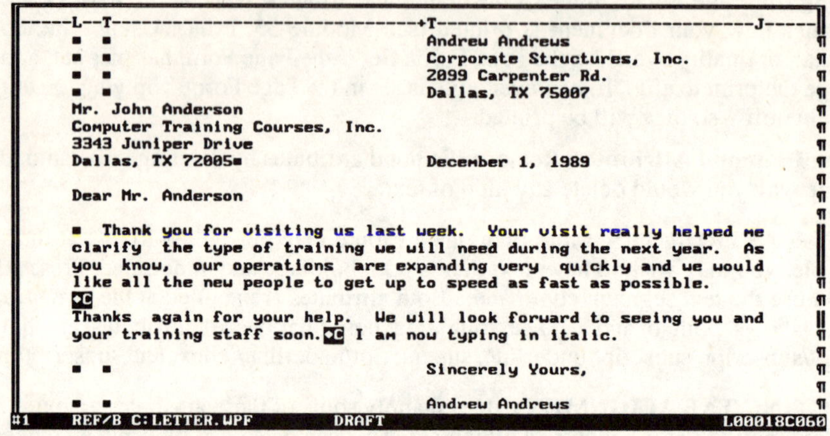

7. Press **F2** followed by **Home** to move the cursor to the top of the document. Press **Alt-S** to turn on the Show Attribute mode.
8. Press **Ctrl-Right Arrow** to move the cursor through the letter, word by word. Notice that when the cursor passes over characters that are bold, underlined, or italic a letter b, u, or i appears in the status line. No letter appears when the cursor passes over a diamond attribute.
9. Press **F10** and type **QY** abandon the document without saving.
10. Turn to Module 18 to continue the learning sequence.

Module 46
WINDOWS

DESCRIPTION

One of Enable's great strengths is that it allows you to open up to eight windows at one time. You could be working on a word processing file while referring to another word processing file and several spreadsheets and databases. The windows are numbered, in the left corner of the status line, in the order in which they are opened, except if you close a window. For example, you have four windows open, and you close number two. The next window you open is number two, not number five.

TIP: Save your file before you open another window, to make sure you don't forget to save it or lose it if you run into problems in another file.

To access window commands, press F10 and type M1 (MCM;Windows). Enable displays the following options:

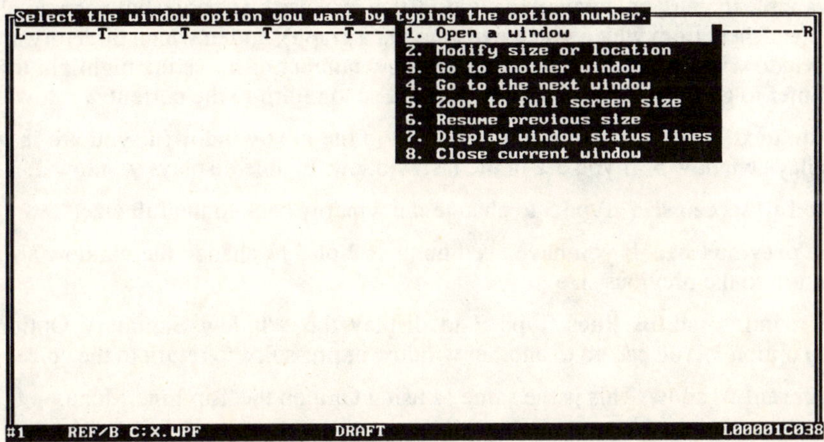

1. Open a window Type 1 to open another window. Enable displays the Main Menu and lets you open any sort of window; word processing, spreadsheet, database, graphics, and so on.

2. Modify size or location Type 2 if you want to change the size of the window or move it to a different place on the screen. Enable displays instructions in the status line, telling you to type M (move), S (shrink), or E (expand) and then press the arrow keys to actually move, shrink, or expand the window. Instead of using the arrow keys, you can press and hold the R key to rapidly shrink or expand the window equally in all directions. You can carry out multiple operations, shrinking and then moving a window, for example. When you have finished the operation, press Esc.

3. Go to another window Type 3, and Enable displays the System Status screen.

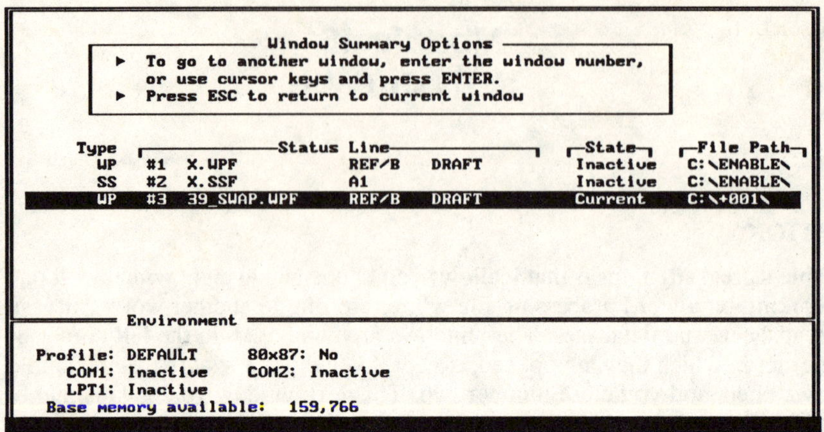

This screen lists all the open windows. It shows the window type (for example, WP is word processing, SS is spreadsheet); the window number (1 to 8); the filename; status-line information (Ref and B, for example, and whether the file is in draft or final mode); whether the window is Current (the window you were in before displaying the System Status screen), Inactive (another window available to you), or Notavail (a window that is in use by Enable, but not available to you, such as a spreadsheet from which you are displaying a graph); and in which directory and disk the file in the window is stored. You can type a window number or move the highlight to a window and press Enter to go to another window, or press Esc to return to the current window.

4. Go to the next window Type 4 to go straight to the next window; if you are in window 4, Enable displays window 5. If you are in the last window, Enable displays window 1.

5. Zoom to full screen size Type 5 to change the window back to the full size.

6. Resume previous size If you have used number 2 or 5 to change the window size, you can type 6 to return to the previous size.

7. Display window status lines Type 7 to display the Window Summary Options screen, described in option 3. You can go to another window or press Esc to return to the current window.

8. Close current window This is the same as using Quit on the Top Line Menu.

CAUTION

Remember to save your file before closing the window.

COPYING DATA FROM ONE WINDOW TO ANOTHER Module 31 explains how to copy text from one word processing document to another. When copying between windows, set the block first, go to the window that will receive the text, and use the copy command. Enable displays the Interwindow Copy Options screen (which looks the same as the Window Summary Options screen). Select the window with the block set and when Enable displays that window press Alt-F5.

Spreadsheets To copy data from a spreadsheet, place the cursor on the line you want to place the data, and press Alt-F5. Enable displays the Interwindow Copy Options screen. Type the window number, or select the window and press Enter, and Enable displays the spreadsheet. Press Enter to copy the entire spreadsheet. To copy just one part of the spreadsheet, select the range by "pointing" to the range, typing its address, or typing its name. Then press Enter. (You will learn how to define ranges when you learn about the spreadsheet in Section 3.)

Graphics You can also copy graphics into your document. You will learn how to do this when you learn about building graphs in Section 4.

Databases You can also copy data from databases. Module 56 explains how to copy data into an ASCII file. This data can then be converted to Enable format and copied into your word processing document.

EXPERT COMMANDS There are several expert commands for windows that are worth learning quickly. Alt-Up Arrow and Alt-Down Arrow display the next window in that "direction" (with a higher or lower window-number). And Alt-Home displays the Main Menu, so that you can open a new window.

APPLICATIONS

Enable's window operations make true application-integration possible. Opening several windows at the same time allows you to refer to information in another window, or even copy information from one to the other. A section of a spreadsheet can be included in a memo or letter, or a list from a database could be added to a document. You can choose to leave the windows full size, and display another window when you need it, or you can display several smaller windows at the same time.

TYPICAL OPERATION

In this activity you open the files named LETTER and LEARN, created in Modules 6 and 29 respectively, and carry out various windows operations. Begin at the Main Menu.

1. Open the file named LETTER.
2. Press **F10**, and type **M12** to modify the size and location of the window. When Enable displays the instructions in the status line, type **S**, and press and hold **R** until the window is about half the original size. Type **M**, and press **Left Arrow** and **Up Arrow** until the window is in the top left corner. Press **Esc**.
3. Press **F10** and type **M11** to open a window. Enable displays the Main Menu. Open the file named LEARN.
4. Press **F10** and type **M12** to modify the size and location. Type **S** and press **Down Arrow** until the top border of the window is in the middle of the screen. Press **Esc**. Your screen looks something like the following, depending on its size.

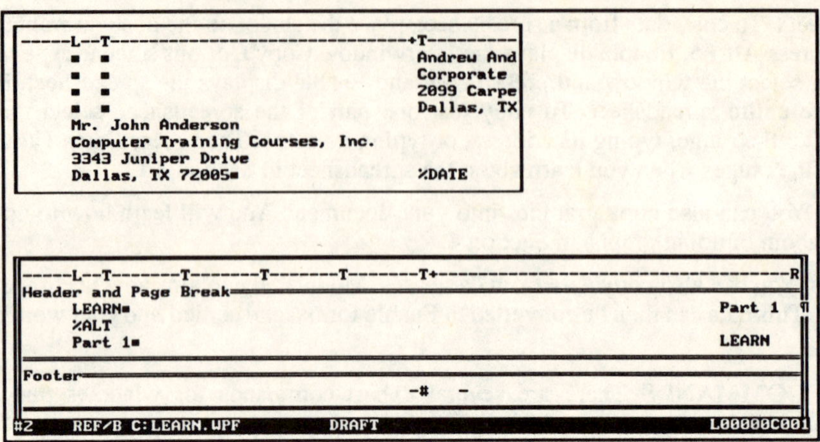

5. Press **F10** and type **M13** to go to another window. Enable displays the System Status screen. Notice that window 2 is highlighted, and is "Current."

6. Press **Up Arrow** to highlight window 1 and press **Enter**. Enable displays both windows, but notice that the cursor is now in window 1, that window 1 has a double line around it, and that "#1" is displayed in the status line.

7. Press **F10** and type **M15**. Enable zooms window 1 to full size, obscuring window 2. Press **F10** and type **QY** to quit window 1. Window 2 is displayed again. Press **F10** and type **M18Y** to quit window 2.

8. Turn to Module 40 to continue the learning sequence.

Module 47
DATABASE OVERVIEW

INTRODUCTION

Enable's DBMS (Database Management System) is a method for handling large amounts of information, allowing you to convert raw data into a useful format. You can take information from spreadsheets, word processing files, Enable database files, other database programs, or information typed into the database, and put the information into reports displayed on your monitor, printed on paper, or stored on floppy disk.

DATABASE FORMAT

A database consists of related information. It may be names and addresses of a company's clients or of your friends and relatives, a list of the books you own, or of your stocks and shares.

This information is broken down within the database into records. Each record is also related information, but at a finer resolution. It may contain the name, address, telephone number, and contact name of one company or one relative; the title, author, subject, and price of one book; or the name, purchase date and price, and current price of one share. Many database programs have limits on the number of records, but Enable has no such limit—you can have as many records as your computer can accomodate in its memory.

Each record is further broken down into fields. The field is the smallest piece of information in the database, and could be the address of a company or the name of a book. However, you can be as specific as you want; instead of creating one field for an address you may want to create four fields (street, city, state, zip), or even five if you want to add a country name.

Breaking the data down like this makes it easier to use. You can ask Enable to list all the books you own by Salman Rushdie, or all your friends and relatives that have birthdays in June. A business may want to list all its clients in Portland, or all of them that owe money.

The following screen shows how data is broken down into fields.

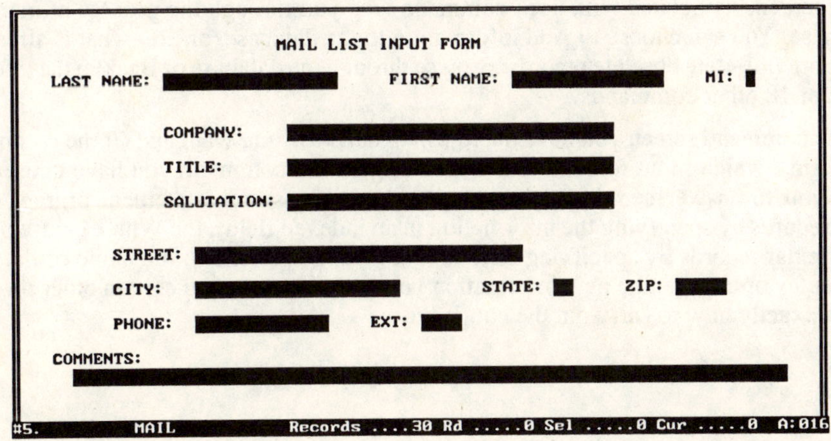

DATABASE FILES

Enable has a number of different types of database files. As the following screen shows, the database is made up of two different files.

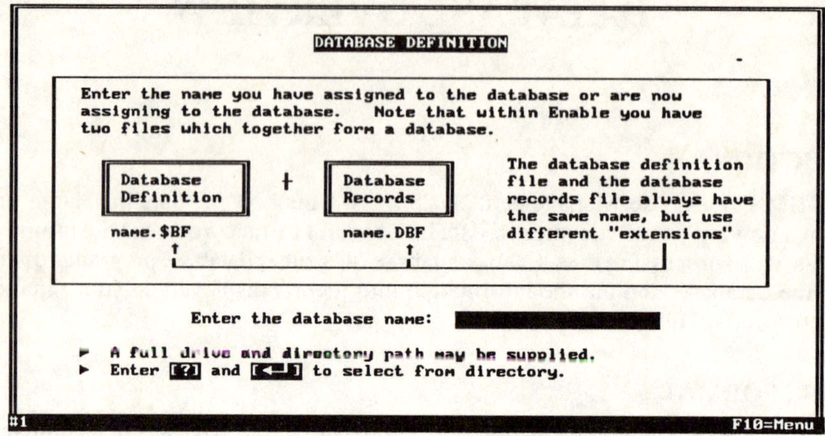

Enable stores the actual information in the *database record* file which has a .DBF extension. The *database definition* file contains instructions to Enable explaining what sort of data to allow in each field, and how to use it. (This file has a .$BF extension.) When you create a database you actually create the .$BF file, and Enable builds the .DBF file when you add data.

Another file you use is the *input form* file. This file tells Enable what to display on the screen when you are adding or editing records; exactly where each field is, and what titles to display next to each field. This file has a .$IF extension. If you don't build an input form, Enable will build one for you the first time you use the database.

Other files are used: files with lists of records you have sorted into a specific order, with "problem" records, with formats for printing data, and so on.

THE INTERACT SCREEN

After you build a database you use the Interact (DBMS Command Chart) screen and the command screens to control your database. The Interact screen is a menu of command choices, and the command screens associated with each command lead you through the process of manipulating your database. You can choose to Add information to the database, or Edit what is already there; print a Report, or Delete obselete records; Browse through the database or Backup the information; or use one of 18 other commands.

Once in the command screen you tell Enable which database you want and (if the command uses an input form), which input form to use. Depending on the command you have chosen, Enable then asks you to answer certain other prompts: the Index search statement prompt (to select particular records by specifying the information in an indexed field); the Where clause prompt (to select particular records by specifying criteria that must be matched); the name of the field you want to display or change; the new information you want to input; and certain other prompts that tell Enable exactly how to carry out the command.

These prompts let you not only select the database you want to use, but the actual records. If your database has 500 records and you only want to edit or print 4, you don't need to go through the entire database to reach them; specify the four records you want using the Index or Where prompts.

WINDOWS The database screens have the same Top Line Menu window commands as the word processing screens. See Module 46 for information.

THE TOP LINE MENU The Top Line Menu available in both the Interact and the command screens is shown in the following screen.

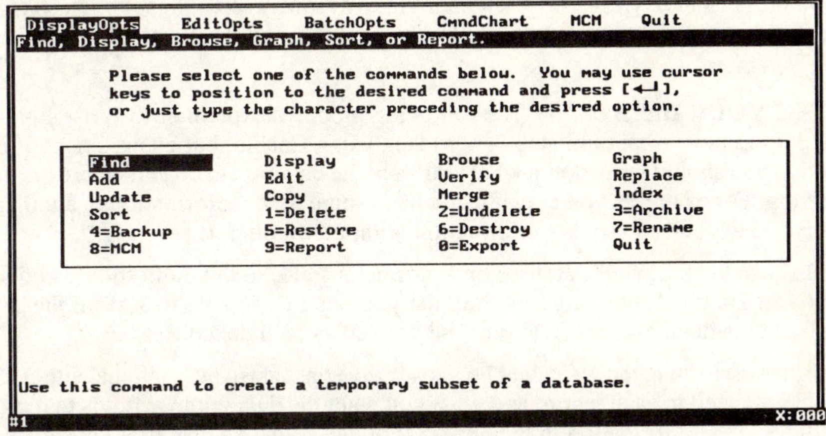

DisplayOpts, EditOpts, and BatchOpts These options duplicate the commands in the Interact screen. Press F10, type the first letter of one of the options, and select one of the displayed commands. For example, if you press F10 and type E (EditOpts), Enable displays six commands, with short descriptions; Add, Edit, Verify, Replace, Delete, and Undelete.

CmndChart This option displays the Interact screen again (so it has no function in the Interact screen).

The MCM Option MCM has three options associated with it: Windows, which lets you view other windows (see Module 46); Files, which displays a list of database and database definition files (Module 114); and Screen, which lets you change the monitor mode (see Module 2).

Quit Selecting Quit closes the command screen or the Interact screen and displays the Main Menu, and saves the data in the buffers to disk. Make sure you have saved the last record you worked on before you use this command. (Enable does not ask you to confirm the Quit before closing the screen). You can also select the Quit command from the Interact screen's list of commands to return to the Main Menu. Pressing Esc twice while in a command screen returns you to the Interact screen.

STATUS LINE The status line at the bottom of the screen shows the name of the database, the total number of records in the database (Records), the number of records read or checked to see if they fit your criteria (Rd), the number of records matching the criteria (Sel), and the sequence number of the record displayed on the screen (Cur). This sequence number is not the same as the Sys:record number; it shows the number within the selected records, so in a database with 500 records, if you use the Index or Where prompts to select 10 records, the Cur. number goes from 1 to 10. The status line also shows the window number (left side). The number at the right end of the status line has the format *x:nnn*, where *x* shows the input form status, and *nnn* is a system-generated code; E:*nnn* for example, is Edit mode. (A is Add mode, V is Verify mode, ? is Query mode.)

DATABASE BUFFERS While you are working in a database Enable stores the information you enter or modify in a series of buffers. The default size of a buffer is 512 bytes, but you can select other buffer sizes using the expert commands listed in Appendix C. The information in the buffers is not actually written onto a disk until one of the following happens: the buffer fills up; you exit the database screens, returning to the Main Menu; you enter a different name in the Database prompt; you press F9 and type U; or you add or modify more records than the "flush to disk" limit you set in your user profile (see Appendix B—this feature is not used unless you select it in your profile).

DESIGNING YOUR DATABASE The following modules explain how to use Enable to build databases, but the most important step is not taken using Enable, but using a pencil. Before you begin building you should write down what you want the database to do and where the information will come from. For example, you may already have some of the information in another database; you will learn how you can use this information without retyping it.

You may also want to sort your database on a particular field, so this field should be indexed. For example, if you are building a large mailing list you need to be able to sort on the Zip code, so when you build the database that field must be defined as an indexed field.

Consider the report format you want, and how to arrange the data to best suit the output; the number of fields you will need in each record and what you want the data in those fields to look like when it is printed. Read the information in the DBMS modules to get an idea of what can be done with your data; then spend some time thinking about how to build your database. Enable's features may be powerful, but they are only as good as the planning that goes into using them.

Turn to Module 50 to continue the learning sequence.

Module 48
ADD RECORDS (ADD)

DESCRIPTION

The data entry procedure consists of typing information into an input form, one record at a time.

NOTE

Before you read this module you should read Module 60 to learn how to use the Interact and command screens.

You add information to your database using the Add screen. At the Main Menu type UDB (Use System;DBMS;Build). (You can also reach this screen from the Interact screen; see Module 60.) Enable displays the Add command screen, like this:

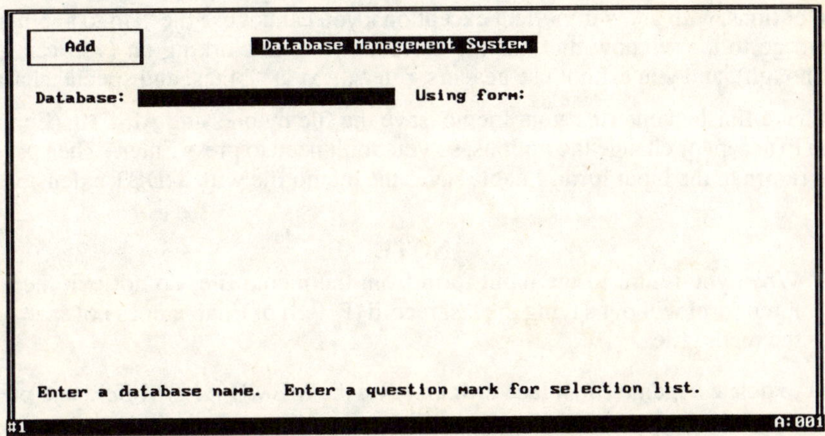

Select the database and the input form and Enable displays a blank input form of the type you specified.

NOTE

Although you are in Add mode when you enter the database using this method you may swap between Add and Edit modes while inputting data. (See this module's text.) If you are in Edit mode when you Quit the database you do not return to the Add screen; you go to the Edit screen.

INPUTTING DATA TO THE INPUT FORM Whether you are using a standard input form, or one you designed for yourself, you input data in the same way. When Enable first displays the form, the cursor is in the first field. Type until you reach the end of the field, or until you have input all the information. If you reach the end of the field the cursor jumps to the next field (unless you specified, when you designed the input form, that the cursor must not move out of that field automatically). You can move to the next field at any time by pressing Enter, Down Arrow, or Tab. Pressing Shift-Tab or Up Arrow moves the cursor to the preceding field. If the form is a multi-screen form, the PgUp and PgDn keys move the cursor between screens. The Home key returns the cursor to the beginning of the form.

If you don't add data to a field, Enable automatically fills in the default value: blanks in text fields, 0 in numeric fields, and F (or N) in logical fields. You can change the default when you design the input form (Module 59).

When you have finished inputting data, press F5 to move to the next record's input form.

INVALID DATA If you type data that is incorrect, Enable displays an error message: system-generated, database-defined, or input form message, in that order of preference. (Only system-generated error messages are displayed if you are using a standard input form.) Re-type the information, or press Tab to override the database definition and "force" the information into the field. (This feature is especially useful if you find that you defined a field too strictly; override the definition using Tab, and when you have finished inputting data, revise the database definition.)

MEMO FIELDS If your input form has memo fields, the field contains the words "MEMO ALT/M." Place the cursor in the field and press Alt-M. Enable displays an empty word processing file. You can use most of the usual word processing tools, and you have access to all the usual Top Line Menu options, with a few important exceptions; you cannot use the "Go to another window" command to go to the window that has the database you are working on (you can go to other windows, though), and you cannot use headers, rulers, text attributes, and special characters.

When you have finished entering your memo, save the file by pressing Alt-F10. (Enable doesn't prompt you to accept or change the options, so you don't need to press Enter.) Then press F10 and type QY to return to the input form. Enable saves the memo file with a .DBT extension, in ASCII format.

NOTE

> When you return to the input form from the memo file, do not exit the input form without saving the last record (F10 S) or Enable does not save the memo file.

If you want to delete a memo file, place the cursor on the MEMO ALT/M field and press Alt-F3. (You cannot retrieve a memo file that has been deleted, unlike records that are deleted.)

If you modify a memo field the old text in the .DBT file is not copied over—Enable just adds the new data to the end of the file. Even if you delete a record, the memo text remains in the file. This text is no longer accessible as memo text, but if you want to remove it entirely you must use the Copy command to copy your records into a new database named TEMP.DBF (the new .DBT will only have the latest information). Then delete the TEMP.$BF database definition and the original .DBF and .DBT files. Then rename TEMP.DBF and TEMP.DBT. See Module 57 for more information.

SPECIAL FUNCTIONS AND THE TOP LINE MENU Other features of the input form are available using function keys and the Top Line Menu. Press F10 to see the Top Line Menu, as shown in the following screen.

```
Next  Previous  Save  Ignore  1=Query  2=Index  Where  Quit
Save this record and display next record (same as F5)

LAST NAME:                    FIRST NAME:                 MI:

          COMPANY:
          TITLE:
          SALUTATION:

     STREET:
     CITY:                          STATE:        ZIP:
     PHONE:              EXT:
COMMENTS:

#1.     MAIL1       Records .....2 Rd .....0 Sel .....0 Cur .....0  A:016
```

The options are described next, with the applicable function key in parentheses after the option name.

NOTE

> Using the Save command or any command that displays a record that has already been created (Previous, Query, Index, Where) automatically changes the form to Edit mode (the status line has an E:*nnn* number on the right side). See Module 55 for information.

Next (F5) This option saves the data from the input form in the database buffer, updates the appropriate indexes, and displays a blank input form to let you enter the next record's data.

Previous (F6) This option saves the data, updates the indexes, and displays the previous record, changing to Edit mode.

Save (Alt-F10) This option saves the data, updates the indexes, and continues displaying the same record so that you can add more information or Quit.

NOTE

> The preceding options save the data in the database buffers. The data is not saved on disk until the buffer is full, you press F9 and type U, you leave the Database application, or you use another database. You can also change your user profile to make Enable automatically save records—see Appendix B.

Ignore (Alt-F6) This option erases the data you have just entered, leaving the input form blank.

Query (Shift-F1) This option lets you search the database for records that fit certain criteria. Select Query from the Top Line Menu (or press Shift-F1), and Enable displays a blank input form. The database is now in Query mode, with "?:" displayed in the status line. (This form has its own Top Line Menu, with three options: Find [F5], Add [Ctrl-F5], and Quit.) Type the search criteria. For example, you could type "Anderson" in the LAST NAME field and "75007" in the ZIP field.

Press F5 (Find) and Enable finds the first record with a Zip code of 75007 and a last name of Anderson. (If you type "And" Enable searches for Anderson, Andrews, etc.) The database is now in Edit mode, with "E:" displayed in the status line. Make your edits and then press Ctrl-F5 (Add) to go back to the Add mode—Enable displays a blank input form so you can add data. If Enable does not find a record matching your criteria it displays a message (No records found) and prompts you to press Enter; it then displays a blank form so you can type another search criteria.

If you are searching on a logical field, you can only search for T (Y).

NOTE

Before selecting Query, save your current record.

Index (Shift-F5) The Index feature is another way to search the database for specific records. Select Index and Enable saves the record you were working on and displays a prompt at the bottom of the screen. Type an index search statement and press Enter. (The field must be an indexed field. Index commands are described in detail in Module 60.) For example you might type SYS:RECORD=15 or ITEM="Nails." Enable displays the first record that fits the Index command (putting you in Edit mode), or tells you that there is no matching record. The Index prompt remains displayed. Type another index search statement or press Esc.

Where (Shift-F6) The Where feature works in the same way as the Index feature, except you type a where clause instead of an index search statement. See Module 60 for information about where clauses.

NOTE

If you use a Query, Index, or Where command, the Next and Previous options will only access records in the selected set. If you want to use other records you must use another command or select Add to go back to Add mode.

Quit Press F10 and type Q to display an Add or Edit command screen; Enable displays the Add screen if you were in Add mode when you selected Quit, or the Edit screen if you were in Edit mode. Remember to save your last record before quitting (F10 S).

NON-KEYBOARD DATA FIELDS The fields that you did not define as keyboard-data fields when you created the database are automatically filled in by Enable, in the manner you specified. (See Module 50.)

APPLICATIONS

Adding data to your database is the primary task in using a database. Once you have built a database you can use the data in ways described in the other modules.

TYPICAL OPERATION

In this activity you add a record to the database named SUPPLYX that you created in Module 5.

1. At the Main Menu, type **UDB**. Enable displays the Add command screen. In the Database field type **?** and press **Enter**. Enable displays a list of databases. Move the cursor to SUPPLYX.DBF and press **Enter**. Enable displays the Add command screen again.
2. Press **Enter** twice to accept the standard input form. Enable displays the following screen.

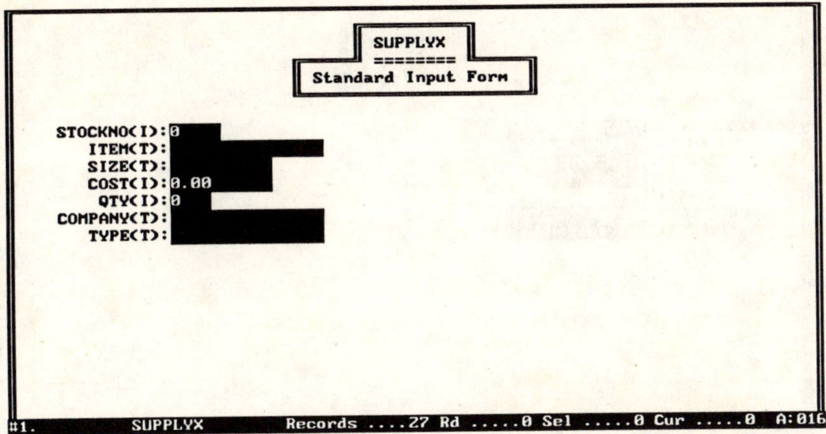

Notice that the status line says that there are 27 records. Also, there is an A: near the right corner, indicating that the input form is in Add mode.

3. Type **11983** in the first field. Notice that the cursor automatically moves to the next field. Type **Piping** in the next field, press **Enter**, and type **8'**. Press **Tab**, type **5.85**, and press **Enter**. Type **10** and press **Down Arrow**. Type **Dallas Plumbing**. The cursor automatically moves to the next line. Type **1"**.

4. Press **F5**. Enable displays another blank input form so that you can add another record. Notice that the status line now shows that there are 28 records.

5. Press **F10** and type **P** to go back to the previous record. When Enable displays the previous record, notice that the A: has changed to E:, indicating that you are now in Edit mode.

6. Press **F10** and type **P** again. Enable beeps and tells you that there are no more records in this direction. There are more records in this direction, of course, but Enable will not let you see them unless you select Query, Where, or Index from the Top Line Menu. Enable will only let you use the records you selected when you were at the Add command screen, that is, the records that you want to add.

7. Press **Enter** and then press **F10** and type **1** to select Query. Enable displays a blank input form. Notice that the E: in the status line has now changed to ?:, showing that you are in Query mode.

8. Type **Nails** in the second field. Press **F10** and type **F**, and Enable displays a record with Nails in the Item field.

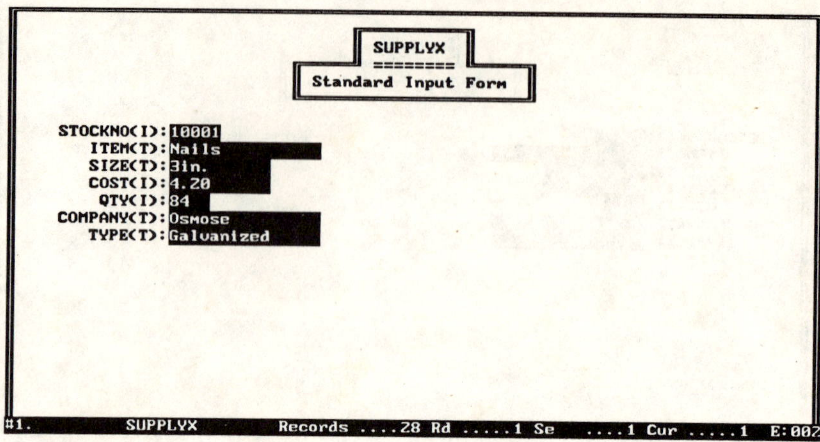

Notice that you are in Edit mode again (E:).

9. Press **Down Arrow** to move the cursor to the Cost field, and press **Right Arrow** three times, moving the cursor to the last digit. Type **5**, changing the value to **$4.25**.
10. Press **F10** and type **S** to save the record, and then press **F10** and type **Q** to exit. Notice that Enable has displayed the Edit screen, not the Add screen, because you were in Edit mode when you quit.
11. Press **F10** and type **Q** to return to the Main Menu.
12. Turn to Module 55 to continue the learning sequence.

Module 49
BACKUPS (BACKUP, ARCHIVE, RESTORE)

DESCRIPTION

DBMS has three commands that help you backup and restore data. The Backup command makes a copy of your database and its associated database definition and index files. The Archive command copies deleted records into a special archive file. And the Restore command brings backed-up or archived data back into use.

NOTE

Before you read this module you should read Module 60 to learn how to use the Interact and command screens.

THE BACKUP COMMAND This command copies a database, its definition file, and its indexes, to another disk drive. (It does not copy input and report form files) You can use the command to store a copy in case the original is damaged or lost, or as a convenient way to transmit the file to another location. Select Backup from the Interact screen.

NOTE

The Backup command only works if Enable is installed on a fixed disk. If not, use the DOS DISKCOPY command.

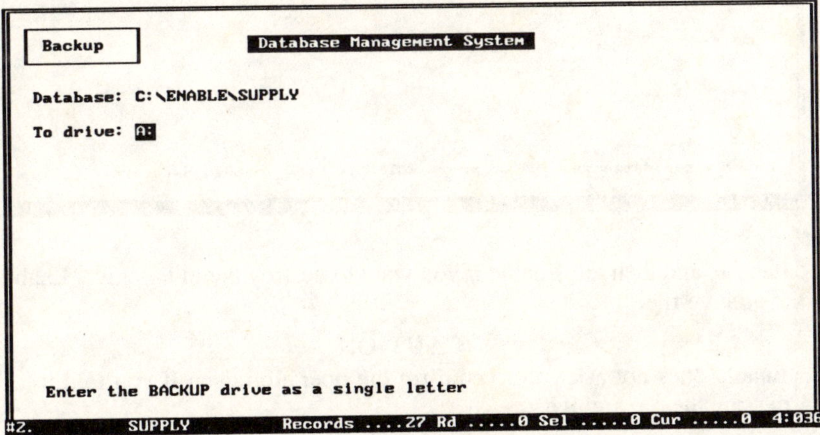

Select the database, and then type the name of the drive to which the files should be copied. You can only copy to a floppy disk drive.

CAUTION

Other files on the floppy disk are destroyed when Enable makes a backup.

Press Enter and Enable tells you to put a floppy disk in the drive. Press any key and Enable warns you that other files on the disk will be deleted. Press Esc to abort, or any key to continue. Enable copies the files onto the disk and displays "BACKUP completed." You can backup more files if you want (if you do not leave the Backup command screen you can backup more files onto the same disk; Enable will not delete the files already backed up).

THE ARCHIVE COMMAND This command copies deleted records from the database to a special archive file. The archive file has the same name as the database, but with an .ARC extension. (See Module 51 for information on deleted records.) If you ever need to use the records again you can restore them to the database.

You have the choice of adding the deleted files to the beginning of the archive file, or creating a new file. For example, if you always destroy the deleted records after archiving them you will probably want to add the new set of deleted records to those already archived. On the other hand, if you add deleted records to the archive without destroying them afterwards, you may want to archive all the deleted records to a new archive file (the previous one is deleted). Select Archive from the Interact screen.

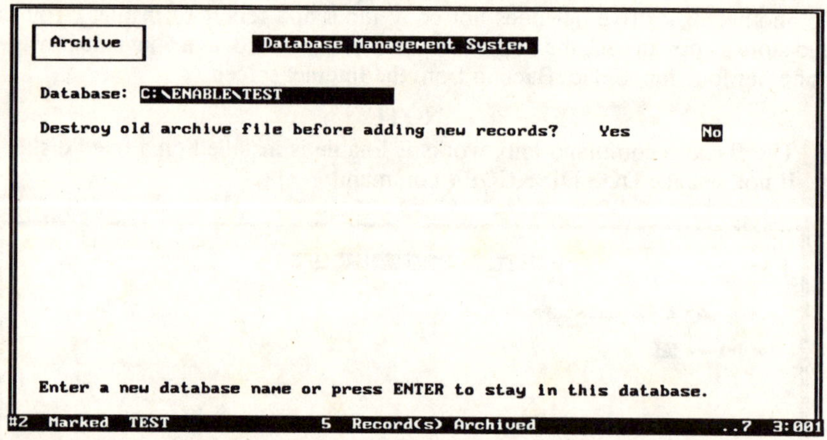

Select the database, and then tell Enable if you want to destroy the old archive. Enable copies the records to the archive file.

CAUTION

Enable does not ask you to confirm the operation even if you told it to destroy the old archive.

THE RESTORE COMMAND This command brings records back from an archive file or copies a backup file into the current data directory. Select Restore in the Interact screen.

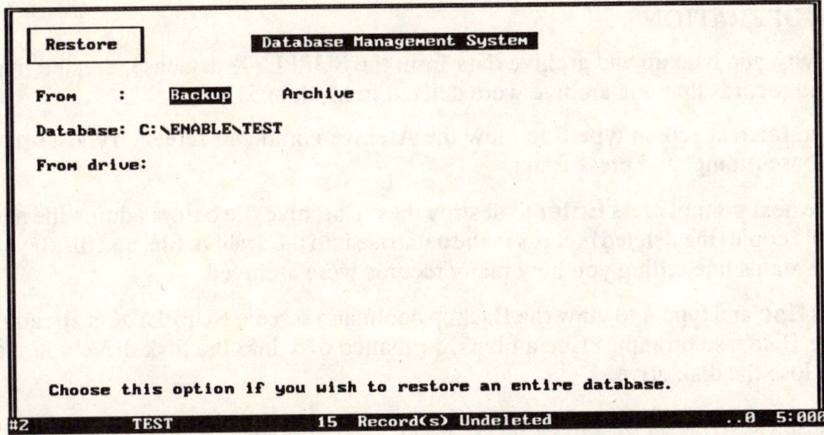

```
Restore            Database Management System

From     :    Backup    Archive

Database: C:\ENABLE\TEST

From drive:

Choose this option if you wish to restore an entire database.
#2        TEST          15  Record(s) Undeleted          ..0  5:000
```

Backup Files Select Backup, the name of the database being copied back into the data directory, and enter the disk drive name. If you try to restore a backed-up file while a file with the same name remains in the data directory Enable displays a message telling you to destroy the database in the data directory. You must destroy both the .DBF and .$BF files or change the names.

Archived Records The following screen shows the prompts you see when you select Archive.

```
Restore            Database Management System

From     :    Backup    Archive

Database: C:\ENABLE\TEST

Where    :

------------------------------------------------------------------------
Operators are:
AND OR NOT   < > = <= >= <>   LT GT EQ LE GE NE   + - * / ** ()   & &- &+
------------------------------------------------------------------------
Fields are:
 SYS:RECORD   DELETED     MEMO       VERIFY      DUPES

 Press PgDn to select from above
#2.      TEST        Records ....19 Rd .....0 Sel .....0 Cur .....0  5:003
```

The where clause lets you selectively restore the records. The restored records are added to the database, but remain marked as deleted files. If you choose to undelete them any duplicate records are put in an error set. (See Module 51.)

APPLICATIONS

The Backup, Archive, and Restore commands are security measures. You can use them to ensure that data you are currently using can be restored if you lose or damage your working copy, and to store data that you do not currently need but may require in the future, freeing disk space.

TYPICAL OPERATION

In this activity you backup and archive data from the SUPPLYX database, created in Module 5. (The deleted records that you archive were deleted in Module 51.)

1. At the Interact screen type **3** to view the Archive command screen. Type **supplyx** at the Database prompt and press Enter.
2. At the next prompt press **Enter** to destroy the old archive file before adding the new records. Enable copies the deleted records in the database into the archive file, and displays a message in the status line telling you how many records were archived.
3. Press **Esc** and type **4** to view the Backup command screen. SUPPLYX is already displayed at the Database prompt. Place a blank, formatted disk into the disk drive you want to use, and close the disk drive.
4. Press **Enter** to accept SUPPLYX. At the To Drive prompt type the name of the disk drive and press **Enter**. Enable reminds you to insert a disk.
5. Press **Enter** again, and Enable warns you that any other data on the disk will be erased. Press **Enter** again and Enable copies the SUPPLYX.DBF, .$BF, .ARC, and .SS files.
6. Press **Esc** twice and press **Enter** to return to the Main Menu.
7. Turn to Module 58 to continue the learning sequence.

Module 50
CREATE A DATABASE (DATABASE DEFINITION)

DESCRIPTION

The first step in using a database is creating the database, telling Enable what the database will look like and how it works. The database is made up of records and fields. A *record* is a grouping of information—the name, address, and purchasing history of a particular client, for example, or the description and part number of an item in your store's inventory.

Fields are the individual pieces of information in each record. For example, a record with client information will have separate fields for the customer's name, street address, city, zip, phone number, and so on. You may even have several fields for the customer's name; one each for the first name, middle initial, and last name, and possibly a special "salutation" field. The salutation field can be used in form letters, and may say "Ms. Jones," "Mrs. A. Jones," or "Andrea," depending on what is most appropriate. You have to tell Enable how many fields each record must have, how large each field is, and what type it is.

There are two stages in the creation of a database; "defining" the database (naming and describing it) and "defining" the fields.

DATABASE DEFINITION

At the Main Menu type UDDD (Use System;DBMS;Design;Database-Definition). Enable displays the Database Definition screen, as shown below. (F10 has been pressed, so the Top Line Menu is also displayed.)

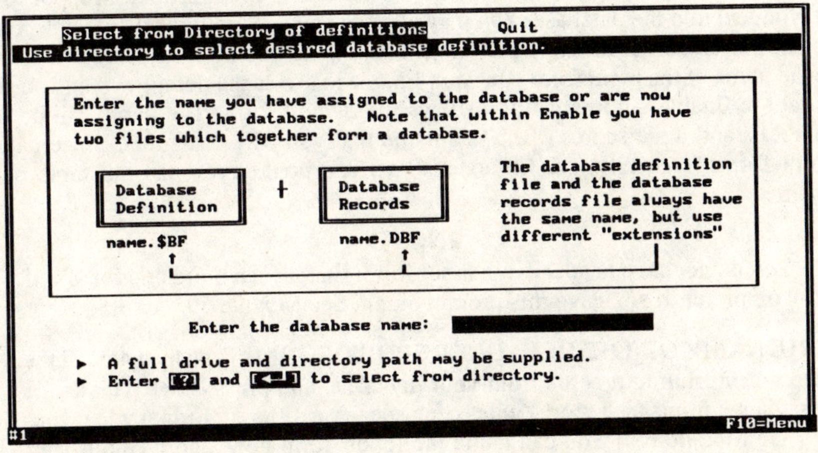

Enter the filename you want to give the database and press Enter. The filename can be up to eight letters, numbers, or underscores (_). Use a name that will remind you of what is in the database, such as CLIENTS or INVENTRY. Don't give the file an extension. If you are building a database in a different directory or drive you must include the drive letter and directory. For example, type a:\databs\clients.

After you press Enter, Enable displays "File Not Found. Your choices: New file List dir Re-enter." Type N (New file) and Enable displays the second Database Definition screen. As you can see in the following screen, the display is in two parts; the top has the prompts, and the bottom has instructions that change as you move the cursor through the screen. The Top Line Menu, accessed by pressing F10, is also shown.

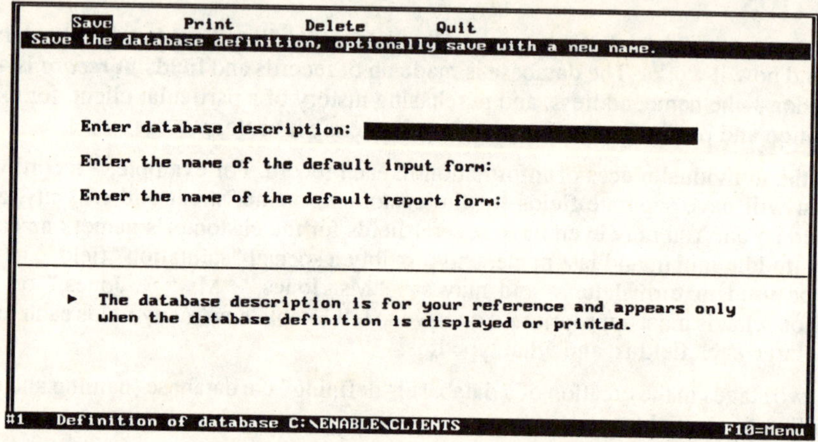

ENTER DATABASE DESCRIPTION Type a description that will help you remember what is in this database, such as "A list of customers," and press Enter.

ENTER THE NAME OF THE DEFAULT INPUT FORM Type the name of the *input form* you want to use when you add records to this database, and press Enter. An input form is used when you type text into the database. You may already have an input form available, one that you used for a similar database, for example, or you can name one now and create it later. In either case, type the name of the input form you want Enable to use as the default; when you add records to your database Enable automatically displays the default form. The name can be up to eight letters, numbers, and underscores (_). Use a name that you will remember. Since databases and default input forms have different file extensions, you could even use the same name as the database name.

NOTE

You do not have to specify an input form. Enable can build one for you if you prefer. If so, leave this prompt blank. See Module 59.

ENTER THE NAME OF THE DEFAULT REPORT FORM Type the name of the *report form* you will use when printing records from your database, and press Enter. This is the format that Enable uses when it prints the reports, unless you specify a different format when you use the Print command. (See Module 62.) You can name the report form now, and create it later. The report form name can be up to eight numbers, letters, or underscores. Pick a name that you will remember, the same name as the database name if you want. You can also specify an extension if you want, but Enable will use .$RF if you don't. After you press Enter, Enable displays the Field Definition screen. If you don't want to specify a report form leave this prompt blank.

FIELD DEFINITION

Enable displays the Field Definition screen next. The following screen shows two fields that have already been defined: FNAME and LNAME. The headers at the top of the page refer to the fields' characteristics, which will be explained later in this module. The screen also shows the number of fields already defined (Total flds), and the total lengths of the fields (Total len). The Real flds and Real len values refer to the number of fields that are not external or derived fields (explained later in this module).

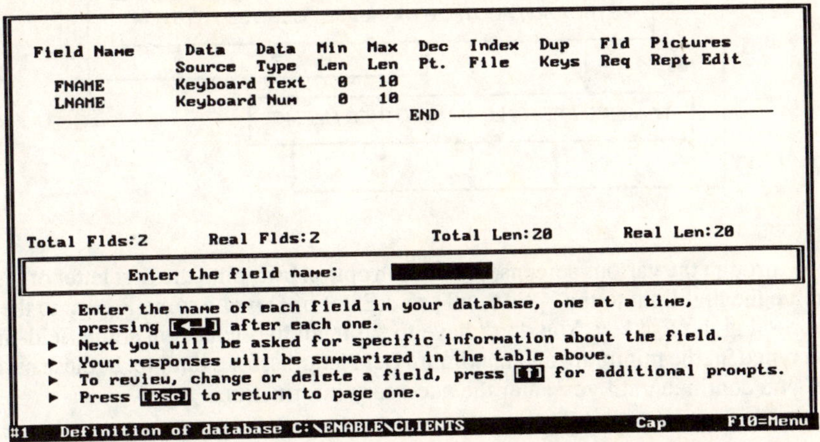

You can define up to 254 fields, each with room for up to 254 characters. Begin defining each field at this screen by typing a field name and pressing Enter. (When you finish defining a field Enable returns to this screen, allowing you to define another field.) Field names can be up to ten characters long. The first character must be a letter; following characters can be letters, numbers, underscores, and colons.

CAUTION

Enable reserves the following words for its own use. Do not use them for field names. AND, AS, DIV, E, EQ, ERR, FALSE, GE, GT, IN, LE, LINK, LT, NE, NO, NOT, OR, PI, TRUE, USING, YES. Do not begin names with MNU: or SYS:

NOTE

If you enter an incorrect or contradictory response during this procedure, Enable may beep and display an error message at the bottom of the screen. Enable may not recognize the error until you have finished the definition and tried to save it; Enable returns you to the Field Definition screen so that you can find and correct the problem. Remember to save the information when you have finished.

When you press Enter, Enable displays a screen with a prompt at the top that asks "What method do you wish to use? Quick Detailed." Type Q or D to select one of these.

There are several routes through the field definition procedure, as the following chart shows (all routes return to the Field Definition screen):

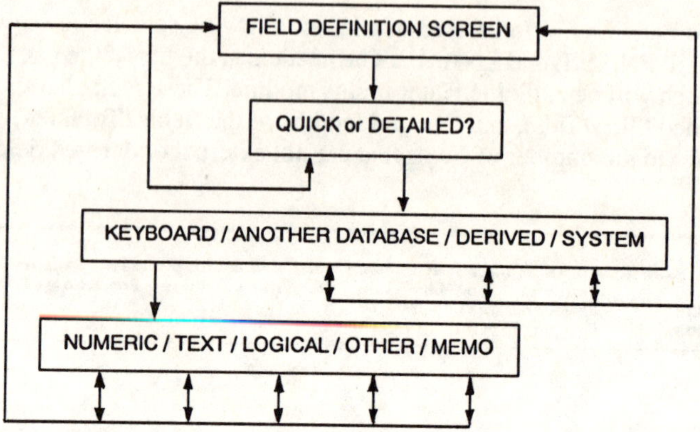

As you move through the various screens, select each option by typing the first letter of the option's name, or move the highlight to the option and press Enter or Down Arrow. Return to the previous prompt by pressing the Esc key. You don't have to fill in all the fields, but some fields must have information typed in; the minimum and maximum field lengths, for example. In these cases Enable does not let you continue until you enter the necessary information.

QUICK FIELD DEFINITIONS

If you type Q for the quick method of field definition, Enable lets you select from the following pre-defined data types.

INTEGER An integer field accepts numbers without decimal points. Enable prompts you to enter the field length.

DECIMAL This type of field accepts numbers with decimal points. Enable prompts for the number of decimal positions, that is, the number of digits to the right of the decimal point. Enable then prompts for the length of the field (including the decimal point and places).

TEXT This type of field accepts any characters. Enable prompts for the field length.

LOGICAL Enable asks if you want to use T or Y to mean True. Type T to use T (True) and F (False); or type Y to use Y (Yes) and N (No).

MEMO Enable sets the Memo field to ten characters long, and displays the Field Definition screen again. This field is a "pointer" to an ASCII memo file. (See Module 48.)

When you have finished the quick field definition, Enable displays the Field Definition screen again, allowing you to enter another field name.

DETAILED FIELD DEFINITIONS

Using the detailed definition method provides more options for a field. When you select "Detailed" from the "Which method do you want to use" prompt, Enable displays the following screen. The prompts are explained after the screen.

```
What method do you wish to use?    Quick        Detailed

Do you wish to copy an existing field definition?  No  Yes

Is this an indexed field?    No Yes

Is this a required field?    No Yes

Source of data: Keyboard   Another database   Derived   System

▸  You may use a field definition you created for another database
   to supply the answers to the remaining questions.

▸  If you want to use a field definition from this database, it must
   first be saved to disk.

#1   Defining field FNAME for Database   C:\ENABLE\CLIENT
```

Do you wish to copy an existing field definition: No/yes If you have an identical field in another database you can copy it instead of redefining it. Type Y (Yes) and Enable asks you for the name of the other database and the name of the field you want to copy. Enter the names, press Enter, and Enable copies the field and returns you to the "What method do you wish to use?" prompt.

The screens now show the same options as the screens for the field in the other database, with one exception; even if the field in the other database is indexed, the new one is not. You can use the Down Arrow to move through the screens, (explained in the following text), changing options where necessary.

Is this an indexed field? No/yes If you define a field as an indexed field, each time you add information to the database Enable builds an index with the information you type into it. For example, if the field is CITY you may want to index it. This will allow you to sort the list in city-groups. On the other hand, you probably wouldn't want to index the MI (middle initial) field, as you are unlikely to have a reason to sort the database in the order of your client's middle initial! You should only index fields that really need it, because building indexes uses up disk and memory space, slowing down the system. If you decide not to index this field you can always change your mind later, by modifying the definition or using the Index command (see Module 58). Enable only indexes the first 100 characters in the field.

Type Y at this prompt and Enable asks you to enter the name of an index file. This is the file where Enable stores the index. Enter an 8-character name. Try to make the name similar to the field name. The name must be unique—you cannot use a name already used by another database. Try combining the database name with the field name (e.g., CLNTLNAM). You can specify a drive name, but not a directory name. If you create an index on a drive other than the default drive, remember to use the drive name when using the index name in any DBMS commands.

When you define a field as indexed, Enable also asks if duplicates are allowed in the field. Type Y (Yes) if the field is one in which different records could have the same value. For example, more than one record could have the same Zip code. Type N (No) if only one record can have the value; you may not want duplicates in a field for social security numbers. When you add data to your database Enable checks to see if any of the other records have the same value. If one does, Enable displays an error message and doesn't let you continue to the next field until you change or remove the number.

Is this a required field: No/yes If you type Y, when you input data to the database Enable will not let you continue past this field without entering data. The ZIP field in a database used only for mailing lists would be a required field, for example.

Source of data: Keyboard/Another database/Derived/System Type K, A, D, or S to tell Enable where the data is coming from. Select Keyboard if you are going to type the data; select Another Database if you want Enable to get the data from another database; select Derived if you want Enable to input the data by manipulating or calculating data in other fields; and select System if you want Enable to automatically input the date or time.

DATA FROM THE KEYBOARD If you type K at the "Source of data:" prompt Enable asks you for information about the type of data that will be typed into the field. The first prompt is "Select the data type: Numeric Text Logical Other Memo." (See the following screen.)

Numeric	Numbers and special characters
Text	Letters, numbers, and special characters
Logical	True or False, Yes or No
Other	Date, time, State code, Zip code, or telephone number
Memo	A pointer to an associated text file

Numeric Data If you type N at the "Select data type" prompt, Enable displays the following screen:

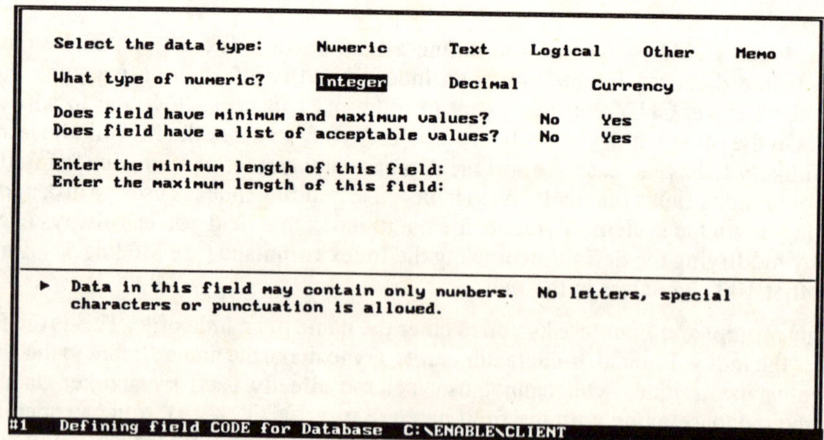

What type of numeric? Select Integer (a number without a decimal point), Decimal (a number with a decimal point), or Currency (a number with a dollar sign, one or more commas, and an optional decimal point).

Does the field have minimum and maximum values? No/Yes Select Yes, and Enable prompts for the minimum and maximum values and the minimum and maximum reasonable values. When you are inputting data to your database, Enable will not let you type in data outside the minimum to maximum range. Also, if you type in a value that is not within the "reasonable" range, Enable displays a warning, but accepts the value. For example, in a sales commissions field you might set reasonable values to warn you if the commission you are typing appears too high; the value might be correct, but the warning reminds you to check your figures.

Does the field have a list of acceptable values? No/Yes You can limit the values that may be input. For example, in a database being used for a limited-area mailing list you could specify the Zip codes that are allowed, so that you cannot accidentally type an incorrect Zip code. Separate the values with commas and don't leave spaces (75006,75007,75008).

Enter the minimum/maximum length of this field: The next two prompts ask for the size of the field. It must be at least one and no more that 16 characters long. Include space for decimal points, dollar signs, minus signs, and commas. Currency values use parentheses for negative values, so leave space for these if necessary.

Enable displays the following screen after you input the maximum length:

```
Enter report picture:

Columnar report heading:

Error msg:

▶ Enter the format Enable should use to display data from this field.
  Type an "N" in the position of each numeric digit.

#1   Defining field P for Database   C:\ENABLE\P
```

NOTE

Enable also displays the picture, heading, and error prompts at the end of the Text, Logical, Other, and Memo field-definition procedures. These fields are only described in detail once in this module, as follows.

Enter report picture: Use the letter N to represent numbers or letters, and type a sample field, exactly as you want to see it in the database report. For example, type "nnn,nnn.nn" or "$nnnnnnn.nn." (In currency format the commas are automatically included, so the second example includes an extra n instead of a comma. You can type a comma instead if you want.) Type "*$nnn,nnn.nn" to insert asterisks in all of the blank spaces in front of the dollar sign (e.g., ****$12.54). If the field will have some negative currency values, put parentheses in the picture; "($nnn,nnn.nn)." Although negative integer and decimal fields usually have a minus sign to show negative values, put parentheses in the picture if you want to use them instead. If the value is a percentage, type a % at the end of the field. Enable will multiply the value in this field by 100; for example, .89 typed into the field becomes 89% in the report. If you want to make sure that empty fields are left blank (rather than displayed with a zero), enter Z at the beginning of the report picture.

Data in a field that is longer than the report picture is printed as asterisks.

Columnar Report Heading: One of Enable's report formats is a standard columnar format. Type in the title that should appear at the top of the field's column. If you don't type a name, Enable uses the field name.

Error Msg: Type an error message for Enable to display if you enter inappropriate or incorrect data to this field. For example, if you have specified that the field must only be zip codes 75006 and 75007 you could use "Incorrect Zip Code" as an error message.

When you press Enter at the Error Msg prompt Enable displays the Field Definition screen again.

Text Data If you type T at the "Select the data type:" prompt, Enable displays the following screen:

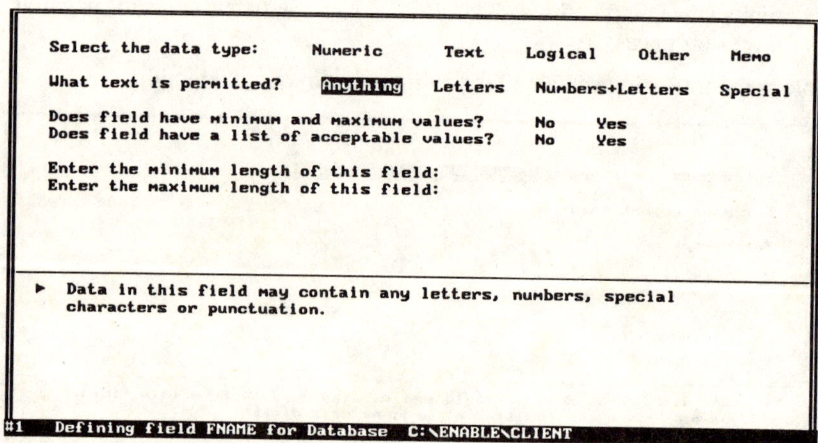

What text is permitted? Anything/Letters/Numbers+Letters/Special Type A, L, N, or S to select one of the following types of text:

Anything—any letters, numbers, special characters, and punctuation. Enable prompts for the minimum and maximum values and the reasonable value range, as described in the section on numeric data. In this case the values may be alphabetical values.

Letters—any letters or specified punctuation. Enable prompts for the permitted punctuation (type ".,&" for example). It also asks if the text will be uppercase, lowercase, or both, and if blanks (spaces) can be entered. Enable then prompts for the minimum and maximum values and the range of reasonable values.

Numbers+Letters—numbers, letters, and specified punctuation. The prompts are the same as the ones for Letters.

Special—a very specific format of any characters. Enable prompts you for the "edit picture." For example, you might want to see only serial numbers with the format "SN: 999-99/99." Use the following characters to build the edit picture.

l	Lowercase letters
u	Uppercase letters
a	Uppercase or lowercase letters
n	Numbers
x	Numbers or letters (uppercase or lowercase)
?	Any letter, number, or character
'	Any letter, number, or character in single quotes will always print in that position.
, . -	Commas, periods, dashes, and spaces may also be included.

SN: 999-99/99 is specified in this manner; 'SN:' nnn'-'nn'/'nn.

Report Picture After you enter information about the text fields, Enable prompts for the report picture, the columnar report heading, and the error message. These are described in the preceding section on numeric data. The report picture for text fields is different though. Specify the picture using the characters shown at the preceding text on Special fields.

When you have finished entering the text-field information, Enable displays the Field Definition screen again.

Logical Data If you typed L at the "Select the data type:" prompt, Enable asks if you want to use Y or T for true. Type Y if you want to use Y (Yes) and N (No), or type T if you want to use T (True) and F (False). An example of a logical field is a field for CLIENT? in a mailing list. Assuming you decided to use Y and N, you could type Y in the field if the person has purchased from you or N if the person had not. Later you could use this field to print a report on buyers.

Enable then prompts for the columnar report heading and the error message, as described in the earlier section in this module on numeric data. When you have completed these fields, Enable displays the Field Definition screen.

Other Data If you typed O at the "Select the data type:" prompt, Enable displays the following screen:

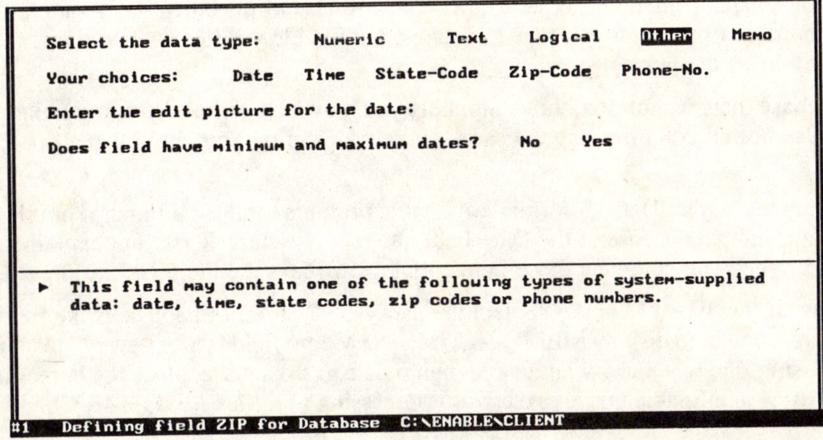

Date Enable asks you to specify the format. Use mm (month number), dd (day number), yy and yyyy (year), dashes, periods, colons, and slashes. For example, mm/dd/yyyy.

NOTE

Think about how you want to sort the database. If you want to sort by year, use a date with the year first (e.g., yy:mm:dd). If you want to sort by the month, put the month first.

Enable also asks you for the earliest and latest dates, and the range of reasonable dates, in the same format. (Enable displays a warning when you type a date outside the reasonable range).

When you have finished inputting the Date information, Enable prompts for the report picture format. The picture may be the same as the field format, but you could build a different picture, and include *mon* (month name abbreviation), or *month(mm)* (month name). For example, type "month(mm) dd, yyyy" for "September 19, 1989."

Time Enable asks you for the time format. Use hm (hours in 24-hour format), hh (hours in 12-hour format), mm (minutes), ss (seconds), x (A or P, i.e., a.m. or p.m.), dashes, slashes, colons, and periods. For example, "hm:mm" for (18:45). If you are indexing this field you will probably want to use military time or put x (A or P) at the beginning of the field so you can sort the file in a sensible order. Enable also asks for the earliest and latest times, and the range of reasonable times.

State-Code If you select this option Enable uses the US Postal Service list of State abbreviations. Enable will not allow you to input any data to this field that is not on the list.

Zip Code Enable asks if you want to use 5- or 9-digit Zip codes. If you are building a mailing list with foreign addresses you should build your own Zip code field, or have a separate field for foreign postal codes. Also, if you want to set limits on the valid Zip codes you should build your own field; the only validation Enable does is to ensure that the code you enter is on the US Postal Service list of Zip codes.

Phone-No Enable asks you for the phone number format. Use cc (country code), aaa (area code), n (digits in the number), x (digits in the extension number), parentheses (around the area code), dashes, slashes, backslashes, periods, colons, and spaces. For example, cc-aaa-nnnnnn-xx for 44-243-874861, extn 23. If you have also added a State-Code field to this database, whenever you type an area code into a phone number field, Enable checks to see if that code is in the specified state. If it isn't, the information is rejected. (Enable also checks the other way around. If you input the phone number first, when you type the state code Enable verifies against the area code, and rejects it if it does not match.)

If your database includes foreign phone numbers you may have to build your own phone number field, because not all countries use the same number of digits. You could use a Special or Text field.

After entering the "Other Data" information, Enable prompts for the columnar report heading, the error message, and, in the case of the Date field, the report picture. These are explained earlier in this module. When you complete these fields, Enable displays the Field Definition screen.

Memo Data If you typed M at the "Select the data type:" prompt Enable sets the field length to 10 characters, enough to display MEMO ALT/M. The Memo field is a "gateway" to an associated word processing file; when you want to add memo data to a database, place the cursor in the field and press Alt-M and Enable displays the word processing file. (See Module 48.)

If you select Memo, Enable prompts for the columnar report heading and the error message. (When the Memo field is used in a report the first 10 characters are displayed.) When you press Enter at the Error Msg field Enable displays the Field Definition screen.

NOTE

When you are adding or editing data you can override restrictions on inputs by pressing Tab.

DATA FROM ANOTHER DATABASE Typing A at the "Source of data:" prompt displays the following screen:

```
Enter the database name:

Name of lookup field in other database:

Name of indexed linking field in other database:

Name of linking field in this database:

Columnar report heading:

Error msg:

▶  Enter the name of the database in which the field containing the
   data you want to include is located.
▶  The data will NOT be copied.  Enable will read data from
   this "other" database, using it as required in the database
   you are now defining.

#1   Defining field PRICE for Database  C:\ENABLE\CLIENT
```

These prompts allow you to link databases; the data in the field you are defining will come from another database. The field you are defining is known as an *external* field; that is, it gets its information externally. The field in the other database that provides the data is known as a *lookup* field. Both databases also have *link* fields, identically defined fields that join the two databases. The link field in the other database must be indexed, or Enable is not able to search the database for the field.

For example, you are building a database with your clients' purchasing histories (CLIENTS). You want to include a list of the items that your clients have purchased, along with the current price and description. You also have a database of your product line (PRODUCTS). You could use the serial number fields as link fields, and define the cost and description fields in CLIENTS as external fields. When you type a serial number into CLIENTS, Enable searches PRODUCTS for a matching serial number; when it finds one it transfers information from the cost and description fields to CLIENTS.

NOTE

Enable does not store this information in the database that it transfers it to. It retrieves the information each time it needs it (when printing reports, for example). So, both databases must be in the same directory.

Enable prompts for the name of the database that has the information this field needs: the name of the field in the other database that has the required information, and the names of the identically defined fields that link the two databases. Enable then prompts for the optional columnar report heading and error message, and finally returns you to the Field Definition screen.

NOTE

There are other ways to link databases. You can use a derived data field with an .updatekey command (see the following text), you can select ANOTHER DATABASE as the source of data in an input or report form (Modules 59 and 62), and you can use Procedural Language commands (Modules 52 and 53).

DERIVED DATA If you typed D at the "Source of Data:" prompt Enable displays the following screen:

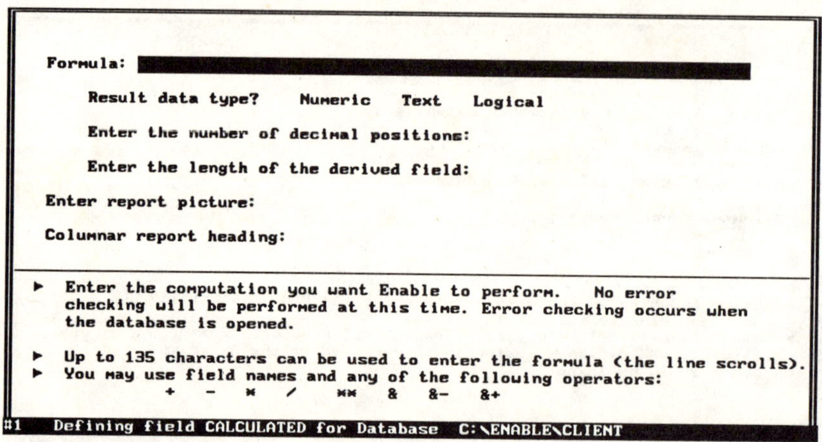

Formula Derived data fields are the result of a calculation using the formula you type in the first field on this screen. You can use any of the following operators:

+	Addition
–	Subtraction
*	Multiplication
/	Division
**	Exponentiation
&	Concatenation (Append one value to the other.)
&–	Concatenation and trim (Append and remove spaces.)
&+	Concatenation, trim, and add one space between.

Any spreadsheet functions that do not take a range as an argument. Functions that take a list of arguments in the spreadsheet take a list of fields, all in the same record. Functions that work only within records include AVG, SUM, COUNT, MAX, MIN, STD, and VAR. See Section 3, Spreadsheets, for more information.

AND/OR/NOT Boolean operators

For example, in an inventory database each record may have the item's cost and the number in stock. It could also have a field that shows the total value of the stock of that one item. The TOTALVAL field could be a derived data field, using the formula "cost*number." Enable derives the total value by multiplying the values in the COST and NUMBER fields.

Linking Databases With Derived Fields You can use the derived data field to retrieve data from another database. You enter a command in this format:

LOOKUPFLD IN DB2 LINK *LINKFIELD=LINKFIELD*

where *LOOKUPFLD* is the field in the other database (DB2) that has the information you want. The *LINKFIELD*s are the fields in each database that have the same information. So, when you enter a value into the linkfield in the first database Enable looks for the same data in the linkfield in the other database. When Enable finds the value it copies the information from the lookupfield in the same record. That information is transferred to the lookupfield in the first database.

For more information on using this type of database link, see Module 59.

Result data type: Numeric/Text/Logical Enable asks what format the derived data should be in. If you select Numeric, Enable asks the number of decimal places and the field length; if you select Text Enable asks for the length of the field; and if you select Logical Enable asks if you want to use Y or T for True.

After these prompts Enable prompts for the report picture (except for Logical) and the columnar report heading. After the report heading Enable returns you to the Field Definition screen.

SYSTEM DATA If you type S at the "Source of data:" prompt, you can define the type of system data that will appear in this field; the date or the time. The first prompt is "Date or time of: ADDition-of-record EDIT-of-record." If you type A, Enable fills in the field when you create a new record. If you type E, Enable fills in the field when you edit any of the information in the record.

The next prompt is "Which? Date Time." Type D, and the field will contain the date. Type T, and the field will contain the time, to a fraction of a second. (The date and time must be entered when you first log on to Enable.)

After these two prompts, Enable prompts for the report picture, the columnar report heading, and the error message, and then returns you to the Field Definition screen.

SAVING OR DELETING YOUR DATABASE AND FIELD DEFINITIONS When you have finished defining fields, press F10. Enable displays a Top Line Menu, with the options Save, Print, Delete, and Quit. Type S, and Enable asks if you want to use the same name or a new name. Type S, and Enable saves the file with the name you gave it when you entered Database Definition. You can now continue with the the definition procedure, adding more fields, or press F10 and type Q to return to the Main Menu.

If you press F10 and type D Enable deletes the entire database definition.

CAUTION

This deletes the database definition file, not just the information you added or modified during this Database Definition session.

PRINTING YOUR DATABASE AND FIELD DEFINITIONS Press F10 and type P to print a report on the database you have created. Enable displays a number of screens, running through the report procedure; but you don't need to take any action; Enable automatically prints the report. The report describes every field in the database. You must have the file named DBMSDEF.$RF on your data disk (if using floppy disks) or data directory (if using hard disk). This is normally loaded when you install Enable. Enable may not be able to print the report if any other windows are open.

EXITING THE DATABASE DEFINITION When you have finished, save your work and print a report if required, and then press F10 and type QY. Enable closes the Field Definition screen and displays the Main Menu.

DBASE II AND DBASE III DATABASES You can use dBASE II and III database files with Enable's DBMS. Simply type the name of an existing dBASE file at the database-name prompt on the first Database Definition form, and press Enter. Enable uses the quick-definition method to build a database definition for the file. It can then be used like any Enable database file, or modified (see Module 61).

APPLICATIONS

As you can see from the text in this module, Enable's database creation (definition) procedure allows you to create a database to fit just about any possible situation. Time spent designing your database, ensuring that each field does exactly what it needs to do, can save much time and trouble later, when you discover the limitations that you built into your database.

TYPICAL OPERATION

Because creating a complete database is a long process, this activity shows you how to define two fields. The database you define is then deleted; later modules use Enable's ready-made databases for examples.

1. At the Main Menu, type **UDDD**. Enable displays the first Database Definition screen. Type **CLIENTS** at the database name prompt, and press **Enter**.
2. Enable displays the "file not found" prompt. Press **Enter** to accept "New File." When Enable displays the next Database Definition screen, type **A list of current clients** and press **Enter**.
3. The cursor moves to the next prompt; press **Enter**. Type **CLIENTS** at the "default report form" prompt. Your screen looks like this:

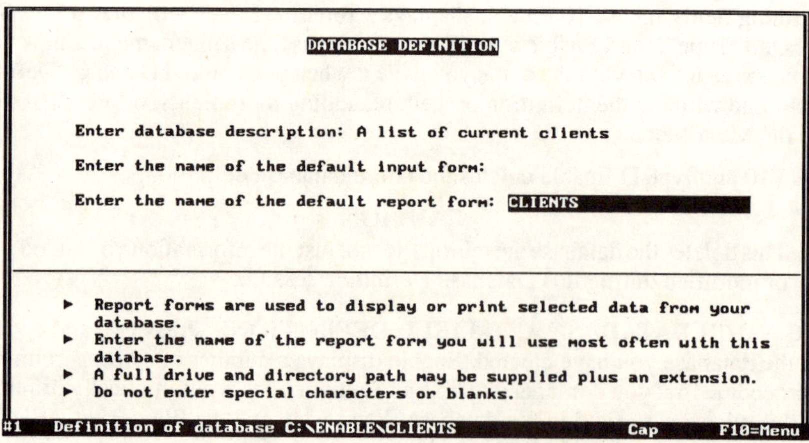

DATABASE DEFINITION

Enter database description: A list of current clients

Enter the name of the default input form:

Enter the name of the default report form: CLIENTS

- Report forms are used to display or print selected data from your database.
- Enter the name of the report form you will use most often with this database.
- A full drive and directory path may be supplied plus an extension.
- Do not enter special characters or blanks.

#1 Definition of database C:\ENABLE\CLIENTS Cap F10=Menu

4. Press **Enter** and Enable displays the Field Definition screen. Type **LAST NAME** in the field name field and press **Enter**. Enable beeps and displays a message telling you that you have typed an invalid character.
5. Press **Enter**, and remove the space from between LAST and NAME. Press **Enter** again.
6. When Enable displays the "Which method" prompt, press **Enter** to select Quick. Type **T** to select text, and type **20** at the length prompt.
7. Press **Enter** and Enable displays the Field Definition screen again. Notice that the LASTNAME field has been added to the top of the screen.
8. Type **LASTPURCH** for the next field name, and press **Enter**. Enable displays the "Which method" prompt. Type **D** and press **Down Arrow**. Type **Y** at the "Is this an indexed field" prompt. Your screen looks like this:

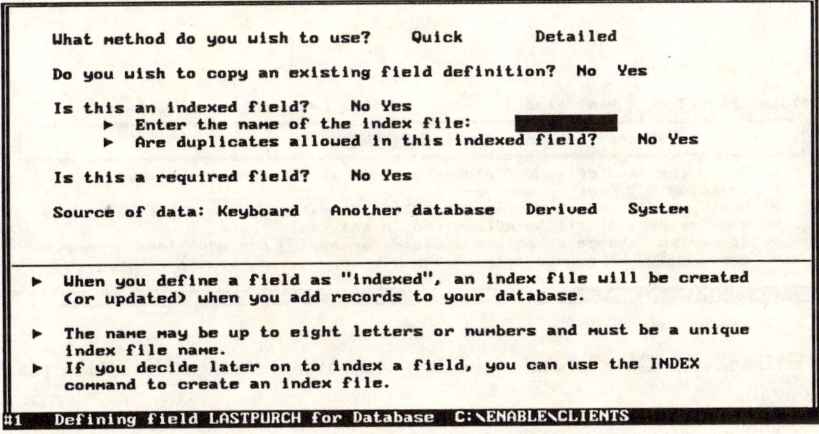

```
What method do you wish to use?    Quick      Detailed

Do you wish to copy an existing field definition?  No  Yes

Is this an indexed field?    No Yes
     ► Enter the name of the index file:
     ► Are duplicates allowed in this indexed field?    No Yes

Is this a required field?    No Yes

Source of data: Keyboard   Another database   Derived   System

► When you define a field as "indexed", an index file will be created
  (or updated) when you add records to your database.

► The name may be up to eight letters or numbers and must be a unique
  index file name.
► If you decide later on to index a field, you can use the INDEX
  command to create an index file.
#1   Defining field LASTPURCH for Database   C:\ENABLE\CLIENTS
```

9. Type **LPURCH** as the name of the index file, and press **Enter**. At the "duplicates" prompt press **Enter**, to accept Yes. At the "required field" prompt type **N**.
10. At the "source of data" prompt press **Enter** to accept Keyboard. Enable displays the following screen.

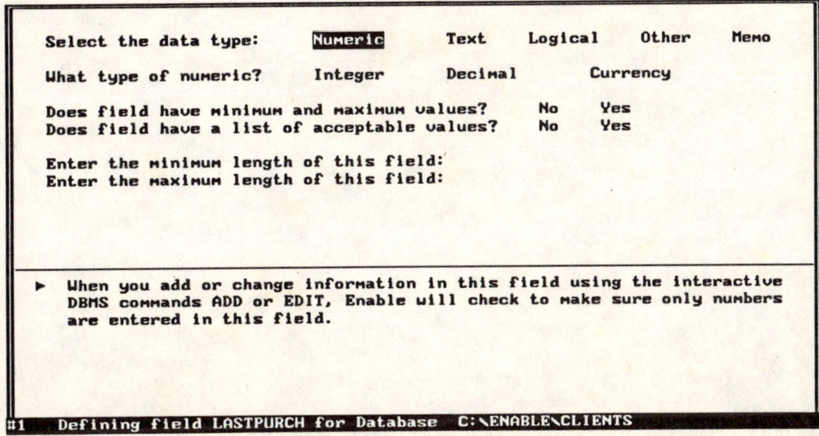

```
Select the data type:     Numeric      Text    Logical    Other    Memo

What type of numeric?     Integer      Decimal        Currency

Does field have minimum and maximum values?     No     Yes
Does field have a list of acceptable values?    No     Yes

Enter the minimum length of this field:
Enter the maximum length of this field:

► When you add or change information in this field using the interactive
  DBMS commands ADD or EDIT, Enable will check to make sure only numbers
  are entered in this field.
#1   Defining field LASTPURCH for Database   C:\ENABLE\CLIENTS
```

11. Press **Enter** to select Numeric, and type **C** to select Currency. Type **2** at the "number of decimals" prompt, and press **Enter**. Press **Enter** twice to select No for minimum and maximum values and for acceptable values.

12. Type **1** at the minimum length prompt and press **Enter**, and type **11** at the maximum length prompt and press **Enter**. Enable displays the "report picture" prompt.

13. Type **$nnn,nnn.nn**, and press **Enter**. At the "columnar report heading" prompt type **Last Purchase**, and press **Enter**. Press **Enter** again to skip the Error message. Enable displays the following Field Definition screen.

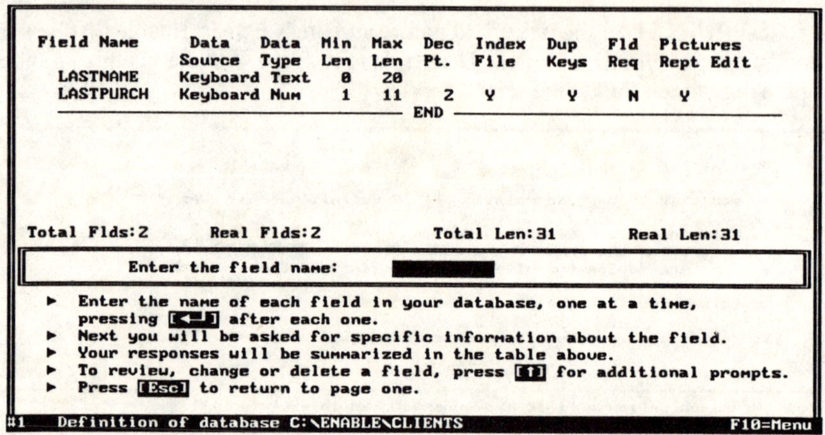

Field Name	Data Source	Data Type	Min Len	Max Len	Dec Pt.	Index File	Dup Keys	Fld Req	Pictures Rept	Edit
LASTNAME	Keyboard	Text	0	20						
LASTPURCH	Keyboard	Num	1	11	2	Y	Y	N	Y	

END

Total Flds:2 Real Flds:2 Total Len:31 Real Len:31

Enter the field name:

- Enter the name of each field in your database, one at a time, pressing [↵] after each one.
- Next you will be asked for specific information about the field.
- Your responses will be summarized in the table above.
- To review, change or delete a field, press [↑] for additional prompts.
- Press [Esc] to return to page one.

#1 Definition of database C:\ENABLE\CLIENTS F10=Menu

14. Press **F10** and type **QY** to abandon the database without saving it. Enable displays the Main Menu again.

15. Turn to Module 59 to continue the learning sequence.

Module 51
DELETE DATA (DELETE, UNDELETE, DESTROY)

DESCRIPTION

The Delete command lets you temporarily remove records that you no longer need. These records are not deleted in the usual sense of the word though. If you delete a line in word processing it's gone, except for a minor Undo feature that lets you recover a recently deleted line—you can't recover a line you deleted two months ago. But DBMS' Delete command is different. The deleted records remain in the file, but unused. You can recover deleted records using the Undelete command days or years later, as long as you haven't used the Destroy command. The Destroy command actually does remove the record; once destroyed the record is gone for good.

NOTE

Before you read this module you should read Module 60 to learn how to use the Interact and command screens.

DELETING RECORDS Select Delete from the Interact screen. The following screen shows the Delete command screen.

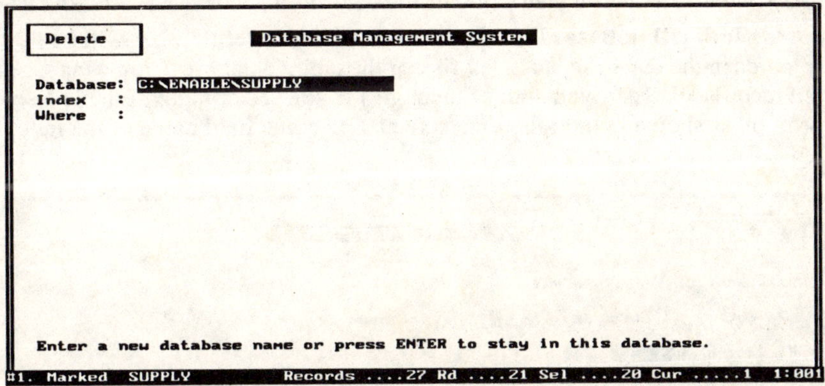

Use the Database, Index, and Where prompts to select the records you want to delete. When you press Enter at the Where prompt Enable deletes the records, and displays a message in the status line telling you how many were deleted. Alternatively, you may want to mark the records in the Display or Browse screens (see Module 64). Then, when you enter the Delete command screen just press End to bypass the prompts and delete the marked records.

NOTE

If you mark records, delete them, and return directly to the Display screen you still see the marked records. They are no longer displayed once you change the records you have selected at the Index or Where prompt.

Deleted records retain their sys:record numbers; you will see a jump in sys:record numbers in the Display screen where the deleted records were, for example.

Using Deleted Records Enable will not use deleted records in any of the commands, unless you specify them. For example, if you select the entire database for editing, Enable shows you all the records except the deleted ones. However, if you type DELETED in response to the Where prompt Enable uses all the deleted records.

UNDELETING RECORDS If you later decide that you want to restore the deleted records, use the Undelete command. Select Undelete from the Interact screen. Select the database and press End to undelete all of the deleted records in the database. Or, use the Index or Where prompts to specify which deleted records you want to undelete.

You can also mark the records you want to undelete. Type DELETED in the Where prompt on the Display command screen to view all the deleted records, and mark the ones you want to restore.

Duplicate Records Restoring deleted records may cause unacceptable duplicates. (You can specify in the database definitions if you will allow the same value to occur in more than one record; see Module 50.) If duplicates occur Enable builds an error set file (see Module 63).

DESTROY RECORDS The Destroy command totally removes deleted records.

CAUTION

The Destroy command can delete records, databases, and index files, and they cannot be restored or undeleted. Use this command with extreme caution. You may want to make a backup or archive data before using the command. See Module 49 for more information.

Select Destroy from the Interact screen and type the name of the database at the Database prompt.

Target: Records/Index/Database The Target options let you define what will be destroyed; all the deleted records in the database, an index file, or the entire database. (You cannot select which of the deleted records are destroyed—all of them go.) If you select Index, Enable also displays a fieldname prompt, as shown in the following screen. Select the field name of the index you want to destroy.

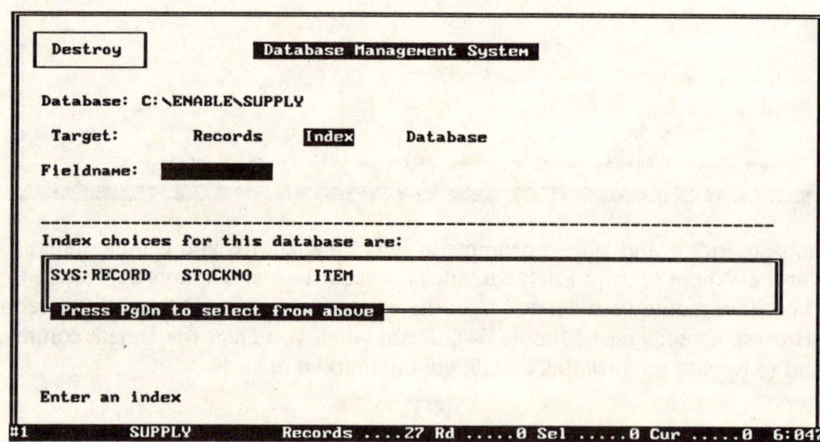

When you have pressed Enter or Down Arrow at the last prompt, Enable warns you that you are destroying data, and asks you to confirm.

CAUTION

Enable uses two confirmation procedures, depending on what you are destroying. If you are destroying a database you must press Y to continue; any other key will abort the operation. If you are destroying records or an index file, however, you can press any key to continue; if you want to abort you must press Esc.

APPLICATIONS

The Delete command is a convenient way to remove records from your database without totally destroying them; you can use this command when you think you may need the records later. Perhaps you haven't had any orders from a client in a long time; delete the record and if the client ever returns you can undelete the client's data. Destroy is only used when you are completely sure you will never need the information again, and would rather have the disk space available for other uses.

TYPICAL OPERATION

In this activity you delete and undelete records in the SUPPLYX database.

1. At the Interact screen type **D** to select the Display command screen. At the Database prompt type **supplyx** and press **End** to display the entire database.
2. Press **F7**, press **Down Arrow**, and press **F7** again. Press **Down Arrow** five times to move the cursor to record 7 and press **F7**.
3. Press **Down Arrow** twice to move to record 9 and press **F7** again. Press **Down Arrow** eight times to move to record 17 and press **Alt-M**.

SYS:RECORD	DELETED	STOCKNO	ITEM..........	SIZE.....	......COST	.QTY	COMPANY
1	No	10001	Nails	3in.	4.25	84	Anderso
2	No	10002	Nails	4in.	4.74	51	Anderso
3	No	40144	Suppt. Lumber	2x4x8	2.35	805	Pine Cr
4	No	40149	Suppt. Lumber	2x4x12	4.02	401	Pine Cr
5	No	61844	Plywood	4x8x.5	11.22	953	Gerrity
6	No	60012	Plywood	4x8x.75	13.24	662	Gerrity
7	No	11227	Nails	2in.	3.33	67	Hawthor
8	No	11239	Nails	1in.	2.49	99	Hawthor
9	No	11234	Nails	3in.	3.49	43	Anderso
10	No	91432	Door	32x80	119.00	35	ThermSa
11	No	93356	Door	36x80	121.00	40	ThermSa
12	No	84432	Window	6x3	202.01	17	Malta
13	No	84435	Window	6x5	262.78	23	Malta
14	No	82333	Window	5x8	213.44	19	Malta
15	No	41222	Suppt. Lumber	2x4x16	6.07	555	Arlingt
16	No	67745	Plywood	4x8x.25	8.29	322	Gerrity
17	No	12222	Nails	5in.	6.66	77	Anderso
18	No	50001	Sheetrock	4x8x.5	4.79	300	Lufkin
19	No	53344	Sheetrock	4x8x1	5.33	233	Lufkin
20	No	55501	Sheetrock	4x10x.5	7.49	130	Lufkin

Use cursor keys to page through display. Press ESC when done.

#2. Marked SUPPLYX Records ....28 Rd ....28 Sel ....28 Cur 9 D:000

4. Press **Esc** twice and type **1** to go to the Delete command screen. Press **End**. Enable deletes the six records and displays a message in the status line.

5. Move the cursor to the Where prompt, type **COMPANY="And$"** and press **End**. Enable deletes all remaining records with the company name Anderson.
6. Press **Esc** and type **D** to go to the Display command screen. Press **End** to display all the records in the database with the name Anderson (the COMPANY="And$" is still displayed). Enable beeps and displays "No Record Found."
7. Move the cursor to the Where prompt, press **Alt-F3** to clear it, and enter **DELETED**. Press **Enter** twice and Enable displays a list of the deleted records.

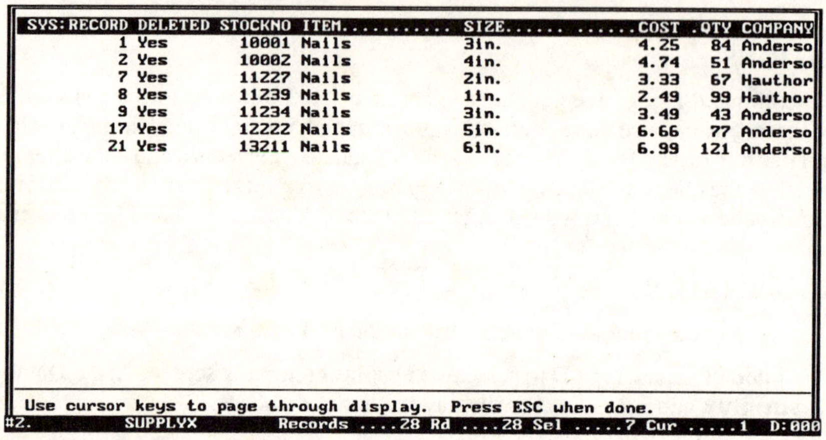

SYS:RECORD	DELETED	STOCKNO	ITEM..........	SIZE.....	......COST	.QTY	COMPANY
1	Yes	10001	Nails	3in.	4.25	84	Anderso
2	Yes	10002	Nails	4in.	4.74	51	Anderso
7	Yes	11227	Nails	2in.	3.33	67	Hauthor
8	Yes	11239	Nails	1in.	2.49	99	Hauthor
9	Yes	11234	Nails	3in.	3.49	43	Anderso
17	Yes	12222	Nails	5in.	6.66	77	Anderso
21	Yes	13211	Nails	6in.	6.99	121	Anderso

Use cursor keys to page through display. Press ESC when done.
#2. SUPPLYX Records ....28 Rd ....28 Sel .....7 Cur 1 D:000

8. Press **Esc** twice and type **2** to go to the Undelete command screen. Move the cursor to the Where prompt, press **Alt-F3** to clear it, and type **COMPANY="And$"**.
9. Press **End** and Enable undeletes (restores) all the deleted records with the company name Anderson and displays a message in the status line.
10. Press **F10** and type **Q** to return to the Main Menu.
11. Turn to Module 49 to continue the learning sequence.

Module 52
DOT COMMANDS (PROCEDURAL LANGUAGE) — REPORTS

DESCRIPTION

Dot commands (Procedural Language commands) are used mainly to produce reports in word processing format. For example, the letter used in the Mail Merge module in the Word Processing section was produced using dot commands. But these commands are also used at the Where and Fields prompts in the command screens, and in input-form macros to link databases, define new fields, and specify if-then conditions.

Enable's procedural language is a simple programming language. It is not the intention of this book to teach how to program, but the commands are summarized and several applications are discussed. This module describes the commands and describes how to use them to produce database reports. Modules 53 and 54 explain how to build input-form macros and use the commands at the Where and Field prompts.

DESIGNING REPORTS WITH DOT COMMANDS Module 62 explains how to generate reports; this module explains how to design those reports using dot commands. Dot-command reports give great flexibility in producing reports; they can be written to allow the user to enter information to the report, to manipulate the data in the report, and even to modify the database with the resulting information.

You type the report design into a word processing document (or in the "Put it Here!" document; see Module 62). Open a word processing file and use the extension .RPT to show that it is a report (you don't have to give it an extension if you don't want to—Enable will apply a .WPF extension.) Set the initial ruler to maximum width. (You will set other rulers later to narrow the text for your paper or screen.)

NOTE

> You can also include spreadsheet @FUNCTIONS in Procedural Language reports. See Module 74 for more information.

The Command Format Dot commands all begin with a period (hence, "dot" command). They can be uppercase or lowercase, and may begin at the left margin or be indented. (You will probably want to indent multiple-command procedures such as .if, to make them easier to read.) Each command appears on a line by itself.

You can add "internal documentation," (notes to yourself) telling what the report is doing, by typing two semicolons (;;). Enable ignores all text begun this way.

When Enable sees a field name in brackets ([ ]) it prints the field's current value. Leave enough spaces between the braces for Enable to print the value. Make sure you don't have any dot commands on the same line as a field you want printed. You can define the alignment of the values within the bracketed space by typing one of the following codes in braces: ^ (center), < (left justified), or > (right justified). For example, [COST   {^}].

When you create a report with the Report definition screen (Put it Here!), automatic reformat is turned off, but when Enable processes a report created in a word processing file it turns automatic reformat on. You can turn it off with the ".reformat off" command if you want your data aligned in columns, and back on (.reformat on) to eliminate extra spaces between values in blocks or paragraphs of text.

The following screen shows an example of a dot-command report.

```
.REFORMAT OFF
.DEFINITIONS
.DEFINE COST1=COST*1.2
.DEFINE TIME=SYS:TIME
.DEFINE DATE=SYS:DATE
.MAP SECTION
.INTRO
                    BUILDING MATERIALS INVENTORY

This is the introduction to the report.

REPORT DATE  [DATE]■        REPORT TIME [TIME]

STOCK #■     ITEM■          COST■     TOTAL COST■      SUPPLIER
.BODY
[STOCKNO{<}]■[ITEM  {<}]■   [COST{<}]■[COST1{<}]■      [SUPPLIER  {<}]
.BREAK 01 PROCEDURE
.BREAK ON ITEM
.BREAK SUMMARY
.REFORMAT ON
Total number = [ITEM{t}]

.BREAK END
#2    REF/B C:SUP.RPT              DRAFT                          L00001C001
```

Dot-command reports can begin with the .Report Division command, although this is not essential. This "command" simply states that the document is a dot-command report. The reports then have the following sections: definitions, map, introduction, break, body, conclusion, and subroutines.

The Definitions Section This section begins with the command .Definitions, and is used to define fields that are not in the database you specify when you use the Report command screen. (You can refer to the fields in the specified database by field name alone.) These fields may be from another database, derived from a calculation, a system field (date or time), or provided during the running of the report (local field). You can also change a field's report picture. Non-definition commands and blank lines entered in the definitions section are assumed to be part of the introduction section.

Enable assumes that field names are from the database you are working in, unless another database has been linked to the current database with a .open or .read command, or a field name has been defined in the definitions section. When refering to a field name that appears in more than one database, distinguish between the two by typing the database name first (*dbname.fieldname*; for example, CLIENTS.LNAME). If you are referring to a field name in a user-defined menu, type MNU first (for example, MNU.FILE). See Module 116 for more information on the Menu Generator.

The Map Section The .Map Section command simply shows the beginning of the section that includes the introduction, body, conclusion, and subroutines. You do not have to use the command.

The Introduction Section This section follows the definition section, and begins with the .Intro command. Commands in this section are processed before any records, may include a header or introductory text, and may be used to initialize local values.

The Break Section Breaks can be used to print column headings, force a page break, insert blank lines or text, and to calculate column totals and summary values. The section is not begun with a command, but can be recognized by its individual component .Break commands.

The Body Section This section begins with the .Body command, and is the only section that is required. You can omit all other sections if you want. The body section is processed once for every record.

The Conclusion Section This section, like the introduction section, is processed only once. It begins with the .Conclusion command and appears at the end of the report.

The Subroutine Section Begun with the .Subroutine command, this section divides a large report into easier to handle components. Subroutines are commands that are used more than once within the report. Instead of entering the commands each time, you use a .Label command to name the subroutine, and a .Gosub command to call the subroutine at the places you need it. The .Return command at the end of the subroutine returns the report processing back to the command immediately after the .Gosub command.

NOTE

For examples of dot commands, some of which may be used in reports, see Modules 53 and 54.

MEMO FIELDS When including memo fields in a report the reformat status has an important effect. If automatic reformat is turned off the memo field appears as a block of text, in the format it appears in the memo file. This allows you to include fields either side of the memo field. However, if automatic reformat is turned on, the memo field text conforms to the ruler in the report form.

THE COMMANDS The following is a list of the procedural language commands. These commands cannot all be used in reports, but are applicable to macros and Where and Field prompts.

.add ***dbname***—Adds current field values from the specified database to the end of the current database, creating a new record. (See .update and .write.)

.autolock ***dbname***—LAN command which turns on automatic single-record locking for the specified database.

.body—Typed at the left margin, indicates the beginning of the first record in a report. The body of the report is repeated for each record. Information that is not repeated (such as a header page) is entered before .body or in a break (.break). Type field names in brackets exactly as you want them to appear, for example, [LNAME], and leave enough space for field length (see .reformat). Put as many fields as you want on a line, up to 160 characters. Use the brace codes explained in Module 62 to indicate computations. Fields are normally left justified. You can change justification with these brace codes: {<} left justified; {>} right justified; {^} centered. When specifying computations with length or justification, always put the computation code first, for example, [CNAME{T1,^}]. The computation codes are as follows:

Numeric fields only:

The total value (sum)	{s}
The highest value	{h}
The lowest value	{l}
The average value	{a}

Any fields:
The tally (number of records) {t}
The number of different values {c}

.break *nn* procedure—*nn* is the break number, 1 to 16. Interrupts printing to add blank lines, labels, explanatory text, page break, and computations. Followed by some of the other break commands. See the report shown near the end of this module for an example.

.break on (*condition or filename*)—Tells Enable when to break. Typing .BREAK DATE means insert a break whenever the DATE field changes.

.break *nn* heading—Allows you to enter a heading to appear above the break. You enter labels, field names, page breaks, etc.

```
.BREAK 01 HEADING
NAME            COMMISSION
.BODY
[NAME    ]      [COMMIS    ]
```

.break summary—Summaries appear at the end of the report, and typically include computations (see computation codes at .body).

```
.BREAK SUMMARY
    [COST {S}]
```

means sum the values in the specifed break fields since the last break.

.break end—Indicates the end of a break procedure.

.case *condition*—Used with .do case and .otherwise to check multiple conditions and execute subsequent conditions. See .do case.

.checkkey—Only used in input form ADD macro procedures to avoid modifying the lookup database when searching for data in a second database linked to the first through the sys:record. An error is displayed if no matching data is found. The .passthru command must be off. See Module 53.

.close—Closes a file opened with .open. This command doesn't work with a primary database, or during execution of a report or .perform file.

.clrscreen—Clears the entire screen. Also, .clrscreen(*row*) clears the specified row, and .clrscreen(*row,column,row,column*) clears a block where the first *row/column* pair is the top left corner and the second pair is the bottom right corner. Rows are numbered 1 to 22 and columns from 1 to 78.

.conclusion—Beginning of the text to be added to the end of a file.

.define—Creates *local* fields, that is, fields with data from another database, data derived from a formula, or data from an .input command. Enter the .Definition command first, then begin the .Define commands on the next line. (Fields created with .define cannot be used with .break.)

.define *fieldname = lookupfld* in *db2* link *link2 = link1* pulls data from another database (*db2*). The *link* field in the other database (*db2*) must be indexed. For example, .DEFINE COMMIS=COMMIS IN SALES LINK LNAME=LNAME.

.define ***fieldname=formula*** calculates the value. For example, .DEFINE COMMIS= SALES*0.1.

.define ***fieldname*** **as** ***type length.decimals*** defines the type and length of a field. You can then supply the data with the .input or .let command. Types are data, time, text, integer, decimal, logical y, and logical t. After text and integer specify the field length, and after decimal the length and decimals. For example, DEFINE COMMIS AS DECIMAL 11.2. You can also combine this command with the next.

.define ***fieldname*** **using** ***picture*** lets you define a picture other than the default report picture. For example, .DEFINE COMMIS USING "$NNN,NNN,NN"

.definitions—Begins the section of a report where you .define local fields or modify previously defined fields.

.do case—Begins a .case or .otherwise condition. Allows you to define a condition or series of conditions. For example:

```
.DO CASE
      .CASE CITY1="A"
      .LET ADDRESS3="ALBANY"
.ENDCASE
```

You can combine more than one condition (just continue on the line after "ALBANY" with .CASE, etc.

.otherwise is used after the .case command, to specify what is done if the .case condition is not met, as in this continuation of the previous command.

```
      .LET ADDRESS3="ALBANY"
.OTHERWISE
      .LET ADDRESS3="NEW YORK"
.ENDCASE
```

.endcase is always used to end the .do case conditions.

.echo on/.echo on—Diagnostic command. The dot commands will be printed with the report.

.else/.elseif/.endif—See .if

.endwhile—Indicates the end of a .while condition. See .while.

.error—Only used in ADD and EDIT macro procedures. When the error command is encountered Enable stops and displays an error message.

.escape on/.escape off—Overrides the Esc key/turns Esc key on. Used to define sections of a report that cannot be exited by pressing Esc.

.exit—Used with .if to abort the report. For example,

```
.IF COMMIS>10,000
***ABNORMALLY HIGH COMMISSION***
.EXIT
```

This prints the message and aborts the report if a commission is greater than 10,000.

.getchar—Interrupts the report; the report continues when you press a key, and Enable stores (in variable sys:1char) the scan-code value of the key pressed. You can then use .if to define the next step, depending on the key pressed.

```
.GETCHAR
.IF SYS:1CHAR=7181
.INPUT "What is your ID?" field 1
.ELSE
.EXIT
.ENDIF
```

will make Enable display "What is your ID" if the Enter key is pressed (scan code 7181). If another key is pressed the report is aborted. The .getchar command is similar to .input, but any key restarts, so you can't write data to a local field.

.gosub ***label name***—Begins the .subroutine commands indicated by the *label name*. When Enable sees .return, it returns to the command following the .gosub command.

.goto ***label name***—Continues the report at the .label *label name*. The .label command must be in the same section as the .goto command, unlike .gosub and its .label.

.if ***condition***—Used to establish a condition or, in conjunction with .elseif, .else, and .endif commands, to build if-then conditions. The .else command tells Enable what to do if the condition is not met, and the .elseif specifies another condition to check for if the first condition is not met.

```
.IF COST GE 10,000
     ******EXCESSIVE COST******
.ELSEIF COST LE 2,000
     ******THIS MAY BE INCORRECT; CHECK DATA*****
.ELSE
.ENDIF
```

means that if the cost is over 10,000 or under 2,000 Enable prints a warning, but if it is within these two, Enable continues.

.if commands are always ended with .endif.

.input ***text field name***—Used to make Enable stop and prompt you to input information before continuing with the report.

```
.INPUT "ENTER COMMISSION RATE" RATE
```

Enable stops at this point, displays "ENTER COMMISSION RATE" at the bottom of the screen; the user inputs a value and presses Enter, and Enable puts the value in RATE.

NOTE

The .input command only works if you are displaying a report on screen, writing it to a disk file, or spooling it to a printer. (Your user profile must be set to Spool Report. See Module 62.)

You can specify where the user must input the data using .input(*row*/*column*,*len*) where *row* is the row, from 1 to 22, *column* is the column, from 1 to 78, and *len* is the length of the input field, up to the default length of the field. If you don't enter a *len*, Enable uses the default length.

Use .input *memofield* to let the user input data to a memo field.

.intro—Marks the begining of the introduction section of the report, the text to be added to the report before the .body. This section is also used to set intial field-values for the report.

.label ***label name***—Used with a .goto or .gosub, the .label provides a name for a .subroutine. The name is a single word.

.let ***fieldname=expression***—Used with .if, .else, and .elseif to insert the expression in a specific field.

```
.LET COMMISS=SALES*0.1
```

.lockwait ***dbname sys:record#***—LAN command locking individual records.

.macro ***macro statement***—Used to create a keystroke sequence in input-form macros (see Module 53).

.map section—Begins section of report where you lay out the appearance of the report, including the introduction, body, and conclusion. This is an optional, informational command.

.maxscreen—Allows access to the entire 22-line screen without the status line and system command line; if you try to go beyond line 22 Enable displays an End of Screen message, obscuring data in the last line.

.noautolock ***dbname***—LAN command turning .autolock off.

.open ***dbname***—Opens another database for use with the .read or .write commands. Closed with .close.

.open ***dbname*** **index** ***fieldname***—Opens another database (for use by .read and .write) that is accessed in index order of the specified field. Closed with the .close command. When you use this command in a report form, don't use the Index prompt in the Report command screen.

.otherwise—Used after .case to determine what Enable should do for conditions not satisfied. See .do case.

.passthru on/.passthru off—Used in an input-form macro, it allows changes made to an external field in one database to be passed through to the next. When data is keyed into the link field in database 1 Enable finds the matching record in database 2, and displays the data from the lookup field in the external field in database 1.

If passthru is set on (and if you defined the field in the input-form design as one that can be "keyed over"), typing over the displayed data in the external field also passes the data back to database 2, changing the data in the lookup field.

If no match was found in database 2, a new record is created when you key-over the external field. See Module 53 for more information.

NOTE

The default profile has passthru set on. It remains on until Enable sees the first .passthru off command. You can change your profile to set passthru to normally off.

.perform ***filename %on***—Runs the dot commands in the specified word processing file, letting you build a library of often-used commands. You can use this when building macros over 135 characters long, or to save repeating commands in reports. Segment commands (.intro, .body, etc.) have no meaning, and bracketed field names are ignored. Local fields should be defined in the main report or input form so the perform file can access them by name.

You can use up to nine replaceable variables, %1 to %9. After the .perform command and filename, type the names of the variables separated by spaces.

```
.PERFORM CITY.PRM "ALBANY" "BOSTON" "BUFFALO"
calls the file CITY.PRM.
.IF CODE=1
  .LET CI=%1
.ELSEIF CODE=2
  .LET CI=%2
.ELSEIF CODE=3
  .LET CI=%3
.ENDIF
```

Thus, if CODE is 3 the field CI is given the value BUFFALO.

.position ***dbname expresssion***—Positions the pointer on a specified record as a starting point, and establishes the order of access of subsequent records.

```
.POSITION CLIENT SEQ SYS:RECORD=5
.READ CLIENT NEXT
```

positions the pointer on sys:record 5 in the CLIENT database, and then reads records sequentially (6, 7, etc.).

```
.POSITION CLIENT INDEX=CNAME SYS:RECORD=5
```

positions the pointer on sys:record 5, but continues in the index-order of the CNAME field.

.read ***dbname expression***—Opens a secondary database and accesses a specific record. The database may have any of these extensions: .DBF, .SS, .ERR, .ASC, .SSF, .WKS, .WK1, .DEF, .DTA, .DAT.

The command is normally used in a where clause.

```
.READ DBASENAME FIRST SOCSEC=SOCSEC
```

positions you in the first record of the DBASENAME database that has the same SOCSEC field as the one in the current database. Or specify the values in the field (SOCSEC =411-1522-123), or omit the field name to position on the first record in the database. Replace FIRST with NEXT or PRIOR to use the next or prior record that satisfies the condition.

The .read command only reads one record. Create a loop to ensure you read all the necessary records.

```
.BODY
.READ DB2 FIRST DB2.ACCTNUM=DB1.ACCTNUM
.WHILE DB2.SYS:RECORD<>0
     [NAME]      [ADDRESS]      [CITY]      [STATE]      [ZIP]
.READ DB2 NEXT DB2.ACCTNUM=DB2.ACCTNUM
.ENDWHILE
```

reads the first record in DB2 where ACCTNUM has the same value as an ACCTNUM in DB1. If the record number in DB2 is not zero, Enable prints the name and address. Then Enable searches for the next ACCTNUM field in DB2 that matches an ACCTNUM field in DB1. When you use this command in a report form, don't use the Index prompt in the Report command screen.

CAUTION

Read dot commands are intended to read secondary databases. You should never attempt to .read primary databases while in the body of the report.

.read *dbname* index *fieldname=expression*—Reads a record in the specifed database in the index order of the specified field.

```
.READ DB1 INDEX MONTH="MAY"
```

searches the DB1 database in index order of the MONTH field, and reads the first field with MAY as a value. If no match is found the pointer is set to sys:record = 0.

Replace the = sign in the command with >= to set the pointer to the first sys:record with an index value higher than the value being searched for.

```
.READ DB1 INDEX LASTNAME>="JONES"
```

If Enable does not find a record with Jones, the pointer is positioned on the next name in alphabetical order.

.reformat on/.reformat off—Turns reformat on and off in a report. In Put it Here! reports, reformat is off unless turned on, but in word processing reports it is on unless turned off. Keep it on for form letters and paragraph-style reports, because trailing blanks in fields are removed. If it is off you can set field length by showing the spaces in the brackets ([LNAME]) or by putting the number of spaces in braces to keep the columns aligned ([LNAME{18}]). Allow enough room for commas in currency fields.

.report division—Identifies reports designed with dot commands. Put this command at the top of the report, or omit it entirely (it is optional).

.return—Used with .gosub to indicate the end of a .subroutine. See .subroutines.

.screenpos (*row,column*)—Controls where fields are displayed on the screen, where *row* is the row, from 1 to 22 and *column* is the starting column, from 1 to 78. You do not need to use both *row* and *column*.

.status *text* [*field name*]—Displays the text above the status line on your screen while the report is being written to disk so that you can monitor the report's progress.

```
.STATUS COMPANY NAME: [CNAME] CONTACT: [LNAME]
```

When Enable reaches the company names in report it displays the text, names, and contacts on your screen.

.subroutines—Begins the section of the report where subroutines are listed, groups of commands called from another area of the report by .gosub. The Subroutine section comes after the Conclusion section.

```
.SUBROUTINES
.LABEL LABELNAME
(command)
.RETURN
```

The .subroutine command indicates the beginning of the commands, the .label indicates that the next word is the name of the subroutine, and the .return command returns Enable to the command immediately after the .gosub command that called the subroutine. After the .return start the next subroutine command with another .label.

.unlock ***dbname sys:record#***—LAN command unlocking record locked with .lockwait.

.update ***dbname***—Modifies the record on disk to match current field values. It will not add a new record to the database.

.updatekey ***field name***—Only used in an input-form ADD macro, looks up data in a second database linked to the current database by the sys:record field. If matching data is not found in the second database, the second database is updated with the entered data as a new record. See Module 53.

.while *condition*—Begins statements that are performed as long as the stated *condition* exists. The condition includes a variable that is altered by one or more of these statements. Once the condition is no longer met Enable continues with the command after the .endwhile command.

```
.WHILE X<100
.READ DB2 NEXT
.LET DB1.FIELD1=DB2.FIELD1
.LET X=X*DB1.FIELD1
.ENDWHILE
```

If X is less than 100 Enable reads values sequentially from database DB2. Field1 in the first database is updated with data from Field1 in DB2. X is then multiplied by the new value in Field1. If it is still less than 100 Enable goes to the next record in DB2.

.write ***dbname***—Adds records to (or updates) the database with information from the specified database. If the sys:record equals 0 the record is added. If the sys:record is any other value the data from the record is used to update the record in the first database.

SYSTEM-SUPPLIED FIELDS The following system-supplied fields can be read by dot commands.

sys:record—The number of the current record.

sys:screen—A number from 0 to 20 can be assigned to sys:screen. Any print commands that follow the command will begin on that assigned line. (If you have used .maxscreen you can enter 0 to 22.)

```
.LET SYS:SCREEN=10
  [CNAME]
```

This command prints the CNAME field on line10 of the report screen. Clear the value by assigning 0 and leaving a blank line.

sys:1char—Stores the scan-code of the last key pressed. See .getchar.

sys:date—The system date (YY/MM/DD).

sys:time—The system time (HM:MM:SS) in military (24-hr.) format.

INCLUDING MEMO FIELDS You can put memo fields in reports. If you leave reformat turned off the text in the memo field will be printed as it appears in the memo file; this allows you to place other fields to the right and left of the memo field. If you turn reformat on the text prints according to the ruler in the report form.

GENERATING THE REPORT When you have written the report, use the Report command to print it (see Module 62). If your file has a .WPF or .RPT extension you must use the extension when you enter the report name.

APPLICATIONS

Procedural language commands let you design almost any report format you could possibly need. The commands give you the power of a programming language to build the commands you want; to let you enter information and update the database while you run a report; to design complicated form letters that manipulate the data, not just print it; and to use the reports to make calculations with the data.

These commands can also be used to build input-form macros, to link databases together, and to write complex where clauses and Field commands (see Modules 53 and 54).

TYPICAL OPERATION

In this activity you build a simple dot-command report for the SUPPLYX database created in Module 5. You must understand how to use the word processing features to build this report.

1. At the Main Menu type **UWC**. When Enable prompts you to enter a filename type **SUP.RPT** and press **Enter**. When Enable shows you the default ruler, change it; put the left margin at column 1, and tabs at columns 14, 29, 39, and 56. (See the column indicator at the far right of the status line.) Place the right margin at 77. Press **Enter** when you finish.
2. Delete the Document Title entry space (press **Up Arrow** three times and press **Alt-F3**). Enter the report exactly as shown in the following screen.

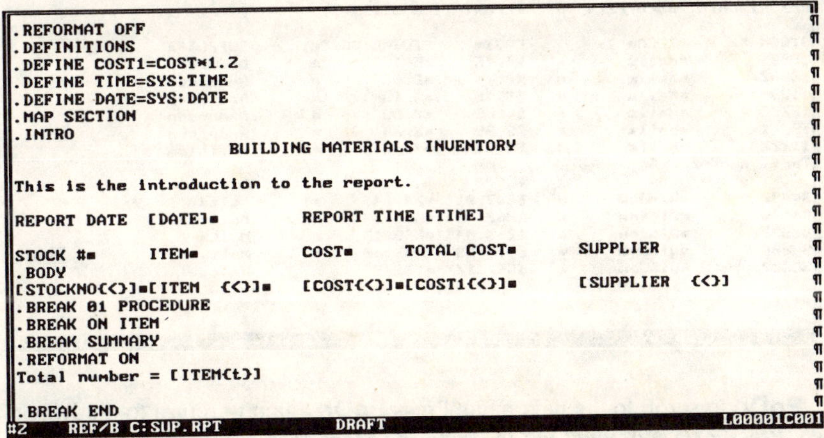

```
.REFORMAT OFF
.DEFINITIONS
.DEFINE COST1=COST*1.2
.DEFINE TIME=SYS:TIME
.DEFINE DATE=SYS:DATE
.MAP SECTION
.INTRO
                    BUILDING MATERIALS INVENTORY

This is the introduction to the report.

REPORT DATE  [DATE]         REPORT TIME [TIME]

STOCK #      ITEM           COST     TOTAL COST      SUPPLIER
.BODY
[STOCKNO{<}][ITEM  {<}]     [COST{<}][COST1{<}]      [SUPPLIER  {<}]
.BREAK 01 PROCEDURE
.BREAK ON ITEM
.BREAK SUMMARY
.REFORMAT ON
Total number = [ITEM{t}]

.BREAK END
#2    REF/B C:SUP.RPT          DRAFT                         L00001C001
```

3. Delete all the blank lines between the last line of the report and the end-of-file marker (the double line). When you have finished typing the report press **Alt-F10** and press **Enter** to save it. Press **F10** and type **QY** to exit.
4. At the Main Menu type **UDI** and at the Interact screen type **9** to see the Report command screen. At the Database prompt type **SUPPLYX** and press **Enter**. At the "Using form" prompt press **Alt-F3** to clear the default report name and type **SUP.RPT**. Press **Enter**.
5. At the Index prompt type or select **ITEM**, to put the records in alphabetical order by item. (The Item field must be indexed. This was done in Module 58.) Press **Enter** and type **S** to select Screen. At the Where prompt type **ITEM="N$" OR ITEM="W$"**.

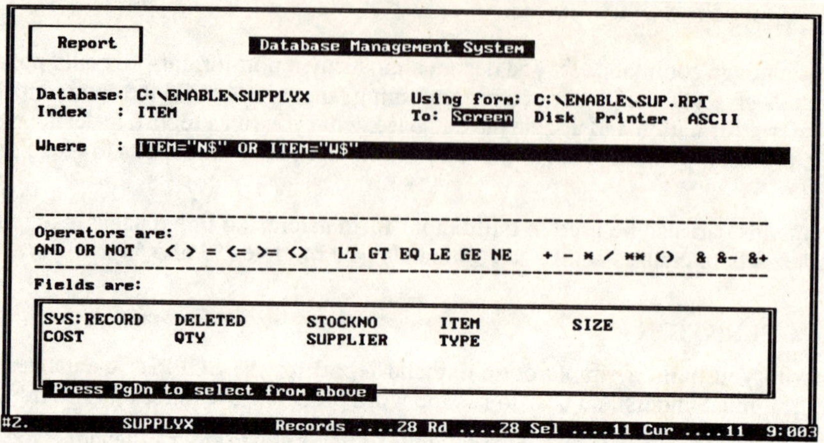

6. Press **Enter** and Enable generates the report, using all the records with an ITEM beginning with the letter N or W, as shown in the following screen.

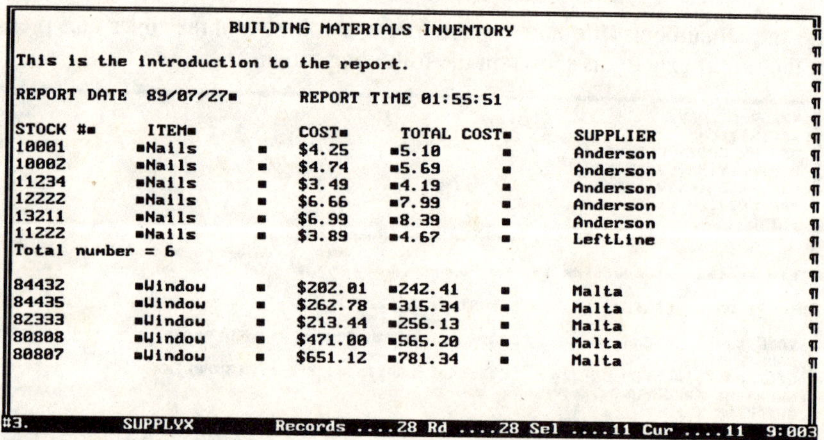

7. Press **PgDn** to scroll to the next page. Press **PgDn** again to return to the Report command screen. Press **F10** and type **Q** to return to the Main Menu.

8. Turn to Module 53 to continue the learning sequence.

Module 53
DOT COMMANDS — INPUT-FORM MACROS

DESCRIPTION

Input-form macros can be built to look up data from another database, to perform conditional testing to control the input-form flow, to update related databases while you enter data in the input form, and so on. For example, you might use a .read command and a .let command to enter data from another database, or use an .update command to change data in another database. Input-form macros can include dot commands (described in Modules 52 and 54) or macro commands (described in Module 115). This module describes the different types of input-form macros and how to enter them, and gives three examples.

Input-form macros are entered when you design the input form (see Module 59). Position a field, press Shift-F9, enter the name of a field, press Enter, and answer Yes to the "Special processing options" prompt. Enable displays several processing options. The eighth option is "Does this field have a macro procedure?" Answer Yes and the following screen is displayed.

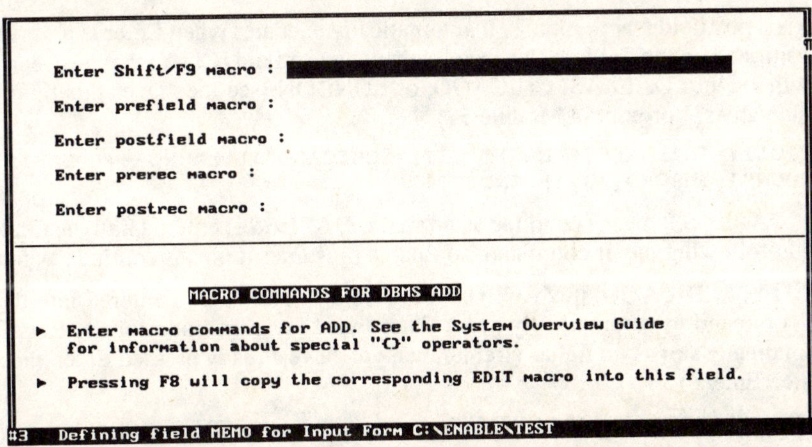

This first screen contains the ADD macros, the macros that will operate when you are adding records. (After you complete this page the same questions are asked for the EDIT macros, those that operate when you are editing data.)

Macros work at five different points.

Shift-F9	executes when you press Shift-F9.
Prefield	automatically executes when the cursor is placed on a particular field. A macro could automatically look up data from another database, for example.
Postfield	automatically executes after data is entered in a field and Enter is pressed. For example, the data entered could be used to update a field in another database.

Prerecord automatically executes when a record is first read; a prerecorded macro could increment a field each time a record is added for example.

Postrecord automatically executes when the record is saved. Could be used to update a record in another database.

You can type the macro or press F8 to copy the corresponding macro from the EDIT macros (if you are in ADD) or ADD macros (if you are in EDIT). If the field already has a macro statement, pressing F8 copies the one from the other set over the current one (so if the current macro is longer than the one from the other set, Enable leaves the remainder of the original macro at the end of the new one — make sure you delete this). When you have finished entering the EDIT macros the input form is displayed again.

MACRO FORMAT Macros can be up to 132 characters, although you can bypass this limit using a .perform command to perform operations specified in another file; these commands may be much larger (see .perform in Module 52).

Macro statements include text; macro codes in braces {}; and field names, expressions, and dot commands in brackets [ ]. Macro codes are discussed in detail in Module 115. Bracketed field names are replaced by the field contents, bracketed expressions are replaced by the results, bracketed commands are executed, and text is displayed as entered.

A POSTFIELD MACRO — CONTROLLING CURSOR POSITION This example shows how to control where the cursor goes after finishing a field and pressing Enter; to the next field, to a specified field, or to the next record.

This macro is a postfield macro, that is, it automatically executes when Enter is pressed while the cursor is positioned on the field. In this example you have a field (CITY) that has been defined to accept only the values DALLAS, CHICAGO, or LONDON (see the "Does this field have a list of acceptable values?" prompt in Module 50).

```
[.IF CITY="DALLAS"][.ELSIF CITY="CHICAGO"][.MACRO~~][.ELSIF CITY=
"LONDON"][.MACRO{F5}][.ENDIF]
```

[.IF CITY="DALLAS"] means continue as normal if DALLAS is entered into the field. (There is no instruction following the .if command, so Enable presumes it means continue as normal.)

[.ELSEIF CITY="CHICAGO"][.MACRO~~] means if CHICAGO is entered into the field use the .macro command to automatically press Enter twice (~ is the code for the Enter key). The cursor automatically skips two fields. (Remember, you have already pressed Enter once, so this is a total of three Enters.)

[.ELSIF CITY="LONDON"][.MACRO{F5}] means if LONDON is entered use the .macro command to automatically save the record and continue to the next one, skipping all the subsequent fields in this record.

[.ENDIF] ends the .if command.

.UPDATEKEY This command copies information from a *lookup field* in a record in another database (DB2) into a specially defined *external field* in the current database (DB1). In order to do this you must know the information in a *link field* in DB2. For example, two databases have CNAME (company name) fields. One database (DB2) stores the client names, addresses, and account numbers. The other database (DB1) is a record of sales. You could set up the CNAME fields as link fields, and the account number (ACCTNUM) field as an external field in DB1 and as the lookup field in DB2. Then, when you type the CNAME into DB1, Enable automatically looks in DB2 for the company name. When it finds the same name it copies the account number in DB2 into the ACCTNUM field in DB1. (In fact you could use this method to copy the company's entire address.)

Use this procedure to set up the .UPDATEKEY procedure.

Defining the Database The link field (the field in DB2 that contains the data you know) must be indexed and contain no duplicate records. The link field in DB1 is the field into which you enter data. This field does not require any special format. In our example the CNAME fields are the link fields.

The external field (the field in DB1 that will receive the data from the lookup field in DB2) must be defined as a Derived field when you create the database. (In our example the external field is ACCTNUM.) Select Derived at the "Source of Data" prompt, and enter the following at the formula prompt:

```
Lookupfld IN DB2 LINK Linkfield=Linkfield
```

For example:

```
ACCTNUM IN SALES LINK CNAME=CNAME
```

means "look at the CNAME fields in the database called SALES. When you find a name that matches the CNAME field in the current database (DB1), copy the value from the ACCTNUM field in the same record."

See Module 50 for information on defining a database.

Designing the Input Form When you enter the external field (ACCTNUM) into the input form select Yes at the "special processing options" prompt. You then have a choice. You can answer Yes at the "Can this field be keyed over" prompt. This allows you to type new information into the ACCTNUM field; this information is then put into a new record in DB2.

Then enter an ADD postfield macro; type [.UPDATEKEY *Fieldname*]

The *Fieldname* is the name of the field you are defining as the external field; in this example ACCTNUM.

Then enter a prerecorded macro; type [.PASSTHRU OFF] This stops the data you entered in DB1 being used to change the record in DB2.

Then move on through the prompts to the EDIT macros. Press F8 at the postfield and prerecord macros to add the macros you entered at the ADD page.

See Module 59 for information on creating an input form.

NOTE

> Linked databases must be in the same directory, because the looked-up data is not stored in both databases.

.CHECKKEY The .checkkey command works with the .updatekey command, but it stops Enable from adding a new record if you enter a value into the external field. In the previous example, when you type a company name in the CNAME field, Enable displays the corresponding ACCTNUM. If you then type over the ACCTNUM, Enable clears the CNAME field and searches for that ACCTNUM. If Enable finds the ACCTNUM it displays the corresponding CNAME. However, if it cannot find the ACCTNUM and if you now save the record, Enable adds a new record with the new ACCTNUM to DB2. You can use the .CHECKKEY command to stop Enable from updating DB2.

Simply type [.CHECKKEY *Fieldname*] at the postfield macro prompt when you are defining the input form. (In this example you type [.CHECKKEY ACCTNUM].)

NOTE

See Modules 52 and 54 for examples of other dot commands, some of which may be used in input forms.

APPLICATIONS

Input-form macros give you the flexibility to design forms to do almost anything. They can pull information from other databases, make calculations with the information you type in, move the cursor to another part of the form depending on your input, and so on.

TYPICAL OPERATION

In this activity you add an input-form macro to the MAILIN input form. This is loaded when you install Enable.

1. At the Main Menu type **UDDI**. When Enable displays the "input form name" prompt type **MAILIN** and press **Enter** four times. Enable displays the input form.
2. Place the cursor on the diamond in the field after the word CITY:. Press **Shift-F9** and Enable displays the "special processing" prompt. Type **Y** and then type **N** seven times. At the "macro procedure" prompt type **Y**.
3. Press **Enter** twice to move to the "postfield" prompt. Type **[.if city="Johnson"][.let state="TX"][.let zip="75111"][.macro ~~][.endif]**. As you type, the command scrolls to the left.

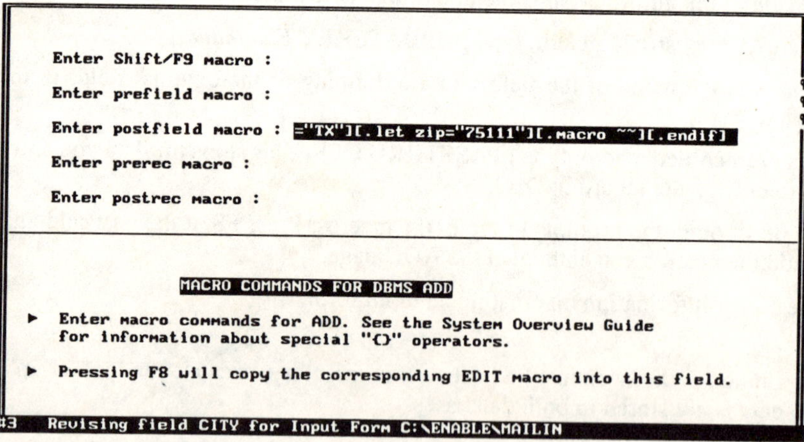

4. Press **Enter** five times, and press **F8** to copy the macro into the EDIT postfield prompt. Press **Enter** three times, and the input form is displayed.
5. Press **F10** and type **FSS** to save the form. Press **F10** and type **Q** to exit and return to the Main Menu. Type **UDI** to go to the Interact screen, and type **A** to go to the Add command screen.

6. Type **Mail** at the Database prompt and press **Enter**. Enable displays the name of the default input form, MAILIN. Press **Enter**. Enable displays the input form.
7. Press **Enter** seven times to move to the CITY field, and type **Johnson**. Press **Enter** and Enable enters TX in the STATE field, 75111 in the ZIP field, and moves the cursor to the PHONE field.

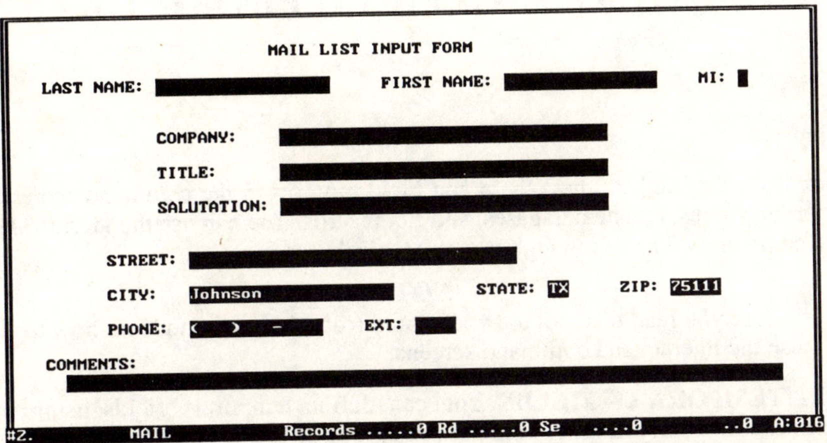

8. Press **F10** and type **Q** to go to the Add Command screen. Press **F10** and type **Q** to go to the Main Menu.
9. Turn to Module 54 to continue the learning sequence.

Module 54
DOT COMMANDS — WHERE AND FIELD PROMPTS

DESCRIPTION

You can use dot commands at the Where and Field prompts in the command screens to define variables, assign values, update databases, and run macros. You can use the .define, .let, .update, and .macro commands. The following are a few typical uses.

NOTE

Before you read this module you should read Module 60 to learn how to use the Interact and command screens.

DEFINING TEMPORARY FIELDS You can define temporary fields using the .define command. These temporary fields remain defined as long as you are working in that database. For example, type the following at the Where or Field prompt.

```
.DEFINE ITEM1=ITEM&+SIZE
```

This combines the two fields ITEM and SIZE into one field called ITEM1. The "&+" (concatenate, trim, and add) means join the two values together, remove blank spaces, and put one blank space between the two values. Press Enter and Enable adds ITEM1 to the list of fields at the bottom of the page and displays Enter in the status line. Enable will not let you combine text and numeric data fields.

Press Alt-F3 to remove the command from the prompt (if you press Enter, End, or Down Arrow before clearing the command you add another field with the same name). Proceed with the command screen as normal. You can use the field at any point and in any command until you leave the database. The new field takes the length of the longest field in the expression.

Another command might be

```
.DEFINE COMMISSION=SALES*0.1
```

This defines a new field COMMISSION that is the SALES field multiplied by 0.1.

CHANGING THE REPORT PICTURE You can change the way a field is displayed in a report or in the Display screen by typing

.DEFINE *FIELDNAME* USING "*PICTURE*"

See Module 50 for information on report pictures. For example, typing

```
.DEFINE COST USING "$NNN,NN"
```

changes the display to five numbers and a comma, but no decimal point.

You can combine type and length commands, as follows:

```
.DEFINE COMMISSION AS DECIMAL 11.2 USING "$NNN,NNN.NN"
```

NOTE

This does not work for memo fields.

.DEFINING LENGTHY WHERE CLAUSES You can use the .define command to store lengthy where clauses. The clauses can then be used by typing one word, and remain stored until you leave the database. For example, type the following at the Where prompt:

```
.DEFINE FIND=COMPANY="JONES" AND (ITEM="NAILS" OR STOCKNO=21452)
```

Press Enter, and when Enable displays READY in the status line press Alt-F3 to delete the command. Then type FIND at the Where prompt and press Enter. Enable adds FIND to the list of fields.

You have built a command called FIND which selects all the records that have a company name of Jones and either the Item Nails or the Stock Number 21452. Instead of typing the entire where clause each time you want to use it you can just type FIND.

USING .DEFINE TO LINK DATABASES The following command can be used to define a field using data from another database.

```
.DEFINE FIELDNAME=LOOKUPFLD IN DB2 LINK LINKFLD=KEYFLD
```

where *FIELDNAME* is the name of the field being defined, *LOOKUPFLD* is the name of the field in the other database that you want to copy data from, *DB2* is the name of the other database, *LINKFLD* is the name of an indexed field in the other database (that does not allow duplicates), and *KEYFLD* is the name of a field in the current database. For example,

```
.DEFINE ITEM=NAME IN DB2 LINK SERNO=NUMBER
```

means that Enable will look at the value in NUMBER in the first database, and search the second database (DB2) for the same value in the field SERNO. When it finds the same value it copies the value from the field NAME (in the same record) to the field ITEM in the first database.

USING .OPEN AND .READ TO LINK DATABASES Instead of defining new fields you can open a database and read information from it.

```
.OPEN DBASENAME
.READ DBASENAME
```

opens a database named DBASENAME and reads the first record. You can bypass the .open command by just typing

```
.READ DBASENAME FIRST
```

This reads the first record in the database. You can also specify the particular record.

```
.READ DBASENAME FIRST LINKFLD=KEYFLD
```

tells Enable to read the first record in the second database with a linkfield that has the same value as the keyfield in the first database. If the linkfield and keyfield have the same names, specify which database by typing the database name, a period, and the field name.

```
.READ DBASENAME FIRST COMPANY.NAME=CLIENT.NAME
```

NOTE

The .read command does not actually modify data in the databases, it just reads it in temporarily.

RETRIEVING DATA WITH .LET If you want to update a field using data from another database you must use the .let command. For example, use the .read command to position the pointer on the record you are looking for, and then type

```
.LET COMPANY.ADDRESS=CLIENT.ADDRESS
```

This copies the address from the second database into the first database.

USING .DEFINE WHEN IMPORTING DATA The .define command is used to name fields imported from word processing files. See Module 57 for more information.

APPLICATIONS

Dot commands used at Where and Field prompts let you build reports and displays the way you want them, and make complicated where clauses easier to use.

TYPICAL OPERATIONS

In this activity you use dot commands when working with the SUPPLYX database, created in Module 5.

1. At the Interact screen type **D** to view the Display command screen. Type **SUPPLYX** at the Database prompt, and press **Enter** twice to move the cursor to the Where prompt.
2. Type **.DEFINE TCOST=COST*1.23** and press **Enter**. Enable adds TCOST to the list of fields, and displays READY in the status line.

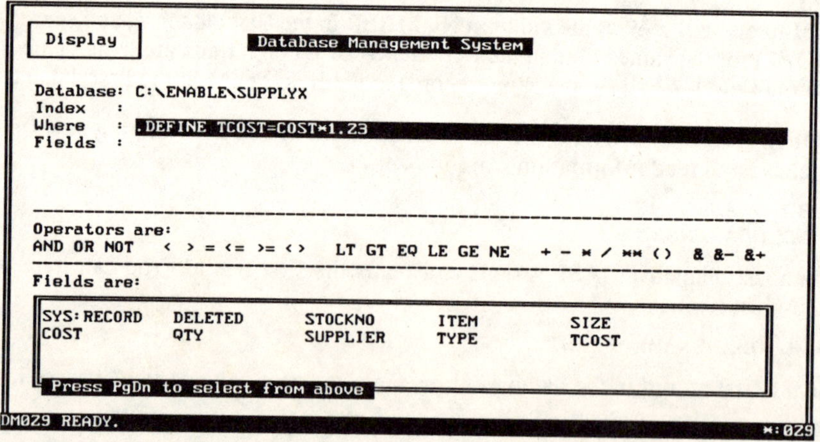

3. Press **Alt-F3** to clear the command from the Index prompt, and press **Down Arrow**. At the Fields prompt press **PgDn** to move the cursor into the list of fields. Move the cursor to each of these fields, pressing **,** (comma) after each one: STOCKNO, ITEM, and COST. Move the cursor to TCOST and press **Enter**. The line at the Fields prompt is as follows: STOCKNO,ITEM,COST,TCOST.

4. Press **End** and Enable displays the fields, as shown in the following screen.

```
STOCKNO ITEM.................COST .......TCOST
  10001 Nails              $4.25        5.23
  10002 Nails              $4.74        5.83
  40144 Suppt. Lumber      $2.35        2.89
  40149 Suppt. Lumber      $4.02        4.94
  61844 Plywood           $11.22       13.80
  60012 Plywood           $13.24       16.29
  11234 Nails              $3.49        4.29
  91432 Door             $119.00      146.37
  93356 Door             $121.00      148.83
  84432 Window           $202.01      248.47
  84435 Window           $262.78      323.22
  82333 Window           $213.44      262.53
  41222 Suppt. Lumber      $6.07        7.47
  67745 Plywood            $8.29       10.20
  12222 Nails              $6.66        8.19
  50001 Sheetrock          $4.79        5.89
  53344 Sheetrock          $5.33        6.56
  55501 Sheetrock          $7.49        9.21
  13211 Nails              $6.99        8.60
  80808 Window           $471.00      579.33

Use cursor keys to page through display.  Press ESC when done.
#2.      SUPPLYX        Records ....28 Rd ....22 Sel ....20 Cur .....1  D:000
```

5. Press **Esc** to display the Display command screen, and press **Enter** twice to move to the Where prompt. Type **.DEFINE FIND=ITEM="N$" AND SUPPLIER="A$"** and press **Enter**. Enable adds a field named FIND to the list of fields. Press **Enter** again, and notice that Enable adds yet another field named FIND to the list of fields.

6. Press **Alt-F3** to delete the command. Press **End** and notice that the display is the same as before. Press **Esc**, press **Down Arrow** twice, and type **FIND**.

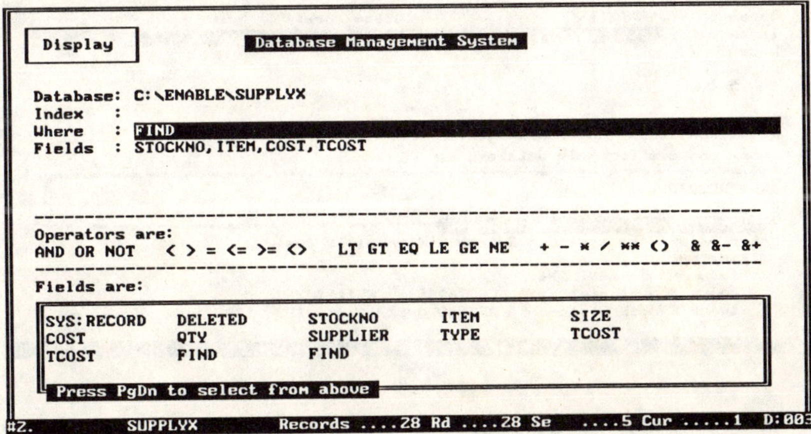

7. Press **End** and Enable displays the records that have an item starting with N and a supplier starting with A.

8. Press **Esc**, press **F10**, and type **Q** to return to the Main Menu.

9. Turn to Module 6 to continue the learning sequence.

Module 55

EDIT (EDIT, VERIFY, REPLACE, RENAME)

DESCRIPTION

There are several ways to change the information in your database: the Edit, Verify, and Replace commands, the F4 function in Display mode, and the Rename command. You can use all of these commands through the Interact screen.

NOTE

Before you read this module you should read Module 60 to learn how to use the Interact and command screens.

Select Edit, Verify, or Replace from the Interact screen. In the command screen select the database and input form you want to use. Use the Index and Where prompts to specify the records you want to edit, or leave them blank to use the entire database or the marked records. The following screen shows the Edit command screen.

```
 Edit                  Database Management System

Database: C:\ENABLE\A                   Using form:
Index    :
Where    :

------------------------------------------------------------------------
Index choices for this database are:

SYS:RECORD

 Press PgDn to select from above
Enter Index Name or Index Search Statement if desired.
  Examples:
    Index Name: LASTNAME
    Index Search Statement: LASTNAME = "Smith$"
    Index Search Statement: ACCTNO = 123, 127, 130..139, 145
#1.        A          Records .....17 Rd .....0 Sel .....0 Cur .....0  E:002
```

EDIT The Edit command lets you change the information in the records by typing new data into the fields. Refer to the module on Adding data (Module 48) for information on entering data in the input form.

If you use the Index prompt to select a group of records, when you come to the end of that group Enable displays a prompt over the input form asking for another index search statement. You can enter the search statement and continue without returning to the Edit command screen. (You can stop Enable from displaying this prompt by pressing F9 and typing IE, and turn it back on by pressing F9 and typing ID.)

Top Line Menu The Top Line Menu is the same as that already described for the Add mode, except it has one more option, Add. Select Add or press Ctrl-F5 to change from Edit to Add mode; Enable lets you type data into a blank input form. (If you are in Add mode when you Quit, Enable displays the Add command screen, not the Edit command screen.)

VERIFY The Verify screen looks like the Edit screen, and the Top Line Menu works the same. Any of the fields you defined as Verify fields when you created the database are blanked out, that is, the data that was originally typed into those fields cannot be seen. Move the cursor into the field and type the data. Enable compares the data you type with the data already in the database. If you type a character that is not in the original field, in the position you typed it, Enable beeps and will not accept the data. Try typing the data again or press F8 to display the original data. Once the original data is displayed you can change it if necessary. Then select Next from the Top Line Menu to verify the next record (this saves the change you made). When you have finished, save the changes to the last record and select Quit.

Changing Modes The status line displays a V:*nnn* number at the right side when in Verify mode. You can change to Add mode by selecting Add from the Top Line Menu. You can change to Edit mode by selecting Query and searching for a record. To return to Verify you must quit, display the Interact screen, and select Verify again.

REPLACE If you want to put the same value in a field in several records you can use the Replace command to change all of them at once. Use the Index or Where prompts to specify exactly which records should be changed. Use the Fields prompt to specify which field should be changed, and the With prompt to specify what should replace the old data. (All data except for logical and numeric data must be entered in quotation marks.) For example, the following screen shows that the company name Osmose is being replaced with Anderson.

```
 Replace            Database Management System

 Database: C:\ENABLE\SUPPLY
 Index    :
 Where    : COMPANY="Osmose"
 Field    : COMPANY
 With     : "Anderson"

 --------------------------------------------------------------------
 Operators are:
 AND OR NOT    < > = <= >= <>   LT GT EQ LE GE NE    + - * / ** <>   & &- &+
 --------------------------------------------------------------------
 Fields are:
  SYS:RECORD   DELETED     STOCKNO     ITEM      SIZE
  COST         QTY         COMPANY     TYPE

  Press PgDn to select from above
#1.       SUPPLY       Records ....27 Rd .....0 Se   ....0       ..0  R:005
```

NOTE

Press Enter and the changes are made.

EDITING RECORDS IN DISPLAY MODE You can also edit records using the Display command (Module 64). However, Enable does not enforce all field restrictions and specifications. (For example, you could type numbers into a text-only field.) And, you cannot edit fields of more than 148 characters.

Use the arrow keys to move the cursor to the record you want to edit; as the fields extend past the limits of your screen, when necessary Enable moves the fields onto your screen, scrolling the data to the left. Press F4 and a prompt appears at the bottom of the screen, as shown in the following screen:

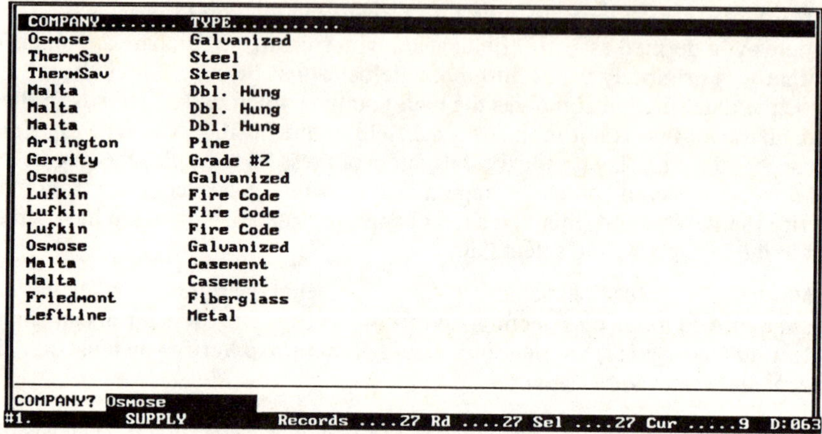

Make your changes and press Enter.

RENAMING A DATABASE Use the Rename command to change a database's name. Select Rename from the Interact screen. The screen has two prompts, Database and New Name. Type the names and press Enter. Remember, a name can be up to eight numbers, letters, or underscores. Enable changes the name of the database definition (.$BF) and database (.DBF) files and displays the new name at the Database prompt.

If you type the name of another database at the New Name prompt Enable displays an error message and tells you to try again.

APPLICATIONS

You will need to edit data often. Clients change their addresses, make new purchases, or appoint new buyers. A patient's health status and insurer change. As circumstances change the database must be updated. You may even want to change the database's name; for example, the name might include the year, so you would want to change the name at the beginning of the new year and continue using the same database.

TYPICAL OPERATION

In this activity you edit a record in the database named SUPPLYX, created in Module 5.

1. At the Main Menu, type **UDI**. Enable displays the Interact screen. Type **E** to select Edit, and Enable displays the Edit screen. Type **SUPPLYX** at the Database prompt and press **Enter**.
2. Press **Enter** again, to bypass the "Using form" prompt, and again to bypass the Index prompt. At Where press **PgDn**. The cursor moves to the list of fields. Use Right Arrow and Down Arrow to move the cursor to COMPANY and press =. Enable displays COMPANY= at the Where prompt.

3. Type **"Osm$"** and your screen looks like this:

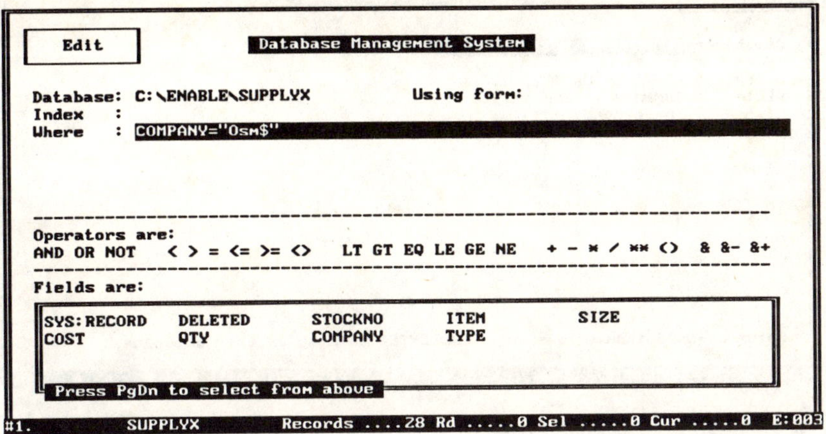

4. Press **Enter** and Enable asks you if you want to use the existing standard form or create a new one. Press **Enter** to use the existing one and Enable displays the first record with the name Osmose in the COMPANY field.

5. Press **F5** twice. Enable moves through the records with the name Osmose. Press **Down Arrow** twice and type **3**, replacing the 2.

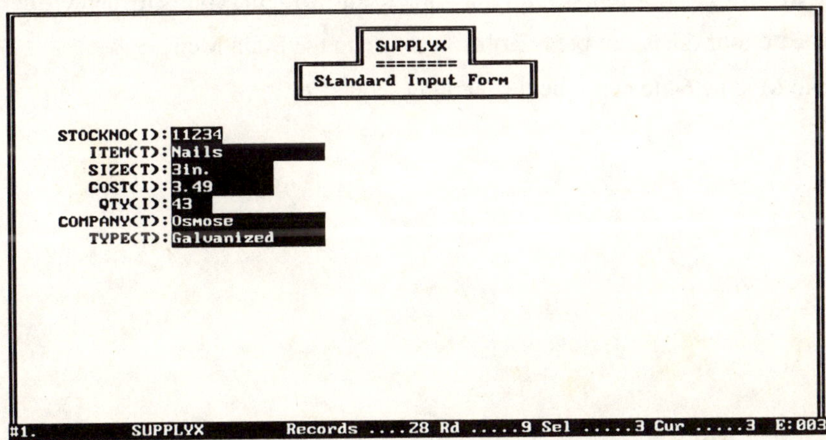

6. Press **F10** and type **S** to save the edit, and press **Esc** three times to return to the Interact screen. Type **R** to select Replace. Notice that the Database and Where fields in the Replace command screen have the same information as in the Edit command screen.

7. Press **Down Arrow** three times and type **COMPANY** at the Field prompt. Press **Down Arrow** and type **"Anderson"** at the With prompt. Press **Enter**. Enable makes the changes.

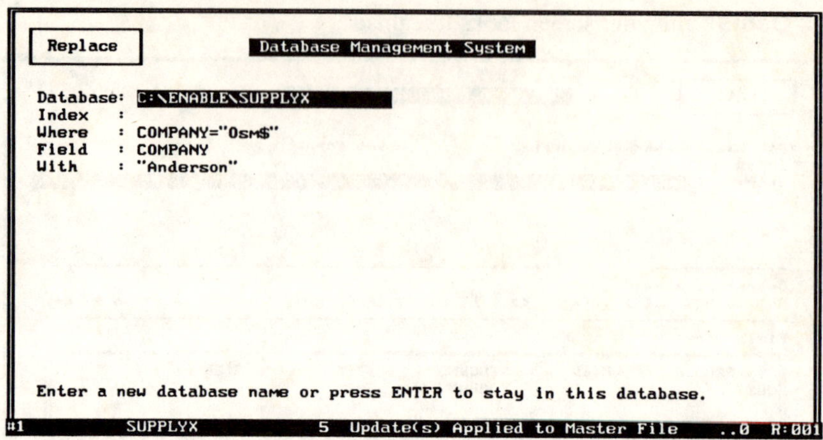

Notice the message in the status line telling you how many records have been changed.

8. Press **Esc** to return to the Interact screen and **E** to go to the Edit command screen. The Database prompt still says SUPPLYX and the Where prompt still says COMPANY= "Osm$". Press **End**. Enable beeps and displays the No Record Found message in the status line.
9. Move the cursor to the Where prompt. Change the command to **COMPANY="And$"** and press **Enter** twice. Enable displays the first record with the company name Anderson.
10. Press **Esc** four times and press **Enter** to return to the Main Menu.
11. Turn to Module 64 to continue the learning sequence.

Module 56
EXPORT DATA TO AN ASCII FILE (EXPORT)

DESCRIPTION

The Export command lets you copy Enable database files or records to ASCII files. You can specify columnar or comma-separated formats.

NOTE

Before you read this module you should read Module 60 to learn how to use the Interact and command screens.

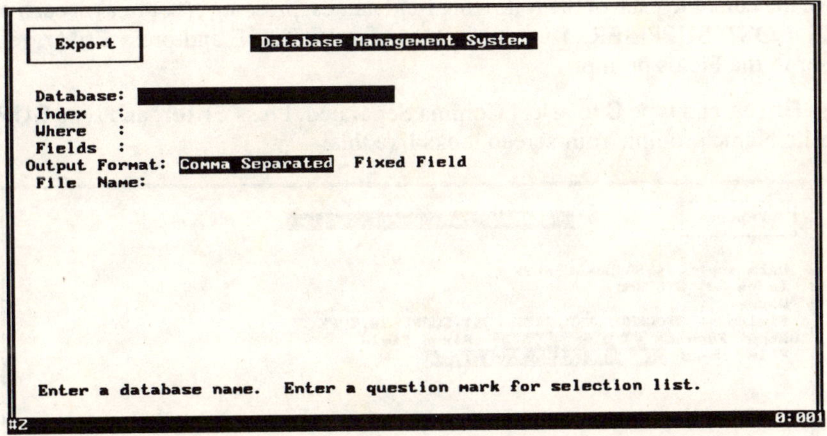

Use the Database, Index, Where, and Fields prompts to specify the data you want to put into ASCII format.

The Output Format prompt allows you to select Comma-separated or Fixed Field (columnar). See Module 57 for examples of these formats. The comma-separated format eliminates trailing blanks, but the columnar or fixed-field format maintains the same field lengths. Enter a filename (Enable adds the .ASC extension), press Enter, and Enable builds the ASCII file.

CAUTION

Enable makes the file only 80-characters wide, so if your fields amount to more than this some data is lost.

APPLICATIONS

ASCII files can be used to transfer data to other database formats, or to transfer data into word processing documents. You can then use the data in those particular programs. For example, if you have a series of form letters written in WordStar you could produce an ASCII file that WordStar could use instead of rewriting the letters in Enable. Or if you have to send data to a person but you don't know what type of database the person uses, change it into ASCII—most databases can accept ASCII data.

TYPICAL OPERATION

In this activity you make an ASCII copy of SUPPLYX, created in Module 5.

1. At the Interact screen type **O** to select Export. Type **SUPPLYX** at the Database prompt and press **Enter**. Type (or use the box to select) **STOCKNO** in the Index field, to put the records in the file in stock-number order. Press **Enter** twice.
2. At the Fields prompt press **PgDn** and move the cursor to STOCKNO and press **,** (comma). Move the cursor to each of the following field names, pressing **,** (comma) at each one: ITEM, SIZE, COST, SUPPLIER. Then move the cursor to TYPE and press **Enter**, returning the cursor to the Fields prompt.
3. Press **Enter**, and type **C** to select Comma Separated. Press **Enter**, and type **SUP_ASCI** at the File Name prompt. Your screen looks like this:

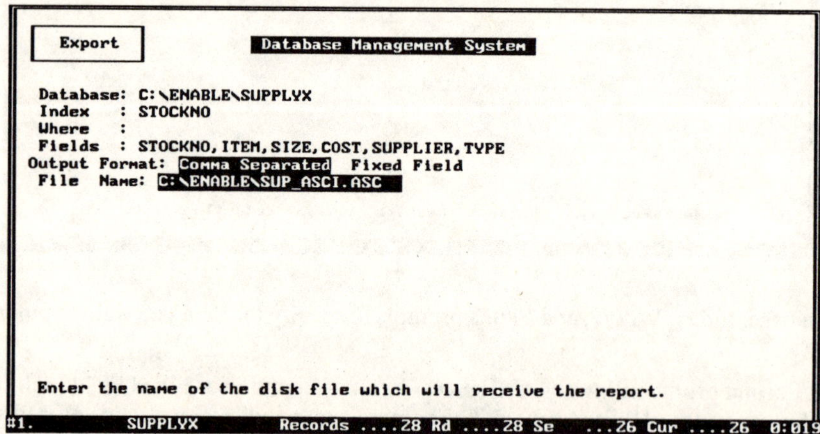

4. Press **Enter**. Enable builds an ASCII file. Press **Esc** and type **Q** to return to the Main Menu.
5. Type **UWR** and type **SUP_ASCI.ASC** at the "Enter name" prompt. Press **Enter** and Enable displays a list of different file formats. Press **Enter** to accept ASCII, and the following screen is displayed.

```
L-------T-------T-------T-------T--+----T---------------------------R-------
10001,"Nails","3in.",4.25,"Anderson","Galvanized"
10002,"Nails","4in.",4.74,"Anderson","Galvanized"
11221,"Steps, preform","8'",500.00,"Crown Steps Co.","Concrete"
11222,"Nails","2in.",3.89,"LeftLine","Metal"
11234,"Nails","3in.",3.49,"Anderson","Galvanized"
11983,"Piping","8'",5.85,"Dallas Plumbing","1" Plastic"
12222,"Nails","5in.",6.66,"Anderson","Galvanized"
13211,"Nails","6in.",6.99,"Anderson","Galvanized"
22344,"Step Ladder","8'",48.00,"Jones","Wood"
30001,"Shingles","Bundle",7.19,"Friedmont","Fiberglass"
40144,"Suppt. Lumber","2x4x8",2.35,"Pine Crest","Pine"
40149,"Suppt. Lumber","2x4x12",4.02,"Pine Crest","Pine"
41222,"Suppt. Lumber","2x4x16",6.07,"Arlington","Pine"
50001,"Sheetrock","4x8x.5",4.79,"Lufkin","Fire Code"
53344,"Sheetrock","4x8x1",5.33,"Lufkin","Fire Code"
55501,"Sheetrock","4x10x.5",7.49,"Lufkin","Fire Code"
60012,"Plywood","4x8x.75",13.24,"Gerrity","Grade #2"
61844,"Plywood","4x8x.5",11.22,"Gerrity","Grade #2"
67745,"Plywood","4x8x.25",8.29,"Gerrity","Grade #2"
80807,"Window","8x6",651.12,"Malta","Casement"
80808,"Window","6x4",471.00,"Malta","Casement"
82333,"Window","5x8",213.44,"Malta","Dbl. Hung"
#3        /B C:SUP_ASCI.ASC        DRAFT                          L00001C001
```

6. Press **F10** and type **QY** to exit the file and return to the Main Menu.
7. Turn to Module 57 to continue the learning sequence.

Module 57
IMPORT DATA (UPDATE, COPY, MERGE)

DESCRIPTION

You can import data to a database from another database, an Enable or Lotus spreadsheet, an ASCII text file, a telecommunications text file, or an open Enable window.

NOTE

If you want to import data from an Enable word processing file you must open the file and import it from the open window, or convert it to ASCII and then import it.

You can update specific records, add records, or create new databases. You can also use spreadsheet and text data as read-only data in several command screens.

NOTE

Before you read this module you should read Module 60 to learn how to use the Interact and command screens.

PREPARING DATA FOR IMPORT Before you import data it must be in a format Enable can recognize.

Spreadsheet Data Row 1 must contain the names of the database fields. Up to 254 fields (columns) can be used. Row 2 must contain the data-type identifier; C (character, that is, text), N (numeric), or L (logical). (Numbers in scientific notation are text.) Row 3 must contain the maximum field length, up to 254 characters for text or 16 for numeric. Numeric fields use the format *n.d* (*n* = total length including decimal point and places, *d* = number of decimal places). Each record uses one row, from row 4 on. Fields are arranged in columns, and must begin at column A. See the following screen for an example.

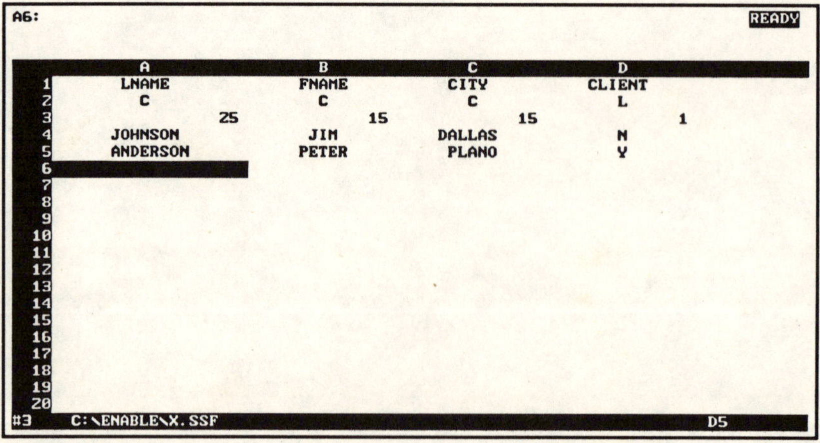

NOTE

If you do not use this format Enable automatically assigns 254 fields, starts the data in row 1, and defines the fields as COL_A, COL_B, etc.

Enable 2.0 Spreadsheets If you want to import an Enable/OA spreadsheet you must either open the spreadsheet and copy from the window, or save it in Enable/OA format and use the Copy command.

Word Processing or ASCII Data Enable word processing data and ASCII data are prepared in the same way. The data may be in columns, or lines of data with the fields separated by commas. The following screen shows a line of data. No spaces are left between fields, and any fields that require a comma inside must be enclosed within quotation marks.

The following shows the same data in the column format.

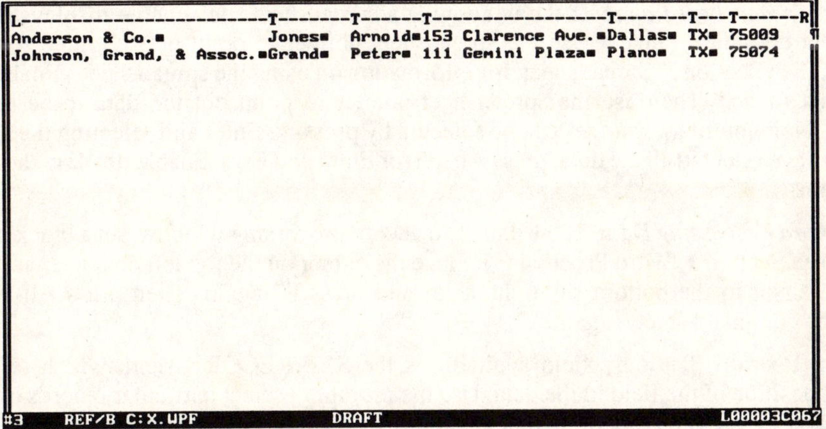

dBASE II and dBASE III Database Files These files can be used by Enable's DBMS without any modifications, and the file formats are maintained. Type the filename at the Database prompt in any command screen. You can use Enable's database definition procedure to build a definition for these files.

Condor3 Database Files These files can be used by Enable's DBMS without any modifications; enter the filename with the extension .DAT at any Database prompt. Condor3 databases contain the following files: field values (.DAT), field characteristics (.DEF), field names and lengths (.FRM), index files (.NDX), and a file listing the other file names (DATA.DIC). If Enable can't find the .FRM file it supplies field names (C000001, C000002, etc.). If it does find .FRM it changes any names with more than ten characters, special characters, or blanks. Condor3 allows one field of more than 254 characters; Enable breaks this field into separate fields. And, although Condor3 has up to 20 significant digits in numeric fields, Enable only allows 14 and displays a warning if a field contains too many digits.

If you want to give a Condor3 file all the features of an Enable file you must convert it to Enable format. Use the Copy command to copy the database to a new database name.

IMPORTING READ-ONLY DATA You can use the prepared data as read-only data in the Find, Display, Sort, Report, and Export command screens. You can use this data in the normal way, for example you could sort the data into select sets; however, the data cannot then be edited or added to. The following text explains how to use the command screen prompts when using read-only data.

The Database "Name" Prompt Enter the name of the data file with one of the following extensions: .WK*n* (a Lotus worksheet, where *n* is a number or character, .WK1 being the default); .SSF (an Enable spreadsheet); .ASC (ASCII text data); .DEF (to use a database definition as a database).

Or, to use data from an Enable window, press Alt-F5 at the database prompt, and select the window, or type WINDOW*n.m*, where *n* is the window the command screen is in, and *m* is the number of the data window. The data window is displayed.

Marking a Spreadsheet Range If the window is a spreadsheet file, Enable displays the prompt "Enter Data definition range." Use the spreadsheet pointer to point out the three rows of data definition. (See Section 3, Spreadsheet, for information on using the spreadsheet.) Enable displays "Enter Data range." Then use the spreadsheet pointer to point out the data to be used in the command. Non-continuous ranges can be selected by pressing Enter and selecting the next range. When you have selected all the data, press Alt-F5 (or Enter and Esc). Enable displays the command screen again.

Marking Word Processing Data If the data is in a word processing window, set a block on the data using F7 (see Section 1, Word Processing). Place the cursor on the top left character and press F7. Move the cursor to the bottom right character and press F7 again. Then press Alt-F5. Enable displays the command screen again.

The Index Prompt The only field available is the SYS:RECORD field, which refers to the sequential position of the field in the data. Use the prompt to select particular records or ranges of records. (You have effectively done this already if you marked the data correctly in the previous step.)

The Where and Field Prompts You can use either of these prompts to define the field names and lengths for the text files you are importing. Type ".define *fieldname*=F*n*L*n*" or ".define *fieldname*=C*n*L*n*" and press Enter. The actual code you use depends on the type of the text data.

Fields Separated With Commas F*n*L*n*, where F*n* is the position of the field in the line, and L*n* is the maximum length of the field. F1L13 means first position, 13 characters long.

Columnar fields C*n*L*n*, where C*n* is the column number, and L*n* is the maximum length of the field.

NOTE

Don't get these mixed up! C*n*L*n* is for columnar fields (not for comma-separated fields, as Enable calls the other type). F*n*L*n* is for fields separated with commas (not for columnar fields, called fixed length fields by Enable).

Enable enters the field name in the list of field names at the bottom of the screen. For example (using the word processing screen shown earlier in this module, with the data separated by commas), type ".DEFINE CNAME=F1L25" and press Enter. Then clear the text and type ".DEFINE LNAME=F2L5" and press Enter. Continue the procedure until you have defined all the fields. When you have finished, press Alt-F3 to clear the prompt, and press End to import the data.

PC-File III Database Files Enable can use these as read-only files. Enter the filename with the .DTA extension. Both .DTA and .HDR files must be present in your default data directory.

THE UPDATE COMMAND The Update command lets you change the contents of specified fields in a database (the master file) by replacing them with fields from another database, a data file, or an open window (the transaction file), or by replacing them with the result of a formula that uses fields from both files. There must be a link field (a field that is the same in both files), and it must be indexed in the master file; ideally the field in the master file does not have duplicates.

Select Update from the Interact screen. Enter the name of the master file at the first Database prompt, the file that will be modified. Enter the name of the link field.

With: Database/Window/File You can select Database (Enable, dBASE, or Condor3 files), Window (database, spreadsheet, or text data in another window), or File (text or spreadsheet data in a file).

Database Select Database and Enable displays the Database name and Index, Where, and Link Field prompts, as shown in the following screen.

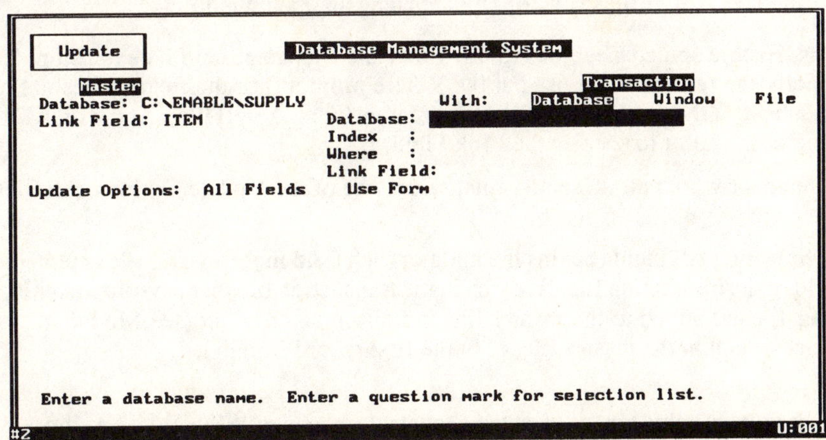

Type the name of the database the data is coming from, and use the Index and Where prompts to select specific records. At the Link Field prompt type the name of the field that links the two databases (the field with data that matches the field you named at the first Link Field prompt).

Window If you select Window, Enable displays the Window Summary screen. Select the window that has the data (the transaction file). Mark the data (as described in Importing Read-Only Data earlier in this module). Press Alt-F5; Enable displays the Update command screen again, with "Window*n.m*" at the Database prompt (*n* is the Update command screen window; *m* is the transaction file window), and Index, Where, and Link Field prompts displayed. Use the F*n*L*n* or C*n*L*n* position and length codes (see Importing Read-Only Data, earlier in this module) to specify at the Index and Where prompts the records you want to use, or leave the fields blank to use them all. Use the codes at the Link Field prompt to define one of the fields as the linking field.

File Select File to use data from a disk file with ASCII text or spreadsheet data in Enable or Lotus 1-2-3 format.

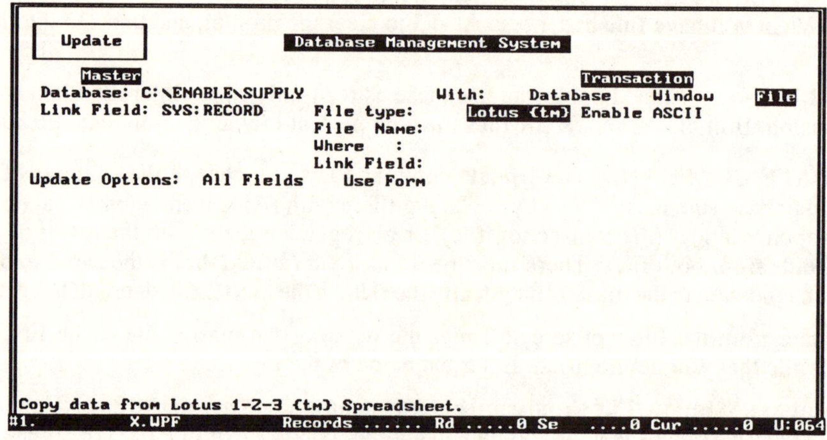

NOTE

Although Enable word processing files can be used in Update commands if they are in open windows, they cannot be used from closed files. Save them as ASCII files first, or Update using an open window.

Select Lotus, Enable spreadsheet, or ASCII. Enter the filename, with its extension. If you want you can specify the records to be used at the Where prompt (use the field names in the first row of the spreadsheet, or the position and length indicators for an ASCII file). At the Link Field prompt use the name or indicator to specify the Link Field.

When you have answered all these prompts, select one of the Update Options; All Fields or Use Form.

All Fields Selecting All Fields begins the update; each field in the master file is replaced with the selected field in the transaction file. Records in the transaction file that have no matching link field in the master file are added to the master file and put in an error set (see Module 63). If there is more than one match in the master file, only the first record is updated.

NOTE

If you are using text or spreadsheet data do not select All Fields. You must select Use Form.

Use Form If you select Use Form, Enable prompts you for a filename for the Update Transfer form. Type the name or press Enter to use the standard form (Enable applies a .UTF extension). Enable displays the Update Transfer Form.

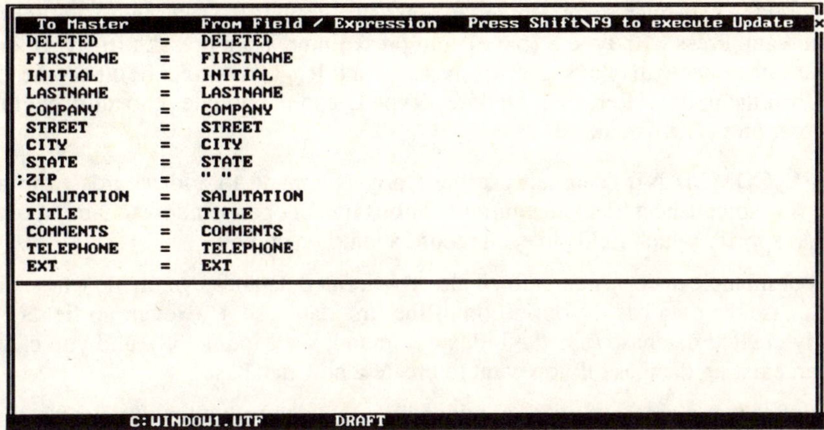

To Master		From Field / Expression	Press Shift\F9 to execute Update
DELETED	=	DELETED	
FIRSTNAME	=	FIRSTNAME	
INITIAL	=	INITIAL	
LASTNAME	=	LASTNAME	
COMPANY	=	COMPANY	
STREET	=	STREET	
CITY	=	CITY	
STATE	=	STATE	
:ZIP	=	" "	
SALUTATION	=	SALUTATION	
TITLE	=	TITLE	
COMMENTS	=	COMMENTS	
TELEPHONE	=	TELEPHONE	
EXT	=	EXT	

C:WINDOW1.UTF DRAFT

The fields on the left are in the master database, the ones being updated. The fields on the right are in the transaction database, the one the new data is coming from. If fields don't match, Enable displays quotation marks (for a text field) or a zero (for a numeric field) in the right column, and a semicolon in column one.

You can type formulae in the right column, (for example, COST*2) and the result of the formula is entered into the master database field. You can specify which database the information comes from by typing MASTER. or TRANS. For example, MASTER.INVEN+TRANS.INVEN means sum the values in the INVEN fields in the two databases and enter the result into the specified field in the master database. And TRANS.COST*2 next to a field means multiply the COST field in the TRANS database and enter the value in the master database field.

Use the F*n*L*n* and C*n*L*n* codes to specify fields coming from text files, as shown in the following screen.

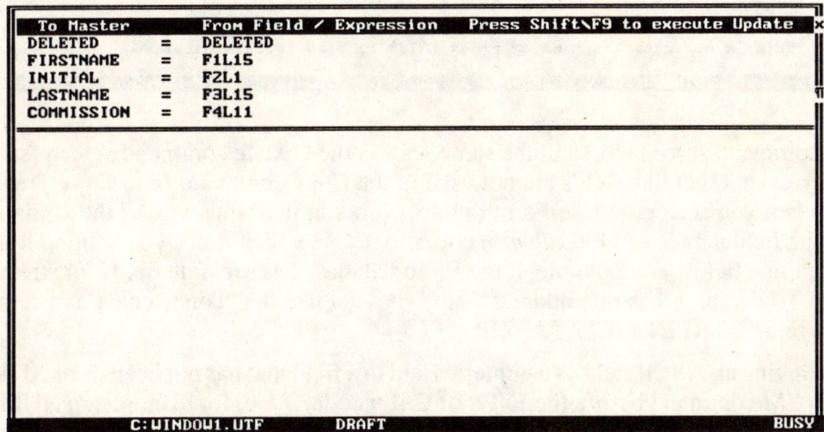

To Master		From Field / Expression	Press Shift\F9 to execute Update
DELETED	=	DELETED	
FIRSTNAME	=	F1L15	
INITIAL	=	F2L1	
LASTNAME	=	F3L15	
COMMISSION	=	F4L11	

C:WINDOW1.UTF DRAFT BUSY

You can select fields not to be updated by typing a semicolon in column one, or by deleting the line by pressing Alt-F3.

You can now save the transaction form if you wish; this lets you use the same form later, without having to enter the data over again. However, you can complete the transaction without saving the form if you want. Press F10, type S (Save), and press Enter. Then press Shift-F9. If there are any errors in the form Enable displays an error message and lets you correct it; otherwise Enable asks you to confirm the update (Return or Update). Type U and the update procedure begins. To abort the procedure, press Ctrl-Break.

THE COPY COMMAND You can use the Copy command to add records from a database, ASCII text file, spreadsheet file, telecommunications file, or open window to the end of a database. You can also specify which fields in each record should be copied.

The Copy command can copy data into an already-defined database, or create a new database for it, in which case the data has the definition of the first database. However, no fields are indexed in the newly created database (use the Index command, see Module 58), and you can only copy data from an existing database if you want to create a new database.

If you copy data into a database with an indexed file that does not allow duplicates, duplicates in the copied data are put into an error set.

Select Copy from the Interact screen.

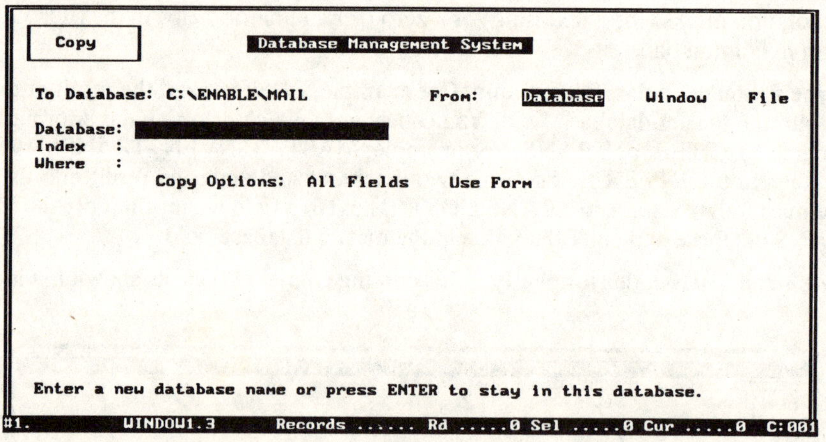

The Copy command screen works in the same way as the Update command screen (see previous description), except that link fields are not used in the Copy command. The Copy Transfer form, displayed when you select the Use Form option, works in the same way as the Update Transfer form. Use the field names and F*n*L*n*/C*n*L*n* codes to define which fields you want to transfer. You can also combine fields. For example, if the From database has separate fields for street, city, and zip, but the To database has one address field, you can use the "concatenate and remove extra spaces" operator: STREET&-CITY&- ZIP.

If you are copying an ASCII field as a numeric field to a field that has not been defined as numeric, use the @NUM command before the F*n*L*n* or C*n*L*n* code. Type, for example, @NUM(F10L11) {11.2} to denote a numeric field in position 10 on the line, with 11 characters, including two decimal places.

Converting Enable 2.0 Files to 3.0 Files If you convert a file to Enable 3.0 format you can include up to 65,535 records in the database. Before converting, your user profile must be set to Enable 3.0/dBASE III (see Appendix B). Make a backup copy of the database. Using the Copy command screen, type TEMP.DBF as the "To Database," and the name of the 2.0 file as the "From Database." Bypass the Index and Where fields, and select All Fields.

Enable builds the TEMP.DBF file, and a TEMP.$BF definitions file which you do not need (because the original definitions file remains effective). Delete the original 2.0 file and the TEMP.$BF file, and rename the TEMP.DBF file. No indexes have been built for the new file, so use the Index command if you need any.

Converting Files To Other Database Formats You can convert any database format that Enable recognizes into any of the other formats. For example, you can convert Condor3 files to dBASE III. Simply create a database definition file in dBASE III format, and then copy the Condor3 data into it using the Copy command.

THE MERGE COMMAND The Merge command is similar to the Copy command, except that a third database is built, consisting of the specified records from the first two.

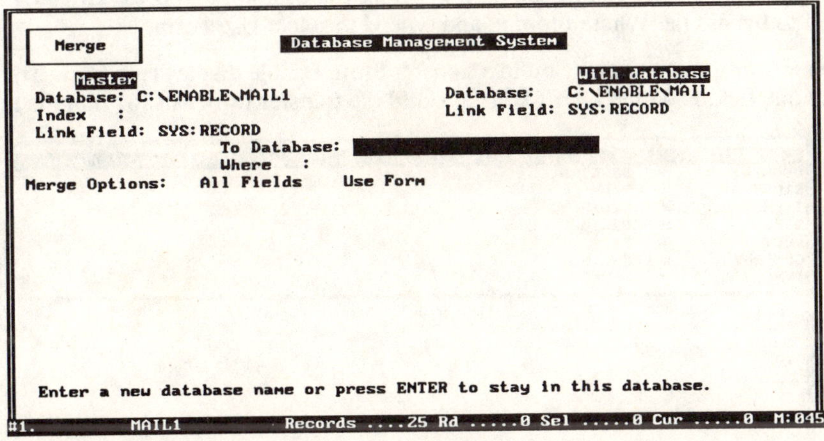

Both databases must have one common link field. In the "with" database the link field must be indexed, and not allow duplicates.

When merging fields of the same name, Enable uses the length of the field in the master database. The new database will not have any indexes—use the Index command to build them.

You can enter a select set name as the master database, or use a database with marked records. But the "with" database may not use either a select set or marked records. The Merge Transfer form works in the same way that the Update and Copy Transfer forms work.

What is Merged? Think of the master database as DB1, the "with" database as DB2, and the third database as DB3. Enable places the following records in the third database: any record in either database with no match in the other; if a record in DB1 has a matching record in DB2, the data from DB1 is placed in DB3; if a record in DB2 has a matching record in DB1, but includes extra fields not in the DB1 record, those fields are added to the record copied from DB1 into DB3.

APPLICATIONS

These commands give you a great deal of flexibility, allowing you to transfer data from entirely different formats into a database. The ability to use spreadsheet and word processing data is extremely useful and saves a lot of time that might have been spent rekeying data. Bringing data in from other database programs, in particular the dBASE databases, allows you to use information entered by other people on their systems, or entered by you before you began using Enable; you don't need to rebuild a database just because you've started using Enable. And combining and merging databases allows you to keep up with changes in your data applications.

TYPICAL OPERATION

In this activity you import the ASCII file you built in Module 56.

1. At the Interact screen type **C** to view the Copy command screen. At the To Database prompt type **SUPPLY2** and press **Enter**.
2. At the From prompt type **F** to select file, and then type **A** to select ASCII at the File type prompt. Type **SUP_ASCI.ASC** at the File Name prompt, and press **Enter**. Press **Enter** again to bypass the Where prompt, and type **U** to select Use Form.
3. Press **Enter** to make Enable build a transfer form. Enable displays the Copy Transfer form. Only one field is defined, DELETED. Build the transfer form as shown in the next screen.

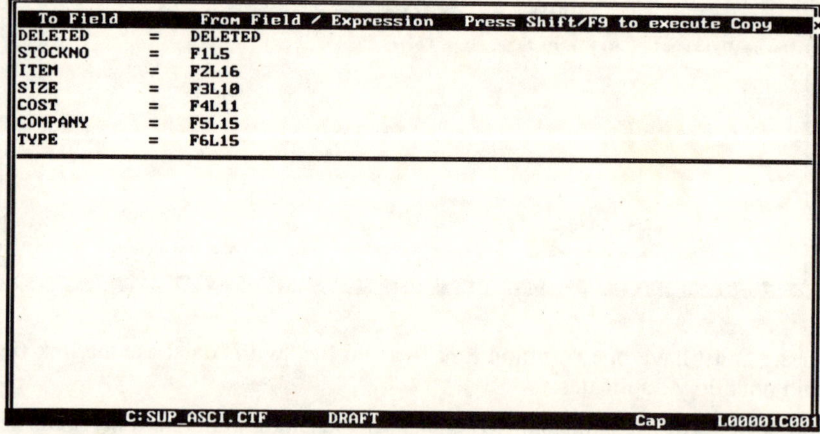

4. Press **Shift-F9** and type **C** to copy. Enable copies the data into the new file.
5. Press **Esc** and type **D** to go to the Display command screen. Type **SUPPLY2** at the Database prompt. Press **End**, and Enable displays the new file.
6. Press **Esc** twice and type **Q** to return to the Main Menu.
7. Turn to Module 52 to continue the learning sequence.

Module 58
INDEX A FIELD (INDEX)

DESCRIPTION

Indexes are normally built during database creation. The Index command, however, lets you build an index at a later date. Indexes let Enable quickly search all the indexed fields in a database, and are needed for index search statements, linking databases using link fields, and avoiding duplications. (You can also build an index when you modify a database—see Module 61.)

NOTE

> Before you read this module you should read Module 60 to learn how to use the Interact and command screens.

A database can have up to ten indexes, but remember that indexes take up memory and slow the system down. Indexes are stored in index files, with the extension .NDX. Enable indexes all records, even deleted ones (although deleted records are not used in other commands unless specifically requested). The indexes treat lowercase and uppercase letters differently, with uppercase coming first.

Select Index from the Interact screen.

```
 Index                  Database Management System

 Database: C:\ENABLE\TEST

 Fieldname:                           Index File Name:

 Allow Duplicates?        Yes         No




 Enter a new database name or press ENTER to stay in this database.
#2.        TEST           Records ....19 Rd .....0 Se    ....0 Cur .....0   I:001
```

Select the database and the name of the field to be indexed. Enter the index filename you want to use (up to eight letters, numbers, or underscores). The name should be the same or similar to the field name, but you cannot use a name that has already been used by an index in another database. Select No at the Allow Duplicates prompt if you don't want Enable to allow duplicate values to be typed into this field. For example, a doctor's office has one record for each patient. The Social Security field should not allow duplicates. If a duplicate value is typed Enable does not let you leave the record without changing or removing the value.

After you answer all the prompts Enable builds the index file, and displays the number of records processed in the status line.

DUPLICATES If you selected No at the Allow Duplicates prompt and the existing records include some duplicate entries, when Enable builds the index it displays an error message and builds an error set, a list of the duplicate records (see Module 63). The records can then be deleted from the database, or edited to remove duplicate values.

APPLICATIONS

If you discover that you can use your database more efficiently if a non-indexed field could be converted to an indexed field, you can use this command to build an index. You may have simply made a mistake and not realized that the field needs an index, or you may have started using the database in a way you didn't forsee when you created it. For example, you originally built your database of customers for internal use—reports on purchases and outstanding invoices, for example. Now you want to mail promotional material to them each month, so the Zip code field should be indexed. This allows you to pay lower postal rates by putting the letters in Zip code order.

TYPICAL OPERATION

In this activity you add two indexes to the database named SUPPLYX, created in Module 5.

1. At the Interact screen type **I** to select the Index command screen. Type **supplyx** at the Database prompt and press **Enter**.
2. Type **ITEM** at the Fieldname prompt and press **Enter**. At the Index File Name prompt type **ITEM** and press **Enter**. Your screen looks like this:

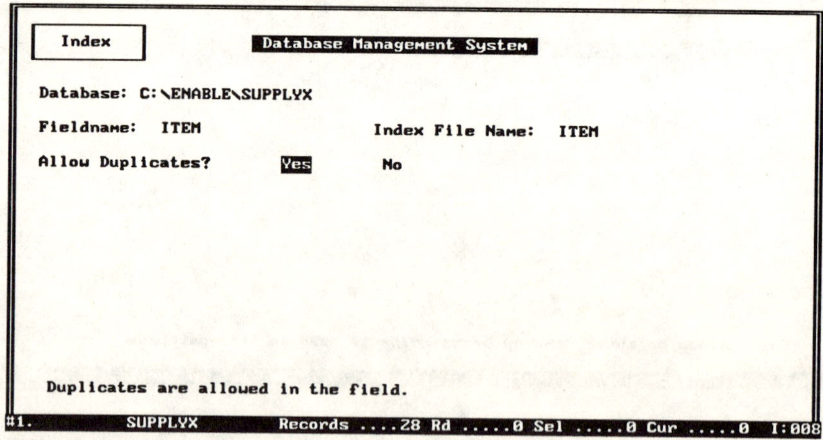

3. At the Allow Duplicates prompt press **Enter** to accept Yes. Enable builds the index for the ITEM field and puts the cursor back on the Database prompt.
4. Press **Down Arrow** and **Alt-F3** to delete **ITEM** from the Fieldname prompt. Enter **STOCKNO** in its place. Press Enter, type **STOCKNO** at the Index File Name prompt, and press **Enter** again.

5. At the Duplicates prompt type **N** to disallow duplicate stock numbers. Enable builds the index.
6. Press **Esc** and type **B** to view the Browse command screen. Press **Enter** and notice that there are now three indexed fields listed in the box. Press **Alt-F3** to clear the Index field and enter **ITEM** in its place.
7. Press **End**, and Enable displays the following Browse screen, showing the number of each type of ITEM.

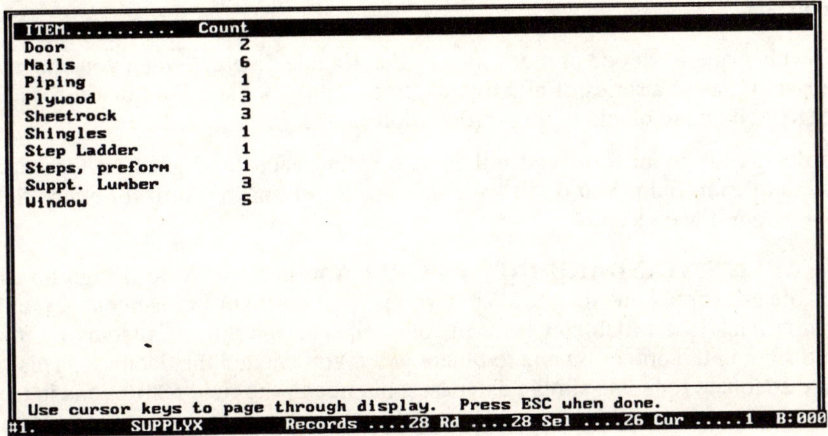

8. Press **F10** and type **Q** to return to the Main Menu.
9. Turn to Module 61 to continue the learning sequence.

Module 59
INPUT-FORM DESIGN

DESCRIPTION

An *input form* is made up of one or more screens that Enable displays when you are entering data in the database. It has of a series of highlighted blocks, one for each field in a record. You move your cursor from block to block, typing information as you go.

When you design the input form you tell Enable where each field goes on the page, and the characteristics of each field. You don't have to place a field in the form for every field in your database if you don't want to.

USING ENABLE'S STANDARD INPUT FORM You don't have to design an input form, because Enable can supply one for you. When you go to the Add or Edit screens leave the "Using Form" prompt blank (see Module 60) and Enable builds an input form, placing all the fields on the left hand side, in the order you entered them when you created the database. This input form may be quite adequate for some simple databases, but not all the field restrictions in the database definition are enforced, and only system-supplied error messages are displayed. Also, you may want to input data in a different order from that in which the fields were created. If so you may have to build an input form.

The standard input form uses the name of the database with a .$IF extension.

DESIGNING AN INPUT FORM At the Main Menu, type UDDI (Use System;DBMS; Design;Input-Form). Enable displays the Input Form Definition screen. Type an input form name (up to eight letters, numbers, or underscores) and press Enter.

If you are designing an input form for a database that you have already created, make sure you use the same name you entered in the database.

Enable displays "File not found. Your choices: New file List dir Re-enter." Type N and Enable displays "Enter the name of the database associated with this form." Type the database's name, press Enter, and Enable diplays "Enter input form description." This optional field is a description that is displayed when you print the input form design report. Type the description and press Enter. Enable then displays a page of instructions. Press Enter to display the blank input form.

Word Processing Input You can use all the usual word processing features to design a form. For example, you could start by printing a bold title at the top of the page, and centering it. You can then type field labels for each field you want on the form. These labels can be as large as you want; you might type Zip code as the label for the field named ZIP. The Word Processing Top Line Menu is available by pressing F10 and typing W.

TIP: If you want to see a list of the fields in the database, press F10, type 1, and press Enter. Enable prompts you for the name of the database. Type the name and press Enter and Enable displays a list of field names at the top of the screen. Select one and press Enter to insert the name at the cursor position.

The following screen shows Enable's mailing list input form, after the word processing step is complete.

```
                       MAIL LIST INPUT FORM
LAST NAME:                     FIRST NAME:                  MI:

           COMPANY:
           TITLE:
           SALUTATION:

       STREET:
       CITY:                              STATE:        ZIP:
       PHONE:                  EXT:
COMMENTS:
#1         C:MAILIN           DRAFT                     L00021C076
```

"Put It Here!" Command The next step is to place the actual fields after each field label. This is done using Enable's "Put it here!" command. Put the cursor where you want the field to start and press Shift-F9. Enable displays the "Enter field name" prompt. You can type the field name and press Enter, or type ? and press Enter, in which case the following screen is displayed.

```
                       MAIL LIST INPUT FORM
LAST NAME:                     FIRST NAME:                  MI:

              Enter field name : ?

 ▶  Enter the field name which corresponds to the label you just placed
    on the input form. To choose from fields in the definition, type "?".

FIRSTNAME      INITIAL        LASTNAME       COMPANY        STREET
CITY           STATE          ZIP            SALUTATION     TITLE
COMMENTS       TELEPHONE      EXT

   Use Arrow Keys or Press Return or ESC
 ▶  Press [Esc] to return to the form screen
#1.TEXT     17
```

Enable displays a list of the field names. Select a field name by moving the highlight and pressing Enter. Enable asks if "you wish to select special processing options." If you press Enter or type N, Enable displays the input form again, with a block the length of the specified field inserted where the cursor was. If you type Y, Enable displays a series of prompts, as follows.

Should this field be verified? No/Yes Typing Y allows you to use the Verify command later (see Module 55). This command lets you check the data in the field by rekeying it.

Should this field be copied to the next ADD screen? No/Yes Type Y if you want Enable to copy the value in this field into the same field in the next record and subsequent records. For example, you have a list of addresses in Zip-code order that you are typing into a database. Using this option you only have to type a Zip code each time you reach a new code in the list, not for each record.

Should this field be protected from update? No/Yes Type Y if you don't want to allow this field to be edited once it has been entered.

Does this field require an [ENTER]? No/Yes If you type Y the cursor will not move out of this field if the data you input fills the field. You must press Enter, Tab, or Down Arrow to move out of the field.

Do you want to provide default data for this field? No/Yes Type Y to specify a value that Enable will automatically display in this field. Enable prompts for the value. For example, most of your customers are in the 75007 Zip code. Type in that value, and every record automatically has the Zip code 75007, unless you choose to type over it.

Is there a special message if invalid data is entered? No/Yes This is another way to define an error message, similar to the ones that can be defined in database creation (Module 50). The message defined here takes precedence over the one defined in the database definition and the system error message.

Does this field have a "GO TO field IF" condition? No/Yes You can use where clauses (Module 60) to tell Enable to automatically move the cursor to a specific field if certain values are input here. For example, if the value in the field is the amount of money owed by a client, you could make the cursor move to another field if the amount is above a specified amount; the other field might ask if further action has been taken (Y/N). Type Y, and Enable prompts for the condition (a where clause such as OWED GE 2000) and the field to go to.

Does this field have a macro procedure? No/Yes Input form macros can be used to look up data in another database, update a field in another database, perform conditional testing, and so on. If you select Yes, Enable displays two more pages of prompts—these are explained in Module 54.

When you have finished answering these prompts Enable displays the input form again, with a block the length of the specified field inserted where the cursor was. The following screen shows the input form MAILIN once it has been finished.

```
                        MAIL LIST INPUT FORM
 LAST NAME:                      FIRST NAME:                   MI:

           COMPANY:
           TITLE:
           SALUTATION:

      STREET:
      CITY:                              STATE:        ZIP:
      PHONE:                 EXT:
COMMENTS:

#1   Definition of input form C:\ENABLE\MAILIN                  L00001C001
```

If you want to confirm the field positions, place the cursor on the diamonds in the blocks; the status line displays the database field name.

"Put It Here!" Command; Non-Typed, Display-Only Fields Press Shift-F9 and Enable displays the "Enter field name:" prompt. If you type a name that isn't used in the database, Enable prompts you for the "Source of data: Another Database/Derived/Local/System." These are display-only fields; the information is not added to the database.

Another Database Type A to make Enable display a value from a field in another database. Enable prompts for the name of the other database, the name of the field you want to look up, and the name of the linking fields. The link field in the other database must be indexed. Enable also asks if this field can be "keyed over," allowing you to change the data in the field. This can allow you to update information in the other database.

NOTE

For more information on linking databases in input forms, see Module 53.

Here is an example of using a field from another database. When you are typing data into a mailing list database you might want to see the "date of last purchase" from another file; if the customer had not purchased within a certain period you could decide to remove him from the list. You define a field in the input form (LASTPURCH), tell Enable the name of the database that has the field, and tell Enable the linking fields (CUSTMRNAME). When you are adding information to the form Enable looks at the information in the linking field, searches the second database for a record with the same name, and copies the last-purchase information from that record back to the LASTPURCH field in the first database.

Derived Type D to make this a derived-data field. Enable prompts for the formula to be used, the result type (numeric, text, or logical), and whether the field can be typed over.

TIP: Enable does not display the sys:record number in the screens that use the input form. The sys:record number is a number assigned to the record by Enable, in the order you add it. As this number can be used in index search statements and where clauses you might want to add it to the input form. Type a name (such as SNUMBER) at the "Enter field name:" prompt (do not use SYS:RECORD). Press Enter and select Derived. Type SYS:RECORD into the Formula field. Then select Numeric, 0 decimal places, 7 characters long, No to "can this field be typed over," and No to "special processing."

Local Type L to make this a local field. Local fields can be used to temporarily store data or calculations without entering them in the database. You could type "go-to-field-if" conditions and run macros. Enable prompts for the data type (numeric, text, or logical).

System Type S if you want to display the current date or time on your input form. Enable asks which you want, and the format in which it will be displayed.

TOP LINE MENU To view the Form Design Top Line Menu, shown in the following screen, press F10 and type F.

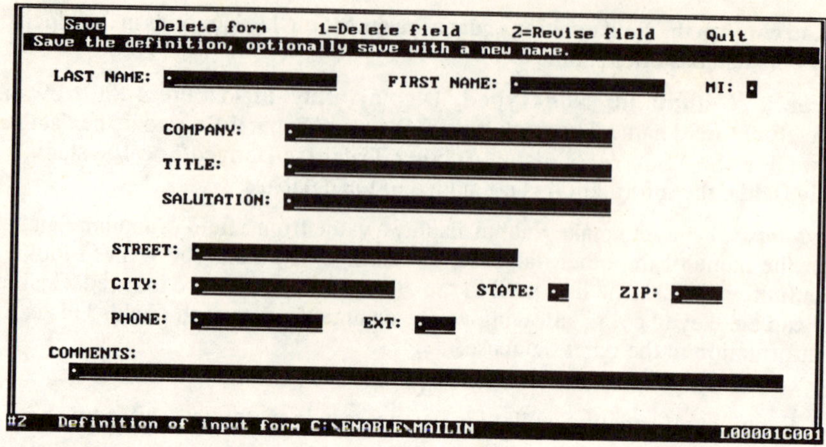

The options let you save or delete the input form, or exit the input form. Options "1=Delete field" and "2=Revise field" display instructions.

DELETING AND REVISING FIELDS Delete a field with any of the word processing deletion functions; the Spacebar may be the best way to delete fields, because the other fields are not moved up to take the place of the deleted characters.

To revise a field, place the cursor on the diamond at the beginning of the field and press Shift-F9. Enable displays the "Put it here!" prompts so that you can change the options.

SAVING THE INPUT FORM When you have finished designing the form, press F10 and type FSS (Form Design Options;Save;Same name and disk). Then press F10 and type FQY to exit.

REVISING THE INPUT-FORM DESIGN You can return to the input form and modify it at any time. Use the word processing tools and the special features already described in this module to change the form.

If you change the database definition you should modify the input form as well. Delete all the fields you modified in the database definition, and re-enter them using the "Put it here!" command. Then save the input form again. If you want you can save the form with a different name, which produces a new file and leaves your original form unchanged; press F10 and type FSD (Form Design Options;Save;Different name or disk).

APPLICATIONS

You need a method to get your information into the database, and the input form is that method. Adding information to the input form is just like typing information onto a paper form in a typewriter, except the information is electronically stored and manipulated. The features explained in this module make adding data to the database quick and efficient.

TYPICAL OPERATION

Rather than going through the lengthy process of building an entire input form, in this activity you modify MAILIN, Enable's standard mailing-list input form. This file is on disk 10 of the Enable disks, and should have been copied to your default data directory during installation. Begin at the Main Menu.

1. Type **UDDI**. Enable displays the Input Form Definition screen. Type **MAILIN** and press **Enter**. Enable searches for the file, and then displays the "name of associated database" prompt.
2. Press **Enter** to accept the filename MAIL, and Enable displays the "input form description" prompt.
3. Press **Enter** twice, and Enable displays the MAILIN input form. Move the cursor to the space below the L in LAST NAME and type **SALUTATION:**. Press **Spacebar**, and press **Shift-F9**. Your screen looks like this:

```
LAST NAME:                    FIRST NAME:                   MI:
SALUTATION:
              COMPANY:

              Enter field name :

 ▶ Enter the field name which corresponds to the label you just placed
   on the input form. To choose from fields in the definition, type "?".

 ▶ When you press [↵] Enable will attempt to locate this field within
   the database definition associated with this form.

     If the field is found, the information regarding the field
     will be obtained from the database definition.
     Otherwise you will be prompted for additional information.

 ▶ Press [Esc] to return to the form screen
#2  Definition of input form C:\ENABLE\MAILIN                 Cap
```

4. Type **?** and press **Enter** and Enable displays a box with a list of the field names in the database MAIL. Move the highlight to SALUTATION and press **Enter**.
5. Enable asks if the field needs "special processing options." Type **N**, and Enable displays the input form again; a new SALUTATION field has been added where you placed the cursor.
6. Move the cursor down to the original SALUTATION field and press **Alt-F3** twice, to delete that line and one other. Move the cursor to the space after the MI field, and press **Ctrl-Enter** to move the new SALUTATION field. Your screen looks like this:

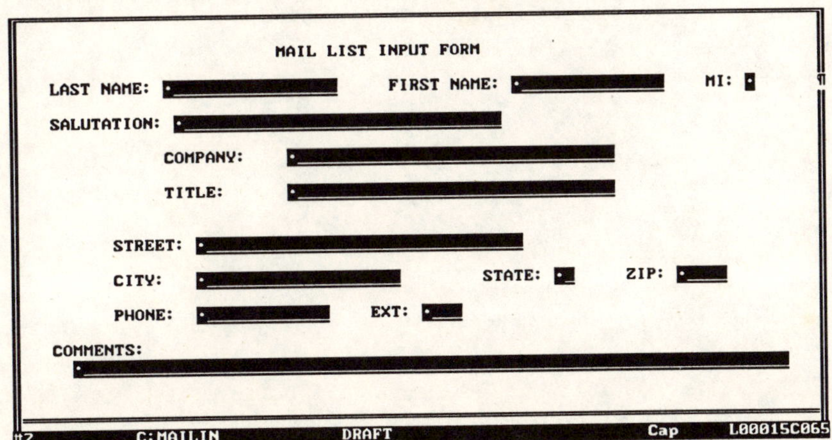

7. Place the cursor on the diamond at the beginning of the ZIP field. Press **Shift-F9** and Enable displays the "special processing" prompt. Type **Y**. At the "verify" prompt type **N**, and at the "copied to next ADD screen" type **Y**.
8. Type **N** six times to return to the input form. The Zip code will be automatically copied into subsequent records' ZIP field.
9. Press **F10** and type **FQY** to exit the input form without saving the changes. (You would normally type FSS to save the changes).
10. Turn to Module 60 to continue the learning sequence.

Module 60
INTERACT AND COMMAND SCREENS

DESCRIPTION

Enable has many ways of using the database information. You can display the information on your screen, print a report, or draw a graph (the graphics commands are described in Section 4 of this book). You can add, edit, or replace information, or sort it into a different order. And you don't need to use the whole database all the time. Enable has special commands that let you decide exactly which records will be used; you might tell Enable to print a report on all your friends and relatives that have birthdays in June and live in Texas, for example.

Enable also has other ways to keep information up to date, apart from editing data. You can delete records, make backups of whole databases or single records, and restore information that has been deleted or backed up.

THE INTERACT SCREEN

The Interact screen (DBMS Command Chart) is Enable's DBMS "control panel."

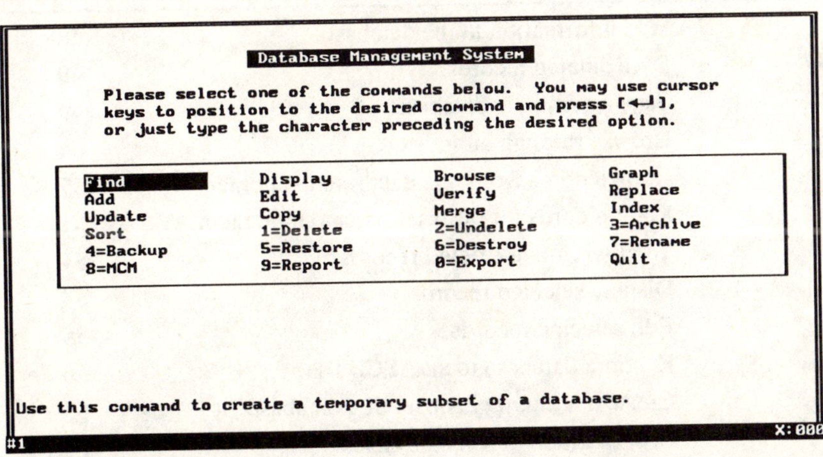

All the DBMS commands are selected from this screen, except for the commands used to create a database or design an input or report form (these are accessed from the Main Menu). You can also use the ADD and REPORT commands from the Main Menu, even though these commands are also on the Interact screen.

To use the Interact screen, move the highlight to the command you want and press Enter, or simply type the first character of the command (F for Find or 1 for Delete, for example). Enable displays a description of the highlighted command at the bottom of the screen. When you select a command, Enable displays the applicable command screen.

THE COMMAND SCREENS

A typical command screen (Edit), is shown in the following screen.

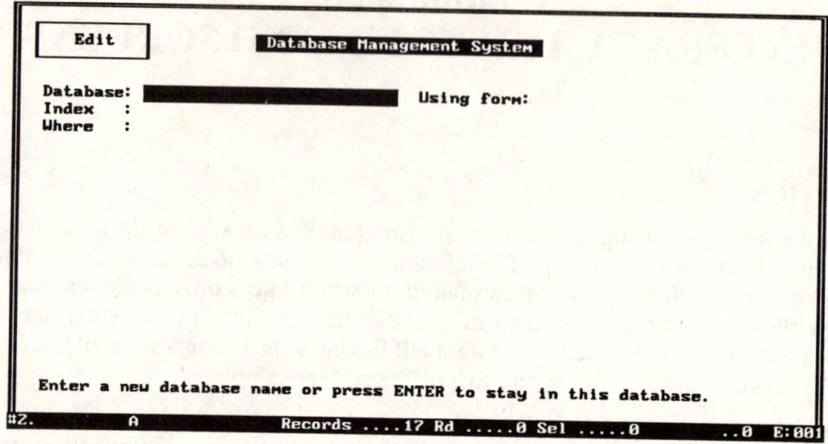

The command name is displayed in the box at the top left of the screen. All the command screens are similar in format, with variations that are described in the applicable modules. The following table refers you to the applicable module for each command:

Command	*Purpose*	*Module*
ADD	Add information to the database	48
ARCHIVE	Save deleted records	49
BACKUP	Save a complete database	49
BROWSE	Browse through an index	64
COPY	Copy records from one database to another	57
DELETE	Mark records for destruction, and hide them	51
DESTROY	Totally remove deleted records	51
DISPLAY	Display selected records	64
EDIT	Edit selected records	55
EXPORT	Export a database to an ASCII file	56
FIND	Create a temporary subset of a database	63
GRAPH	Draw a graph of selected fields	Part 4
INDEX	Create a new index	58
MCM	MCM; Windows, Files, and Screens commands	47, 114, 2
MERGE	Merge two databases into one	57
QUIT	Return to the Main Menu	This Module
RENAME	Rename a database	55
REPLACE	Replace information in specific fields	55
REPORT	Print a report	62

Command	Purpose	Module
RESTORE	Restore archived or backed-up data	49
SORT	Sort the data into a different order	63
UNDELETE	Restore deleted records	51
UPDATE	Update with data from another file	57
VERIFY	Type over data to verify data is correct	55

Move from prompt to prompt on a command screen by pressing Enter or Down Arrow (or use Shift-Tab or Up Arrow to move backwards). Some prompts are optional, but others do not let you past without entering data (Database, for example). Prompts with data already displayed can be cleared by pressing Alt-F3. (Enable automatically displays the most recently entered data at each prompt.)

TIP: If the information at the command screen's prompts is exactly as you need it, press End to bypass the prompts and start the command. Or if you enter information at the first prompts but do not need to answer the subsequent prompts, press End to bypass them and start the command.

DATABASE Type the name of the database with which you want to work at the Database prompt. To display a list of available databases, type ? at the blank prompt and press Enter. Select a database from the list by moving the cursor to the name and pressing Enter, or press Esc to return to the command screen without selecting a name. (You can select either the .DBF or $BF filename.) You can also enter a window number or the name of a read-only file. See Module 57 for information on importing read-only data. When you have entered a name, press Enter; the cursor moves to the next prompt in the screen.

USING FORM This prompt requires the name of the input form. If, when you created the database, you defined an input form as the default form, Enable displays the name of the form at this prompt. Accept the form by pressing Enter or clear the name (Alt-F3) and type another name. Type ? and press Enter to display a list of input forms (select a form from the list and press Enter). If you want Enable to provide the standard form, leave the prompt blank.

Standard Input Form If you leave the "Using form:" prompt blank, once you complete the remaining prompts on the command screen Enable displays a prompt asking if you want to build a new standard input form. The first time Enable builds a standard input form for a database it saves the form for future use; press Enter to use the saved form. However, if you have changed the database definition since the last time you used it (for example, added fields or changed field lengths) press C to build a new input form. The following screen shows a standard input form for Enable's MAIL database.

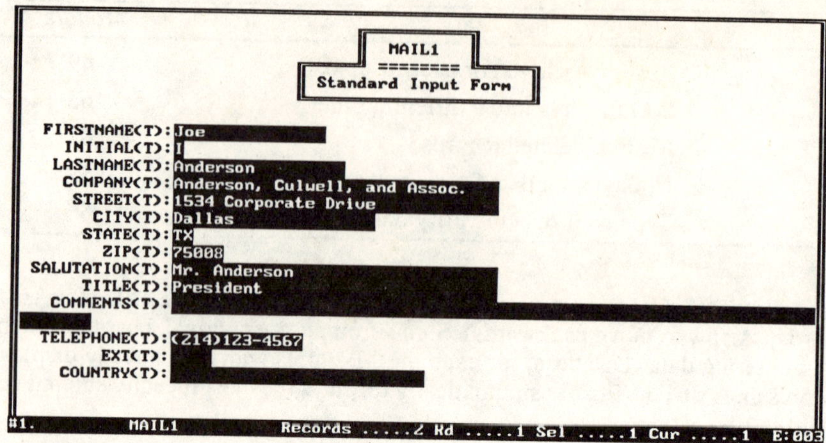

Notice that the field names are aligned on the left side of the screen, and each one has a letter in parentheses to show the field type (T = text, S = state, Z = zip, and so on). Not all field restrictions and specifications in your database definition will be enforced in a standard input form.

INDEX The Index prompt lets you tell Enable which records you want to work with. For example, you have a salesperson visiting a customer in another town. You would like him to visit other customers while he is there, so you want to print a report on all your customers in that particular city. If you type CITY="CHICAGO" at the Index prompt of the Report command screen, Enable prints a report on all your customers in Chicago.

You can only search fields that you defined as indexed when you created the database. (If you didn't define the field as indexed, but would now like it to be, you can use the Index command to build one or modify the database definition; see Modules 58 and 61.)

When the cursor reaches the Index prompt Enable displays a list of the indexed fields in the database, as shown in the following screen.

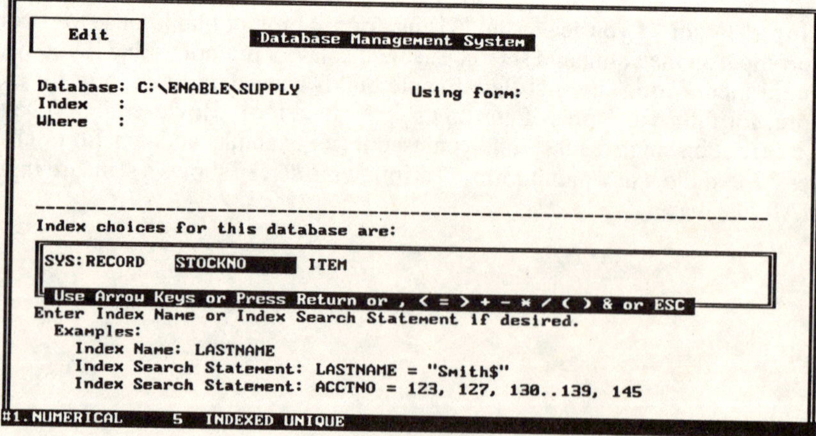

Below the list are several example index search statements. You can type the search statement directly at the Index prompt if you wish, or press PgDn to move the cursor into the list, select a field name, and press Enter. The field name displays at the Index prompt. Or, select a field name and type =; the field name is displayed at the Index prompt with = after it. Pressing Tab at the Index prompt moves the cursor eight characters or to the end of the text, whichever is closest.

The Index Search Statement An index search statement uses the following format: FIELD=*value*. You can type a list of values by separating them with commas (e.g., SERIALNO= 543,544,587), or a range of values by separating them with two periods (e.g., SERIALNO=544.. 587 selects all serial numbers between 544 and 587).

The index search is case sensitive. For example, if you are searching for ITEM="NAILS" Enable will ignore records if the word is spelled "Nails." And Enable searches not only for the word you type, but all words beginning with those characters. For example, typing ITEM="N" finds Nails.

You can specify the number of the record or records you want to use. Enable assigns a sys:record (system record) number to each record, in the order in which you enter the record. Enable automatically builds a SYS:RECORD field for every record. You can use the record number in the same way you use any of the other fields. Type SYS:RECORD=51 to use record 51, or SYS:RECORD=51..58 to use records 51 through 58.

TIP: Enable displays the sys:record number in the Display screen (see Module 64) but it does not display it in the input form; when you are editing, for example, you don't normally see the record number. However, you can make Enable display a SYS:RECORD field by defining a derived field when you are building an input form (see Module 59). You can also see sys:record numbers when you use the Display command.

If you want to see all the records in the order of a particular field, type the name of the field alone. For example, type ITEM to use the records in alphabetical order according to the ITEM field.

When the value being specified is text or a date, you must use quotation marks around it (CITY="CHICAGO"). Numeric and logical (T or F) values do not need quotation marks.

NOTE

You can use only the = operator with the index search statement. Although the screen lists other operators, this is a mistake. Enable lets you type the other characters at the prompt, but does not let you continue.

NOTE

Enable will not be able to use the index search statement if the index file has been damaged or accidentally deleted. If this has happened rebuild the index using the Index command (Module 58).

Descending Order Records are automatically accessed in ascending order, but you can use descending order by typing ",D" after the field name. For example, if you want to edit the records in descending order, type SYS:RECORD,D. or type DATE,D to use the most recent record first, and the oldest last (presuming your date field has the year first followed by the month and day, so that a sensible order can be used).

WHERE When you move the cursor to the Where prompt, Enable displays a list of all the fields, not just indexed fields. (The list looks similar to the index list, and works in the same way, except that all the listed operators are available.)

FIELDS Some command screens have a "Fields:" prompt. For example, if you are exporting data you can tell Enable which fields to export by typing the field names, separated by commas, at the Fields prompt. Or press PgDn to move the cursor to the list of fields, move the cursor to the first field you want, and press Enter. Enable displays the field name at the Fields prompt and lets you make another selection in the list.

OTHER PROMPTS Some command screens have other prompts. These are described in the applicable modules.

LEAVING THE PROMPTS BLANK If you do not enter data at the Index, Where, or Fields prompts, Enable assumes you want to use the entire database, in the system-record-number order.

MARKED RECORDS If you mark some records in the Display or Browse screens (see Module 64) before going to a command screen, the marked records override any index search statements or where clauses that may have already been input. When you reach the command screen, press End to bypass the prompts and use the marked records.

CARRYING OUT THE COMMAND When you press Enter or Down Arrow at the last prompt, or press End at any stage after the required prompts, Enable carries out the command. If Enable needs to refer to another database that is not in the same directory, Enable warns you. You can press Enter to continue, but the records that require the other database will be incorrect.

APPLICATIONS

The Interact screen makes using the DBMS easy; commands are quickly selected by typing one letter or number. The command screens let you type the necessary information without remembering complicated commands. Also, Enable stores the index search statements and where clauses from the previous screens, further simplifying the process.

TYPICAL OPERATION

In this activity you open the Interact screen, enter a command screen, and select records using the Index and Where prompts. You will use the SUPPLYX database created in Module 5. Begin at the Main Menu.

1. Type **UDI**, and Enable displays the Interact screen.
2. Press **E** to select Edit, and Enable displays the Edit command screen. Type **?** at the Database prompt, and press **Enter**. Enable displays a list of databases. Move the cursor to SUPPLYX.DBF and press **Enter**. Enable displays the Edit command screen again, with the disk, pathname, and filename of the selected database.
3. Press **Enter** to bypass the Using Form prompt. The cursor moves to the Index prompt. Press **PgDn** and press = to select SYS:RECORD. Type **20..25** to select records 20 through 25. (Don't leave any spaces.) Your screen looks like this:

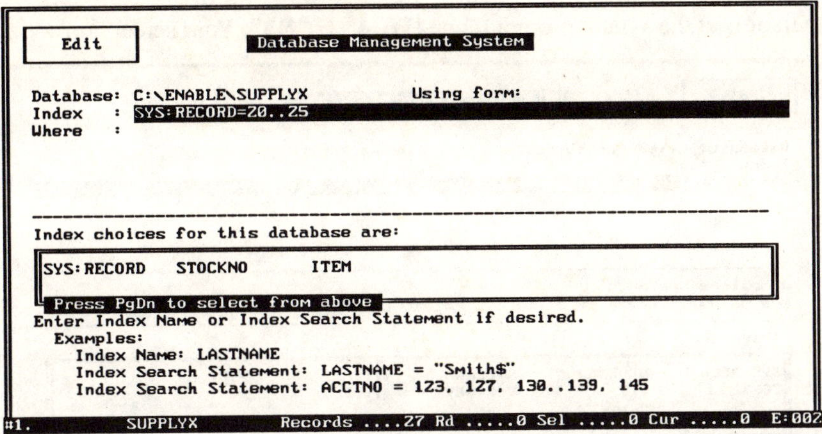

4. Press **Enter** twice (to bypass the Where prompt) Enable asks you if you want to create a new input form, or use the one already created. Press **Enter** and Enable displays the selected record. Press **F5** (Next) several times; each time you press it Enable displays the next record, until you have seen all six. At that point Enable displays a prompt at the bottom of the screen.

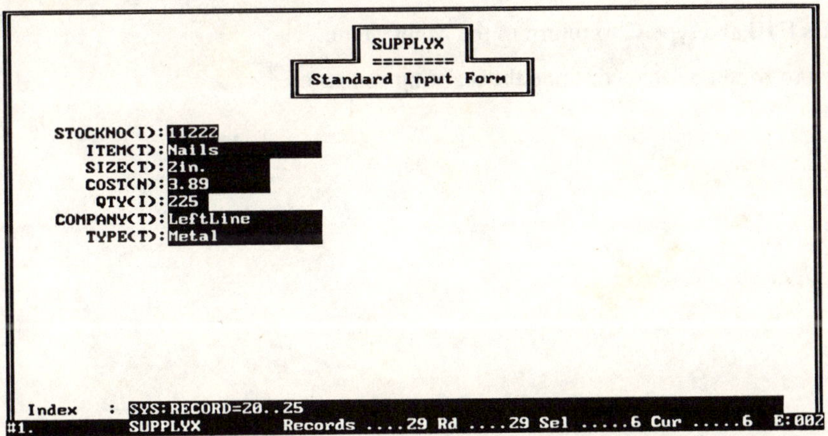

5. Type **11** over the 20 and press **Spacebar** several times to delete the rest of the Index statement. Press **Enter**, and Enable goes to record 11. Press **F10** and type **Q** to return to the Edit command screen. Press **Enter** twice. The cursor moves to the Index prompt. Press **Alt-F3** to delete the index search statement, and press **Enter**.

6. The cursor is at the Where prompt. Type **ITEM LE "N$"**. Your screen looks like this:

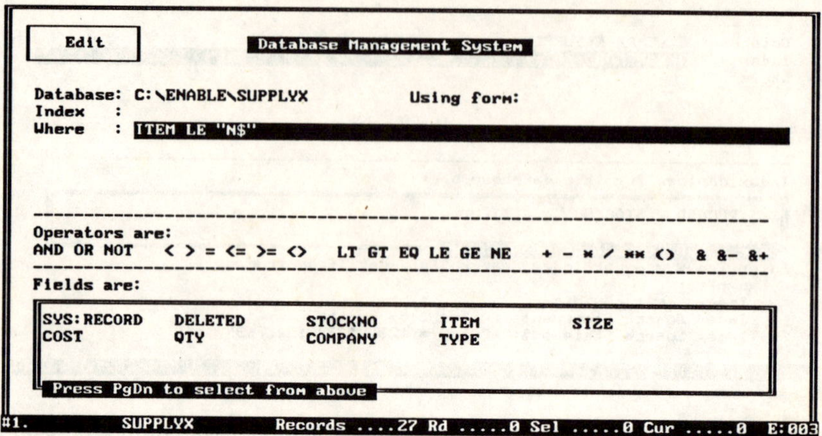

7. Press **Enter** twice. Enable displays the first record that fits the criteria (the word in the ITEM field must be less than or equal to N$, that is, any word beginning with an N or with any letter earlier in the alphabet). Press **Esc** twice to return to the Edit command screen.
8. Press **F10** and type **Q** to return to the Main Menu.
9. Turn to Module 48 to continue the learning sequence.

Module 61
MODIFY A DATABASE

DESCRIPTION

You can return to a database and modify the database and field definitions at any time. You may change a field's specifications, rename it, delete it, or add a new field. Close all the other windows before revising a database, to ensure that there is adequate memory for the operation.

Enter the Database Definition screen the same way you did when you created the database: at the Main Menu type UDDD (Use System;DBMS; Design;Database-Definition). On the first Database Definition page type the name of the database you want to revise, and press Enter (or type ? and press Enter to select from a list of databases).

Enable displays the second Database Definition screen; make any changes you want to the database description and the default input form and report. Enable displays a screen warning you to revise the input and report forms if you change the field definitions. Press any key and Enable displays the Field Definition screen.

RENAMING FIELDS If you want to rename a field press the Up Arrow key to move into the box, press the Down Arrow key to move the highlight onto the name of the field, and type R. Enable displays an "Enter New Field Name" prompt. Type the name and press Enter.

REVISING FIELDS There are two ways to revise fields. The easiest way is to press the Up Arrow and Down Arrow to move the highlight to the field you want to revise and then use the Right Arrow to move it to the item in the field you want to change. Press Spacebar and Enable prompts you to enter the new information, as shown in the following screen.

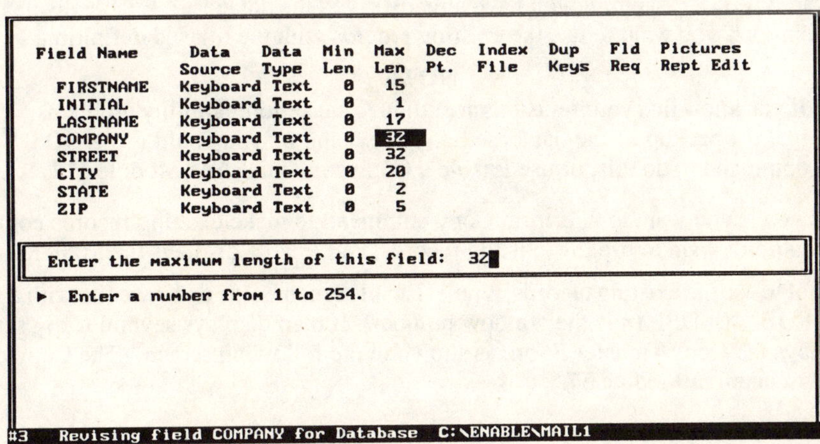

After the field has been changed, you can move to the listed characteristics of another field, but you can't move the highlight to another field name. To do so press Esc (to return to the Field Name prompt) and use the Up Arrow key again.

If you want to change the options available through the Detailed-definition procedure to a field that was defined using the Quick-definition procedure you must use the other revision method; place the highlight on the field name (or type the field name at the Field Name prompt) and press Enter. Enable then takes you through the same sequence of prompts you saw when you created the database, allowing you to make the changes you want (see Module 50).

DELETING A FIELD To delete a field, use the Up and Down Arrow keys to move the highlight to the field name and press Del. Enable asks to confirm the deletion; type Y and the field is removed.

ADDING A FIELD To add a field use the same procedure you used when you created the database; type the new name in the Field Name field, press Enter, and Enable takes you through the definition prompts.

CAUTION

Revising fields, especially deleting and renaming them, may change other, derived fields in this and other databases.

SAVING YOUR REVISIONS When you have finished revising the database, press F10 and type SS to save the revisions (or type SN and Enable prompts you for a new filename and creates a new file, leaving the original unchanged). Then press F10 and type QY to return to the Main Menu. (If a field name is highlighted you must move the cursor back to the Field Name prompt by pressing Esc, before you can save the file.)

REVISING A DATABASE AFTER ADDING RECORDS If you have already added records to your database revising it can cause trouble; some of the revised fields may be incompatible with the data already entered. The data may be longer than the new fields, for example, and changing names means Enable doesn't know where to put data. Some changes have no effect (changing the database description, the default forms, and error messages, for example). But if the changes you made do cause compatibility problems you have to convert the data to the new format; when you press F10 and type QY (assuming you have already saved the database), Enable displays an error message and asks if you want to use the existing records with the revised definition.

NOTE

If you know that your revisions are going to cause compatibility problems, make a backup of the database before revising it. You could use a DOS command to do this, or use Enable's Copy command. See Module 114.

Enable asks you if you want to "Perform Copy command to make existing records compatible?" Type N if you don't want to use the existing records, and Enable displays the Main Menu.

If you do want to use the existing records, type Y. Enable renames the database file with the original records TMPDBXX*n*.DBF (*n* is the window number). It then displays several Copy screens and finally displays the Copy Transfer Form, as shown in the following screen. (The Copy command is described in detail in Module 57.)

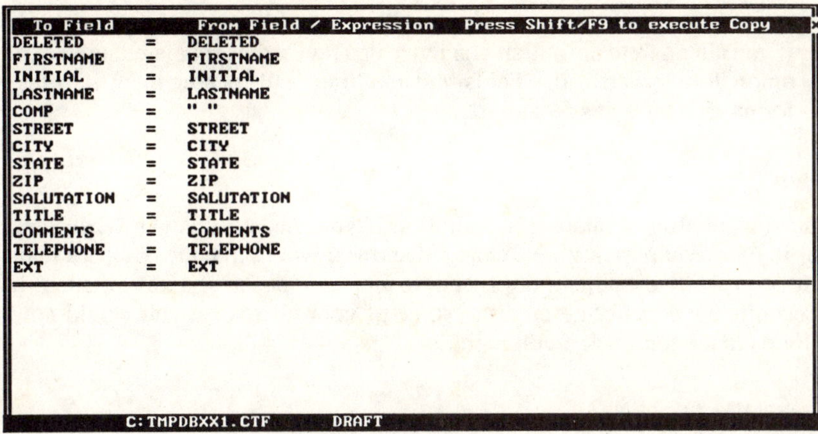

In this screen you can see that Enable knows how to transfer data for all the fields except the COMP field, a field that has been renamed. Because this is a text field Enable has displayed "COMP = ' ' ." If it were a numeric field Enable would display "COMP = 0." Move the cursor to that line and type the old field name after the equal sign. If there are no field names missing in the right column, you don't need to make any changes on this screen.

Press Shift-F9 and type C to select Copy. Enable copies the old records into the new format, updates the database indexes, and deletes the TMPDBXX*n*.DBF file. Enable then displays the Copy screen.

Errors During the Copy If error messages occur during the copy procedure don't accept the changes until you have viewed the database to see if the data was correctly transferred. Press F10 and type M11 (MCM;Windows;Open a Window) and Enable displays the Main Menu. Type UDIE (Use System;DBMS;Build;Edit). When Enable displays the Edit command screen type the name of the original database file. Review the data to ensure that it is correct. If you shortened any fields some of the data may be truncated. When you exit the Edit screen Enable displays the Copy screen again.

Accepting the Changes Press Esc and Enable prompts you to accept or reject the changes. Type Y and Enable displays the Main Menu. If you type N, the records and the database definition remain incompatible and you will not be able to use the database until you rename or delete the .DBF file (using the Delete command in the file directory; see Module 51).

CAUTION

Using the database Destroy command destroys both the database definition (.$BF) and the database records (.DBF) files. If you want to delete the .DBF file only, use the file directory Delete command.

$B@ FILES Enable stores a copy of the last database definition file that is compatible with the database record file. This file has the extension .$B@. If you rename it, changing the extension to .$BF (the extension used by database definition files), the files are compatible again and can be used.

Other changes can be made using the Index command (Module 58) and the Rename command (Module 55).

NOTE

If you alter a field definition you must also revise the associated input and report forms; delete the fields you modified and reenter them into the forms. See Modules 59 and 62.

APPLICATIONS

You may need to modify a database's definition if you made a mistake when you created the database, or if your requirements have changed and you would like the database to do something more than it is presently capable of doing. For example, suppose you have a client-list database. You have recently begun offering credit to some of your clients, so you would now like to add some new fields to let you track credit records.

TYPICAL OPERATION

In this activity you revise the copy of the database named Supplyx, created in Module 5.

1. At the Main Menu type **UDDD**. Enable displays the first Database Definition screen. Type **SUPPLYX** and press **Enter**.
2. When Enable displays the second Database Definition screen type **Training Database** in the "database description" field and press **Enter**. Press **Enter** at the "default input form" prompt and type **suplyrep** at the default report form prompt.

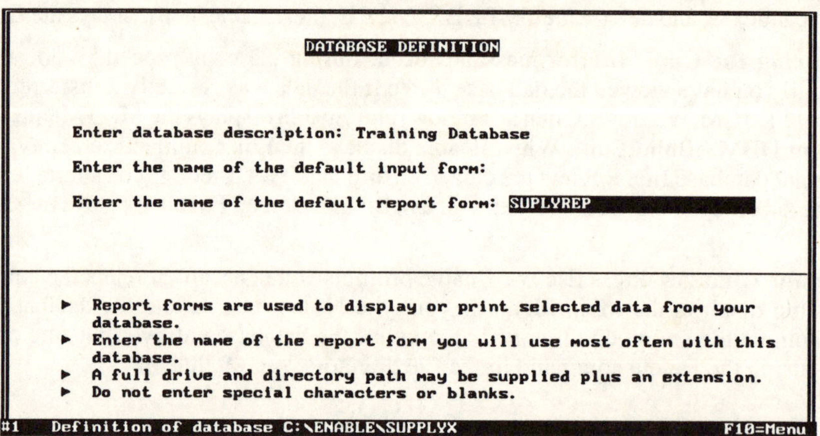

3. Press **Enter** and Enable displays a message telling you to modify the input and report forms if you modify the database definition. Press **Enter** and Enable displays the Field Definition screen.
4. Press **Up Arrow** and then **Down Arrow** to move the highlight to the field named ITEM. Press **Right Arrow** three times until the cursor is over ITEM's field length. Press **Spacebar** and Enable prompts you for the new value. Type **16**.

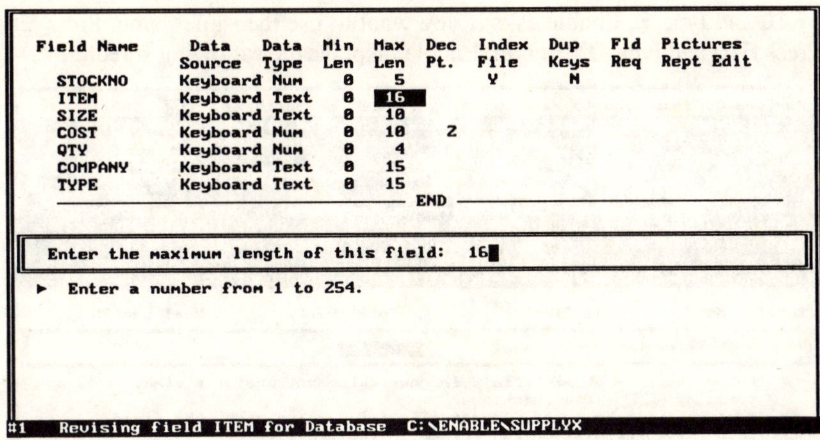
Field Name Data Source Data Type Min Len Max Len Dec Pt. Index File Dup Keys Fld Req Pictures Rept Edit
STOCKNO Keyboard Num 0 5 Y N
ITEM Keyboard Text 0 16
SIZE Keyboard Text 0 10
COST Keyboard Num 0 10 2
QTY Keyboard Num 0 4
COMPANY Keyboard Text 0 15
TYPE Keyboard Text 0 15
END
Enter the maximum length of this field: 16
▶ Enter a number from 1 to 254.
#1 Revising field ITEM for Database C:\ENABLE\SUPPLYX

5. Press **Enter** to change the value and press **Esc** to display the "Enter the field name" prompt. Type **COST** and press **Enter**.

6. When Enable displays the "What method do you wish to use" prompt, type **D** (Detailed). Press **Down Arrow** ten times, until you get to the Maximum length prompt. Type **11** and press **Enter**, and then type **$NNN,NNN.NN** at the report picture prompt.

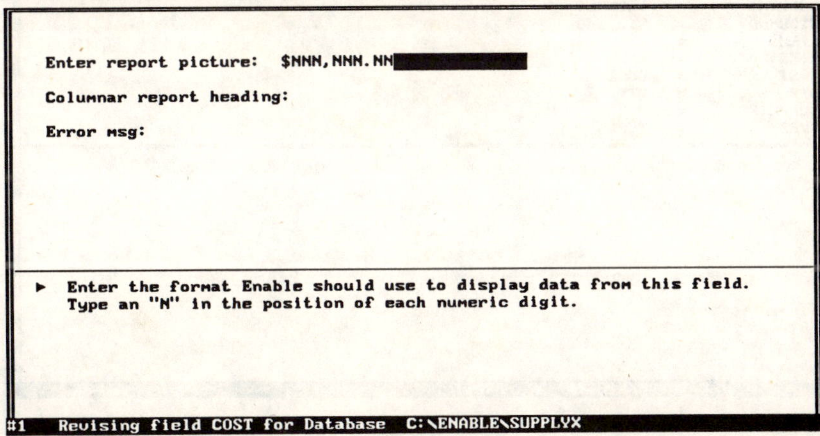
Enter report picture: $NNN,NNN.NN
Columnar report heading:
Error msg:
▶ Enter the format Enable should use to display data from this field.
Type an "N" in the position of each numeric digit.
#1 Revising field COST for Database C:\ENABLE\SUPPLYX

7. Press **Down Arrow** three times. Enable displays the Field Definition screen again; notice that the the COST field definition at the top of the page has changed.

8. Press **Up Arrow** once and **Down Arrow** five times to move the cursor to COMPANY. Press **R** and type the new name **SUPPLIER**. Press **Enter** twice and Enable displays the field definition prompts. Type **Q** (Quick), **L** (Logical), and **Y** (Yes) and Enable displays the Field Definition screen again.

9. Press **F10** and type **S**. Enable asks if you want to use the same name. Press **Enter** to say yes. Press **F10** and type **QY** to quit. Enable displays the following screen.

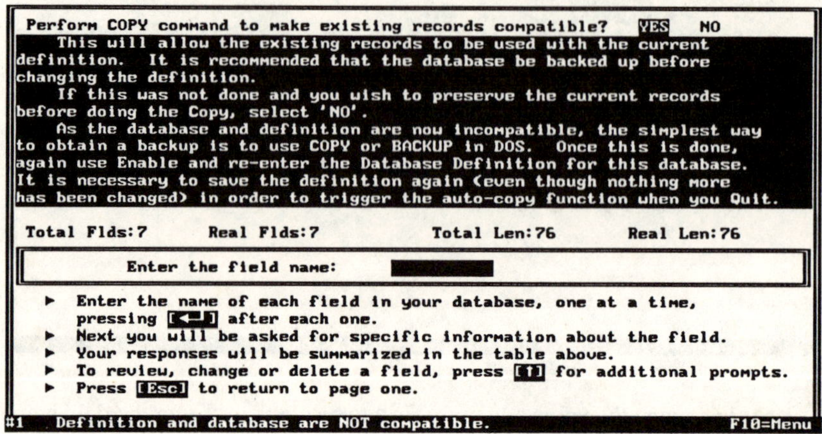

10. Type **Y** to perform the Copy command, and Enable fills in the Copy screen and then displays the Copy Transfer form, as shown in the following screen.

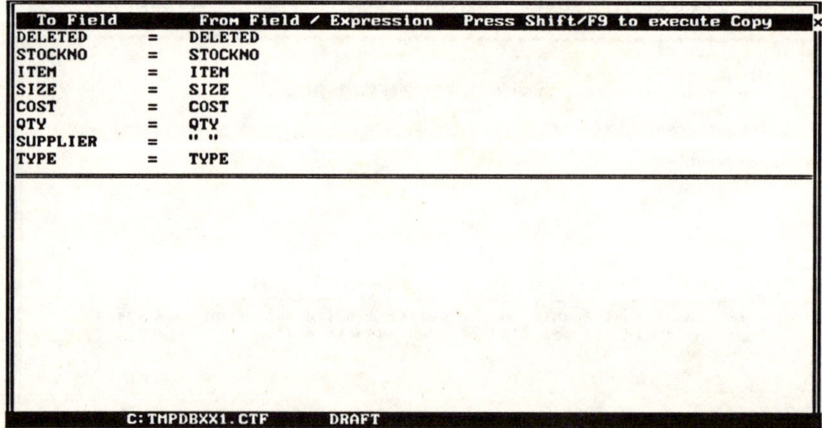

11. Use the arrow keys to move to the quotation marks beside SUPPLIER, and replace them with **COMPANY**.

12. Press **Shift-F9** and type **C** to continue the copy operation. Enable copies the data and displays the Copy screen again. Press **Esc**, and your screen looks like the following.

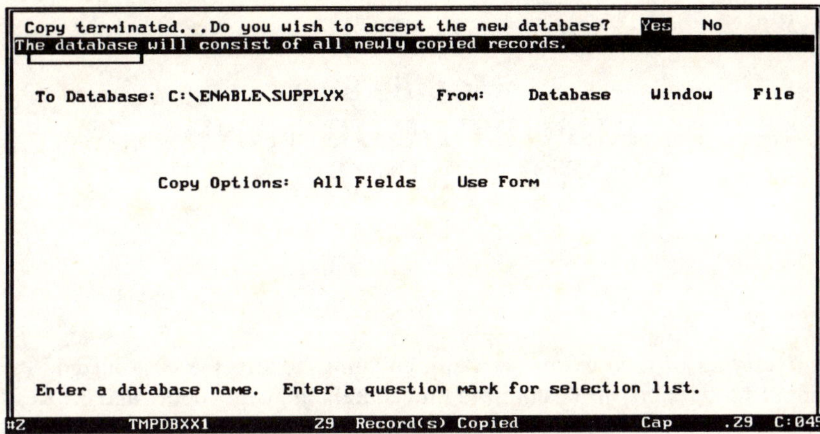

13. Type **Y** to accept the changes. Enable displays the fields and then returns you to the Main Menu.
14. Turn to Module 62 to continue the learning sequence.

Module 62
REPORT DESIGN AND GENERATION (REPORT)

DESCRIPTION

Enable has five types of reports: the standard, columnar report; the customized "Put it Here!" report; the input-form report; the customized Procedural Language report, and the Read-only data reports. Reports can be printed, displayed on the screen, and saved on a disk in Enable's word processing or ASCII format.

NOTE

Before you read this module you should read Module 60 to learn how to use the Interact and command screens.

ORGANIZING YOUR DATA Records are stored in your database in the order you added them, and Enable uses this order when it prints reports. If you want to use a different order you can organize your records in two ways: by typing the name of an indexed field at the Index prompt on the Report command screen (see later in this module); or by using the Sort or Find command (see Module 63). The Index prompt lets you sort the records in one way; for example, you could type ZIP to organize the data in Zip code order. The Sort command allows more detailed, specific organization of the records, with up to nine levels of sorting, and lets you sort on non-indexed fields. (The Sort command produces a select set; when you print your report type the name of the select set at the Database prompt on the Report command screen.)

NOTE

Printing database reports uses a lot of memory. If you have other open windows Enable may tell you to close them first. Sometimes saving the information in the other windows before printing the report will allow Enable to complete the operation.

COLUMNAR REPORTS The columnar report is a standard report format. There are a few format changes you can make, but unlike the Put it Here and the Procedural Language reports you do not design the report before going to the Report command screen; all the work is done at that screen. The following screen shows the prompts that appear when you select Report from the Interact screen. You can also get to the Report command screen from the Main Menu by typing UDR (Use System;DBMS;Report).

```
Report                 Database Management System

Database: C:\ENABLE\TEST                 Using form:
Index    :                               To: Screen  Disk  Printer  ASCII

Where    :
Fields   :
Title    :

Enter a new database name or press ENTER to stay in this database.
#1.        TEST        Records ....25 Rd .....1 Sel .....1 Cur .....1  9:001
```

Enter the database name. (If you used the Sort or Find command, type the name of the select set.) Leave the "Using form:" prompt blank. At the Index prompt type the name of the indexed field on which you would like to sort the records and press Enter, or press Enter to skip the prompt. (You probably won't need to specify the sort if you are using a select set.) This prompt can also be used to select records to be included in the report. (See Module 60 for instructions on index search statements and where clauses.)

To: Screen/Disk/Printer/ASCII Select Screen to see your report on your screen, twenty lines at a time. You display the next twenty lines by pressing PgDn or Enter. When Enable pauses at the end of each block you can see the columns that are "off-screen" by scrolling sideways with the arrow keys. Cancel the display by pressing Ctrl-Break.

Disk or ASCII If you select Disk or ASCII, Enable prompts for a filename. You can use the same filename as the database if you wish; press Enter and Enable assigns a .WPF extension to the file. You can specify the extension if you want but do not use the .DBF extension.

CAUTION

> Do not use the database filename with a .DBF extension or Enable replaces the database file with a word processing file, destroying the database.

If you select Disk the file is in Enable format, allowing you to add notes and embedded print commands into the report. See Section 1, Word Processing, for more information. If you enter the name of an existing file, Enable tells you to press Enter if you want to re-enter the name or type O to write over the file.

Printer Select Printer to print the report. The way this feature operates depends on whether you set up your user profile to use the system queue (see Appendix I).

The default condition is to print immediately, that is, not to use the queue. Enable prints the file immediately without building a temporary print file. If the printer is in use Enable displays an error message and cancels the printout. While printing the document Enable displays another window or the Main Menu; you cannot use the Report command screen or the database the report comes from, but you can still work in other windows.

NOTE

If you are using .input Procedural Language commands in your dot command reports you should use the system queue; otherwise Enable ignores the .input command. (See Module 52.)

If you configured your user profile to use the system queue, Enable creates a temporary print file named TMPDBXX*n*.RPT, where *n* is the window number. Enable prints the report if the printer is not in use. If the printer is in use the report is sent to the system queue and printed when the printer is available. You can continue using the Report command screen and the database while the report is printing.

Where Use the Where prompt to specify the records in the report.

Fields Enter the names of the fields, in the order you want to see them in the report, separated by commas. The easiest way to do this is to press PgDn to move the cursor into the list of fields, select the first field, and press the comma key. The field is displayed at the Fields prompt, and the cursor moves to the next field in the list. You can also define derived fields, such as PRICE-COST or PRICE/WEIGHT. Enable accepts as many fields as you want, up to 160 characters.

Defining Field Length Enable determines the field length from the report picture, field definition, or heading, whichever is longest, up to twenty characters. Override this value by typing the length in braces after the field name (for example, ITEM{6}). If the data in a numeric field is longer than the field length, it is shown in the report as asterisks. You can also define the number of decimal places in the field by including that in the braces. (For example, PRICE/WEIGHT{5.2} means of the 5-character field, one is a decimal point and two are decimal places.)

Use {$} to show the field in currency format. If you want to define the length as well, separate with a comma ({$,5.2} for example), and include the dollar sign in the character count.

Breaks You can enter brace codes after the field names to define breaks in the report. For example, if you wanted a break each time the Zip code changed you could type ZIP{B1}. You can define up to 16 breaks; you could also define a break after the CITY field, for example. The number after the B in the braces indicates the break-order. Each field must have a different number, and the order you use will define the number of blank lines. The more levels you have, the more blank lines that are left.

NOTE

You should use the Sort command if you want more than one break in your report.

Computations You can use brace codes to make calculations at the end of the report or at a break point. The following table shows the codes.

Numeric fields only:

The total value (sum)	{s}
The highest value	{h}
The lowest value	{l}
The average value	{a}

Any fields:

The tally (number of records)	{t}
The number of different values	{c}

These letters are included in the report immediately after the result of the computation.

If you want the computation made at a break point, type the code with the break number. For example, if you want to know how many companies you had in each Zip code you could enter CNAME{C1},ZIP{B1}. Computations are then made at that level and every level lower, with a total at the end. If you want multiple calculations, separate codes with commas (for example, {s2,c4}).

Title This is a line of text printed at the top of the report. Don't exceed the width of the page. If you are printing the report, typing # in the title prints the page number on each page. You can also use the word processing automatic numbering and automatic date features.

Producing the Report When you have completed the entries Enable produces the report. If you are printing the report Enable displays the Print Form first, allowing you to modify the settings. When you are ready to print, press Alt-F2.

CAUTION

Do not press Alt-F10 to save your changes to the Print Form, or the system may crash.

The following screen shows a typical report with breaks and computations.

```
Header and Page Break
STOCKNO  ITEM...........  SIZE......  QTY.  COST......  COMPANY........

  10001  Nails            3in.          84      $4.20   Osmose
  10002  Nails            4in.          51      $4.74   Osmose
  11239  Nails            1in.          99      $2.49   Hawthorne
  11234  Nails            2in.          43      $3.49   Osmose
-------  ---------------
     4T  Nails

  91432  Door             32x80         35    $119.00   ThermSav
  93356  Door             36x80         40    $121.00   ThermSav
-------  ---------------
     2T  Door

  84432  Window           6x3           17    $202.01   Malta
  84435  Window           6x5           23    $262.78   Malta
  82333  Window           5x8           19    $213.44   Malta
-------  ---------------
     3T  Window

  Arrow keys to scroll sideways, PGDN or RETURN to continue, or ESC to cancel.
#1.      SUPPLY          Records ....27 Rd ....27 Sel ....22 Cur .....9  9:053
```

"PUT IT HERE!" REPORTS This procedure is similar to that for designing input forms. At the Main Menu, type UDDR (Use System;DBMS;Design;Report-Form). At the "Enter the report form name:" prompt type a name (up to eight numbers, letters, or underscores). You may have already named a default report form when you created the database, so make sure you use the same name.

When you enter the name and press Enter, Enable displays "File not found. Your choices: New file List Dir Re-enter." Press Enter to select "New file" and Enable asks you to enter the name of the database associated with the form. Enter the name or type ? to see a listing of databases.

The next prompt is the "report description." This is printed if you print a title page with the report. (Answer Y at the "Print a title page" prompt in the Print Form, displayed just before the document prints.) After typing the title, press Enter and Enable displays a page of instructions. Press Enter again to see a blank screen.

Word Processing Format You start designing the form by using all the usual word processing features to input titles and headings, just as you do in the input-form design (see Module 59). You can use footers and headers, the automatic date feature, page numbers, rulers, and so on. If you want each record on its own page, put a page break at the end of the report form. (See Section 1, Word Processing.)

You design the layout for only one record; Enable then repeats that format for each record. It even repeats blank lines, so press Alt-F3 to delete the unwanted blank lines between the fields and the end-of-file marker (the double line). The following screen shows a sample report form.

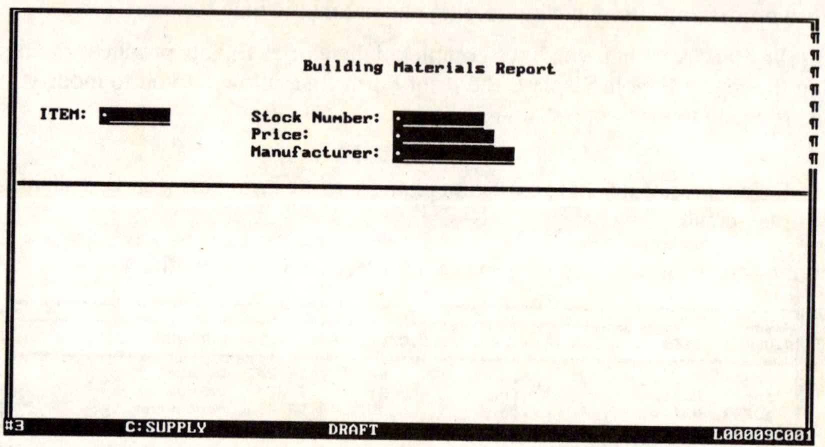

Put it Here! The next step is to place the actual fields after each field label. This is done using Enable's "Put it Here!" command. Put the cursor where you want the field to start and press Shift-F9. Enable displays the "Enter field name" prompt. You can type the field name and press Enter, or type ? and press Enter to display a list of the field names. Select a name by moving the highlight and pressing Enter.

Enable then displays the "Enter the default report picture:" prompt. If you entered a default picture when you created the database it is displayed here. You can change it or enter a new one (see Module 50 for information on report pictures). Enter the picture and press Enter and Enable displays the report form again with the field where you positioned the cursor.

Fields Not In The Database You can add fields that don't appear in the database. At the "Enter field name:" prompt type a name that is not used by any of the fields on the database. Enable displays "Source of data: Another database Derived System." If you select "Another database," Enable prompts for the database name, the lookup field in that database, and the link fields in both this and the other database. If you select "Derived," Enable prompts for the formula, the resulting data type (numeric, text, or logical), the number of decimal positions, the field length, and the report picture. If you select "System," Enable asks if you want to display the date or time, and what report picture to use. (See Module 50 for information on using these field types and defining report pictures.)

Top Line Menu The Top Line Menu is the same as the one used in input-form design, letting you save or delete the input form, or exit the input form.

Deleting and Revising Fields Delete a field with any of the word processing deletion functions; the Spacebar may be the best way to delete fields, because the other fields are not moved up to take the place of the deleted characters.

To revise a field, place the cursor on the diamond at the beginning of the field and press Shift-F9. Enable displays the "Put it Here!" prompts so you can change the options.

Saving The Report Form When you have finished designing the form, press F10 and type FSS (Form Design Options;Save;Same name and disk). Then press F10 and type FQY to exit.

Revising The Report Form Design You can return to the input form and modify it at any time. Use the word processing tools and the special features already described in this module to change the form.

If you change the database definition you should modify the report form as well. Delete all the fields you modified in the database definition, and re-enter them using the "Put it Here!" command. Then save the report form again. If you want you can save the form with a different name, which produces a new form and leaves your original form unchanged; press F10 and type FSN (Form Design Options;Save;New name and disk) and Enable prompts for the new name.

NOTE

You can also use spreadsheet @FUNCTIONS and dot commands in Put it Here! reports.

Generating the "Put It Here!" Report When you have built your report form you can generate the report. Select the Report command screen from the Interact screen, or from the Main Menu by typing UDR (Use System;DBMS;Report). Enter the database name and the report name and you see the following screen.

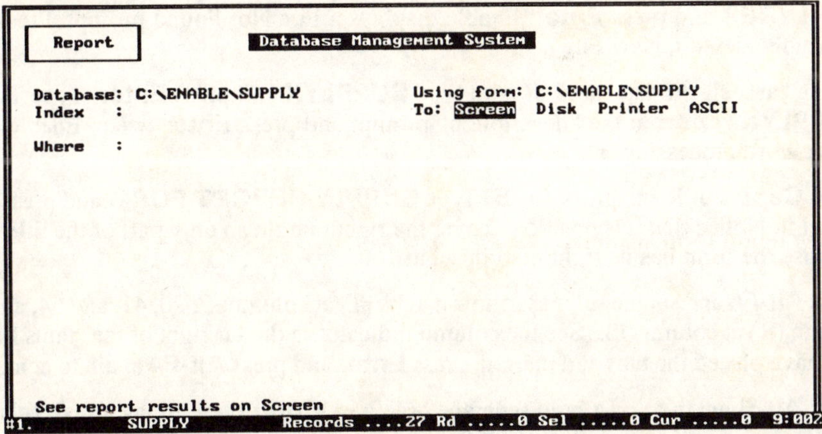

The Index, To, and Where prompts work in the same way described for the columnar reports, earlier in this module.

INPUT-FORM REPORTS You can generate a report in the same format as the input form, the form you see on the screen when you edit or add records. Enter the input form name, with the .$IF extension, in the "Using Form:" prompt. Use the rest of the Report command screen in the same way you would for the "Put it Here!" reports. You might want to put this type of report on disk, so that you can add page breaks.

DOT COMMAND REPORTS Dot command reports are described in Module 52. They are designed in a word processing file and generated in the same way as the Put it Here! reports; enter the name of the dot command file at the "Using Form" prompt (enter the extension with the name).

Dot commands can also be entered in a Put it Here! report.

READ-ONLY DATA REPORTS You can also produce reports with data imported from other databases, spreadsheets, ASCII text files, or open windows. For more information see Module 57.

APPLICATIONS

Your database is no good to you if you can't get useful information out of it. These report formats let you define exactly what information you want, and how you want it presented. You can also define the media you want it on; you can display it on your screen (you will want to do this before using one of the other outputs, to make sure it all looks right), put it on paper, or put it on a floppy disk to use on another machine.

TYPICAL OPERATION

In this activity you design and print a report using the SUPPLYX database created in Module 5.

1. At the Main Menu type **UDDR**. When Enable displays the "report form name" prompt type **SUPLYREP** and press **Enter**. Enable displays a File Not Found prompt. Press **Enter** to accept the default, New File.
2. At the "associated database" prompt type **SUPPLYX** and press **Enter**. Type **This is the SUPPLYX report** at the "description" prompt and press **Enter** twice. Enable displays a blank word processing file.
3. Press **Caps Lock** and press **Alt-B**. Type **SUPPLY REPORT FORM** and press **Alt-F4** to center it. Notice that it is positioned over the right margin so only part of the title is present, because the form has its right margin set at 160.
4. Press **Alt-F6** and set the ruler as follows: Tabs (T) at columns 7, 20, 41, and 54, and the right margin (R) at column 78. (See the column indicator in the far right of the status line.) When you have placed the tabs and margin, press **Enter** and press **Alt-F4** again to center the title.
5. Press **Alt-B** again to turn bold typeface off. Press **Enter** three times, press **Tab**, and type **ITEM:**. Press **Tab** and press **Shift-F9**. Type **?** at the "Enter field name:" prompt and press **Enter**. Select ITEM from the list and press **Enter** twice. You screen looks like the following:

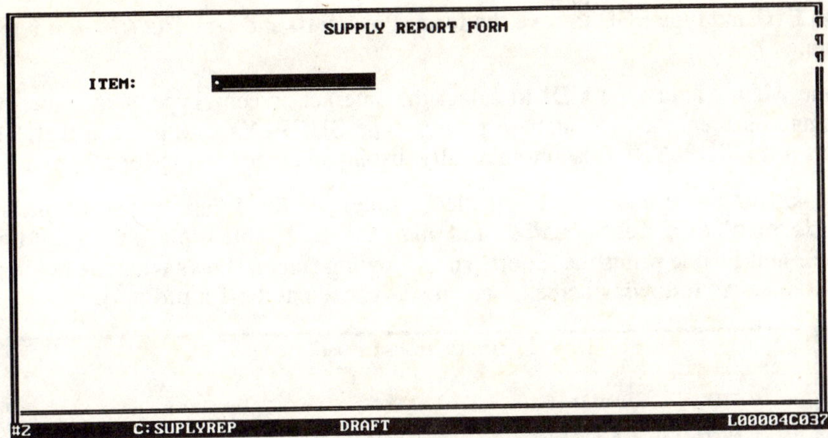

6. Press **Tab** and type **TYPE:**. Press **Tab**, press **Shift-F9**, and type **TYPE** in the "Enter field name" prompt. Press **Enter** twice. Press **Enter** twice more to move the cursor down the page and press **Tab**.
7. Type **SUPPLIER:**, press **Tab**, press **Shift-F9**, type **SUPPLIER**, and press **Enter** twice. Press **Tab**, type **SIZE:**, press **Tab**, press **Shift-F9**, type **SIZE**, and press **Enter** twice.
8. Press **Enter** twice more to move the cursor down the page and press **Tab**. Type **COST:**, press **Tab**, press **Shift-F9**, and type **COST**. Press **Enter**. At the "default picture" prompt delete the last three characters of the picture so that it looks like this: **$NNN,NNN**. Press **Enter** twice.
9. Press **Tab**, type **STOCKNO:**, press **Tab**, press **Shift-F9**, type **STOCKNO**, and press **Enter** twice.
10. Press **Enter** to move the cursor down one line and press **Alt-F3** until only one blank line remains between the fields and the end-of-file marker. Your screen looks like this:

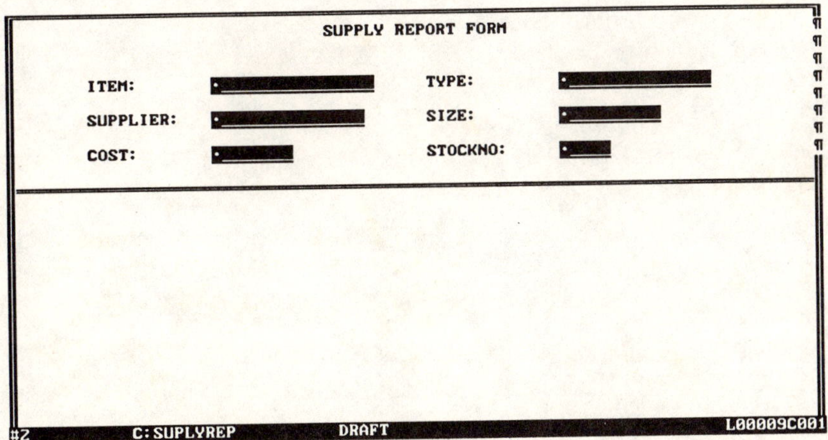

11. Press **F10** and type **FSS** to save the form. Press **F10** and type **FQY** to return to the Main Menu.

12. At the Main Menu type **UDI** to select the Interact screen. Type **9** to select the Report command screen. At the Database prompt type **SUPPLYX** and press **Enter**. The default report form, SUPLYRPT, is automatically displayed at the "Using form" prompt.

13. Press **Enter** twice and type **P** to select Printer. At the Where prompt type **supplier= "Anderson" and item="nails"** and press **Enter**. Enable diplays the Print Form. Press **Alt-F2** and Enable prints the report. The following screen shows what the report looks like (to produce the following screen, Screen was chosen at the To: prompt):

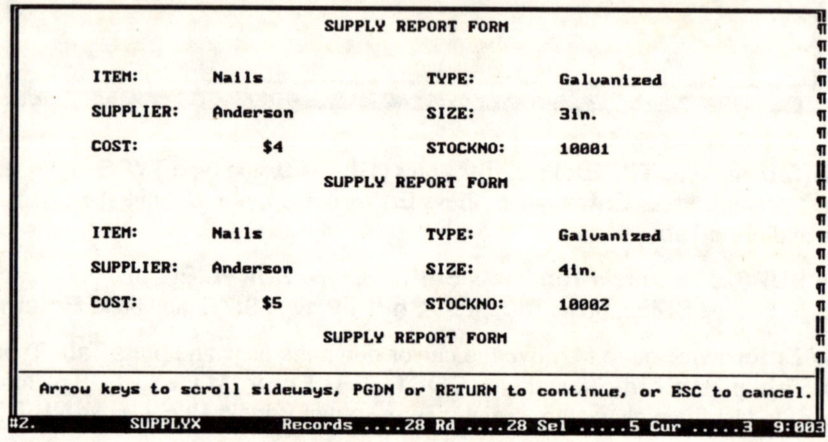

14. Press **Esc** and type **Q** to return to the Main Menu.

15. Turn to Module 56 to continue the learning sequence.

Module 63
SELECT SETS (FIND, SORT) AND ERROR SETS

DESCRIPTION

Select sets and *error sets* are special files that list records in a database. In a way they are like index search statements and where clauses; they let you select the specific records you want to work with, not the entire database. In fact the Find and Sort commands actually use the Index and Where prompts to define which records go into the select set. (Error sets are built automatically by Enable in certain situations).

But sets differ in an important manner. If you use an index search statement or where clause in the Edit or Display command screens Enable quickly searches through the file for the specified records and displays them for use. When you exit the screen all you are left with is the database. When you build a select set (or when Enable builds an error set), you have a separate file in addition to the database.

You can then use the select set or error set in any of the commands. The set has the same name as the database it comes from, but with a .SS (select set) or .ERR (error set) extension. Type the name and extension into the Database prompt on any of the command screens, and Enable uses the set just as if it was actually a database. You can even use the index and where prompts to further define the records you want to use. Any changes made to the sets are actually made to the database; remember, the select set is just a list, a way of selecting the records.

CAUTION

> Records deleted or modified in a select or error set are deleted in the actual database.

Each time you use the Find or Sort command you create a new select set; the previous one is destroyed.

NOTE

> Before you read the descriptions of the Find and Sort commands, read Module 60 to learn how to use the Interact and command screens.

THE FIND COMMAND Select Find from the Interact screen, and at the Database, Index, and Where prompts specify the records you want to appear in the select set.

You can use the Index prompt to specify the order of the select set. For example, type CNAME to put the select set in alphabetical order by company name. (This presumes that you defined your field, CNAME, as an indexed field.)

When you finish with the prompts Enable builds the select set, displays the name of the select set in the Database field, and displays a status line message telling you how many records were selected. You could then use the Find command on the select set to further refine the record selection, which would replace the original select set with another.

THE SORT COMMAND The Sort command not only selects records, but sorts them into a particular order. For example, you could select all the companies in your list of clients that have bought from you in the past year, and list them in the select set in purchase-value order, the largest purchasers at the top of the list, the lowest at the bottom.

Select Sort from the Interact screen. Enable displays the following screen.

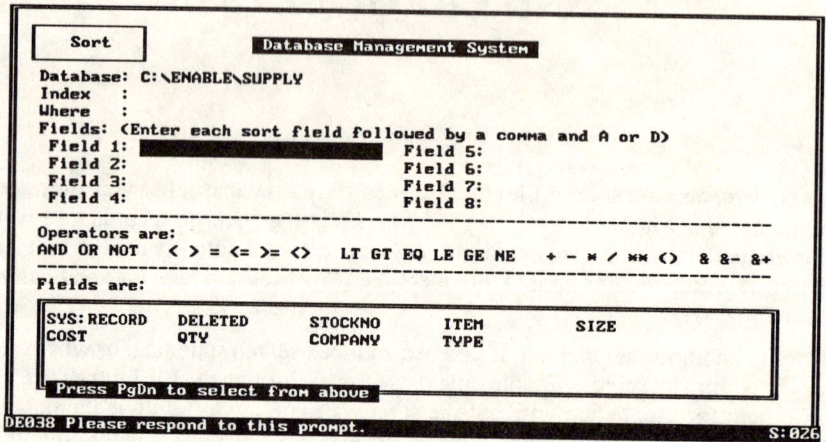

Specify the database name, the index search statement, and the where clauses to define which records will be included in the select set. You can leave these blank, or just type the name of an indexed field at the index prompt, to use the entire database. If you type the name of an indexed field Enable uses it in the same way it uses the Field prompts, as Field number 9.

Fields 1 to 8 Type the fields you want to sort on, in the order you want to use them. For example, if you want to sort a list of clients into Zip-code order, put ZIP in Field 1. Within Zip codes you could list the company names in alphabetical order; put the company name in Field 2. If you have more than one buyer at each company you could list the buyers in alphabetical order by putting that field in Field 3. You can sort on up to nine fields using the eight Field prompts and the Index prompt (type an indexed field name without any operators and the prompt acts as if it is Field 9).

Sorting Order Unless you specify otherwise, Enable sorts the records in ascending order (1,2,3 and a,b,c). ASCII characters ({, [, >, <, etc.) are put in ASCII character-collating sequence. Uppercase and lowercase letters are considered different characters; uppercase precedes lowercase. You can sort in descending order by typing ",d" after the field name.

When you have specified the last field Enable sorts the records, creates a select set, displays the select set filename in the Database prompt, and displays a status-line message telling you how many records were sorted.

ERROR SETS Error sets are built automatically when Enable creates "errored" records during certain commands. If you define fields in your database as non-duplicate fields Enable will not allow you to type duplicate text (see Module 50). For example, a doctor's office may have a list of patients, one record per patient. One of the fields is SOCSEC (social security number). Obviously you would not want two records with the same number; one of the numbers would be incorrect, or you would have two records for the same person. Defining the SOCSEC field as a non-duplicate field stops you typing the same number twice.

However, the Index, Restore, Copy, Replace, and Undelete commands can automatically create duplicates. For example, you deleted a patient's records from the database, but the patient later returned and a new record was mistakenly created. Later still, you decide to undelete certain records, so you end up with duplicates. Error sets are also produced when using the Update and Merge commands if one file has records that do not match the other file.

Error sets operate like select sets; they are lists of selected records, in this case errored records automatically selected by Enable.

Using Error Sets When you use a command that produces duplicate records Enable displays an error message and tells you to press Enter. Press Enter and Enable continues with the operation, adding the records to the database and building an error set file.

You can now use the error set file like a database. Type the name and .ERR extension into the Database field in the command screens. For example, you could edit the error set, changing the duplicate fields. Or you could display the error set, marking records for deletion and editing others. Changes made to the error set are made to the database itself.

READ-ONLY DATA You can also produce select sets from read-only data, data temporarily imported from other databases, spreadsheets, ASCII text files, telecommunications files, and open windows. However, the data cannot then be edited or added to. See Module 57 for more information.

APPLICATIONS

There are several applications for select and error sets. You could use Find to bypass complicated where clauses; produce a select set, and then select from that set to further refine your selection. You can continue selecting as many times as you want. The Sort command is often used before printing reports; produce a select set with all the information in the order you want to see it in the report and then select the Report command.

Enable uses the error set to let you decide what to do about problems in the database, instead of simply not allowing certain operations. For example, instead of only restoring deleted records that do duplicate existing records, Enable restores them all and provides you with a list (the error set) of the problems; you can them make your own decision about what should be done with them.

TYPICAL OPERATION

In this activity you build a select set of records from the SUPPLYX database, which was created in Module 5.

1. At the Interact screen type **S** to select the Sort command screen. At the Database prompt type **SUPPLYX** and press **Enter**.
2. Press **Down Arrow** twice to move the cursor to the Field 1 prompt. Select from the list of fields (or type) **ITEM** and press **Enter**. At Field 2 enter **TYPE**, at Field 3 enter **SIZE**, at Field 4 enter **COST**, and at Field 5 enter **COMPANY**.

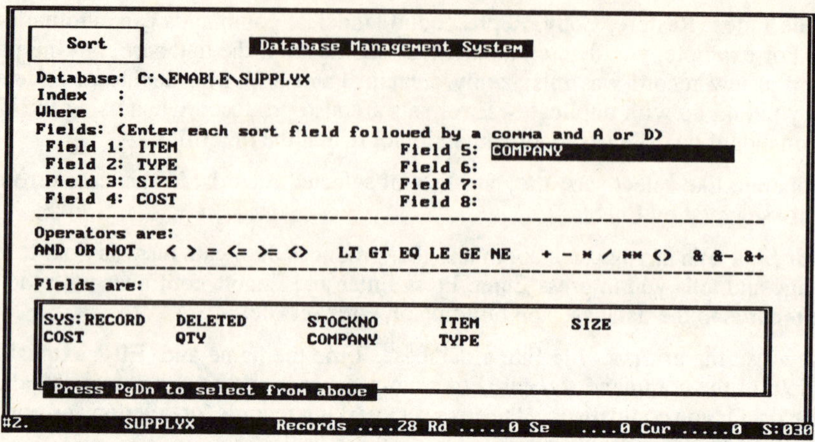

```
Sort                Database Management System

Database: C:\ENABLE\SUPPLYX
Index    :
Where    :
Fields: (Enter each sort field followed by a comma and A or D)
  Field 1: ITEM                          Field 5: COMPANY
  Field 2: TYPE                          Field 6:
  Field 3: SIZE                          Field 7:
  Field 4: COST                          Field 8:
--------------------------------------------------------------------------
Operators are:
AND OR NOT   < > = <= >= <>    LT GT EQ LE GE NE    + - * / ** () & &- &+
--------------------------------------------------------------------------
Fields are:

SYS:RECORD   DELETED    STOCKNO    ITEM     SIZE
COST         QTY        COMPANY    TYPE

 Press PgDn to select from above
#2.      SUPPLYX       Records .....28 Rd .....0 Se   .....0 Cur .....0   S:030
```

3. Press **End** and Enable sorts the records into the order you specified, puts the cursor back on the Database prompt, and displays a message in the status line telling you how many records were sorted.

4. Press **Esc** to return to the Interact screen and type **D** to go to the Display command screen. The Database prompt automatically displays the SUPPLYX.SS name (SUPPLY's select set). Press **End** to view the select set.

SYS:RECORD	DELETED	STOCKNO	ITEM..........	SIZE.....	......COST	.QTY	COMPANY
10	No	91432	Door	32x80	119.00	35	ThermSa
11	No	93356	Door	36x80	121.00	40	ThermSa
9	No	11234	Nails	3in.	3.49	43	Anderso
1	No	10001	Nails	3in.	4.25	84	Anderso
2	No	10002	Nails	4in.	4.74	51	Anderso
17	No	12222	Nails	5in.	6.66	77	Anderso
21	No	13211	Nails	6in.	6.99	121	Anderso
8	No	11239	Nails	1in.	2.49	99	Hauthor
7	No	11227	Nails	2in.	3.33	67	Hauthor
25	No	11222	Nails	2in.	3.89	225	LeftLin
28	No	11983	Piping	8'	5.85	10	Dallas
16	No	67745	Plywood	4x8x.25	8.29	322	Gerrity
5	No	61844	Plywood	4x8x.5	11.22	953	Gerrity
6	No	60012	Plywood	4x8x.75	13.24	662	Gerrity
20	No	55501	Sheetrock	4x10x.5	7.49	130	Lufkin
18	No	50001	Sheetrock	4x8x.5	4.79	300	Lufkin
19	No	53344	Sheetrock	4x8x1	5.33	233	Lufkin
24	No	30001	Shingles	Bundle	7.19	2100	Friedmo
27	No	22344	Step Ladder	8'	48.00	2	Jones
26	No	11221	Steps, preform	8'	500.00	1	Crown S

Use cursor keys to page through display. Press ESC when done.

#2. SUPPLYX.SS Records ....28 Rd ....20 Sel ....20 Cur 1 D:000

The fields are displayed in the normal way (SYS:RECORD followed by the DELETED indicator, and then the fields in the order they were created in the database). However, notice that the order the records are placed in is not the sys:record number order. Rather, they are alphabetically ordered according to the ITEM field. Where there is more than one record with the same data in ITEM, those fields are alphabetically ordered according to the TYPE field. Those of the same type are in size order, and so on.

5. Press **F10** and type **Q** to return to the Main Menu.

6. Turn to Module 51 to continue the learning sequence.

Module 64

VIEW AND MARK RECORDS (DISPLAY, BROWSE)

DESCRIPTION

Enable's Display command lets you view lists of records. Instead of viewing one record at a time, on an input form, you can see one record per line on your screen. And you can then mark the records for further processing.

The Browse command summarizes your database; you select a field, and Enable counts the number of different values. For example, if you select ZIP Enable shows you the different Zip codes that appear, and how many records in each Zip code.

NOTE

Before you read this module you should read Module 60 to learn how to use the Interact and command screens.

THE DISPLAY COMMAND Select Display from the Interact screen. In the Display command screen select the database you want, and then use the Index, Where, and Fields prompts to select the records you want to see.

Field Contents You can specify how the field contents are displayed. After the field name include one of the following brace codes.

{$}	to display a $ in front of the field
{*n*}	to specify a field width (*n* characters)
{*n*.d}	to specify the decimal places (*n* decimal places)
{<}	to left justify
{>}	to right justify
{^}	to center

The DELETED field displays Yes or No, to indicate if the record has been deleted, and MEMO fields display the first 10 characters of the memo file.

After you have completed the responses and pressed Enter, Enable displays the data, as shown in the following screen:

SYS:RECORD	DELETED	STOCKNO	ITEM..........	SIZE..........	......COST	.QTY	COMPANY
1	No	10001	Nails	3in.	$4.20	84	Osmose
2	No	10002	Nails	4in.	$4.74	51	Osmose
3	No	40144	Suppt. Lumber	2x4x8	$2.35	805	Pine Cr
4	No	40149	Suppt. Lumber	2x4x12	$4.02	401	Pine Cr
5	No	61844	Plywood	4x8x.5	$11.22	953	Gerrity
6	No	60012	Plywood	4x8x.75	$13.24	662	Gerrity
7	No	11227	Nails	2in.	$3.33	67	Hawthor
8	No	11239	Nails	1in.	$2.49	99	Hawthor
9	No	11234	Nails	2in.	$3.49	43	Osmose
10	No	91432	Door	32x80	$119.00	35	ThermSa
11	No	93356	Door	36x80	$121.00	40	ThermSa
12	No	84432	Window	6x3	$202.01	17	Malta
13	No	84435	Window	6x5	$262.78	23	Malta
14	No	82333	Window	5x8	$213.44	19	Malta
15	No	41222	Suppt. Lumber	2x4x16	$6.07	555	Arlingt
16	No	67745	Plywood	4x8x.25	$8.29	322	Gerrity
17	No	12222	Nails	5in.	$6.66	77	Osmose
18	No	50001	Sheetrock	4x8x.5	$4.79	300	Lufkin
19	No	53344	Sheetrock	4x8x1	$5.33	233	Lufkin
20	No	55501	Sheetrock	4x10x.5	$7.49	130	Lufkin

Use cursor keys to page through display. Press ESC when done.

#2. SUPPLY Records ....27 Rd ....20 Sel ....20 Cur 1 D:000

Editing Fields You can use the Page, Arrow, Ctrl-End, and Ctrl-Home keys to move vertically and the Tab, Shift-Tab, and arrow keys to move horizontally. Shift-Home returns the top left corner of the display to the screen. Any data that is longer than the space allowed for it is displayed as asterisks.

You can edit records while in Display mode. However, Enable does not enforce all field restrictions and specifications. For example, you could type numbers into a text-only field. And you cannot edit fields of more than 148 characters. Use the arrow keys to move the field you want to edit to the left of the screen, and place the cursor on that line. Press F4 and a prompt appears at the bottom of the screen. Make your changes and press Enter.

You can even edit memo fields in this way. Place the cursor on the memo field, press F4, and Enable displays the memo text on the screen. Edit the text and then use any of the word processing Save commands to save your changes; Enable shows the Display screen again.

Read-only Data You can display data temporarily imported from other databases, spreadsheets, ASCII text files, telecomunications files, and open windows. See Module 57 for more information.

THE BROWSE COMMAND The Browse command builds a list of information from an indexed field. For example, suppose you have a database of sales records, one record per sale and you want to know how many sales you made to each of your clients last month. You can use the Browse command to display two columns, the name of the company in one column and the number of records (i.e., sales) in the other.

NOTE

The field you are browsing must be an indexed field.

Select Browse from the Interact screen and select the database in the Browse command screen. Type the name of the indexed field you want to view at the Fields prompt. (Enable does not let you proceed without specifying a field.) The Where prompt is optional, and is used as described in Module 60.

An example of the Browse screen follows.

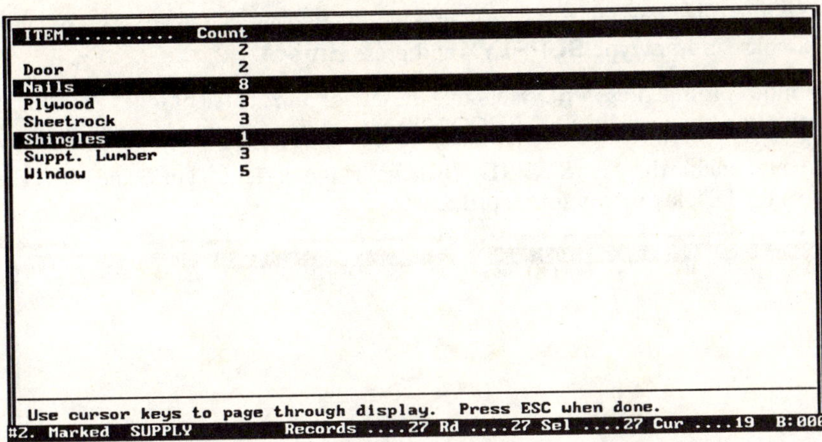

This screen shows two marked records; marking records is described next.

MARKING RECORDS Marking records is a quick way to select records without using index search statements or where clauses. You can Display or Browse your database, mark specific records, return to the Interact screen, and use one of the other commands, such as Edit or Delete.

Mark multiple records by placing the cursor on the first record and pressing F7, and then on the last record and pressing F7; Enable marks all the records from the first to the last. Or, select a record and press Alt-M to mark that one record.

Press Alt-F7 to remove all the markers in the database, or select a record and press Alt-N to remove one marker.

Using the Marked Records Press Esc twice to leave the Display or Browse screen and return to the Interact screen. Select the next command (Edit, for example). When Enable displays the command screen the Index and Where prompts have the same information you typed into those fields in the Display or Browse command screen. Press End to bypass these prompts. Enable displays the Edit screen. The status line says "Marked" on the left side. The only records available are those that you marked, not all those specified by the Index and Where prompts.

If you change the information in the Index or Where prompts the marked group is overriden and no longer available; the markers are actually removed.

APPLICATIONS

The Display and Browse screens are a quick way to get an overview of your database. Seeing just one record at a time is sometimes confusing, so being able to see them all in the Display screen, or a summary in the Browse screen, can give you a better feel for the information in your database. And being able to mark records helps you pick out exactly the records you need, without resorting to complicated where clauses or index search statements.

TYPICAL OPERATION

In this activity you use the Display and Browse screens, and mark several records, using the SUPPLYX database created in Module 5. Begin at the Main Menu.

1. Type **UDI** to select the Interact screen and type **D** to view the Display command screen. At the Database prompt type **SUPPLYX** and press **Enter**.
2. At the Index prompt press **PgDn** to move the cursor into the list of indexed fields. The cursor is automatically placed on SYS:RECORD because it is the only indexed field.
3. Press = and Enable displays SYS:RECORD in the Index field. Type **5** and press **End**. Enable displays the Display screen for record 5.

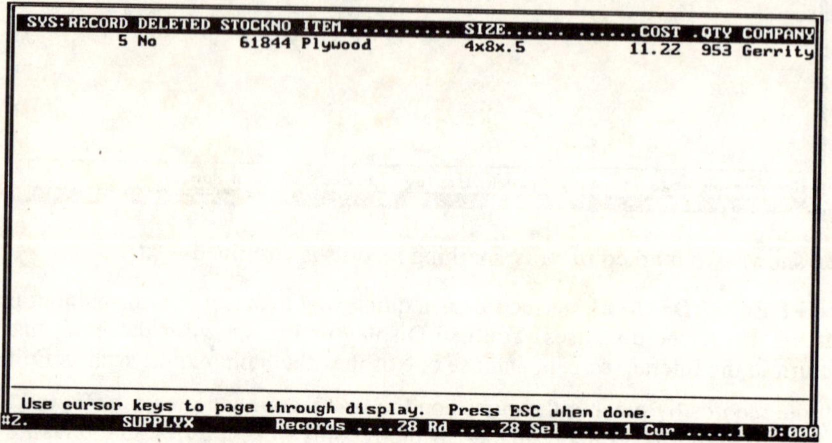

4. Press **Esc** to return to the Display command screen. Press **Down Arrow** to move the cursor to the Index prompt and press **Alt-F3** to remove the index command statement. Press **Down Arrow** and type **COMPANY="And$"** at the Where prompt.
5. Press **Down Arrow** to move to the Fields prompt, and press **PgDn** to move into the list of fields. Type , (comma) and Enable puts SYS:RECORD into the Fields prompt, leaving the cursor in the list.
6. Move the cursor to **STOCKNO** and type **,** (comma), move to **ITEM** and press **,** (comma), and move to **COMPANY** and press **,** (comma). Then move to **COST** and press **Enter**. Enable puts the cursor back in the Where prompt.

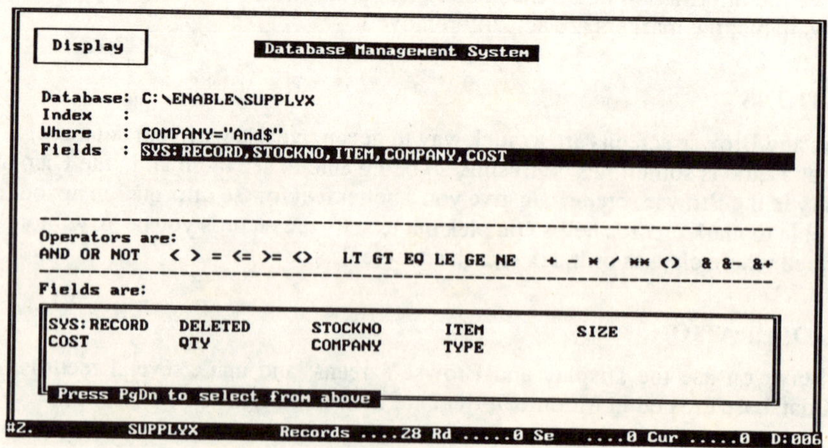

7. Press **Enter** and Enable displays the fields and records you requested.

```
SYS:RECORD STOCKNO ITEM.......... COMPANY....... ......COST
         1   10001 Nails          Anderson              4.25
         2   10002 Nails          Anderson              4.74
         9   11234 Nails          Anderson              3.49
        17   12222 Nails          Anderson              6.66
        21   13211 Nails          Anderson              6.99

Use cursor keys to page through display.  Press ESC when done.
#2.      SUPPLYX        Records ....28 Rd ....28 Sel .....5 Cur .....1   D:000
```

8. Press **Esc** twice to return to the Interact screen and type **B** to view the Browse screen. Press **Down Arrow** to move to the Index field and type or select **SYS:RECORD**.

9. Press **End** to display the Browse command screen, leaving COMPANY="And$" at the Where prompt.

10. Press **F7**, press **Down Arrow** four times, and press **F7** again. You have marked all the records with the company name Anderson.

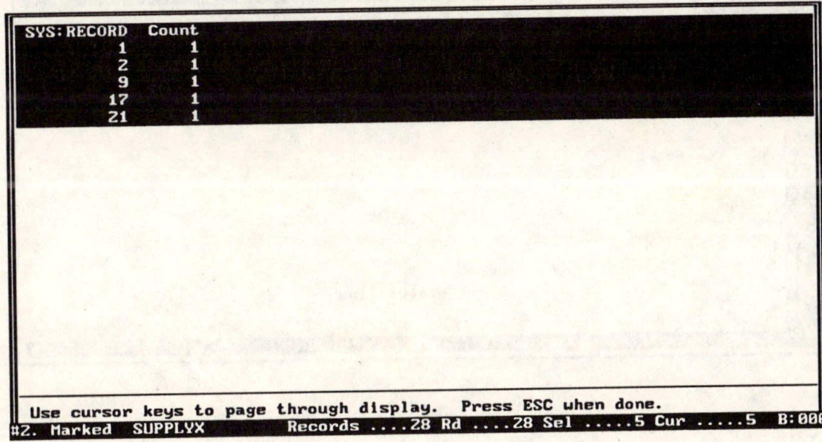

Notice that the Browse screen displays the number (count) of records with the same value in an indexed field. As SYS:RECORD is the only field that is indexed, and as sys:record numbers are all unique, the count is only 1 for each field value.

11. Press **F10** and type **Q** to return to the Main Menu.

12. Turn to Module 63 to continue the learning sequence.

Module 65
SPREADSHEET OVERVIEW

INTRODUCTION

A spreadsheet manipulates numbers. Unlike a database, the primary function of which is to store, sort, and report on both numbers and words, the primary function of a spreadsheet is to perform calculations. The spreadsheet looks much like a paper spreadsheet, consisting of columns and rows on a page. But the electronic spreadsheet's page is far larger than a paper page could ever be, and it uses the power of a computer to take over much of the work of the person entering the data.

Enable's spreadsheet can handle enormous amounts of data. Enable allows 1024 columns and 9999 rows; that is 10,238,976 *cells*, or pieces of information. What normally limits a spreadsheet's size is your computer's memory or your ability to work with such huge files. Luckily Enable provides methods for copying data from other spreadsheets or even linking spreadsheets, so you can break your work into manageable bites.

The following screen shows the main spreadsheet components.

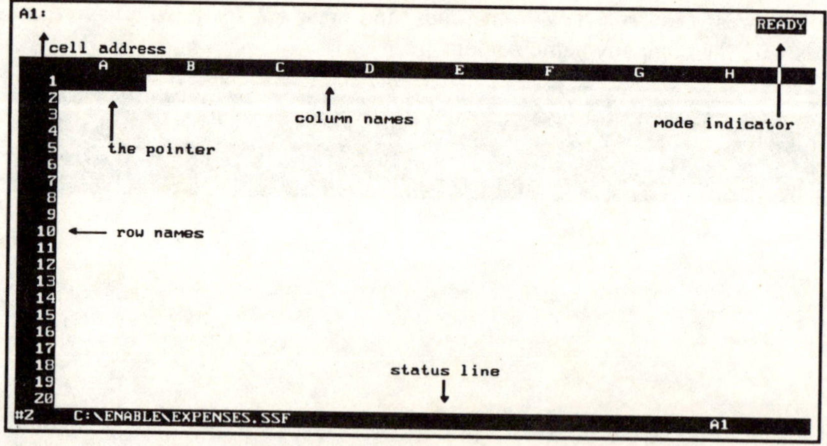

STATUS LINE

The status line at the bottom of the screen works much the same as it does in the other Enable applications. The window number is shown in the bottom left, and the filename, directory, and disk are shown next to that. The letter and number shown on the right side of the status line indicate the current boundary (furthest extent) of the spreadsheet. If Z15 is shown you know that you have data somewhere in column Z and somewhere in row 15, and you have not used any of the spreadsheet further out than that.

COLUMN AND ROW NAMES

Along the top of the spreadsheet are the column names. Columns are named A to Z, and then AA to AZ, and then BA to BZ, and so on, all the way to AMJ (1024 columns). On the left side are the row numbers, 1 to 9999. Using these two components you can build a *cell address.* AA23 for example, is the *cell* at the intersection of column AA and row 23.

CELLS

The cell is the basic unit of the spreadsheet. You can't see a cell until the pointer is on it or there is something in it (the *pointer* is the highlight, the spreadsheet's equivalent of word processing's cursor). But there is a cell at the intersection of each row and column. Imagine fine lines dividing columns from each other and rows from each other — the cells are the spaces between the lines.

You will do the actual work of the spreadsheet inside the cells. You enter the numbers you want to work with, instructions telling Enable what to do with them, and labels that help you make sense of it all.

INFORMATION DISPLAY AREA

Above the column letters is an area used to show what is going on in the spreadsheet. The box in the top right is called the *mode indicator*; it displays one of the following codes:

READY	Waiting for you to do something.
BUSY	Carrying out a procedure; you can't do anything.
CMD	Using a macro.
CMENU	Using a user-defined menu.
COMM	Processing a command.
DBMS	Copying DBMS records.
EDIT	Letting you modify a cell's contents.
GRAPH	Creating a graph.
LABEL	You are entering a label.
MENU	Displaying the Top Line Menu.
POINT	You are pointing to a range.
VALUE	You are entering a value or formula.

On the left side of your screen, opposite the mode indicator, is the cell address. When the pointer is in cell D4, that address is displayed, followed by a colon and the value, label, or formula inside the cell. When you use a formula Enable displays the result of the formula in the cell. If you want to see the formula itself, you can place the pointer in the cell and look next to the cell address, as in the following screen.

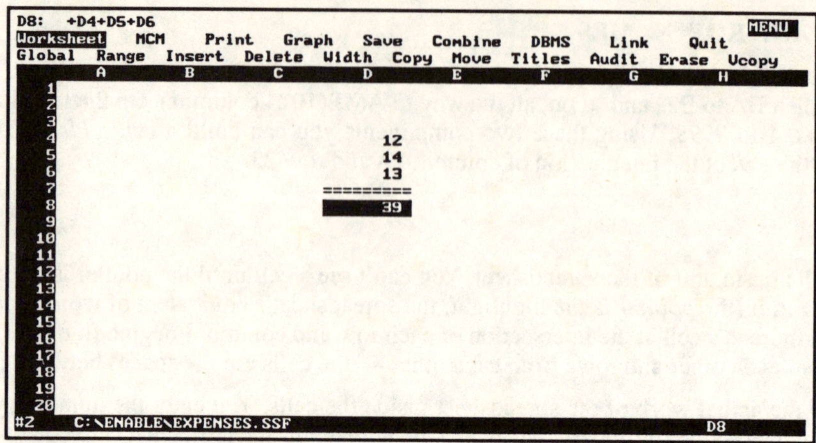

Sometimes Enable displays a code next to the cell address. This code shows if the cell has a special format, alignment, or protection status. For example, if the code is ($,2/C/P) the cell uses currency format, has two decimal places, is centered, and is protected.

TOP LINE MENU

You can display the Top Line Menu in two ways. Press F10 or press / (slash). F10 is used in the other Enable applications to access menus, but / is used in a number of other spreadsheet programs, so both methods are available in Enable's spreadsheet. This book uses F10, to remain consistent with Enable's other menus.

The Top Line Menu does not work like Enable's Word Processing or Database menus; those are "drop-down" menus, because when you make a selection a list of options drops down on the screen. In the spreadsheet, however, choosing an option in one menu replaces the menu with another list of options on the same line. And unlike the other menus, most of the options are not numbered. Select an option by typing its first character, or move the highlight using the arrow keys and press Enter. Notice also that the line below the menu options describes what options are available if you select the highlighted option, or, if there are no more options, what selecting the option will do.

The following table shows the menu choices, and how they are "nested." For example, if you want to set alignment in the specified cell, you press F10, select Worksheet, select Range, and select Alignment (i.e., press F10 and type WRA). The table also shows you in which module you can find information about each command.

Command	*Description*	*Module*
Worksheet		—
Global		—
Format	Define type of values in the cells.	73
Alignment	Set alignment within cells.	66
Width	Set column width.	68
Protection	Protect cells.	80
Recalculation	Define type of recalculation.	83

Command	*Description*	*Module*
Transpose	Swap columns and rows.	88
Range		—
Format	Define type of values in specified cells.	73
Alignment	Set alignment within specified cells.	66
Protect	Protect specified cells.	80
Unprotect	Unprotect specified cells.	80
Erase	Erase specified cells.	72
Data-Fill	Increase or decrease cell values.	70
Name	Name cell ranges.	82
Sort	Sort cells and ranges.	85
Insert	Insert columns and rows.	76
Delete	Delete columns and rows.	76
Width	Set the current-column width.	68
Copy	Copy cells or ranges.	69
Move	Move cells or ranges.	69
Titles	Freeze labels for use as titles.	87
Audit		—
List	List status, formulas, and ranges.	67
Highlight	Highlight dependent/referenced/copied cells.	67
Map	Display a cell-contents map.	67
Erase	Clear the screen.	72
Vcopy	Copy cells without formulas.	69
MCM		—
This Window	Adjust window size and location.	89
Split	Split the screen.	86
Other Windows	Go to another window.	89
Files	List files.	89
Screen	Set the screen mode.	89
Print	Print the spreadsheet.	79
Graph	Draw a graph from the spreadsheet.	Section 4
Save	Save the spreadsheet.	84
Combine	Combine spreadsheets.	75
DBMS	Import data from a database.	75
Link	Link different spreadsheets.	77
Quit	Exit the spreadsheet without saving.	81

NOTE

Some of the Top Line Menu options are different in 3D spreadsheets. See Appendix K for more information.

3D SPREADSHEETS

Later releases of Enable/OA have *three-dimensional (3D) spreadsheets.* These are spreadsheets that allow you to break the information in a large spreadsheet into as many as 32 *levels.* (If your copy of Enable/OA does not include the 3D spreadsheets you may be able to obtain the extra software from Enable Software.) For example, if you want to use a spreadsheet to record your monthly expenses, you could have 12 levels for the monthly expenses and 1 level for a summary of the expenses since the beginning of the year. You may find it easier to work with a 3D spreadsheet than with a one-level, giant spreadsheet. With a 3D spreadsheet you can just view the information for the present month, while data from previous months remains hidden from view—but instantly available when necessary. 3D spreadsheets are easy to use. See Appendix K for more information.

WHAT CAN A SPREADSHEET DO FOR YOU?

Just about any operation you can carry out using numbers can be done on a spreadsheet. You can do your business accounts, calculate you taxes, or balance your checkbook. The spreadsheet commands let you automate mundane and repetitive operations, not only making them thousands of times faster than doing them by hand, but eliminating many errors that otherwise would occur.

Turn to Module 78 to continue the learning sequence.

Module 66
ALIGN DATA

DESCRIPTION

In Module 71 you learned how to align a label when you enter it into a cell. Enable also lets you specify the alignment of values, and lets you define value and label alignment both before and after entering the information into the cells. You can set the alignment for the entire spreadsheet, or individual cells. The default is centered labels and right-justified values.

GLOBAL ALIGNMENT—THE ENTIRE SPREADSHEET Press F10 and type WGA (Worksheet;Global;Alignment). Enable asks if you want to align values or labels. Type V or L to select one, and then type L (Left Justified), R (Right Justified), or C (Centered).

Left-justified values and labels are placed at the left border. Right-justified values are placed one space to the left of the right border, and right-justified labels are placed at the right border.

Decimal-Point Alignment Later releases of EnableOA let you center values on the decimal point, in which case the decimal points in a column are aligned. If a decimal is not typed, all entries are aligned flush right, regardless of the number of characters in each entry. Press F10 and type WGAV (Worksheet;Global;Alignment;Values). Type 0 (Set Decimal Pnt Centered: On) to center on the decimal point, or 1 (Set Decimal Pnt Centered: 1=No) to center according to the number of digits. This alignment affects all centered cells in the spreadsheet; there is no Range command that will let you change the type of centering for one range.

RANGE ALIGNMENT—SPECIFIED CELLS Press F10 and type WRA (Worksheet;Range; Alignment) and Enable displays the same three options shown at Global Alignment, plus one more, 1=Reset. Typing 1 resets the specified cells to the Global Alignment.

When you have selected the option you want, Enable displays "Enter range to align:". Press Enter to align the cell the pointer is on, or select a range using the methods described in Module 82 (typing its coordinates, typing its name, or pointing to it).

NOTE

> A Range Alignment always takes precedence over a Global Alignment. Changing Global Alignment does not change those cells that have been individually set. Using one of the alignment characters (<, >, or ^) overrides both Global and Range Alignment.

CELL INDICATOR The *cell indicator* shows the format, alignment, and protection status that has been set using the Range commands. The cell indicator is a code in parentheses between the cell address and the cell contents display, in the information display area. There are three alignment codes; R (Right), L (Left), and C (Center). For example, ($,1/C) is a cell with currency format, one decimal place, and centered contents.

APPLICATIONS

The Alignment commands are useful for adjusting the "look" of the spreadsheet. You can quickly line up all of a column's labels, for example, or all the values in a column of numbers.

TYPICAL OPERATION

In this activity you align data in cells in the EXPENSES spreadsheet.

1. Open the file named EXPENSES.
2. Press **Home**. Press **F10** and type **WGAVL** (Worksheet;Global;Alignment;Values;Left). All the values in the spreadsheet are now aligned with the left side of the cells.

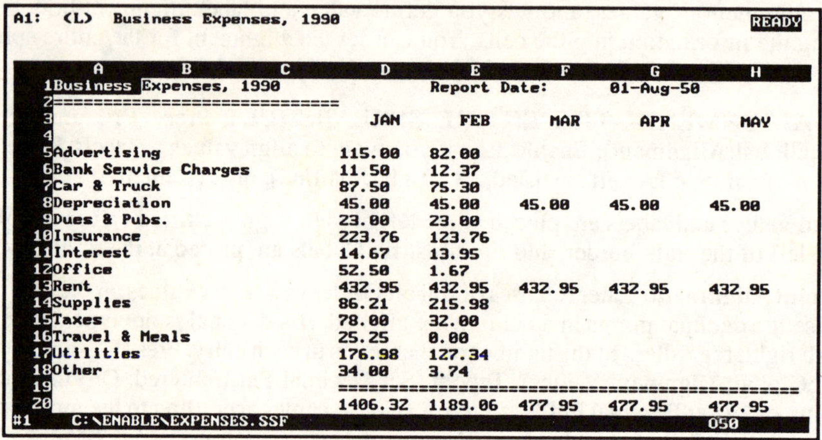

A1: <L> Business Expenses, 1990 READY

	A	B	C	D	E	F	G	H
1	Business Expenses, 1990				Report Date:		01-Aug-50	
2	==============================							
3				JAN	FEB	MAR	APR	MAY
4								
5	Advertising			115.00	82.00			
6	Bank Service Charges			11.50	12.37			
7	Car & Truck			87.50	75.30			
8	Depreciation			45.00	45.00	45.00	45.00	45.00
9	Dues & Pubs.			23.00	23.00			
10	Insurance			223.76	123.76			
11	Interest			14.67	13.95			
12	Office			52.50	1.67			
13	Rent			432.95	432.95	432.95	432.95	432.95
14	Supplies			86.21	215.98			
15	Taxes			78.00	32.00			
16	Travel & Meals			25.25	0.00			
17	Utilities			176.98	127.34			
18	Other			34.00	3.74			
19				==========	==========	==========	==========	==========
20				1406.32	1189.06	477.95	477.95	477.95

#1 C:\ENABLE\EXPENSES.SSF 050

3. Press **F10** and type **WGAVR** (Worksheet;Global;Alignment;Values;Right) to change the alignment back to right-aligned.
4. Press **F10** and type **WRAC** (Worksheet;Range;Alignment;Center). Enable prompts for the range. Type **A5..A18** and press **Enter**. The labels in that range are centered (the labels that overlap onto the next cell do not appear centered).

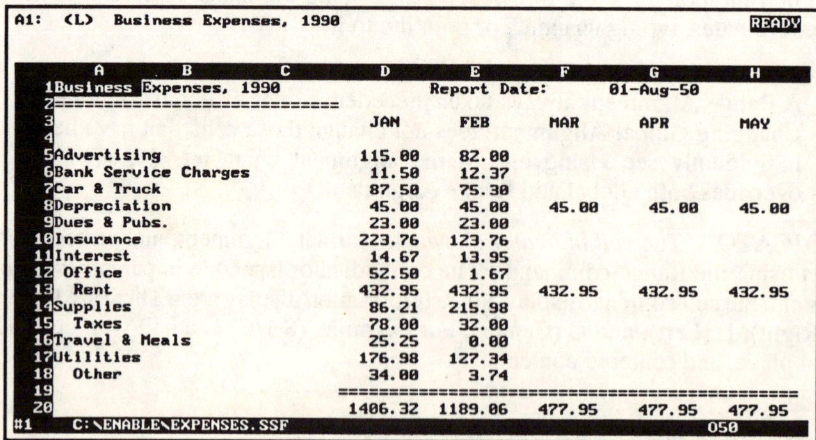

A1: <L> Business Expenses, 1990 READY

	A	B	C	D	E	F	G	H
1	Business Expenses, 1990				Report Date:		01-Aug-50	
2	==============================							
3				JAN	FEB	MAR	APR	MAY
4								
5	Advertising			115.00	82.00			
6	Bank Service Charges			11.50	12.37			
7	Car & Truck			87.50	75.30			
8	Depreciation			45.00	45.00	45.00	45.00	45.00
9	Dues & Pubs.			23.00	23.00			
10	Insurance			223.76	123.76			
11	Interest			14.67	13.95			
12	Office			52.50	1.67			
13	Rent			432.95	432.95	432.95	432.95	432.95
14	Supplies			86.21	215.98			
15	Taxes			78.00	32.00			
16	Travel & Meals			25.25	0.00			
17	Utilities			176.98	127.34			
18	Other			34.00	3.74			
19				==========	==========	==========	==========	==========
20				1406.32	1189.06	477.95	477.95	477.95

#1 C:\ENABLE\EXPENSES.SSF 050

5. Press **F10**, type **WRAR**, type **A5..A18**, and press **Enter**, to change the labels back to right-aligned.
6. Press **F10** and type **QY** to close the file without saving.
7. Turn to Module 68 to continue the learning sequence.

Module 67
AUDIT (LIST, HIGHLIGHT, MAP)

DESCRIPTION

Enable's Audit commands provide tools for managing the data in your spreadsheet. List displays the status of the spreadsheet or a list of all the formulas or range names; Highlight indicates cells that are dependent on or referenced by another cell, or cells copied from another; and Map provides a graphic way to find formulas.

LIST Press F10, type WAL (Worksheet;Audit;List), and Enable provides three options: Status, Formulas, and Range Names.

Status The following screen shows an example of the status display.

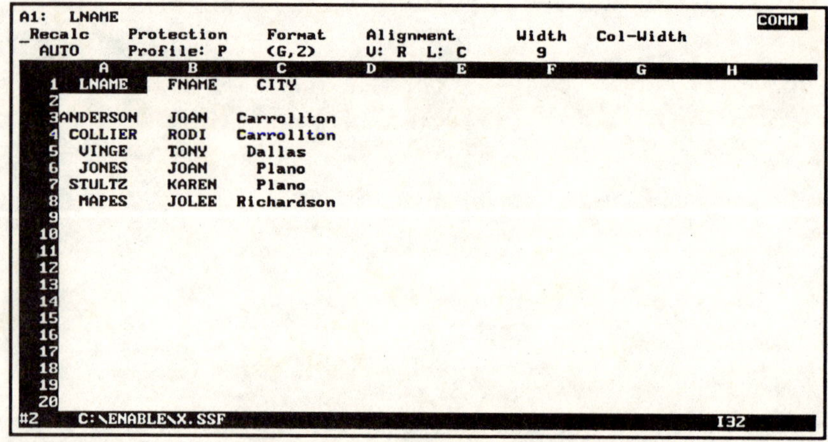

This shows the Recalculation status; the Protection Profile (P is displayed if your user profile is set up to protect all cells); the Global Format (G,2 means General with two decimal places); Global Alignment (V: is values, L: is labels); Global Column-Width; and the Column Width of the column the pointer is in.

Formulas Enable displays two options: Recalculation order and Cell order. Select Recalculation to view a list of all the formulas in the spreadsheet, in the order they are recalculated, or select Cell to view the list in the order the formulas appear in the cells (column A then column B, etc.). Use the PgUp, PgDn, Up Arrow, and Down Arrow keys to move the cursor, and any other key to return to the spreadsheet.

Range-Names Enable displays a list of all the named ranges in the spreadsheet, with the name and cell addresses of each one. Use the PgUp, PgDn, Up Arrow, and Down Arrow keys to move the cursor, and any other key to return to the spreadsheet.

HIGHLIGHT Type WAH (Worksheet;Audit;Highlight) and Enable displays three options: Dependent Cells, Referenced Cells, and Consolidated Formulas (or, in early releases of EnableOA, Copied Cells). In each case Enable highlights the related cells and displays the number in the status line.

Dependent Cells This option highlights cells with formulas that depend on a specified cell. You can make Enable highlight all cells that depend on the specified cell, or just those that directly depend on it, that is, those that have the cell's address in the formula. (Indirect dependency means the formula has the address of another cell that is directly or indirectly dependent on the specified cell.)

Select All or Direct and Enable prompts for the "cell whose related cells are to be highlighted." Type the cell address or move the pointer to the cell and press Enter. Enable displays the dependent cells in boldface and underlines them, and moves the pointer to the first one. You can jump from cell to cell by pressing F2.

To highlight cells dependent on a different cell press Esc and enter another cell address, or press Esc to finish the procedure.

Referenced Cells This option displays all the cells that a formula refers to. Select a cell and Enable highlights those cells whose addresses appear in the selected cell. You can move from cell to cell by pressing F2. To highlight cells referred to by a different cell press Esc and enter another cell address, or press Esc to finish the procedure.

Consolidated Formulas This option displays all the cells with formulas similar to the specified cell—cells that have been copied from the specified cell and those with formulas that have the same structure even though they have not been copied. This works just like the Referenced Cells option.

NOTE

In early releases of Enable/OA this command is called Copied Cells.

MAP Select Map to set or clear the Map display. The Map display changes all the columns to one character wide, and replaces labels with " (quotation mark), values with #, and formulas with +. You can still see the cell contents by moving the pointer to the cell and looking in the Information Display Area at the top of the screen; the contents are displayed next to the cell address.

APPLICATIONS

These features help you troubleshoot your spreadsheet. For example, if the result of a formula does not seem correct you can display all the referenced cells and use the F2 key to move quickly between cells, checking their contents. Or you can use the Map display to find formulas; you cannot normally tell the difference between values and formulas until the pointer is on the cell, but the Map indicates each cell that indicates a formula.

TYPICAL OPERATION

In this operation you experiment with the Audit tools in the file named EXPENSES, created in Module 6.

1. Open the file named EXPENSES. Press **Home**.

2. Press **F10** and type **WAMS** (Worksheet;Audit;Map;Set). Enable displays the spreadsheet in Map mode, as shown in the following screen.

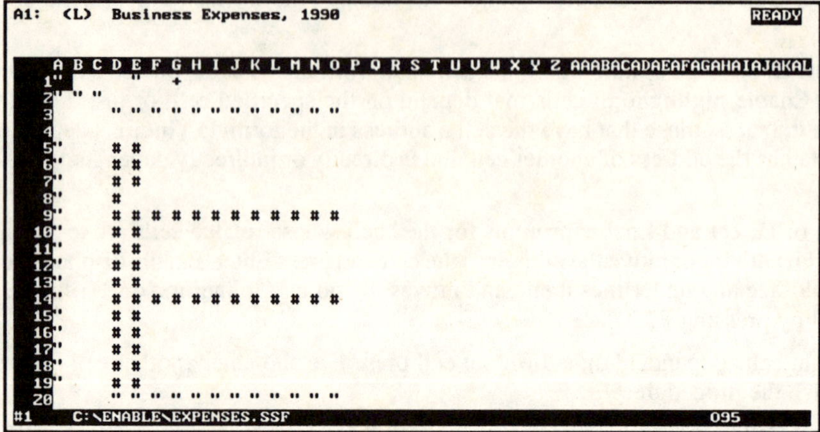

Notice the formulas are shown as + and the values as #.

3. Press **F10** and type **WAMC** (Worksheet;Audit;Map;Clear) to clear the map from the screen.
4. Press **F10** and type **WALFR** (Worksheet;Audit;List;Formulas;Recalculation Order). Enable displays the following list of formulas, in the order that Enable recalculates them.

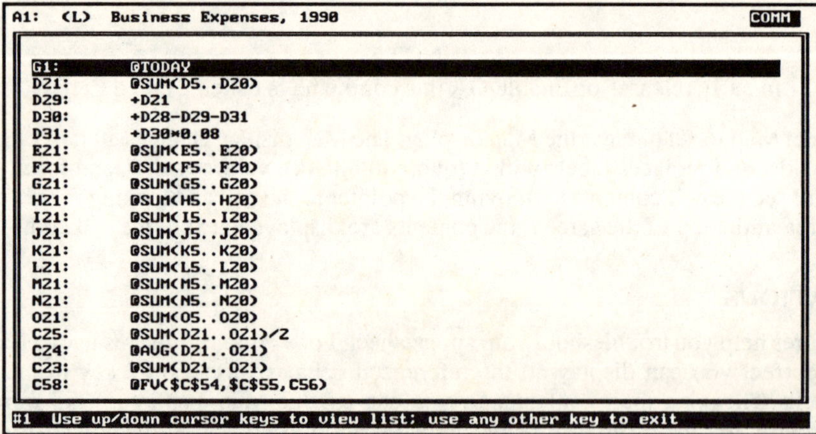

5. Press **Esc** to remove the list.
6. Press **F10** and type **WAHDA** (Worksheet;Audit;Highlight;Dependent;All). Enable prompts for the cell name. Type **D5** and press **Enter**. Enable places the pointer on D21 and highlights all the dependent cells.

7. Press **Left Arrow** three times and **Up Arrow** three times to get a better view of the spreadsheet. Your screen looks like this:

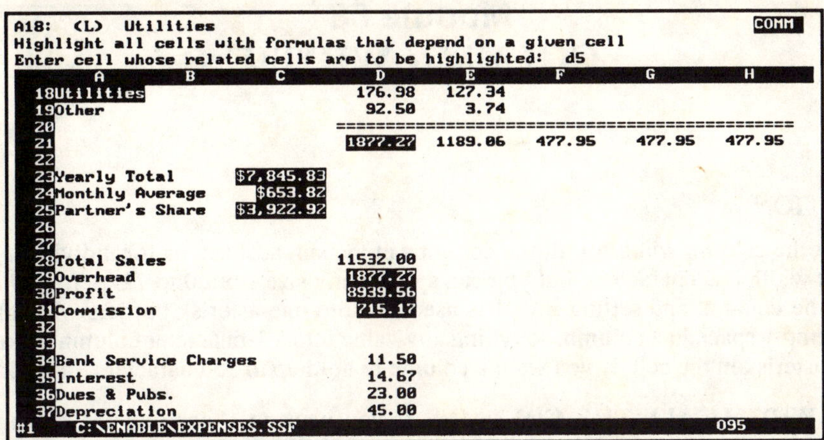

8. Press **F2** several times in succession and the pointer moves to each dependent cell, in recalculation order. Press **Esc** twice.
9. Press **F10** and type **WAHDD** (Worksheet;Audit;Highlight;Dependent;Direct). Enable prompts for the cell name. Type **D5** and press **Enter**. Enable places the pointer on D21.
10. Press **Left Arrow** three times and **Up Arrow** three times to get a better view of the spreadsheet. Notice that the only highlighted cell is D21, because it is the only directly dependent cell. Press **Esc** twice.
11. Press **F10** and type **QY** to close the file without saving.
12. Turn to Module 75 to continue the learning sequence.

Module 68
COLUMN WIDTH

DESCRIPTION

You can set the column width for all the columns in the spreadsheet, or for individual columns. The default width is 9 characters, but you can specify any size from 0 to 72. Setting the column to 0 hides the column, and setting it to 1 is used to build one-asterisk borders—Enable always needs one empty space in a column, so typing any value into a 1-character column makes Enable display an asterisk in the cell. If you want a column to hold up to 15 characters, make it 16 wide.

GLOBAL WIDTH—ALL THE COLUMNS If you want to change all the columns in the spreadsheet, press F10 and type WGW (Worksheet;Global;Width). Enable displays "Enter Global Column Width (1..72)" and shows the current setting. (You cannot set the Global Width to 0.)

Either type the new width or press the Right Arrow or Left Arrow. Using the arrow keys lets you see the width setting; Enable adjusts the width one character each time you press the key. You can use this to see how wide a column needs to be to display a value that was too long to be seen. When you reach the correct size the asterisks are replaced with the actual value.

Once you have selected the width you want, press Enter and Enable adjusts all the columns.

ADJUSTING ONE COLUMN If you want to set one column to a different width, place the pointer in that column and press F10. Type WW (Worksheet;Width) and Enable displays "Set Reset:Current Hidden." Type S, enter a value (type a number or use the arrow keys) and press Enter. If you enter 0, the column is hidden; the column letter is removed from the top of the spreadsheet, and the entire column disappears.

Resetting A Column You can reset a column to the global width setting and recover hidden columns using the reset options. To reset the column the pointer is in, type C and the column is reset to the global width. To reset a hidden column type H. Enable displays "Enter range that includes column to be reset: ALL." Press Enter and all hidden columns reappear, with the global width. Or type the range (for example, A1..A1) and press Enter. (You must type this in range-format. You cannot type A1, even if that is the only column you want to reset. And you must include a row number [A1..A1, not A..A], even though it seems unnecessary.)

NOTE

A width set on an individual column takes precedence over the global width. When you change the global width the individually-set columns are unchanged.

TIP: If individually-set columns are just one or two characters larger or smaller than the global width setting they can be difficult to identify. Change the Global Width to 1. Enable sets all the columns at 1 character except the individually-set ones. Make your changes and then change the Global Width back to its previous setting.

HIDDEN COLUMNS Hidden columns, created by setting a column width to 0 (zero), are affected by some commands and not others. For example, you can draw a graph with information from a hidden column, but you cannot print it.

You *Can* Use These Commands...

> Worksheet;Delete, ;Copy, ;Move, ;Erase, ;Vcopy
> Worksheet;Global;Format, ;Alignment, ;Protection, ;Transpose
> Graph
> Save
> Combine
> DBMS

You *Cannot*...

> copy hidden data to a word processing file.
> print hidden data.
> highlight hidden data, (Worksheet;Audit;Highlight), although the hidden cells are included in the cell count.

APPLICATIONS

Setting the column widths correctly ensures that values are displayed accurately, asterisks are not displayed, and labels do not spill into the next column. It also ensures that labels are not truncated if data in the next cell stops the label from overlapping into that cell.

TYPICAL OPERATION

In this operation you adjust the column widths in the file named EXPENSES, created in Module 6.

1. Open the file named EXPENSES. Press **Home**.
2. Press **F10**, type **WGW** (Worksheet;Global;Width), type **1**, and press **Enter**. All the columns in the worksheet are set to one character wide.

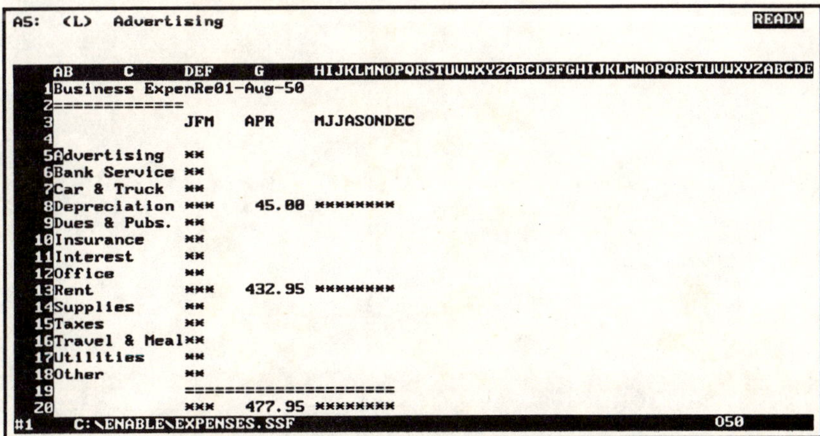

3. Press **F10**, type **WGW**, type **9**, and press **Enter**. The cells return to their former size.

4. Move the pointer to column D. Press **F10**, type **WWS** (Worksheet;Width;Set), type **0**, and press **Enter**. Column D disappears. Move the pointer down until you can see cells C22, C23, and C24. Notice that they are still using the numbers in column D.

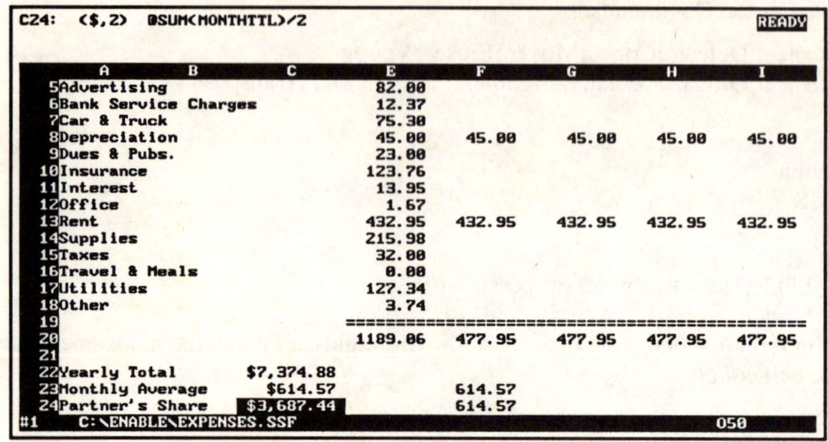

C24: ($,2) @SUM(MONTHTTL)/2 READY

	A	B	C	E	F	G	H	I
5	Advertising			82.00				
6	Bank Service Charges			12.37				
7	Car & Truck			75.30				
8	Depreciation			45.00	45.00	45.00	45.00	45.00
9	Dues & Pubs.			23.00				
10	Insurance			123.76				
11	Interest			13.95				
12	Office			1.67				
13	Rent			432.95	432.95	432.95	432.95	432.95
14	Supplies			215.98				
15	Taxes			32.00				
16	Travel & Meals			0.00				
17	Utilities			127.34				
18	Other			3.74				
19				==========	==========	==========	==========	==========
20				1189.06	477.95	477.95	477.95	477.95
21								
22	Yearly Total		$7,374.88					
23	Monthly Average		$614.57		614.57			
24	Partner's Share		$3,687.44		614.57			

#1 C:\ENABLE\EXPENSES.SSF 050

5. Press **F10**, type **WWH** (Worksheet;Width;Reset:Hidden), and press **Enter** twice. Column D reappears.
6. Press **F10** and type **QY** to close the file without saving.
7. Turn to Module 72 to continue the learning sequence.

Module 69
COPY AND MOVE

DESCRIPTION

Enable has three commands for copying and moving spreadsheet data. Worksheet/Copy copies the contents of a range of cells; Worksheet/Move moves the contents of a range of cells; and Worksheet/Vcopy copies all the contents of the cells except for the formulas. (It copies the result of the formulas instead of the formulas themselves.) The copied cells retain the formats and alignment of the cells they are copied from.

COPY Press F10 and type WC (Worksheet;Copy). Enable asks you for the range of cells to copy. Define the range using one of the methods described in Module 82 (type the address, type the name, or point to it).

Enable then asks for the range to copy to. Move the pointer to the upper left cell of the range you want to copy to (or type the address) and press Enter. Enable copies the cells.

Multiple Copies If you are copying a single cell, row, or column to many cells, rows, or columns, you must specify the entire range you wish to copy to. For example, you could copy a single cell full of = (equal signs) to several cells to build a border. However, a range of cells that spans more than one row or one column can only be copied once each time you use the Copy command.

NOTE

> You cannot copy onto protected cells. Data in the cells that are copied onto is erased and replaced with the new data. Also, in some early Enable/OA releases you cannot overlap the Copy From and the Copy To ranges.

MOVE Press F10 and type WM (Worksheet;Move). The Move command works just like the Copy command, except it moves the values, labels, and formulas, instead of merely duplicating them. Use this command in the same way as the Copy command.

THE EFFECT ON FORMULAS Enable has to make some adjustments when you move or copy cells.

Copying the Formula The adjustments Enable makes when you copy a formula depending on whether the formula uses absolute or relative cell addresses. As explained in Module 71, there are three types of cell addresses used in formulas: relative, absolute, and mixed. (See Module 71 for detailed information.)

When you copy formulas, the formulas in the original cells remain unchanged. Relative or mixed addresses in the copy of a formula, however, are changed to show the new relative or mixed address; absolute addresses in the copy still refer to the same cell as the original formula.

Moving the Formula When you move a cell that contains a formula with a cell address, the address remains the same, regardless of whether it is a relative or absolute address.

Moving the Value If you move a cell that contains a value used by a formula in another cell, Enable does one of three things.

If the formula refers to a cell individually (that is, not as part of a range) the formula is updated with the cell's new address, and the result of the formula remains the same. If the formula refers to a range, and the entire range is moved, the formula is updated with the cell's new address, and the result of the formula remains the same. However, if the formula refers to a range, and only part of the range is moved, the formula keeps the old address; the cells in the range that have been moved now contain 0, so the result of the formula changes.

In these situations, (where the data-cell moves and not the formula-cell), addresses are updated regardless of whether they are absolute, relative, or mixed.

VCOPY—DON'T COPY FORMULAS Press F10 and type WV (Worksheet;Vcopy). Use the command in exactly the same way as the Copy command. Enable copies all the values, labels, and formula-results to the "To" range, but it does not copy the formulas themselves.

No formulas are adjusted using this command, because no formulas are copied and the original data remains in place; the data is copied, not moved.

APPLICATIONS

There are many uses for these commands. You can copy parts of a spreadsheet and make changes to it to see their effects, and still have the original data to return to if you don't like the results. You can spread a large spreadsheet out across a large area, build its component parts, and then move it together when you know how much room each piece requires. And you can use it to "store" calculations off to one side of the main spreadsheet. You don't need to print them or even see them, but they are there if you need them later.

One of the most common uses for the Copy command is to copy formulas instead of rewriting them. For example, you build a table of expenses, with the type of expense down the side and the month across the top. You can type a formula using relative addresses to sum the first column, and then copy the formula to the bottom of the other columns.

Vcopy is used to copy results of calculations, perhaps for use in other calculations.

TYPICAL OPERATION

In this activity you copy cells and ranges in the EXPENSES spreadsheet, created in Module 6.

1. Open the file named EXPENSES.
2. Press **F2**, type **E8**, and press **Enter**. You are going to copy the expenses that are the same each month. Press **F10** and type **WC** (Worksheet;Copy). Enable prompts for the range to copy. Press **Enter**.
3. Enable prompts for the range to copy to. Press **Right Arrow**, type **.** (period), and press **Right Arrow** nine times. Press **Enter** and Enable copies the value to the next 10 months.
4. Repeat this operation with the value in cell E13 (Rent).

5. Move the pointer to E19. Press **F10** and type **WC**. When Enable prompts for the range to move from, type **.** (period) and press **Down Arrow**.

6. Press **Enter** to select cells E19 and E20. Enable prompts for the range to copy to. Press **Right Arrow**, type **.** (period), and press **Right Arrow** nine times. Press **Enter** and Enable copies the dividing line and formula.

7. Move the pointer to F20. Notice that Enable has modified the address in the formula.

```
F20:   @SUM(F5..F19)                                                    READY

      A        B        C        D         E         F         G         H
 1Business Expenses, 1990              Report Date:        01-Aug-50
 2==============================
 3                                 JAN       FEB       MAR       APR       MAY
 4
 5Advertising                     115.00     82.00
 6Bank Service Charges             11.50     12.37
 7Car & Truck                      87.50     75.30
 8Depreciation                     45.00     45.00     45.00     45.00     45.00
 9Dues & Pubs.                     23.00     23.00
10Insurance                       223.76    123.76
11Interest                         14.67     13.95
12Office                           52.50      1.67
13Rent                            432.95    432.95    432.95    432.95    432.95
14Supplies                         86.21    215.98
15Taxes                            78.00     32.00
16Travel & Meals                   25.25      0.00
17Utilities                       176.98    127.34
18Other                            34.00      3.74
19                              ==============================================
20                               1406.32   1189.06    477.95    477.95    477.95
#1     C:\ENABLE\EXPENSES.SSF                                         024
```

8. Move the pointer along the row; notice that each formula has a different address, each one related to the column it appears under.

9. Move the pointer to F23. Type **+**, move the pointer to C23, and press **F7** once. Press **Enter** and the pointer moves back to F23, displaying C23 in the information display area. You have used an absolute address to refer to cell C23.

10. Press **F10**, type **WC**, press **Enter**, press **Down Arrow**, and press **Enter** again. Press **Down Arrow** to move the pointer to the copy. Notice that the formula and value remain the same—copying them did not change the address. (Try this again with +C23, instead of C23, if you want.)

11. Press **Home**. Press **F10** and type **WC**. Type **.** (period) and press **Right Arrow** 15 times. Then press **Down Arrow** 23 times. Press **Enter**.

12. Enable prompts for the range to copy to. Move the pointer to cell A27 and press **Enter**. Enable copys the data. When the mode indicator says READY again, press **PgDn** to see the copied data. Your screen looks like the following:

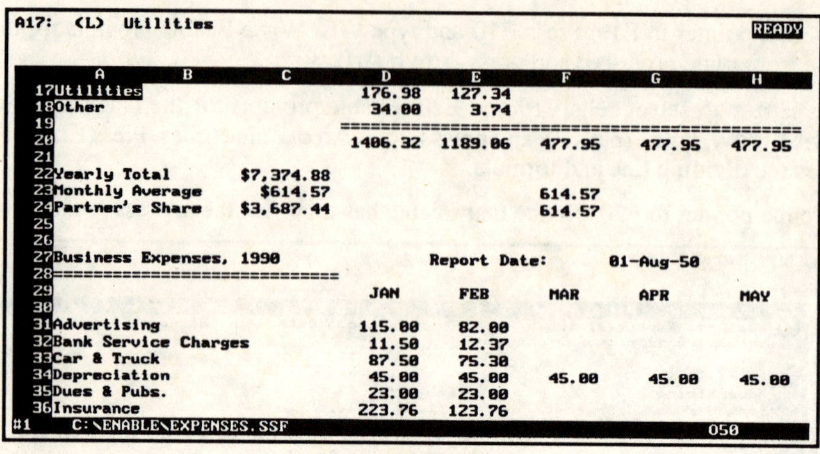

13. Press **Alt-F10**, press **Enter**, and type **R** to save the file.
14. Press **F10** and type **QY** to close the file.
15. Turn to Module 66 to continue the learning sequence.

Module 70
DATA-FILL

DESCRIPTION

Data-Fill lets you enter a value in a cell and then make Enable fill in subsequent cells with that value plus or minus a specified value, so the range is filled with a rising or falling sequence of values. Data-Fill can also modify values in a range of cells by adding, subtracting, multiplying, or dividing the values with a specified value.

Press WRD (Worksheet;Range;Data-Fill) and Enable displays two options: Initialize and Modify.

INITIALIZE The Initialize option fills a range of blank cells with a series of increasing or decreasing values. Enable prompts for the range of cells to be filled. Use one of the methods described in Module 82 to specify the range (type the address, type the name, or point to it). Enable then asks for the first value, the step value, and the stop value. Suppose you type 1, 1, and 20. When you press Enter after typing 20, Enable fills the first cell with 1, the second with 2, the third with 3, and so on, until it reaches 20 or comes to the end of the range. Specify negative values by preceding a number with a minus sign (–20, for example).

If you specify a range that includes more than one column, Enable fills the cells column by column, filling the first column, then the second column, etc.

NOTE

Existing data in the cells is deleted and replaced by the new values.

MODIFY If you select the Modify option, Enable displays four more options: Add, Subtract, Multiply, and Divide. Enable then asks for the range to modify, and the value to use in the modification. For example, if you select Divide, select a range, and enter 5 as the value, Enable divides all the values in all the cells in the range by 5. Blank cells, labels, and formulas are not affected.

APPLICATION

This feature can save typing in some situations. For example, you may want to set up a table with the day of the month down the left side. You can use Data-Fill to quickly build the table. Or in a business plan you may decide that each month's projected income should be 20% lower—use Modify to multiply each value by 0.8. You can even use Data-Fill to build long sequences of numbers to copy into Word Processing to save typing.

TYPICAL OPERATION

In this activity you use Data-Fill to modify values and begin a table in the file named EXPENSES, created in Module 6.

1. Open the file named EXPENSES. Press **F2**, type **C56**, and press **Enter**. The pointer moves to C56.

2. Press **F10** and type **WRDM** (Worksheet;Range;Data-Fill;Modify). Type **S** (Subtract). Enable prompts for the range; type **C56..G56** and press **Enter**. Enable prompts for the value. Type **5**.

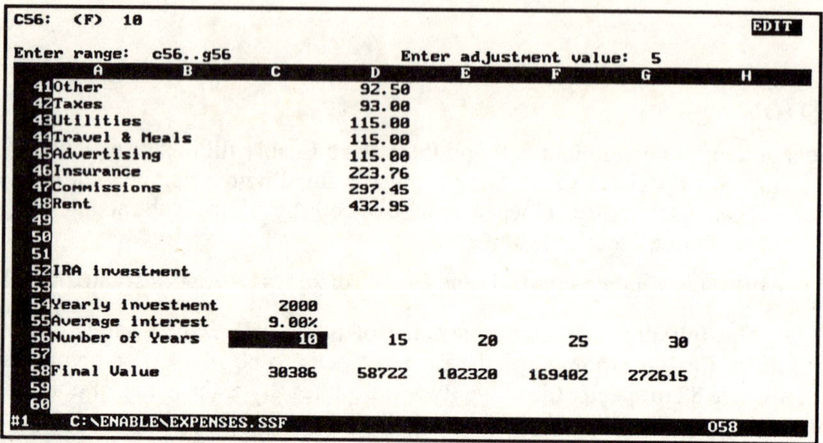

3. Press **Enter** and Enable subtracts 5 from each value; 10, 15, 20, 25, 30 changes to 5, 10, 15, 20, 25.

4. Move the pointer to A62. Type **Daily Expenses** and press **Down Arrow** twice.

5. Press **F10** and type **WRFF** (Worksheet;Range;Format;Fixed). Type **0** (zero) and press **Enter**. Type **A64..A94** and press **Enter**.

6. Press **F10** and type **WRDI** (Worksheet;Range;Data-Fill;Initialize). Enable prompts for the range. Type **A64..A94** and press **Enter**. Enable prompts for the Start; type **1** and press **Enter**.

7. Enable prompts for the Step. Type **1** and press **Enter**. Enable prompts for the Stop. Type **31**.

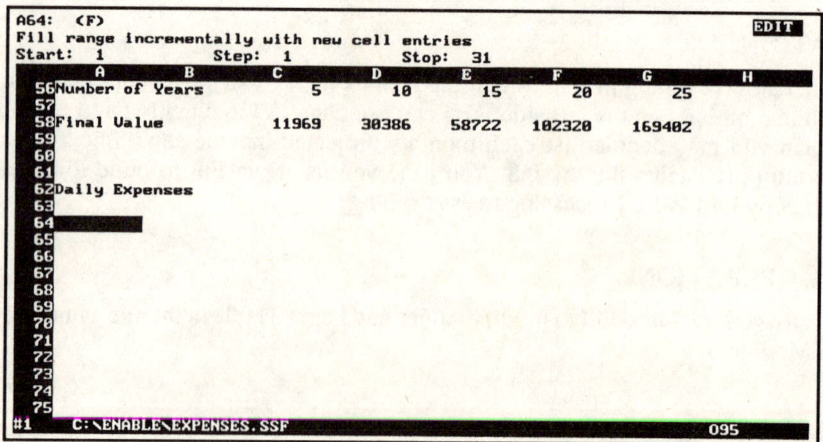

8. Press **Enter** and Enable adds the days of the month, from 1 to 31, in column A.
9. Press **Alt-F10,** press **Enter,** and type **R** to save the file.
10. Press **F10** and type **QY** to close the file.
11. Turn to Module 89 to continue the learning sequence.

Module 71
ENTER AND EDIT DATA

DESCRIPTION

This module explains how you enter data into the spreadsheet. There are three types of data you can enter: a value, a formula, or a label. Place the pointer in the cell, begin typing, and Enable displays what you type in the information display area until you press Enter or move the pointer to another cell. Enable then displays the value, label, or result of the formula in the cell.

VALUES Enable's spreadsheets accept numbers from 1.00E–63 to 1.00E+63. The number may be an integer, a decimal number, or in scientific notation. Enable stores numbers with an accuracy up to 14 digits.

Move the pointer to the cell in which you want the value. The word READY is displayed in the status-indication block at the top right of the screen. Type the value and the status-indication block changes from READY to VALUE. Then press Enter or move the pointer to another cell. In either case Enable displays the value in the cell. (If you press Enter the pointer remains on the same cell.)

You can enter a number in scientific notation in the same way. For example, type 1.23E+23 and press Enter, and Enable displays the value in the cell. If the value can be converted and displayed in the cell as an integer Enable does so; for example, type 1.23E+3 and press Enter and Enable displays 1230 in the cell.

If you enter a number too long for the cell, Enable changes it into scientific notation. For example, the cell is eight characters long and you enter 1000000000. Enable displays 1.00E+09.

The first character you type must be a number (0-9) or one of the following:

+	Indicates a positive number.
–	Indicates a negative number.
.	Indicates a decimal or currency value.
(	Sets a level of precedence in the formula.
$	Establishes an absolute cell reference. (Do not use as a dollar.)
@	Indicates a spreadsheet function.

These characters tell Enable that you are not entering a label, and indicate the type of operation.

NOTE

Do not enter commas in long numbers. Enter 1000000, not 1,000,000.

FORMULAS A formula is a set of instructions for performing a mathematical operation. A formula must begin with one of the characters used to begin values. Formulas vary from simple to highly complex. +10+20 is an example of a simple formula.

Using Cell Address In Formulas Formulas often use the values from other cells. You can type the cell *address*. For example,

```
+115+116+g24-b1
```

adds the values in cells L15, L16, and G24, and then subtracts the value in B1. Note that the formula begins with the +, to indicate that it is not a label. (It could also have read –b1+l15, etc.)

Pointing-Out Cells You can point to cells instead of typing the numbers. Begin the formula. When you come to a point where you need a cell number, move the pointer to the cell and press the operator that will appear after the cell number. For example, begin the formula by typing "+". Move the pointer to L15. Press "+" again and the pointer moves back to the formula-cell; Enable displays "+L15+" in the information display area. You can then point out the next cell in the formula. Do not press Enter until the formula is finished because Enable performs the calculation when you press Enter.

Once you have finished entering the formula press Enter or move the pointer to another cell. Enable makes the calculation and displays the result in the cell.

NOTE

There is also a method for pointing out absolute and mixed addresses. See the discussion later in this module.

Mathematical Operators The following table shows the symbols used as mathematical operators. The level of precedence shows which operations are done first. This can be overridden by putting parts of the formula in parentheses; for example, 10+2/4 = 10.5, but (10+2)/4 = 3.

Symbol	*Operation*	*Precedence*
+	Add	4
–	Subtract	4
–	Negative number	2
*	Multiply	3
/	Divide	3
=	Equal	5
**	Exponentiation	1
< or LT	Less than	5
<= or LE	Less than or equal to	5
> or GT	Greater than	5
>= or GT	Greater than or equal to	5
<> or NE	Not equal to	5
AND	Logical And	7
OR	Logical Or	7
NOT	Logical Not	6
(!)	Precedence level — operations in parentheses are done first.	

Relative, Absolute, and Mixed Formulas There are different types of cell addresses in formulas: those that refer to a cell in a relative position to the formula, such as "the cell three cells above the formula" (*relative* addresses); those that refer to exactly the same cell, even if the formula is moved or copied (*absolute* addresses); and those that refer to a specific row or column, but a position within the row or column that is relative to the formula's position (*mixed* addresses).

A relative address is entered in the format of a normal cell address, such as A1, but it refers to the relative position of the addressed cell to the cell the formula is in. For example, a formula in A5 refers to the cell in A1. A1 really means "4 cells above the formula." If you copy the formula, it changes, taking the cell address of the cell four cells above. Move it to B5, for example, and A1 changes to B1; or if you change it to X15 the address changes to X10.

An absolute reference is in the format A1. It means, "wherever the formula is copied to, always use the value in cell A1." The data in that part of the formula comes from A1 whether the formula is in cell A5, B5, or Z132.

The mixed address uses just one $ to indicate the part of it that is absolute. For example, if the formula in A5 refers to A$1, it means "use the cell that is in row one of the same column as this formula." $A1 means "use the cell in column A that is four cells above this formula." For example, if you copy the formula that has $A1 in it to cell E20, the new formula uses the address $A16, that is, column A, four spaces above the formula's cell.

Moving and copying formulas and values is discussed in more depth in Module 69.

Pointing Out Absolute and Mixed Addresses The method for pointing out cell addresses explained earlier in this module creates relative addresses. You can also point out absolute addresses using the F7 key. Press once to make the entire address absolute (A1), twice to make the row absolute (A$1), three times to make the column absolute ($A1), and four times to return to a relative address.

For example, begin a formula, point to the cell you want, press F7 the appropriate number of times, and press the operator (+ or minus, for example). Enable adds the absolute or mixed address to the formula and waits for you to press Enter or point to another address.

Ranges You can also use ranges in formulas. Ranges specify groups of cells. You can give ranges names, to make then easier to remember. Ranges are normally used in functions, but a range can be used in a formula in one situation; if you have given a single cell a range name. For example, if C20 is named JAN and D20 is FEB, you could type the formula "+JAN+FEB" to sum the two values.

Functions Functions are a form of shorthand. Enable has various ready-made functions available. Typing @ and the name of the function automatically enters the function. For example, if you type "@SUM(A4..A56)" Enable adds all the values in all the cells in column A from row 4 to row 56. Another common function is @AVG that calculates the average value from a range or cells. You can also make Enable displays the current date or time, using functions, or make trigonometric calculations using functions. See Module 74 for more details.

LABELS A *label* is text that is not intended as part of the calculations. It is there for information. It may be a column or spreadsheet heading, an explanatory note, or a value name.

Enable assumes that anything you enter into a cell is a label, unless it begins with a number or one of the value characters listed earlier in this module. As soon as you begin to type a label Enable displays LABEL in the status-indication block at the top of the screen. Labels may be up to 240 characters long. If you enter a label longer than the cell is wide the label overlaps into the next cell or cells to the right, unless those cells have data, in which case Enable truncates the label.

ASCII Characters You can enter ASCII characters into your labels by pressing and holding Alt and typing the ASCII-character code on the numeric keypad. Release Alt and Enable displays the character in the information display area. Press Enter and the character is displayed in the cell. For example, press and hold Alt, type 128, and release Alt. Press Enter and Enable displays Ç in the cell.

NOTE

You can use ASCII decimal values from 32 to 175, except 127. Also, you can use the numeric keypad while Alt is pressed without pressing Num Lock first. Your printer may not be able to print some or all of these characters.

Applying Attributes You can make a label boldface, italic, or underline by pressing Alt-B, Alt-I, or Alt-U, respectively. Press the keys, type the label and press Enter. Or, if you have already entered the label, press F4 to enter Edit mode, press the applicable attribute keys, and press Enter; the attribute is applied to the label. The attribute only lasts for one entry—use the keys again if you want to apply it to another cell.

NOTE

Your printer may not be able to print these attributes (check your manual), and your monitor may not display them (italic may appear as boldface). You can also use your printer's control codes. See Module 79 for more information.

Aligning The Label Use one of the following characters at the beginning of the label to align it within the cell.

>	aligns it with the right margin of the cell
<	aligns it with the left margin of the cell
^	centers it

The character is not displayed in the cell, but a code letter (R, L, C) is shown in the information display area in parentheses in front of the label. You can also align labels, and values, using the Top Line Menu commands. See Module 66.

Repeating A Character If you want to repeat a character until it fills the cell, precede it with the backslash (\). For example, typing "\=" fills the cell with the equals sign. This is a convenient way to build borders and lines under columns of numbers.

Numbers As Labels If you want to enter a label beginning with a number, precede it with one of the alignment characters or press Spacebar and then type the number.

THE NUMERIC KEYPAD You may want to use the numeric keypad to enter numbers. Some keyboards have separate arrow, Page, Home, and End keys, but others use the numeric keypad numbers instead. If you want to use the keypad to enter numbers, press Num Lock (many keyboards have a light to show you when it is in "number" mode).

But if your keypad doesn't have separate pointer-movement keys, how do you move the cursor while you are entering numbers with the numeric keypad? You could keep pressing Num Lock on and off, but you can also use these keys:

Shift-Arrow	Moves to the next cell in the arrow direction
Ctrl-Enter	Moves to the cell below

Perhaps easier still, you can put the numeric keypad in number mode temporarily by pressing Shift. While Shift is held down you can type numbers. As soon as you release it the numeric keypad returns to its pointer-movement function.

EDITING DATA You can edit your cell entries very easily, using several methods. If you make a mistake while you are entering the data, use Backspace to delete the incorrect characters and continue (you can alter the way Backspace works in your user profile; see Appendix B).

If you want to correct data you have already entered, move the pointer to the cell you want to change, type the new entry, and press Enter or move the pointer; Enable replaces the entry with the new one.

You can also correct data already entered by changing to edit mode. Place the pointer on the cell, press F4, and Enable displays the value, formula, or label below the cell number in the Information Display Area. You can then move the cursor and type over characters or use the Delete, Spacebar, and Backspace keys to correct the entry. You can also use Home (to move to the first character in the entry), End (to move to the last character), and Insert (to let you insert characters). Press Enter or move the pointer when you finish (the Right and Left Arrow keys will not move the pointer in Edit mode). Press Esc if you want to leave Edit without making any changes.

DELETING DATA To delete a cell's entry, place the pointer on the cell, press Spacebar, and press Enter. To delete an entire range of cells use the Range Erase command. (See Module 72.)

UNDO If you removed a cell's contents by pressing the Spacebar or typing and then pressing Enter, you can recover the erased value, labels, or formulas by pressing F9 and typing U. This is also a quick way to move things, because if you erase the data, move the pointer, press F9, and type U, Enable enters the erased data into the cell the pointer is on. This command will not restore data removed using the Range/Erase command.

APPLICATIONS

In order to make calculations correctly Enable has to know what each piece of information is; a value, a formula, or a label. These often look very similar, so following the conventions described in this module is essential. The different methods for entering and editing data provided by Enable make using the spreadsheet a very simple procedure.

TYPICAL OPERATION

In this activity you enter data into the EXPENSES spreadsheet created in Module 6.

1. Open the spreadsheet named EXPENSES.
2. Press **F2**, type **E5**, and press **Enter**. The pointer moves to cell E5. Type **82** and press **Down Arrow**. Type **12.37** and press **Down Arrow**. Continue until the column of numbers is complete, as shown in the next screen.
3. When you enter the last number, press **Down Arrow**, press \=, and press **Down Arrow**. Type **@(SUM(E5..E19)** and press **Enter**. Enable adds up all the numbers in the column.

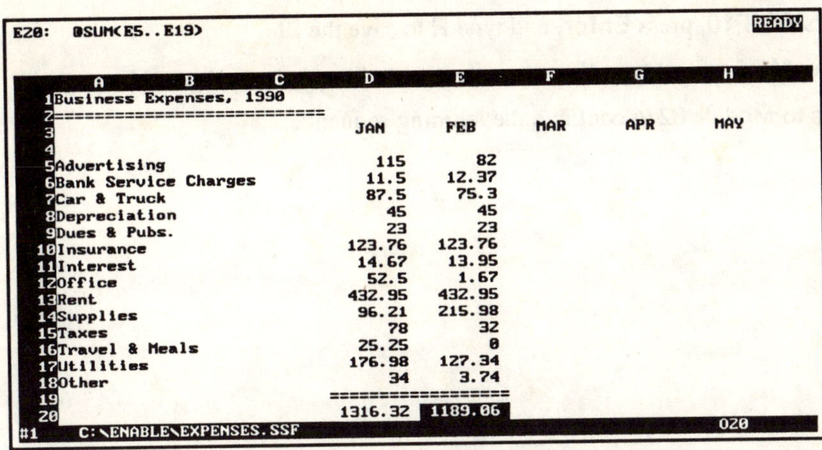

4. Press **Down Arrow** twice and **Left Arrow** four times. Type **Yearly Total** and press **Right Arrow** twice. Type **+D20+E20+F20** and press **Enter**. Notice that the total figures at the bottom of the columns are added up.

5. Type **@sum(D20..O20)** and press **Enter**. Notice that the number doesn't change, but you have added a formula that sums all the monthly totals, without typing all the cell addresses.

6. Press **Down Arrow** once, and **Left Arrow** twice. Type **Monthly Average** and press **Right Arrow** twice. Type **@AVG(D20..O20)** and press **Enter** to calculate the average monthly expenses.

7. Press **F2**, type **D14**, and press **Enter** to move the pointer to cell D14. Type **86.21** and press **Up Arrow** four times. Notice that the number in D14 changes, as do the totals and monthly average.

8. Press **F4** and the number in cell D10 appears below the cell address in the information display area at the top of the screen. Type **2** (replacing the 1) and press **Enter**. Again, notice the value, totals, and average change. You screen looks like this.

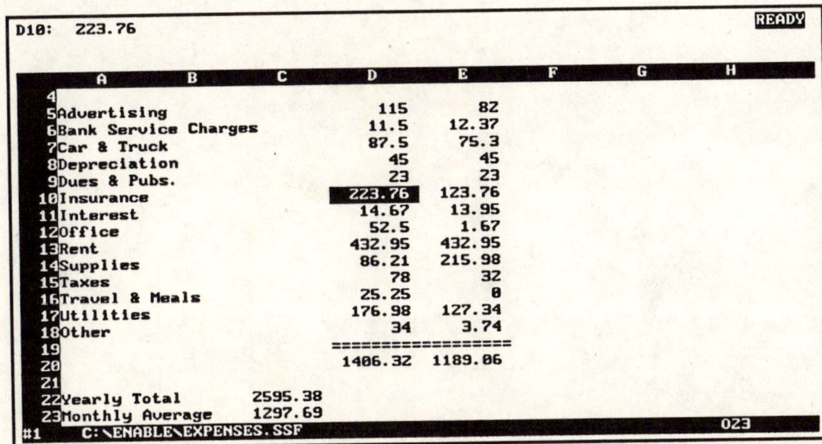

9. Press **Alt-F10**, press **Enter**, and type **R** to save the file.
10. Press **Alt-End** and type **Y** to close the file and return to the Main Menu.
11. Turn to Module 82 to continue the learning sequence.

Module 72
ERASE

DESCRIPTION

The Erase commands let you erase values, labels, or formulas in individual cells, ranges of cells, or the entire screen. Formulas that refer to erased cells display ERR.

ERASE A CELL Place the pointer in a cell, press Spacebar, and press Enter or move the pointer out of the cell and the contents are erased.

ERASE A RANGE Press F10 and type WRE (Worksheet;Range;Erase). Specify the range of cells using one of the methods described in Module 82 (type the address, type the name, or point to the range). When you press Enter Enable erases the information in the cells. You can abort the command by pressing Esc before you press Enter.

CAUTION

Once the data is erased it cannot be retrieved. You may want to use the "point" method of specifying the range to make sure you don't make a mistake.

ERASE A SPREADSHEET Using this command deletes a spreadsheet from the screen and resets all the cell formats to the default settings. This does not delete the file saved on disk. Press F10 and type WE (Worksheet;Erase). Enable asks you to confirm. Type Y to delete the entire worksheet. Enable displays a blank spreadsheet with the name NONAME.SSF. Each time you use this command Enable displays a blank spreadsheet, with the name NONAME.SSF, even if you saved a spreadsheet to this file previously. Saving to NONAME.SSF again replaces the data previously saved.

CAUTION

Save the spreadsheet first if you just want to clear the screen to start another spreadsheet.

TIP: Immediately save the blank spreadsheet with a new name. This stops you from accidentally saving the new spreadsheet with the name NONAME.SSF later on.

CAUTION

Take care not to press F10 and type WE instead of WRE. You might erase your spreadsheet instead of a few cells!

APPLICATIONS

Erasing single cells with Spacebar is the quickest way to correct mistakes and remove unwanted data. The Range Erase command lets you remove large areas of a file. For example, you could copy a file, open the spreadsheet, and delete the areas of it you didn't need.

The Worksheet Erase command is most often used to clear the screen before beginning a new spreadsheet. Save the first spreadsheet before clearing the screen.

TYPICAL OPERATION

In this activity you use several tools to erase data in the EXPENSES file, created in Module 6.

1. Open the file named EXPENSES.
2. Press **F2**, type **F23**, and press **Enter**. The pointer moves to cell F23.

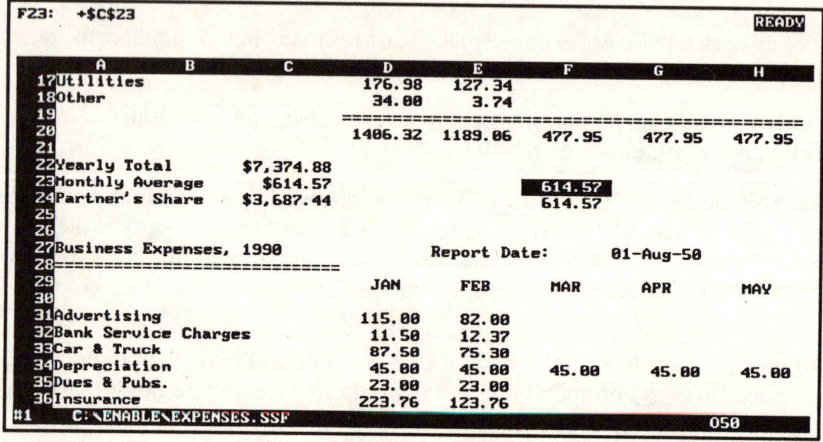

3. Press **Spacebar** and **Down Arrow**, and the formula in F23 disappears. The pointer is in F24. Press **Spacebar** and **Enter**, and the formula in F24 is also erased.
4. Move the pointer to A27. Press **F10**, type **WRE** (Worksheet;Range;Erase), and Enable prompts you for the range to erase. Type **A27..O50** and your screen looks like this:

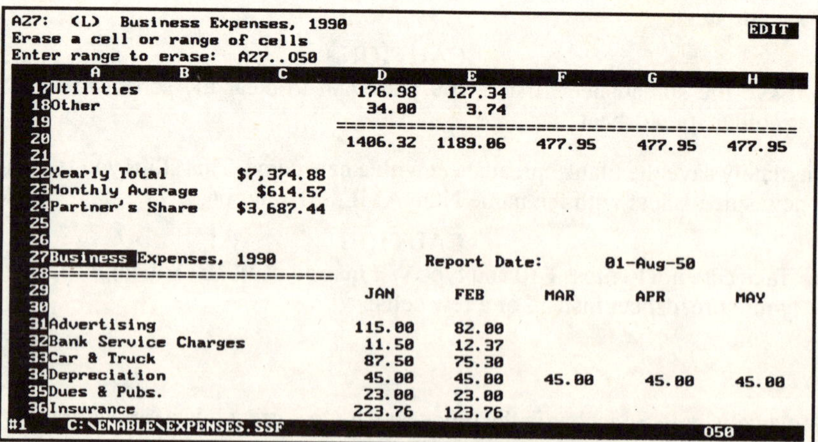

5. Press **Enter**. Enable deletes the range.
6. Press **Alt-F10**, press **Enter**, and type **R** to save the file.
7. Press **F10** and type **WE** (Worksheet;Erase). Enable prompts you to confirm the operation. Type **Y** and Enable removes the file from the screen. It displays a blank spreadsheet with the pointer in A1, allowing you to create a new spreadsheet. The new spreadsheet is named NONAME.SSF until you rename it.
8. Press **F10** and type **QY** to close the new spreadsheet without saving.
9. Turn to Module 76 to continue the learning sequence.

Module 73
FORMAT CELLS

DESCRIPTION

Enable lets you define the format used by the values you enter into the cells. You can define the format for individual cells, ranges of cells, or the entire spreadsheet. This has no effect on labels, only on values you enter, and values that result from formulas.

GLOBAL FORMAT—THE ENTIRE SPREADSHEET Use the Global Format command to set the format for all the cells in the spreadsheet. Press F10 and type WGF (Worksheet;Global; Format) to see the following screen.

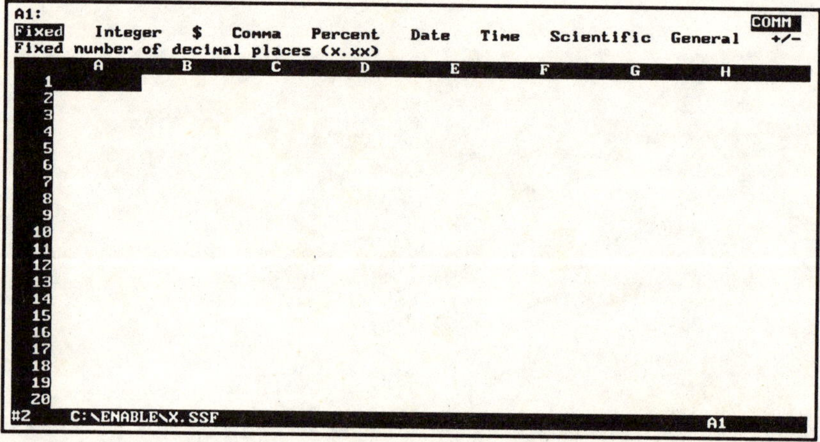

You have ten format options. Type the first letter of the option you want, and Enable prompts you for more information.

Fixed The Fixed format lets you specify how many decimal places are displayed in the cell (Enable saves a number with more decimal places than specified here, but only displays the specified number of places). Type a number from 0 to 14 and press Enter.

Integer The Integer format means whole numbers only. If you enter a decimal number into an integer cell, Enable rounds the number to the nearest integer. 123.50 is rounded to 124, and 123.49 is rounded to 123.

$ This option places a dollar sign in front of all values and separates groups of three digits with a comma. Enter the number of decimal places from 0 to 14 and press Enter. Negative values are displayed in parentheses in currency cells.

Comma Selecting this option displays long numbers with commas separating groups of three digits (123,456,789.00). Type the number of decimal places (0 - 14) and press Enter.

Percent The Percent option multiplies values you enter by 100 and displays them with a % sign. For example, you type 2 and Enable displays 200%. Type .02 and Enable displays 2%. Enter the number of decimal places (0 - 14) and press Enter.

Date Enable displays seven date formats: *DD-MMM-YY* (15-Dec-89), *DD-MMM* (15-Dec), *MMM-YY* (Dec-89), *YY/MM/DD* (89-12-15), *YYDDD* (89349, where *DDD* is the number of the day in the year), *YYYY/MM/DD* (1989/12/15), and *MM/DD/YYYY* (12/15/1989).

NOTE

You can define whether the dates shown here with slashes should use slashes, hyphens, or dots. Go to Page Form in the Profile Definition Screen, select either Numerical or European date pictures, and then select the character you want to use. (See Appendix B.)

If you just want to display a date as a label, do not use this format. This format is intended for use with Date functions. Enable converts each date to a number, the *serial date number*. This is the number of days elapsed since December 31, 1899. If you type 45 into a date-format cell, Enable displays February 14, 1900 (in the chosen format). Or, use one of the Date functions to enter a date. You can use the @TODAY function to automatically enter the current data into the spreadsheet. See Module 74 for information about Date functions.

Time This format converts numbers into time format. Enable has four formats: military (*HH:MM:SS*), standard (*HH:MM:SS X*, where *X* is A for a.m. or P for p.m.), and two elapsed time formats (*DDD HH:MM:SS* and *DDD HH:MM:SS: X*, where *DDD* is the number of elapsed days). These formats are used with date functions. You can use the @NOW function to display the current time each time the F5 key is pressed. See Module 74 for information about Time functions.

Scientific The Scientific format displays all numbers in exponential scientific notation. Type the number of decimal places (0-14) and press Enter. Numbers entered are automatically converted. For example, enter 10 and Enable displays "1.0E+01." Enable displays exponents from –63 to +63.

General The General format displays values as you enter them, removing trailing zeros after a decimal point. Very large and very small numbers are converted to scientific notation. This is the default format, the one all the cells in a spreadsheet have until you change the settings.

+/– This format displays a histogram, indicating positive numbers with plus signs and negative numbers with minus signs. This is a crude form of graphics. For example, entering 4 displays four plus signs, while entering –4 displays four minus signs. Zeros are displayed as periods.

NOTE

If you enter a value too large to display in the cell, Enable fills the cell with asterisks (the value is saved in memory, however, so it can still be used in formulas). You may need to change cell widths to accomodate values when you change to some of these formats. See Module 68.

RANGE FORMAT—SPECIFIED CELLS The Range Format command lets you format specified cells. Press F10 and type WRF (Worksheet;Range;Format). Enable displays the same ten formats described already, plus one more option—Reset. Typing R (Reset) lets you change cells back to the Global Format setting.

When you have selected a format Enable displays "Enter range to format." Press Enter to format the cell the pointer is on, or select a range using the methods described in Module 82 (typing its coordinates, typing its name, or pointing to it).

NOTE

A range format always takes precedence over a global format. If the global format is set to General and you set a cell to Date using Range Format, the global format is not applied to that cell.

CELL INDICATOR The *cell indicator* shows the format, alignment, and protection status that has been set using the Range commands. Slashes divide the format code from the alignment and protection codes. The cell indicator is a code in parentheses between the cell address and the cell contents display, in the information display area. There are ten format codes: F,*n* (Fixed); I (Integer); $,*n* (Currency); C,*n* (Comma); P,*n* (Percent); D,*n* (Date); T,*n* (Time), S,*n* (Scientific); G (General); and + (+/–). (*n* is a number indicating the Date or Time option chosen, or the number of decimal places.) For example, a cell with the indicator ($,1/C) has a currency format with one decimal place, and centered contents. See Modules 66 and 80 for the alignment and protection codes.

APPLICATIONS

These commands let you define the format of each cell in the spreadsheet. Set the format of the majority of the cells using the Global Format command, and then use the Range Format command to set the format of those cells that need a different one. You do not need to set the format of label cells—Enable allows you to type a label into any kind of cell format.

TYPICAL OPERATION

In this activity you format cells in the EXPENSES spreadsheet, created in Module 6.

1. Open the file named EXPENSES.
2. Press **F10** and type **WGF$** (Worksheet;Global;Format;$). Enable prompts for the number of decimal places in the information display area. Type **2** and press **Enter**.
3. All the numbers in the spreadsheet have changed to 2 decimal places, with dollar signs. This looks too messy, so press **F10**, type **WGFF** (Worksheet;Global;Format;Fixed), and press **Enter**. The dollar signs disappear.
4. Move the pointer to cell **C22**. Press **F10** and type **WRF$** (Worksheet;Range;Fixed;$). Press **Enter**. Enable prompts for the range. Type **.** (period), press **Down Arrow** twice, and press **Enter**. The cells fill with asterisks, because they are not wide enough for the numbers. Notice the code ($,2) in the information display area next to the cell address.

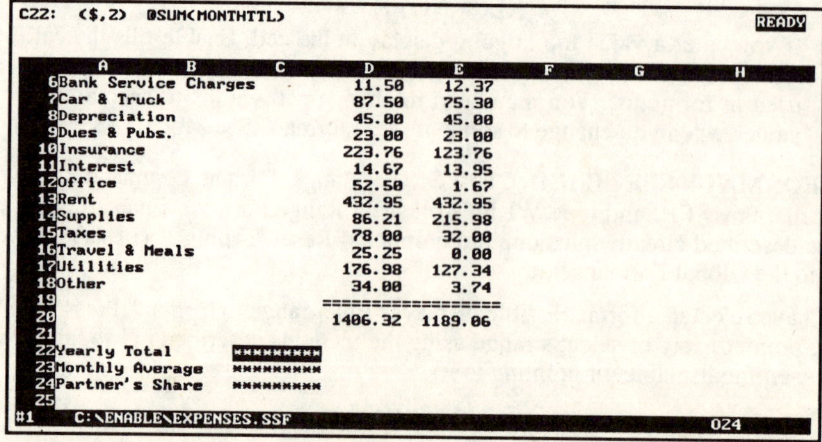

5. Press **F10** and type **WWS** (Worksheet;Width;Set). Enable displays the width in the information display area, 9 characters. Press **Right Arrow** twice. The numbers appear in cells C22, C23, and C24. Press **Enter**.
6. Press **Home**. Press **Right Arrow** four times, type **Report Date:**, and press **Right Arrow** twice.
7. Press **F10** and type **WRFD** (Worksheet;Range;Format;Date). Your screen looks like this:

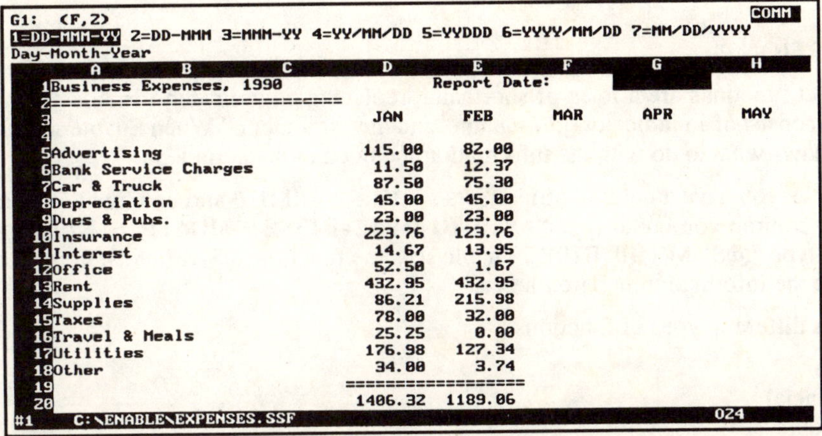

8. Press **Enter** twice to accept the first date format, for cell G1. Notice the code (D,1) displayed next to the cell address in the information display area.
9. Type **55000** and press **Enter**. The cell fills with asterisks. Press **F10** and type **WWS** (Worksheet;Width;Set). Press **Right Arrow** and 01-Aug-50 appears in the cell. Press **Enter**. (Don't worry about this date right now. In a later module you will make Enable automatically enter the current date.)
10. Press **Alt-F10**, press **Enter**, and type **R** to save the file.
11. Press **Alt-End** and type **Y** to close the file.
12. Turn to Module 69 to continue the learning sequence.

Module 74
FUNCTIONS

DESCRIPTION

Spreadsheet functions are a form of shorthand, replacing complicated formulas with one word. Functions consist of an indicator (@), a name, and the "argument." When Enable sees the function name it knows what to do with the information included in the argument.

For example, you have a column of numbers starting at cell B10 and ending at B19. If you want to add the column you could type "+B10+B11+B12+B13+B14+B15+B16+B17+B18+B19" or you could type "@SUM(B10..B19)". Enable sees the function @SUM and automatically knows how to use the information in parentheses.

Enable has different types of functions:

Date
Financial
Link
Logical
Mathematical
Selection
Special
Statistical
String
Time
Trigonometric

For example, you could use @RAND to generate a random number (Mathematical), @ISNUM to check if a cell has a numeric value (Logical), @TERM to calculate the number of payments required for a loan (Financial), or @EXACT to determine if two strings are identical (Logical).

ENTERING FUNCTIONS Functions consist of three parts: the at sign (@), the name, and one or more arguments; @NAME(argument).

The at sign (@) simply tells Enable that the next word is not a label but is a function. The name can be entered in uppercase or lowercase. The argument must be enclosed in parentheses and consists of numbers or letters, depending on the function. It may be a range or list of cells, values, or a filename.

Arguments are separated by commas or semicolons—@SUM(A1,B5,H7). The high and low ends of ranges are separated with periods—@SUM(A1..A5).

A few functions break these rules. For example, @PI takes no argument; it is simply a shorthand way of entering the value of pi, 3.14159. A few functions do not even begin with @. The function &, for example, concatenates (joins together) the entries in selected cells.

Functions can be entered in formulas. For example, "(+V60*10)+@SUM(A20..A25)" takes the value in V60, multiplies it by ten, and adds the total to the sum of cells A20 to A25. You can also use multiple functions in formulas, in the same way you would use multiple cell addresses or values.

You can also use range names with functions. If A20..A25 has been defined as a range with the name EXPENSES, you could enter @SUM(EXPENSES).

NOTE

Many of these functions can also be used by Enable's Word Processing calculator, or in the DBMS when defining a calculated field or producing a report.

The functions are described on the following pages, in groups of related functions. The following list shows how they are grouped and the page number of each description. (Some functions can be written in more than one way—@RAN, @RAND, and @RANDOM, for example. In such cases the names are shown together.)

Mathematical Functions:

Selection Functions:

Special Functions:

Statistical Functions:

String Functions:

DATE FUNCTIONS The date functions let you manipulate dates mathematically. Enable converts each date to a serial date number, with January 1, 1900 being 1; 16798 is the serial number for December 28, 1945. You must change a cell to Date format using Global Format or Range Format to display these serial numbers as dates. See Module 73 for more information about Date format.

@ADDM/@ADDMONTH(*date,months*)—Adds Months to Date
Determines the serial number of the date plus the specified number of months. @ADDM(B1,3) starts with the date in B1, adds three months, and returns either the serial number (if the cell is not in date format), or the date (if the cell is in date format).

@BEGM/@BEG_MONTH(*date-number*)—Calculates Date of Beginning of Month
(You must use the underline to enter this function name.) @BEG_MONTH(16798) = 16771 or 01-Dec-45, because the date 16798 is the 28th of that month.

@DATE(*year,month,day*)—Changes Date to Serial Number
Takes the date and returns the serial number, unless the cell containing the function is in date format, in which case it returns the date in the specified format. @DATE(45,12,28) = 16798. Can also be entered as @DATE("45/12/28").

@DVAL/@DATE(*date-number*)—Changes Serial Number to Date
The opposite of the previous @DATE command, it changes the serial number to date format, even if the cell containing the function is not in date format.

@DATE$(*date-number*)—Changes Serial Number to Date
This is the same as the previous @DATE function, except that it returns the date fully spelled out, as in December 28, 1945.

@DAY(*date-number*)—The Day Of The Month
Returns the day of the month. @DAY(16798) = 28, because 16798 is December 28, 1945.

@ENDM/@END_MONTH(*date-number*)—Calculates Date of End of Month
Works like @BEG_MONTH except it returns the last day of the month.

@JULIAN(*date-number*)—2-digit Year, 3-digit Day
Returns the date in the form YYDDD, where YY is the year and DDD is the number of the day within the year. @JULIAN(16798) = 45362 (1945, 362nd day of the year).

@MONTH(*date-number*)—The Number of the Month
Returns the number of the month in that year. @MONTH(16798) = 12.

@MONTHS$(*date-number*)—The Name of the Month
Works like @MONTH, except the month is spelled out. @MONTH$(16798) = December.

@TODAY—Today's Date
Use this like the word processing automatic date function. @TODAY does not require an argument. The date must be set when you log on to Enable, and if the cell is formatted as a Date cell, today's date is displayed. If not, Enable displays the serial number.

@WEEKDAY(*date-number*)—Day of the Week
Displays the day of the week, as a number. @WEEKDAY(16798) = 5. (Monday is 1.)

@WEEKDAY$(*date-number*)—The Name of the Day of the Week
Like @WEEKDAY except the day is spelled out. @WEEKDAY(16798) = Friday.

@YEAR(*date-number*)—The 2-digit Year
Displays the two-digit year. @YEAR(16798) = 45.

@YEAR$(*date-number*) — The 4-digit Year
Displays the four-digit year. @YEAR$(16798) = 1945.

FINANCIAL FUNCTIONS The following is a list of the financial functions. Interest rates must always be entered as decimal fractions (.125, not 12.5%), and the interest rate and term must always be in the same time units. If you define term in months, the interest rate must be in months.

@CTERM(*interest,future value,present value)*—Compounding Terms
Calculates the number of compounding terms to reach the future value. @CTERM (.1,100000,50000) calculates how long it takes for an investment of 50,000 "units" (dollars, yen, etc.) to grow to 100,000 with an annual percentage rate of 10%. (If the interest compounds monthly, use the monthly interest rate and Enable calculates the number of months.)

@FV(*payment,interest,term*)—Future Value
Calculates the future value of an investment depending on regular and equal payments, the interest rate, and the term. @FV(2000,.08,30) = 226566 where the investment is 2000, the interest rate 8%, and the term 30 payments. If the investment compounds yearly, use the annual percentage, the yearly investment, and the number of years. If it compounds monthly, use the monthly interest rate, the monthly investment, and the number of months.

@IRR(*estimated rate,range with payments*)—Internal Rate of Return
Calculates the expected profit from an investment when a series of unequal payments is expected at regular intervals. You provide an estimate of the rate, and a range of cells that contain the initial investment (as a negative figure) in the first cell and the payments on the investment in the subsequent cells. For example, the range C58 to C63 contains –8000, 1000, 1000, 3000, 3000, 4000. @IRR(.1,C58..C63) returns 12.01%.

@NPV(*interest,range with expected payments*)—Net Present Value
Calculates the present value of an investment discounted at a specified interest rate, when unequal payments are expected at regular intervals. Enable assumes the payments occur at the end of the period.

@PMT(*principal,interest,term*)—Payment Per Period

Calculates periodical payments when you know the principal, the interest rate, and the payment term (the number of payments). Remember the interest rate and the term must use the same time periods, so if you want to use monthly payments, you must provide the monthly interest rate. @PMT(73000,.01,360) = 750.89 means that a $73,000 loan with a monthly interest rate of 1 percent and 360 payments (30 years) requires a $750.89 monthly payment.

@PV(*payment,interest,term*)—Present Value of Annuity or Loan

This is the inverse of @PMT, calculating how much principal you can borrow if you know the term and how much you can pay each pay period. Or it can calculate the value of an annuity; you have an annuity and know how much it will pay you and for how long; @PV tells you how much it is worth.

@RATE(*future value,present value,term*)—Rate Required

Calculates the interest rate at which the present value must grow to reach the future value within the term.

@TERM(*payment,interest rate,future value*)—Number of Payments

Calculates the number of payments required to build an investment (or pay off a loan) when you know the future value you want (or the present value of the loan), the amount of the investment (or payment), and the interest rate.

LINK FUNCTIONS Enable has several functions for linking spreadsheets. These are described in detail in Module 77.

@EXTCOPY(@LINK(*#filename,"range"*),*range*)—Get Contents of Another Spreadsheet Range

Used with @LINK to copy information from a specified range in another spreadsheet.

@ISREF(*cell*)—Check For REF

Checks a cell for the REF indicator, an indication of inactive spreadsheet links.

@LINK(*#spreadsheet,cell*)—Get Contents of Another Spreadsheet Cell

Copies information from a specified cell in another spreadsheet.

@MACRO(*#spreadsheet,"display cell,execute cell"*)—Retrieve A Macro

Uses a macro built in another spreadsheet.

@PRTCL(*#spreadsheet,"code"*)—Retrieve Printer Control Code

Uses a printer control code in another spreadsheet.

@RNGSTR(*range*)—Relative Addresses in @LINK

Builds relative addresses for use in @LINK.

LOGICAL FUNCTIONS The logical functions are used in conditional formulas, where Enable has alternative courses of action depending on the status of conditions in the spreadsheet.

You can substitute the logical operators AND, OR, and NOT for the functions @AND, @OR, and @NOT. For example, you can type (A1=5 OR A1=6) AND (B10<>4) instead of @AND ((@OR(A1=5,A1=6),(B10<>4)). However, Enable processes the @ functions faster than the logical operators.

@ALPHA(*argument*)—Test for Letters
Returns 1 if all the characters in the specified cell are letters or spaces, or 0 if some or all of the characters are numbers or special characters. If cell B3 contains "Monday 9," then @ALPHA(B3) = 0.

@AND(*list of arguments*)—Logical And
Returns 1 if all the arguments are true. For example, B3 contains the value 10, so @AND(B3>0,B3<100) = 1.

@ERR—Error Indication
Used to return ERR if an error condition is present. Usually combined with @If. For example, @IF(C3<15000,@ERR,"CORRECT") means that if the value in C3 is less than 15000 the formula's cell displays ERR, if it is not it displays CORRECT.

@EXACT(*string1,string2*) — Compares Two Strings
Compares two strings (of non-numeric entries) and returns 1 if they are exactly the same or 0 if they are different. Can be used with @IF to "trigger" other actions. For example @EXACT(B2,B18) compares the text or non-numeric characters in B2 and B18). @EXACT(B2,"Paid") looks at B2 and returns 0 if the characters are not "Paid," even if they are PAID.

@EXIST("*filename*")—Determines if File Exists
Returns 1 if the specified file exists. Enter, in double quotation marks, the name of the file, and the disk and path if the file is not in the default data directory. Or enter the address of a cell with the information. @EXIST("A:\DATA\SPREAD.SSF") searches for the file in the DATA directory on disk drive A, and returns 1 if it finds the file.

@FALSE—False
Needs no argument. Returns 0 if a condition is false. @IF(B56>100,@FALSE,@TRUE) means display 0 if B56 is greater than 100 or 1 if it is not. You could substitute 0 for @FALSE, but this method clearly shows that the formula is intended to produce a logical value, making the formula "self-documenting."

@IF(*condition,result,result*)—If-Then Decisions
Lets Enable make a decision depending on the condition; if the condition is true, Enable returns the first result; if it is not, Enable returns the second. For example, @IF(B1= 10000,A15,A16) means that if the value in B1 is equal to 10000 return the value from A15, but if B1 is not equal return the value in A16.

@ISBLANK(*cell*)—Checks if Cell is Blank
Returns 1 if the cell is blank, 0 if it is not. @ISBLANK(F14) = 1 if the cell is blank F14. Blank cells may still contain formulas, as long as they don't display anything on the screen.

@ISEMPTY(*cell*)—Checks if Cell is Empty
If @ISEMPTY finds data, formulas, or cell attributes it returns 0 (no). If the cell is empty it returns 1.

@ISERROR/@ISERR(*cell*)—Checks for ERR
Returns 1 if an error condition (ERR) is found in the specified cell, 0 if it is not.

@ISLABEL(*cell*)—Checks for Label
Returns 1 if the specified cell contains a label, or a formula that returns a non-numeric string, or 0 if it doesn't.

@ISNA(*cell*)—Checks for NA
Returns 1 if the cell contains NA, 0 if it doesn't. See @NA.

@ISNUM(*cell*)—Checks for Number
Returns 1 if the cell contains a numeric value, or a formula that returns a numeric value, and 0 if it doesn't.

@ISREF(*cell*)—Checks for REF
Returns 1 if the cell contains REF, 0 if it doesn't. REF indicates an inactive spreadsheet link. See @LINK in the Linking Functions.

@NA—Not Available
Requires no argument. Returns NA if a value is not available. Cells that reference an NA cell also display NA. @IF(B12<0,@NA,B12) means if the value in B12 is less than 0 return NA, but if it is 0 or more than 0 return the value.

@NO—No or False
The same as @FALSE.

@NOT(*argument*)—Logical NOT
Reverses True=1 and False=0. If the argument has the value 0 (false) @NOT returns 1, and if it has the value 1 (true) it returns 0. Only one argument can be entered. If B12 = 15, then @NOT(B12>10) = 0.

@NUMERIC(*string*)—Determines if String is Numeric
Returns 1 if the string contains only numeric characters. A numeric string is a label consisting of only numbers, no letters or special characters. Returns ERR if the argument is not a string expression (if it is a value or formula) or if the cell is empty.

@OR(*list of arguments*)—Logical OR
Returns 1 if any of the listed arguments are correct. For example @OR(B1>100,B2<100) = 1 if B1 is greater than 100 or if B2 is less than 100.

@TRUE—True
Needs no argument. Returns 0 if a condition is true. @IF(B56>100,@FALSE,@TRUE) means display 0 if B56 is greater than 100 or 1 if it is not. You could substitute 1 for @TRUE, but this method clearly shows that the formula is intended to produce a logical value, making the formula "self-documenting."

@YES—True
The same as @TRUE.

MATHEMATICAL FUNCTIONS The following is a list of Enable's mathematical functions.

@ABS(*argument*)—Absolute Value

Computes the absolute value of an argument, always a positive number. Used to calculate the difference between two numbers. Instead of using the – (minus sign), which may return a negative value, use @ABS to convert negative values to positive. For example, A1=10, A2=35, A3=+A1–A2, so @ABS(A3) = 25.

@E—Natural Number E

This is the base of natural logarithms. Requires no argument. E = 2.7182818284590

@EXP(*argument*)—Exponentiation Of E

The natural number E raised to the power of the value in parentheses. @E(B12) is the power of the value in cell B12. @EXP(10) = 22026.4658.

@EXP10(*argument*)—Exponentiation of 10

10 raised to the power of the value in parentheses. @EXP10(5) = 10000.

@INT(*argument*)—Integer

Truncates the value in parentheses to create an integer. Both @INT(3.99) and @INT(3.01) produce the number 3.

@LN—see @NLOG

@LOG10(*argument*)/@LOG(*argument*)—Logarithm Base 10

Returns the base 10 logarithmic value of the value in parentheses. The argument must be greater than zero or Enable returns ERR. @LOG(G6) returns the log of the value in G6. @LOG(100) = 2.

@MOD(*argument*)—Modulus

The modulus is what is left over after a value has been divided by another. @MOD(17,4) = 1, because four goes into 17 four times, so 1 is left over. If the second part of the argument is zero, Enable returns ERR.

@NLOG(*argument*)—Logarithm Base e

Also entered as @LN, @NLOG returns the logarithm of the natural base e. The argument must be greater than zero. @NLOG(10) = 2.3026

@PRODUCT(*nexp,nexp*)—Product of a List of Numbers

This function multiplies the specified numbers. For example, @PRODUCT(2,4,2,10) returns 160 (2 x 4 x 2 x 10). @PRODUCT(3,F5) multiplies the value in cell F5 by 3.

@RAN/@RAND/@RANDOM—Random Number

Returns a random number from 0.0 to 1.0. Does not require an argument. Add or multiply @RAND by a constant to move the starting point or enlarge the range. (@RAND*10)*B15 multiplies the value in B15 by a random number with a range from 0.0 to 10.0. You can calculate the random number over again by pressing F5 to recalculate.

@ROUND(*value,decimal places*)—Rounds a Value

Rounds the first value to the number of decimal places specified in the second. @ROUND (22.3479,3) = 22.348. @ROUND(22.3479,2) = 22.35. @ROUND(E5,2) rounds the value in E5 to 2 decimal places. You can also round the number to an integer by specifying a negative number. –1 rounds to tens, –2 rounds to hundreds. For example, @ROUND (125.3,–1) = 120, @ROUND(125.3,–2) = 100. Or enter 0 to round a decimal number to an integer. Note that Enable only uses the value immediately to the right of the specified decimal places to determine how to round the number. It will not cumulatively round. For example,

@ROUND(22.3479,3) = 22.348, but @ROUND(22.34745,3) = 22.347, that is, in the second example it will not round the 4 to a 5 and use that number to round the 7 to an 8. If the second number is not an integer, Enable rounds it before using it to round the first number.

@SIGN(*argument*)—Sign of a Value
Indicates the sign of the value in the argument, positive or negative. If the value in B15 is negative, @SIGN(B15) = –1, if the value is positive it equals 1.

@SQRT(*argument*)—Square Root
The square root of the value. @SQRT(16) = 4. The argument must be greater then zero.

@TRUNC(*value,decimal places*)—Truncates a Value
Truncates all the digits past the decimal places specified by the second part of the argument. @TRUNC(22.347987463,3) = 22.347.

@UROUND(*argument*)—Unbiased Rounding
Works like @ROUND, rounding the first value to the number of decimal places specified in the second. However, it works differently in one situation; if the digit to the right of the specified number of decimal places is 5 and the last specified decimal digit is an even number. In this case the number is actually rounded down. For example, @UROUND (1.235,2) = 1.24, but @UROUND(1.245,2) = 1.24.

SELECTION FUNCTIONS The selection functions search for specified values.

@CHOOSE(*position,list*)—Choose From a List
Selects a value or string expression from a list depending on the specified position. Position number 0 is the first position. @CHOOSE(4,A1,A2,A3,A4,A7,A8A,B15) returns the value in A7. The position could be a value in a cell. The list could be a range of cells.

@HLOOKUP(*key value,range,offset*)—Looks Up Value in Table of Rows
Horizontal Lookup retrieves values from a lookup table of rows. The key value is a number, or cell containing a number. The range is the lookup table, and the first cell in the range defines which row is the key row (A5..D12 means that the row 5 is the key row). Enable searches for the cell in the key row with the largest value that does not exceed the key value. When it finds this cell it looks at the column beginning at that cell. The offset tells it how many cells to move down the table. 0 means stay in the cell, so Enable returns the value in the key row (the largest value that does not exceed the key value). If the offset is 1 Enable moves one cell down the table and returns the value in that cell. If the offset is 5 Enable moves down five cells, to the sixth, and returns the value in that cell.

@INDEX(*range,offset column,offset row*)—Lookup Value in Range
Specifies the coordinates of a value in a table. @INDEX(A1..C10,1,4) means go to column B (A is offset 0, B is offset 1), and move four cells down the column to row 5 (row 1 is offset 0, etc.). The offset values could be found in other cells; @INDEX(A1..C10,D5,D6).

@INDEX3D(*range,offset column,offset row,offset level*)—Lookup Value in Range
This function works like @INDEX, but using 3D spreadsheet levels.

@LLOOKUP(*value,range,offset level*)—Look Up a Value in a Table of Columns or a Table of Rows in Different Levels

This function is similar to functions @HLOOKUP, @LOOKUP, and @VLOOKUP, but is used in 3D spreadsheets. For example, @LLOOKUP(13,B:C31..B:C52,2) tells Enable to go to range C31 to C52 in level B; to find the value in the range closest to 13, and to then go down two levels to find the value in the same cell two levels below.

@LOOKUP(*key value,range*)—Lookup Value in a Small Table

This works like @HLOOKUP and @VLOOKUP, except that the table can only be two columns or two rows. The top row or the left column is the key row or column. Enable finds the largest value in the key row or column that does not exceed the key value, and returns the value in the cell immediately below (for rows) or to the right (for columns).

@LOOKUP3D(*value1,value2,comparison row or column,offset*)—Look Up a Value in a Table of Columns or Rows in Different Levels

This function is similar to functions @HLOOKUP, @LOOKUP, @VLOOKUP, and @LLOOKUP, but is used in 3D spreadsheets. You can use this function to do single-level and multiple-level comparisons.

The function will look down a column of numbers listed in ascending order, then across a row of numbers in ascending order, and then down the specified number of offset levels to find the result. For example, @LOOKUP3D(1000,3,B:A3..B:D20,1) tells Enable to search column A in level B and stop at 1000; to search across the row 1000 is in until it finds 3; and then return the value in the same cell one level below. If you want to do a multiple-level comparison, enter a cubic range and an offset column, rather than an offset level. For example, @LOOKUP(1000,3,B:A3..D:B20,1) tells Enable to search column A in level B and stop at 1000; to search down levels below that cell until it finds 3; and then return the value in the cell to the right.

@VLOOKUP(*key value,range,offset*)—Looks Up Value in Table of Columns

Vertical Lookup retrieves values from a lookup table of columns. This works just like @HLOOKUP, except vertically.

SPECIAL FUNCTIONS The special functions perform a variety of tasks, such as returning the current pointer position. They may be useful in macros.

@COLS(*range*)—Number of Columns

Returns the number of columns in the range. @COLS(TEST) = 7, because there are seven columns in the range named TEST. This might be used with @INDEX.

@CURCOL—Current Pointer Column

Requires no argument. This returns a value equivalent to the column that the cursor is currently on; column A = 1, B = 2, etc. This function is often used in macros. The value is constantly updated, but you must press F5 to see the most recent value.

@CURLEVEL—Current Pointer Level

Requires no argument. This function returns a value equivalent to the level the pointer is in (A:, B:, etc.), and may be used in macros. It is updated each time the spreadsheet is recalculated.

@CURPOS—Current Pointer Cell Address

Requires no argument. This function returns the current pointer cell address. It can be used in GOTO macros to tell Enable to go to a specified cell. The value is constantly updated, but you must press F5 to see the most recent value.

@CURROW—Current Pointer Row

Requires no argument. This function returns a value equivalent to the row that the cursor is currently on. It is often used in macros. The value is constantly updated, but you must press F5 to see the most recent value.

@CURVAL—Contents of Current Pointer Cell

Requires no argument. This function returns the contents of the cell the pointer is in. It is often used in macros to tell Enable to carry out a procedure depending on the contents of the pointer cell. The value is constantly updated, but you must press F5 to see the most recent value.

@ID(*1,2*)—User Code

Returns your user code if you are part of a network. 1 is the first character, 2 is the second.

@LASTERR—Last Error Number

Requires no argument. This function returns the last system error number. It is used primarily in macros. Informational errors (such as "circular reference") return 0.

@LEVELS(*range*)—The Number of Levels in the Specified Range

Returns the number of levels in a range. For example, @LEVELS(B:A3..F:A33) returns 5.

@ROWS(*range*)—Number of Rows

Returns the number of rows in the range. @COLS(TEST) = 4, because there are four rows in the range named TEST. Might be used with @INDEX.

@THISCOL—This Column

Requires no argument. This function returns the letter of the column the function is entered in.

@THISLEVEL—Level Where the Formula is Entered

Returns a number related to the level in which the formula is entered. If the formula is in level D:, a 4 displays in the cell.

@THISROW—This Row

Requires no argument. Returns the number of the row the function is entered in.

STATISTICAL FUNCTIONS The statistical functions perform statistical analyses from a list of values.

@AVERAGE/@AVG(*range*)—Average

Calculates the average of a list of numbers. @AVG(B1..B5) sums and averages the values in the cells B1 to B5. @AVG(1,5,21,46) returns the average of 1, 5, 21, and 46.

@AVGPRD(*range,range*)—Average of the Sum of Products

Sums the two lists of numbers and averages the totals. @AVG(B15..B20,B123..B140).

@COUNT(*range*)—Counts Items in List

Adds the number of occupied cells in a range. If A1 and A2 are filled, but A3 is empty, @COUNT(A1..A3) = 2. However, if you name a specific cell, it is counted even if it is empty. If A3 is empty, then @COUNT(A1..A3,A4) = 3, even if A4 is empty.

@CUMPCT(*range,range*)—Cumulative Percentage

Calculates the cumulative or running percentage from the first range and enters the values in the second range. The formula itself must be entered in an unused cell that is in neither range (the function appears in the information display area, but not in the cell). @CUMPCT(A1..A10,C1..C10) totals the values in A1..A10, calculates the percentage of this total that is in each individual cell, calculates the running percentages, and enters them in the range C1..C10. A cumulative percentage is the percentage in A1, then in A1+A2, then in A1+A2+A3, etc.

@CUMSUM(*range,range*)—Cumulative Sum

Calculates the cumulative or running totals from the first range and enters the values in the second range. Works like @CUMPCT. @CUMSUM(A1..A3,C1..C3) puts the value from A1 in C1, A1+A2 in C2, and A1+A2+A3 in C3.

@MAX(*argument*)—Maximum Value in Argument

Returns the maximum value in the argument. The argument could be a list of numbers, a list of ranges, a single range, or a numeric expression. If A1 contains the number 8, and A2 contains 3, then @MAX(A1,A2) = 8.

@MIN(*argument*)—Minimum Value in Argument

The inverse of @MAX. In the example in @MAX, the result would be 3.

@PCT(*range,range*)—Percentage

Sums the values in the first range, calculates the percentage share of each cell in the first range, and enters the resulting percentages in the second range. For example, if A1 = 2, A2 = 2, A3 = 1 , then @PCT(A1..A3,C1..C3) puts 40% in cell C1, 40% in C2, and 20% in C3. The function must be entered in a cell that is not part of either of the ranges; the function appears in the information display area but not in the cell itself.

@STDEV/@STD(*argument*)—Standard Deviation

Calculates the biased standard deviation, the amount that specified data varies from the average. @STD(11,3,5,8,19) = 5.6.

@SUM(*argument*)—Sums the Values

The most commonly used function, this sums the values in the argument; @SUM(1,3,5,6) = 15. Most often used to sum the figures in a range of cells; @SUM(B23..B40) adds all the values in cells B23 to B40. Be careful when you add values to the list. If you add them to the end, the formula is not updated to include the new cell; either edit the formulas or insert a row inside the range.

@SUMPRD(*argument*)—Sum of Products

Multiplies pairs of values together and sums the products. Values must be in pairs, or it returns ERR. @SUMPRD(A1,A2,A3,A4,B1,B2,B3,B4) is the same as (A1*A2)+(A3*A4)+(B1*B2)+(B3*B4). However, @SUMPRD(A1..A4,B1..B4) is the same as (A1*B1)+(A2*B2)+(A3*B3)+(A4*B4).

@VAR(*argument*)—Variance

Calculates the biased variance of the argument, the variation from the average of the data. @VAR(11,3,5,8,19) = 31.36.

STRING FUNCTIONS String functions manipulate labels, non-numeric "strings" of data.

&(*string*)—Concatenate

Combines two strings. If A1 has "Anderson" and A2 has "John", then +A2&A1 = JohnAnderson. If the cells have trailing blanks they are included (the spreadsheet does not leave trailing blanks, but the database does).

&–(*string*)—Concatenate and Trim

This has no real effect in the spreadsheet, but works in the database. It combines strings (see &), but it removes all trailing blanks except one.

&+(*string*)—Concatenate and Trim or Add One Blank

Works like &, but adds a space between the two. Thus the example at & becomes "John Anderson." If the strings have trailing blanks (in the database) all but one blank between the strings are removed.

@CHAR(*argument*)—ASCII Character of Code-Value

Returns the ASCII code of the value in the argument. If C1 contains 41, then @CHAR(C1) =) (right parenthesis). Do not use a value over 240. If the cell is blank or if the value is over 240, Enable returns ERR. Negative values are used as if they were positive, and fractions are rounded.

You can also use this function to hide values in a row. Type @char(0) in a cell to the left of the values you want to hide. Press Tab and press Shift-Tab, and the values in all cells to the right of the function cell disappear. To display them again delete the function and press Tab and Shift-Tab.

@CODE(*argument*)—ASCII Code-Value of Character

Returns the ASCII code of the first character in the text string. If C1 contains LNAME, then @CODE(C1) = 108, the ASCII code for L. If the cell contains a value, a function, or a formula that returns a value, Enable returns ERR.

@DEC(*argument*) — Converts Hexadecimal to Decimal

@DEC(D1) = 209. This converts the hexadecimal number in cell D1 to decimal. The Hex number must be in a non-numeric string, but Enable returns a value. If you enter a hex value into the formula you must enclose it in quotation marks; @DEC("EF2H"), for example. An H at the end of a Hex number is ignored.

@FIXED(*value,decimal places*)—Converts Value to String with Fixed Deximal Places

Rounds a numeric value to a fixed number of decimal places and displays the value as a text string. @FIXED(V1,3) takes the value in V1, rounds it to 3 decimal places, and displays it as a string.

@HEX(*argument*)—Converts Decimal to Hexadecimal @HEX(23) = OF8H.

Converts a decimal value to a hexidecimal value, returned as a non-numeric string. Places 0 in front and H at the end.

@LEFT(*string,number*)—Copies Characters from Beginning of String

Copies characters from the specified string. @LEFT(B4,4) means copy the first four characters from B4. The copy always begins from the first character. See @SUBSTR.

@LC(*string*)—Changes Characters to Lowercase

This changes each word in a text string to lowercase. See @UC and @PROPER. Useful in the database.

@LEN(*string*)—Number of Characters in String
Returns the number of characters in the specified string. A1 contains ANDERSON, so @LEN(A1) = 8. Counts leading blanks.

@MATCH(*string1,string2,start number*)—Matches Characters in Strings
Returns the position at which string 2 begins within string 1. The optional start number tells Enable at which position to begin the search; 0 means start at the first character, 1 means start at the second, etc. @MATCH("johnson","son") = 5. (Unlike the start number, position 1 is the first character, so the s is 5, not 4.)

@NUM(*string*)—Converts String to Numeric Value
If the string contains only numeric characters Enable returns the numbers as a value (i.e., it converts a numeric label to a numeric value). If the string contains non-numeric characters Enable returns ERR. See also @STRING.

@PROPER(*string*)—Changes Characters to Proper Name Format
This changes each word in a text string to proper name format, with the first character being uppercase and the rest lowercase. See @UC and @LC. Useful in the database.

@REPEAT(*argument,number*)—Repeat the Argument
Repeats the characters in the argument. If C1 contains +, then @REPEAT(C1,10) = ++++++++++.

@REPLACE(*string,start position,number,with*)—Replace Characters
This is almost like word processing's Find and Replace function. The first string is the string that contains text to be replaced. @REPLACE(C1,1,4,"ABCD") takes the string in C1, and replaces the four characters beginning to the right of position 1 with ABCD. The result is displayed in the function's cell. If you don't specify a replacement, the characters are removed.

@RIGHT(*string,number*)—Copies Characters from End of String
Copies characters from the specified string. @RIGHT(B4,4) means copy the last four characters from B4. See @SUBSTR.

@STRING(*value*)—Converts Numeric Value to String
The opposite of @NUM. @STRING(4*10) = "40".

@SUBSTR(*string,position,number*)—Copies Characters from String
Copies characters from the specified string. @SUBSTR(B4,1,4) means copy the first four characters from B4. See @LEFT and @RIGHT.

@TRIM(*string*)—Remove Trailing Blanks
Removes trailing blanks, perhaps created by a @STRING function. If the entire string consists of blanks, a single blank is returned. @TRIM(C11) displays the string in C11 without trailing blanks.

@UC(*string*)—Changes Characters to Uppercase
This changes each word in a text string to uppercase. See @LC and @PROPER.

TIME FUNCTIONS The time functions use a serial time number, the number of seconds since midnight. You can display times by using the Time format (Global or Range Format; see Module 73).

@ETIME(*begdate,begtime,enddate,endtime*)—Elapsed Time
Calculates the elapsed time from a beginning date and time to an end date and time, in seconds. To calculate the elapsed time from 00:10 on December 28, 1945 until 01:00 the next day, enter @ETIME(16798,600,16799,3600) = 89400 seconds.

@HOUR(*seconds*)—Converts Seconds to Hours
Can be used to convert seconds or elapsed time (@ETIME) to hours. If the time is under 1 hour, or 24 or more but less than 25, @HOUR returns 0. Otherwise the hours are in 24-hour format, 1 to 23. @HOUR(99000) = 3, because it is over 27 hours.

@MINUTE(*seconds*)—Converts Seconds to Minutes
Can be use to convert the fractions of an hour from @ETIME to minutes. If the time is less than one minute @MINUTE returns 0. @MINUTE(124) = 2.

@NOW—Current Time
Needs no argument. Works like @TODAY, except returns the number of elapsed seconds in the current day. The time must be set when you log onto Enable, and if the cell is formatted as a Time cell the time is displayed. If not, the elapsed seconds are displayed. The time updates each time you press F5. (You could press F5 immediately before printing a file, to "time-stamp" it.)

@SECOND(*seconds*)—Number of Seconds in Last Minute
Returns the number of elapsed seconds in the last minute of the elapsed time. @SECOND(3655) = 55, because 3655 is 60 minutes and 55 seconds.

@TIME(*hours,minutes,seconds*)—Converts Time to Seconds
Takes the time in hours, minutes, and seconds and returns the total number of seconds. @TIME(12,44,56) = 45896. Could also be entered as a label; @TIME("12:44:56").

@TIME(*seconds*)—Converts Seconds to Hours, Minutes, and Seconds
Converts the time in seconds to HH:MM:SS, even if the cell is not formatted as a time cell.

@TIME$(*seconds*)—Elapsed Time in Days, Hours, Minutes, and Seconds
Returns the elapsed time as DD HH:MM:SS, even if the cell is not formatted as a time cell. @TIME$(1253790) = 14 12:16:30. Use with @ETIME.

TRIGONOMETRIC FUNCTIONS The following is a list of trigonometric functions.

@ACOS(*argument*)—Arc Cosine
Calculates the arc cosine of the argument, in radians. This is the inverse of @COS. The returned value is always between 0 and pi. @ARC(0.8) = 0.6435.

@ASIN(*argument*)—Arc Sine
Calculates the arc sine of the argument, in radians. @ASIN(0.8) = 0.9273.

@ATAN(*argument*)—Arc Tangent
Calculates the arc tangent of the argument, in radians. @ATAN(0.8) = 0.6747.

@ATAN2(*value1,value2*)—4-quadrant Arc Tangent
Calculates the angle, in radians, whose tangent is equal to argument2/argument1. @ATAN2(–2,2) = 2.3562.

@COS(*argument*)—Cosine
The cosine of the argument, in radians. @COS(G13) is the cosine of the value in G13.

@PI—Pi

The value of pi. Requires no argument. A shorthand way of entering the value into a calculation. @PI*G10 multiplies pi (3.141592653589794) by the value in G10.

@SIN(*argument*)—Sine

The sine of the value in the argument, in radians. @SIN(23) = –0.8462.

@TAN(*argument*)—Tangent

Calculates the tangent, in radians, of the value in the argument. If the argument is pi/2+(pi**n*), where *n* is an integer, it returns ERR.

APPLICATIONS

The spreadsheet functions range from simple calculation aids like @SUM, to extremely powerful tools that turn your spreadsheet into far more than a simple arithmetic-machine. You can carry out complex statistical analyses, make loan and investment calculations, and build If-Then instructions. You can also use @NOW and @TODAY to time- and date-stamp reports, or use the @LOOKUP functions to build tax tables. The possibilities are limitless.

TYPICAL OPERATION

In this activity you use a few simple functions in the file named EXPENSES, created in Module 6.

1. Open the file named EXPENSES. Press **F2**, type **G1**, and press **Enter**. The pointer moves to G1.

2. Type **@TODAY** and press **Enter**. This cell, which was formatted in Date format in an earlier module, displays today's date (the date you entered when you logged onto Enable).

```
G1:  (D,1)  @TODAY                                                  READY

     A        B        C         D         E          F          G          H
 1Business Expenses, 1990              Report Date:          07-Feb-89
 2============================
 3                                JAN       FEB       MAR        APR        MAY
 4
 5Advertising                   115.00     82.00
 6Bank Service Charges           11.50     12.37
 7Car & Truck                    87.50     75.30
 8Commissions                   297.45
 9Depreciation                   45.00     45.00     45.00      45.00      45.00
10Dues & Pubs.                   23.00     23.00
11Insurance                     223.76    123.76
12Interest                       14.67     13.95
13Office                         52.50      1.67
14Rent                          432.95    432.95    432.95     432.95     432.95
15Supplies                       86.21    215.98
16Taxes                          93.00     32.00
17Travel & Meals                125.25      0.00
18Utilities                     176.98    127.34
19Other                          92.50      3.74
20                            =============================================
#1    C:\ENABLE\EXPENSES.SSF                                        048
```

Notice the function in the information display area next to the code (D,1), to the right of the cell address. (D,1 means Date format 1.)

3. Press **F2**, type **A52**, and press **Enter**. Type the labels shown in the following screen.

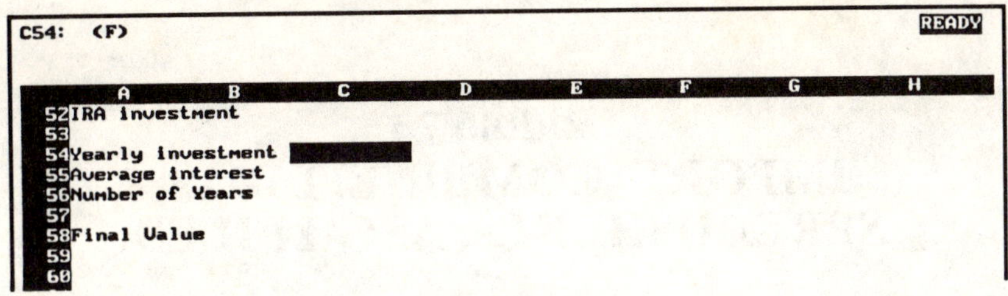

4. Press **F10** and type **WRFF** (Worksheet;Range;Format;Fixed). Type **0** (zero) and press **Enter**. Type **C54..G58** and press **Enter**.

5. Move the pointer to **C55**. Press **F10**, type **WRFP** (Worksheet;Range;Format;Percent) and press **Enter** twice.

6. Enter **2000** in C54 and **0.9** in C55. In cells C56 to G56 enter **10, 15, 20, 25,** and **30**, respectively.

7. Move the pointer to C58. Type **@FV(C54,C55,C56)** and press **Enter**.

8. Press **F10** and type **WC** (Worksheet;Copy) and press **Enter**. When Enable prompts for the range to copy to, press **Right Arrow**, type **.** (period), and press **Right Arrow** three times. Press **Enter**. Enable copies the function, using the absolute cell addresses C54 and C55. The address C56 is changed to use the cell two cells above the function in each place.

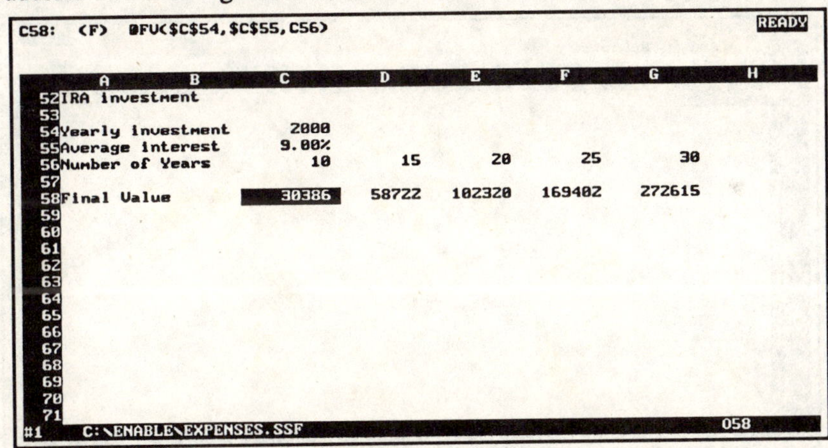

This function calculates the value of your IRA investment, assuming $2000 invested at the same time each year, with an average interest rate of 9%, compounded annually. The final value is calculated for 10 to 30 years.

9. Press **Alt-F10**, press **Enter**, and type **R** to save the file.

10. Press **F10** and type **QY** to close the file.

11. Turn to Module 70 to continue the learning sequence.

Module 75
IMPORT (COMBINE, DBMS, SPREADSHEETS, ASCII FILES)

DESCRIPTION

You can import data from other files in several ways. You can use the Combine command to bring data from another spreadsheet; copy information from a database using the DBMS command; or import non-Enable spreadsheets or ASCII data. If you want to import data from an Enable word processing file, save it as an ASCII file first. (You can also link spreadsheets using @ functions. See Module 77 for more information on these commands.)

COMBINING SPREADSHEETS The Combine command lets you copy data from another spreadsheet into specified cells. You can replace the data in those cells: increase the values in the cells by adding the imported values, or decrease the values by subtracting the imported values.

Press F10 and type C (Combine). You see the following screen:

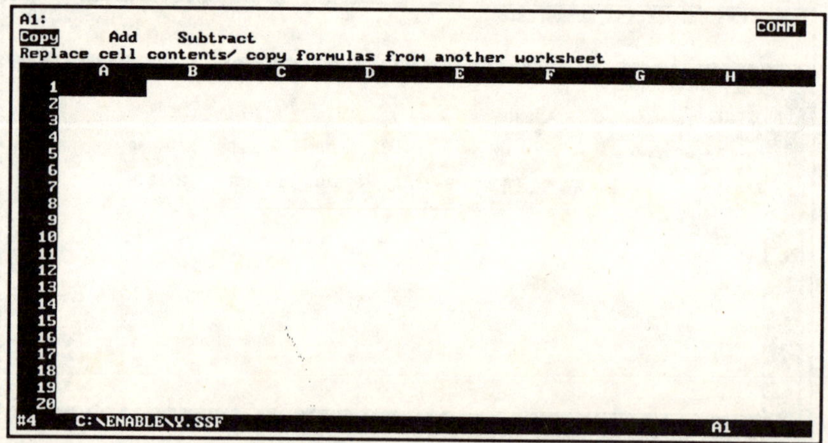

Copy This option copies the values, labels, and formulas from the other spreadsheet, totally replacing the values in the current spreadsheet's cells. Enable will not copy onto protected cells. Copied values bring their worksheet range characteristics with them (format, alignment, etc.), but not their column widths or global characteristics.

Add This option adds the values from the other spreadsheet to the values in the current spreadsheet. It does not copy labels or formulas, but it does add the result of the formulas.

Subtract This option works like the Add option, except that the values are subtracted from the current spreadsheet.

When you have selected one of these options Enable displays the following screen:

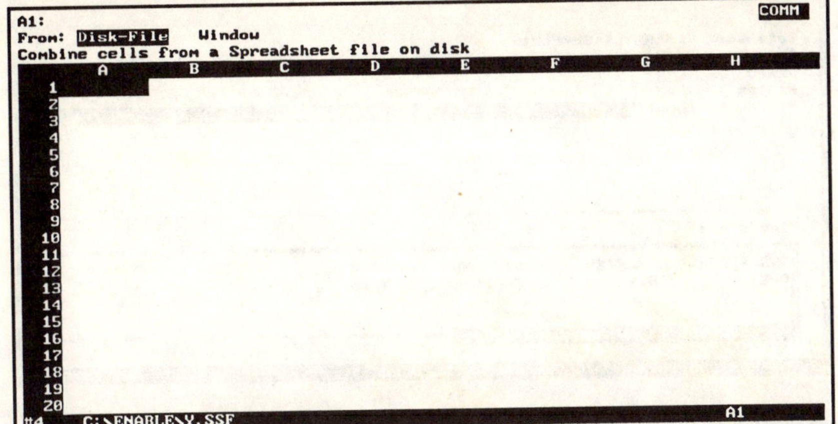

Disk-File This option lets you copy, add, or subtract cells from a spreadsheet file. Enter the filename or type ? and press Enter to select from a list of files. Enable then asks you to specify the range in that file that you want to copy from. Type the range and press Enter. Enable then asks for the "Range starting cell," the cell at the top left of the area into which you want to enter the imported data. Type the cell address, or move the pointer to the cell, and press Enter. Enable imports the data to the range beginning at that cell.

Window Probably the easiest way to import from another spreadsheet is from an open window. Select Window and Enable displays the Window Status screen. Select the window you want to import from and Enable displays that window and prompts for the From range. Use any of the methods described in Module 82 to enter the range (type the address, type the name, or point to the range), and press Enter.

Enable returns you to the original spreadsheet and prompts you for the "Range starting cell," the cell at the top left of the area you want to enter the imported data. Type the cell address, or move the pointer to the cell, and press Enter. Enable imports the data to the range beginning at that cell.

COPYING DATA FROM A DATABASE It's very easy to copy data from a database to your spreadsheet. First, open both the database and the spreadsheet.

Use the DBMS Display command to display the contents of the database in columns (see Module 64), and mark the records you want to export to the spreadsheet. Return to the spreadsheet. (Use the Top Line Menu Windows command or press Alt-Down Arrow or Alt-Up Arrow to move between windows.) Press Alt-F5 or press F10 and type D (DBMS).

Enable displays the Window Status screen. Select the database window, and Enable displays the database columns again, with the records marked. Press Alt-F5 again, and Enable displays the following screen.

```
Database: C:\ENABLE\SUPPLY1
Index    :
Where    :
Fields   :
Fields to copy:

------------------------------------------------------------------------
Fields are:

SYS:RECORD   DELETED    STOCKNO    ITEM    SIZE
COST         QTY        SUPPLIER   TYPE

Press PgDn to select from above
#4. Marked  SUPPLY1      Records ....28 Rd ....23 Se   ...20 Cur ....15  D:044
```

The cursor is at the "Fields to copy" prompt. Enter the names of the fields that you want to export to the spreadsheet and press Enter. You see the spreadsheet, with two options in the information display area: Insert or Overlay. Select Insert if you want Enable to add new rows to insert the data, or Overlay if you want to place the data in existing cells, erasing the contents of those cells.

Enable then asks for the "starting coordinate for DBMS record insertion." Type the cell address, or move the cursor to the top left cell of the area to be copied to, press Enter, and Enable copies the data.

You don't have to mark the records before the import procedure; you can mark them when you return to the database if you want, just before going to the "Fields to copy" prompt.

You can use the Index, Where, and Fields prompts to specify exactly which records are displayed, and in which order. Read the Database section of this book for more information.

IMPORTING VERY LARGE ENABLE 2.0 SPREADSHEETS If you try to import very large Enable 2.0 spreadsheets into a system without EMS hardware or EMS simulation software such as LIMSIM you may run into memory problems. Sign on to Enable using the Disk-EMS parameter (see Appendix J). When you try to open the document Enable builds a file called PGLIB_.TSG. You must copy this file into several smaller files before you exit Enable, becuase Enable will not save the file.

USING NON-ENABLE SPREADSHEETS Enable allows you to import non-Enable spreadsheets or data in non-spreadsheet format. The files may be ASCII, Lotus 1-2-3 (release 1A or 2) or Symphony, DIF, Multiplan (SYLK format), or SuperCalc3 (.CAL format, release 2).

At the Main Menu type USR (Use System;Spreadsheets;Revise). Type the filename, including the extension. Because Enable does not recognize the file as being in Enable format, it displays the following prompt;

> Spreadsheet format; 123 VisiCalc DIF ASCII SYLK 3=SCalc3

Select the appropriate file type.

Lotus 1-2-3 If you select 123, Enable asks if you want to "Convert LIC characters?" This converts the Lotus International Character Set characters to the ASCII characters that Enable uses, except for a few characters not supported by Enable. Say No if you intend to save in Lotus format, or you may lose some characters. Enable also asks if you want to "Convert Lotus 1-2-3 Macros?"

Also, you should set your user profile to "protect all cells" before importing Lotus files—see Module 80.

Enable does not import the Lotus print and graph settings. Functions that Enable cannot recognize and formulas referencing cells not within the spreadsheet are entered as labels. The functions are highlighted, and formulas depending on them are turned into labels. Other non-supported features are ignored.

VisiCalc When Enable converts a VisiCalc file it creates a conversion file called TSGVC. There must be enough room on disk for both the conversion file and the newly created Enable file, if you intend to save the file in Enable format.

ASCII ASCII data must be in comma-separated rows, each row ended with a carriage return (press Enter after typing each row), and each individual "cell" in the rows enclosed by commas. You can enclose labels in quotation marks. To include quotation marks in the label, use single quotes and enclose the entire label with double quotes; " 'LABEL' ". The only other character that may appear is the Ctrl-Z end-of-file character.

TIP: If you want to enter lists from Enable Word Processing, put the lists in comma separated rows, save the file in ASCII, and then import the ASCII file.

SYLK Functions that Enable does not support are displayed as labels. Cells containing LOOKUP and NPV functions are highlighted so that you can change the arguments to the Enable format. Enable truncates range names over 15-characters long and highlights the range. You should rename the range names used in formulas.

If non-contiguous ranges have been named, Enable highlights the cells, but ignores the range and does not display the name. Formats for whole rows and columns, and Multiplan window features, are ignored.

SuperCalc3 Not all SuperCalc commands are supported. PRINT and GRAPH are ignored.

Also, you should set your user profile to "protect all cells" before importing SuperCalc 3 files—see Module 80.

APPLICATIONS

Sometimes it is easier to build several small spreadsheets, and combine data where necessary, than to build one huge, unwieldy file. Importing data from databases saves you duplicating work; you enter the data just once, and use it in both the database and spreadsheet. And importing from other formats lets you use other people's data, or data you entered before you began working with Enable.

TYPICAL OPERATION

In this activity you import data from a database and from another spreadsheet. You use the spreadsheet named EXPENSES (created in Module 6), the Enable sample spreadsheet named A (one of the tutorial samples), and the Enable example database file named SUPPLY. You should have loaded the last two files when you installed Enable. If you didn't load these files use any other files; the steps will be the same, just substitute the correct cell addresses and filenames.

1. Open the file named EXPENSES. Press **F2**, type **A100**, and press **Enter**. The pointer moves to A100.

2. Press **F10** and type **MOO** (MCM;Other Window;Open). At the Main Menu type **UDI** (Use;DBMS;Interact) and Enable displays the Interact screen. Type **D** (Display) and the Display command screen appears.

3. Type **SUPPLY** and press **End**. Enable displays the database.

4. Press **Alt-Down Arrow** to move to the spreadsheet. Press **Alt-F5**. Enable displays the Window Status screen. Select the window that has the database and press **Enter**.

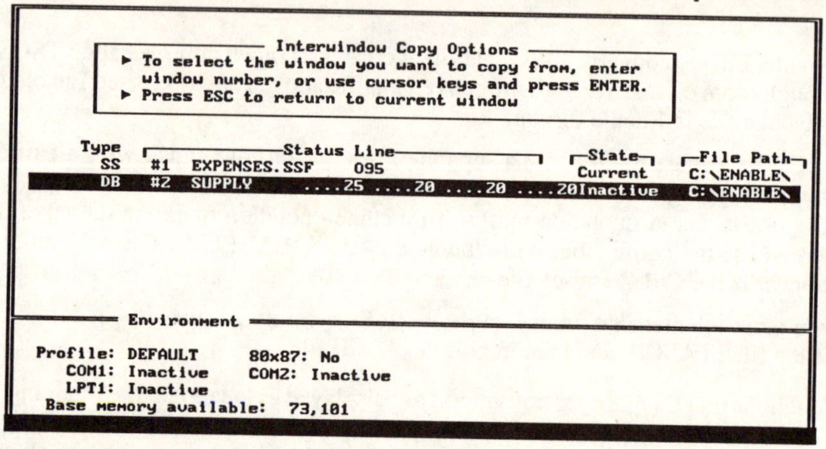

5. Press **Enter**. Enable displays the database. Use the arrow keys to move to the first record, press **F7**, move to record 20, and press **F7** again. You have highlighted 20 records.

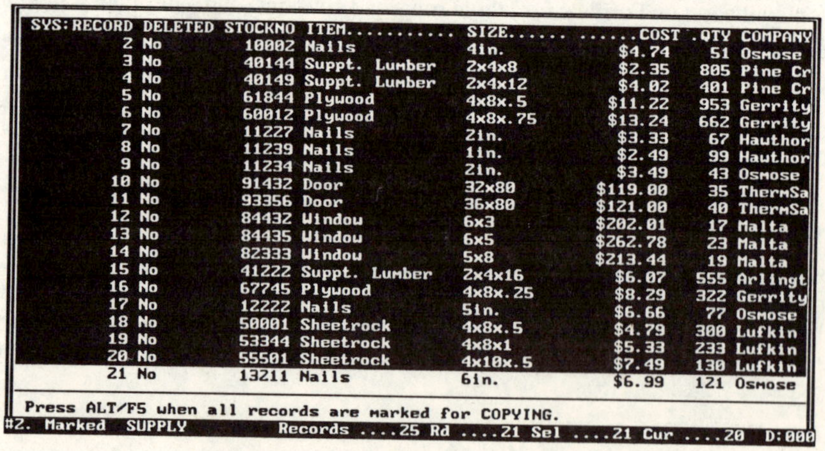

SYS:RECORD	DELETED	STOCKNO	ITEM..........	SIZE.....	......COST	.QTY	COMPANY
2	No	10002	Nails	4in.	$4.74	51	Osmose
3	No	40144	Suppt. Lumber	2x4x8	$2.35	805	Pine Cr
4	No	40149	Suppt. Lumber	2x4x12	$4.02	401	Pine Cr
5	No	61844	Plywood	4x8x.5	$11.22	953	Gerrity
6	No	60012	Plywood	4x8x.75	$13.24	662	Gerrity
7	No	11227	Nails	2in.	$3.33	67	Hawthor
8	No	11239	Nails	1in.	$2.49	99	Hawthor
9	No	11234	Nails	2in.	$3.49	43	Osmose
10	No	91432	Door	32x80	$119.00	35	ThermSa
11	No	93356	Door	36x80	$121.00	40	ThermSa
12	No	84432	Window	6x3	$202.01	17	Malta
13	No	84435	Window	6x5	$262.78	23	Malta
14	No	82333	Window	5x8	$213.44	19	Malta
15	No	41222	Suppt. Lumber	2x4x16	$6.07	555	Arlingt
16	No	67745	Plywood	4x8x.25	$8.29	322	Gerrity
17	No	12222	Nails	5in.	$6.66	77	Osmose
18	No	50001	Sheetrock	4x8x.5	$4.79	300	Lufkin
19	No	53344	Sheetrock	4x8x1	$5.33	233	Lufkin
20	No	55501	Sheetrock	4x10x.5	$7.49	130	Lufkin
21	No	13211	Nails	6in.	$6.99	121	Osmose

Press ALT/F5 when all records are marked for COPYING.
#2. Marked SUPPLY Records ....25 Rd ....21 Sel ....21 Cur 20 D:000

6. Press **Alt-F5** and Enable displays a screen with a "Fields to copy" prompt. Type **item,size,cost**, as shown in the following screen.

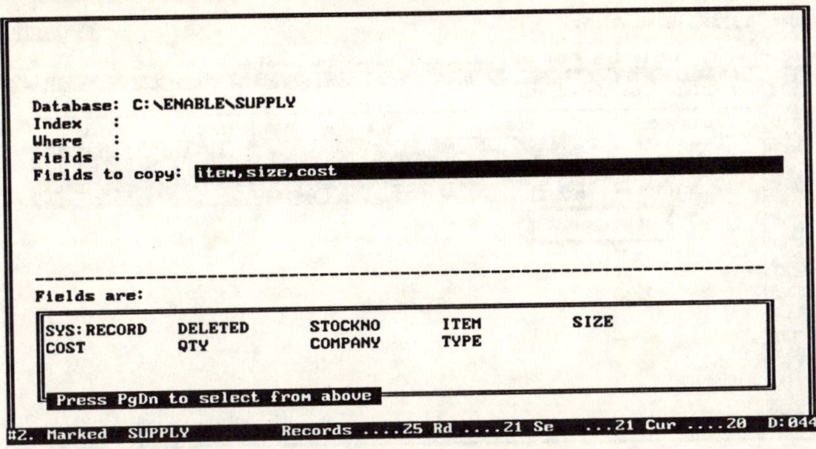

7. Press **Alt-F5**, and Enable displays the spreadsheet again, with a prompt asking if you want to insert or overlay the data. Type **O** and press **Enter** to confirm the copy-to position, and Enable copies the data, as shown in the following screen.

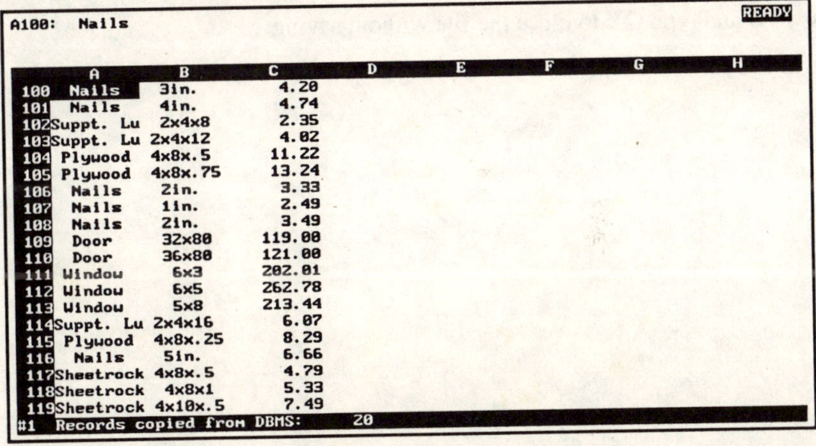

8. Press **F10** and type **MOO** (MCM;Other Windows;Open). At the Main Menu type **USR** (Use;Spreadsheet;Revise). When Enable prompts for the filename type **A** and press **Enter**. Enable displays the spreadsheet. Press **Alt-Up Arrow** to go to the other spreadsheet.

9. Move the pointer to E100. Press **F10** and type **CCW** (Combine;Copy;Window). Enable displays the Window Status screen. Select spreadsheet A, and press **Enter**.

10. Enable displays the spreadsheet, and prompts for the range to copy. Select the range as shown in the following screen.

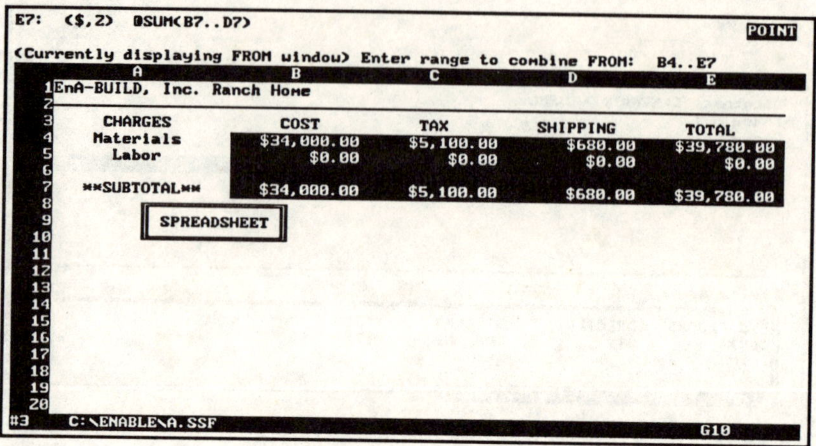

11. Press **Enter** and Enable displays the other spreadsheet and prompts for the starting cell. Press **Enter** and Enable copies the data. Notice that some of the values are displayed as asterisks, because they are too wide for the current column width.

12. Press **F10** and type **QY** to close the file without saving.

13. Turn to Module 77 to continue the learning sequence.

Module 76
INSERT OR DELETE ROWS AND COLUMNS

DESCRIPTION

Enable lets you insert or delete rows and columns, and automatically adjusts the entire document to fit the new cell addresses; all the formulas are modified, for example, so that they still refer to the cell with the appropriate data.

NOTE

Cells that are inserted into ranges that are named, formatted, aligned, or protected automatically assume the characteristics of that range.

INSERTING ROWS AND COLUMNS Position the pointer in the column that will be moved to the right, or the row that will be moved down. Press F10 and type WI (Worksheet;Insert). Then type C (Column) or R (Row). Type the number of rows or columns you want to insert, and press Enter.

DELETING ROWS AND COLUMNS Press F10 and type WD (Worksheet;Delete). Then type C (Column) or R (Row). Enable prompts you for the range to delete. Type in a range (for example, B1..B5 to delete rows one to five), or point out the rows or columns. As long as the row or column is specified it doesn't matter which address you use; you could also type A1..A5 or Z1..Z5 to do the same thing. (Enable requires the full address—typing 1..5 is not sufficient, even though it might appear to be enough information to complete the operation.)

NOTE

Enable does not let you delete rows or columns that have protected cells. Formulas dependent on values in deleted cells display "ERR."

APPLICATIONS

As a spreadsheet grows you will find new requirements and discover unintentional limitations. These commands let you shift entire blocks of the spreadsheet to one side so you can insert more data, or remove data that is no longer needed.

TYPICAL OPERATION

In this operation you insert and delete rows in the file named EXPENSES, created in Module 6.

1. Open the file named EXPENSES. Press **F2** and type **A8.**
2. Press **F10** and type **WIR** (Worksheet;Insert;Row). Enable asks you for the number of rows. Type **4** and press **Enter**. Enable inserts the rows.

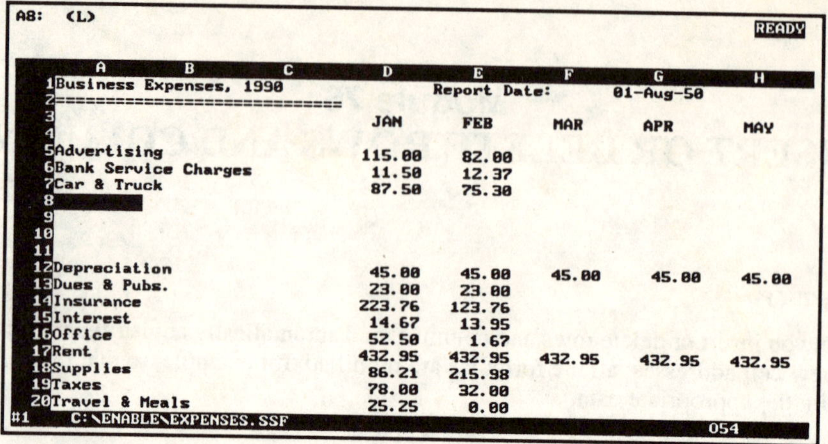

3. Type **Commissions,** press **Right Arrow** three times, and type **297.45**. Move the pointer to A9. Press **F10** and type **WDR** (Worksheet;Delete;Row). Enable prompts for the range to delete. Type **.** (period) and press **Down Arrow** twice. Your screen looks like this:

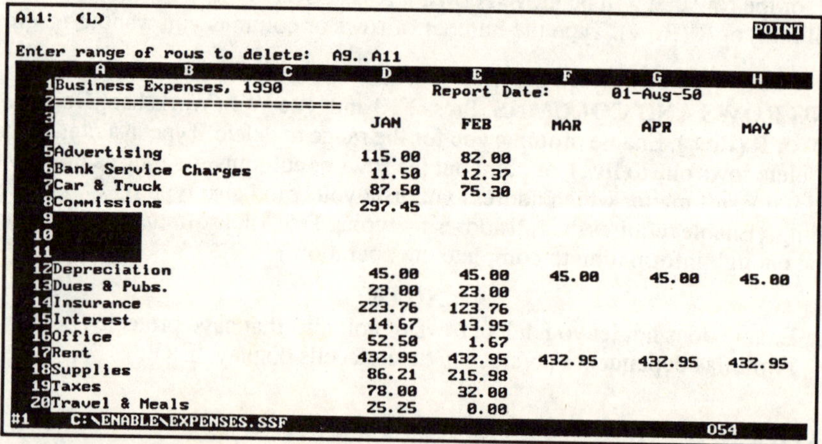

4. Press **Enter** and Enable deletes the rows. Notice that the new monthly total figure now includes the inserted value.
5. Press **Alt-F10**, press **Enter**, and type **R** to save the new file.
6. Press **F10** and type **QY** to close the file and return to the Main Menu.
7. Turn to Module 79 to continue the learning sequence.

Module 77
LINKING SPREADSHEETS

DESCRIPTION

Enable has several functions used for linking spreadsheets. Unlike copying data directly, these functions tell Enable to look up information in another spreadsheet for you. You tell Enable where the information is, and Enable retrieves it—you don't even have to open the other spreadsheet. The spreadsheet receiving the data is called the *dependent* spreadsheet. The one supplying the data is the *supporting* spreadsheet.

There are many reasons to link spreadsheets. You may have a spreadsheet for each month's expenses, for example, and want to copy totals into a yearly spreadsheet. You can also nest spreadsheets; a yearly expenses file might get information from 12 monthly expenses files, which in turn get information from several weekly expenses files.

NOTE

> Later releases of Enable/OA have 3D spreadsheets. These allow you to break complicated spreadsheets into as many as 32 different *levels*. You may find 3D spreadsheets easier to work with than linked spreadsheets. See Appendix K for more information.

@LINK(filename.ext,"*location*") This function retrieves data from the cell in the specified file. For example, type @LINK(#expenses,"B15") to copy the information from cell B15 of the spreadsheet called "expenses." The filename must be preceded by #. The file must have a .SSF extension, but you don't need to type the extension—Enable adds it automatically. Include the directory if it is in a different directory from the dependent spreadsheet. The cell address must be in quotation marks.

When you enter a @LINK function linking to a new filename, Enable displays "Activate this external link? No File." Type N if you do not want to activate the link now (Enable displays REF in the cell); you may want to enter all the linking formulas and then activate the link, or enter the formulas before you have even created the supporting file. If you do want to make the link now, type F, and Enable retrieves the information.

NOTE

> You cannot open and edit a supporting spreadsheet while the dependent spreadsheet is still open. Enable lets you open a read-only version, and you can make changes, but you will not be able save them unless you use a different name or close the dependent spreadsheet.

Each time you add a @LINK statement referring to the same spreadsheet, Enable uses your first answer to the "Activate external link?" prompt; if you answered No, Enable continues without retrieving the information, but if you answered Yes, Enable immediately retrieves the data. When you enter a @LINK function referring to a different spreadsheet, Enable asks the question again.

If you answered No, you can use the Top-Line Link command to retrieve the data later.

Combining @LINK Functions You can combine @LINK functions in various ways. You could add the values from two different cells; @LINK(*#FILENAME*,"A1")+@LINK (*#FILENAME*, "B1"). These cells could even be in different spreadsheets.

You can also combine with different functions. For example, @SUM(@LINK (*#FILENAME*, "C4..E5")).

LINK OPTIONS SCREEN Press F10 and type L (Link) to view the Link options screen.

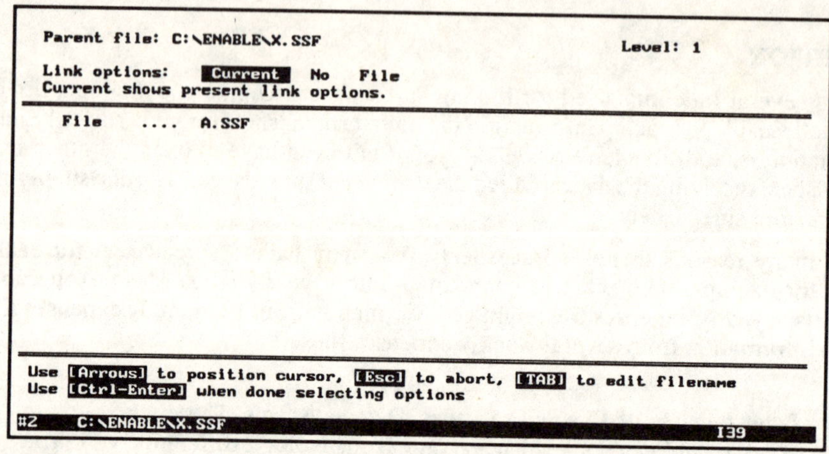

This shows the name and directory of the current spreadsheet (the dependent spreadsheet) with its link level to the right (its level in a hierarchy of "nested" spreadsheets). It also shows a list of all the supporting spreadsheets, and has three options. Select Current to leave the link settings as they were, No to disable all links to all supporting spreadsheets, or File to activate all links to all spreadsheets.

You can also select individual supporting spreadsheets. Press Down Arrow or Enter to move the cursor to the list of spreadsheets. At the one you want to change, press Right Arrow or Left Arrow to change between No and File. For example, selecting No disables all the links to that one supporting spreadsheet.

Press Tab if you want to edit the supporting spreadsheet's name. The highlight moves to the filename, letting you type over it.

When you have set all the options, press Ctrl-Enter. If you have activated any links, Enable retrieves the information. Enable then displays the spreadsheet again.

LINKING RANGES Use the @EXTCOPY command to retrieve entire ranges from another spreadsheet. For example,

@EXTCOPY(@LINK(#EXPENSES,"JULY"),B51..E70)

tells Enable to look at the range named JULY in the spreadsheet called EXPENSES, and to place the data in the range B51..E70 in the dependent spreadsheet. (You could, of course, enter the range address instead of the name.) The *target range*, the cells in the dependent spreadsheet, does not have to be the same shape as the range in the supporting spreadsheet; Enable copies the range column by column, wrapping the data into the next column if necessary.

CELL REFERENCES The @LINK command is an *absolute* cell reference. If, for example, it refers to cell B10 in the supporting spreadsheet, it always refers to B10, regardless of where you copy the function to. @RNGSTR lets you build relative references. For example, if you enter

@LINK(#EXPENSES,@RNGSTR(B51..B51))

Enable links with cell B51 in the EXPENSES file (the cell must be entered as a range, although you cannot use the range name). You can now copy (F10; Worksheet;Copy) this function to another cell in the dependent spreadsheet; for example, copy it to the cell two below the original position. Enable automatically adjusts the cell address to show (B53..B53). Or copy it four columns to the right; Enable changes the address to (F51..F51).

However, if you move (F10-Worksheet;Move) the function, the address is not modified.

CHANGES TO SUPPORTING SPREADSHEET When you have made changes to the supporting spreadsheet (in cells that link with the dependent spreadsheet) and saved the spreadsheet, reopen the dependent spreadsheet, display the Link Options screen, and set the link to No. Press Ctrl-Enter, display the Link Options screen again, and set the link to File. Press Ctrl-Enter and Enable retrieves the new data.

Pressing F5 (the recalculate key) does not normally retrieve data from supporting spreadsheets, because it only recalculates circular references and changed data. However, you can change your user profile such that pressing F5 recalculates everything, including retrieving data from other spreadsheets. See Appendix B for more information.

PASSWORD-PROTECTED SPREADSHEETS If you enter a @LINK function that refers to a spreadsheet requiring a password, you are prompted for the password when you select File, whether you select it when you first enter the @LINK or in the List Options screen. Also, when you enter the dependent spreadsheet you are prompted for the passwords of all the supporting spreadsheets (Enable displays the filenames in the status line, one after another as you enter the passwords). If you make more than three mistakes entering a password the spreadsheet is still opened, but the link is set to No. See Module 114 for more information on passwords.

MOVING CELLS AND RENAMING FILES If you move the data in the supporting spreadsheet, the @LINK function is not corrected to use the new address. You must enter the new address yourself. And if the supporting filename is changed, you must enter the new name at the @LINK function, or in the Link Options screen.

These functions link spreadsheets for very specific purposes; @MACRO links a spreadsheet to a macro library, and @PRTCTL links to a printer control code library. See Modules 115 and 79 for more information.

NOTE

If you use a lot of @LINKs you may need to increase the number of files stated in your CONFIG.SYS file. Enable recommends defining 40 when you install Enable, but this may not be enough.

APPLICATIONS

Computer spreadsheets have a tendency to grow larger than you can handle; there always seems to be something else that can be added. Use the link functions to retrieve data from other files when it is needed, and keep the individual file sizes small and easy to work with. For example, don't put all the year's expenses in one giant file; rather, break it down into twelve smaller files plus one summary file that is linked to the other twelve.

TYPICAL OPERATION

In this example you link the EXPENSES spreadsheet, created in Module 6, with the spreadsheet named A, loaded when you installed Enable.

1. Open the file named EXPENSES. Move the pointer to E25.
2. Type **^1990 Construction** and press **Right Arrow** twice. Type **@link(#a,"e4")** and press **Enter**.
3. Enable displays a prompt asking if you want to activate the link now.

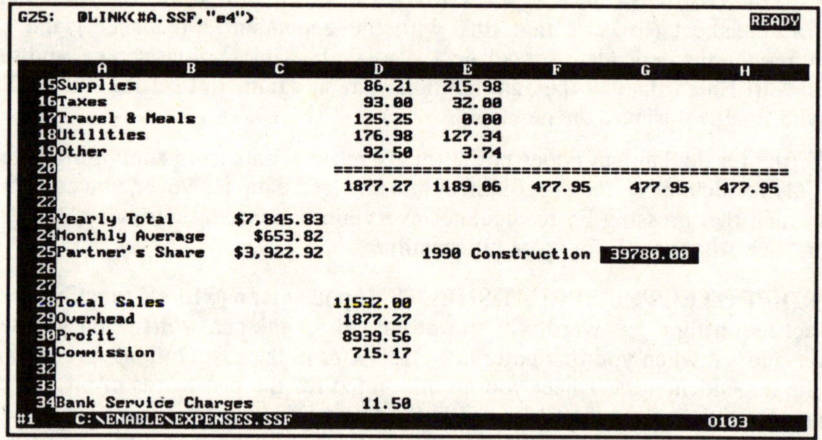

4. Type **N** and Enable displays REF in cell E25. If you had typed F Enable would have immediately retrieved the data.
5. Press **F10** and type **L** (Link). Enable displays the Link Options screen. Type **F** to activate all file-links. Press **Ctrl-Enter**. Enable displays the spreadsheet again, with the data from spreadsheet A in cell E25.
6. Press **F10** and type **QY** to close the file without saving.
7. Turn to Module 7 to continue the learning sequence.

Module 78
OPEN SPREADSHEET AND MOVE POINTER

DESCRIPTION

You can create a new spreadsheet, or open a spreadsheet that has been created previously, from the Main Menu. Type US (Use System;Spreadsheeet). Then, to open a new file, type C (Create); to open an existing file, type R (Revise). In either case Enable prompts for a filename. Type the name and press Enter to open the file. (The filename is up to eight letters, numbers, or underscores.) If you are not sure of the name of a file you want to revise, type ? and press Enter; Enable displays the file directory, allowing you to select a file. (See Module 114 for more information on the file directory.) Enable displays the spreadsheet, similar to the following screen:

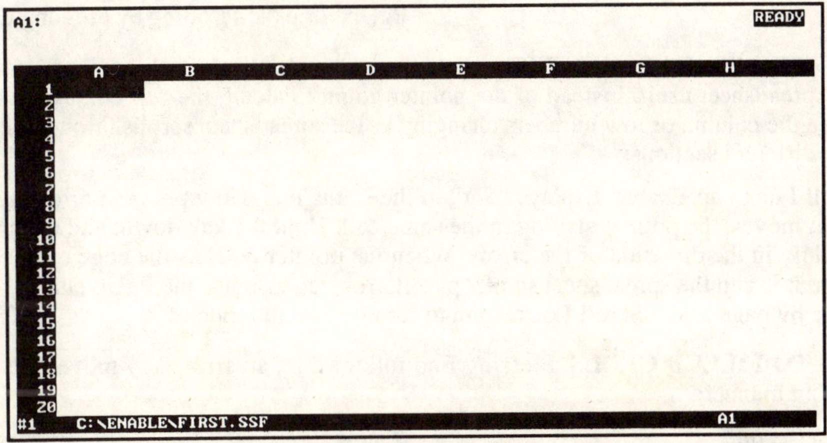

When you open an existing file the pointer is on the cell it was on when you last saved the file. There are several ways to move around in the spreadsheet. You can move the pointer, or move the spreadsheet itself. Note that you are moving the *pointer*, not a *cursor*. The spreadsheet has a highlighted block (the pointer) that indicates which cell you are working in. The cursor doesn't appear until you type a character, at which time Enable displays the cursor in the top left corner (in the information display area) to the right of the typed character.

The following shows the different ways to move around in the spreadsheet.

To Move To...	*Press...*
The next cell	An arrow key.
The next page (screen)	PgUp, PgDn, Tab (to the right), or Shift-Tab (to the left).

A particular cell	F2. Enable displays "Enter address to go to." Type a cell number (L5, for example) and press Enter. If you type the address of a range the pointer goes to the first cell in the range.
The top left corner (A1)	Home. (The cursor will move as close to the top left corner as it can if you have "frozen" titles there; see Module 87 for information.)
The bottom right corner	End and Home (moves to the intersection of the highest row and column in use).

You can also *scroll* the pointer through the spreadsheet. This means that the pointer moves continuously.

To Move...	*Press...*
Rapidly in one direction	An arrow key, and hold it down.
Rapidly page by page	PgUp, PgDn, Tab, or Shift Tab and hold it down.
Continuously in one direction	Alt-F9 followed by an arrow key, PgUp, or PgDn. Stop the scrolling by pressing Ctrl-Break.

MOVING THE SPREADSHEET The preceding methods all move the pointer. You can also move the spreadsheet itself. Instead of the pointer going to a cell, the cell comes to the pointer. You can see the column or row numbers changing as the spreadsheet scrolls through your screen, displaying different sections.

Press Scroll Lock and Enable displays "Scr" in the status line. Now press an arrow key and the spreadsheet moves, the pointer staying in the same cell. Hold the key down, and the spreadsheet moves rapidly in the direction of the arrow. When the pointer reaches the edge of the display, it stays where it is and the spreadsheet scrolls past it. You can also use the PgUp and PgDn keys to scroll, page by page. Press Scroll Lock again to turn the Scroll mode off.

MOVING TO FILLED CELLS Pressing End followed by an arrow key moves the pointer in the following manner:

If the pointer is in...	*It moves to...*
An empty cell	the next filled cell in that direction.
A filled cell at the end of several filled cells	the next filled cell in that direction.
A filled cell within a group of filled cells	the last filled cell in the group.

If there are no filled cells between the pointer and the edge of the spreadsheet in the direction of the arrow key, the pointer moves to the edge of the spreadsheet.

SKIPPING PROTECTED CELLS In Module 80 you will learn how to protect cells. You can skip over protected cells by pressing Alt-F6; when you press an arrow key the pointer moves only to unprotected cells. "Skip" is displayed in the status line. Press Alt-F6 again to turn Skip off.

APPLICATIONS

The methods for moving the pointer make using the spreadsheet quick and efficient. You can go directly to the cell you want if you know its number. If you don't, or if the cell is close by, you can use one of the other methods. Scrolling is especially useful when you know the data you need is in a particular direction, but you are not sure exactly where.

TYPICAL OPERATION

In this activity you open the file EXPENSES created in Module 6 and practice moving the pointer.

1. At the Main Menu type **USR** (Use;Spreadsheet;Revise). Enable prompts for the filename. Type **EXPENSES** and press **Enter**. Enable displays the file, with the pointer in the cell you left it in when you saved the file.
2. Press **Home**, and the cursor moves to cell A1. Press **F2**, type **AMJ9999**, and press **Enter**. The pointer moves to cell AMJ9999. Press **Right Arrow** and **Down Arrow**. The pointer cannot move any further.

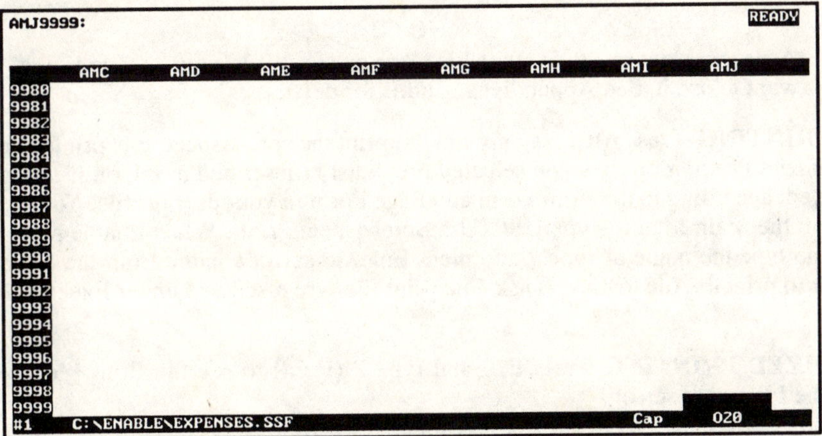

3. Press **Home** to return to A1. Press **PgDn** once. Notice the pointer jumps to the next page. Press and hold **PgDn**. Notice the row numbers changing as you rapidly move from page to page. Release **PgDn** and press **Right Arrow**. The pointer moves to the next cell to the right.
4. Press and hold **Right Arrow**. Notice the column numbers at the top changing as the pointer moves. Release **Right Arrow**.
5. Press **Home**. Press **Scroll Lock**. "Scr" is displayed in the status line. Press and hold **Down Arrow**. Notice that instead of the pointer moving down, the spreadsheet moves up to meet it. Release **Down Arrow**, and press and hold **Up Arrow**. Release **Up Arrow.**
6. Press **Scroll Lock** again. Press **End** and then press **Home**. The pointer moves to the intersection of the highest column in use and the highest row in use.
7. Continue using the pointer-movement tools for a few minutes to get the feel for the different ways to move around the spreadsheet.
8. Press **F10** and type **QY** to exit the spreadsheet without saving.
9. Turn to Module 81 to continue the learning sequence.

Module 79
PRINT

DESCRIPTION

You can print all or part of your spreadsheet. If the spreadsheet is too wide to fit on one printer page Enable divides it into pages, and prints all the pages at the top of the spreadsheet first (left to right), then the pages below them (left to right), and so on.

NOTE

A system print queue is available. You must set it in your profile if you want to use it. See Appendixes I and B for details.

QUICK PRINTING Press Alt-F2 at any time to print the spreadsheet. It is printed according to the Customized Printing options you selected previously (described next), or, if no options have been selected, according to the Print Form and Page Form in your user profile. You can also print to disk from the Main Menu—type USP (Use;Spreadsheet;Print). When Enable prompts you for the filename type the name or type ? and press Enter to select a name from the directory. Then press Enter to print the file to disk. (Disk-File print files are discussed under Execute, later in this module.)

CUSTOMIZED PRINTING Press F10 and type P (Print) to see the Print Menu options, as shown in the following screen:

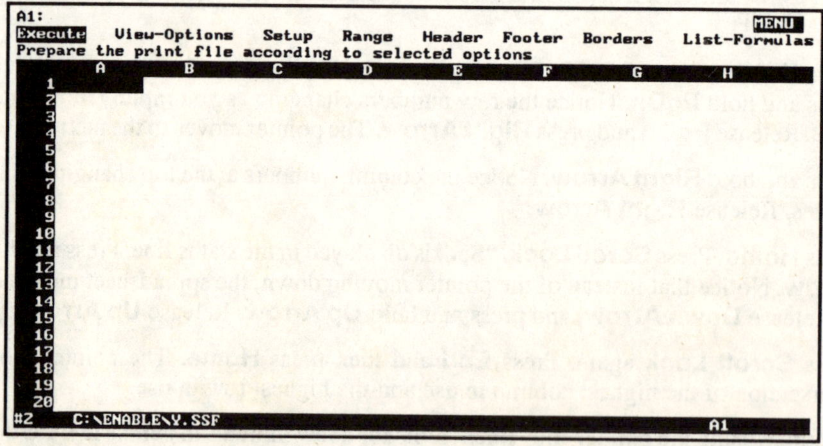

Execute Enable gives you two options if you select Execute: Disk-File and Printer. Select Disk-File if you want to save the spreadsheet in a file so that you can print it later; Enable prompts for the filename, and adds a .SSP extension. Select Printer if you want to print the document now.

NOTE

If you previously selected options from this Print Menu those options are used to print the spreadsheet. If you haven't it is printed according to the options set in your user profile.

View-Options This selection displays a screen showing the printer options you have already chosen. Nothing is displayed if you haven't chosen any options.

Setup Choose Setup to display the Print and Page Forms, allowing you to modify the page dimensions, margins, number of copies, printer information, and so on. These forms are described in detail in Module 35, so they are not discussed here.

Range You can specify the area of the spreadsheet to print or to save in a disk-file. Select the range using one of the methods described in Module 82 (typing the address, typing its name, or pointing to it).

TIP: The easiest way to select the entire spreadsheet as the range is to anchor the pointer in cell A1, press End, and then press Home. Enable highlights a rectangle with A1 in the top left corner and the furthest used cell in the bottom right corner.

Printing Non-Contiguous Ranges Enable allows you to print up to 10 non-contiguous ranges at the same time. First create a range named PRINT_RANGE_*xn*, where *x* is a letter, A to Z, and *n* is a number, 0 to 9. For example, create a range named PRINT_RANGE_A0. Then create a name for the next range, using the same letter but a different number; PRINT_RANGE_A1 in this example. Repeat this until you have named up to ten ranges. Next, name a "phantom" range, PRINT_RANGE_A, press F10, type WRNC (Worksheet;Range;Name;Create), type PRINT_RANGE_A, and press Enter twice. You don't enter a cell addresses for this range.

When you are ready to print press F10, type PR (Print;Range), type PRINT_RANGE_A, press Enter twice, and Enable prints the non-contiguous ranges. Because the range sets can be named PRINT_RANGE_A to PRINT_RANGE_Z you can have up to 26 different sets of non-contiguous ranges.

Header This selection gives you the options of specifying or deleting a header. The header is one line, and prints on each page of the spreadsheet. You can add automatic page numbering by typing a # symbol in the header. For example, type "page #." This overrides page numbering set in the Page Form.

Footer This selection works the same as the header, letting you specify or delete a one-line footer.

Borders This selection lets you specify which rows or columns to reprint on each page, allowing you to repeat cells containing labels and column or row headings. Enable gives you three options: Row-borders, Column-borders, and ID-borders.

Select Row- or Column-borders and Enable asks if you want to set or clear a border. To set a border you specify the range of cells to be printed at the top or side of each page, and the number of blank lines inserted between the border and the rest of the spreadsheet.

If you want to print the column letters along the top of each page and the row numbers along the left edge, select ID-borders.

List-Formulas Selecting this option specifies a printout of all the formulas in the spreadsheet. This is used for tracking problems in your calculations. Enable asks if you want to print them in the Recalculation order (the default, the order in which Enable calculates the formulas) or in Cell order. The next time you press Alt-F2 or select Printer or Disk-File, a list is printed or saved on a Disk-File.

PRINTER-CONTROL CODES You can use your printer's control codes to apply attributes to printouts. Use the %CONTROL command, as shown in the following screen. Insert lines to hold each command (these lines are not printed). This example shows Overstrike mode being turned on and off for the title line.

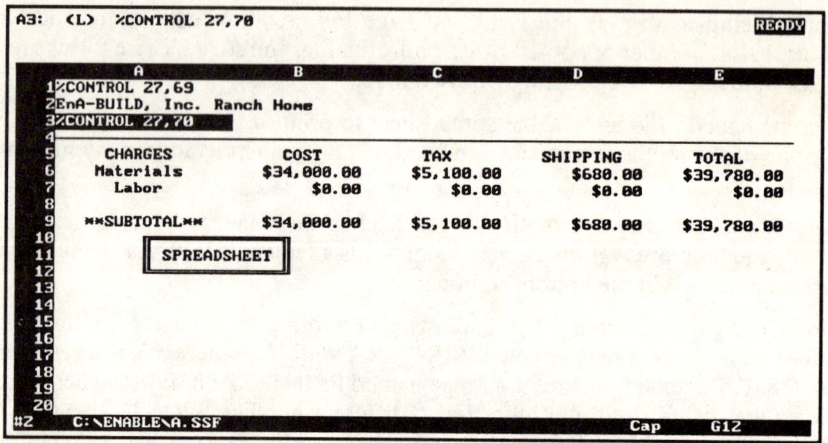

The %CONTROL command must be left justified, and the decimal printer-control codes begin immediately after %CONTROL or after a space. The codes are separated by commas, and you can put more than one control code after the %COMMAND.

NOTE

The control code must be decimal, not Hex or ASCII.

Printer-Control Code Files If you use printer-control codes in more than one spreadsheet you may want to build a special spreadsheet to keep them in. Name the file something you'll remember (PCODES, for example) and enter the codes exactly as shown above. You can leave a line below each one to put a description so that you'll know what each one does. Then name a range for each one (F10, Worksheet;Range;Name;Create). Again, name the range something obvious, BOLD for example. Put the range name in the line below the %CONTROL command.

Now, instead of searching for your printer's manual each time you want to add printer attributes, or searching through other spreadsheets to see how you did it before, use the @PRTCTL function. In the place of the %CONTROL command, type @PRTCTL(#FILENAME,"RANGENAME"); Enable automatically searches for the file and uses the attribute specified in that range. For example:

```
@PRTCL(#PCODES,"BOLD")
```

goes to the file named PCODES and uses the command in the range named BOLD. Of course you then need a @PRTCTL(#PCODES,"BOLDOFF") command to use the printer control code that turns boldface off. If the file is not in the same directory as the spreadsheet you are going to print, include the directory with the filename.

APPLICATIONS

Printing the spreadsheet gives you a working copy for inclusion in reports for distribution to other people, and makes it easier for you to study your work.

TYPICAL OPERATION

In this activity you print the file named EXPENSES, created in Module 6.

1. Open the file named EXPENSES.
2. Press **F10** and type **P** to see the Print options. Type **BIS** (Borders;ID-Borders;Select ID-Borders).
3. Type **HS** (Header;Specify). Type **This is the first two months' expenses for '90.**

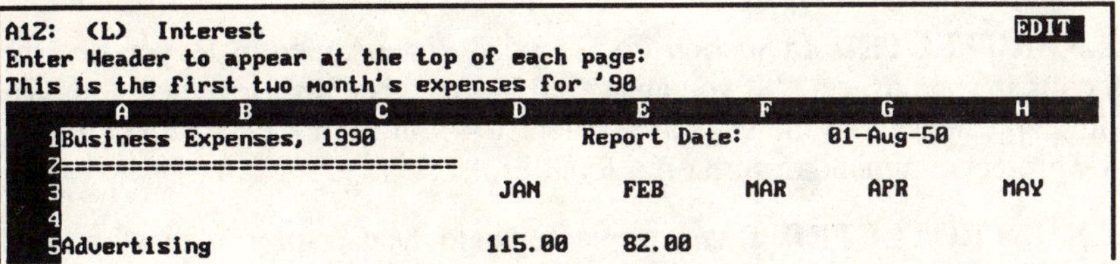

```
A12:  (L)  Interest                                                        EDIT
Enter Header to appear at the top of each page:
This is the first two month's expenses for '90
        A         B          C          D          E          F          G          H
 1Business Expenses, 1990                         Report Date:          01-Aug-50
 2==============================
 3                                      JAN        FEB        MAR        APR        MAY
 4
 5Advertising                          115.00      82.00
```

4. Press **Enter**. Type **R** (Range). Press **Home**, type **.** (period), and press **Down Arrow** until the highlight reaches row 25. Press **Right Arrow** until the highlight covers column E. Press **Enter**.
5. Type **V** (View-Options). You see the following screen.

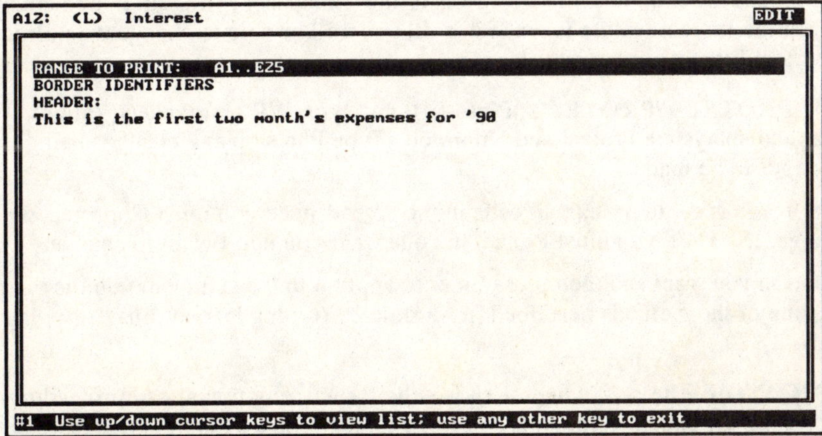

```
A12:  (L)  Interest                                                        EDIT

  RANGE TO PRINT:    A1..E25
  BORDER IDENTIFIERS
  HEADER:
  This is the first two month's expenses for '90

#1  Use up/down cursor keys to view list; use any other key to exit
```

6. Press **Enter** to return to the Print Options. Type **EP** (Execute;Printer). Enable prints the file.
7. Press **Alt-F10**, press **Enter**, and type **R** to save the print options you have set.
8. Press **F10** and type **QY** to close the file.
9. Turn to Module 83 to continue the learning sequence.

Module 80
PROTECT CELLS

DESCRIPTION

Use the Global and Range Protection commands to ensure a cell's data is not accidentally changed. These commands work in conjunction and there are two ways for them to work, depending on how you set your user profile.

ALL CELLS PROTECTED In Section 7 of the profile (see Appendix B) you find this question: "Protect all cells in spreadsheet?" If you answered Yes to this question, when you turn on Global Protection in a spreadsheet all the cells are protected—you cannot change a cell unless you use the Range Unprotect command or turn off Global Protection.

ALL CELLS UNPROTECTED If you answered No to the user-profile question, when you turn on Global Protection none of the cells are protected, until you use the Range Protect command. This is the default condition, i.e., the way the profile is set up if you haven't changed it.

GLOBAL PROTECTION Press F10 and type WGP (Worksheet;Global;Protection). Enable displays two options, Allow Changes and Disallow Changes. Type A to turn the Global Protection feature off, or D to turn it on. When the feature is on, "Prot" is displayed in the status line.

If your user profile is set up to protect all cells in the spreadsheet you will not be able to change any data when the Protect feature is on. If it isn't, you will be able to change data. Proceed to the Range Unprotect/Protect commands.

RANGE UNPROTECT/PROTECT Press F10 and type WR (Worksheet;Range). Two of the options Enable displays are Protect and Unprotect. Type P to stop any changes being made, or U to allow changes to be made.

If your user profile is set to protect all cells in the spreadsheet, you must Unprotect the ones you want to change. If it isn't, you must Protect the ones that you don't want to change.

Select the option you want and then press Enter to apply it to the cell the pointer is on, or select a range using one of the methods described in Module 82 (typing its coordinates, typing its name, or pointing to it).

CELL INDICATOR The *cell indicator* shows the format, alignment, and protection status that has been set using the Range commands. The cell indicator is a code in parentheses between the cell address and the cell contents display, in the information display area. There are two protection codes; P (Protected) and U (Unprotected). P only displays if the profile was set to "No" and the cell is protected. U only displays if the profile was set to "Yes" and the cell is unprotected. For example, ($,1/C/U) is a cell with currency format, one decimal place, and centered contents that is unprotected.

SKIPPING PROTECTED CELLS Press Alt-F6 to skip over protected cells. When you use any of the pointer movement commands Enable moves the pointer to the next unprotected cell, jumping over protected cells. If there are no unprotected cells in the direction you try to move, Enable displays a status-line message or beeps. When this feature is turned on "Skip" is displayed in the status line. Press Alt-F6 again to turn the feature off.

SAVING AND RETRIEVING FILES The protection status is saved when you save the file, so when you reopen the spreadsheet, previously protected cells are still protected.

NOTE

The way the command works depends on how your profile was set when you created the spreadsheet. Changing the profile does not change existing files. Also, before the change to your profile takes effect you must exit Enable and log on again.

If you want to use Lotus 1-2-3 or SuperCalc3 files, set your user profile to "protect all cells," because that is how those programs operate. You can change your profile back once you have opened and saved the file.

APPLICATIONS

The Protect commands are especially useful if other people are using your spreadsheets. You can protect the entire spreadsheet, so they can refer to it but not change it, or protect selected cells, so that they can change only the cells that you want them to change. For example, you might want a clerk or secretary to add data to certain cells once a month, but not be able to accidentally damage the formula cells.

TYPICAL OPERATION

In this activity you practice protecting cells in the spreadsheet named EXPENSES, created in Module 6.

NOTE

This Typical Operation assumes that your user profile has "No" set at the "Protect all cells in spreadsheet?" question in section 7 of the Profile setup. See the discussion of profiles earlier in this module.

1. Open the file named EXPENSES.
2. Press **F10** and type **WGPD** (Worksheet;Global;Protection;Disallow). Notice that Enable displays "Prot" in the status line.
3. Move the pointer to cell D5. Type **100** and press **Enter**. The value in the cell changes to 100.
4. Press **F10** and type **WRP** (Worksheet;Range;Protect). Enable prompts for the range to protect. Type **.** (period) and press **Down Arrow** until the cells from D5 to D19 are highlighted. Press **Enter**.
5. Try to enter a value into D5. Enable does not accept the value. Notice that Enable displays the code (P) next to the cell address in the information display area.
6. Move the pointer up and down the column, trying to enter data. All the cells are protected and do not accept changes.

7. Place the pointer on D5 again. Press **F10** and type **WRU** (Worksheet;Range;Unprotect). When Enable prompts for the range to Unprotect, type **.** (period) and press **Down Arrow** until the pointer is on D11. Press **Enter**.

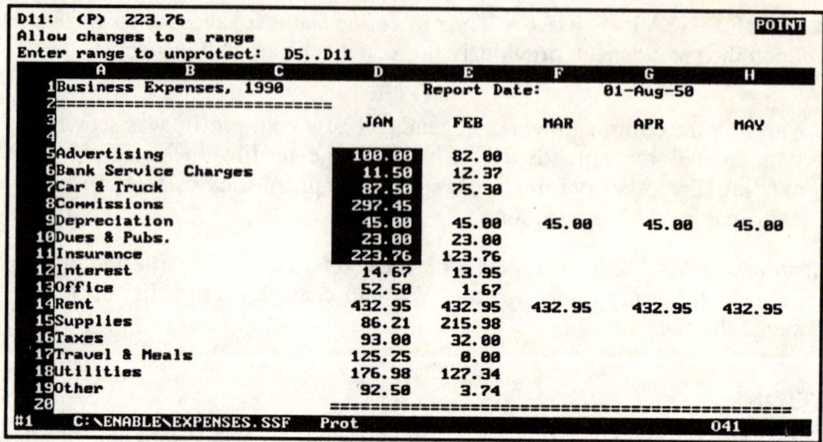

D11: (P) 223.76 POINT
Allow changes to a range
Enter range to unprotect: D5..D11

	A	B	C	D	E	F	G	H
1	Business Expenses, 1990				Report Date:		01-Aug-58	
2	===========================							
3				JAN	FEB	MAR	APR	MAY
4								
5	Advertising			100.00	82.00			
6	Bank Service Charges			11.50	12.37			
7	Car & Truck			87.50	75.30			
8	Commissions			297.45				
9	Depreciation			45.00	45.00	45.00	45.00	45.00
10	Dues & Pubs.			23.00	23.00			
11	Insurance			223.76	123.76			
12	Interest			14.67	13.95			
13	Office			52.50	1.67			
14	Rent			432.95	432.95	432.95	432.95	432.95
15	Supplies			86.21	215.98			
16	Taxes			93.00	32.00			
17	Travel & Meals			125.25	0.00			
18	Utilities			176.98	127.34			
19	Other			92.50	3.74			
20				=========	=========	=========	=========	=========

#1 C:\ENABLE\EXPENSES.SSF Prot 041

8. Type **111** and press **Enter**. The value is entered into D5.

9. Move the pointer down the column of numbers; notice that the (P) code has gone. When you get to D13 the code reappears. Try to enter a value. The cell is protected.

10. Press **F10** and type **WGPA** (Worksheet;Global;Protection;Allow). Place the pointer on cell D18. Type **156.27** and press **Enter**. The cell contents change. Notice that even though the cell is now unprotected, the (P) code remains.

11. Press **F10** and type **QY** to exit the file without saving it.

12. Turn to Module 87 to continue the learning sequence.

Module 81
QUIT

DESCRIPTION

To exit a file press F10 and type Q (or use the expert command, Alt-End). Enable shows two options, No and Yes.

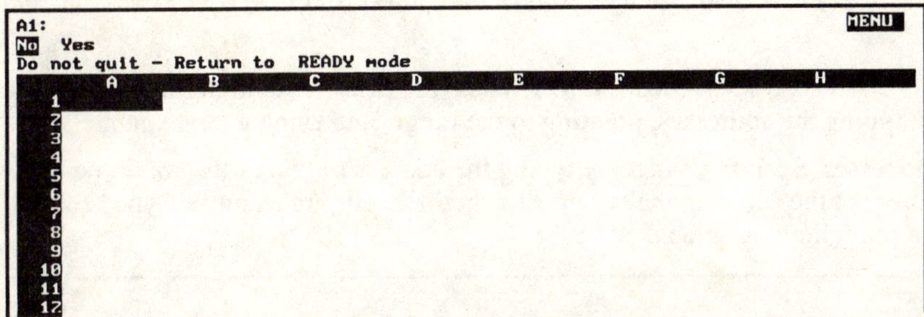

Type N or press Enter to remain in the spreadsheet without closing it, or type Y to close the spreadsheet.

CAUTION

> Typing Y at this point closes the spreadsheet without saving data. Enable does not warn you that you will lose data. Save your spreadsheet before using the Quit command.

APPLICATIONS

When you have finished working with your spreadsheet save it using the Save command, and then use Quit to close it. If you need to view another file and return to your spreadsheet, you do not need to close this one. Use the MCM command to open another window.

TYPICAL OPERATION

In this activity you open the spreadsheet named EXPENSES, created in Module 6, and exit without saving.

1. At the Main Menu type **USR**. When Enable prompts for the filename type **EXPENSES** and press **Enter**. Enable displays the spreadsheet.
2. Press **F10** and type **Q**. Enable displays the two options, No and Yes.
3. Type **Y** and Enable closes the file, returning you to the Main Menu.
4. Turn to Module 84 to continue the learning sequence.

Module 82
RANGE SELECTION

DESCRIPTION

Enable has several methods for selecting *cell ranges*. Many of Enable's commands and functions require that you specify a cell range. A *range* of cells is a square or rectangular group, that may be one cell or many cells wide. In fact, some commands prompting for a cell range *require* a one-cell range.

DEFINING RANGES IN COMMANDS There are three ways to define ranges in spreadsheet commands: typing the addresses, pointing to the range, and using a range name.

Typing Addresses Specify a range by typing the address of one of the corner cells, two periods, and the address of the cell diagonally opposite the first cell. For example, type "B2..E7" to define the range in the following screen.

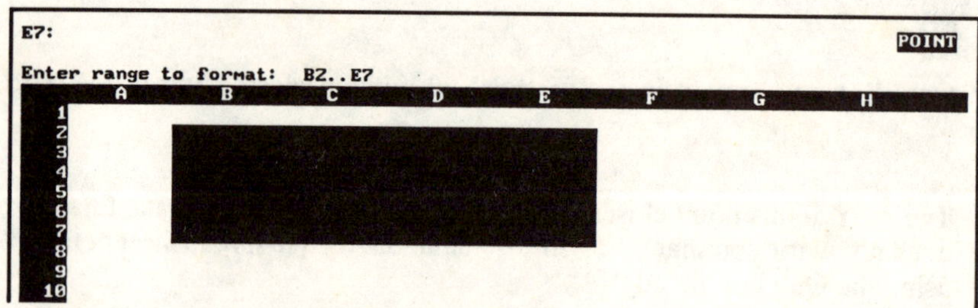

You could also type E7..B2, B7..E2, or E2..B7.

Pointing to Ranges Sometimes the easiest way to define a range is to point to it with the pointer. When Enable prompts you for the range move the pointer to one of the corner cells and press . (period), "anchoring" the range on that cell. Then move it to the corner of the range that is diagonally opposite and press Enter.

As you point out the range, the range addresses displayed in the information display area change to conform to the cells already pointed out.

If you change your mind about the range you can redefine it any time before you press Enter. Press Backspace to return to the anchor position, or move the cursor to another cell and press . (period) to re-anchor the range in that cell. If you want to cancel the command altogether press Esc.

You can select all the information in the spreadsheet by anchoring the range on cell A1, pressing End, and then pressing Home. Enable highlights all the cells inside a rectangle with A1 in the top left corner and the furthest used cell in the bottom right corner.

Naming Ranges Use the Range Name command to name a frequently used range of cells. Then, when you need to specify a range in a command, type the name and press Enter. This saves having to remember the actual address.

To name a range, press F10 and type WRN (Worksheet;Range;Name). Enable displays five options: Create, Delete, Modify, Labels, and Reset.

Create If you select the Create option, Enable prompts you for the name. Type a name up to 15 characters and spaces long. Use a name you can easily remember and associate with the cells. If the name is going to be used in formulas (discussed later in this module), do not include special characters, spaces, and numbers. Press Enter and Enable prompts you for the range. Type the address or point out the range, and press Enter. Enable stores the name and displays "Enter name:" again. Create a new name, or press Esc.

Delete The Delete option deletes a range name. Enable prompts you for the name. Type the name and press Enter. Enable deletes the name and the "Enter name:" prompt remains displayed. Delete another name or press Esc.

Modify The Modify option lets you change the range address. Type the name of the range and press Enter. Enable displays the range address. Point out a new address and press Enter. Then modify the name of another range or press Esc to exit.

Labels The Labels option lets you use cell labels to name a range of cells. For example, down the left side of the EXPENSES spreadsheet you have typed the months of the year. To the right of the months you have entered expenses across several columns.

Select Label and tell Enable which cells you want named: those to the right of the labels (Right), those below the labels (Down), those to the left of the labels (Left), or those above the labels (Up). Of course in this case the cells to the right of the labels will be named.

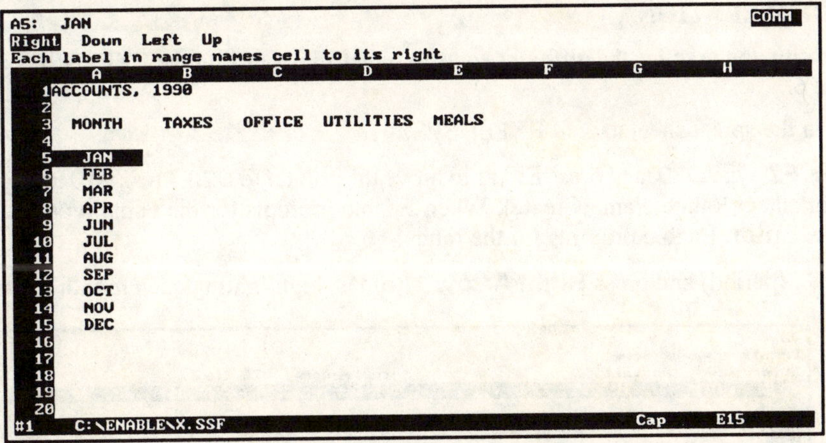

Enable then prompts you to enter the range of cells with labels. In this case you point out or type the range from A5 to A16 and press Enter. Enable then names 12 ranges. Cell B5 is JAN, B6 is FEB, B7 is MAR, etc. Unfortunately Enable stops here; it defines each range as only one cell, it doesn't let you define how large each range should be. This feature is only useful if you want one-cell ranges. If you want multi-cell ranges you could use Modify to add the other cells, but it is quicker to use Create in the first place.

Reset This option deletes all the range names in the spreadsheet. Enable prompts you to confirm; type Y to delete the names or N to keep them.

LISTING RANGE NAMES Press F10 and type WALR (Worksheet;Audit;List;Range-Names) to see a list of all the range names.

USING A RANGE IN A FORMULA You can type range addresses or range names into formulas. For example, typing @SUM(B5..E5) sums all the values in the range B5, C5, D5, and E5. If you name this range JAN, you could type @SUM(JAN) to sum the values in range B5..E5—in fact, if you enter the range address Enable replaces it with the range name.

You can also point out a range while you are typing the formula. In this example, place the pointer where you want the result of the formula to appear. Type @SUM(and move the pointer to the first cell. Press . (period) and move the pointer to the last cell (the one diagonally opposite the first). Press) (right parenthesis) and Enable completes the formula.

Notice that a range name can generally be used in a formula only if it is combined with a function. For example, you could enter "@SUM(INCOME)–@SUM(EXPENSES)" to subtract the sum of the EXPENSES range from the sum of the INCOME range, but you couldn't enter "+INCOME–EXPENSES" *unless* the ranges are one-cell ranges.

APPLICATIONS

The range selection commands provide several easy ways to tell Enable which cells to use. Perhaps the most commonly used method is pointing, but naming ranges you use frequently can save a lot of time.

TYPICAL OPERATION

In this activity you practice the different ways to select a range using the EXPENSES file, created in Module 6.

1. Open the spreadsheet named EXPENSES.
2. Press **F2**, type **D20**, and press **Enter** to move the pointer to D20. Press **F10** and type **WRNC** (Worksheet;Range;Name;Create). When Enable prompts for the name type **monthttl** and press **Enter**. Enable prompts for the range.
3. Type **.** (period) and press **Right Arrow** 11 times, highlighting each month's total cell.

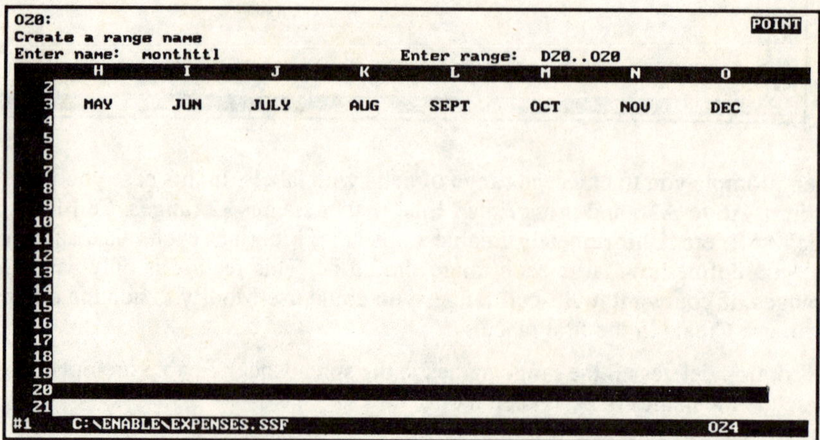

4. Press **Enter** to name the range. Enable lets you name another range if you want to. Press **Esc** to exit the Range Menu options.

5. Move the cursor to **C22**, the Yearly Total cell. Look at the cell contents in the information display area. Notice that Enable has rewritten the formula "@SUM(MONTHTTL)" because the original formula used the same range.

6. Press **Down Arrow**. Notice that the formula in the next cell has also been rewritten. Press **Down Arrow** and then press **Left Arrow** twice. Type **Partner's Share** and press **Right Arrow** twice.

7. Type **@SUM(MONTH)/2** and press **Enter**. Enable beeps and displays "Range name not defined" in the status line. It also puts the spreadsheet in Edit mode (see the mode indicator in the top right). Change the name to **MONTHTTL** and press **Enter**. Enable adds all the values in the MONTHTTL range and divides the total in two.

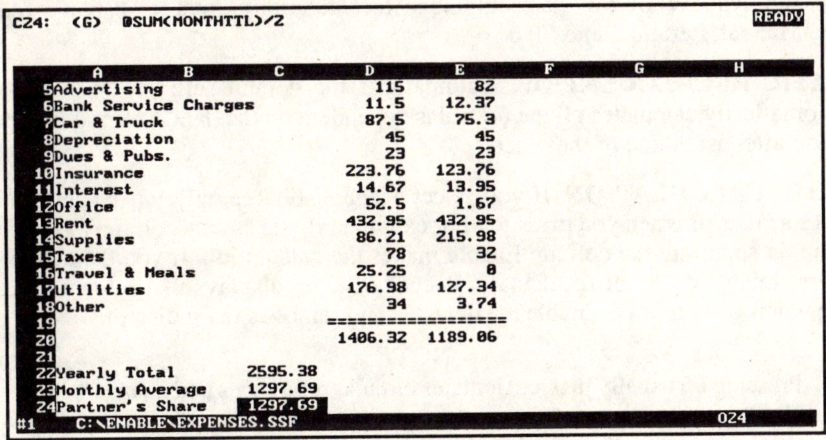

8. Press **Alt-F10**, press **Enter**, and type **R** to save the file.

9. Press **F10** and type **QY** to close the file.

10. Turn to Module 73 to continue the learning sequence.

Module 83
RECALCULATE

DESCRIPTION

When data is entered into a cell Enable automatically calculates all the formulas dependent on that data. Sometimes you don't want Enable to make the calculations, so it has a Recalculate feature that lets you define how and when calculations are made.

Press F10 and type WGR (Worksheet;Global;Recalculation). Enable displays four options: Automatic, Manual, Iteration, and Step.

AUTOMATIC RECALCULATION Automatic is the default setting. When you enter data Enable automatically calculates all the formulas dependent on the data. Select this option to reset recalculation after using one of the others.

MANUAL RECALCULATION If you select Manual, Enable only makes calculations when you enter a formula, or when you press F5. For example, if you enter a column of figures and then enter a formula summing the column Enable makes the calculation. If you then change some of the numbers, Enable does not recalculate. Instead, Enable displays the indicator "Calc" in the status line; when you press F5 Enable recalculates and removes the indicator.

NOTE

Pressing F5 usually just recalculates circular references and changed data. However, you can change your user profile to make pressing F5 recalculate everything in the spreadsheet. This is especially useful if you are linking spreadsheets, because pressing F5 will update the spreadsheet with new data from the supporting spreadsheets.

ITERATION The Iteration feature is used to resolve *circular references.* A circular reference occurs when you create a formula that depends on it's own value. For example:

Cell Number	*Formula or value*
A1	100
A2	50
A3	2*A4
A4	+A1+A2+A3

In this calculation A4 is the sum of the values in A1, A2, and A3. However, A3 is A4 multiplied by two. Circular references like this are usually the result of mistakes. As soon as Enable finds one it displays "Circular reference found" in the status line.

Because these types of formulas are usually mistakes Enable only calculates them once. However, it is sometimes necessary to make circular references, so Enable lets you calculate them up to 51 times each time you press F5 (the original calculation plus 50 iterations). When you select Iteration at the Recalculation options, Enable prompts you to enter the number of recalculations (0-50).

There are two types of circular reference. The one just described is a diverging circular reference—the difference between calculations becomes greater and greater each time a new one is made. With converging references, however, the difference becomes less and less until eventually there is no perceived change.

Why would you want to use a circular reference? For example, a company wants to pay its sales people a commission based on profits. Profit is defined as the sales price minus commission and overhead. Obviously the profit then is dependent on the commission, which depends on profit. This is a converging circular reference that can be solved using multiple iterations.

TIP: Although Enable displays a message telling you if you have circular references, it doesn't tell you where they are. Set the Iteration value to 50, press F5 several times, and watch for the cells recalculating over and over (cells in non-circular formulas will not change or will only change once). Of course this doesn't work once a converging reference has converged too close. You can also use the Audit commands to help you find related cells (see Module 67).

STEP RECALCULATION Step calculations allow you to increase the value in a cell until the value in another cell (the target cell) reaches or exceeds a specified goal. For example,

Cell..	*Value*
A1 (source)	13.57
A2	25.3
A3 (target)	A1+A2*5.7

You can make Enable calculate the value of A1 when a specified value in target A3 is reached.

NOTE

Step Recalculation only works when Recalculation is set to Automatic.

Select Step at the Recalculation options and Enable provides two more options: Manual and Automatic.

Manual Step-Recalculation Enable prompts you for the address of the source cell (the cell that you want to change the value of). Press Enter if the pointer is on the cell, or type the address and press Enter. Then Enable prompts for the adjustment value, the amount to add to or subtract from the cell. Enter the value, press Enter, and press Right Arrow to increase the cell's value, or Left Arrow to decrease it. Watch the target cell as it gets closer to the value you are looking for. Press Esc when you have finished.

Automatic Step-Recalculation Enable prompts you for the address of the source cell (the "cell to be adjusted"), the adjustment value, the target cell, and the "completion value." When you enter the completion value and press Enter Enable begins the calculation. You see the values change as they get closer to the targets. As soon as the target value is reached or exceeded Enable stops. If the value is not reached or exceeded within 100 calculations Enable asks if you want to continue; press Esc to cancel or any other key to continue.

NOTE

When Enable makes a Step-Recalculation it displays "Circular reference found" in the status line. Ignore this message.

APPLICATIONS

Recalculating each time you enter a number can really slow you down in large, complicated spreadsheets and on slow computers. Setting the spreadsheet to manual recalculation speeds things up. The iteration feature helps when you are making complicated circular-reference calculations with percentages, and the Step feature lets you make projections. For example, you want to know the before-tax income you need to make a particular after-tax sum. You can build the tax tables to calculate the taxes, and then specify the after-tax sum as the target, and the before-tax sum as the source.

TYPICAL OPERATION

In this activity you experiment with recalculation in the file EXPENSES, created in Module 6.

1. Open the file named EXPENSES. Move the pointer to a position where you can see the totals cells and the column of figures, as shown in the following screen.

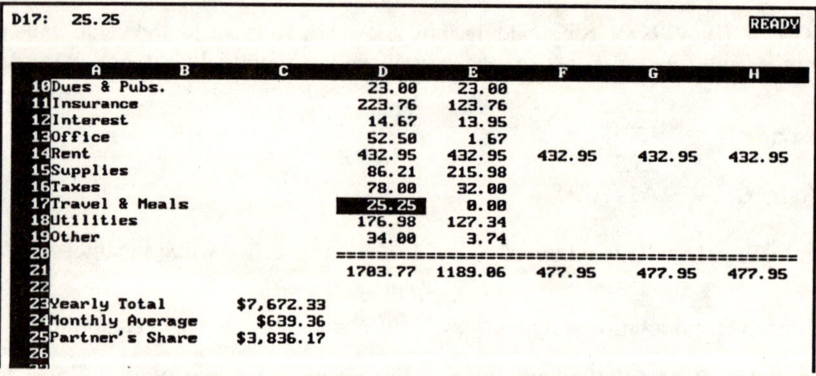

2. Press **F10** and type **WGRM** (Worksheet;Global;Recalculation;Manual).
3. Move the cursor to cell D16. Type **93** and press **Enter**. Notice that the totals do not change, and that Enable has displayed Calc in the status line. Enter **125.25** in the Travel & Meals cell for January, and **92.50** in the Other cell.
4. Press **F5** and the totals are recalculated.

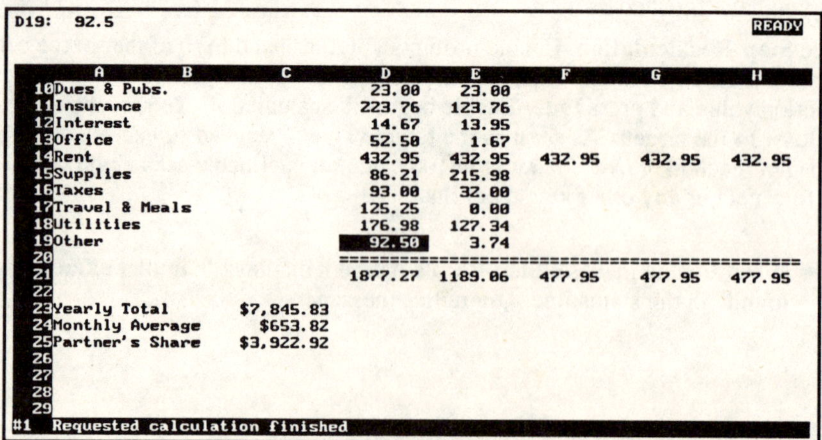

5. Press **F10** and type **WGRA** (Worksheet;Global;Recalculation;Automatic) to reset the recalculation mode.

6. Move the cursor to A28. Add the labels in A28 to A31 as shown in the following screen. Enter **11532** into D28. The other three cells have formulas; D29 has **+D21**, D30 has **+D28-D29-D31**, and D31 has **+D30*.08**. When you finish, Enable displays "Circular reference found" in the status line.

```
D31:  +D30*0.08                                                    READY

      A            B          C          D          E          F          G
13Office                                52.50       1.67
14Rent                                 432.95     432.95     432.95     432.95
15Supplies                              86.21     215.98
16Taxes                                 93.00      32.00
17Travel & Meals                       125.25       0.00
18Utilities                            176.98     127.34
19Other                                 92.50       3.74
20                                  ==========================================
21                                    1877.27    1189.06     477.95     477.95
22
23Yearly Total              $7,845.83
24Monthly Average             $653.82
25Partner's Share           $3,922.92
26
27
28Total Sales                         11532.00
29Overhead                             1877.27
30Profit                              9654.73
31Commission                           772.38
32
#1  Circular reference found
```

7. Press **F10** and type **WGRI** (Worksheet;Global;Recalculation;Iteration). Type **5** and press **Enter**.

8. Press **F5** and watch as the numbers in cells D30 and D31 change rapidly, recalculating the circular reference. Press **F5** again. The numbers change very slightly. Press again, and they don't appear to change at all.

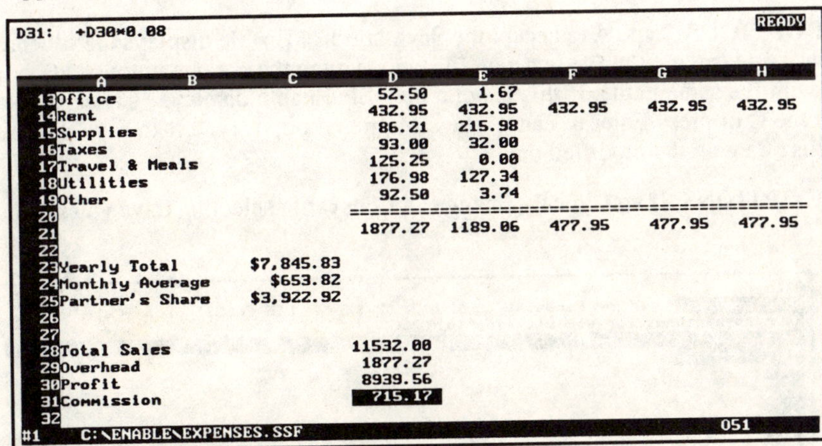

```
D31:  +D30*0.08                                                         READY

      A            B          C          D          E          F          G          H
13Office                                52.50       1.67
14Rent                                 432.95     432.95     432.95     432.95     432.95
15Supplies                              86.21     215.98
16Taxes                                 93.00      32.00
17Travel & Meals                       125.25       0.00
18Utilities                            176.98     127.34
19Other                                 92.50       3.74
20                                  =====================================================
21                                    1877.27    1189.06     477.95     477.95     477.95
22
23Yearly Total              $7,845.83
24Monthly Average             $653.82
25Partner's Share           $3,922.92
26
27
28Total Sales                         11532.00
29Overhead                             1877.27
30Profit                              8939.56
31Commission                           715.17
32
#1     C:\ENABLE\EXPENSES.SSF                                               051
```

9. Press **Alt-F10**, press **Enter**, and type **R** to save the file.

10. Press **F10** and type **QY** to close the file.

11. Turn to Module 80 to continue the learning sequence.

Module 84
SAVE

DESCRIPTION

Enable lets you save your spreadsheet in several different formats. Apart from using Enable's own spreadsheet format you can also use Lotus 1-2-3 (release 1A or 2), Symphony (the same format as Lotus 1-2-3 release 2), DIF, ASCII, or SuperCalc3 (release 2, .CAL format).

You can save in two different Enable formats; with all the values and formulas, or with only the values. You should only use the second format if you don't want to use the formulas again, or if you have saved them in a separate file.

To save a file press F10 and type S (Save). You see the following Top Line Menu.

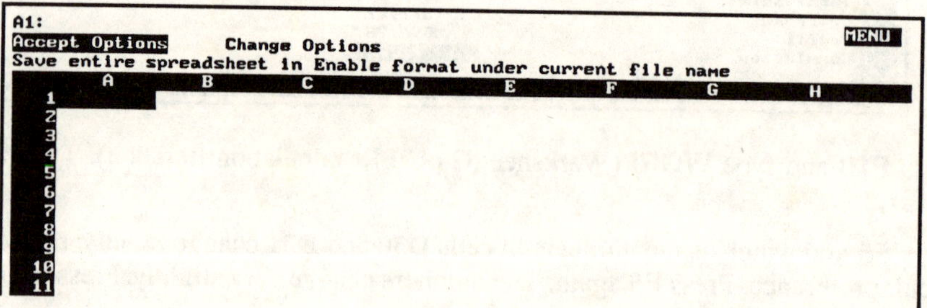

ACCEPT OPTIONS Type A to accept the Save options; Enable displays the filename. You can enter a new name (saving the file in a new file, and leaving the old one untouched), or press Enter to save it with the same name. If this is not a new file Enable displays "Cancel Replace" on the top line. Type C or press Enter to cancel the save operation, or type R to save the file, replacing the previous one with the modified one.

CHANGE OPTIONS If you type C (Change Options) after selecting Save you see the following screen.

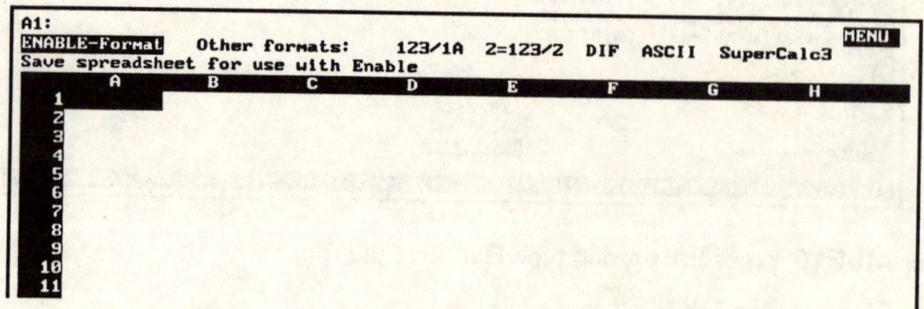

Enable Format If you press Enter or type E, Enable displays two additional options, All or Values. Typing A (All) saves all the values, formulas, and labels. Typing V saves only values and labels, saving disk space. (Enable saves both the values you input and the results of the formulas, but not the formulas themselves, so you can't return to the file later to make recalculations.)

Enable then displays "Enter range to save: ALL" allowing you to define the cells you want to save. Press Enter to save the entire file. Or define a range to save by moving the pointer to one corner of the range of cells to save and pressing . (period). (As soon as you begin moving the pointer the display in the information display area changes. ALL becomes A1..A1 and then changes depending on the position of the pointer.) Then move the pointer to the diagonally opposite corner of the range and press Enter.

Enable displays the filename. Press Enter to accept that name, or type a new name. Whether you save the entire file or select a range, if the filename is of an already existing file, Enable displays the "Cancel Replace" prompt, allowing you to abort the operation or continue and replace the existing data with the new data.

NOTE

There are two other methods for selecting ranges. See Module 82 for more information.

Other Formats If you select one of the other formats Enable saves the entire file; you do not have the option of specifying a range. The following table shows what to type at the prompt, and what data is saved, when you save a file in a different format.

To Save In...	*Type*	*To Save...*
Lotus 1-2-3, 1A	1	Formulas, numbers, cell formats, labels, range names
Lotus 1-2-3, 2	2	Formulas, numbers, cell formats, labels, range names
Symphony	2	Formulas, numbers, cell formats, labels, range names
DIF	D	Numbers, labels
ASCII	A	Numbers, labels, in a comma-separated list
SuperCalc3	S	Formulas, numbers, cell formats, labels

Lotus 1-2-3 If you save a file in Lotus 1-2-3 format Enable changes the integer-format cells to fixed-format, because Lotus 1-2-3 does not have integer-format. Any value-cells that have used Global or Range Alignment commands are right-justified.

When you save a file in Lotus 1-2-3 Release 2 format Enable displays "Convert LICS characters? Yes/No." Selecting Yes changes the characters from ASCII (used by Enable) to the Lotus International Character Set, used by Lotus. Say No if you want to use the file in Enable again, because several characters cannot be converted to LICS, so you may lose some.

When you select a format Enable prompts you for the filename. Enter a name up to eight letters, numbers, and underscores long. If the filename is of an already existing file, Enable displays the "Cancel Replace" prompt, allowing you to abort the save or continue and replace the existing data with the new data.

FILENAME EXTENSIONS The extension with which Enable saves the spreadsheet file depends on the format:

Enable	.SSF
Lotus 1-2-3, 1A	.WKS
Lotus 1-2-3, 2	.WK1
Symphony	.WK1
DIF	.DIF
ASCII	.ASC
SuperCalc3	.CAL

NOTE

If the spreadsheet being saved has a function that has no equivalent in the other format Enable displays @ERR in the cell.

SHORTCUT To use the expert command, press Alt-F10. Enable displays the filename. Press Enter or type the new name.

TIP: Save your document before going to another window, printing, or doing any major operation such as copying large amounts of data from another spreadsheet. That way, if anything goes wrong (and it will, now and again), you can always back up one step.

AUTOMATIC BACKUPS You can make Enable automatically back up files each time it saves a spreadsheet file. See the "Backup existing spreadsheet files when saving?" prompt in Section 7 of the user profile (see Appendix B).

If you select this option, each time you save a file Enable makes a backup copy of the file being replaced. It replaces the last letter in the extension with @, so the backup of an ASCII file called ACCOUNTS.ASC is ACCOUNTS.AS@. Only one backup is kept, so the next time you save the .SSF file, the .SS@ file is replaced by the .SSF file that was saved the previous time.

APPLICATIONS

The Save command lets you save all or a portion of an Enable spreadsheet, or save an entire spreadsheet in one of the other formats. You may need to send a portion of a spreadsheet to someone else, or send a spreadsheet to someone who is using Lotus 1-2-3, for example. You can also convert data into ASCII format so that you can import it into another database program.

The automatic backup feature can save files from being accidentally destroyed; you will always have a copy of the most recently replaced version of each file.

TYPICAL OPERATION

In this activity you open the spreadsheet named EXPENSES, created in Module 6, and save part of it. Begin at the Main Menu.

1. Type **USR**. Type **EXPENSES** and press **Enter**.
2. Press **Alt-F10** and press **Enter**. Enable asks if you want to replace the file on disk. Type **R**, and Enable saves the spreadsheet.

3. Press **F10**, type **SC**, and press **Enter**. Enable asks if you want to save all the file or only labels and values (no formulas). Press **Enter** to accept All. Enable prompts you for the range to save.
4. Press **Home**, type **.** (period), press **Down Arrow** 3 times, and press **Right Arrow** 14 times.

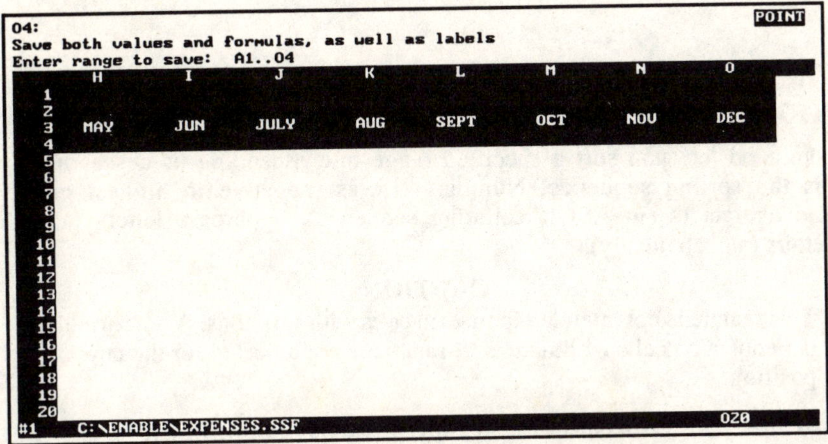

5. Press **Enter** and you have specified the range A1 to O4.
6. Enable displays the filename and the directory name. Change the filename to **LABELS.SSF** and press **Enter**. Enable saves the range in the new file named LABELS.SSF.
7. Press **F10** and type **QY** to return to the Main Menu.
8. Turn to Module 71 to continue the learning sequence.

Module 85
SORT RANGES

DESCRIPTION

The Sort command lets you sort a specified range into ascending or descending order. The following is the sorting sequence: Numbers (lowest negative to highest positive), non-alphanumeric characters (in ASCII collating sequence), uppercase letters (alphabetically), lowercase letters (alphabetically).

CAUTION

This feature is not intended for use on cells with formulas. Also, formulas dependent on cells within the sort-range are not adjusted for the new cell position.

Press F10 and type WRS (Worksheet;Range;Sort) to see the following screen.

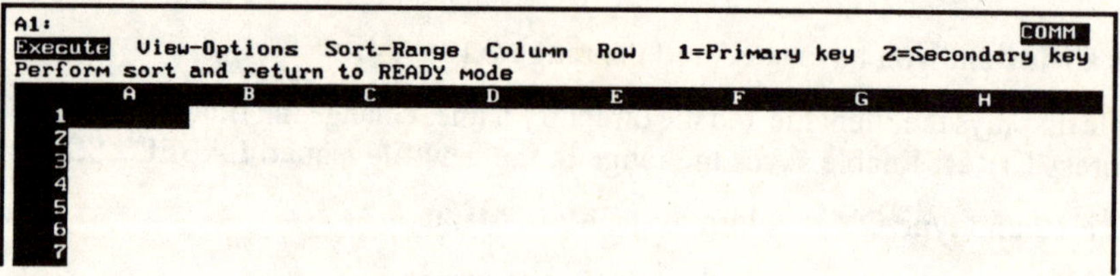

The options are described in the order you are most likely to use them.

COLUMN/ROW Type C or R to tell Enable whether the information is in columns or rows. (The menu line flashes momentarily and Enable stores the information you have given it, but otherwise Enable does not display any kind of response when you press C or R.)

1=PRIMARY KEY You must select a primary key. This tells Enable how to do the primary sort of the data. For example, in the following screen you could have Enable put the list into last-name order, or into city order.

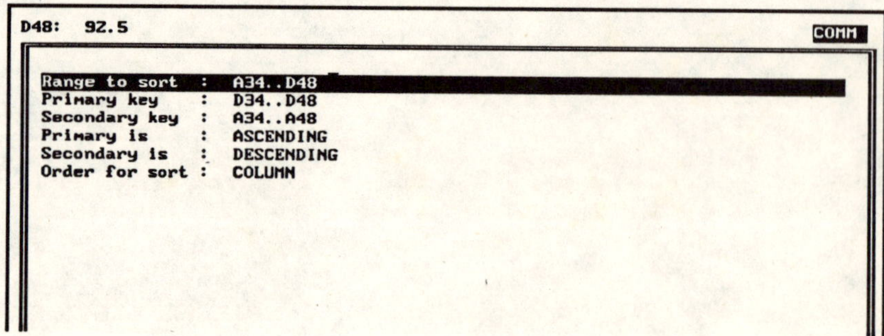

Enable shows you three options: Ascending (1 to 100 and a to z), Descending (100 to 1 and z to a), and Clear. You don't really need Clear, because it removes the primary key, and you cannot sort without a primary key. When you have selected Ascending or Descending, Enable prompts you to enter the range. For example, in the previous screen, if you want to put the names in city order the range is C3..C8.

Actually you can enter C3 and press Enter twice. Enable can calculate the full range when you enter the Sort-Range later.

2=SECONDARY KEY You can specify another range to sort on. For example, if you sort the previous screen in city order you will have two listings in Carrollton. What order should they be in? If you tell Enable to do a secondary, ascending sort on range A3..A8, JONES comes before STULTZ. The Clear option does have a purpose for the Secondary Key, because you may not want a secondary sort.

SORT-RANGE Enable prompts for the range to sort. If you entered C3..C8 for the previous screen, only the cities are sorted—the names remain in the same order. The correct range is A3..C8.

VIEW-OPTIONS This selection displays a window showing your options. Use this just before the sort to make sure it is all set up correctly. Press any key (except the arrow keys) to return to the spreadsheet.

EXECUTE When you have finished selecting the options, type E to sort the cells. If one of the sort keys is not specified correctly Enable displays an error message in the status line.

APPLICATIONS

This feature lets you move your data into easier-to-use formats. You may want to sort a list of expenses into alphabetical order, or set up a list of clients with the highest purchase at the top of the list.

TYPICAL OPERATION

In this activity you copy some cells in the EXPENSES file, created in Module 6, and sort the rows.

1. Open the file named EXPENSES.
2. Press **F10** and type **WC** (Worksheet;Copy). When Enable prompts for the range to copy, type **A5..D19** and press **Enter**. Enable prompts for the range to copy to. Move the pointer to A34 and press **Enter**. Enable copies the cells.
3. Move the pointer to cell D46. Type **115** and press **Down Arrow**. Type **115** again and press **Down Arrow**.

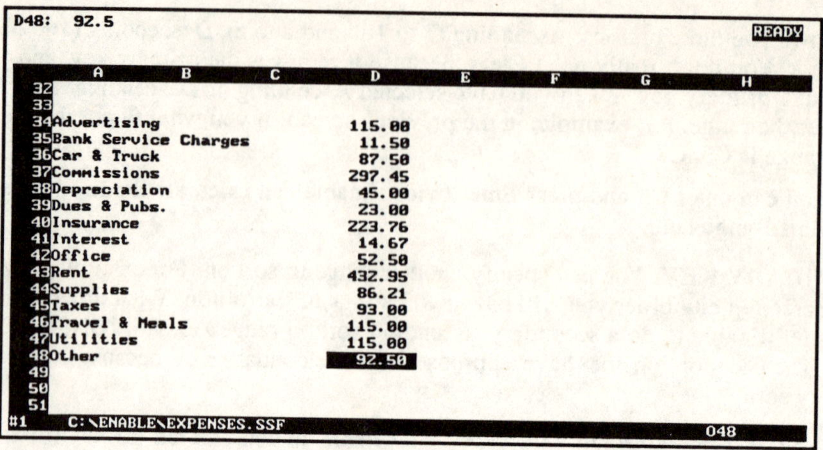

4. Press **F10** and type **WRS** (Worksheet;Range;Sort). Type **R** (Row). Type **1A** (1=Primary key;Ascending). When Enable prompts for the range type **D34..D48** and press **Enter**.
5. Type **2D** (2=Secondary key;Descending). When Enable prompts for the range type **A34..A48** and press **Enter**.
6. Type **S** (Sort). Type **A34..D48** to define the total range to be sorted. Press **Enter**.
7. Type **V** (View-Options). Your screen looks like this:

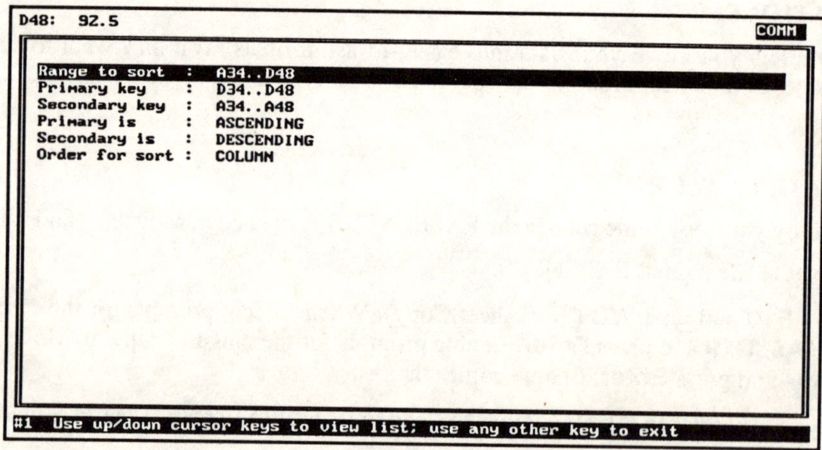

8. Press **Enter** (or any other key, except the arrow keys) to display the Top Line Menu again, and type **E** (Execute) to sort the rows. Your screen looks like this:

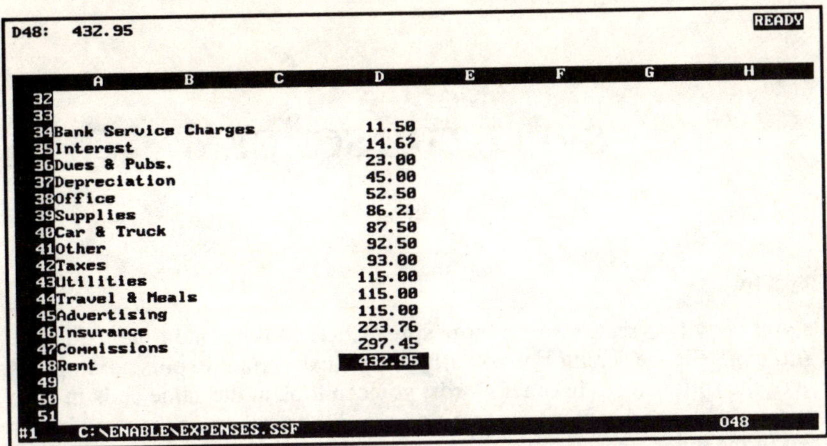

The rows are in value order, with the lowest value at the top. Notice also that the three rows with the same value, 115, are in reverse alphabetical order.

9. Press **Alt-F10**, press **Enter**, and type **R** to save the file.
10. Press **F10** and type **QY** to close the file.
11. Turn to Module 88 to continue the learning sequence.

Module 86
SPLIT THE SCREEN

DESCRIPTION

Enable lets you view two sections of a large spreadsheet at the same time using the split-screen function. You can split the screen horizontally or vertically. Enable puts a complete spreadsheet in each side of the split screen. In other words, you can look at the same cells in both sides of the screen. However, you only have one pointer, and changing a cell in one side of the screen changes the same cell in the other side.

First, position the pointer in the middle of the screen, Press F10 and type MTS (MCM;This Window;Split). Enable displays the options Horizontal, Vertical, Sync, Unsync, Clear.

Select Horizontal if you want one screen above the other, or Vertical if you want the screens side by side. You can move the pointer from one screen to the other by pressing F6. To clear screens, leaving only the top or left screen, select Clear.

SIMULTANEOUS SCROLLING Use Sync and Unsync to turn simultaneous scrolling on and off. When it is on, and the screens are split horizontally, moving one screen laterally also moves the other. If the screens are split vertically, moving one screen vertically also moves the other.

For example, if you want to view both ends of a very wide table, split the screens vertically, press F6 to move the pointer into the right screen, move the pointer to the right side of the table, set Sync on, and then move the pointer up and down the table. As the cells in the screen on the right move up and down, so do the ones on the left screen.

CELL CHARACTERISTICS You can set the new screen's Global Alignment and Global Format independently of the first screen's. However, you cannot set titles once the screen is split (do it before splitting), and the Global Width setting is the same for both screens. However, you can think of the left or upper side of the screen as the master. When you remove the split screen, the cell settings all return to those of the master side.

APPLICATIONS

This feature is useful when you are working in very big spreadsheets and need to see data in areas that are far apart. Split the screen and move one of the areas close to the other.

TYPICAL OPERATION

In this activity you split the screen using the EXPENSES file, created in Module 6.

1. Open the file named EXPENSES. Press **F2**, type **F4**, and press **Enter**. The pointer moves to cell F4.

2. Press **F10** and type **MTSV** (MCM;This Window;Split;Vertical). The screen is "split" in two. Press **F6** and the pointer moves into the right hand screen. Press **Tab**. Your screen looks something like this:

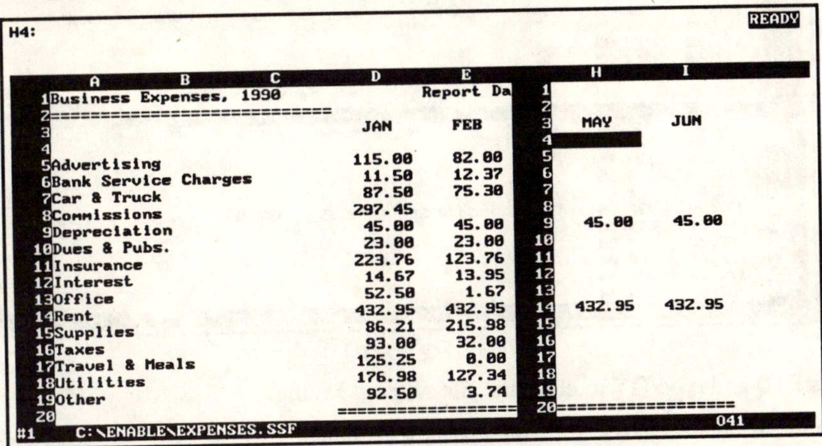

3. Press **Home**. The pointer moves back to cell A1.

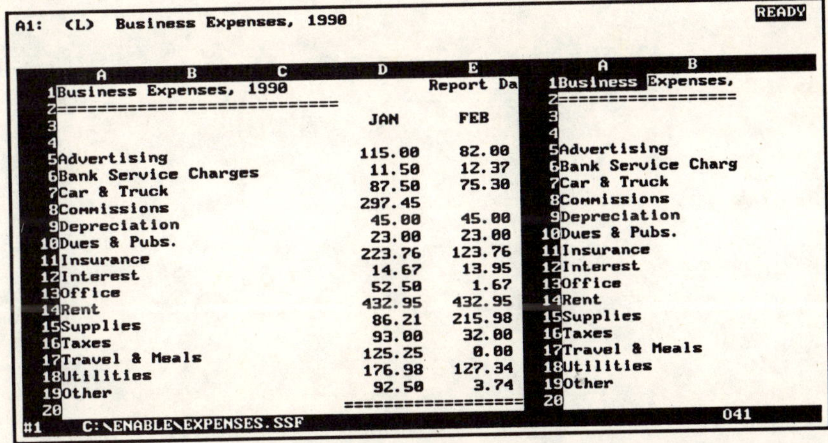

4. Press **F10** and type **MTSC** (MCM;This Window;Split;Clear) to clear the split. Move the cursor to **A9**. Press **F10** and type **MTSH** (MCM;This Window;Split;Horizontal).

5. Press **F10** and type **MTSS** (MCM;This Window;Split;Sync) to set synchronized scrolling. Press **Right Arrow** and watch as both sides of the screen scroll together.

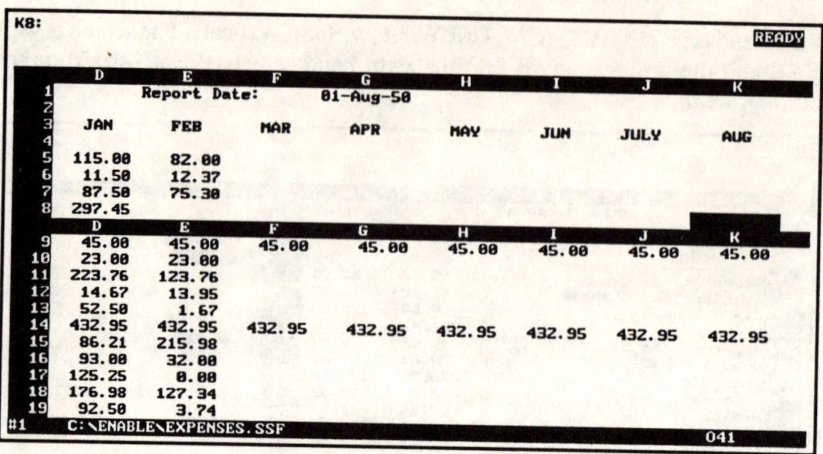

6. Press **F10** and type **QY** to close the file without saving.
7. Turn to Module 85 to continue the learning sequence.

Module 87
TITLES

DESCRIPTION

You can add titles to your spreadsheet by simply typing them where you need them. Enable has a special command called Titles that "freezes" these labels into position on the screen. Whichever section of the spreadsheet you display, the titles remain on your screen.

For example, you might have column headers and row titles that you want to see wherever you are in the spreadsheet. Start by positioning the pointer immediately below the rows, and to the right of the columns you want to freeze. Press F10 and type WT (Worksheet;Titles). Enable displays four options: Both, Horizontal, Vertical, and Clear.

Select Both to freeze the rows above and columns to the left. Select Horizontal to freeze only the rows above, and Vertical to freeze only the columns to the left.

You can select Clear to unfreeze the titles, regardless of the pointer position.

APPLICATIONS

This feature is very useful in large spreadsheets, when the row titles and column headers may be off-screen. Freeze them into position so you always know what each cell's data is.

TYPICAL OPERATION

In this operation you freeze the titles in the file named EXPENSES, created in Module 6.

1. Open the file named EXPENSES. Move the pointer to cell C4.
2. Press **F10** and type **WTB** (Worksheet;Titles;Both). Press **Up Arrow** and **Left Arrow**. Enable beeps and does not move the pointer into the titles.
3. Press **Tab**. Cells from the right of your spreadsheet move into view, but the left hand column remains in place. Your screen looks something like this:

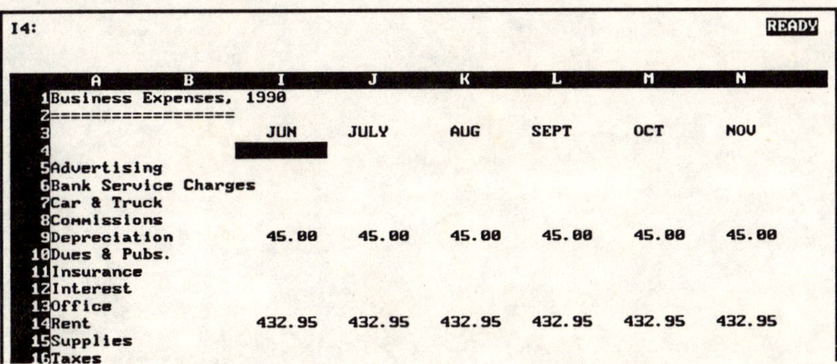

4. Press **Home**. The pointer returns to cell C4. Press **PgDn** several times. Notice that although the cells from lower in the spreadsheet are displayed, the top three rows remain in view.
5. Press **F10** and type **WTC** (Worksheet;Titles;Clear). Press **Home** and the pointer moves back to cell **A1**.
6. Press **F10** and type **QY** to close the file without saving.
7. Turn to Module 86 to continue the learning sequence.

Module 88
TRANSPOSE ROWS AND COLUMNS

DESCRIPTION

You can adjust a spreadsheet format by switching rows of data into columns, or vice versa. Unlike the Move command, which moves data from a row into another row, or a column into another column, the Transpose command moves the data from a row into a column, or from a column into a row.

Press F10, type WGT (Worksheet;Global;Transpose) and Enable asks you to enter a "From" range. Enter the range using one of the methods described in Module 82 (typing the adress, typing the name, or pointing to the range). Enable then prompts you for the first cell of the "To" range. Type the cell address or move the pointer to the cell, and press Enter (this is the top left cell of the "To" range). Enable moves all the data from the cells in the "From" range and puts it in the "To" range.

CAUTION
Data in the To-range cells is replaced by the new data.

FORMULA ADJUSTMENTS Formulas that refer to data in cells that are transposed are adjusted in the same way formulas are when values are moved or copied. See Module 69.

ABORTED TRANSPOSITIONS In some cases Enable cannot move the cells. If the To and From ranges overlap, Enable displays an error message. Press Esc and Enable displays "Enter from range" again. However, Enable does complete transpositions if you are only transposing one row or column.

TIP: If you need to move the data into a position that overlaps the original position, transpose it into a different position and then move it using Worksheet/Move (see Module 69). Or, insert rows or columns, transpose the data, and then delete the extra rows or columns (see Module 72).

Enable cannot transpose data if the To range overlaps the edge of the spreadsheet; Enable displays "To range limits wraparound." Press Esc and the "Enter from range" prompt is redisplayed.

You cannot transpose cells onto protected cells.

APPLICATIONS

Transposing rows and columns is a convenient way to change the format of your spreadsheet, allowing you to move data if you think it could be better presented in another way.

TYPICAL OPERATION

In this activity you open the file named EXPENSES and transpose a column.

1. Open the file named EXPENSES. Press **F2**, type **A34**, and press **Enter**. The pointer moves to A34.

2. Press **F10** and type **WGT**. Enable prompts for the range to transpose. Type **D34..D48** and press **Enter**. Enable prompts for the starting cell. Type **A51**.

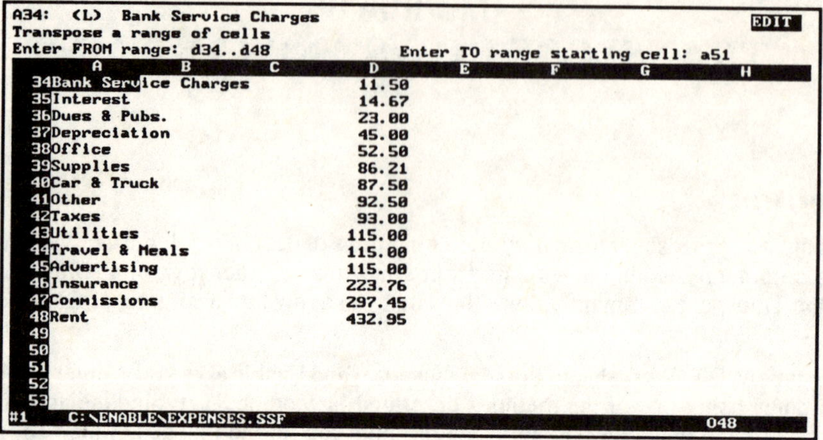

3. Press **Enter** and Enable transposes the column.

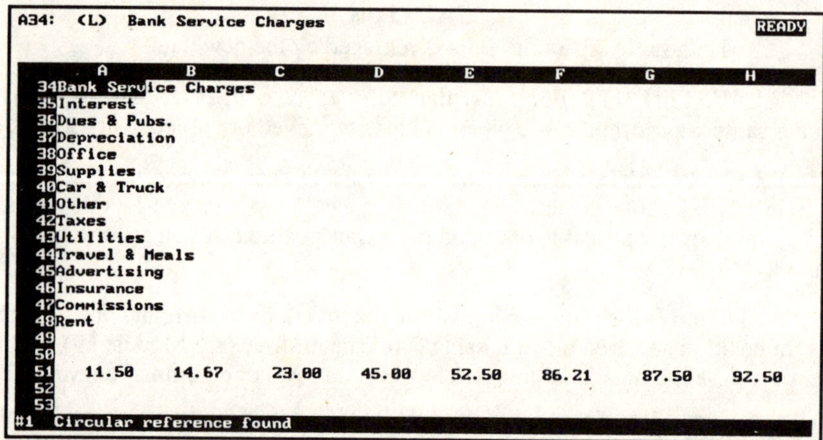

4. Press **F10** and type **QY** to close the file without saving.
5. Turn to Module 74 to continue the learning sequence

Module 89
WINDOWS AND FILES

DESCRIPTION

Enable's spreadsheet window commands are very similar to those in Word Processing. Up to eight windows can be opened. The windows are numbered, in the left corner of the status line, in the order in which they are opened, except if you close a window. For example, you have four windows open, and you close number two. The next window you open is number two, not number five. You could be working on a word processing file while referring to another word processing file and several spreadsheets and databases.

You can also see a list of spreadsheet or print files (Disk-Files) using the Files option.

To access window commands, press F10 and type M (MCM). Enable displays the following options:

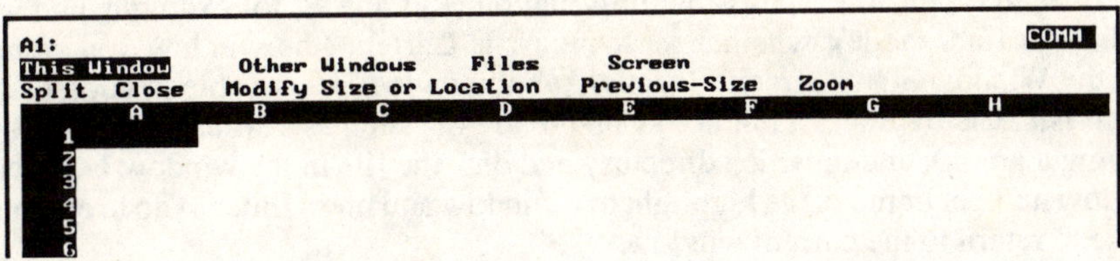

Select This Window if you want to split the screen, close the window, or change the window size or location. Select Other Window if you want to go to another window or view the Window Summary screen.

THIS WINDOW The following screen shows the This Window options:

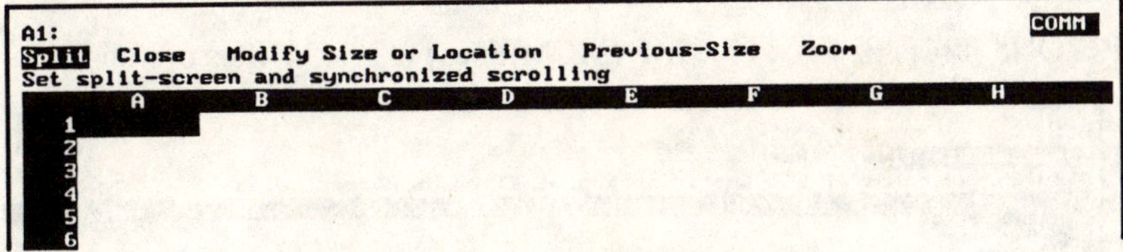

Split See Module 86 for information on splitting the screen.

Close This option is the same as using Quit on the Top Line Menu.

Modify Size or Location This option changes the size of the window, or moves the window to a different position on the screen (if it is less than full-size). Enable displays instructions in the status line, telling you to press M (move), S (shrink), or E (expand) and then press the arrow keys to actually move, shrink, or expand the window. Instead of using the arrow keys, you can press and hold the R key to rapidly shrink or expand the window equally in all directions. You can carry out multiple operations, shrinking and then moving a window, for example. When you have finished the operation, press Esc.

Previous-Size If you have changed the window's size by using Modify or Zoom, you can select this option to return to the previous size.

Zoom Select this option to change the window back to full-screen size.

OTHER WINDOW Select Other Window to see the following options:

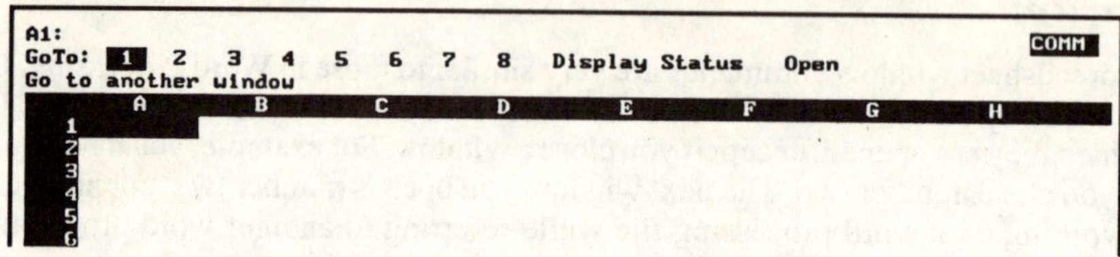

Go To: 1 2 3 4 5 6 7 8: Select a window number and Enable displays that window.

Display Status This option displays the Window Status screen, which lists all the open windows. It shows the window type (for example, WP is word processing, SS is spreadsheet); the window number (1 to 8); the filename; status-line information (Ref and B, for example, and whether the file is in draft or final mode); whether the window is Current (the window you were in before displaying the Window Status screen), Inactive (another window available to you), or Notavail (a window that is in use by Enable, but not available to you, such as a spreadsheet from which you are displaying a graph); and in which directory and disk the file in the window is stored. You can type a window number or move the highlight to a window and press Enter to go to another window, or press Esc to return to the current window.

Open Enable displays the Main Menu and lets you open any sort of window; word processing, spreadsheet, database, graphics, and so on.

EXPERT COMMANDS Press Alt-Up Arrow or Alt-Down Arrow to move directly to the previous or next window in sequence, bypassing the menus. You can also press Alt-Home to display the Main Menu so that you can open another window.

FILES OPTIONS Press F10 and type MF (MCM;Files) to see the files options.

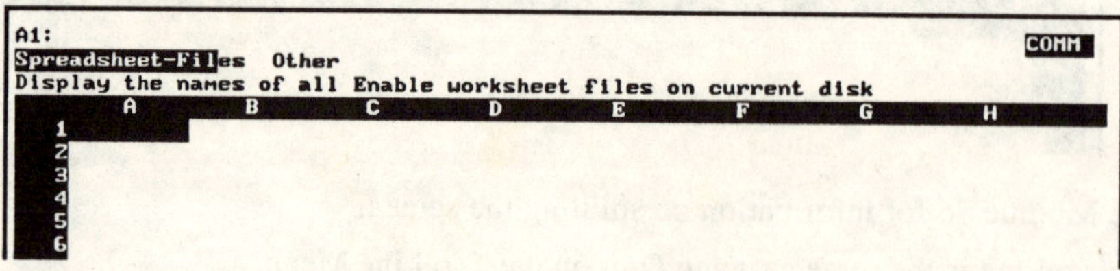

Spreadsheet-Files This option displays a list of spreadsheet files, those files with a .SSF extension.

NOTE

In some releases of Enable/OA this option is called Worksheet-Files.

You can use any of the file directory commands, or select a file and press Enter. Enable prompts you to confirm the "retrieve" operation. If you answer Yes the retrieved file replaces the spreadsheet you were just in.

CAUTION

If you do not save the first spreadsheet, any changes you have made are lost when the second file is retrieved.

Other Enable prompts for a filename, and then replaces the current spreadsheet with the specified spreadsheet. (Enable prompts you to confirm the retrieve first.) If the file has a .SSF extension you don't need to enter the extension. If Enable doesn't recognize the spreadsheet format it asks you to select the format: ASCII, DIF, or VisiCalc.

NOTE

These options work differently in 3D spreadsheets. See Appendix K for more information.

Print-Files Earlier releases of Enable/OA (the releases in which the Spreadsheet-Files option is called Worksheet-Files), contained another option, Print-Files. You can use this option to view print files, files created when you select Disk-File from the print option. You cannot retrieve these files.

APPLICATIONS

Enable's window operations make true application-integration possible. Opening several windows at the same time allows you to refer to information in another window, or even copy information from one to the other. A section of a spreadsheet can be included in a memo or letter, or a list from a database could be added to a document. You can choose to leave the windows full size, and display another window when you need it, or you can display several windows at the same time.

You can use the Files options to open a spreadsheet and close the current one in a single operation.

TYPICAL OPERATION

In this activity you experiment with the windows commands while in the EXPENSES file, created in Module 6.

1. Open the file named EXPENSES and press **Home**.
2. Press **F10** and type **MFS** (MCM;Files;Spreadsheet-Files) [Type MFW (MCM;Files; Spreadsheet-Files) in earlier release of Enable/OA]. Enable displays a list of spreadsheets, similar to the following screen.

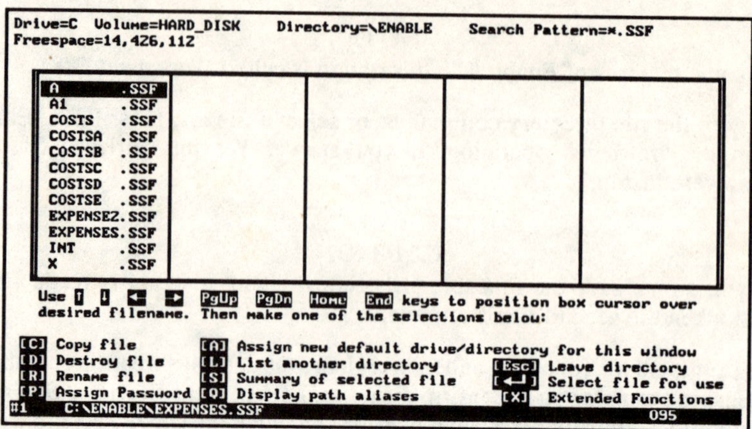

3. Press **Esc** to clear the screen. Press **F10** and type **MTM** (MCM;This Window;Modify). Type **S** and hold **Up Arrow** down until the screen is about half size. Press **Esc**. Your screen looks like this:

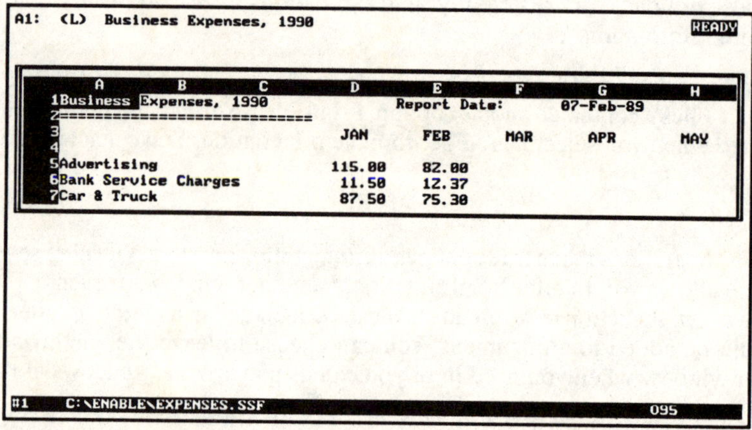

4. Press **F10** and type **MTMM** (MCM;This Window;Modify;Move). Press **Down Arrow** until the window is in the bottom of the screen. Press **Esc**.

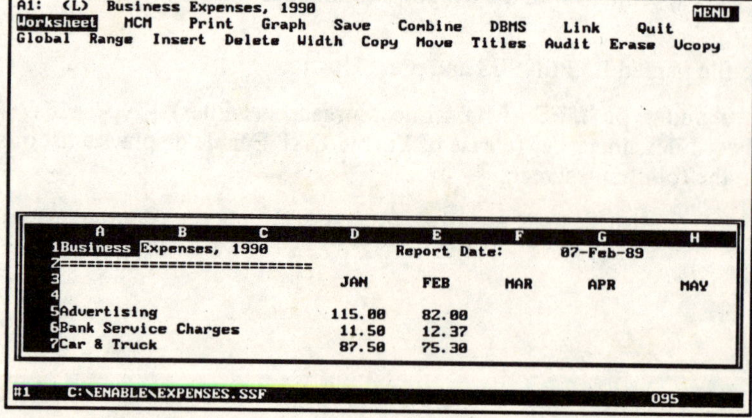

5. Press **F10** and type **MOD** (MCM;Other Window;Display Status). Enable displays the Window Status screen.

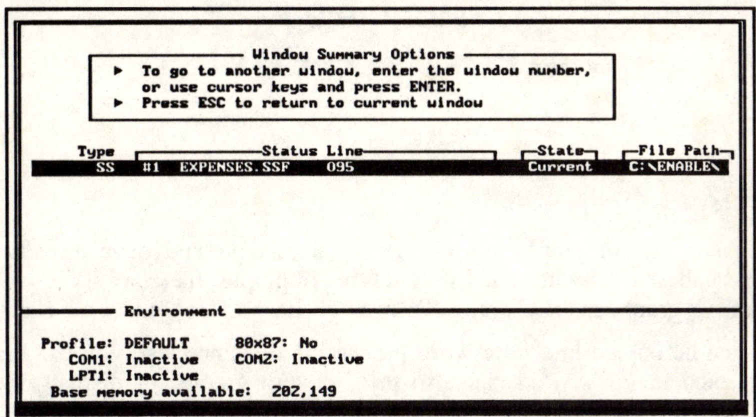

6. Press **Esc** to return to the spreadsheet. Press **F10** and type **QY** to close the file without saving.
7. Turn to Module 67 to continue the learning sequence.

Module 90
GRAPHICS OVERVIEW

INTRODUCTION

Enable has an easy-to-use graphics package that uses data you have already entered in a spreadsheet or database to produce ten different types of graphs; there are six types of bar graphs, a line graph, an XY graph, an HLC graph (Open-High-Low-Close), and a pie chart.

These graphs can be copied into your word processing documents so you can include them in letters, reports, and manuals. You can also print or plot graphs, or display one alongside a spreadsheet so you can watch it change as you change the values in the spreadsheet.

FORMAT OPTIONS

Enable has a number of format options that let you change the way the graph looks. You can add legends and titles, and even select from a list of nine different fonts. You can select the type of shading to be used in bar graphs or the lines and symbols used in line and XY graphs. You can also select the colors used when a graph is plotted or displayed on a color graphics monitor.

GRAPH SETTINGS

Enable saves *graph settings* so that you don't have to re-design a graph each time you want to produce one. Graph settings are sets of instructions that tell Enable exactly how to build the graph; where to find the data to go in the graph, the type of graph, what scale to use, etc. Each graph setting describes one file. Once you have designed the settings, you can save them. Then you can come back later and produce the same graph again using just four or five keystrokes. For example, suppose you design and print a graph. A month later, when you have modified some of the data in the spreadsheet you were working with, you want to print an up-to-data version—just press F10, type GS (Graph;Select), select the settings, type P (Print) and another graph is on its way. You can design up to eight different graph settings for each spreadsheet or database graph-settings file.

Unlike spreadsheet graph settings (which are stored with the spreadsheet), the database settings are stored in a separate file. This allows you to build graphs using data from more than one database.

HARDWARE

You need the right hardware to work with Enable's graphics. First, you need a graphics monitor and a graphics card. An inexpensive monochrome graphics card is sufficient. If you want to print the graph, you need an Enable-compatible graphics printer (a dot-matrix or laser printer, for example). Enable shows you a list of the compatible printers when you use the Install program. And of course, if you want to plot, you need an Enable-compatible plotter.

IMPORTING GRAPHICS TO WORD PROCESSING

You can copy Enable's graphs to your word processing documents, but you can also import other types of graphics into your documents. You can use MacPaint, PC Paintbrush, and IBM 6180 Plotter files (from Perspective). (Perspective is a more advanced graphics package that is now packaged with Enable. Because of its large number of features and capabilities it was not possible to include it in this book). You can also import Enable Graphics' plot files, files stored on disk when you use the Plot command.

MENU CHOICES

The Enable graphics menu system seems complicated at first, but once you understand it you will have no trouble finding your way around. Module 99 describes the menu system, with a flow diagram showing you the structure, to help you understand it. Some of the confusion arises because the terms are not always consistent, and they are sometimes ambiguous. There are two Scale options, although perhaps one of them could have been called Multiplier or Scale-Factor. The Headings option is inconsistent with other terminology, because elsewhere the headings are actually called Titles; and the Shade option could have been called Shade&Lines to be more descriptive.

But when you finish Module 99 in this book you will understand what each option does, and you can always use the flow diagram to find your way around until you are totally familiar with how it all works.

THIS BOOK

Data for graphics comes from a spreadsheet or a database. Whichever one of these you use for your graphics, this section of the book is written with the assumption that you know how to use it. While we explain how graphics interact with the database and spreadsheet, we do not include detailed instructions on preparing your data—these can be found in the other sections of this book.

There is no single way to build a graph. You can begin the procedure many different ways, and carry out the various operations in many different sequences. For the purpose of explaining how to use the graphics features this book suggests the following learning sequence.

Module 101—Select Graphics Mode; how to begin the operation from the spreadsheet or database.

Module 100—Save; how to save the graph settings.

Module 99—Menus; how to find your way around the graph-system menus.

Module 96—Graph Type; how to select the type of graph.

Module 95—Graph Format; how to define the overall format of the graph.

Module 91—Axes; how to define the format of the graph's axes.

Module 92—Data Groups; how to select the data and define what it looks like.

Module 97—Headings; how to enter titles and subtitles.

Module 93—Display (and Copy to Word Processing); how to display the graph and copy it to a word processing file.

Module 94—Draw and Print; how to plot and print the graph.

Module 98—Import Graphics; importing other graphics files to word processing.

DEFAULTS

All the graphics options have defaults—if you don't make a selection Enable chooses for you. For example, the default Grid setting is Neither, that is, Enable does not display a grid unless you choose one. In some of the modules' Typical Operations you may be choosing options that are actually the default choices, but we have still included these steps to illustrate the different choices available.

REMEMBER!

Of course we all know this, but... the y-axis is vertical; the x-axis is horizontal.

Turn to Module 101 to continue the learning sequence.

Module 91
AXES

DESCRIPTION

There are several ways to format the labels on the axes. The following options affect all the graphs, even the pie chart (the labels next to the Pie chart slices come from the X-axis-data option). From the Task Options Menu type OGA (Options;Global;Axis) to see the following screen.

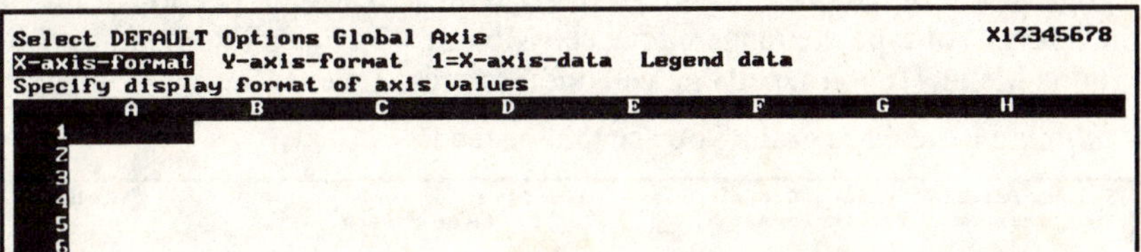

X-AXIS-FORMAT This option defines the format of the labels on the horizontal (x) axis. Enable displays the following options:

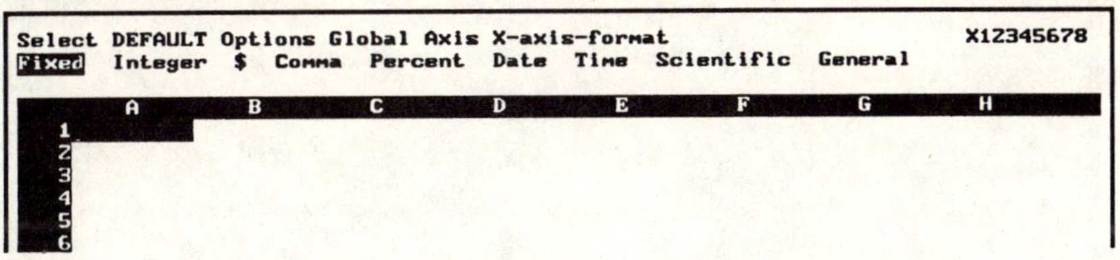

You probably recognize these formats from the spreadsheet Global and Range Format commands; they work the same here. For example, select Integer if you want the labels to be whole numbers, or Date to convert a number into a date. See Module 73 for more information.

You need to define the X-axis format if you are building an XY graph (because you will have data on both axes), or if you are using numerical data (from the X-axis-data option) to provide labels for the x-axis of a line graph or bar graph or the slices of a pie graph. You define the source of the numerical data for the x-axis at the X-axis-data option, described later in this module.

Y-AXIS-FORMAT This option defines the format of the labels on the vertical (y) axis. The options are the same as for the X-axis-format. You have y-axis data on all the graphs except the pie graph.

1=X-AXIS-DATA This is used in two ways: to provide the values for the x-axis on XY graphs, and to provide labels for slices of a pie graph or the x-axis on all other types of graphs. Enable asks you to define the spreadsheet cells or database fields that provide the X-axis-data.

NOTE

If you are building an XY graph you *must* define X-axis-data, and that data must be *numerical.*

The values used for X-axis data in any graph other than an XY graph may be numbers or words. For example, if you are graphing your company's monthly income, you might use the row labels from the spreadsheet (Jan, Feb, etc.).

If you select the X-axis-data option while you are building a spreadsheet graph you see the following:

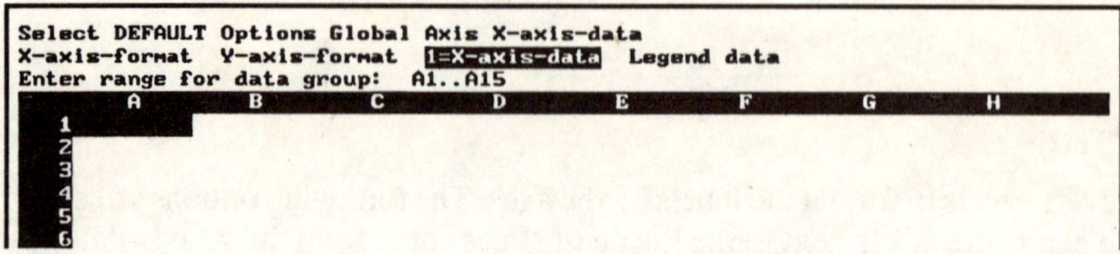

Define the range in one of the three ways described in the spreadsheet section of this book (point to it, type the address, or type the range name; see Module 82). Press Enter and Enable returns to the Axis Options Menu. (If you typed one cell address press Enter twice.)

If you are designing a database graph you see this instead:

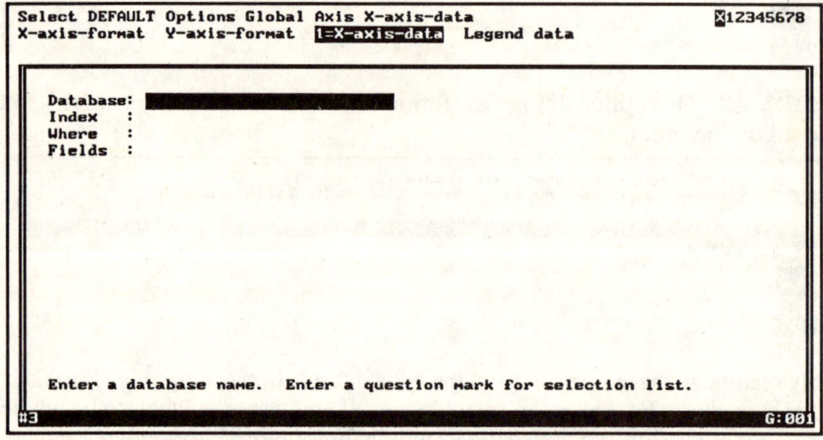

Enter the database name and use the Index prompt to define the order the records will be used in, the Where prompt to define which records will be used, and the Fields prompt to tell Enable from which field to take the data to put on the x-axis. A simpler method may be to use the Sort command to build a select set, enter the select set name at the database prompt, and then skip the other prompts. When you finish specifying the range Enable returns to the Axis Options Menu.

Pie Chart If you are building a pie chart you must also select Data-Labels at the Pie options (Options;Global;Type;Pie;Format;Data-Labels). Otherwise the X-axis-data selected here is not used.

LEGEND DATA This option is not used by Enable graphics—it is used to define legends from spreadsheet cells or database records when you are using the Perspective graphics system, which is not covered in this book.

APPLICATIONS

The axis options let you tell Enable what to display on the left side of the graph and underneath it. These labels tell the person looking at the graph what the data means.

TYPICAL OPERATION

In this activity you set the format of the y-axis numbers and tell Enable where to get the labels for the x-axis, using the spreadsheet named GRAPH, which you created in Module 96.

1. Open the spreadsheet named GRAPH. Press **F10**, type **GS** (Graph;Select), select **BAR**, and press **Enter**.
2. At the Task Options Menu type **OGA** (Options;Global;Axis). Enable displays the following menu.

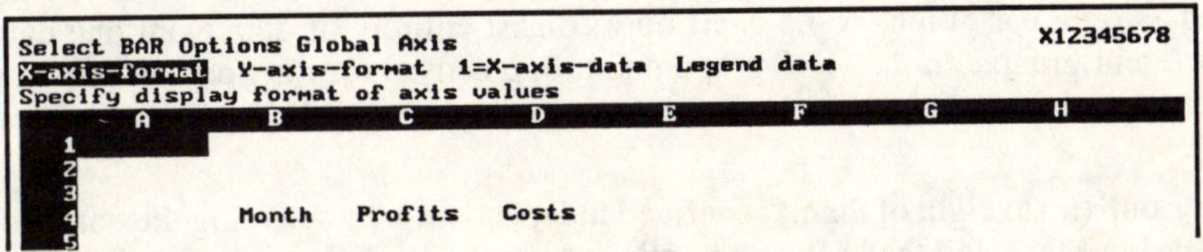

3. Type **Y** (Y-axis-format) and type **I** (Integer) to specify that the numbers on the Y axis are integers.
4. Type **1** (1=X-axis-data). Enable prompts for the range. Move the pointer to cell B6 and type . (period). Move the pointer to B17.

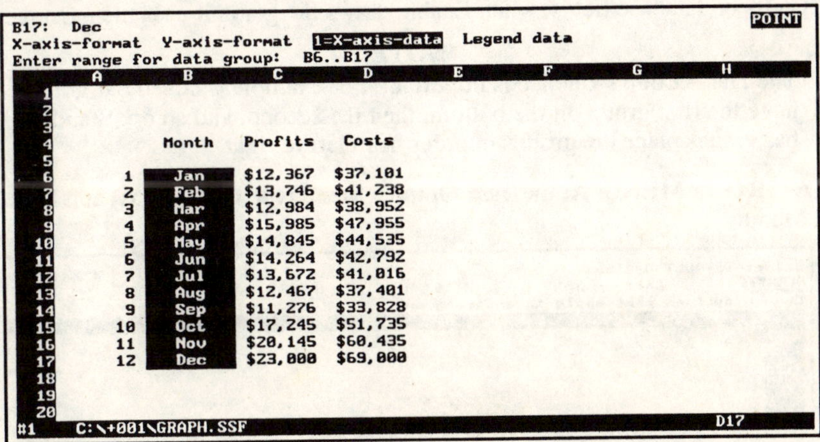

5. Press **Enter**. These labels are used for the bottom (x-axis) labels.
6. Press **Esc** five times to remove the graph menus from the spreadsheet.
7. Press **Alt-F10**, press **Enter**, and type **R** to save the spreadsheet.
8. Press **F10** and type **QY** to close the file.
9. Turn to Module 92 to continue the learning sequence.

Module 92

DATA GROUPS

DESCRIPTION

This module explains how to select the data used in each data group, and how to format the data; which scale, color, shade, and legend to use, for example.

A data group is one element of the graph. It may be one line on a line graph or XY graph or one group of bars on a bar graph. A pie chart may consist entirely of data from one data group, or several different groups. In the HLC graph one group is used for the opening prices, one for the closing prices, one for the highs, and one for the lows (see Module 96 for a discussion of the HLC graph).

Each data group (up to eight of them) is defined independently by selecting the data group number from the Design Menu and then selecting options from the Data Group Menu. When you have set up one data group, return to the list of data groups and select the next one. You can return at any time to change any of the settings described in this module. For example, you may have made a mistake when you defined the spreadsheet range; just come back to the Data Group Menu option and do it again. Also, remember that these are only graph "settings." You are telling Enable what to do *when* it draws the graph. It does nothing now. So if you change the data in the specified spreadsheet cells or database fields, when Enable draws the graph it uses the most recent data.

NOTE

The Data Group sequence is important. For example, stacked bar graphs have the first group on the bottom, then the second, and so on. Standard bar graphs place the groups in order from left to right.

THE DATA GROUP MENU At the Task Options Menu type O (Options) and Enable displays the Design Menu:

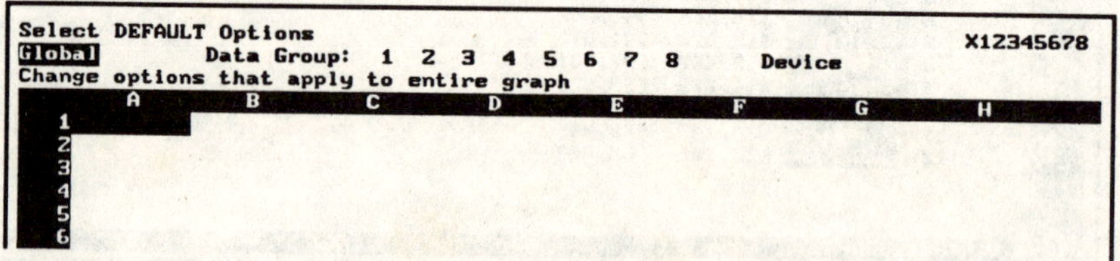

The numbers after "Data Group" are the individual groups. Type 1 to select the first group and Enable displays the Data Group Menu:

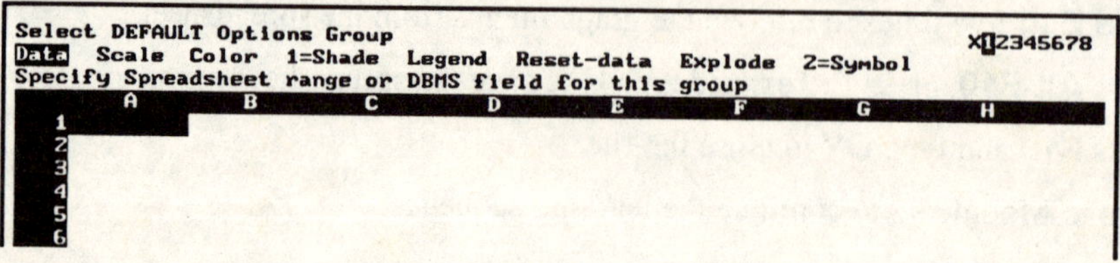

NOTE

The option in the menu is Data Group: 1. Don't type D (which selects Device); type the group number.

Notice that the 1 in the group of numbers in the top right of the screen is highlighted, indicating that you are working with group 1. Any data groups that have already had their data specified are underlined.

DATA—SELECTING DATA FROM A SPREADSHEET Select Data to tell Enable which data is going to be used for this data group. If you are working with a spreadsheet Enable prompts you for the range of cells to be used as group 1. For example, you might want to select the cells that hold the income totals for each month.

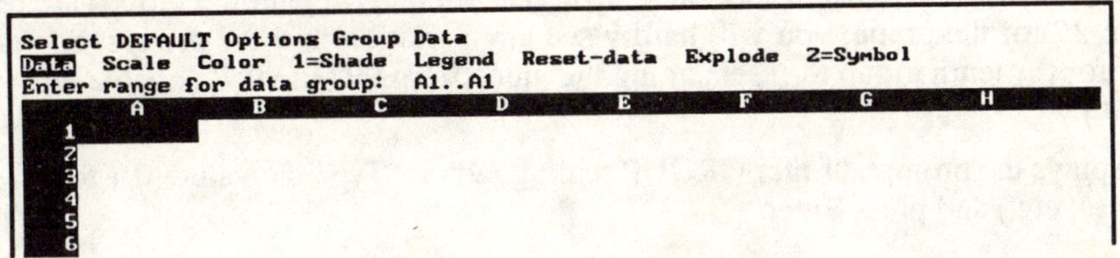

Define the range in one of the three ways described in the Spreadsheet section of this book (point to it, type the address, or type the range name; see Module 82). Press Enter and Enable returns to the Data Group Menu.

NOTE

If you move spreadsheet ranges specified in a graph setting Enable automatically updates the setting with the new addresses.

DATA—SELECTING DATA FROM A DATABASE Enable displays the following screen if you select Data while working with a database.

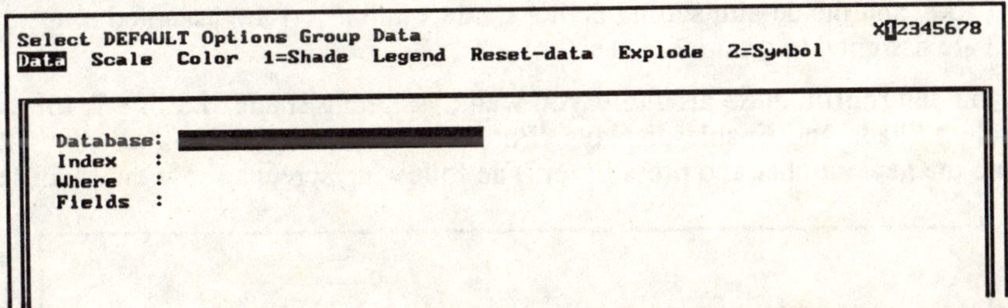

Enter the database name, use the Index prompt to define the order the records will be used in, the Where prompt to define which records will be used, and the Fields prompt to tell Enable from which field to take the data. When you finish specifying the range, Enable returns to the Axis Options Menu.

Probably the best way to prepare database data for graphing is to build a select set first using the database Sort command. Use Sort to put the ranges in order, and to select exactly the records you want to graph. Then, when you select Data from the Data Groups Menu you can enter the select set name (the filename with a .SS extension) at the Database prompt. You can then skip the Index, Where, and Fields prompts.

The database graphing procedure allows you to select information from different databases to go on one graph. You should read and understand the database section before trying to use database data for graphing.

SCALE This option lets you specify a multiplier for the data group. Use this if the group's values are much higher or lower than those of the other groups. Enable automatically sets the scale beginning at 0 and ending high enough to fit the largest value. You can specify your own scale (Options;Global;Scale—see Module 95), but you can also adjust the data group to bring it closer to the other groups.

For example, suppose you have ten groups, nine of which lie in the range of 20 to 30. The last group has a value of 997. Enable sets the scale at 0 to 1000, so nine of the groups are relegated to the bottom 3% of the graph; you will hardly see any variation in these groups. So set the scale multiplier for the tenth group to .1, changing the value from 997 to 99.7. (Enable will use a scale of 0 to 100.)

Enable displays the prompt, "Enter GROUP scaling factor." Type the value (0.1 for one tenth, 10 for ten times, etc.) and press Enter.

NOTE

Enable makes no indication on the graph that one of the data groups is scaled. You can do this yourself by adding a note to the legend (discussed later in this module) or entering a title or subtitle (Options; Global;Headings).

COLOR This option lets you specify the color used for the line, bar, or pie wedge and corresponding legend when you plot the graph or display it on a color monitor. This overides the Shade option. You can select from a list of ten colors.

1=SHADE This option not only controls the shading used in bar graphs, but also the lines used in line and XY graphs. Enable has eight types of shading and eight types of line. Both groups are numbered 1 to 8, and the default setting is that shade 1 and line 1 are assigned to group 1, shade 2 and line 2 are assigned to group 2, and so on.

However, you can shuffle these around if you want, assigning shade and line 7, for example, to group 3. Select Shade and Enable displays "Enter shade value (1-8)" and displays the current setting. Type the new number and press Enter. The following screens show the shades and lines.

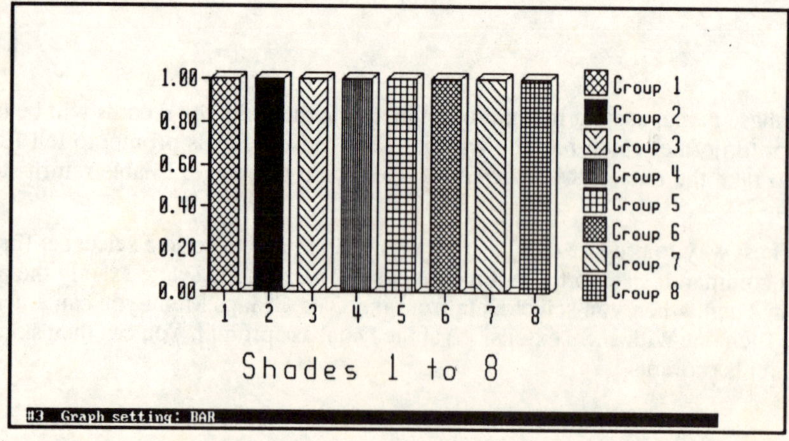

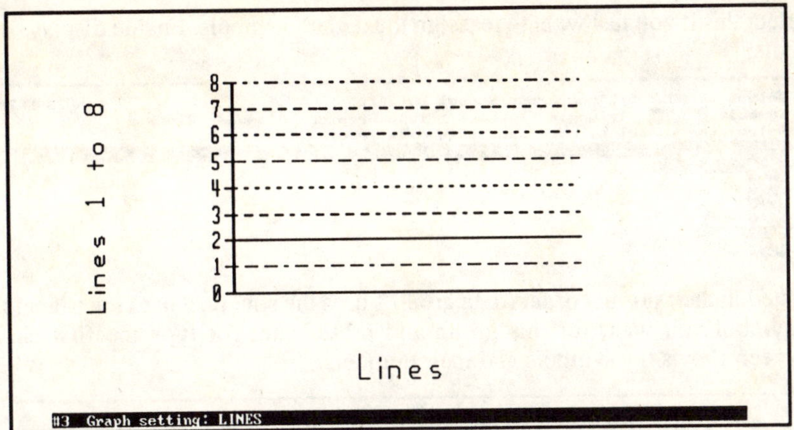

LEGEND Enable displays legends on the right side of the screen to show what each color, symbol, shading, or line used in the graph represents. The graph showing the bar graph shades, earlier in this module, is an example of the use of legends. Enable prompts you for the legend; type up to ten characters. You can include ASCII special characters as well. Press and hold Alt and type (on the numeric keypad only) the ASCII decimal value of the character you want—you can use any value from 32 to 175, except 127. Release Alt and Enable displays the special character. You can only use special characters with the Default font (see Module 97).

RESET-DATA This option turns off the data group. Data from this group is not used in the graph, and the underline is removed from below the data group's number in the list of numbers at the top right of the menu. However, it does not change the other settings back to their defaults. For example, if you entered a Scale multiplier or a Legend they remain. To turn the group back on again, reselect the data.

EXPLODE Enable displays two more prompts: No and Yes. Select Yes if you want this data group's values to be "exploded" or slightly removed from a pie chart. You can use this to add emphasis to a particular group of data. This option has no effect on any other types of graph. If you select Yes here, you must also select Exploded at the pie graph Type options (Options;Global; Type;Pie;Type;Exploded).

2=SYMBOL Enable has a group of eight symbols used in the line and XY graphs, but you can change the symbols in three ways; you can reassign symbols (so that, for example, symbol 1 is assigned to group 8), you can type a character from the keyboard, or you can select a special character. Enable displays the following menu when you select Symbol.

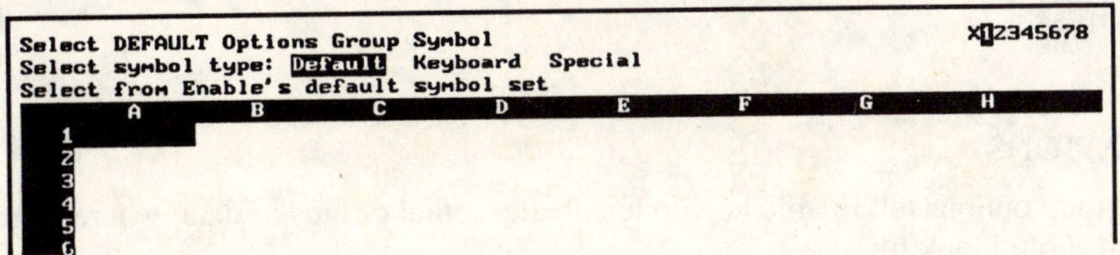

Default Select this if you just want to reassign the default symbols. Enable displays the following list of symbols:

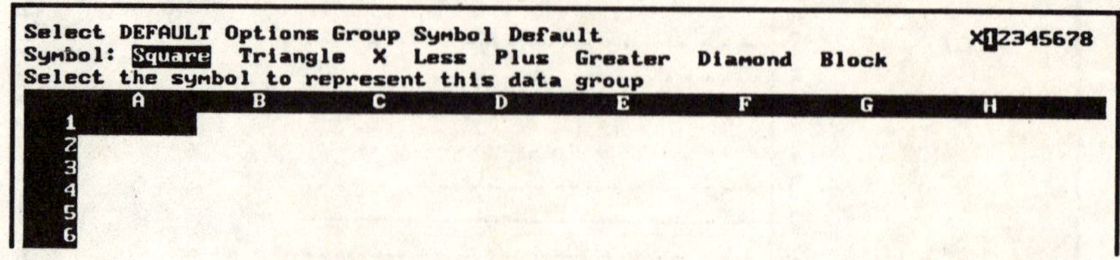

These are listed in their normal order (data group 1 uses the square, 2 uses the triangle, and so on). Select the symbol you want for this group and press Enter (or type the first character). The following screen shows the symbols and their numbers.

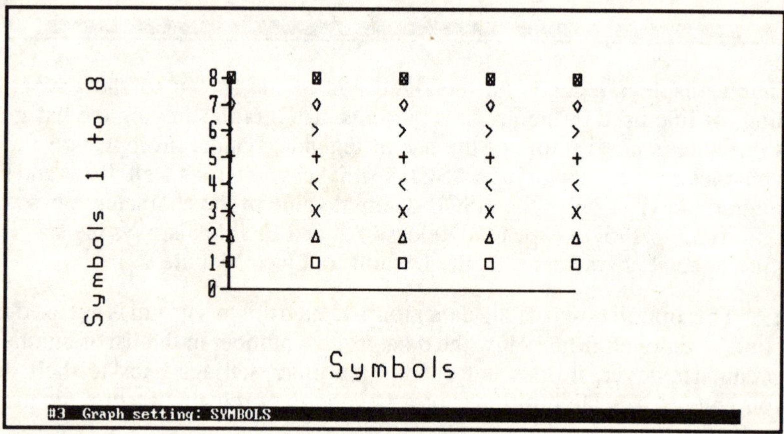

Keyboard Enable prompts you to "Enter the desired keyboard character." Type any character and press Enter. (Do not use this option if you are building an HLC graph.)

Special Enable displays the following screen. Use the arrow keys to select a symbol and press Enter. (Do not use this option if you are building an HLC graph.)

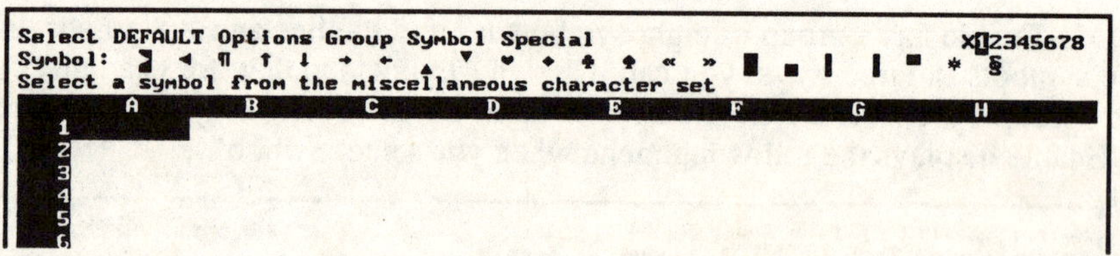

APPLICATIONS

The data group options tell Enable how to handle the actual groups of data; where to get the data, and what it should look like.

TYPICAL OPERATION

In this activity you select the data for the graph, using the spreadsheet named GRAPH, created in Module 96.

1. Open the spreadsheet named GRAPH. Press **F10**, type **GS** (Graph;Select), select **BAR**, and press **Enter**.
2. At the Task Options Menu type **O1** (Options;Data Group:1).

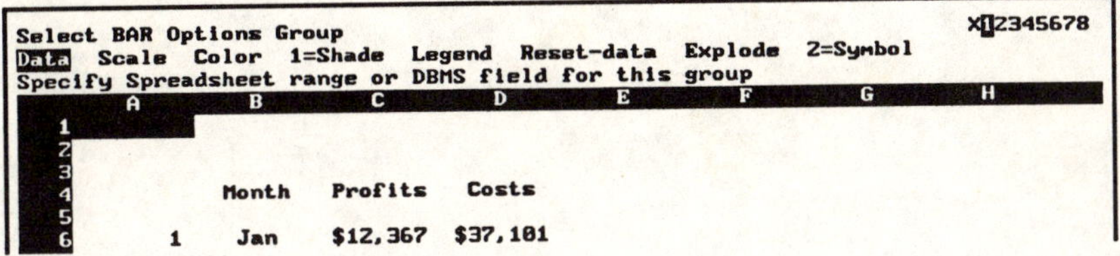

Notice that number 1 in the list of numbers in the top right of the screen is highlighted, indicating that you are working on data group one.

3. Type **D** (Data). Enable prompts for the range. Move the pointer to cell D6. Type **.** (period) and move the pointer to D17.

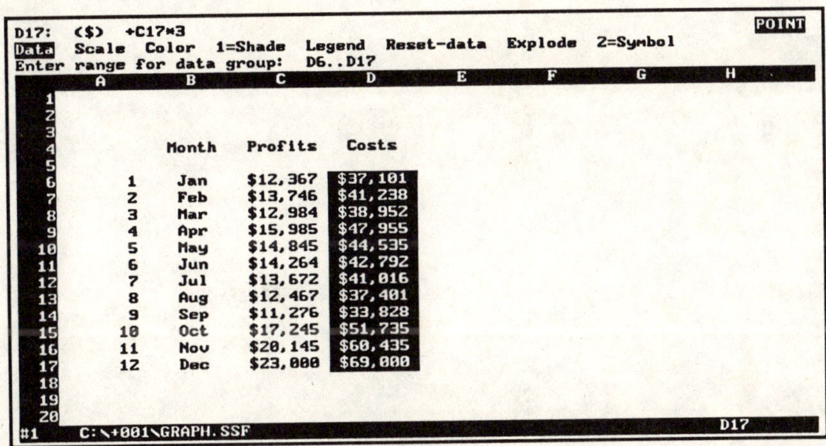

4. Press **Enter**. Type **L** (Legend) and type **Costs**.

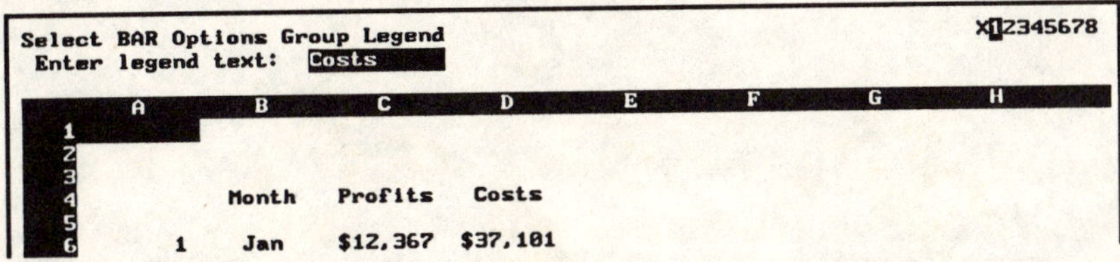

5. Press **Enter** and **Esc**. Type **2** to select data group 2. Type **D** (Data) and type **C6..C17** to define the range. Press **Enter**.
6. Type **L** (Legend) and type **Profit**. Press **Enter**.

7. Press **Esc** four times to remove the graph menus from the spreadsheet.
8. Press **Alt-F10**, press **Enter**, and type **R** to save the spreadsheet.
9. Press **F10** and type **QY** to close the file.
10. Turn to Module 97 to continue the learning sequence.

Module 93
DISPLAY (AND COPY TO WORD PROCESSING)

DESCRIPTION

There are three good reasons to display a graph on your screen: to make sure the graph looks right before you plot or print it; to copy it to a word processing file; and to display it beside a spreadsheet so that you can watch it change as you modify the spreadsheet's data.

DISPLAY MODE Before you display the graph, you can select the graphics-display mode; Primary or Secondary. (Primary is the default mode). At the Task Options Menu type ODS (Options;Device;Screen) to see the following menu.

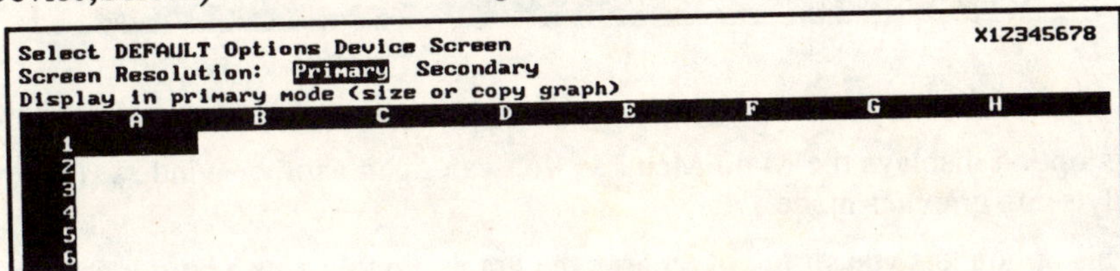

Primary Mode While in this mode you can copy the graph to a word processing file or change its size using the Window options (displayed when you display the graph). Always select this mode if you have a monochrome (single-color) graphics board.

Secondary Mode Select this mode if you have a color graphics board and want to see the graph in color. This is a medium-resolution display. You cannot size or copy the graph when it is in secondary mode. Enable displays two color-palette options; 1 is green, red, and brown, while 2 is cyan, magenta, and white—both use a blue background. The brown and white are used for the axes, grids, and lettering.

NOTE

Different color graphics boards react in different ways in these modes. Although the secondary mode is usually the color mode, some boards will display monochrome in the secondary mode.

DISPLAY THE GRAPH To see the graph on your screen select Display from the Task Options Menu (the following menu). (If you don't have a graphics card Enable displays an error message. Press Esc to continue.)

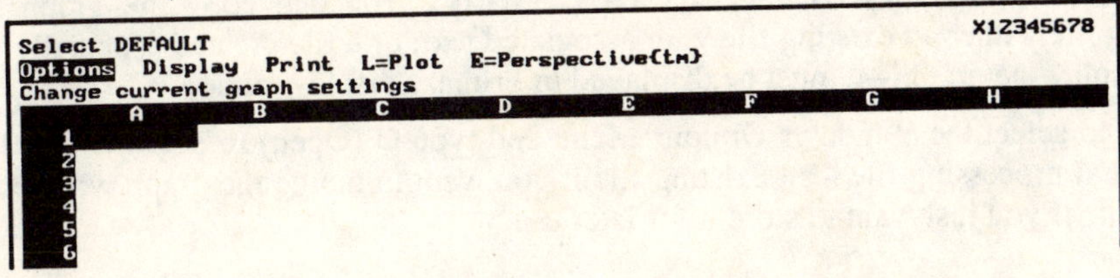

WINDOW OPTIONS The Window Options Menu lets you open windows, change the graph size, go to other windows, and so on. Press F10 to display the menu, as shown in the following screen.

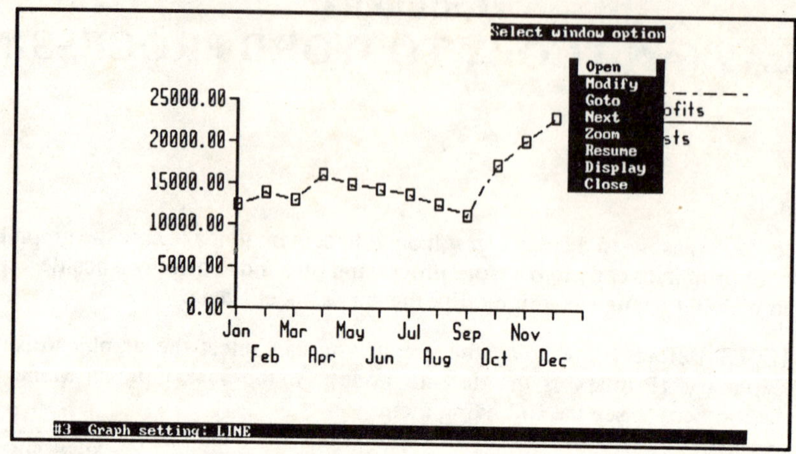

These options work in a similar way to the windows options in word processing or the spreadsheet.

Open This option displays the Main Menu so you can open another window. (The window is automtically set to graphics mode.)

Modify This option lets you shrink or enlarge the graph. Enable puts a border around the graph; type M (move), S (shrink), or E (expand), and then use the arrow keys to indicate the direction. Or, type S or E and type and hold R to shrink or expand in all directions at once.

GoTo This option displays the Window Status screen so you can select another window.

Next This option displays the next open window.

Zoom This option returns the graph to full size, if you previously reduced it.

Resume This option returns the graph to the previous size.

Display This option displays the Window Status screen, letting you select another window. This is the same as the GoTo command.

Close This option closes the graphics window and returns to the Task Options Menu. This is the same as pressing Esc when the graph is not displayed.

NOTE

You can only use the size-modification options if the graph is displayed in Primary display mode.

COPY TO A WORD PROCESSING DOCUMENT You can copy the graph to a word processing file, either an existing file with associated text, or a file created especially to hold the graph. Display the graph—it must be displayed in Primary display mode.

Press F10 to select the Windows Options Menu and type O (Open) to display the Main Menu. Open a word processing file—an existing file if you want to merge the graph with existing text, or a new file if you just want to store it for later use.

Place the word processing cursor where you want to place the graph. Press Alt-F5. Enable displays the Interwindow Copy screen. Select the graph's window by typing the window's number or moving the highlight to it and pressing Enter. (The listing says "Graph Setting.") Enable displays the graph. Press Alt-F5 again, and Enable copies the graph into the word processing file. Enable automatically changes the word processing document into graphics mode.

The main title is copied as a comment line, so Enable does not include it in printouts. Tabs have no effect on graphs, but you should make sure the graph fits within the margins; if the file has narrow margins, shrink the graph to fit before you copy it.

Start In Word Processing You can also carry out this procedure the other way around, beginning the process from the word processing file by pressing Alt-F5. You can change to graphics mode before beginning, but if the word processing file is in text mode when you copy the graph it will appear as a shaded box. Change your screen to graphics mode by pressing F10 and typing M34 (MCM;Screen;Graphics). You can now see the graph and enter text around and even over the graph. When you have finished, change back to text mode by pressing F10 and typing M33 (MCM; Screen;Co80), or M31 (MCM;Screen;Mono) if you have a monochrome-graphics board. (Entering text and editing is very slow in graphics mode.)

You can use word processing embedded commands to adjust your graph. For example, you can use the %LINES command to shorten the graph, or use the %DENSITY command to darken the graph.

DISPLAY SPREADSHEET AND GRAPH SIMULTANEOUSLY This feature places the graph and associated spreadsheet together on the screen. (An example is shown near the end of this module, in the Typical Operation.)

When you have selected a graph and defined what goes into it return to the spreadsheet (press Esc or Up Arrow until the graphics menus disappear). Move the pointer to the area of the spreadsheet that you want to see.

Press Shift-F7 and Enable converts the spreadsheet to graphics mode, reduces it in size, and displays the graph to the right of the spreadsheet. You can now work in the spreadsheet; as you change data, Enable automatically redraws the graph. This is a great way to see "What-If" procedures at work, to change data and see the effect of the changes you make in a graphic form.

Press Shift-F7 (or press F10 and type G (Graph)) to remove the graph and redisplay the full spreadsheet. If the spreadsheet screen is split before you change to simultaneous display, the split is removed, but you can split again after you change to simultaneous mode.

Using the spreadsheet is very slow in this mode, so you won't want to work in this mode for very long. You can speed things up a little by using only the default fonts in the graph's titles and legends.

APPLICATIONS

The ability to copy graphs to word processing files lets you include graphs in your memos, reports, letters, manuals, and so on. (If you need a good print of a graph, print it using the Graph menu; the printouts of graphs in word processing are not very high quality.)

And the simultaneous display with the spreadsheet lets you see the effect of changes in a graphic form. Sometimes it is difficult to really understand the changes that will occur when you modify a few numbers among dozens or hundreds. For example, what effect will increasing your sales force have on your sales, income, and expenses, and how much must your factory increase output to meet the extra demand. With simultaneous display you can compare different scenarios, watching a bar graph being modified each time you try a new number.

TYPICAL OPERATION

In this activity you display the graph you have defined, and copy it into an empty word processing file. You use the spreadsheet named GRAPH, created in Module 96.

1. Open the spreadsheet named GRAPH. Press **F10**, type **GS** (Graph;Select), select **BAR**, and press **Enter**.
2. At the Task Options Menu type **ODSP** (Options;Device;Screen;Primary) to set the display to Primary mode, allowing you to copy the graph to a word processing file.
3. Press **Esc** twice and type **D** (Display). Enable displays your graph on your screen.
4. Press **F10** to see the window options.

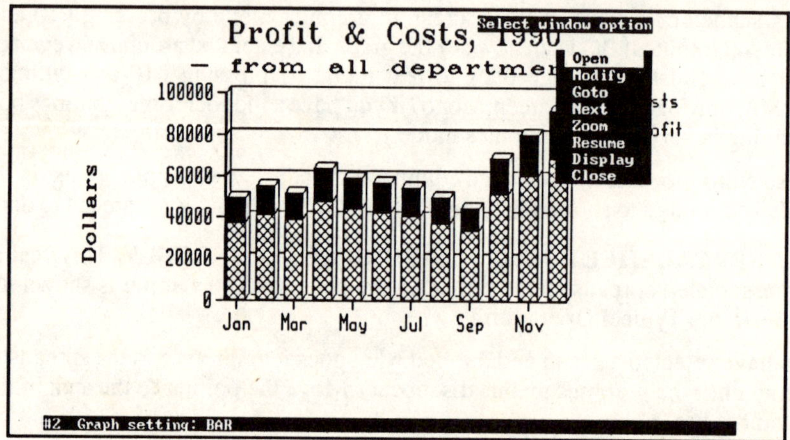

5. Type **O** (Open). When Enable displays the Main Menu type **UWC** (Use;Word Processing; Create). When Enable prompts for the filename type **Graph** and press **Enter**.
6. Enable opens the file. Press **Enter** and **PgDn**. Press **Alt-F5** and Enable displays the Interwindow Copy screen.

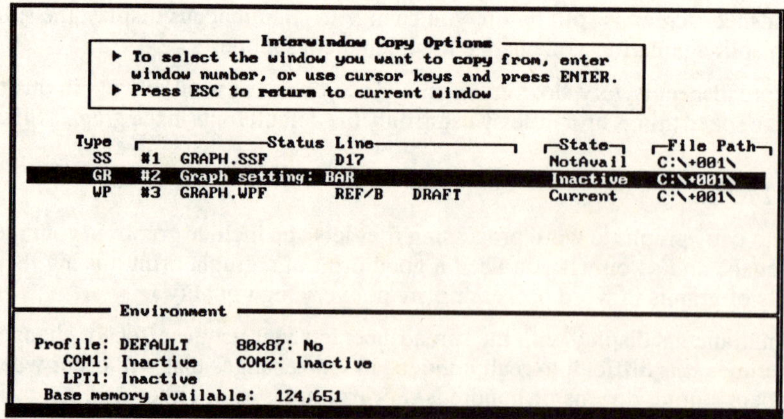

7. Type the number of the window that has the graph (it says "Graph Setting: BAR") and Enable displays the graph.

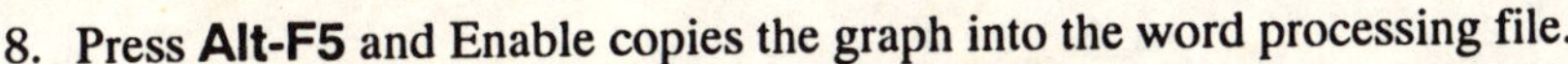

8. Press **Alt-F5** and Enable copies the graph into the word processing file.

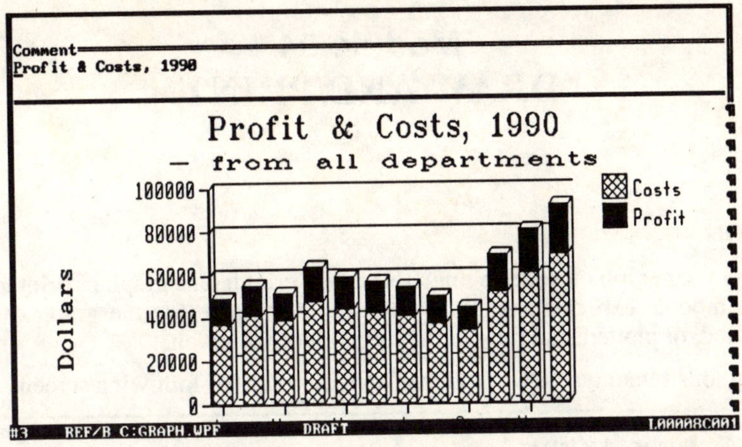

9. Press **Alt-F10** and press **Enter** to save the file. Press **F10** and type **QY** to close the file.
10. Enable displays the graph again. Press **Esc** three times to display the spreadsheet again.
11. Press **Shift-F7** and Enable displays the spreadsheet on the left of the screen, with the graph on the right side.

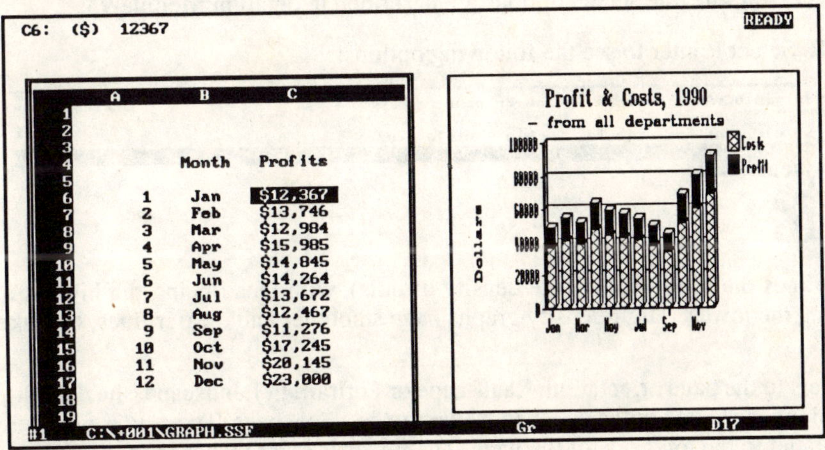

12. Use the arrow keys to move the pointer to the cells in column C. Try changing the values, and watch as Enable redraws the graph.
13. Press **Shift-F7** to display the spreadsheet full-size again.
14. Press **Alt-F10**, press **Enter**, and type **R** to save the file.
15. Press **F10** and type **QY** to close the file.
16. Turn to Module 94 to continue the learning sequence.

Module 94
DRAW AND PRINT

DESCRIPTION

You can display your graph on your computer's screen, print it on a graphics printer, or draw it on a plotter. This module explains how to set up each device so that the graph can be properly displayed, printed, or plotted, and how to finally produce the graph.

At the Task Options Menu type OD (Options;Device) to see the following screen.

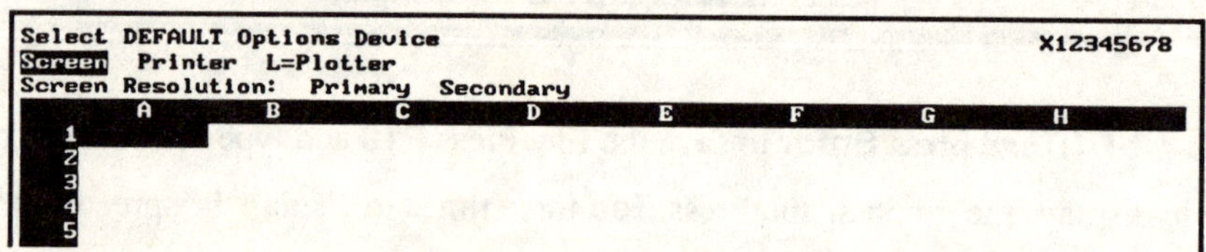

SCREEN Because there are several things you can do with a displayed graph, such as copy it to a word processing file, the screen options are described in detail in Module 93.

PRINTER Select Printer to see the following options:

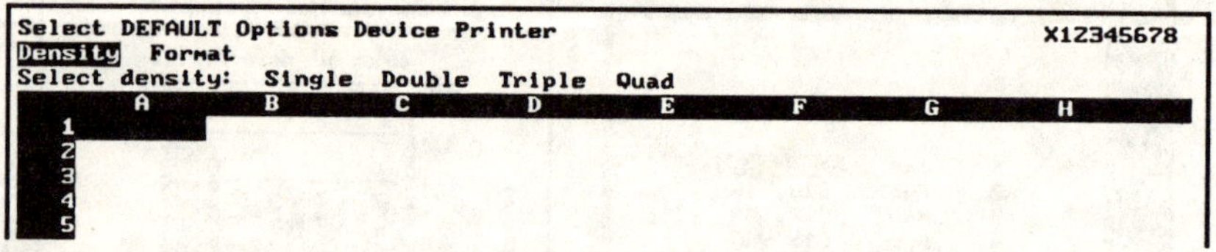

Density defines the print quality (the density of dots), with Quad being the highest quality and Single being the lowest. High-density graphs have smoother and clearer lines, but take longer to print.

Format refers to the page orientation; Landscape or Portrait. In Landscape (the default), the graph is printed along the length of the paper and takes up the whole page. The x-axis, which is ten inches long, is parallel to the long side of the page. The y-axis is eight inches long.

In portrait mode the graph has an eight-inch x-axis, parallel to the short side of the page, and a ten-inch y-axis, so the graph takes up the whole page.

L=PLOTTER Select Plotter to see the following menu:

```
Select DEFAULT Options Device Plotter                          X12345678
Pen-width  Speed  Direct Output
Specify thickness of plotter pen points being used
        A        B        C        D        E        F        G        H
 1
 2
 3
 4
 5
```

Choosing Pen-width gives you two options; Narrow or Wide. Narrow is size P.3, and Wide is size P.7. Select Wide if you are making transparencies or if the pen is worn.

The Speed option has two choices; Fast and Slow. Fast is the default, but pick Slow if you are making transparencies or if the pens are worn—this gives a smoother line.

Select Direct Output and Enable displays several choices; COM1, COM2, COM3, and FILE. Although your user profile defines which port your plotter is connected to, you can tell Enable to send this particular graph to a different communications port. You can also send the graph to a file (Enable automatically adds the .PLT extension). This file can be plotted later, or imported to a word processing file.

PRODUCING THE GRAPH Once you have set up the output device, you can produce the graph. Return to the Task Options Menu (press Esc or Up Arrow).

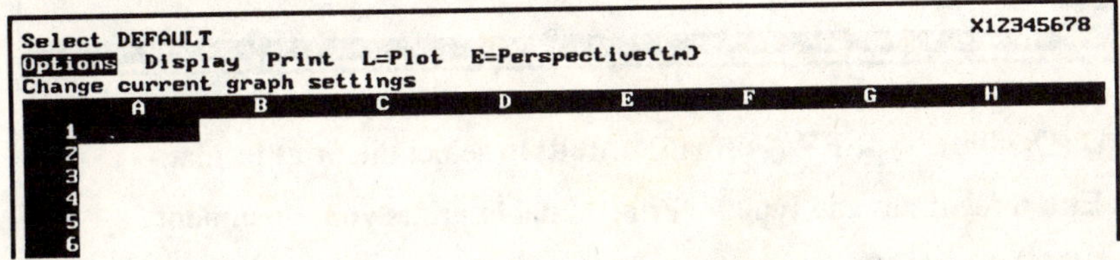

Select Display to view the graph on your screen, Print to print the graph, and L=Plotter to plot the graph. Using the displayed graph is described in more detail in Module 93.

If you select Display and you don't have a graphics card in your computer Enable displays an error message. Press Esc to return to the Task Options Menu. Printouts and plots can be cancelled by pressing Ctrl-F2.

If you select Plot, and had told Enable to produce a plot file (Device;L=Plotter;Direct Output;File), Enable prompts for the filename. Enable automatically adds the .PLT extension.

APPLICATIONS

The options described in this module let you define how the output devices handle the graph. If you intend to copy the graph into a word processing file, for example, you select Primary screen mode. You can use the low quality printouts to make a quick review copy of the graph, and then print the final copy in the highest quality. You may want to use a plotter that you have temporarily connected to your computer, or make a plot file that you can add to a word processing file later.

TYPICAL OPERATION

In this activity you print a graph using the spreadsheet named GRAPH that you created in Module 96.

1. Open the spreadsheet named GRAPH. Press **F10**, type **GS** (Graph;Select), select **BAR**, and press **Enter**.
2. At the Task Options Menu type **ODPD** (Options;Devices;Printer;Density). Enable displays the following options.

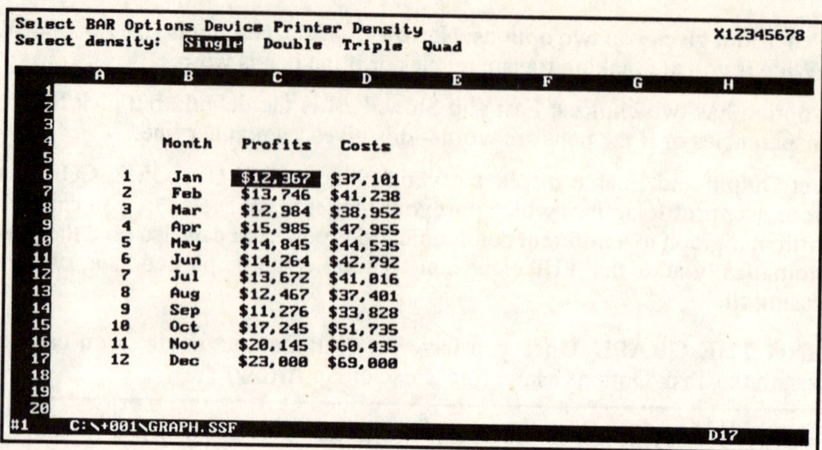

3. Type **D** (Double). Type **FP** (Format;Portrait) to select the print format.
4. Press **Esc** three times and type **P** (Print). Enable prints your document.
5. Type **ODL** (Options;Device;L=Plotter). Type **DF** (Direct Output;File).
6. Press **Esc** three times. Type **L** (L=Plot). Enable prompts for the filename. Type **Bar**.

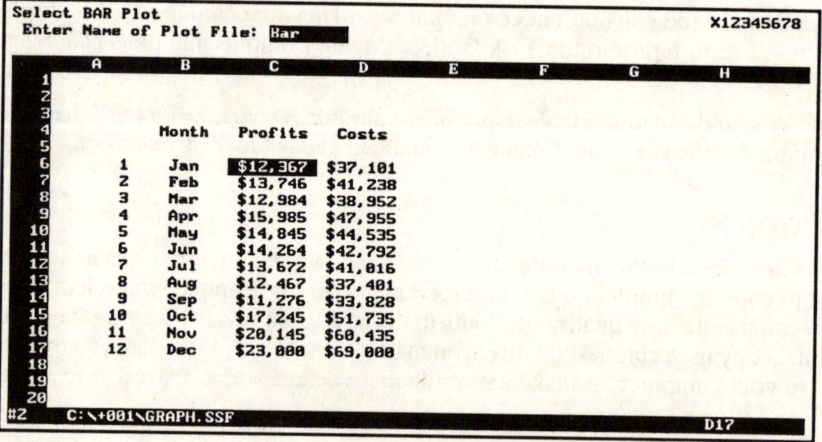

7. Press **Enter** and Enable creates a plot file.
8. Press **Esc** twice to remove the graphics menus from the spreadsheet.
9. Press **Alt-F10**, press **Enter**, and type **R** to save the spreadsheet.
10. Press **F10** and type **QY** to close the file.
11. Turn to Module 98 to continue the learning sequence.

Module 95
GRAPH FORMAT

DESCRIPTION

This module explains how to set up the graph's format (its "look"); the type of grid to use, the headings, color, layout, and so on.

Begin by typing OG at the Task Options Menu (Options;Global) to see the following menu (the Global Options Menu).

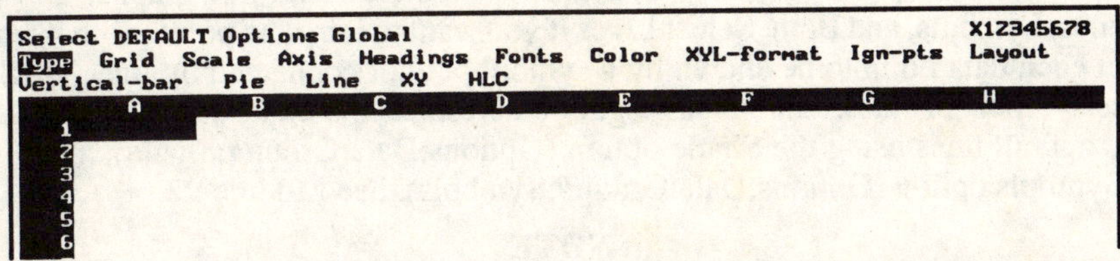

TYPE This option lets you select the graph type. See Module 96.

GRID You can display horizontal and/or vertical lines over your graph, making it easier to read. You can choose Horizontal, Vertical, Both, or Neither. Your choice is ignored if the graph is a Pie chart. The following screen shows horizontal grid lines.

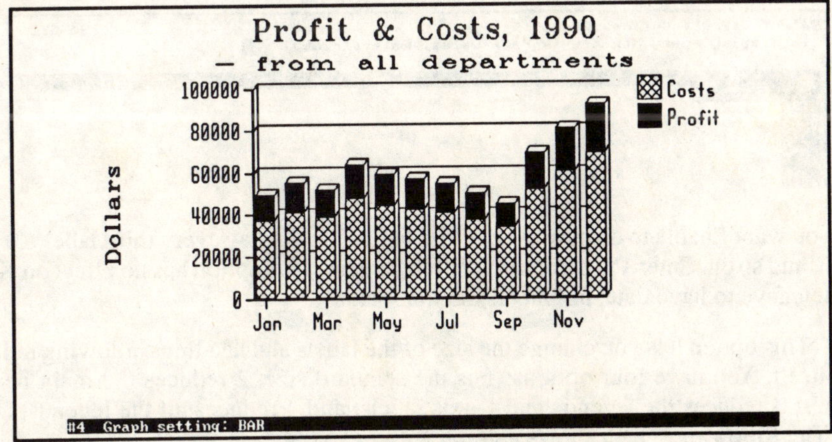

SCALE This option lets you define the type of y-axis scaling: Automatic or User-Specified. If you select Automatic Enable begins the graph at 0 (or the lowest negative value), and chooses a maximum value large enough to accomodate the largest value in the data groups. This is not always appropriate. If you were graphing sales for the month, and the sales ranged from $4,000 to $4,125, the variation in the figures would be dwarfed by the scale, which would begin at $0. Select User-Specified and Enable prompts for the lowest and highest values, and the increments; you could enter 3,800, 4,200, and 100, for example.

Your choice is ignored if you are building a pie, XY, HLC, 2D-stacked, or 3D-stacked graph.

AXIS Defines the type of x- and y-axis labels and the x-axis data. See Module 91 for details.

HEADINGS This option adds graph and axis titles. See Module 97 for details.

COLOR This option defines the background color used when you plot the graph or view it on a color monitor. The color is used on the title, grid, headings, and x-axis data. Enable displays a list of ten colors you can select from. The pie graph Shade option must be set to User (Options; Global;Type;Pie;Shade;User) to make the color option work.

XYL-FORMAT This option defines how data appears on XY and line graphs. You have three options: Lines, Symbols, and Both. Select Lines if you want to join data points with lines, Symbols if you want each data point to be shown by a symbol but not connected by lines, or Both if you want to use symbols or lines. Enable has eight default lines and eight default symbols. You can change the default lines using the Shade option (Options;Data Group#;Shade), and the symbols using the Symbols option (Options;Data Group#;Symbols). See Module 92.

NOTE

The XY graph Linearfit option overrides the choice made here (Options;Global;Type;XY;Linearfit).

IGN-PTS This option lets you ignore x-axis labels. If there are a lot of labels on the x-axis they may be so close together that some of them are truncated. Although this option is called Ignore Points (Ign-pts), you actually tell Enable which labels to use.

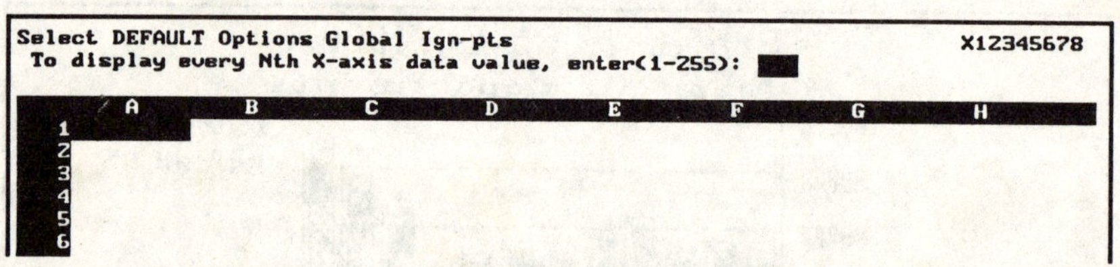

Enter 2 if you want Enable to display every other label, 3 to display every third label, 10 to display every tenth, and so on. Enter 1 to display every label again. This option has no effect on XY graphs, because they have to have data, not labels, on the x-axis.

LAYOUT This option lets you change the size of the labels and headings, allowing more size for the graph itself. You have four options: 1 is the standard size, 2 reduces the main heading and x-axis labels; 3 reduces the legends and y-axis labels; and 4 reduces all the legends, labels, and headings. The following screen shows a graph with Layout 4.

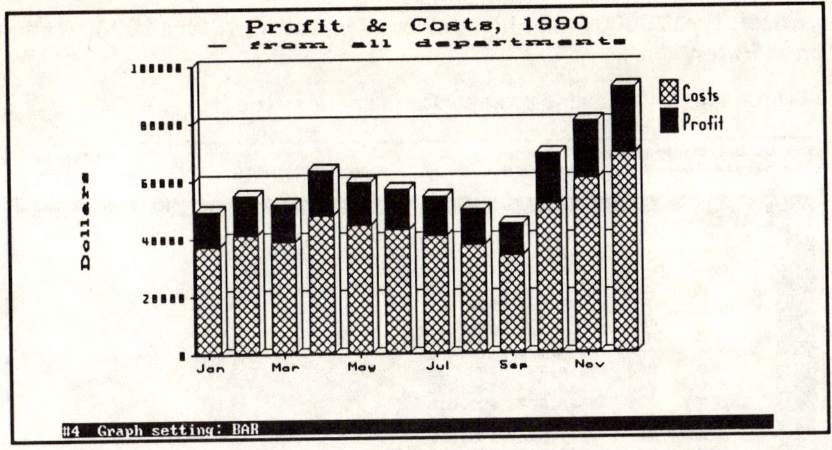

APPLICATIONS

The Global options are mostly cosmetic, allowing you to change the look of the graph, and the way the data is presented.

TYPICAL OPERATION

In this activity you modify some of the graph format options, using the spreadsheet you created in Module 96.

1. Open the spreadsheet named GRAPH. Press **F10**, type **GS** (Graph;Select), select **BAR**, and press **Enter**.
2. At the Task Options Menu type **OG** (Options;Global). Enable displays the following menu.

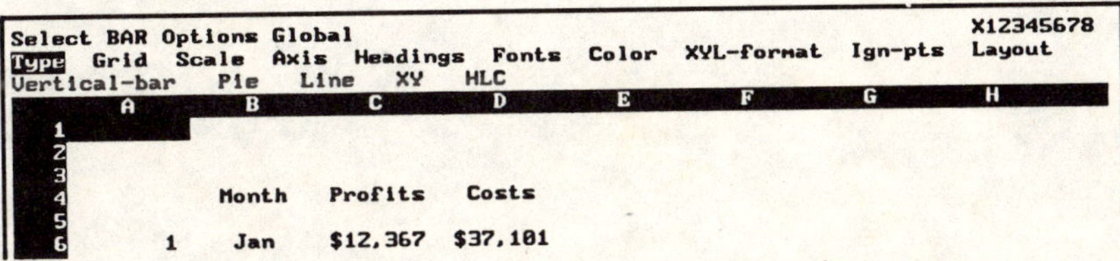

3. Type **GH** (Grid;Horizontal) to tell Enable to display horizontal grid lines on your graph.
4. Type **S** (Scale). Enable displays two options; type **U** (User Selected). Enable prompts for the starting value. Type **10000**.

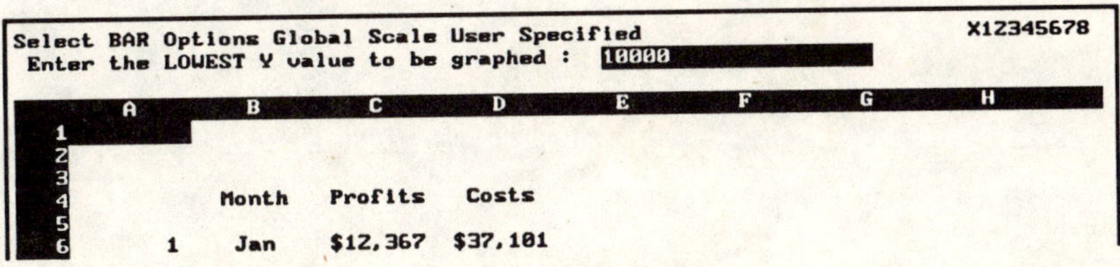

5. Press **Enter**. Type **70000** for the high value and press **Enter**. Type **10000** for the increment and press **Enter**.
6. Type **I** (Ign-pts). When Enable prompts for the points, type **2**.

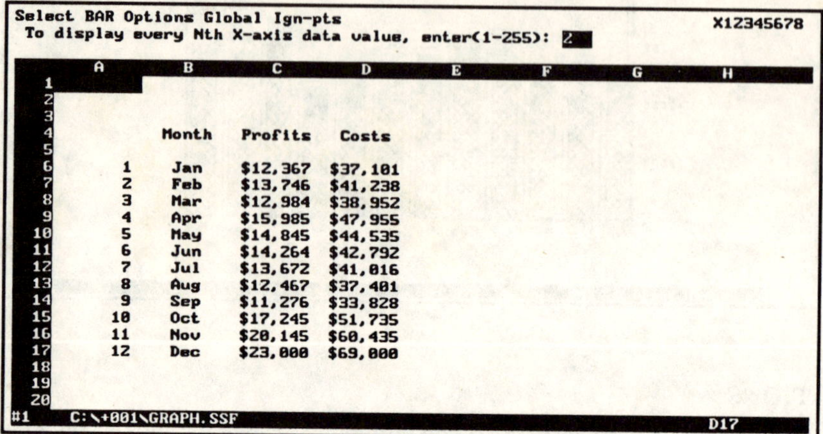

```
Select BAR Options Global Ign-pts                                   X12345678
 To display every Nth X-axis data value, enter(1-255): 2

          Month   Profits    Costs
    1     Jan     $12,367    $37,101
    2     Feb     $13,746    $41,238
    3     Mar     $12,984    $38,952
    4     Apr     $15,985    $47,955
    5     May     $14,845    $44,535
    6     Jun     $14,264    $42,792
    7     Jul     $13,672    $41,016
    8     Aug     $12,467    $37,401
    9     Sep     $11,276    $33,828
   10     Oct     $17,245    $51,735
   11     Nov     $20,145    $60,435
   12     Dec     $23,000    $69,000

#1   C:\+001\GRAPH.SSF                                                  D17
```

7. Press **Enter**. You have told Enable to display only every second x-axis label on the graph.
8. Press **Esc** four times to remove the graph menus from the spreadsheet.
9. Press **Alt-F10**, press **Enter**, and type **R** to save the spreadsheet.
10. Press **F10** and type **QY** to close the file.
11. Turn to Module 91 to continue the learning sequence.

Module 96
GRAPH TYPE

DESCRIPTION

Enable has six types of vertical bar graphs, two types of pie charts, a line graph, an XY graph, and an HLC graph. These options are buried near the bottom of the menu structure for some reason. Select the graph settings at the Graphics Selection Menu to display the Task Options Menu. Then type OGT (Options;Graphics;Type) and Enable displays the following options.

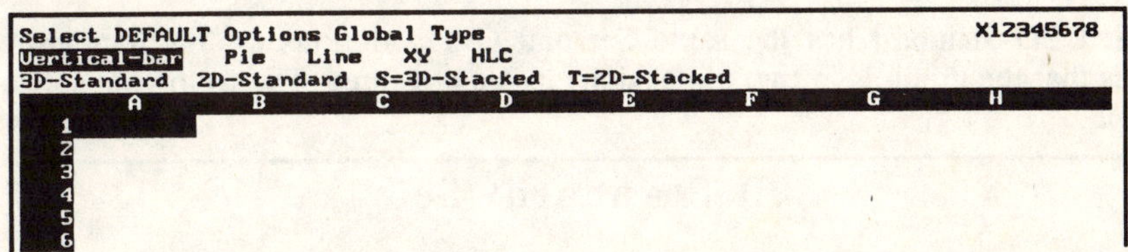

VERTICAL BAR GRAPHS There are six types of vertical bar graph. Select this option and Enable displays the four main options.

3D-Standard A "three-dimensional" graph is simply one that *seems* to have a third dimension. It is drawn so that each bar looks like a box, projecting "behind" the front of the graph. There are two types of 3D-Standard graphs: Set and Group. Set interlaces data, with bars from each group of data being displayed in sequence: the first value from Group1, the first value from Group2, the second value from Group1, the second value from Group2, etc. Group displays all the bars in one group together. The following screens show the two types.

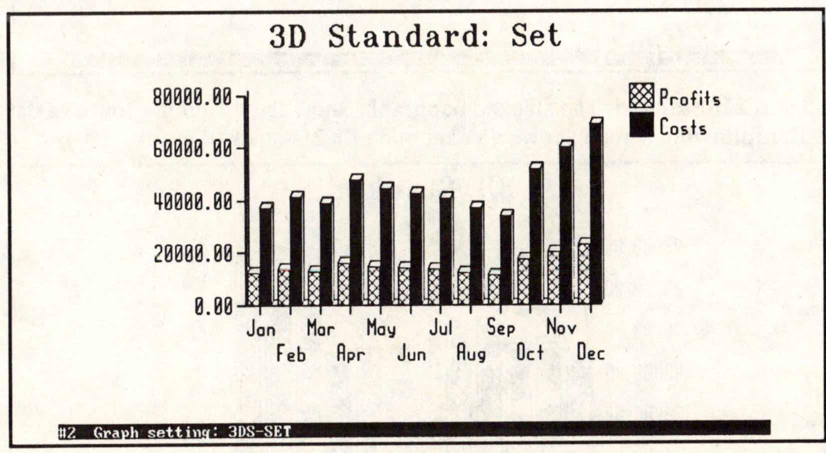

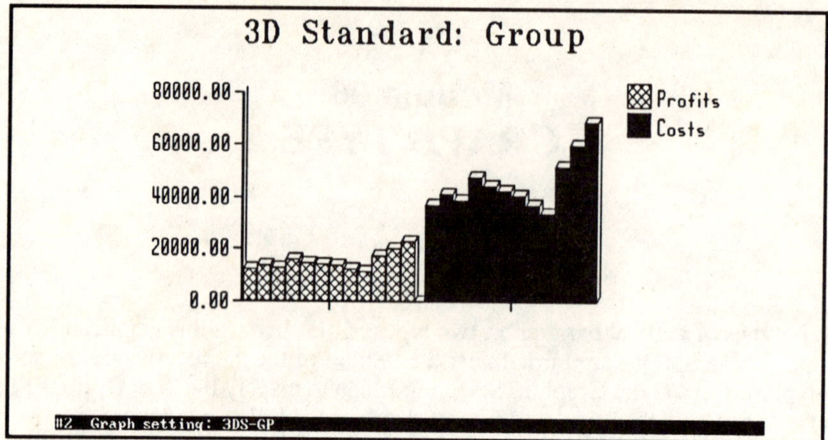

2D-Standard 2D-Standard has the same Set and Group options as 3D-Standard. The only difference is that the graph is in two dimensions instead of three. The following screen shows a 2D Set graph.

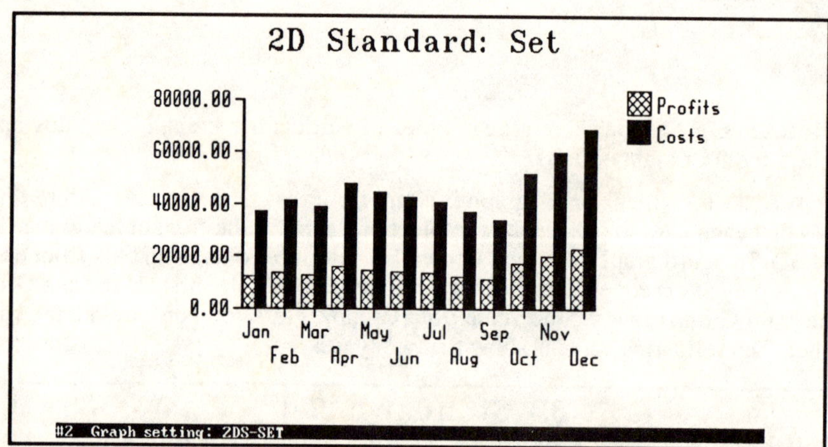

3D-Stacked and 2D-Stacked The stacked bar graphs show the different groups of data on top of each other. The following screen shows an example of a 3D-stacked graph.

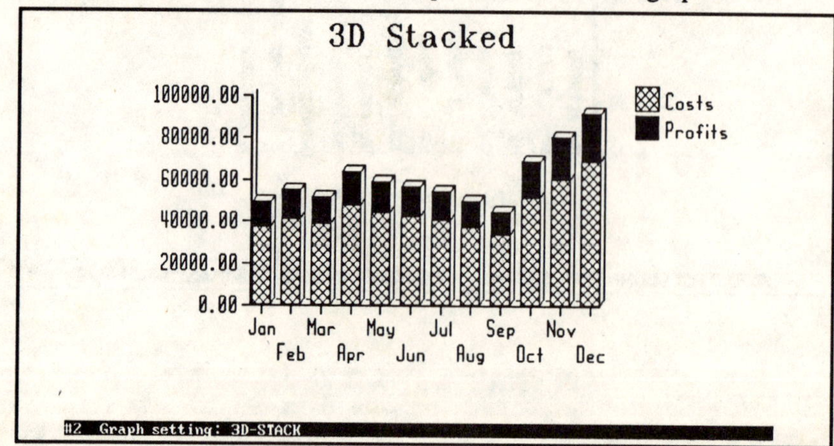

PIE Selecting Pie displays three more options: Type, Format, and Shade.

Type You can select Standard or Exploded. The *exploded* pie chart has one or more pieces of the pie that have been "moved" away from the pie itself. You must also define one of the Data Groups as Exploded (Options;Data Group#;Explode; see Module 92). The following screen shows an exploded pie chart.

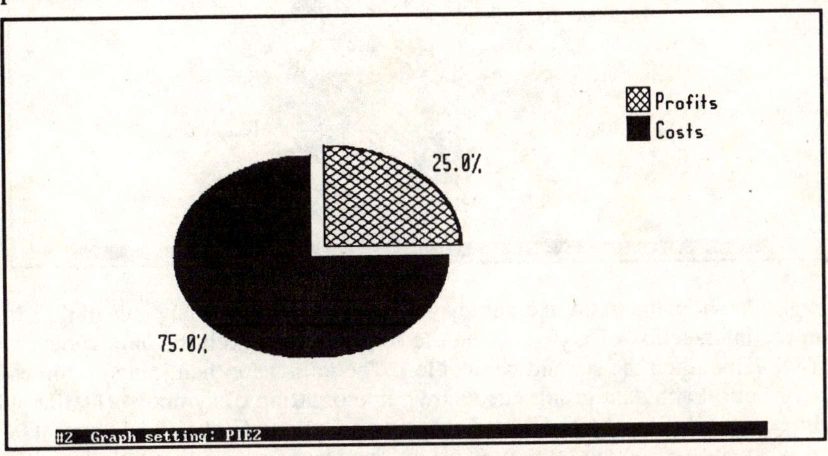

NOTE

If type is set to "Standard" the pie chart is not exploded, even if a data group is set to "Explode."

Format This defines how Enable labels each piece of the pie. Enable always prints the percentage of each portion of the pie, but you also have the choice of including Data-labels or Legends (you must include one; Data-labels is the default).

If you select Data-labels Enable places the X-axis-data labels from the spreadsheet or database next to each piece of pie (Options;Global;Axis;1=X-axis-data; see Module 91). Select this option if you are using one data group with multiple spreadsheet fields or database fields.

Select Legend to place the legends next to the pie chart. Legends are entered for each data group individually (Options;Data Group #;Legend; see Module 92).

Shade You have two options; User and Enable. If you select User Enable uses the shade (printing) and color (plotting) you define for each Data Group (Options;Data Group#;Color and ;Shade; see Module 92).

If you select Enable, Enable chooses the shade or color. Select this option if you have one data group with multiple cells or fields of data. If you select User in this situation all the slices are drawn with the same color or shade, but if you select Enable two shades or colors are alternated between slices.

The following graph shows a pie chart using one data group, with Shade set to Enable, and Format set to Data-labels.

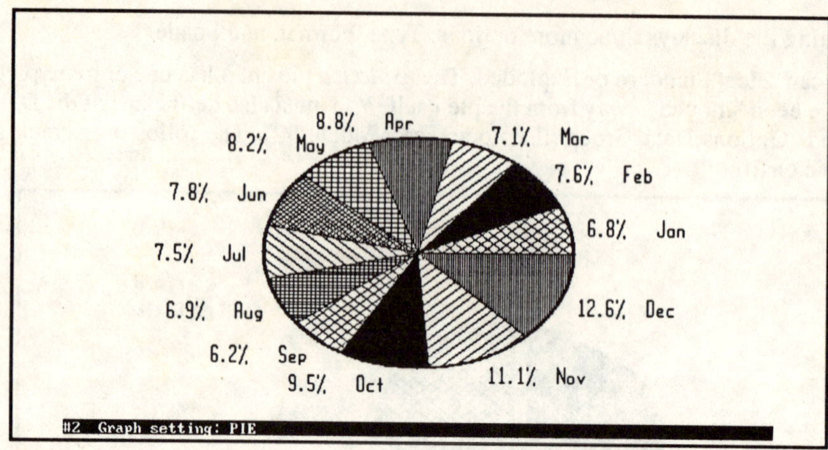

LINE Line graphs show the trend of a value over time. Each individual piece of data in the group is plotted on the intersection of a y-value, in the sequence in which the data appears in the data group (the first value, then the second value, etc.). The points are then joined by lines, indicated by symbols, or both. Each data group has its own line or string of symbols. (Define whether the graph uses lines or symbols at the XYL-format option—Options;Global;XYL-format [see Module 95]. You can also choose the symbols used—Options;Data Group#;Symbols [see Module 92].) The following screen shows a line graph with both symbols and lines.

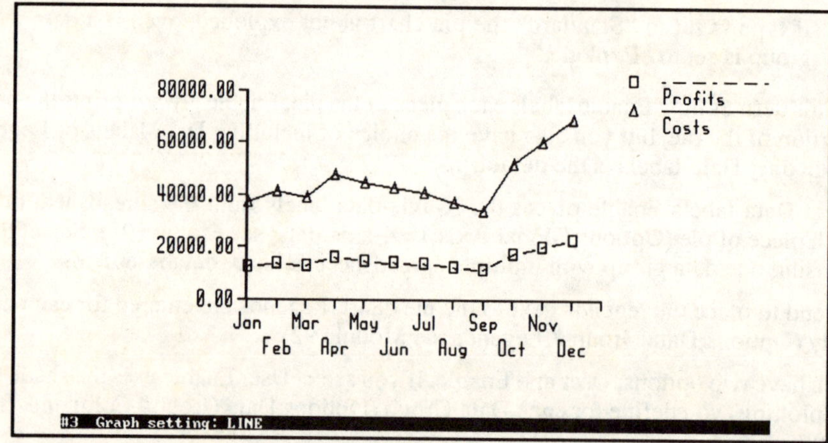

XY The XY graph looks like a line graph, but works differently. It "shuffles" data into the numerical order of the X-axis-data. (You *must* define X-axis-data or Enable will not draw the graph; Options;Global;Axis;1=X-axis-data.) For example, suppose you want to correlate telephone sales-calls against the number of sales. Each day you record two numbers; the number of sales and the number of calls. At the end of the month you build a graph. Data group 1 is the number of sales. The X-axis-data is the number of calls.

When Enable draws the XY graph it puts calls into order, with the lowest number at the left and the largest at the right of the graph. It then plots the corresponding sales-numbers on the graph above each call-number.

You have two options when you choose XY; Connect and LinearFit. Select LinearFit to draw a straight line that "averages" the data. (The line is drawn through the least-squares linear fit of the data.) This line does not necessarily pass through data points, but it passes through the middle of them, smoothing out the fluctuations.

Select Connect to draw lines between all the data points. The problem with Connect is that the lines are drawn depending on the order of the values in the data group, but because the values are re-ordered when the graph is drawn the connecting line may zig-zag all over the place. You can avoid this problem by making sure that the X-axis-data is in ascending order. Also, the choice you make here overrides your choice at XYLformat; if you choose Linearfit here, and Lines at XYL-format (Options;Global;XYL-format;Lines), the symbols are not connected by a line.

The XY lines and symbols can be changed in the same way they are for the line graph (see the earlier topic "Line" in this module). The following screen shows an XY graph with Linearfit.

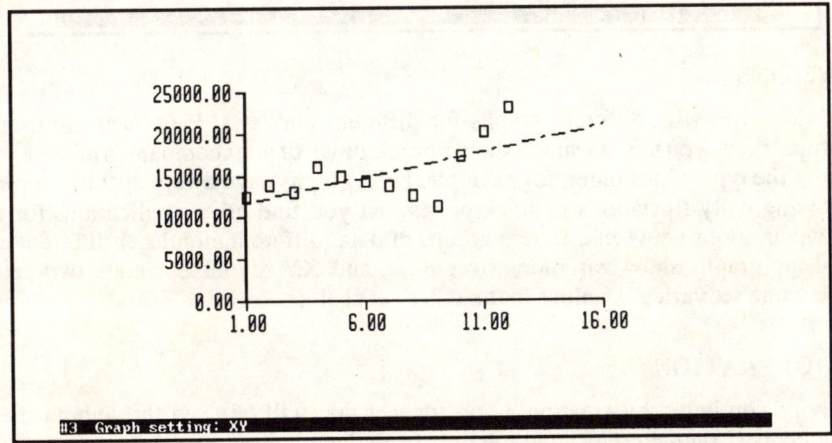

HLC The Open-High-Low-Close is most commonly used to represent daily fluctations in a stock's price, showing the opening price, the day's high and low, and the closing price. The High and Low values are indicated with dashes, and connected with a line. The Open, Close and any intermediate values are indicated using the default symbols or those selected when you define the data group (Options;Data Group#;Symbols (Module 92)).

Each data group you define includes values from different stocks, or the same stock on different days. For example, suppose you want to plot the changes in 10 stocks on one day. Data group 1 consists of the high values for all 10 stocks. Group 2 is the low values, group 3 is the closing values, group 4 is the opening values, and subsequent groups are intermediate values during the day. (Enable assumes that the groups are defined as described here, so it draws a line from each value in group 1 to its corresponding value in group 2, even if other groups have higher or lower values; so make sure you assign the groups correctly.) The following screen shows an example of an HCL graph.

NOTE

To avoid confusing Enable, start designing the HCL with a "clean slate" (i.e., with no data groups defined), and define the groups in numerical order.

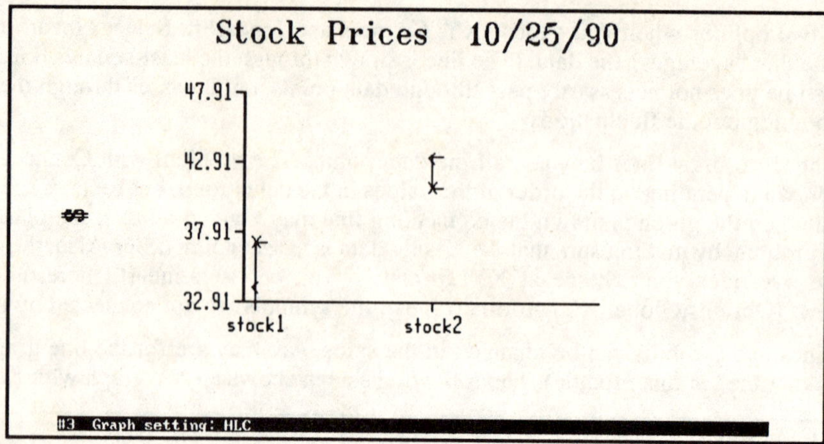

APPLICATIONS

Enable provides you with different graphs for different purposes. Pie charts are used to show different proportions; you might want to show a break-down of your company's income into groups depending on the type of customer, for example. HCL graphs have a very specific application, of course, showing daily fluctations in stock prices, but you find other applications for them. Bar graphs show variations between different groups of data (different months or different clients, for example). Line graphs show variations over time, and XY graphs correlate two sets of data, showing how one set varies as values in the other set change.

TYPICAL OPERATION

In this activity you begin by creating a spreadsheet that will be used throughout the graphics learning sequence. You then select a graph type from the graphics menus.

1. Create a spreadsheet called GRAPH.
2. Enter the values as shown in the following screen, in exactly the same cells. (The two columns of numbers are formatted (Worksheet;Range;Format) in currency format with no decimal places.)

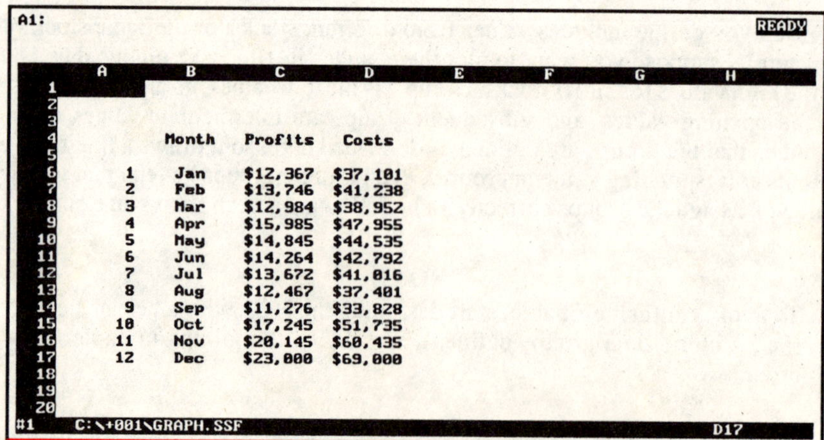

A1: READY

	A	B	C	D
4		Month	Profits	Costs
6	1	Jan	$12,367	$37,101
7	2	Feb	$13,746	$41,238
8	3	Mar	$12,984	$38,952
9	4	Apr	$15,985	$47,955
10	5	May	$14,845	$44,535
11	6	Jun	$14,264	$42,792
12	7	Jul	$13,672	$41,016
13	8	Aug	$12,467	$37,401
14	9	Sep	$11,276	$33,828
15	10	Oct	$17,245	$51,735
16	11	Nov	$20,145	$60,435
17	12	Dec	$23,000	$69,000

#1 C:\+001\GRAPH.SSF D17

3. Press **F10** and type **G** (Graphics) to see the following menu.

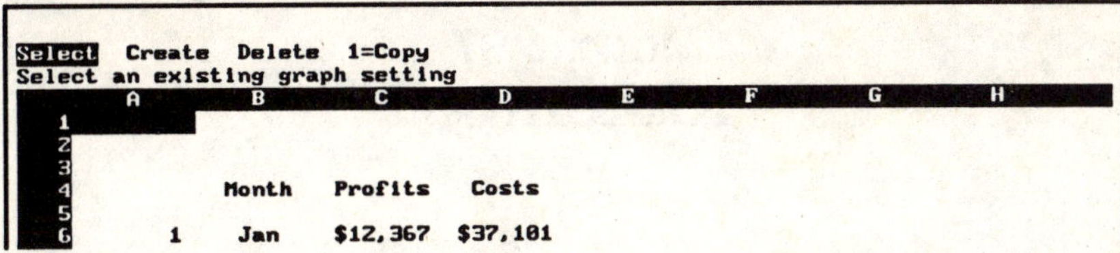

4. Type **C** (Create) and Enable prompts for the graph settings name. Type **Bar**.

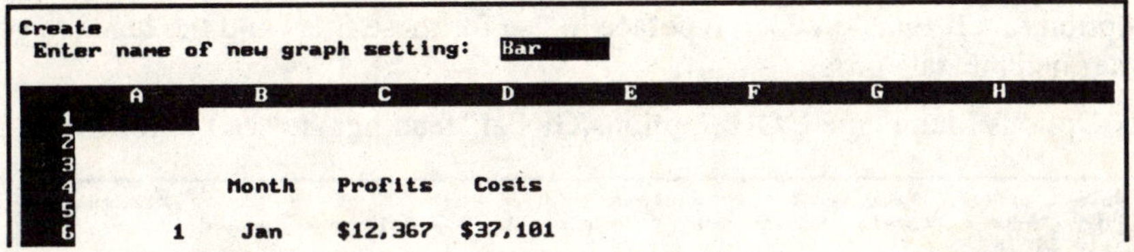

5. Press **Enter** and type **OGTV** (Options;Global;Type;Vertical Bar). Enable displays the following menu.

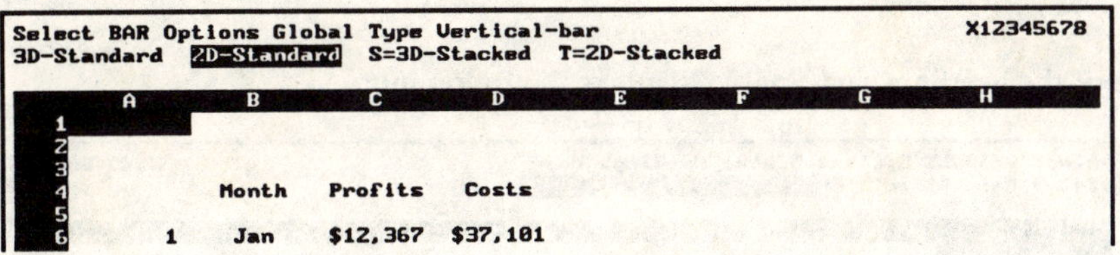

6. Type **S** (S=3D-Stacked). You have selected a three-dimensional, stacked bar graph, that is, one data group is stacked on top of the other.
7. Press **Esc** four times to remove the graph menus from the spreadsheet.
8. Press **Alt-F10**, press **Enter**, and type **R** to save the spreadsheet.
9. Press **F10** and type **QY** to close the file.
10. Turn to Module 95 to continue the learning sequence.

Module 97
HEADINGS

DESCRIPTION

Enable lets you add titles and subtitles to your graph using the Headings option. You can also use the Fonts option to tell Enable which typeface to use for these titles and the legends you entered when you defined the data group.

At the Task Options Menu type OGH (Options;Global;Headings) to see the following menu.

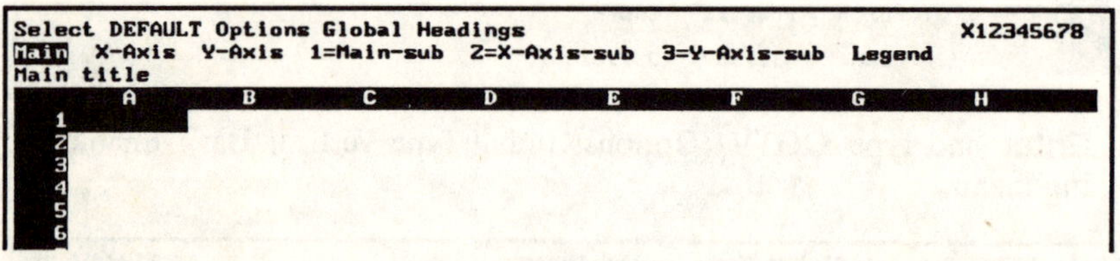

Select one of the headings and Enable displays the following:

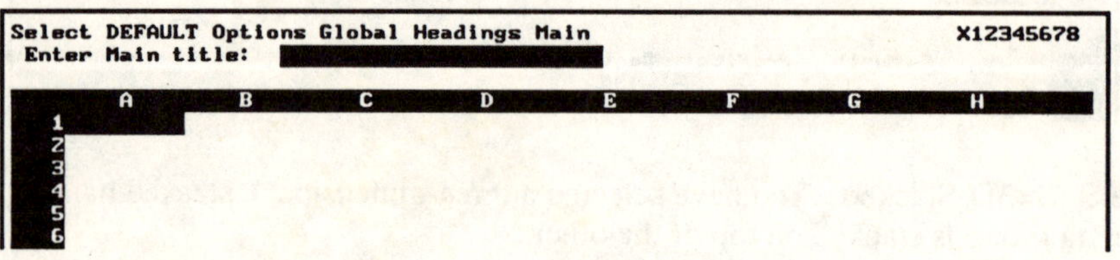

Type the heading and press Enter. The heading is up to 19 characters, although Enable may truncate the last character, depending on the width of the font you use. You can include ASCII special characters as well. Press and hold Alt and type (on the numeric keypad only) the ASCII decimal value of the character you want—you can use any value from 32 to 175, except 127. Release Alt and Enable displays the special character. You can only use special characters if you are using the Default font (discussed later in this module).

The titles are as follows:

Main:	The top of the graph.
X-Axis:	The bottom of the graph.
Y-Axis:	The left side of the graph, with the text on its side.
Main-sub:	Subtitle below the Main title.
X-Axis-sub:	Subtitle below the X-Axis title.
Y-Axis-sub:	Subtitle below the Y-Axis title (on its side).
Legend:	Used for legend titles in Perspective, which is not covered in this book.

Only the Main and Main-sub titles are used in pie charts.

FONTS Enable has nine fonts you can use for the graph's titles and legends. At the Task Options Menu type OGF (Options;Global;Fonts) to see the following screen.

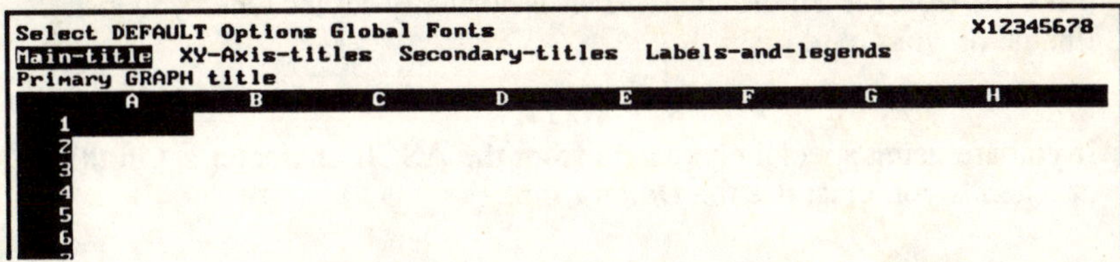

Main-title:	The title at the top of the graph.
XY-Axis-titles:	The primary titles at the side and bottom.
Secondary-titles:	All the subtitles.
Labels-and-Legends:	All x- and y-axis labels and the legends.

Select one of the headings or titles and Enable displays the following:

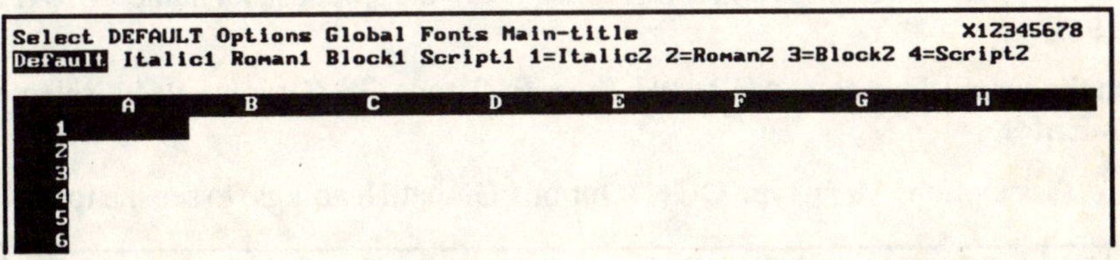

The following illustration shows the different fonts.

Default Font

Italic1 Font

Roman1 Font

Block1 Font

Script1 Font

Italic2 Font

Roman2 Font

Block2 Font

Script2 Font

Select a font and press Enter.

NOTE

If you want a font other than the default font you must copy the appropriate .FNT file from the Tutorial Disk. This is normally copied when you install Enable on your hard disk.

NOTE

If you are using special characters from the ASCII character set in titles or legends you must use the Default font.

APPLICATIONS

The headings options let you add explanatory text and select the font that looks best in your particular application.

TYPICAL OPERATION

In this activity you enter headings and select fonts, using the spreadsheet named GRAPH, created in Module 96.

1. Open the spreadsheet named GRAPH. Press **F10**, type **GS** (Graph;Select), select **BAR**, and press **Enter**.

2. At the Task Options Menu type **OGH** (Options;Global;Headings) to see the following menu.

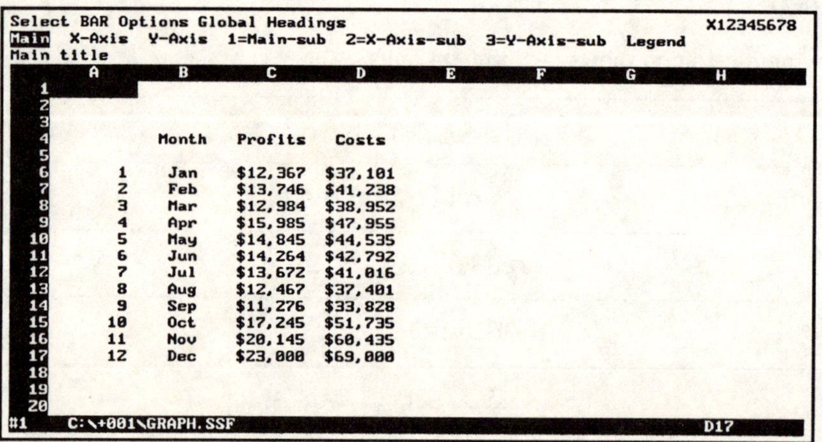

3. Type **M** (Main). Enable prompts for the Main heading. Type **Profit & Costs, 1990**.

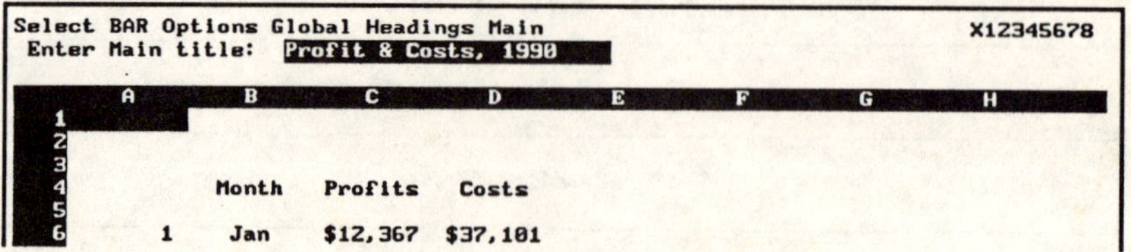

4. Press **Enter**. Type **3** (3=Y-Axis-sub) and type **Dollars.** Press **Enter.**
5. Type **1** (1=Main-sub) and type **- from all departments**. Press **Enter.**
6. Press **Esc** and type **FM** (Fonts;Main-title). Enable displays the following menu.

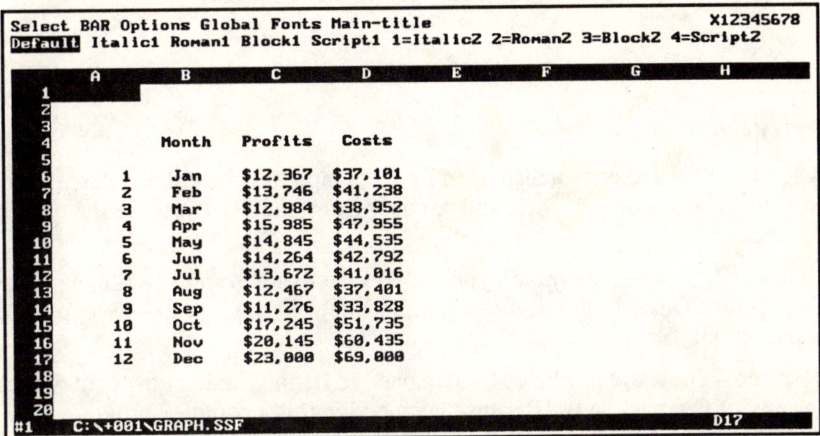

7. Type **2** (2=Roman2).
8. Type **SR** (Secondary-titles;Roman2).
9. Press **Esc** five times to return to the Task Options Menu.
10. Press **Alt-F10**, press **Enter**, and type **R** to save the spreadsheet.
11. Press **F10** and type **QY** to close the file.
12. Turn to Module 93 to continue the learning sequence.

Module 98
IMPORT GRAPHICS

DESCRIPTION

Module 93 describes how to copy a displayed Enable graph into a word processing document, but there are other ways to import graphics, and not only from Enable. These are the types of graphics that you can import:

Enable Plotfiles—Remember the option you had to save a plot graph in a file, with the extension .PLT? (Options;Device;Plotter;Direct Output;File). Well, you can later copy that file into a word processing file.

IBM 6180 Plotter—These are produced by Perspective II, and Enable now comes packaged with a free copy of Perspective II. (Because Perspective II is a complex program in its own right, this book does not describe it— there simply isn't enough space to do it justice.) These files have a .3PP extension. You can also use this format to import AutoCAD HPPL plotfiles.

PC Paintbrush—You can import MicroSoft v2.01/ZSoftv3.11 Paintbrush files. These have a .PCX extension. However, you cannot import Paintbrush files created using a Hercules graphics card. Also, you can only import a file that was created with the same type of video display as your terminal. For example, if you have a CGA display you cannot import a .PCX file produced in VGA.

Macintosh MacPaint—These files have a .MAC or .PIC extension.

Enable Graphics—Enable graphs that have already been imported into a word processing file are stored in .GO*n* files (see this module). Later you can import a .GO*n* file directly into another wordprocessing file. Like PC Paintbrush, .GO*n* files can only be imported if they were created using the same type of video display that your computer has.

Some of these formats are not graphs. For example, you can import pictures produced in PC Paintbrush or MacPaint.

IMPORTING THE FILE Open the word processing file you want to copy the graph into. This may be an existing file with related text, or a blank file you are going to use to store the picture for use later. Place the cursor in the position you want to insert the picture.

Press F9 Ins D (the expert command for inserting a file). Enable displays the following prompt.

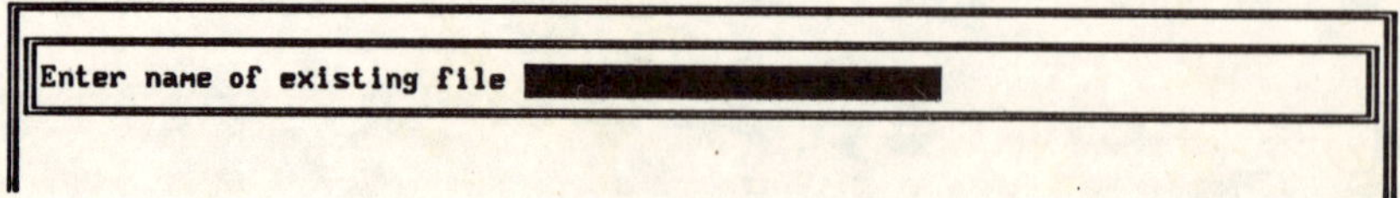

Type the filename and press Enter. Remember to include the disk and pathname, if necessary, and always include the extension (such as .PCX for PC Paintbrush, .PLT for an Enable Plot File, or .3PP for a Perspective file).

Enable displays the following:

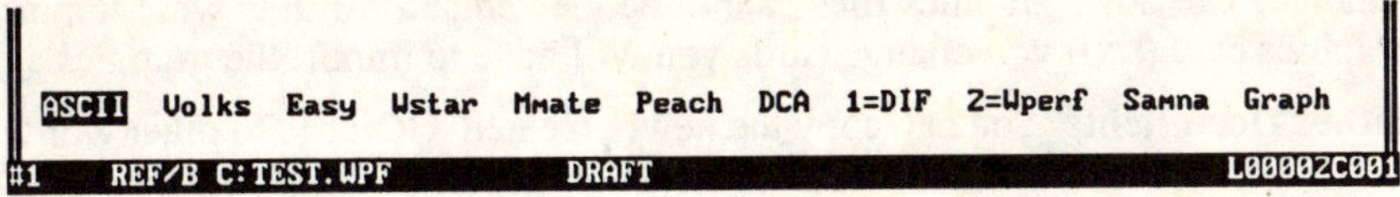

Type G to select graphics, and Enable displays a list of the graphics options, as shown in the following screen.

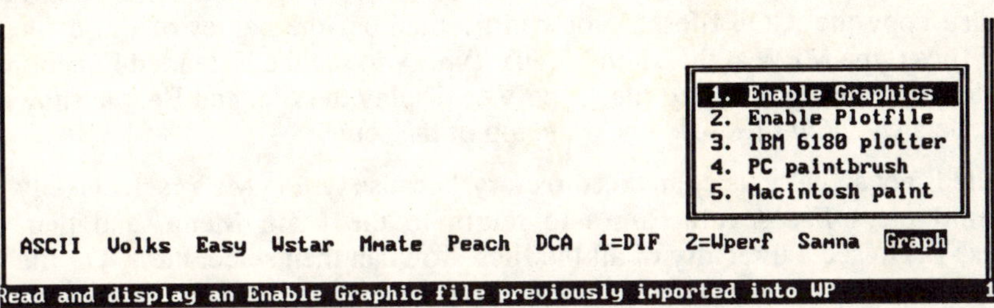

Select the appropriate graphics file, and Enable changes to graphics mode and copys the graphics file into the document. (If you are importing an IBM 6180 format file, see the special instructions later in this module.)

Enable also creates a special graphics file with the same name as the original and the extension .GO*n*, where *n* is the number of graphics files associated with the word processing document. For example, you have a PC Paintbrush file called CAR.PCX. You copy it into the word processing file, and Enable builds a file called CAR.GO1.

When you save the word processing document the picture is not actually stored in the word processing file (the .WPF file); each time you open the word processing document Enable redraws the picture from CAR.GO1, so the .WPF file and the .GO*n* files must be in the same directory when you reopen the .WPF file.

You can move and copy the picture in your document by inserting it again using this same F9-Insert-D procedure—use the .GO*n* extension this time. You can type over and around the picture, but if you want to do a lot of work with text, change back to text mode—press F10 and type M33 (MCM;Screen;Co80) or M31 (MCM;Screen;Mono) if you have a monochrome-graphics board; the picture turns into a shaded block.

IBM 6180 Format (Perspective II) These files use the .3PP extension, and Persective II creates them in its Print-To-Disk procedure. If you import this type of file Enable displays the picture before copying to the word processing document. You can now press S (Shrink), E (Expand), or M (Move) to modify the picture's size and location. Press Esc to return to the original size and location. Press Enter when you are ready to import it and Enable copies it into the document.

REVISING WORD PROCESSING FILES When you reopen a word processing file Enable automatically retrieves the pictures from the .GO*n* files. (Remember, they must be in the same directory as the .WPF file.) However, you will not see the picture right away—you see a shaded block that shows where the picture is placed. To see the picture in graphics mode press F10 and type M34 (MCM;Screen;Graphics).

If the picture was imported from an Enable plot file using a different graphics board the color attributes change. The other graphics files cannot be viewed at all if they were imported using a different graphics card (so if you change cards you will have to import the graphics again).

Copy To Other Documents You can copy the newly created .GO*n* file to other word processing documents using the procedure outlined in this module; use the filename and the .GO*n* extension. When Enable lists the acceptable graphics files, select Enable Graphics. Enable builds another .GO*n* file associated with the second word processing file.

Lost .GOn Files? If you want to copy or move a word processing file to another disk or directory you must also copy the .GO*n* files. If you can't remember the names of those files, go to the directory of files (type MFW at the Main Menu). Type X to see the Extended Functions Directory and then select the word processing file. Type V to display the file, and Enable shows the names of all the associated .GO*n* files listed near the top of the screen.

The .GO*n* file is not actually listed in this directory, because typing MFW selects only .WPF files, but you could press Esc several times to return to the Main Menu, and then type MFA (MCM;Files;All) to see a directory of all the files. You can then select the .GO*n* file and type V to view the picture that the file contains.

APPLICATIONS

The ability to import graphics files from other programs allows you to incorporate not just graphs but actual pictures. Using PC Paintbrush or MacPaint files you can add any kind of hand drawn picture, or even photographs and clip art originally scanned into a computer and modified with those programs.

TYPICAL OPERATION

In this activity you copy a .GO*n* file from the plot file created in Module 94.

1. Create a word processing document named **BARGRAF**.
2. Press **Enter** to accept the margins and press **PgDn**.
3. Press **F9**, press **Insert**, and type **D**. Enable prompts for the filename. Type **Bar.plt**, the name of the plot file created in Module 94.

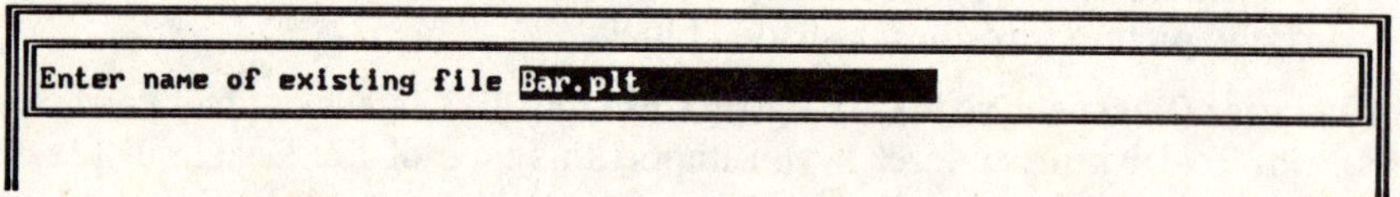

4. Press **Enter**, and Enable displays the file options. Type **G** and Enable displays the graphics file options.

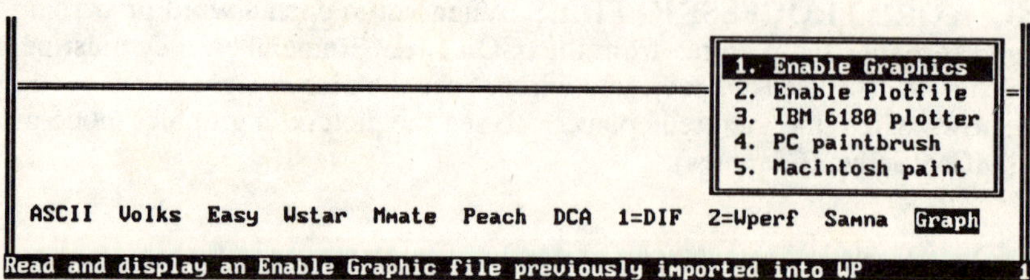

5. Type **2** and Enable imports the graph.

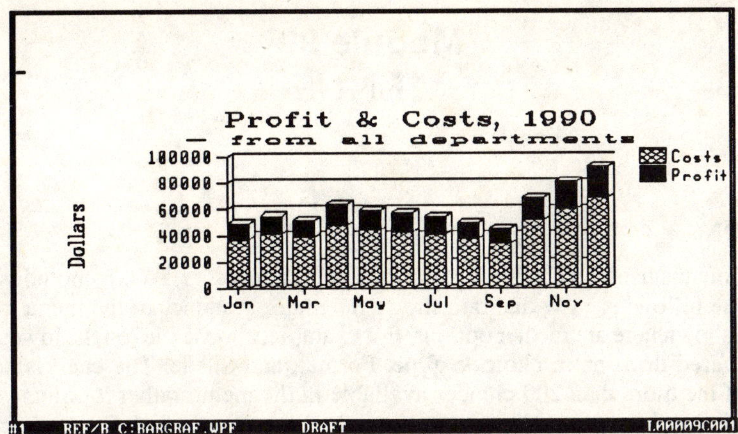

6. Press **F10** and type **QY** to close the file without saving.
7. Turn to Module 8 to continue the learning sequence.

Module 99
MENUS

DESCRIPTION

The system of menus used by Enable's graphics is a bit confusing, so this module describes how to use them. The following flow diagram shows the major branches of the menu tree. At the end of each branch shown here are further options. For example, choose Pie (on the lowest level shown) and you are offered three more choices: Type, Format, and Shade. The chart is not intended to show you all of the more than 200 choices available in the menu, rather it points you in the right direction. You know from the chart, for example, that if you want to define a pie chart you must select Options, Global, Type, and Pie.

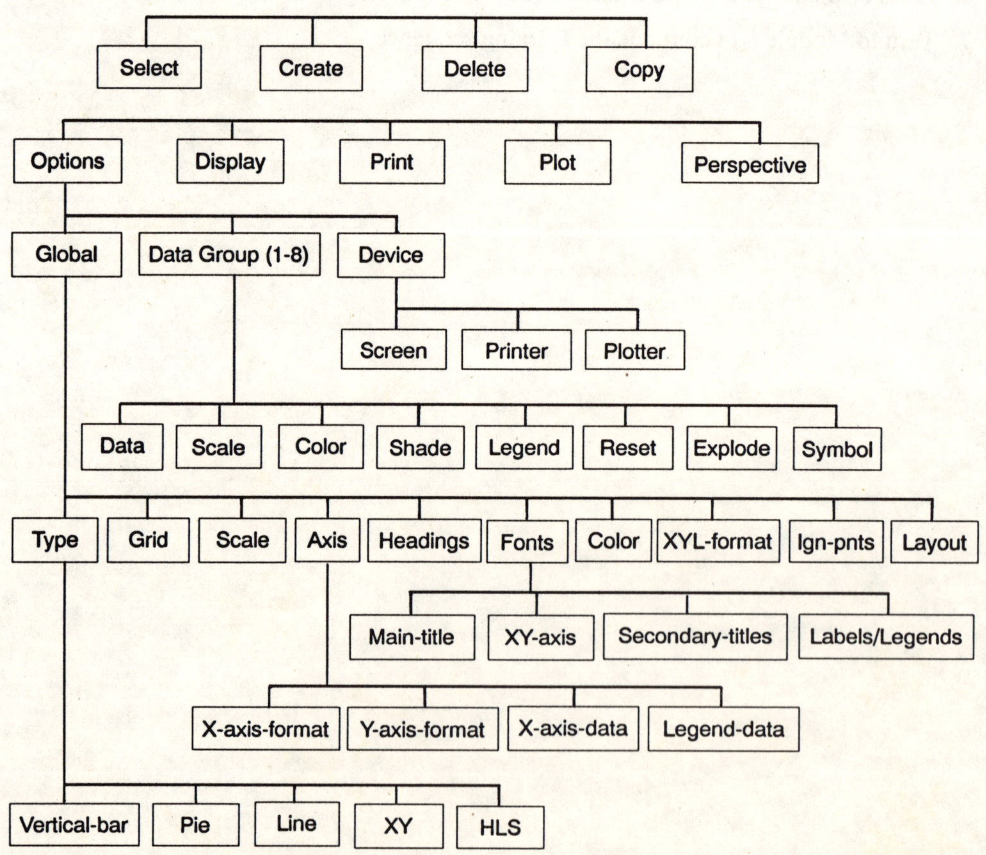

USING THE MENUS The graphics menus work like the spreadsheet menus; Enable displays a row of choices on the middle line of the three-line menu area at the top of the screen. Below the choices is a description of what the highlighted choice does. Select an option by typing the first character of its name or by moving the highlight to it (by pressing Spacebar or an arrow key) and pressing Enter or Down Arrow.

Unlike the Spreadsheet menu though, these menus tell you where you have come from; on the top line is a list of the menu choices you made. For example, in the following screen the top line, "Select DEFAULT Options Group Scale" tells you that you chose Select, picked the DEFAULT graph setting, and then chose Options, one of the data Groups, and Scale to get where you are now. The highlighted number on the right side of the screen shows that you selected data group 2.

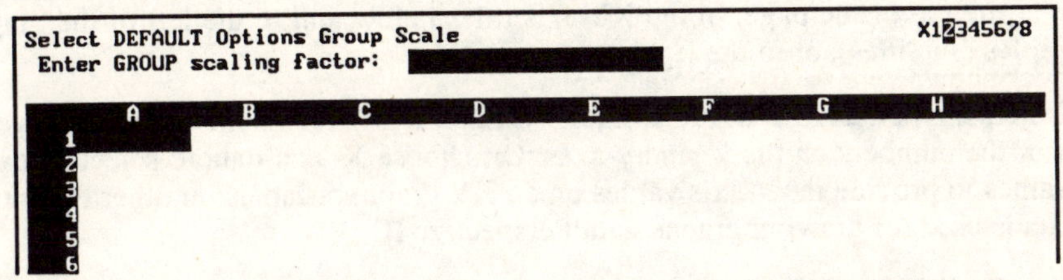

Enable underlines the numbers of any data groups that have been defined already; the previous screen shows that group 1 has been defined. To back up a menu level, press Esc or Up Arrow.

SELECT/CREATE/....COPY The Graphics Selection Menu lets you select an already-built graph setting, create a new setting, delete a setting, or copy a setting. These options are described in Module 101.

OPTIONS/DISPLAY/....PERSPECTIVE When you Select, Create, or Copy a graph setting at the first level of the menu, Enable displays this second level. This menu level is not only the beginning of the graph design procedure, but also where you tell Enable to go ahead and actually display, print, or plot the graph. Select Options when you want to begin designing the graph. Select Perspective when you want to use the Perspective II program to design and draw the graph. (Perspective II, packaged with Enable, is not described in this book).

GLOBAL/DATA GROUP/DEVICE The design procedure is broken into three parts. Global tells Enable what the overall look of the graph is; the type, colors, fonts, legends, and so on. Data Group lets you define the data that will be used (you can define up to eight groups of data to put on each graph) and what each group of data will look like; its scale, color, whether it is "exploded" out of the graph (that is, shown apart from the pie, like a slice of cake), and so on. The final part of defining the graph is telling Enable how the output device works; the print density and orientation of the paper for example.

DATA/SCALE/COLOR/.....SYMBOLS This is where you choose the data to go in the graph and describe what it looks like. To get to this menu level choose one of the Data Groups from the previous level. The changes you make from here on down through the menu levels affect only that data group; you must repeat the procedure for each group.

Choose Data to select the data from the spreadsheet or database; Scale to select a scale-multiplier for the data group; Color to select the color; Shade to select from eight types of shading or lines (for line-graphs); Legend to enter the label used to describe the data group; Reset-data to remove the data group from the graph; Explode to show the group in the pie chart as a slice removed from the pie; and Symbol to change the symbols used on Line and XY graphs.

TYPE/GRID/SCALE/.....LAYOUT This is where you define the overall look of the graph. Choose Type to select the type of graph; Grid to define the type of grid used on any of the graphs (except the Pie); Scale to set the scale-labels on the y-axis; Axis to select the format of the numbers on the axes; Headings to enter the graph title; Fonts to select the type of print used for the headings and legends; Color to add color to the title, grids, headings, and x-axis data in plots and color displays; XYL-format to define how data is displayed in XY line graphs; Ign-pts to remove certain labels from the x-axis so the other labels fit better; and Layout to increase the size of the graph and reduce the size of the titles, labels, and legends.

MAIN-TITLE/XY-AXIS/.....LABELS-AND-LEGENDS The menu that Enable displays when you choose Fonts at the previous level lets you choose which fonts you want to change; in the Main Title at the top of the page, in the XY-axis titles below and to the left of the graph, in the secondary titles (subtitles), or in the legends.

X-AXIS-FORMAT/Y-AXIS-FORMAT/.....LEGEND DATA This menu level lets you choose the format of the numbers on the x- and y-axes. Or, choose X-axis-data to select spreadsheet or database values to provide the x-axis values on an XY graph, or labels on other types of graphs. Legend Data is used for drawing graphs with Perspective II.

VERTICAL-BAR/PIE/.....HLC This is where you choose the type of graph you want to draw. There are six types of vertical bar graphs: the standard or exploded pie chart, the line graph (showing a changing value over time), the XY line graph, (showing a correlation between two types of data), and the HLC graph (the open-high-low-close graph) which shows a value's ranges (for example, a stocks daily high and low, and opening and closing value).

APPLICATIONS

The graphics menu system is the path through the graphics procedure. Although it seems complicated at first glance, once you get the feel for it you will soon know where to find everything. Use the flow diagram in this module as a road map to the menus.

TYPICAL OPERATION

In this activity you create a spreadsheet and enter the graphics menu "tree." You select various options, moving around the structure between the various levels.

1. Create a spreadsheet. (At the Main Menu type **USC**, type a name, and press **Enter**.)
2. When Enable displays the blank spreadsheet press **F10** and type **G**. Enable displays the Graphics Selection Menu.

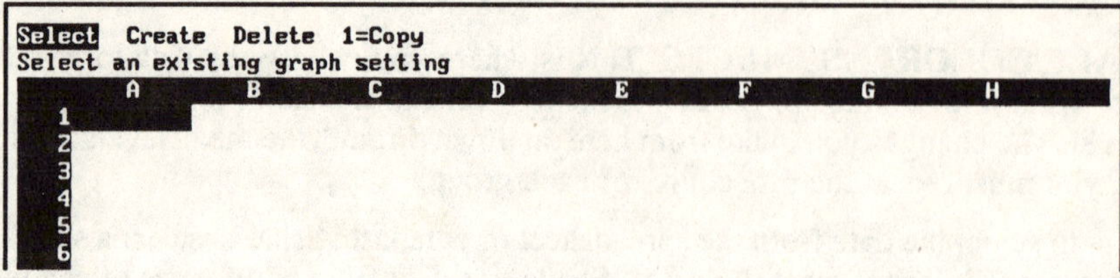

3. Type **S** and Enable displays the list of graph settings; only DEFAULT is displayed because you haven't created any others. Press Enter to select DEFAULT. Enable displays the Task Options menu.

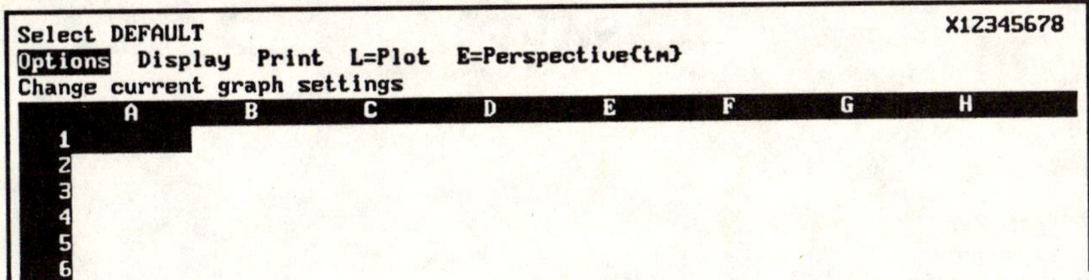

4. Type **OGT** (Options;Global;Type). Enable displays the menu with the graph-type choices.

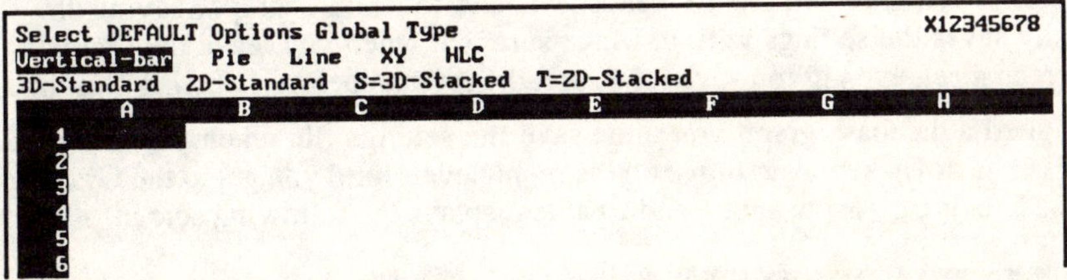

5. Press **Esc** twice and type **1D** (Data Group:1;Data). Enable prompts for the range of cells that contain the data.

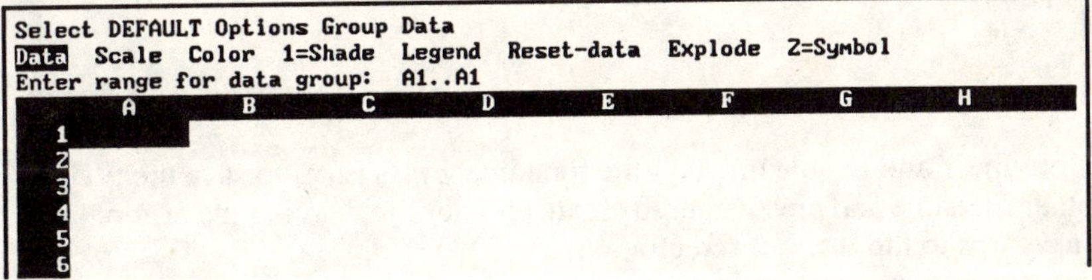

6. Continue moving through the menu structure until you understand it. (Refer to the flow diagram earlier in this module.) Press Esc to move up the tree, and type the first character of a choice to move down.
7. When you have finished, press **Esc** until the menus are no longer displayed above the spreadsheet.
8. Press **F10** and type **QY** to close the file without saving.
9. Turn to Module 96 to continue the learning sequence.

Module 100
SAVE

DESCRIPTION

You can save graphs in a couple of ways; you can save the graph settings, or you can save the graph itself in a word processing file.

GRAPH SETTINGS If you used spreadsheet data to build a graph, saving the spreadsheet automatically saves the settings with it. Make sure that when you leave the Graphics mode you save the spreadsheet, even if you saved the spreadsheet data before selecting Graphics.

If you designed a database graph you must save the settings file when you leave the Graphics menus. Press Esc or Up Arrow to move up the menu levels until you get to the Graphics Selection Menu. Press Esc or Up Arrow again, and Enable displays the following screen.

```
Do you want to save the graph settings file? Yes  No

 Database:
 Index   :
 Where   :
 Fields  :
```

Press Enter or type Y and Enable displays the filename. Press Enter to save the file with that name, or type another filename and press Enter to create another file, leaving the original file unchanged. Enable then returns to the Interact screen.

WORD PROCESSING FILES You can also save the graph in a word processing file; either an existing file with associated text, or a file created especially to hold the graph. This procedure is described in Module 93. This is not a substitute for saving the graph settings. Saving a graph in a word processing file saves a picture of the file, not the instructions, or settings, for building one. You must save the settings if you want to draw the same file later, perhaps with updated information.

APPLICATIONS

Remember to save your graph settings, or you will have a lengthy procedure to repeat the next time you want to display or produce a graph.

TYPICAL OPERATION

In this activity you open a graph settings file from the database Interact screen, and save the file.

1. Open the Interact screen.

```
Database Management System

Please select one of the commands below.  You may use cursor
keys to position to the desired command and press [↵],
or just type the character preceding the desired option.

Find          Display       Browse        Graph
Add           Edit          Verify        Replace
Update        Copy          Merge         Index
Sort          1=Delete      2=Undelete    3=Archive
4=Backup      5=Restore     6=Destroy     7=Rename
8=MCM         9=Report      0=Export      Quit

Use this command to graph selected fields from a database.
#3                                                        X:000
```

2. Type **G** (Graph). Enable prompts for the name of the graph settings file. Type **testfile**.

Enter the name of the graph settings file: testfile

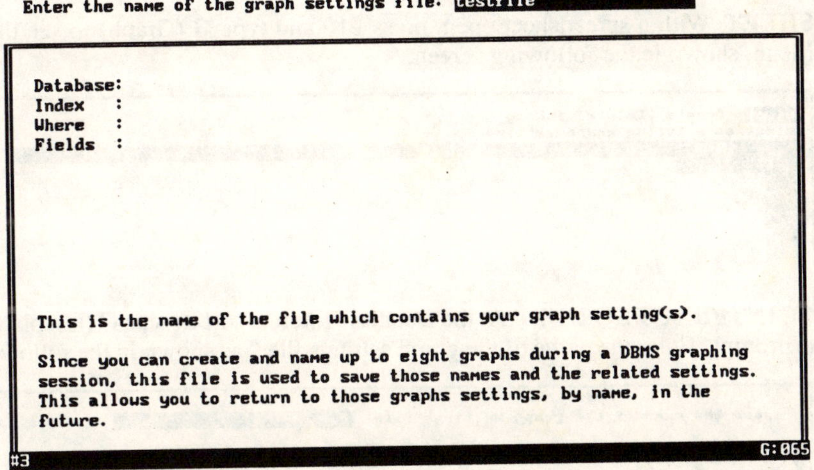

3. Press **Enter** and Enable displays the Graphics Selection Menu. You would normally continue designing your graphs at this point.
4. Press **Esc**. Enable asks if you want to save the graph settings file.
5. Type **Y** and Enable displays the name of the file. Press **Enter** and Enable saves the graph settings and displays the Interact screen again.
6. Type **Q** to return to the Main Menu.
7. Turn to Module 99 to continue the learning sequence.

Module 101
SELECT GRAPHICS MODE

DESCRIPTION

Graphics mode can be entered from two places; a spreadsheet and the DBMS Interact screen. The methods used to enter graphics are slightly different because of the way *graph settings* are stored. If you design a graph using *spreadsheet* data Enable stores the settings in the same file as the spreadsheet, but if you design a *database* graph the settings are stored in a separate file that you name when you enter graphics mode. This allows you to build a graph using data from more that one database.

The graph settings describe what a graph looks like; the information used to draw it, the type of graph (pie or bar, for example), the types of axes used, the device it is drawn on, and so on. Because you may want several different graphs from one spreadsheet or group of databases, you can create several different graph settings in each spreadsheet or graph settings file (up to eight).

SPREADSHEET With a spreadsheet open, press F10 and type G (Graph) to see the Graphics Selection Menu, shown in the following screen.

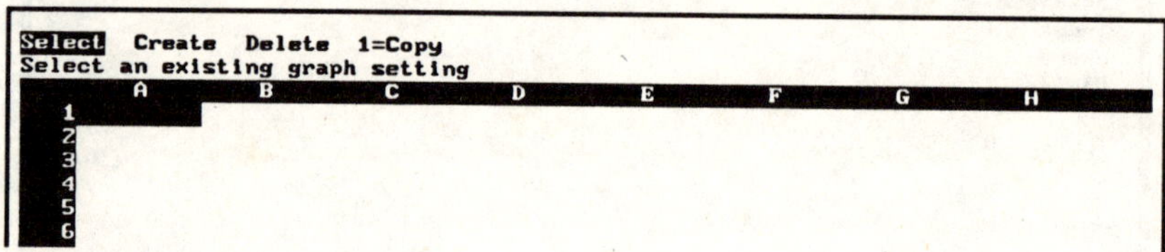

DATABASE INTERACT SCREEN At the Database Interact screen type G (Graph) and Enable displays the prompt "Enter the name of the graph settings file," as shown in the following screen.

```
Enter the name of the graph settings file:

Database:
Index    :
Where    :
Fields   :

This is the name of the file which contains your graph setting(s).

Since you can create and name up to eight graphs during a DBMS graphing
session, this file is used to save those names and the related settings.
This allows you to return to those graphs settings, by name, in the
future.
#4                                                                G:065
```

Enter a name, or type ? and press Enter to view a list of graph settings files. Use a name you will remember, something associated with one of the databases providing data to the graph, for example. Enable will store the file with a .GRF extension. Press Enter and Enable displays the Graphics Selection Menu, as shown in the next screen.

```
Select  Create  Delete  1=Copy
Select an existing graph setting

   Database:
   Index    :
   Where    :
   Fields   :
```

NOTE

Both the database file and the graph settings file must be in the same directory when you try to draw a graph.

Select This option displays a list of the existing graph settings (each graph setting, remember, defines one graph). Select one and Enable continues to the Task Options Menu, where you can modify the graph setting. If you have not yet built a graph setting Enable displays a setting called DEFAULT. (The default graph is a two-dimensional bar graph.)

Create This option displays a prompt asking you for a graph setting name. The name is up to eight letters, numbers, commas, periods, carets (^), backslashes (\), and tildes (~). Do not include spaces. Press Enter and Enable displays the Task Options Menu, where you can modify the graph setting. Enable stores up to eight graph settings.

Delete This option displays a list of the existing graph settings. Move the highlight to a setting and press Enter to delete that setting.

Copy This option displays a list of the existing graph settings. Move the highlight to a setting and press Enter. Enable prompts for the name of the new setting. Enter the name and press Enter. Enable creates the new setting and displays the Task Options Menu, where you can modify the graph setting.

EXIT THE GRAPHICS SELECTION MENU If you want to exit the Graphics Selection Menu displayed above a spreadsheet, press Esc and Enable removes the menu from the spreadsheet. To exit from the database Graphics Selection Menu press Esc and Enable displays a prompt asking if you want to save the graph settings file. When you answer the question Enable displays the Interact screen.

APPLICATIONS

Enable lets you use spreadsheet or database data in a graph. These procedures let you go directly from working with a spreadsheet or database to designing a graph.

TYPICAL OPERATION

In this activity you enter Graphics mode from the spreadsheet named INT, used in Module 7.

1. Open the spreadsheet named INT.
2. Press **F10** and type **G** (Graphics). Enable displays the Graphics Selection Menu.

3. Type **1** (1=Copy) and select the graph settings named BUILD. Press **Enter**, and when Enable prompts for a new graph settings name type **build2**.

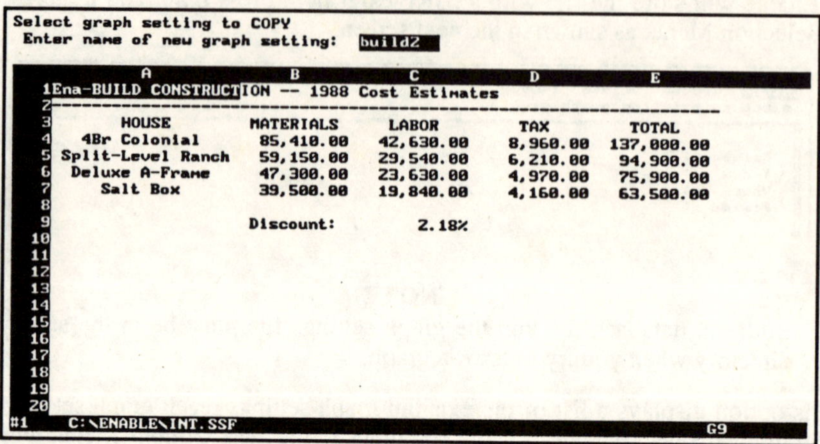

4. Press **Enter**. Enable displays the Task Options Menu. Press **Esc** to return to the Graphics Selection Menu.
5. Type **D** (Delete). Select Build2 and press **Enter** to delete it.
6. Enable displays the Graphics Selection Menu again. Press **Esc** to remove the graphics menu system from the spreadsheet. Press **F10** and type **QY** to close the spreadsheet without saving.
7. Turn to Module 100 to continue the learning sequence.

Module 102
TELECOMMUNICATIONS OVERVIEW

INTRODUCTION

Enable's telecommunications features let you do everything from making simple connections to bulletin boards or information services, to building complicated scripts instructing Enable to transmit or retrieve files when you are not even present.

You can use telecommunications for a wide variety of purposes. You can call other computers within your company to deliver or retrieve files; call business and personal bulletin boards to keep up with what's going on in your industry or play computer games; call electronic mail services to transmit messages to other users; call electronic databases to find information from an encyclopeadia or search through magazine articles. The uses for computer telecommunications are varied and growing every day—there is even a network linking grassroots political groups in the U.S. with groups in the U.S.S.R.

Closer to home, you may want to use Enable Software's bulletin board to ask questions about Enable and read messages from other users. The number is 1-518-877-6316. Module 111 (Setup) describes how to prepare to call the Enable bulletin board.

TELECOMMUNICATIONS BASICS

This book does not say much about how telecommunications work—follow the instructions in the modules and you can make calls without really understanding the technical aspects. But there are a few terms you need to understand in a general way.

A *modem* is an instrument that takes your computer data and turns it into the sort of signal that can travel down phone lines. (One day soon we won't need modems, because all phone lines will be digital; but for the moment most phone lines are analog so we have to convert the digital computer signal into an analog phone signal.) The modem also takes the information coming back from the modem at the other end and converts it into information that your computer understands. The modem may be an *auto-dial* modem (give Enable the telephone number and Enable and the modem will dial the call for you), or a *manual-dial* modem (you have to dial the call yourself and then pass the line back to Enable). The modem may be built into your computer or in a separate box next to it. Because of all these variations, you need to read your modem's instructions for specific requirments.

Another word you will see now and again is *protocol*. Think of this as the language that the computers use to talk to each other, a set of instructions that tell them what sort of signals to transmit to say "hello," to say "stop sending me data," to check for problems, and so on. It also tells the computers how fast to send information, and what size "packets" or "words" it should send. You must get all this information before you try to call another computer. For example, if you subscribe to an information service the information package you receive tells you what *baud rates* (speeds) you can use. You need to pick a speed that your modem can use, and enter that information into Enable's setup. (Generally speaking faster is better because it is cheaper—the less time you are online the less the telephone company and database service charge. However, some databases charge more if you use a high speed. If you are going to spend a lot of time reading while on line, the lower speed may be cheaper.)

Telecommunications networks (such as Telenet, CompuServe Network, Tymnet) are special phone networks that specialize in transmitting data rather that voice signals. They are usually cheaper than using ordinary phone lines. To call another computer using a network you call the network first (with a local number), and then give the network the information it needs to send your data to the right place. When you sign up with an information service they will usually provide one or two networks you can use.

THE SETUP

Enable lets you build up to 256 *setups*—sets of instructions that tell Enable how to "set up" a call—which telephone numbers to call, what type of modem you will use, the protocol, and so on. Then, when you are ready to call, you tell Enable to use the applicable setup. Depending on how you built your setup and the type of modem you have, Enable dials the number, makes the connection, and even transmits your password and log on information. If you need to take any action Enable lets you know.

QUICK-CONNECT

You don't have to build a setup if you don't want to. You may want to call a computer that you will probably never have to call again. In such a case you can use Quick-Connect. This lets you give Enable the most basic protocol information necessary and the telephone number to call just before making the call.

ONCE YOU ARE CONNECTED

There are a number of things you can do once you are connected. You can make Enable save all or part of the data you receive—either directly in an ASCII file on a disk, or in your computer's RAM memory (when you end the session Enable can save that data in a word processing file). You can use a word processing screen to edit the data you are receiving at the same time that Enable continues saving incoming data.

You can also make Enable print the information for you as it arrives. And you can transmit data to the other computer. You can transmit blocks you mark in a word processing file, or entire files that you name when you are ready to send them.

ADVANCED FEATURES

Enable also has several features (as briefly described here) that most users do not need, but which are very useful in certain applications. Unattended File Transfers are described further in Module 112 and the last four advanced features are further described in Appendix H.

UNATTENDED FILE TRANSFERS You can transmit files when you are not even present—you write a *script* telling Enable which computer to call, how to log on, which files to send, and how to log off. The script can include several different operations, and can instruct Enable to send files or request files from the other computer.

TERMINAL EMULATION You may want to *emulate* a terminal so you can use your computer to call a mainframe computer or minicomputer. Enable lets you emulate three common terminal types: the VT-100, VT-52, and AT&T4410.

TRANSMIT/RECEIVE MAPPING TABLES Enable has a special feature that allows you to *filter* data arriving at your terminal, or change the data being transmitted. For example, suppose the computer you are communicating with uses certain characters that your computer cannot use; you can build a *mapping table* to convert those characters to an equivalent character. Or, if you want to include incoming data in an outgoing Telex (which requires all the characters in uppercase), you can make Enable automatically convert all incoming characters to uppercase for you.

Some computers may also require that you transmit certain special characters in commands and responses. It would be difficult to use Enable's special character set each time you wanted to send the character, so use a mapping table to convert another character (@, for example) to the one you need.

KEYBOARD MAPPING TABLES These are keyboard macros. You can assign a whole sequence of operations to one key, speeding up the telecommunications session and saving time. You might assign a log on procedure or password to a key so you could press that one key instead of actually typing the entire procedure. Or, you can use one key to begin the file transmission procedure, or begin capturing data. This feature is one that you will probably want to take advantage of if you use telecommunications a lot, because it makes communications easier and quicker (and, therefore, cheaper).

MODEM TABLES You can build modem tables that give Enable special instructions in how to use your modems; you can even use these tables to work with modems that Enable does not usually support.

WINDOWS

You can use windows while you are working with telecommunications. Press F10 and type M1 (MCM;Windows) to access the windows features. Because these features are exactly the same as those in Word Processing, they are not described again in this section. See Module 46 for more information.

Turn to Module 111 to continue the learning sequence.

Module 103
CALLING USING QUICK-CONNECT

DESCRIPTION

If you want to call a system you use infrequently or are unlikely to use again, use Quick-Connect to make the call. You don't have to build a setup—Enable prompts you for a few details before making the call.

Make sure your modem is turned on (and set to Originate if necessary). At the Main Menu type UTCQ (Use;Telecom;Communicate;Quick-Connect) and Enable displays the Quick-Connection Form.

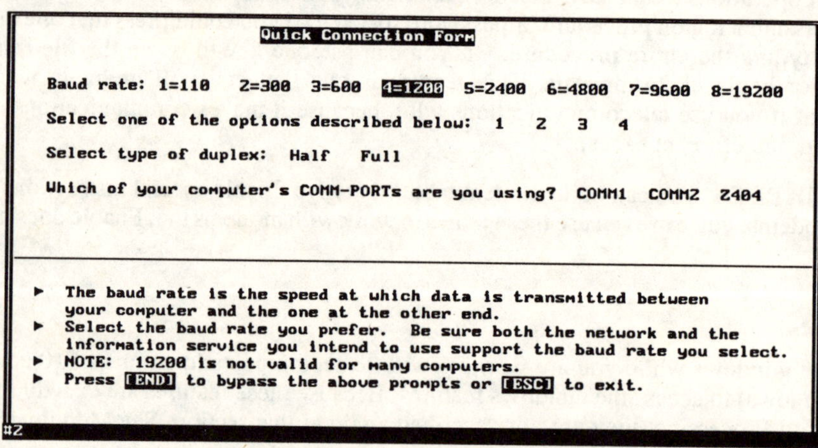

Select the correct options at the prompts in this screen. (For more information on these options see Module 111, and the documentation for your modem and the service or device you are calling.) You can change the default settings in your user profile. For example, if you have your modem connected to COMM2 you can set your profile to use that port as the default, so you will not have to select it each time you use Quick-Connect. See Appendix B for more information about profiles.

When you have completed this form Enable displays the Word Processing Interface screen.

```
TELEPROCESSING SYSTEM

Establishing Interface With Word Processing

▶  You may capture all or portions of the data displayed on your
   screen during your telecommunications session.
▶  This feature allows you to review data which has scrolled off
   the screen.  Also, you may edit this data using all of the Word
   Processing functions.
▶  At any time during the session (or at the end of the session)
   you may save this data on disk as a Word Processing document.

If you wish to immediately begin capturing data, enter a file name
in the area below.  Otherwise just press ENTER.

   Enter file name (or just press ENTER):

#2   If you are using a modem, please make sure the modem has been turned on.
```

If you want to capture data in a word processing file, type a filename and press Enter. If you enter an existing name Enable asks if you want to add the data to the end of the file, or re-use the file (erasing the existing data). Leave the prompt blank and press Enter if you don't want to capture data. (Capturing data is described in Module 105.)

Enable now displays the Quick-Connection screen, as shown in the following illustration.

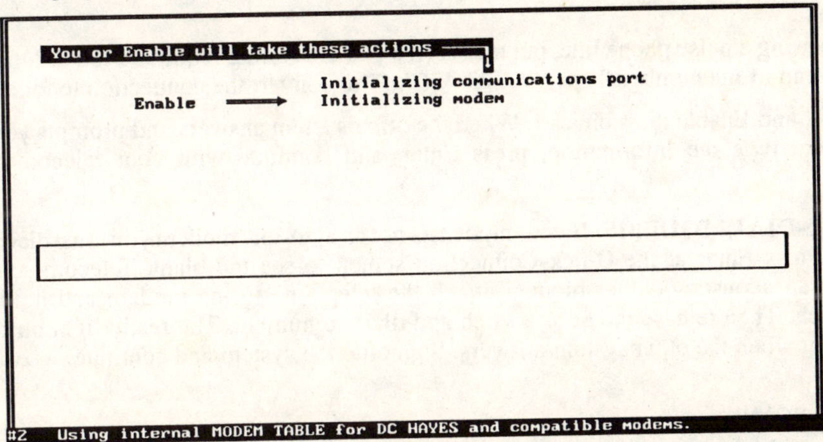

Once Enable has initialized the modem it displays the following instructions screen. Your subsequent actions depend on whether you are using an auto-dial or manual-dial modem.

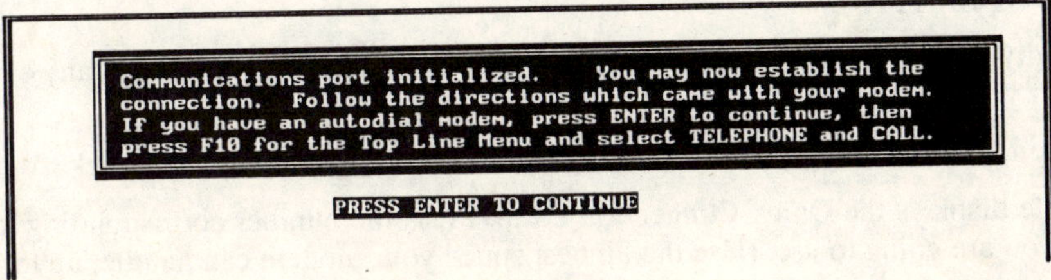

AUTO-DIAL MODEMS Press Enter to see the blank Telecom screen, and press F10 and type TC (Tele;Call) to see the the following menu.

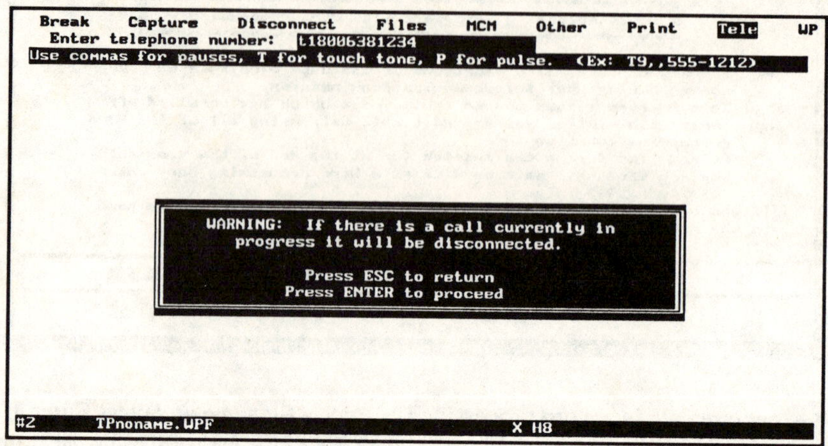

Type the number you want to call, preceded by T (tone) or P (pulse) depending on the type of phone line you are using. You can include numbers required to get an outside line, and commas to insert two-second pauses. T9,,123-4567 tells Enable to dial 9, wait four seconds, and then dial 1234567.

If you are using a pulse phone line, but the service you are calling requires a touch-tone line, enter a T at the end of the number. Type P9,,123-4567,,,T to convert the connection to tone.

Press Enter and Enable dials the call. When the other system answers and prompts you for logon information, type the information, press Enter, and continue with your telecommunications session.

MANUAL-DIAL MODEMS If your modem is not an auto-dial modem you must dial the number yourself. Press Enter at the Quick-Connection screen to see the blank Telecom screen. If the modem is an acoustic-coupler modem attach the telephone to the modem and hold down the hook-switch. Then release the hook-switch and dial the number. The ready light on the modem should light when the other system answers. Sign onto the system and continue.

APPLICATIONS

Use Quick-Connect if you don't want to spend time building a setup for a call that you are unlikely to make again.

TYPICAL OPERATION

In this activity you use Quick-Connect to call the Enable bulletin board. (Or call any other service or computer you want.)

1. At the Main Menu type **UTCQ** (Use System;Telecom;Communicate;Quick Connect).
2. Enable displays the Quick Connection Form. Press the number corresponding to the baud rate you are going to use. (Use the highest speed your modem can handle, up to 2400.)
3. Type **3** and type **F**. At the COMM-PORT prompt move the highlight to the port you are using.

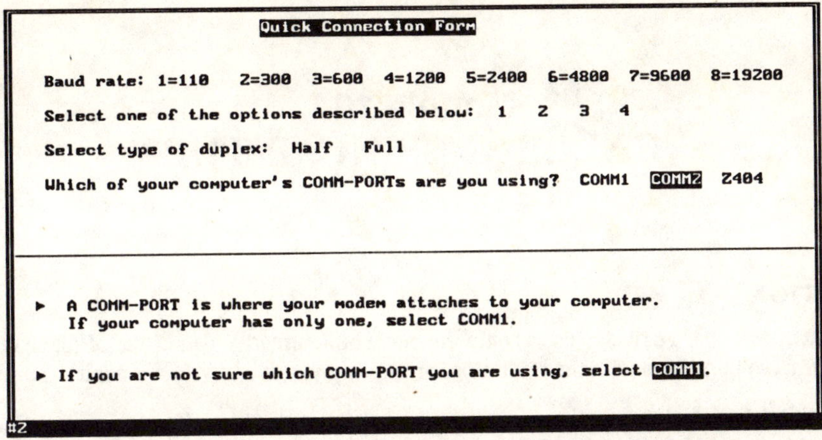

4. Press **Enter** and Enable initializes the port and modem and displays a reminder. Press **Enter** to display the blank Telecom screen.

5. Dial the number:

   Manual-Dial Modems Dial **1-518-877-6316** (plus any other numbers required to get an outside line or use a long distance service).

   Auto-Dial Modems Press **F10** and type **TC**. Type **T** if you have a tone line, or **P** if you have a pulse line. Type the number required to dial an outside line or use a long distance service, if neccessary. Put two commas between the different numbers, and then type **1-518-877-6316**.

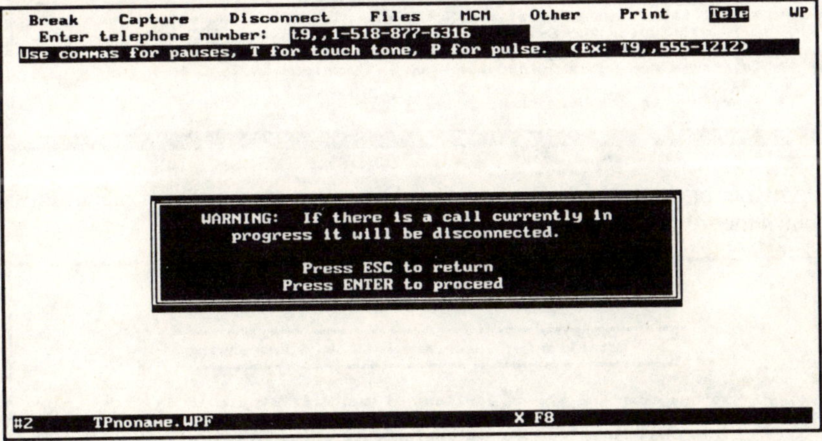

6. If you have an auto-dial modem press **Enter** and Enable dials the number. When the call is connected you see the logon screen.

7. Continue with a bulletin board session if you wish. When you are finished press **F10**, type **DY** to disconnect, and type **N** when Enable asks if you want to save data. Press **Enter** and Enable ends the session.

8. Turn to Module 108 to continue the learning sequence.

Module 104
CALLING USING SETUP

DESCRIPTION

The easiest way to make a call is to use a setup you have built already. You just tell Enable which setup to use, and Enable continues with the operation, prompting you if and when it needs your input.

SELECTING A SETUP Make sure your modem is turned on (and set to Originate if necessary). At the Main Menu type UTCU (Use;Telecom;Communicate;Use Setup). Enable displays the Setup Selection screen, which is very similar to the Initial Setup screen.

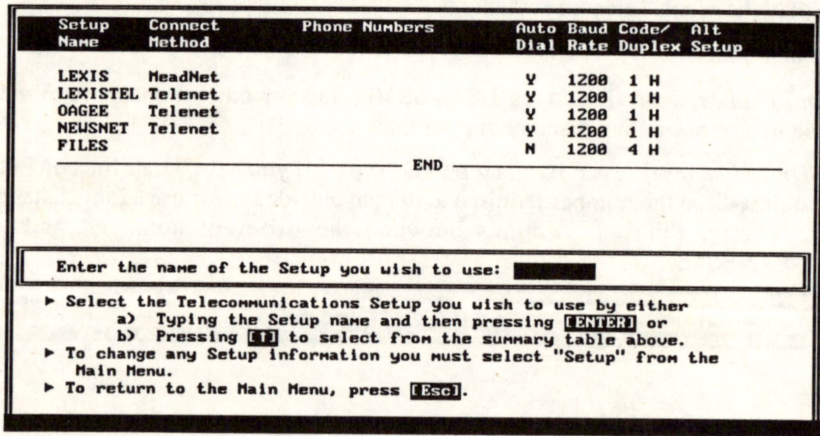

Type a setup name, or press Up Arrow and then Down Arrow to select a name. Press Enter and Enable displays the following screen.

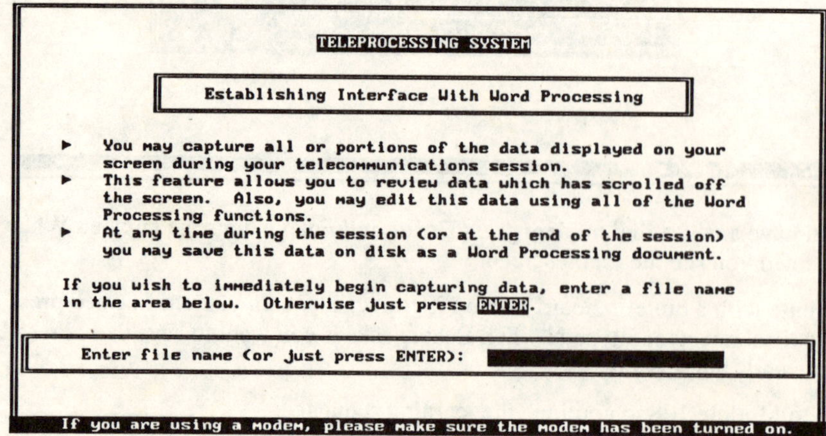

If you want to capture data in a word processing file, type a filename and press Enter. If you enter an existing filename Enable asks if you want to add the data to the end of the file, or re-use the file (erasing the existing data). Leave the prompt blank and press Enter if you don't want to capture data. (Capturing data is explained in Module 105.)

THE SETUP CONNECTION SCREEN Enable now displays the Setup Connection screen. An example is shown in the following illustration, but the steps listed on the screen vary depending on the setup you have chosen.

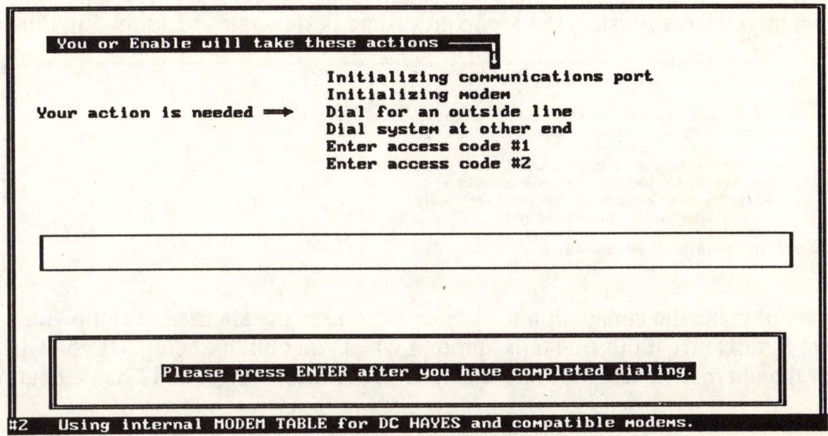

If you have an acoustic-coupler modem attach the telephone to the modem now and hold down the hook-switch. When Enable tells you to dial, release the hook-switch and dial the number. The Ready light on your modem lights when the other system answers.

Enable indicates on the Setup Connection screen which step it is carrying out by displaying "Enable" to the left of the step and drawing an arrow to the step. If you need to do something Enable displays "Your action is needed" to the left of the step, with an arrow pointing to it. For example, if you are not using an auto-dial modem Enable prompts you to dial the number. Dial the number and press Enter.

Once you or Enable have dialed the number, Enable waits for a reply. If the number is busy you can type R to redial or Q to quit. If you hear the system at the other end answer, but Enable doesn't respond, type C (Connect). When Enable makes the connection it displays the first Telecom screen, as shown in the following illustration.

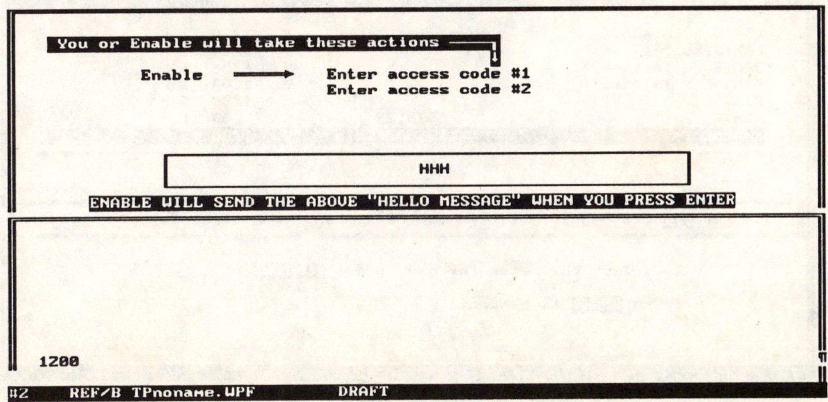

THE TELECOM SCREEN This screen lists the steps you must take once a connection is made. (If you didn't enter any logon information into the setup, Enable bypasses this screen.) The screen in our illustration lists two access codes, but you may also need to enter the "terminal type" code and the "connection address," depending on how you built your setup. Enable displays, in the box in the center of the screen, the message or code that will be transmitted the next time you press Enter. Wait for the system you have called to prompt you, press Enter, and Enable sends the code or address. Enable then moves the pointer to the next step, and waits for you to press Enter again.

If your logon messages are correct the other system lets you continue. An example of the screen displayed when you have finished the logon procedure is shown in the following illustration.

```
          Copyright (C), 1989

GEnie Logon at: 16:03 CDT on: 890816
$ PRIME TIME Rate in Effect ($18/hr) $

         Your GEnie account will be
    unavailable until a representative
   contacts you by phone to confirm your
          account information.

OFF AT 16:03CDT 08/16/89
```

If Enable cannot make the connection it automatically uses the alternative setup you specified at the "name of Setup to try if this one fails" prompt when you built the setup. (If you typed ? before the name of the alternative setup Enable asks you to confirm; type A and Enable continues.)

APPLICATIONS

If you need to call a system more than just once or twice you should build a setup for it. You have more flexibility in the way the call is made, and you save time each time you call that computer.

TYPICAL OPERATION

In this activity you call the Enable bulletin board using the setup you built in Module 111. Or use any other setup you have built.

1. At the Main Menu type **UTCU** (Use System;Telecom;Communicate;Use Setup).
2. Press **Up Arrow** and then press **Down Arrow** until the cursor is on the setup named ENABLE.

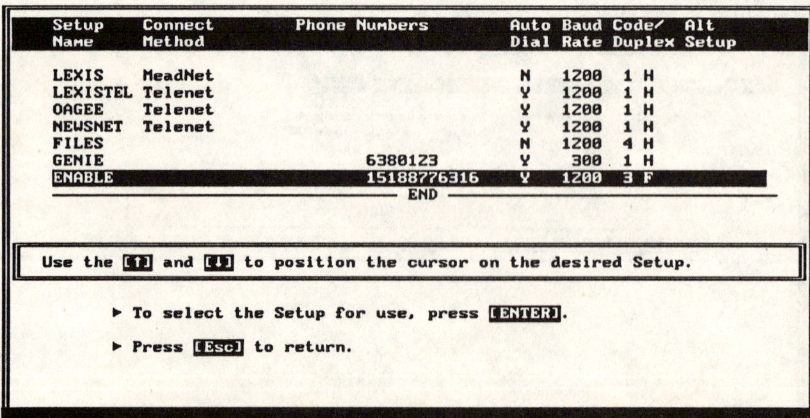

3. Press **Enter** twice to bypass the filename prompt. Enable initializes the modem. If you have an auto-dial modem Enable dials the call; if not Enable asks you to dial.

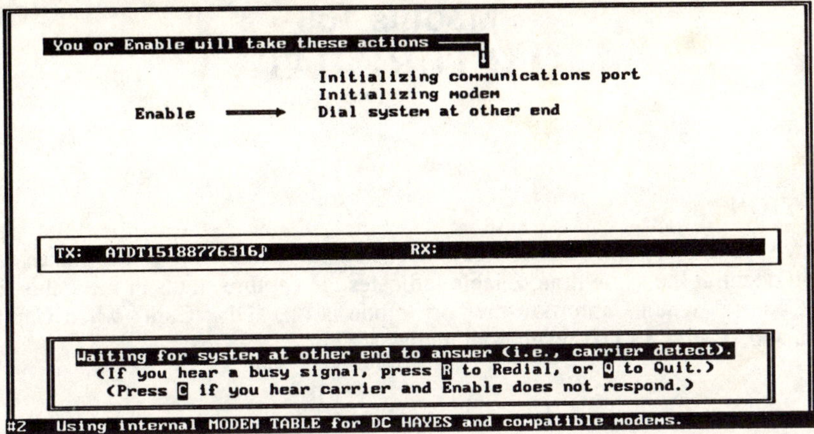

4. When the call is connected you see the logon screen.

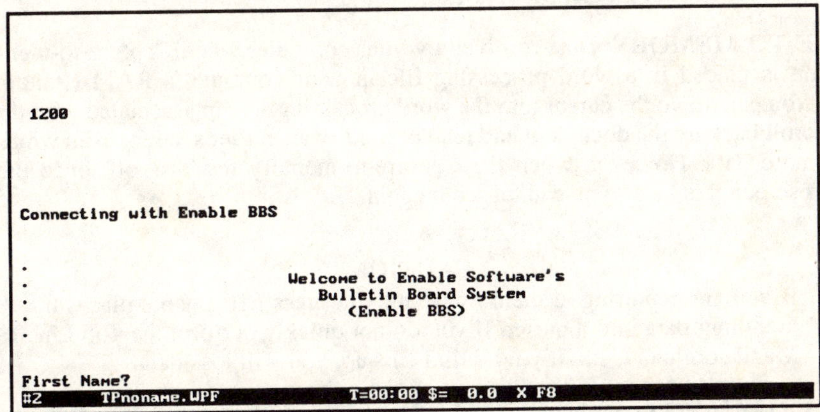

5. Continue with a bulletin board session if you wish. When you are finished press **F10** to see the following menu.

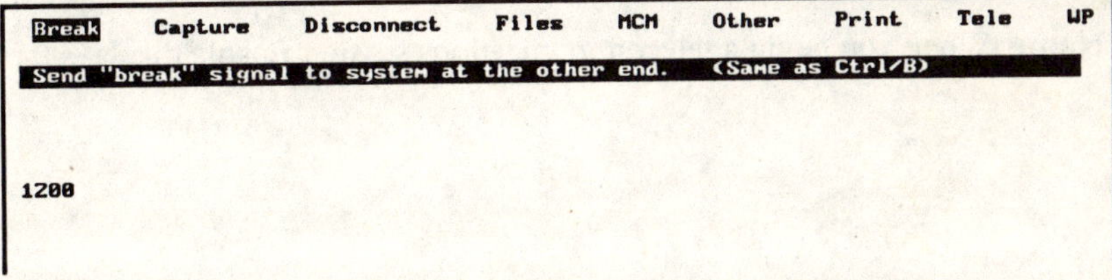

6. Type **DY** to disconnect, and type **N** when Enable asks if you want to save data. Press **Enter** and Enable ends the session.

7. Turn to Module 107 to continue the learning sequence.

Module 105
CAPTURE DATA

DESCRIPTION

There are two ways to capture data. The data can be *captured to memory* or *captured to disk*. Both of these can occur at the same time. Enable indicates the capture status in the status line. Enable displays "Capture" when Capture-to-memory mode is on, "Disk Capt" when Capture-to-disk mode is on, and "Capt (W+D)" when both modes are on.

NOTE

In addition to capturing data Enable can automatically save transferred files. Because this is a totally different type of procedure it is explained in a different module, Module 112.

CAPTURE-TO-MEMORY Data received by your computer when Capture-to-memory mode is turned on is placed in a word processing file in your computer's RAM (Random Access Memory). You can move the cursor into the word processing screen associated with the Telecom screen to scroll back up the document and read or modify an earlier section, even while Enable is receiving more data. However, when the Capture-to-memory mode is off, once the data has scrolled off screen it is lost—you cannot see it again.

CAUTION

If you are capturing to memory, when you press F10 Enable places the incoming data into a buffer. If you do not quickly perform the Top Line Menu command, and if your buffer fills up, you will lose data.

The data captured in your computer's RAM is lost when you turn off your computer. However, when you end a telecommunications session Enable lets you save the word processing file. You can then return to the document later.

There are two ways to turn on Capture-to-memory.

Enter File Name When you begin a telecommunications session Enable displays the following screen.

```
TELEPROCESSING SYSTEM

Establishing Interface With Word Processing

▶  You may capture all or portions of the data displayed on your
   screen during your telecommunications session.
▶  This feature allows you to review data which has scrolled off
   the screen.  Also, you may edit this data using all of the Word
   Processing functions.
▶  At any time during the session (or at the end of the session)
   you may save this data on disk as a Word Processing document.

If you wish to immediately begin capturing data, enter a file name
in the area below.  Otherwise just press ENTER.

Enter file name (or just press ENTER):

If you are using a modem, please make sure the modem has been turned on.
```

Type a filename and press Enter to begin the session. Enable builds a file in the computer's RAM with the name you give it, and adds the extension .WPF. (If you enter an existing filename Enable asks if you want to re-use the file—that is, erase the existing data—or add data to the end of the file.) The data your computer receives is immediately captured in the file without any further command by you.

If you don't enter a name now you can still capture data using the method described next—Enable will capture the data in a file called TPNONAME.WPF.

NOTE

Enable writes over the same TPNONAME file each time it uses it, so if you save data in the TPNONAME file instead of entering a filename, previously saved data is lost.

Press F10 CW or Press F7 These commands toggle the Capture-to-memory mode on and off. If you entered a filename when you began the telecommunications session you can press F7 to turn off Capture-to-memory mode. If you didn't enter a filename, pressing F7 turns on Capture-to-memory mode using the TPNONAME.WPF file. When you turn on Capture-to-memory mode Enable captures all the data on your screen and all subsequent data.

Or press F10 and type CW (Capture;Word Processing (ON/OFF)) to use the Top Line Menu to turn Capture-to-memory mode on or off.

NOTE

You cannot Capture-to-memory during terminal emulation.

CAPTURE-TO-DISK If you have a large amount of incoming data you might want to capture it on disk—your computer's RAM may not be large enough to store it all in Capture-to-memory mode. The data is stored in ASCII format, not Enable word processing format (of course, Enable can use ASCII text files in word processing).

To capture to disk press F10 at the Telecom screen and type CO (Capture;Open). Enable prompts for a filename.

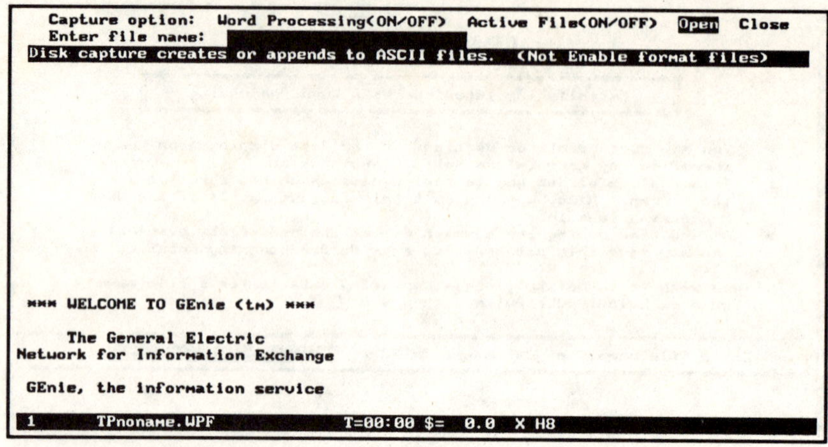

Type the filename and press Enter. (Include a disk drive and directory if necessary. Enable automatically adds a .TPF extension.) If you enter the name of an existing file Enable adds the data to the end of the file (although it doesn't warn you or ask you to confirm this.)

NOTE

This file is not the same as the Capture-to-memory filename you may have entered when you began the session. Use a different name.

You now have a file ready to receive data, but Enable does not begin capturing data until you tell it to. Press F10 and type CA (Capture;Active File (ON/OFF)) to turn Capture-to-disk on and off. Enable captures the data that arrives after you turn Capture-to-disk on, not what is already on the screen. You can also close the file by pressing F10 and typing CC (Capture;Close). You must open another file if you want to Capture-to-disk again.

Expert Commands Because time may be very important when you are trying to capture data to disk, you may want to use these expert commands:

Open a file:	F9 T Home, type a filename, press Enter
Turn mode on and off:	F9 T F7
Close a file:	F9 T End

SAVING CAPTURED DATA Data captured to disk is automatically saved—you don't have to take any further action. However, data captured to memory is stored in a word processing file, and, like any word processing document, you must save the data before you leave it.

You use the same Save command as any other word processing document. Press Alt-F10 and press Enter to save using the default options, or press Alt-F10 and type C to change those options.

You can save at any time during the telecom session, and at the end of the session.

When you end the session by pressing F10 and typing D (Disconnect) Enable asks you if you want to save the data. Type Y. If Capture-to-memory mode is on Enable displays the word processing screen with the Accept/Change Save-Options box at the top of the screen. If Capture-to-memory mode is off and the screen has lines of data that have not been captured, Enable asks if you want to capture them. Press F7 to capture these lines and Enable then displays the word processing screen with the Accept/Change Save-Options box at the top of the screen.

TIP: If you did not enter a filename when you began the session the word processing file is called TPNONAME.WPF. Rename the file before you save it, so that you do not accidentally erase data by using TPNONAME in another telecommunications session.

Press Enter to save the data. Then press F10 and type QY to close the file, or continue editing the file.

APPLICATIONS

When you use telecommunications you normally want to save information you receive, whether it is a telex, electronic mail, or information from an encyclopedia. Even if you are only receiving a short message it is probably best to save it, especially if you are using a fast baud rate, because you may not be able to read it as it arrives.

The Capture options let you save data directly into a word processing file, or an ASCII disk-file if you are going to receive a lot of data. You can turn capture on and off during transmission to capture only the information you need.

TYPICAL OPERATION

In this activity you capture data to memory and to disk, using the ENABLE setup you built in Module 111.

1. At the Main Menu type **UTCU** (Use System;Telecom;Communicate;Use Setup).
2. Press **Up Arrow** and then press **Down Arrow** until the cursor is on the setup named ENABLE.
3. Press **Enter** and Enable displays the filename prompt. Type **CAPTURE** and press **Enter**.

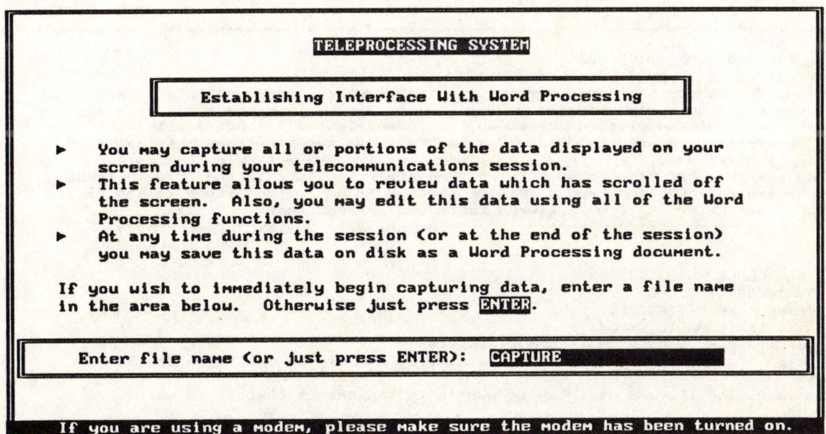

TELEPROCESSING SYSTEM

Establishing Interface With Word Processing

- ► You may capture all or portions of the data displayed on your screen during your telecommunications session.
- ► This feature allows you to review data which has scrolled off the screen. Also, you may edit this data using all of the Word Processing functions.
- ► At any time during the session (or at the end of the session) you may save this data on disk as a Word Processing document.

If you wish to immediately begin capturing data, enter a file name in the area below. Otherwise just press ENTER.

Enter file name (or just press ENTER): CAPTURE

If you are using a modem, please make sure the modem has been turned on.

4. Enable initializes the modem. If you have an autodial modem Enable dials the call; if not Enable asks you to dial.
5. When the call is connected you see the Enable Bulletin Board System (BBS) logon screen. Log on and go to the BBS Main Menu. (Tell Enable not to pause after each display page.)

6. At the BBS Main Menu type **E** (for the Enable message boards), **M** (for the Main Message board), **R** (to Read messages), and **F** (for Forward).

7. When Enable asks if you want to pause, type **N**. When Enable asks which message you want to start with press **Enter**.

8. The messages begin scrolling across your screen. Press **F10**, type **CO** (Capture;Open) and type **CAPT1**, as shown on the next screen.

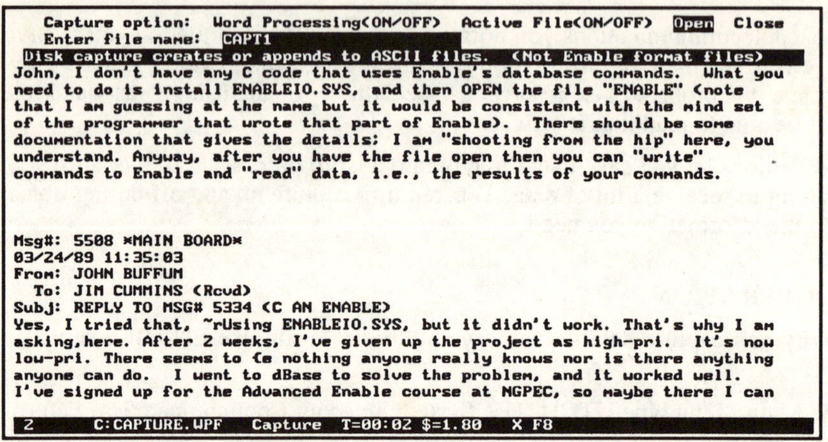

```
   Capture option:  Word Processing(ON/OFF)  Active File(ON/OFF)  Open  Close
   Enter file name: CAPT1
 Disk capture creates or appends to ASCII files.  (Not Enable format files)
John, I don't have any C code that uses Enable's database commands.  What you
need to do is install ENABLEIO.SYS, and then OPEN the file "ENABLE" (note
that I am guessing at the name but it would be consistent with the mind set
of the programmer that wrote that part of Enable).  There should be some
documentation that gives the details; I am "shooting from the hip" here, you
understand. Anyway, after you have the file open then you can "write"
commands to Enable and "read" data, i.e., the results of your commands.


Msg#: 5508 *MAIN BOARD*
03/24/89 11:35:03
From: JOHN BUFFUM
  To: JIM CUMMINS (Rcvd)
Subj: REPLY TO MSG# 5334 (C AN ENABLE)
Yes, I tried that, ~rUsing ENABLEIO.SYS, but it didn't work. That's why I am
asking,here. After 2 weeks, I've given up the project as high-pri.  It's now
low-pri. There seems to (e nothing anyone really knows nor is there anything
anyone can do.  I went to dBase to solve the problem, and it worked well.
I've signed up for the Advanced Enable course at MGPEC, so maybe there I can

 2          C:CAPTURE.WPF    Capture  T=00:02 $=1.80    X F8
```

9. Press **Enter** and you have specified a Capture-to-disk file. To begin capturing press **F10** and type **CA** (Capture;Active File (ON/OFF)). Notice the status line changes to indicate that both types of capture are working.

```
From: SKIP HULTS
  To: JIM CUMMINS (Rcvd)
Subj: REPLY TO MSG# 5051 (MEMORY ISSUES)
Jim, Thanks for the speedy reply.  I'm using OA at the present time, and I
know that the system recognizes that the extra 2MB is present (it does list
it in the window display screen on the lower right side) but I still get
"Insufficient Memory to Proceed" error messages and know that this extra RAM
isn't being used.  I'm trying to figure out if  there is a switch to add to
my startup .BAT file to do this or some other way to tell the program to use
the memory?  OR: is there a problem perhaps in my system either in the lack
of a proper driver for Enable/OA to access the EMS board? OR ???
-------------------------------------Thanks: Skip Hults, NapaCA -----


Msg#: 5063 *MAIN BOARD*
03/14/89 10:27:46
From: MARK FITZGERALD
  To: SKIP HULTS (Rcvd)
Subj: REPLY TO MSG# 5057 (MEMORY ISSUES)
Skip, if it shows up in the window display summary screen, then Enable
is
recognizing it, and will try to use it to the extent that it is able.
The
problem is that you are running out of base before you run out of
#2         C:CAPTURE.WPF    Capt(W+D)T=00:03 $=3.00    X F8
```

10. Continue with a bulletin board session if you wish. When you are finished press **F10** and type **DY** to disconnect. Type **Y** when Enable asks if you want to save data and Enable displays the word processing screen with the data in it, and the Save options displayed on the screen.

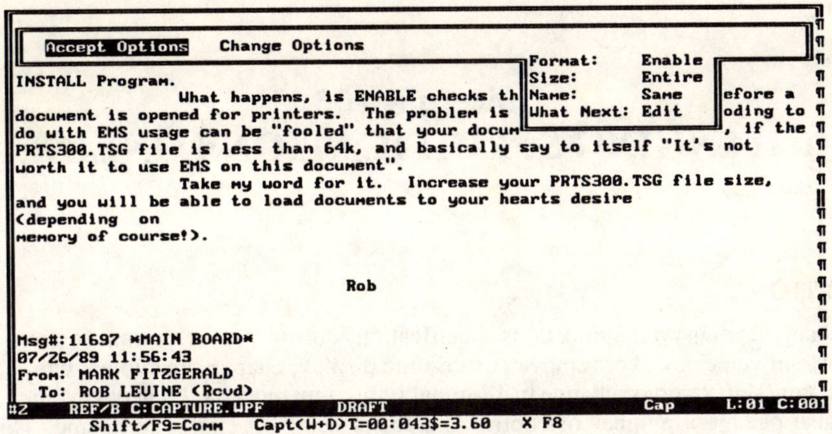

11. Press **Enter** to save the data. Press **F10** and type **QY** to close the file.
12. You can now view either of these files; at the Main Menu type **UWR**, type **CAPTURE**, and press **Enter** to view the Capture-to-memory file; or type **CAPT1.TPF**, and press **Enter** twice for the Capture-to-disk file.
13. Turn to Module 110 to continue the learning sequence.

Module 106
CHANGING SPECIFICATIONS ONLINE

DESCRIPTION

You can change certain communications specifications during your telecomm session. Using the Top Line Menu you can add or remove cost or time display; change the duplex, line-feed, pause, break, and Xon/Xoff settings; change to Terminal Emulation mode; and select keyboard mapping. You can also change a number of control characters using an expert command. This module explains how to change these specifications, but for more information about what the specifications actually do, refer to the module on Setup—Module 111—and to your modem's documentation.

At the Telecom screen press F10 and type O (Other) to see the following options.

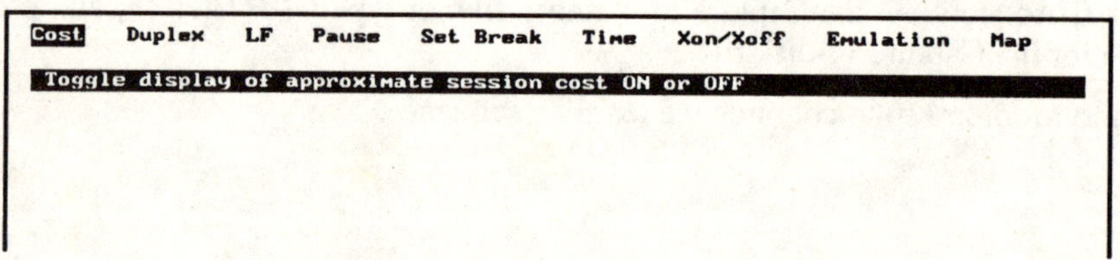

Cost Shows you two options: Cost (ON/OFF) (turns the status line cost display on and off), and Set (prompts you to specify the cost per hour used in the cost calculation).

Duplex Changes the current duplex setting (Half or Full) and changes the status line indicator accordingly.

LF Lets you add a line feed to the end of all transmitted lines, so that the receiving terminal advances one line each time it receives a line (some terminals must receive a line feed character to advance).

Pause If the system to which you are transmitting cannot handle the lines of data as quickly as Enable sends them you can specify the length of time Enable should pause before sending the next line. You may need to use this if the other system does not use Xon/Xoff.

Set Break The break signal sends a message to the other computer to stop transmitting (press Ctrl-B or select Break from the Top Line Menu to send a break signal). The break signal is usually 350 milliseconds long, but some systems may need a longer break signal. You can enter a new value here, or enter 0 to revert back to 350 milliseconds.

Time Turns the status line time display on and off.

Xon/Xoff Turns the Xon/Xoff status on and off.

Emulation Lets you choose to emulate a terminal (a VT-100, VT-52, or AT&T 4410). Lets you turn emulation on and off.

Map Turns the Keyboard Mapping Table on and off.

RECEIVING LINE FEEDS, TABS, AND CONTROL CHARACTERS You can use an expert command to modify the way Enable handles certain incoming characters. Press F9 and type TO*n*, where *n* is one of the following numbers:

0 Ignore all line feeds occurring with carriage returns.
1 Convert all line feeds to carriage returns.
2 Ignore all line feeds.
3 Ignore all tabs.
4 Convert all tabs to a single space.
5 Move the cursor to the next tab position when the tab is received.
6 Accept tabs without modification.
7 Accept keyboard characters only. Ignore ASCII characters with codes 0-6, 12, 14-25, 27-31, and 127-255.
8 Substitute a tilde (~) for the ASCII characters listed in 7.
9 Accept all characters except those with ASCII codes 240-255.

All of these options can also be modified in the setup. These are the corresponding prompts in Setup:

- Specify how received linefeeds will be handled—prompts 1, 2, and 3.
- Specify how received tabs will be handled—prompts 4, 5, and 6.
- Enter receive filter option—prompts 7, 8, and 9

8TH BIT CONVERSION To convert the 8th bit of each incoming data word to zero, press F9 and type T8. You might try this if your are getting a lot of scrambled characters on the screen.

See the expert commands in Appendix F for more ways to change specifications online.

APPLICATIONS

You may need to use the Top Line Menu options for a number of reasons. You might build a setup, make the call, and discover that one of the settings is incorrect. (For example, you may find that each time you type a character it appears twice on your screen. This is probably because you selected Half Duplex instead of Full Duplex in your setup—use the Top Line Menu to change to Full Duplex, and modify the setup when you have finished). You can also use these options to turn mapping and emulation on and off, or to temporarily display the cost or time indicators.

TYPICAL OPERATION

In this activity you use Quick-Connect to display a blank Telecom screen and to change specifications.

1. At the Main Menu type **UTCQ** (Use System;Telecom;Communicate;Quick-Connect).
2. At the Quick-Connection Form type **43F**, position the cursor on the COMM port you are using, and press **Enter**.
3. Enable displays the filename prompt. Press **Enter** and Enable initializes the modem and displays the instructions screen. Press **Enter** to see the blank Telecom screen.

4. Press **F10** and type **O** to see the Other Menu options.

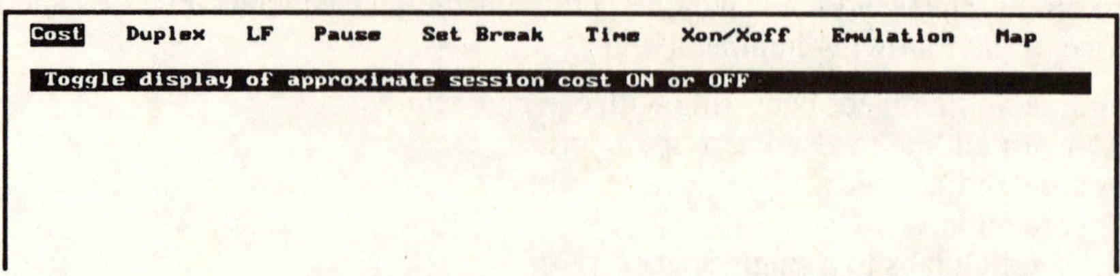

5. Type **CS** and type **65** to add a cost/hour value.

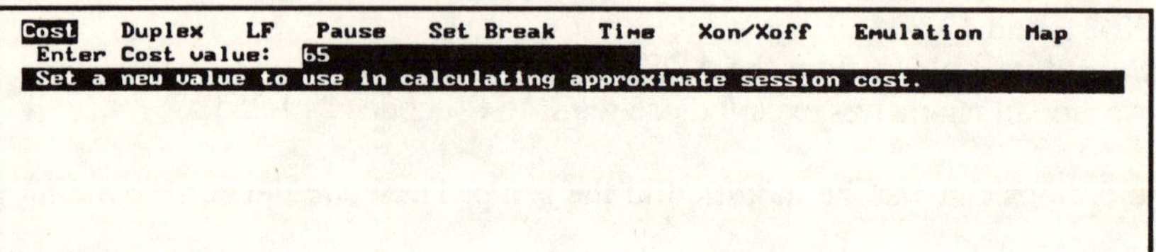

6. Press **Enter**. Press **F10**, type **OC**, and press **Enter** to turn on the Cost display. Notice that "$= 0.0" is displayed in the status line.
7. Press **F10** and type **OX** to turn Xon/Xoff mode off.
8. Press **F10** and type **OLY** to add a line feed to each transmitted line.
9. Press **F9** and type **TO2** to ignore all incoming linefeeds.
10. After you have finished your session press **F10**, type **DYN**, and press **Enter** to terminate the session without saving data.
11. Turn to Module 113 to continue the learning sequence.

Module 107
DISCONNECT AND END SESSION

DESCRIPTION

This module describes the correct way to end a telecommunications session. Some computers and services that you call may require a special sign-off message before you disconnect. Enter any such message and then follow one of these termination procedures.

HANGING-UP Follow this procedure to disconnect a connection, but remain in Telecom mode (so you can dial a new number using the Top Line Menu options Tele/Call, or answer a call by selecting Answer mode). Make sure you are in telecommunications mode before hanging up. If you are in word processing mode (the screen has a border around it) press Shift-F9 to switch modes. Then press F10 and type TH (Tele;Hang-Up).

TERMINATING TELECOM MODE Follow this procedure to disconnect a call and end the session. Make sure you are in telecommunications mode before hanging up. If you are in word processing mode press Shift-F9 to switch modes. Then press F10 and type D (Disconnect). Enable asks if you are sure—type Y (Yes). Enable asks if you want to save captured data.

NOTE

This affects data captured to memory, not data captured to disk or data in files received during file-transfer.

No—Don't Save Captured Data If you type N (No), Enable closes the telecommunications window. (Enable may, if capture-to-memory mode is turned off, ask if you want to save the data on the screen. This is a programming mistake and can be ignored; press any key to end the session.)

Yes—Save Captured Data If you type Y (Yes) one of two things happens; if capture-to-memory mode is on, Enable displays data in a word processing screen, with the Save options shown at the top of the screen. If capture-to-memory mode is turned off and there are lines of data on the screen that have not been saved, Enable asks if you want to save the data—press F7 to save the data, or Enter to continue. Either way Enable displays data in a word processing screen, with the Save options shown at the top of the screen.

Press Enter to save the captured word processing data. (You can also change the save options—see Module 39 in the Word Processing section.)

APPLICATIONS

The methods described in this module are the correct methods for ending telecommunications sessions.

TYPICAL OPERATIONS

In this activity you call the Enable bulletin board with the ENABLE setup built in Module 111, end the call using the Hang Up command, and then terminate the session. (Use another setup if you wish.)

1. At the Main Menu type **UTCU** (Use System;Telecom;Communicate;Use setup).
2. Press **Up Arrow** and then press **Down Arrow** until the cursor is on the setup named ENABLE.
3. Press **Enter** twice, to bypass the filename prompt. Enable initializes the modem. If you have an autodial modem Enable dials the call; if not, Enable asks you to dial.
4. When the call is connected you see the logon screen.
5. Continue with a bulletin board session if you wish. When you are finished press **F10** to see the following menu.

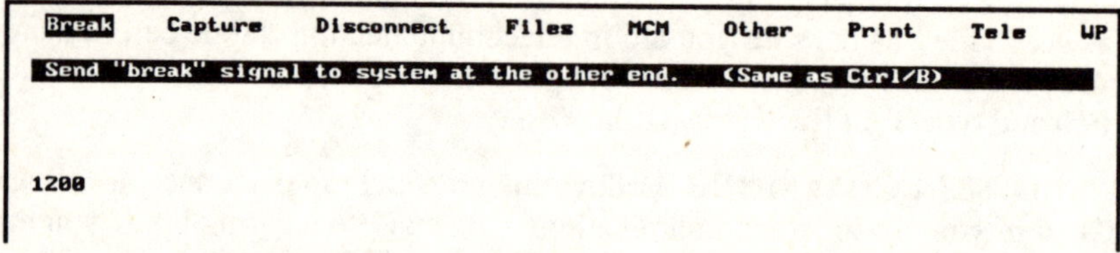

6. Type **TH** to hang up the call. (If you want you can now press F10 and type TC to make another call, or type TA to place the computer and modem in Answer mode).
7. When you are completely finished with your telecom session press **F10**, type **DYN** and press **Enter**.
8. Turn to Module 103 to continue the learning sequence.

Module 108
INTERACTING ONLINE

DESCRIPTION

Once you have connected with another device you can transmit typed text to the other end or transfer and receive files. You need to respond to prompts the other system sends, and perhaps ask questions of the other system. This module explains what the Telecom screen looks like, and how to carry out simple interactions.

THE TELECOM SCREEN The Telecom screen is where you work once you have established a connection with another system. The text transmitted from the other system enters the screen at the bottom and is scrolled or "pushed" up the screen as more lines enter at the bottom. The Telecom screen has a Top Line Menu and a status line.

Top Line Menu Press F10 to see the Top Line Menu, as shown in the following illustration.

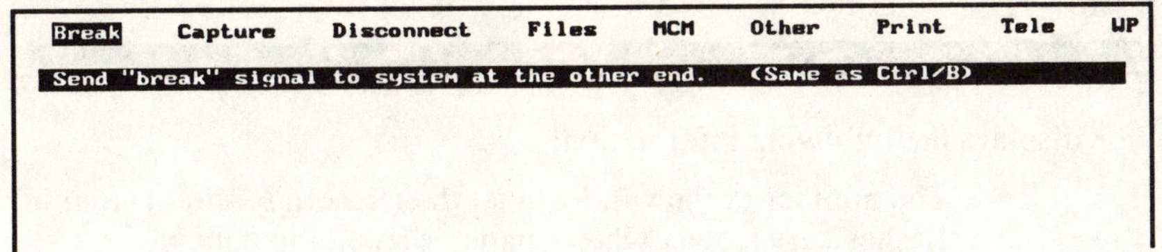

CAUTION

When you press F10 Enable continues receiving data, placing it in a special buffer. Once the buffer is full you lose the incoming data. When you finish using the Top Line Menu Enable sends the information from the buffer to the screen, and continues normal operations.

The following list describe the Top Line Menu commands. The keys in parentheses can be pressed instead of selecting the command from the menu.

Break (Ctrl-B) Sends an interupt signal telling the other system to stop processing data. For example, if you asked the other system to send you a magazine article, and then realized you selected the wrong one, use Break.

Capture Turns the two capture modes on and off. See Module 105.

Disconnect (Alt-End) Hangs-up the connection and terminates the telecom session. See Module 107.

Files Transmits or receives entire disk files. See Module 112.

MCM Enable places the screen in word processing mode and displays the MCM menu options. See the word processing section for information on using these options.

Other Lets you change communications specifications while online. See Module 106.

Print Prints the received data, as you receive it. You can specify the printer port and turn the printer on and off.

Tele Sends messages to your modem telling it what to do. Select Answer-mode, Hang-up, or Call.

Answer-mode tells the modem to wait for a call. (This is a toggle, so it turns Answer-mode on and off.) Enable doesn't indicate Answer mode in any way at present. Answer mode is cancelled any time you select Call, Hang-up, or Disconnect.

Hang-up terminates the call but does not end the telecom session, so you can make another call.

Call lets you enter a telephone number. When you press Enter Enable calls the number.

WP Displays the word processing window and the word processing Top Line Menu. This is the same as pressing Up Arrow (or PgUp in emulation mode).

The Status Line The status line, shown in the following screen, provides information about the telecom session.

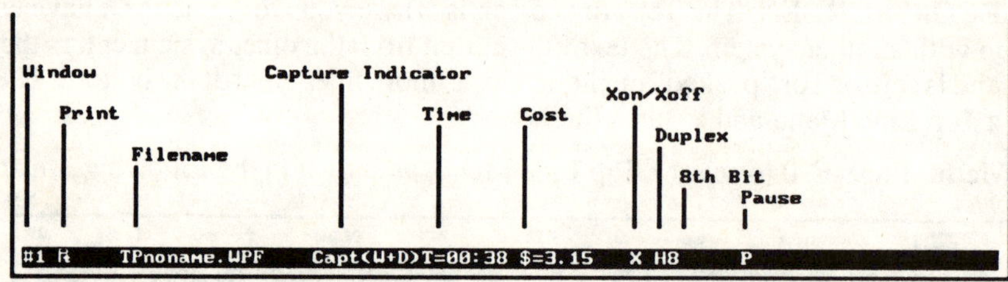

The status line displays the following information:

#1	The number of the window that the telecom session is running in. The # flashes very slowly when Enable is receiving data.
Pt	Indicates that print mode is on.
Filepath and filename	Displays the name of the file and its path (the directory in which the file is found).
Capture Indicator	Displays "Capture" if Capture-to-memory is on, "Disk Capt" if Capture-to-disk is on, and "Capt (W+D)" if both are on.
Time Indicator	The time online, if you specified this in the setup.
Cost Indicator	The cost, if you specified this in the setup.
X	Indicates that Xon/Xoff is turned on.
F or H	Indicates Full or Half Duplex.
8	Indicates that Enable is converting the eighth bit of each incoming data word to 0. This is turned on when you enter Telecom. Turn it off by pressing F9 T 8.
P	Indicates you have specifed a pause time, the time between the transmission of lines of data.

Answering Prompts When you have finally established a communication link you can begin actually communicating with the other system. For example, you might call an information service such as NEXIS/LEXUS or COMPUSERVE to read a magazine article. You have to tell the service which article or subject you want.

Each time the other system asks you for information you see the question on your screen; simply type the answer (each character is transmitted as soon as you type it, not when you press Enter, so if you make a mistake pressing delete does not "erase" it). In some cases the other computer will expect to see a carriage return (press Enter) so it knows when you have finished your answer.

Capturing Data You can capture data so that you can use it or refer to it later. Capturing data is discussed in detail in Module 105.

THE WORD PROCESSING SCREEN The Telecom screen has a word processing screen linked to it. This screen lets you edit captured data while Enable is still receiving more data. You can get to the screen at any time during a telecom session by pressing Up Arrow. (If you are emulating a terminal press PgUp instead.) You can also press F10 and type W (WP) to see the word processing screen with the Top Line Menu already displayed.

If Capture-to-memory is off and there are lines of data on the screen that have not been captured, Enable asks if you want to capture them. Press F7 to capture them and Enable displays the word processing screen. The data that was scrolling across the screen is now frozen in the word processing screen. The following screen is an example of the word processing screen.

```
Please download the manual, available from the <N>ew users menu.  It
contains
instructions, tips and shortcuts that will save you quite a bit of
connect
time.

Some of the older messages on this system have been deleted.  They are
available for downloading in the File transfer section, in the text
files
area.

Comments are welcome.  Just leave a <M>essage to Sysop.



Msg#: 4549 *MAIN BOARD*
03/03/89 17:39:28
From: JAMES BROCK
  To: CUSTOMER SUPPORT
Subj: DISK MEMORY
.I installed 3.0 and decided I was better off with 2.0.  I then
#2    REF/B C:CAPTURE.WPF          DRAFT                          L:21 C:001
        Shift/F9=Comm    Capture  T=00:00 $=  0.0  X F8
```

The word processing screen shares the same window as the Telecom screen (the status line shows the same window number), but unlike the Telecom screen it has a border around it and an extra line under the status line that shows some of the telecom indicators. It also displays "Shift/F9=Comm," a reminder of how to return to the Telecom screen (press Shift-F9).

You can use all the word processing features and the word processing Top Line Menu.

NOTE

Quitting the word processing screen or closing the window while in word processing is the same as the Telecom Disconnect command. The call is disconnected and the session ended.

Using the word processing screen is only really practical if you have turned on Capture-to-memory; if it is off data is not added to the word processing screen as the data is received, and all you see in the screen is the data that was in the screen at the moment you pressed Up Arrow.

With Capture-to-memory on, however, Enable adds the data to the end of the word processing file. It doesn't automatically scroll into the screen, but you can use the cursor-movement keys and commands to move down the file to the new data. You can then edit the data. You can return to the Telecom screen, to see the data as Enable receives it, by pressing Shift-F7.

APPLICATIONS

Enable's Telecom and word processing screens make interacting with other systems easy. The word processing screen is especially useful, letting you begin working with the information before Enable has even received it all.

TYPICAL OPERATION

In this activity you use the word processing screen associated with the Telecom screen during a session with the Enable bulletin board. (You use the setup created for Enable in Module 111.) This typical operation assumes you have already completed the typical operation that describes logging on to the Enable bulletin board using a setup, so the logon procedure is not explained.

1. At the Main Menu type **UTCU** (Use System;Telecom;Communicate;Use Setup).
2. Press **Up Arrow** and then press **Down Arrow** until the cursor is on the setup named ENABLE.
3. Press **Enter** and Enable displays the filename prompt. Type **CAPTURE**.

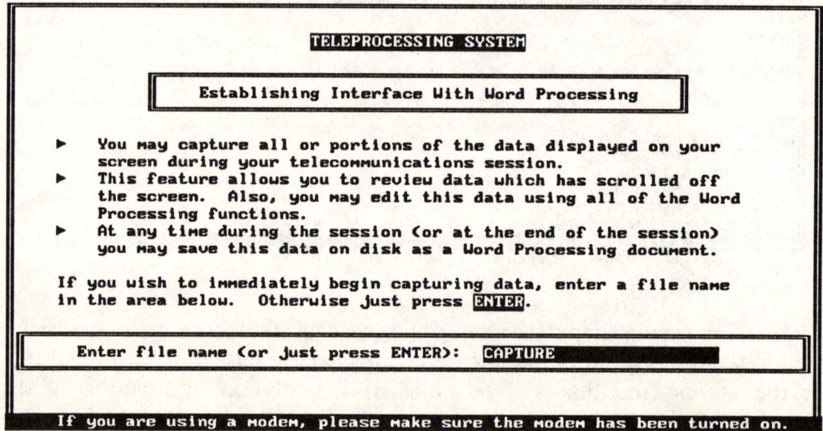

4. Press **Enter** and Enable initializes the modem. If you have an autodial modem Enable dials the call; if not Enable asks you to dial.
5. When the call is connected you see the Enable Bulletin Board System (BBS) logon screen. Log on and go to the BBS Main Menu. (Tell Enable not to pause after each display page.)
6. At the BBS Main Menu type **E** (for the Enable message boards), **M** (for the Main Message board), **R** (to Read messages), and **F** (for Forward).
7. When Enable asks if you want to pause, type **N**. When Enable asks which message you want to start with press **Enter**.

8. The messages begin scrolling across your screen. Press **Up Arrow** and Enable displays the word processing screen (it puts a border around the text, and expands the status line to two lines. The text stops scrolling onto the page.

```
Please download the manual, available from the <N>ew users menu.   It
contains
instructions, tips and shortcuts that will save you quite a bit of
connect
time.

Some of the older messages on this system have been deleted.  They are
available for downloading in the File transfer section, in the text
files
area.

Comments are welcome.   Just leave a <M>essage to Sysop.



Msg#: 4549 *MAIN BOARD*
03/03/89 17:39:28
From: JAMES BROCK
  To: CUSTOMER SUPPORT
Subj: DISK MEMORY
.I installed 3.0 and decided I was better off with 2.0.   I then
#2     REF/B C:CAPTURE.WPF          DRAFT                          L:21 C:001
          Shift/F9=Comm    Capture  T=00:00 $=  0.0  X F8
```

Notice that the receive light on your modem continues flashing, and the # sign on the status line flashes very slowly, indicating that data is still being received.

9. Press **PgDn**. The cursor moves into the text that has been received since you changed to word processing. Try editing text—you can insert, delete, modify, and so on.
10. Press **Shift-F9** to change back to the Telecom screen. The text begins scrolling again.
11. Continue with a bulletin board session if you wish. When you are finished press **F10** and type **DY** to disconnect. Type **N** when Enable asks if you want to save data. Press **Enter** and Enable ends the session.
12. Turn to Module 105 to continue the learning sequence.

Module 109
PRINT

DESCRIPTION

You can print received data in two ways: you can print all of the data as it arrives, or you can print all the data captured to memory so far. Enable prints information both received and transmitted (such as your responses).

PRINT ALL DATA While in the Telecom mode press F10 and type P (Print) to see the Top Line Menu print options.

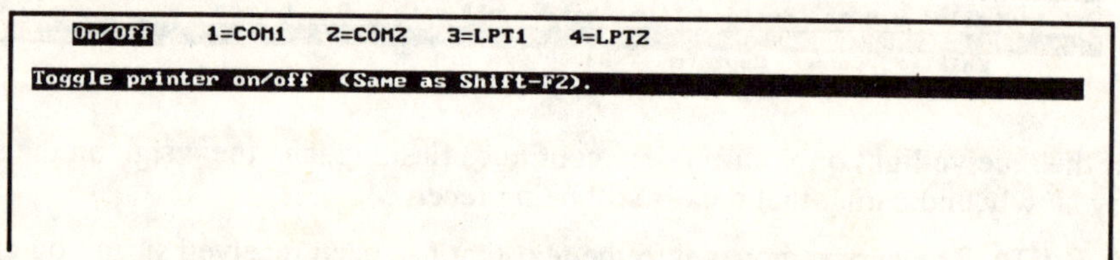

Select the printer port the printer is attached to (the default is LPT1). Then press Enter to select On/Off. Enable begins printing all the data received and transmitted until you turn printing off. The P_t indicator is displayed in the status line. Use the same sequence to turn printing off. You can also press Shift-F2 to turn printing on and off.

Your printer will have to accept data as fast as it arrives. Enable Software recommends that you set your modem to 1200 baud, because most printers can handle a transmission rate that fast, but you may have to experiment with your printer to get the right speed.

PRINT CAPTURED DATA Press Up Arrow to display the word processing screen. Press Alt-F2 to print all the data captured to memory up until that moment. Data received after you use the command is not printed.

CAUTION

If the system from which you are receiving data does not use Xon/Xoff, and if it transmits data faster than your printer prints it, you will lose data.

APPLICATIONS

You can print data if you want to use the information you have received immediately. You may even want to refer to the data while you are online. For example, you are searching an online database for a particular piece of information. The first response you get may determine the subsequent direction of the search.

TYPICAL OPERATION

In this activity you use Quick-Connect to display a blank Telecom screen and turn on printing.

1. At the Main Menu type **UTCQ** (Use System;Telecom;Communicate;Quick-Connect).
2. At the Quick-Connection Form type **43F**, position the cursor on the COMM port you are using, and press **Enter**.
3. Enable displays the filename prompt. Press **Enter** and Enable initializes the modem and displays the instructions screen. Press **Enter** to see the blank Telecom screen.
4. Press **F10** and type **P** to see the Print Menu options.

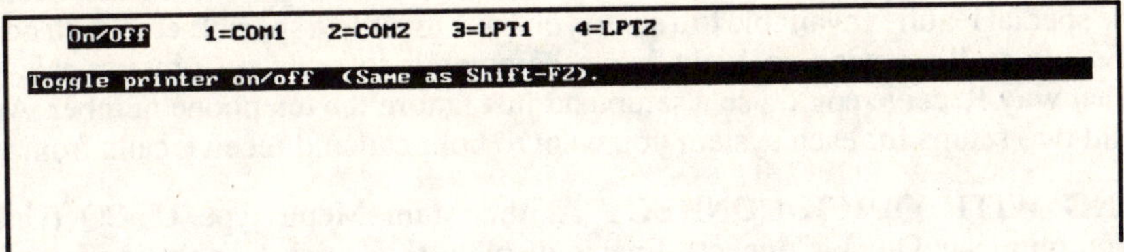

5. Type the number of the COMM or LPT port your printer is attached to. (For example, type 3 for LPT1.)
6. Press **Enter** to turn printer mode on. Notice the small print indicator next to the window number in the status line.

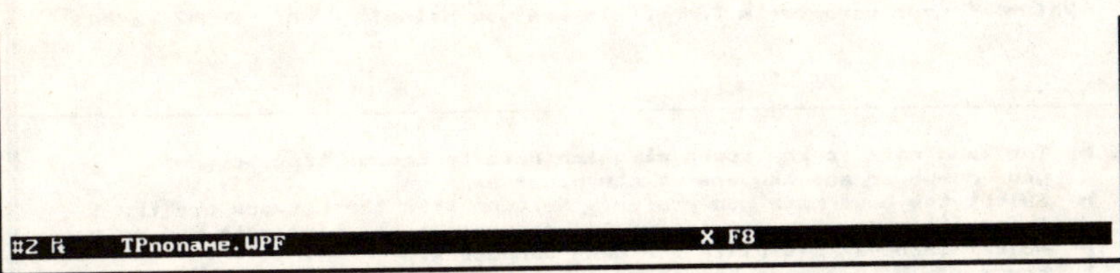

7. After you have finished your session press **F10**, type **DYN**, and press **Enter** to terminate the session without saving data.
8. Turn to Module 112 to continue the learning sequence.

Module 110
RECEIVING CALLS

DESCRIPTION

Enable doesn't receive calls very well. You can use Quick-Connect to receive calls, but if you want to use all the special features available to a setup you have to build a special setup with no telephone number. (Enable really needs two Main Menu commands to replace Communicate—Call and Receive. That way Receive could use a setup and just ignore the telephone number. As it, is you have to build two setups for each system you want to both call and receive calls from.)

RECEIVING WITH QUICK-CONNECT At the Main Menu type UTCQ (Use System; Telecom;Communicate;Quick-Connect). Enable displays the Quick-Connection Form.

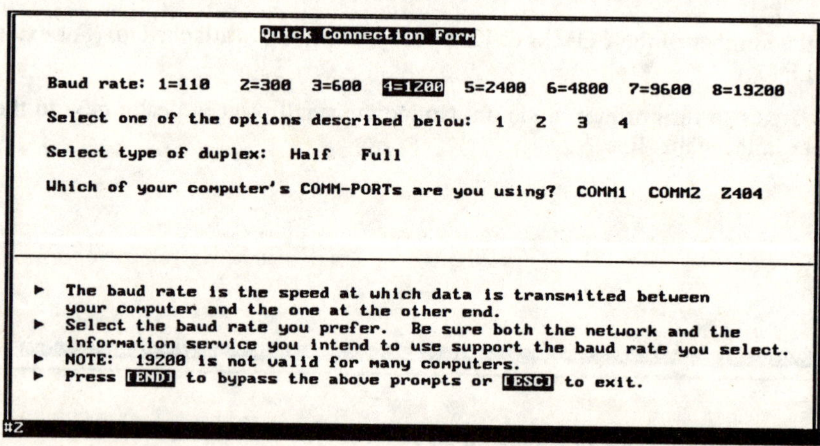

Quick Connection Form

Baud rate: 1=110 2=300 3=600 4=1200 5=2400 6=4800 7=9600 8=19200

Select one of the options described below: 1 2 3 4

Select type of duplex: Half Full

Which of your computer's COMM-PORTs are you using? COMM1 COMM2 Z404

- The baud rate is the speed at which data is transmitted between your computer and the one at the other end.
- Select the baud rate you prefer. Be sure both the network and the information service you intend to use support the baud rate you select.
- NOTE: 19200 is not valid for many computers.
- Press [END] to bypass the above prompts or [ESC] to exit.

#2

Select the correct options at the prompts in this screen. (For more information on these options see Module 111, and the documentation for your modem and the service or device you are calling.) You can change the default settings in your user profile. For example, if you have your modem connected to COMM2 you can set your profile to use that port as the default, so you do not have to select it each time you use Quick-Connect. See Appendix B for more information about user profiles.

When you have completed this form Enable displays the Word Processing Interface screen.

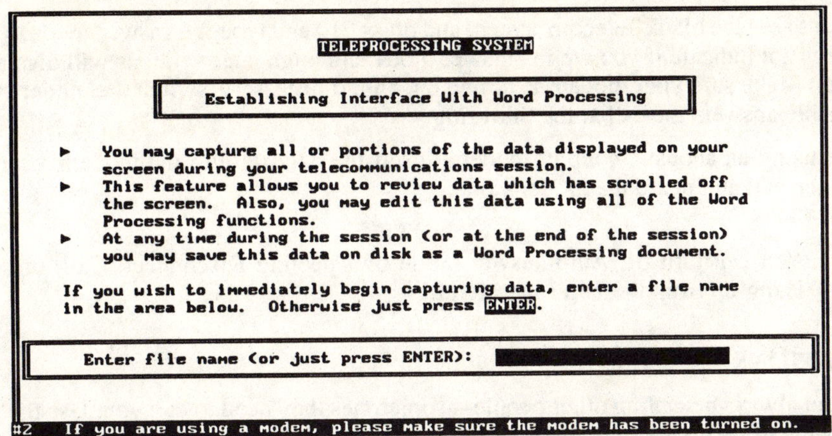

If you want to capture data in a word processing file, type a filename and press Enter. If you enter an existing name Enable asks you if you want to add the data to the end of the file, or re-use the file (erasing the existing data). Leave the prompt blank and press Enter if you don't want to capture data. (Capturing data is described in Module 105.)

Enable now displays the Quick-Connection screen, as shown in the following illustration.

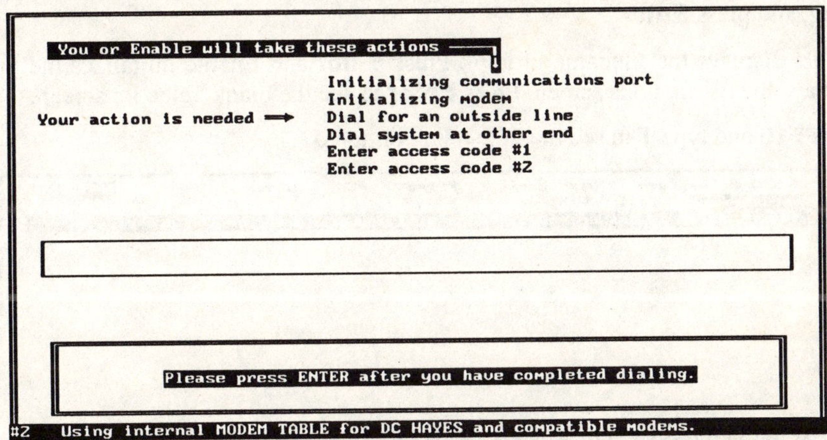

Once Enable has initialized the modem it displays the following instructions screen. Your subsequent actions depend on whether you are using an autodial or manual dial modem.

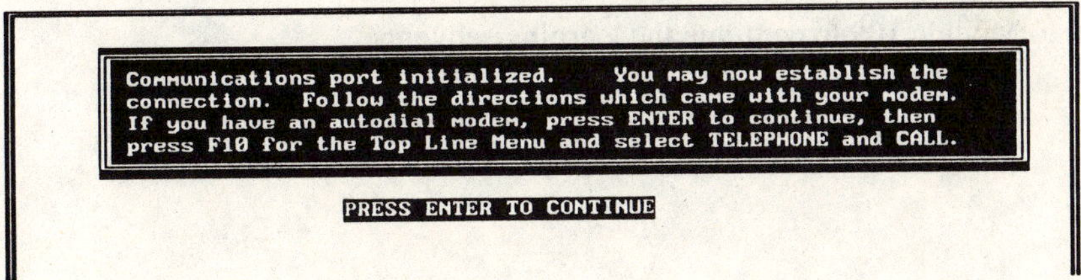

Press Enter to see the blank Telecom screen, and press F10 and type A (Answer-mode). (At present Enable does not indicate if you are in Answer mode, although later versions will display A in the status line.) Make sure your modem is turned on, and, if necessary, switch the modem to Answer mode. Enable answers the call at the third ring.

If you are using an acoustic-coupler modem, insert the handset into the modem after you have answered the call and heard the modem tone.

NOTE

You can turn off Auto-answer mode by selecting Disconnect, Call, or Hang-up from the Top Line Menu.

APPLICATIONS

You will not always be calling other people—sometimes they need to call you. Use the procedure in this module to set up your computer to receive those calls.

TYPICAL OPERATION

In this activity you use Quick-Connect to put your computer into Receive mode.

1. At the Main Menu type **UTCQ** (Use System;Telecom;Communicate;Quick-Connect).
2. At the Quick-Connection Form type **43F**, position the cursor on the COMM port you are using, and press **Enter**.
3. Enable displays the filename prompt. Press **Enter** and Enable initializes the modem and displays the instructions screen. Press **Enter** to see the blank Telecom screen.
4. Press **F10** and type **T** to see the Tele menu options.

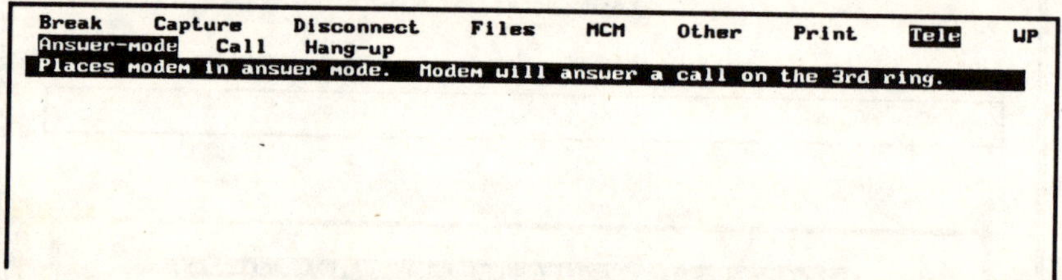

5. Type **A** to put the system in Answer mode. You are now ready to receive calls from another system.
6. After you have finished your session press **F10**, type **DYN**, and press **Enter** to terminate the session without saving data.
7. Turn to Module 109 to continue the learning sequence.

Module 111
SETUP

DESCRIPTION

The *setup* is a list of information telling Enable how to make a telecommunications link. When you select Communicate from the Main Menu you can tell Enable which setup to use. Enable then makes the call and connects the computers using the specifications in that setup.

You can build up to 256 setups, all of which are stored in a file called TPSETUP.$TP. (If you use Enable on floppy disks, put this file on a data disk, and use this disk when you communicate using the setups.)

CHECK YOUR DOCUMENTATION You need a lot of information for the setup procedure. You can find this information from your modem documentation (is it auto-dial, and what baud rate does it use?) or from information provided by the data communcations network (what is the telephone number, what connection address?). Collect all the information together before you begin.

CREATING A SETUP To access the Telecommunications Setup screen, close all files and windows. Then, at the Main Menu, type UTS (Use;Telecom;Setup). Enable displays an instructions screen. Press any key, and Enable displays the Initial Setup Screen.

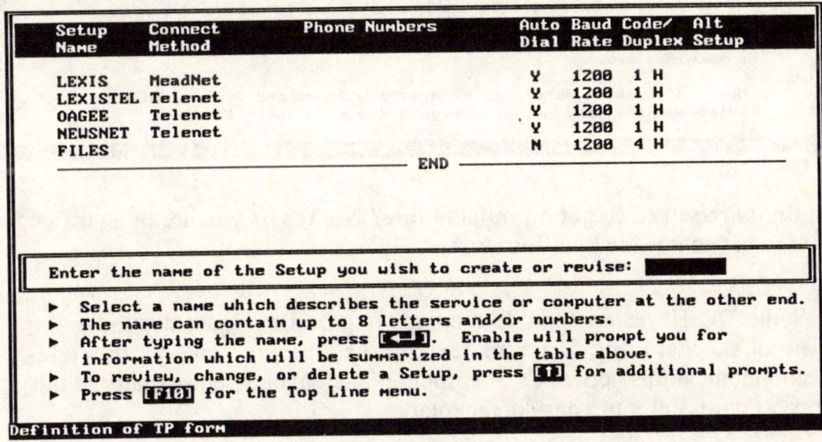

This screen is very similar to the screen used for designing databases, and it works in a similar way. The top half of the screen lists the first eight setups (Enable comes with five partly built setups), and displays some information about each one.

The bottom half of the screen displays instructions, and in the middle is the prompt for the setup name. You can enter a new name, or an existing name if you want to edit a setup, and press Enter; or press Up Arrow, select a setup name, and press Enter. (Setup names are up to eight letters, numbers, colons, and underscores.) Enable displays the first in a series of screens prompting for information. The bottom of the screen contains information about the prompt the cursor is on. Move through the screens by pressing Down Arrow or Enter, and select options by moving the arrow to them and pressing Enter or by typing the first character of the option.

The following screens are not exactly as they appear when you first enter them; some of the questions only appear when you select a previous option. For example, the prompt "Enter the number(s) to dial for an outside line:" only appears if you answered Yes to the previous question.

ENABLE'S SAMPLE SETUPS Enable provides five setups partially built. The setups are LEXIS (connects to LEXIS/NEXUS, an information service, through Meadnet, a telecommunications network owned by Mead Data Central); LEXISTEL (connects to LEXIS/NEXUS through Telnet); OAGEE (connects to the Official Airlines Guide-Electronic Edition); NEWSNET (connects to a major business- and industry-news service); and FILES (a setup used for transmitting files to other computers). If you want to use any of these setups you must add the telephone numbers, your modem information, and your logon codes.

THE SETUP SCREENS The following screen shows the first Setup Information screen.

```
Are special digits required to get an outside line?   No   Yes

Enter the number(s) to dial for an outside line:

Will you use an alternative telephone system?  No   Yes

Enter the telephone number:

Will you use a telecommunications network?  No   Yes

Enter the computer's telephone number:
------------------------------------------------------------------
▶ Examples of telecommunications networks are Telenet and Tymnet.

▶ These networks are designed to handle only non-voice (data)
  communications.

▶ Most information services, such as Dow Jones and Dialog, include
  telecommunications network usage charges in their invoices.
 Revising NEWSNET Setup        Esc=Exit Menu     F10=Exit Setup
```

Are special digits required to get an outside line? No/Yes If you are in an office and need to dial a number to get an outside line, answer Yes.

NOTE

Some DC Hayes-compatible modems require that you enter the entire number, including the number for the outside line, at the telecommunications network's or computer's telephone number later in this procedure. Refer to your documentation.

Enter the number(s) to dial for an outside line: If you answered Yes to the previous question, enter the number here. If you have an auto-dial modem Enable automatically waits two seconds after dialing this number to allow the switchboard to make an outside connection. You can add an extra two seconds of pause by typing a comma after the number. For example, "9,," dials 9 and then waits six seconds. Enter only numbers and commas here, no other characters.

Will you use an alternative telephone system? No/Yes Answer Yes if you use a long distance service that requires you to dial another sequence of numbers.

Enter the telephone number: If you answered Yes to the previous question, enter the number here. Use hyphens if you want. Include the authorization code, separated by commas if you are using an autodial modem. For example, if your long distance service number is 876-5432 and your authorization code is 198765, type "876-5432,,,198765" to leave a six second pause between the numbers.

Will you use a telecommunications network? No/Yes Many information services use special communications networks to provide cheap data communications. If you are using one of these to communicate with a service, answer Yes.

Enter the computer's telephone number: This only appears if you answered *No* to the previous question. Enter the telephone number of the information service, bulletin board, electronic mail service, personal computer, or other device you are calling. You can use hyphens to separate numbers if you want, and commas to pause before connecting to the remote device.

If the service you are dialing requires that you use a touch tone telephone and you are using a rotary (pulse) telephone with an auto-dial modem, enter T at the end of the number (for example, 123-4567,,,T).

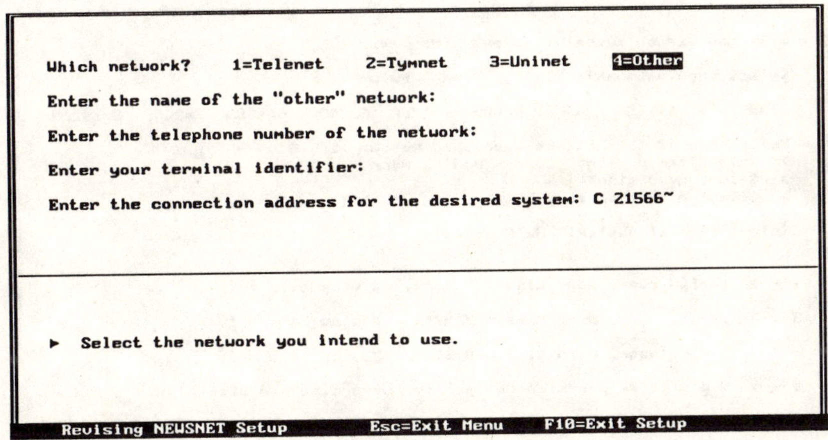

TIP: Call waiting can sometimes cause problems with data transmission. If someone calls you while you are in the middle of a telecom session the "click" from call waiting may cause a glitch. If you find this to be a problem, check the phone company to see if they have a code to turn this feature on and off (some companies do). Enter this code into the setup where it will be the first thing dialed once you get an outside line. You could put it at the end of the number you dial to call an outside line, in front of the number you dial for a long distance company, in front of the network's number, or in front of the computer's number.

Which network? 1=Telenet/2=Tymnet/3=Uninet/4=Other This prompt and the next four prompts only appear if you answered Yes to the question, "Will you use a telecommunications network?" Select one of these three popular networks, or select Other.

Enter the name of the "other" network: Only appears if you selected "Other" at the previous prompt. Type the name of the network you are using.

Enter the telephone number of the network: Enter the network's telephone number, using hyphens if you want. The networks generally have several numbers, one for each baud rate the network uses. Make sure you use the number for the baud rate you are going to enter later in the setup.

Enter your terminal identifier: When you sign up with a network they tell you the terminal identifier you must use. This tells the network how your computer is going to operate. Enable automatically enters the identifiers if you selected Telenet, Tymnet, or Uninet. Otherwise, enter it yourself.

NOTE

If your identifier specifies a carriage return, enter ~ (tilde) instead. Other special characters can also be entered using the macro codes. See Module 115.

Enter the connection address for the desired system: The address tells the network which service or computer you want to connect to. Enable automatically enters the address if you select Telenet, Tymnet, or Uninet. If you have problems getting through via Tymnet, try adding one tilde (~), two tildes (~~), or two semicolons (;;) after the address.

```
Will you use an autodial modem?   No   Yes

Select type automatic dial:   Tone   Pulse

Baud rate: 1=110  2=300  3=600  4=1200  5=2400  6=4800  7=9600  8=19200

Select one of the options described below:  1  2  3  4
>  Select the parity:  Even  Odd  None
>  Select word size:  5  6  7  8
>  Select number of stop bits:  1  2  X=½

Select type of duplex:  Half  Full

1 -->  parity even, word size = 7 bits,  # stop bits = 1.

2 -->  parity odd,  word size = 7 bits,  # stop bits = 1.

3 -->  parity none, word size = 8 bits,  # stop bits = 1.

4 -->  You will be prompted for parity, word size and stop bits.

  Revising NEWSNET Setup        Esc=Exit Menu     F10=Exit Setup
```

Will you use an autodial modem? No/Yes Answer yes if you are using an autodial modem (a modem that dials the call for you).

Select type automatic dial: Tone/Pulse This appears if you answered Yes to the previous question. This tells Enable the type of telephone line you are using; tone (you press the telephone button and it beeps) or pulse (a rotary phone, or a push-button phone that click-click-clicks when you press a button).

Baud rate: 1=110/2=300/3=600/4=1200/5=2400/6=4800/7=9600/8=19200 The baud rate (transmission speed) must be compatible with both the modem you are using and the device or service you are calling. (19200 baud is not valid for standard IBM PC/XTs.)

Some modems have "auto-shift." If you begin a call with 2400 baud and the computer that answers only uses 1200 baud, the modem changes to 1200. Enable displays the message "Enable has auto-shifted to 1200 baud." This only works if you are using a setup to make a call.

Select one of the options described below: 1/2/3/4 When you reach this question Enable displays four different transmission protocols, as shown in the preceding screen. Check your modem and telecommunications network documentation for this information. If you are unable to find the information, try option 1, the most common specifications. If you are communicating with another system using Enable and the Xmodem or Enable protocol, select option 3.

Select the parity: Even/Odd/None

Select the word size: 5/6/7/8

Select number of stop bits: 1/2/X=1/2 These three prompts appear if you selected option 4 at the previous question. They let you specify your own transmission protocol.

Select type of duplex: Half/Full This lets you specify if the computer simultaneously transmits and receives data. The most common setting is Full, but if you are communicating with another computer using Enable select Half.

```
Inter-character transmission delay:  0  1  2  3  4  5

Does the system at the other end support Xon/Xoff?  No    Yes

Does the system at the other end use turnaround character(s)?  No   Yes

Enter the turnaround character(s):

Enter the password or first response:

Enter the second response:

▶  See the System Overview Guide for the correct way to indicate
   special function keys and special characters in your entry.

Revising NEWSNET Setup          Esc=Exit Menu      F10=Exit Setup
```

NOTE

A common problem during telecom sessions is an "echo" — each character you type is displayed on your screen twice. Try changing to Full Duplex in this situation.

Inter-character transmission delay: 0/1/2/3/4/5 This slows down the transmission if the modem or computer system you are communicating with is unable to handle the speed. You should normally select 0 (no delay).

Does the system at the other end support Xon/Xoff? No/Yes Xon/Xoff is a system used to tell another computer to stop sending data for the moment, a convenient way to slow transmission down if the computer is unable to handle all the data. Most information services use it. Select Yes if you are not sure.

Does the system at the other end use turnaround character(s)? No/Yes This prompt appears if you answered No at the previous prompt. The turnaround character used by some systems is usually a question mark or exclamation point. It indicates that the system is ready for your system to transmit data, rather like saying "roger" in a radio conversation. It says "I'm finished, its your turn."

Enter the turnaround character(s): This appears if you answered Yes at the previous prompt. Enter the turnaround character used by the system with which you are communicating. Some systems use a sequence of special characters. You can enter these using the macro codes (see Module 115).

Pause time: 0/1=0.5/2=1.0/3=1.5/4=2.0/5=2.5/6=3.0/7=3.5/8=4.0 This prompt only appears if you answered No at both the Xon/Xoff and Turnaround characters prompts. This lets you specify a pause between each line of data transmitted, from one to four seconds. Select 0 if you don't know that a pause is required. Some auto-dial modems might need to complete the connection within a specific time, so you may need to set the pause to 0; you can always set another pause time using the Top Line Menu once you have made a connection.

Enter the password or first response: Many services give you a password or identification code that lets you sign on. Some require two pieces of information; the terminal-type you are using followed by your password, for example. Enter the first response here. You can enter up to 120 characters. Enter a tilde (~) in place of a carriage return. (You can enter other special characters using the macro codes in Module 115.) You can make sure your password does not appear on your screen when you call a service by entering "{echo off}" before you enter your password.

Enter the second response: The second response, if any. See the previous prompt for more information. You can enter up to 130 characters here.

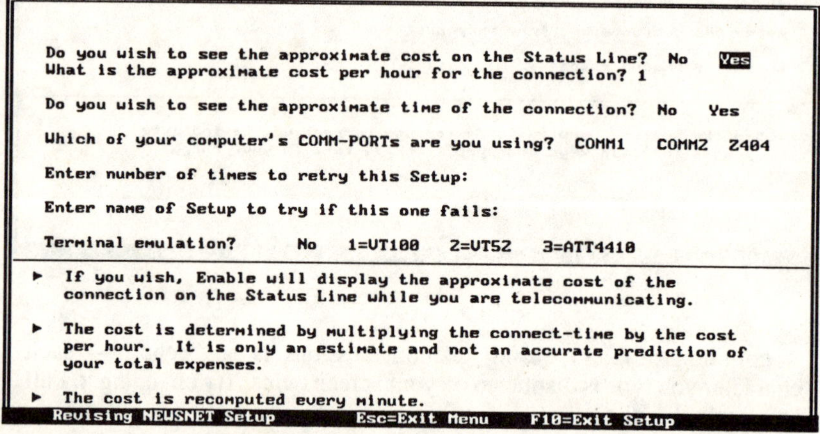

Do you wish to see approximate cost on Status Line? No/Yes Select Yes and Enable displays the approximate cost, to the nearest minute, in the status line while your computer is telecommunicating.

What is approximate cost per hour for connection? Displays if you answered Yes at the previous prompt. Enter the cost per hour. The cost depends on several factors; the network's charge, the time of day, the information service's charge, and so on. Do not enter a dollar sign.

Do you wish to see approximate time of connection? No/Yes Select Yes if you want Enable to display the connection time, to the nearest minute, in the status line.

Which of your computer's COMM-PORTs are you using? COMM1/COMM2/Z404 Select the asynchronous, serial-communications port that your modem is connected to. The Z404 option is a Zenith Z404 or Z304 board. If you have an internal modem check your modem's documentation for the COMM port—the modem may have switches that allow you to change the

COMM port. If you have an external modem your computer must have COMM ports; if it doesn't, you can buy an inexpensive serial interface board.

(If you have a Zenith board make sure that the Carrier Detect pin on the RS-232-C cable is set high.)

Enter the number of times to try this Setup: Enter the number of times that your autodial modem should call if it is unable to get through the first time.

Enter the name of Setup to try if this one fails: Enter the name of another setup to try if Enable cannot get through using this one. For example, you may be able to use two or three different networks to get through to an information service. You could try the cheapest network first, but if you can't get through using that one Enable can automatically try the next cheapest.

Precede the name of the other setup with a question mark (?) if you want Enable to wait for confirmation before proceeding with that setup. If it is unable to get through using the first setup Enable waits for you to type the letter A before proceeding.

Terminal emulation? No/1=VT100/2=VT52/3=ATT4410 Terminal emulation lets your computer call a mainframe computer and act just like one of the mainframe's terminals. Select the type of terminal. (Terminal emulation is discussed in detail in Appendix H.)

```
Do you wish to select any of the options listed below?  No  Yes

Length of Break signal in milliseconds:

Enter receive filter option: 1    2    3    Use Filter/mapping table

Specify how received linefeeds will be handled:  1    2    3

Specify how received tabs will be handled:  1    2    3    4

► Use transmit or receive mapping tables or keyboard mapping table.

► Change default length of the Break signal (350 milliseconds).

► Change default display options for characters, linefeeds and tabs.

► Disable automatic adjustment of communication parameters for Xmodem
  and Enable file transfers.
 Revising NEWSNET Setup          Esc=Exit Menu    F10=Exit Setup
```

Do you wish to select any of the options listed below: No/Yes When you reach this prompt the information area in the screen lists various parameters you can modify. If you answer No and press Enter or Down Arrow Enable leaves the setup prompts and displays the Initial Setup screen again. If you answer Yes, Enable continues with the sequence of prompts. (As these parameters are all fairly advanced, you normally answer No at this prompt, accepting Enable's defaults.)

Length of Break signal in milliseconds: Lets you change the Break signal length (usually 350 milliseconds). This is like pressing Esc—it cancels an operation. Some computers require a longer signal.

Enter receive filter option: 1/2/3/Use Filter, mapping table Enable can ignore or replace characters received during communications, or use a Transmit/Receive Mapping Table (see Appendix H for information about the Mapping Tables.) Option 1 processes keyboard characters only. ASCII characters with codes 0-6, 12, 14-25, 27-31, and 127 to 255 are ignored. Option 2 substitutes a tilde (~) for the characters ignored by option 1. And option 3 processes all characters except those with decimal values from 240 to 255.

Name the receive filter/mapping table This prompt appears if you selected User Filter/mapping table at the previous prompt. Enter the name of the mapping table (the .TPT file).

Specify how received linefeeds will be handled: 1/2/3 Specifies what to do with linefeeds received by your computer. 1, the default, ignores line feeds if they appear with carriage returns. 2 converts all line feeds to carriage returns, and 3 ignores all line feeds. This is done after the received data has gone through the mapping table selected at the previous prompt.

Specify how received tabs will be handled: 1/2/3/4 Enable handles received tabs in four ways. 1, the default, ignores them. Choosing 2 converts them to single spaces. Choosing 3 converts the tab to a space and moves the cursor to the next column position that is a multiple of eight (column 8, 16, 24, etc). And 4 accepts the tab and moves the cursor to the next tab position. This procedure is done after the received data has gone through the mapping table specified at the next prompt.

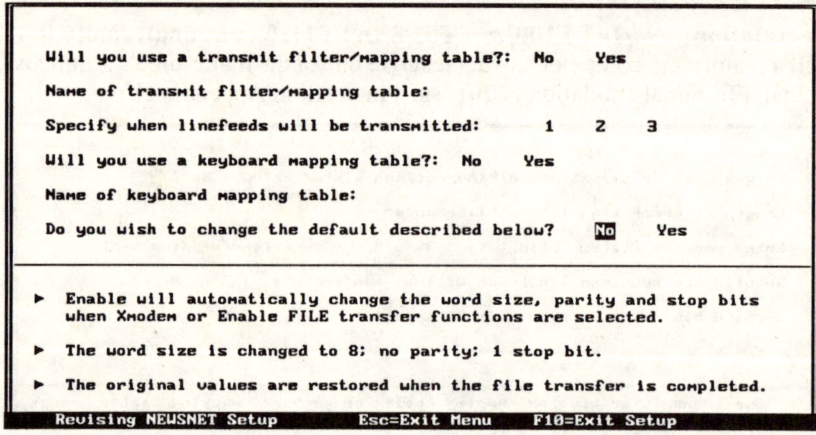

Do you wish to use a transmit filter/mapping table?: No/Yes Uses a table to make Enable ignore or replace certain characters before transmitting them. See Appendix H for details.

Name of transmit filter/mapping table: This prompt appears if you answered Yes to the previous prompt. Enter the name of the mapping table (the .TPT file).

Specify when linefeeds will be transmitted: 1/2/3 1, the default, tells Enable not to transmit linefeeds. 2 transmits a linefeed with every carriage return, and 3 transmits only linefeeds (no carriage returns). This procedure is carried out before the data is sent to the Transmit Mapping Table specified at the previous prompt.

Will you use a keyboard mapping table?: No/Yes Select Yes if you want to use a keyboard mapping table, a macro table that lets you define a single key as a series of characters. See Appendix H for more information.

Name of keyboard mapping table: This prompt appears if you answered Yes to the previous prompt. Enter the name of the mapping table.

Do you wish to change the default described below? No/Yes This prompt affects file transfers made using Xmodem or Enable protocols after you have already made a connection. If you select No Enable automatically changes the settings to a parity of none, an 8-bit word, and 1 stop bit whenever Xmodem or Enable protocols are selected. When Enable has completed the file transfer it restores the original values you entered into the setup. If you select Yes at this prompt Enable does not carry out this procedure.

When you answer this prompt and press Enter or Down Arrow Enable displays the Initial Setup screen again.

SAVE THE SETUP Save the setup by pressing F10 and typing S (Save). Exit the setup routine by pressing F10 and typing QY (Quit;Yes). You can save at any time during the prompts or when you have finished answering all the questions.

NOTE

> If you place the cursor on an option with the arrow keys you must then press Enter or Down Arrow before using Save, or your selection is ignored.

REVISING A SETUP You can return to the setup and revise it at any time. Enter the Initial Setup screen and type the name of the setup you want to revise (or press Up Arrow and select the setup displayed in the top half of the screen). Press Enter and Enable displays the prompts.

You can also make minor revisions in the following manner. Press Up Arrow and select the setup in the top half of the screen. Press Right Arrow to select the data you want to change (the Connect Method, Phone number, Auto Dial, Baud Rate, Protocol Code, Duplex type, and Alternative Setup). Press Spacebar and Enable prompts for the data. When you have entered the data press Esc to return to the "name of the Setup" prompt. Remember to save the setup before leaving the Initial Setup screen.

RENAME A SETUP To rename a setup press Up Arrow and highlight the name. Type R and Enable prompts for the name. Type the new name and press Enter. Remember to save the setup before leaving the Initial Setup screen.

DELETE A SETUP To delete a setup press Up Arrow and highlight the name. Type D and Enable asks you to confirm. Type Y and Enable deletes the setup. Then press F10 and type S to save the changes.

CALLING THE ENABLE BULLETIN BOARD Enable Software has an Enable Bulletin Board System (BBS). You can read other people's questions about special applications, and Enable Software's responses; communicate with other Enable users; read articles about Enable and improvements being made to the program; and leave questions for the Enable customer support group.

If you want to use this BBS, build a setup with the following characteristics: call 1-518-877-6316; Full Duplex; any baud rate up to 2400 baud; and protocol-option 3 (at the prompt immediately after the baud rate prompt). The Typical Operation in this module describes building the Enable BBS setup.

APPLICATIONS

Building a setup saves you time. Instead of using Quick Connect, where you have to enter transmission data before you can make a call, you can tell Enable to use a setup to make the call. Enable then uses all the information you entered previously. You also need to build a setup if you want to use advanced communications tools, such as mapping tables.

TYPICAL OPERATION

In this activity you build the setup used to dial the Enable Bulletin Board Service (Enable BBS).

1. At the Main Menu type **UTS** (Use System;Telecom;Setup). Press **Enter** and Enable displays the Initial Setup screen.
2. Type **ENABLE**. Your screen looks like this:

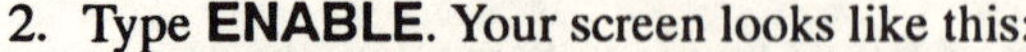

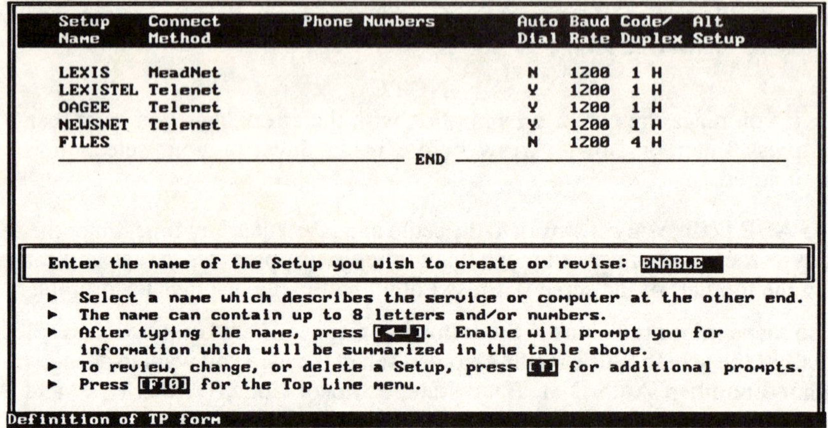

Setup Name	Connect Method	Phone Numbers	Auto Dial	Baud Rate	Code/ Duplex	Alt Setup
LEXIS	MeadNet		N	1200	1 H	
LEXISTEL	Telenet		Y	1200	1 H	
OAGEE	Telenet		Y	1200	1 H	
NEWSNET	Telenet		Y	1200	1 H	
FILES			N	1200	4 H	

END

Enter the name of the Setup you wish to create or revise: ENABLE

▶ Select a name which describes the service or computer at the other end.
▶ The name can contain up to 8 letters and/or numbers.
▶ After typing the name, press [<—┘]. Enable will prompt you for information which will be summarized in the table above.
▶ To review, change, or delete a Setup, press [↑] for additional prompts.
▶ Press [F10] for the Top Line menu.

Definition of TP form

3. Press **Enter** and Enable displays the first setup screen. If you need to dial a number to get an outside line type **Y** (otherwise go to the next step). At the next prompt type the number you have to dial, plus three commas, and press **Enter**.
4. At the "Will you use an alternative telephone system?" prompt type **Y** if you have to dial a long distance company to make the call (otherwise skip to the next step). At the next prompt type the number, plus three commas, and press **Enter**.
5. At the "Will you use a telecommunications network?" prompt type **N**.
6. Type **1-518-877-6316**. (If you are using another long distance service you may not need to dial the 1; check with your service.) Your screen looks like this:

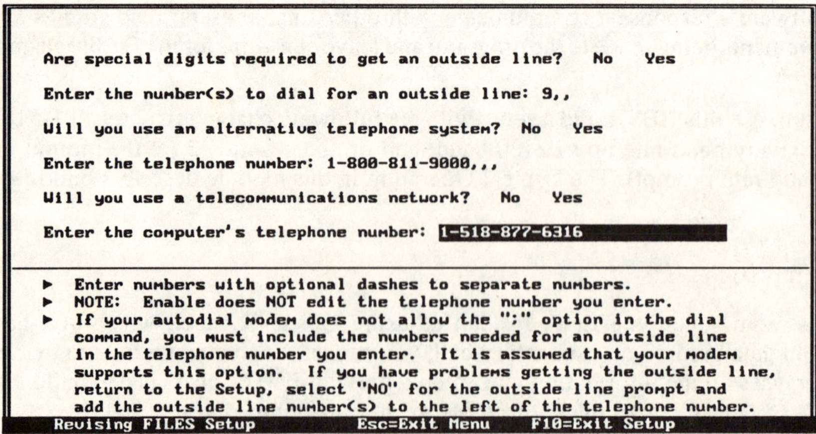

Are special digits required to get an outside line? No Yes

Enter the number(s) to dial for an outside line: 9,,

Will you use an alternative telephone system? No Yes

Enter the telephone number: 1-800-811-9000,,,

Will you use a telecommunications network? No Yes

Enter the computer's telephone number: 1-518-877-6316

▶ Enter numbers with optional dashes to separate numbers.
▶ NOTE: Enable does NOT edit the telephone number you enter.
▶ If your autodial modem does not allow the ";" option in the dial command, you must include the numbers needed for an outside line in the telephone number you enter. It is assumed that your modem supports this option. If you have problems getting the outside line, return to the Setup, select "NO" for the outside line prompt and add the outside line number(s) to the left of the telephone number.

Revising FILES Setup Esc=Exit Menu F10=Exit Setup

7. Press **Enter**. The first prompt on the next screen is "Will you use an autodial modem?" Type **N** if you have a manual-dial modem and skip to the next step. If you have an autodial modem type **Y**, and then select the type of dialing: T for tone or P for pulse.
8. At the "Baud rate:" prompt type the number corresponding to the fastest baud rate that your modem will handle, up to 2400.
9. At the "Select one of the options" prompt type **3**. Your screen looks like this:

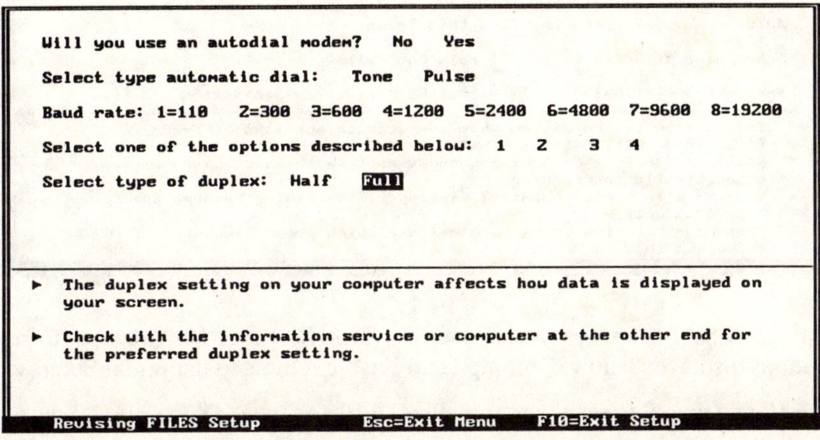

10. At the "Select type of duplex:" prompt type **F** and Enable displays the next screen.
11. Type **0Y** and press **Down Arrow**. Your screen looks like this:

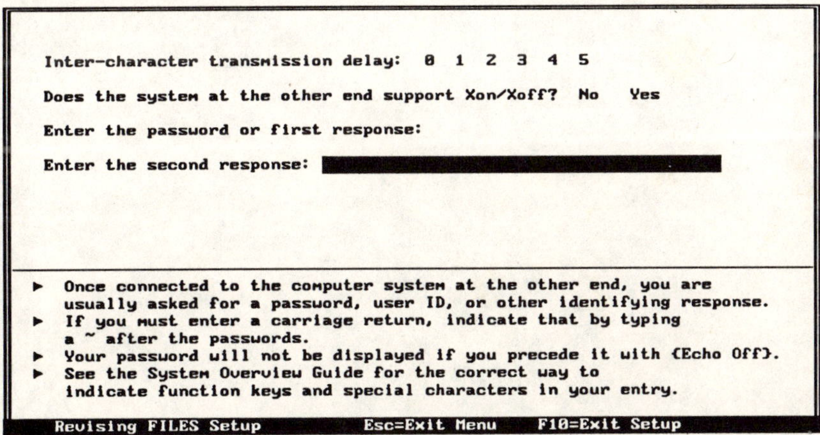

12. Press **Down Arrow** and Enable displays the next screen. Type **Y** and then type the cost per hour for the long distance call to area code 518 (Ballston Lake, New York state). Make an estimate if neccessary. You can always change it later. Press **Enter**.

13. Type **Y** and then move the cursor to the COMM port your computer is using. Press **Down Arrow** three times. Your screen looks like this:

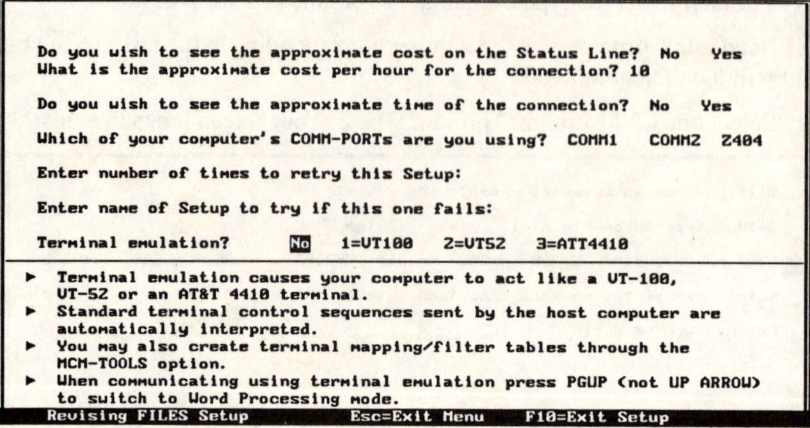

14. Type **N** and Enable displays the next screen. Type **N** at the "Do you wish to select any of the options displayed below?" prompt, and Enable returns to the Initial Setup screen.
15. Press **F10** and type **S** to save the setup. Press **F10** and type **QY** to return to the Main Menu.
16. Turn to Module 104 to continue the learning sequence.

Module 112
TRANSMIT DATA

DESCRIPTION

In addition to typing messages to another system you will sometimes need to transmit previously created data—word processing files or spreadsheets, for example. There are several ways to do this.

You can transmit word processing data from the Telecom window's Capture-to-memory file, transfer an entire file while you are present, or make an "unattended" transfer (a transmission while you are not present).

THE CAPTURE-TO-MEMORY FILE Capture-to-memory is described in Module 105. You can use the following method to transmit word processing data from the file in which you told Enable to place the captured data.

Select the File When you begin a telecom session Enable prompts you for the name of a file in which to store the captured data. Type the name of the file that has the data you want to transmit and press Enter. (You can also type ? and press Enter to see a list of word processing files in the data directory.) Enable asks if you want to add data to the file or re-use the file. Select Add Data and Enable displays the end of the file in the Telecom screen.

CAUTION

Do not enter Re-use or Enable writes the new data over the old file, erasing the original data.

Select the Text If you are receiving a call, making a call with Quick-Connect, or using a setup with a manual-dial modem Enable initializes the modem and then waits for you to continue. Press Up Arrow and Enable displays the word processing screen. Set a block on the text you want to transmit, as shown in the following screen. (Place the cursor at one end of the block, press F7, move the cursor to the other end, and press F7 again.)

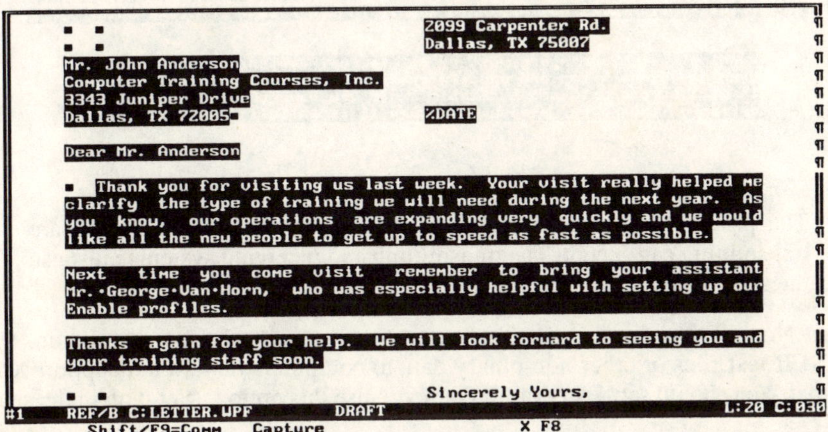

If Enable is automatically dialing a call for you, wait until you have made your connection to mark the block. When you have marked the block go back to the Telecom screen by pressing Shift-F9.

Transmit the Data When you are ready to transmit the marked block of text, press F8 (to copy the block onto the Telecom screen and transmit it), or press Alt-F8 (to transmit the text without copying it to the Telecom screen.)

After the Session If you don't want to append the data you received to the end of the file you used for Capture-to-memory, do not save the data when you Disconnect.

Other Uses You can also use this method to transmit data received during the current telecom session (as long as capture-to-memory is turned on). You might receive information from one source, hang-up the call without terminating the session, and make another call. You could then transmit the data received during the first call. You may also want to use data received during a database search in a search statement during the next phase of the search.

TRANSMITTING FILES You can transmit entire files at any time during a session by selecting the protocol and the file. Your modem must be set to full duplex, although if you have an auto-dial modem Enable sets it for you.

Preparing to Transmit When you are ready to transmit press F10 and type FT (Files;Transmit) to see the following menu options.

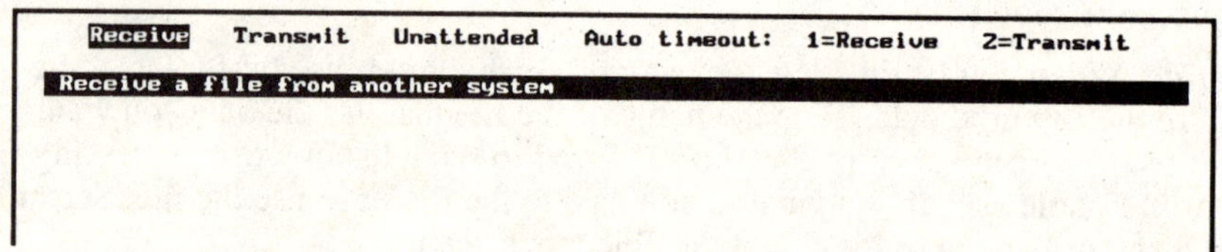

The Auto timeout options specify what Enable does during transmission problems. Type 1 (1=Receive) to make Enable wait for a response from the other system for one minute before terminating the procdeure. Type 2 to make Enable transmit the last block of data ten times before terminating.

Type T (Transmit), and Enable displays the following options, which allow you to select the protocol you want to use.

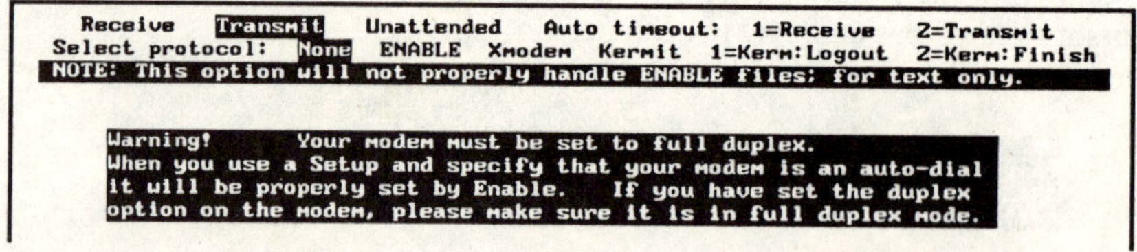

NOTE

The protocol you use depends on what the system to which you are transmitting can accept. The transmitting and receiving systems must use the same protocol.

None Select None if you don't want to use a protocol to control the transmission. Use this to transmit ASCII text files or other non-binary data to computers that do not support Xmodem or Enable format. You should set Xon/Xoff to On if you use this option. (Set it on in the setup, or use the Top Line Menu by pressing F10 and typing OX (Other;Xon/Xoff); when the feature is on Enable displays X in the status line.) The receiving system must also set this feature on. Failure to use Xon/Xoff may lead to loss of data. Do not use None when transmitting binary data, including Enable-format files.

Use messages typed at the keyboard to make sure the receiving end is ready, and then select the protocol. The transmission will begin as soon as you select the name of the file you are transferring (the step after selecting protocol).

Enable This is an advanced Xmodem protocol. The receiving system begins the transmission by transmitting a Hello message every ten seconds for a minute. The transmitting computer begins when it sees the Hello message. If transmission does not begin during the Hello message period Enable cancels the transmission, so it is important that both sides coordinate when they select the protocols and file.

Xmodem This is a very common error-checking protocol. Enable uses the same Hello-message procedure as that described at Enable protocol.

Kermit/1=Kerm:Logout/2=Kerm:Finish The Kermit protocol is an error-checking protocol designed at Columbia University and widely used by mainframes and minicomputers. This is an advanced data-communications procedure that few Enable users will need. To use it you must understand the other computer's Kermit procedures. Enable's Kermit features are outlined later in this module.

After you select the protocol Enable prompts for the name of the file you want to send. Type the name and extension and press Enter. If you do not include an extension Enable assumes the .TPF extension. You can also type ? and press Enter to see a list of files with the .TPF extension.

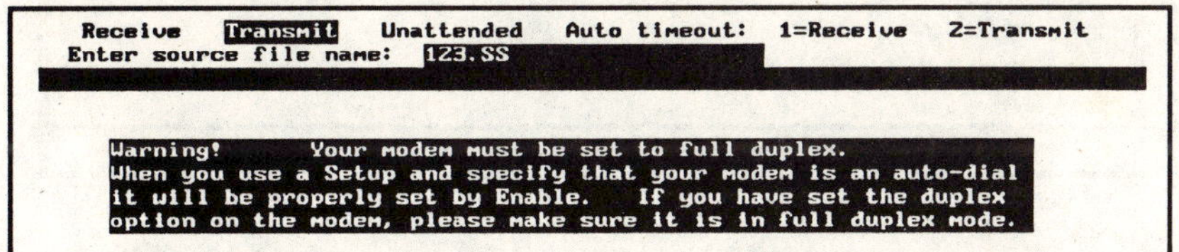

Beginning Transmission If you are using no protocol (the None option) Enable begins transmitting as soon as you type the filename and press Enter. If you are using Enable or Xmodem protocols Enable begins transmission as soon as the transmitting end sees the Hello message. Enable displays the following message:

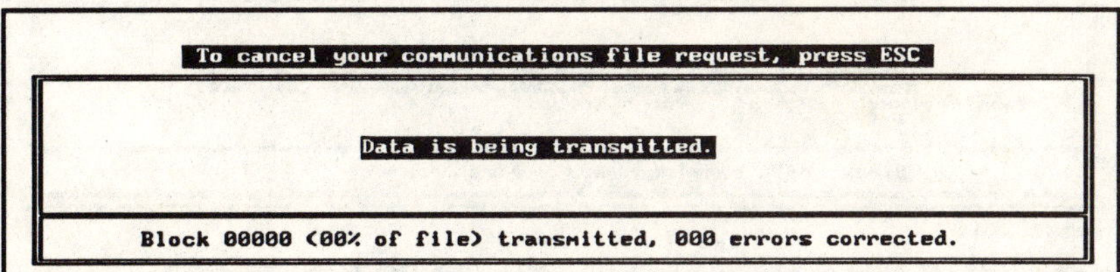

This screen shows the number of blocks and the percent of the total file transmitted and the number of errors corrected.

Blocks In Xmodem or None a block is 128 characters. In Enable protocol the block is usually 256 characters, but may vary depending on errors.

Errors Because None protocol does not check for errors this number remains 0 during None transmissions. During Enable and Xmodem transmissions each block is checked for errors and retransmitted if necessary. This number indicates the number of retransmissions. If you get a lot of errors you may have a bad line; try calling the system again, perhaps with a lower baud rate.

Ending a Transmission With Enable or Xmodem transmissions the sending system automatically informs the receiving end when the transmission is complete, and removes the transmission message. With None press Esc when the transmission is over. You can tell by watching the Blocks-transmitted number—when it stops changing, the transmission is over.

Transmitted files are automatically saved, without any further action by you.

NOTE

The Software Group does not recommend that you use None protocol. Instead you could use the Capture-to-disk method.

RECEIVE DATA If you are at the receiving end of the file transfer you follow a similar preparation procedure, with slight differences. When you first select the Top Line Menu, choose Receive. Pick the protocol, and then enter a name with which to save the incoming file. Add the appropriate extension (depending on the type of file), or Enable adds .TPF.

When you press Enter Enable displays the following transmission message.

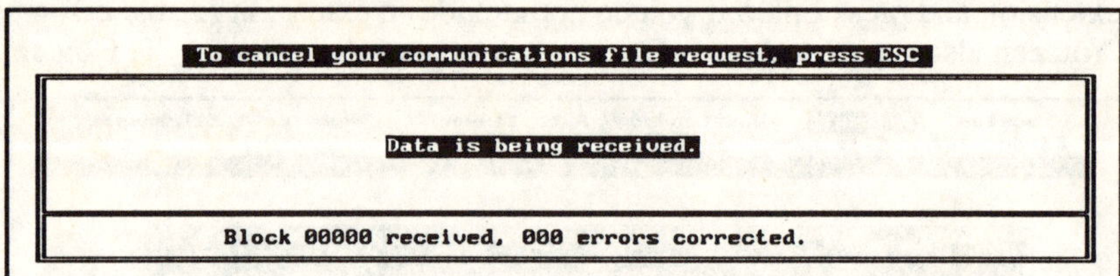

Enable displays this even though initially data is not being received. In a None transmission the system waits for the sender to begin, but in Enable and Xmodem transmissions the system sends a Hello message telling the sender it is ready. In either case if the transmission doesn't begin within a minute Enable displays the following message.

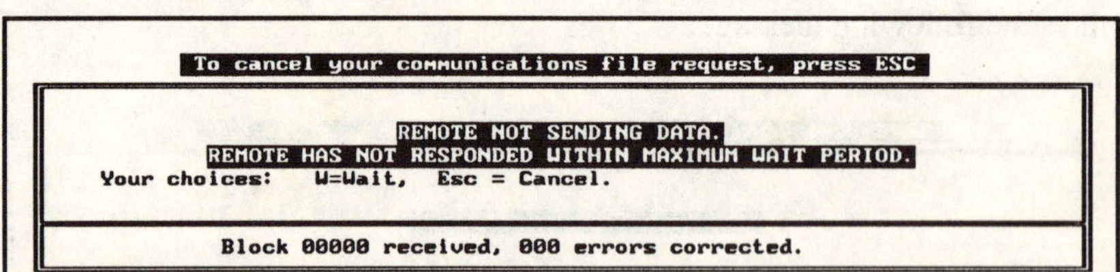

Press Esc to abort, or W to continue waiting (and sending the Hello message).

TRANSMISSION PROBLEMS If a problem stops Enable from sending data it displays a message in the Telecom screen. The problem may be with the telephone line, modems, or computers, or the receiving computer's disk may be full (if so, the Disk Is Full message displays on the receiving computer).

Enable transmits the last block of data ten times, or the receiving computer sends a NAK signal (negative acknowledgment), a signal requesting retransmission. If the data cannot be retransmitted Enable aborts the procedure. Exactly how Enable operates is determined by the Auto timeout selection you made at the Files Options Menu described earlier.

KERMIT PROTOCOL The following is an outline of the Kermit procedures available on Enable. After selecting Transmit or Receive at the Files Options Menu, select Kermit.

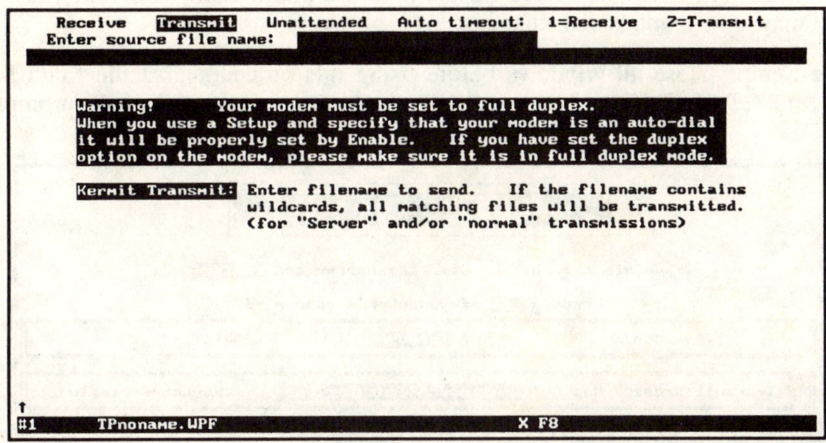

If you are transmitting, type a filename and press Enter. You can use the * (multiple-character) and ? (single-character) wild cards if the other computer supports them. If you are receiving data do not type a filename; press Enter if you want to rewrite any files with the same name, or type /r and press Enter if you want to rename the incoming files. (Enable renames by adding a number to the end of the name, or by changing the name's eighth character to a number.) Use /r to be sure you don't delete any existing files.

Server Mode If you are connecting to a computer with Kermit operating by itself and want to download files, you have to tell the transmitting computer which files to send. In this case the receiving computer does enter a filename. You can use the other computer's wild cards, if any. Use the other computer's syntax for naming files. Add /r to rename the files, to avoid deleting files with the same names as the incoming files.

Enable displays the following box during Kermit transmissions.

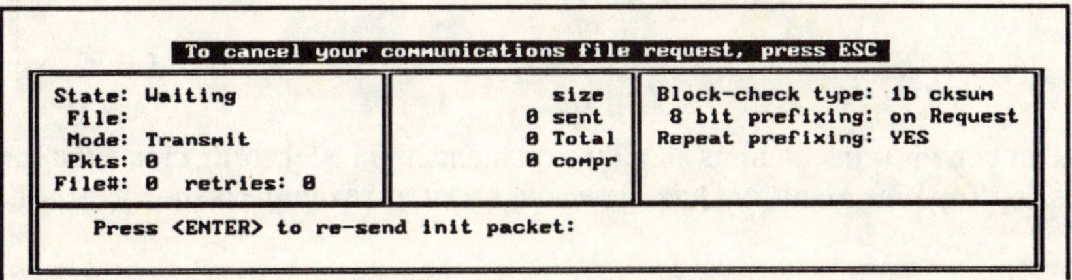

Once the transfer is complete Enable displays a message telling you that the operation is finished and removes the Kermit file transfer box, unless you are in Server mode. To terminate transfers during Server mode press F10, type FR (Files;Receive) and select 1=Kerm Logout (exit server mode and terminate Kermit) or 2=Kerm Finish (Exit server mode but remain in Kermit program).

UNATTENDED FILE TRANSFERS This feature lets you transfer files when you are not present, allowing you to transmit them later using lower telephone-line rates or transfer them at a time when you don't need to use your computer. You must build a script to tell Enable when and how to make the transfer.

NOTE

You must have an auto-dial modem to use this feature. Also, it doesn't work well unless you have Enable loaded on hard disk—if it isn't you may have to make disk changes.

Create the Script Close all windows before using this procedure. At the Main Menu type MTTUC (MCM;Tools;Telecom;Unattended Transfer Form;Create). Enable prompts for the filename.

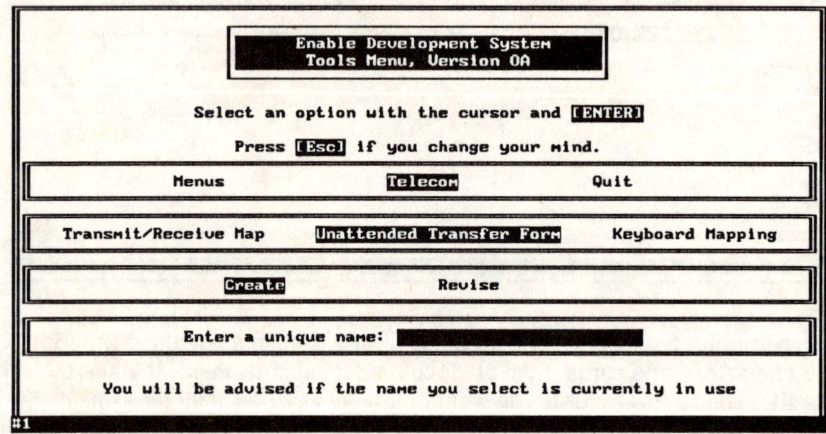

Enter the name (Enable adds .WPF) and press Enter. Press Enter again at the instructions screen, and Enable displays a blank form. This form has a special Top Line Menu, shown in the following screen.

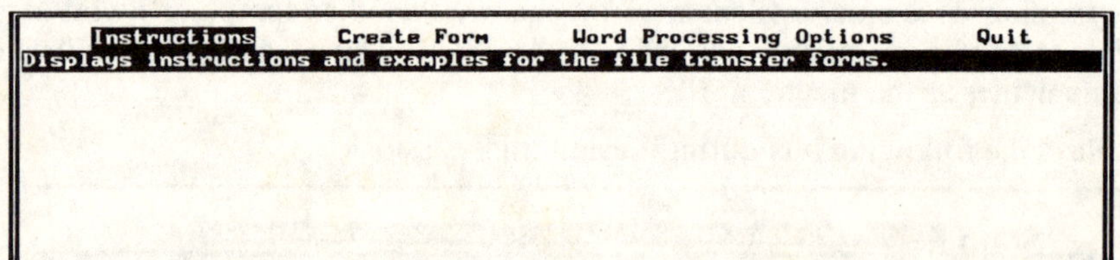

The options let you view instructions about the unattended transfer form, create the form, see the word processing Top Line Menu, or Quit. Type your script. An example is shown in the next screen.

```
L-----------------------------------------+----------------------------------------
.TELECOMMUNICATIONS DIVISION. VER=1                                              ¶
:This script will transmit to the Main Office mainframe at 11:00 p.m.           ¶
.TIME 23:00                                                                      ¶
.SETUP Mainoff                                                                   ¶
.SEND "FILETRANS~"                                                               ¶
.WAIT4 15, "Go Ahead"                                                            ¶
.TX X,ACCOUNTS                                                                   ¶
.SEND "BYE"                                                                      ¶
.EXIT                                                                            ¶
.END

#1    REF/B C:UNATTEND.WPF      DRAFT                          Cap      L00010C006
```

The script is a dot command form, as described in this book's Database section. All commands begin with a period (.), and comments begin with a semicolon. The script must always begin with the following command in the first column of line one: .TELECOMMUNICATIONS DIVISION. VER=1.

Follow the first line with commands and comments, and end the form with .END. The form usually includes the following commands: .TIME (the transfer time); .SETUP (the setup used to make the call); .TX or .RX (the protocol to use and the name of the file to transfer or receive); .END (the end-of-transmission command). You also include sign-on and sign-off information, instructions, and responses to prompts.

Save the Script When you have finished the script press F10 and type C (Create Form). Enable prompts for a filename. Enter a filename (not the same as the one you used when you opened the Transfer Form). Enable automatically adds the extension .TPU. Press Enter and Enable saves the Transfer Form.

You cannot edit or change this form—it is strictly for use in telecommunications. However, you can also save the form as a word processing form. Press F10 and type W (Word Processing Options) to see the word processing Top Line Menu. Type S (Save) and press Enter to save the file. Enable saves the file using the name you entered when you first opened the Transfer Form. Press F10 and type QY to close the file. Type Q to return to the Main Menu.

You can revise the script by typing MTTUR (MCM;Tools;Telecom;Unattended Transfer Form;Revise) at the Main Menu and following the same procedure.

Begin Unattended File Transfer You can begin the session from the Main Menu or from the Telecom screen. You can cancel the session by pressing Enter.

At the Main Menu type UTCF (Use System;Telecom;Communicate;File Transfer). When Enable prompts for the filename enter the name you gave the .TPU file (at the Create Form command). Press Enter and Enable initializes the modem, displays the Telecom screen, and waits for the time specified in the script.

To begin at the Telecom screen press F10 and type FU (Files;Unattended). Type the filename and press Enter.

You can view a log-file that reports on the session. This file is a word processing file named TPLOG.WPF.

The Commands The following lists the script commands. If you need to transmit a carriage return with any of these commands type a tilde (~). Strings of characters must be enclosed in quotation marks. Use right quotation marks to enclose double quotation marks, and vice versa.

Initiate the Connection

.DATE ***day,labelname***—Passes control to the specified *.LABEL* on a particular day. Use the first three letters of the day of the week. See *.LABEL*.

.TIME ***time***—Specifies the time to begin, in 24-hr time. Usually the first command in the script. (If you don't use .TIME Enable begins as soon as you select Unattended Transfer.)

.SETUP ***name***—The name of the setup to use, if you want to use one.

.KEY ***macro statement***—Uses a macro to perform a task, such as to make a connection. For example, type .KEY {F10}TCT9,,5551234 to press F10, type TC (Tele;Call), tone-dial an outside line, wait four seconds, and dial the number.

Specify Filenames

.TX ***protocol,filename***—Specifies the protocol (X=Xmodem, E=Enable, K=Kermit, N=None) and the filename and extension. (.TX X,FILE.WPF).

.RX ***protocol,filename***—Works like .TX, but specifies what to name the file that will be received. With Kermit you do not need to name a file unless you are in Server mode, or want to use Rename (.RX K,/R).

Send Characters

.PASSW ***"string"***—Sends your password. Displays x's on your screen when it transmits. If you are using a setup do not include your password in your setup and use PASSW.

.SEND ***"string"***—Transmits characters, such as commands.

Aids For the User

.BEEP—Makes your computer beep.

.LOCAL ***"string"***—Displays messages on your screen and in the TPLOG file. They are not transmitted.

Pauses

.DELAY ***number***—Pauses for the specified number of seconds.

.WAIT4 ***number,"string",labelname***—Waits for the specified number of seconds and looks for the other computer to transmit the string. If the string is not transmitted in that time, control is passed to the *.LABEL*. If the string is sent, or if you do not include a labelname, Enable moves to the next command. See .LABEL.

Transfer Program-Control

.LABEL ***labelname***—Transfers control to the line of the script immediately below this line. Commands such as .WAIT4 and .GOTO use the labelname to call this location.

.GOTO ***labelname***—Transfers program-control to the command immediately below the specified labelname.

.GOSUB ***labelname***—Tells Enable to perform the subroutine below the labelname. You can build nested subroutines up to 10 levels deep. You must end the subroutine with .RETURN.

.RETURN—Used at the end of a subroutine, it returns Enable to the line in the script below the line that called the subroutine.

Establish Conditions

.IF ***number,"string",action***— You can use up to 50 .IF commands, numbered 0 to 49. Tells Enable that if it sees the string it should carry out the action.

.CLEARIF ***number,number,...***—Cancels the specified .IF command(s). If you don't use an .IF number Enable clears all previous .IFs.

Execute Another Script

.RUN ***scriptname,labelname***—Calls another script, optionally specifying a label. Doesn't return to the original script.

.SUBFILE ***scriptname,labelname***—Like .RUN, except that Enable returns to the original script when it is finished. You could build a script with commonly used commands.

Terminate Script

.EXIT—Saves the TPLOG file and closes the Telecom window.

APPLICATIONS

Enable offers several convenient methods for transferring large or small amounts of data to other computers. The Capture-to-memory file method is the quickest and easiest method, but you need the other methods for larger transfers and for multiple files.

TYPICAL OPERATION

In this activity you transfer data from a Capture-to-memory file. It is not specified where you should send this data—use a bulletin board or another computer.

1. Use a setup or Quick-Connect to begin the call procedure. When Enable prompts for a filename type the name of the word processing file that has the message you want to transmit. Enable asks if you want to add to the end of the file or re-use it.

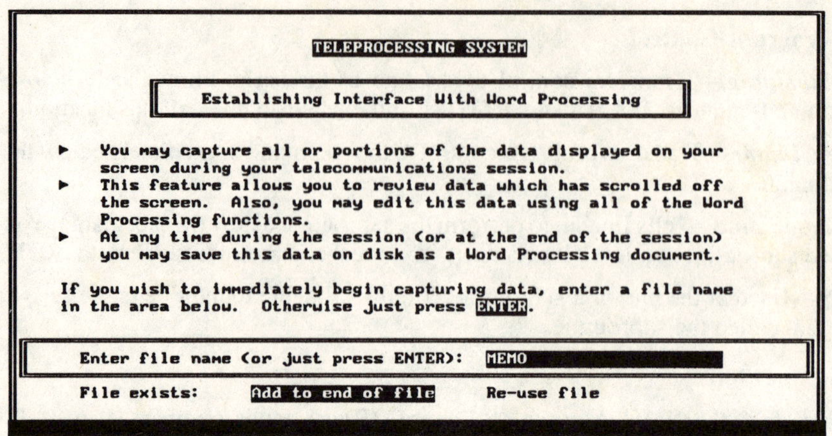
TELEPROCESSING SYSTEM

Establishing Interface With Word Processing

► You may capture all or portions of the data displayed on your screen during your telecommunications session.
► This feature allows you to review data which has scrolled off the screen. Also, you may edit this data using all of the Word Processing functions.
► At any time during the session (or at the end of the session) you may save this data on disk as a Word Processing document.

If you wish to immediately begin capturing data, enter a file name in the area below. Otherwise just press ENTER.

Enter file name (or just press ENTER): MEMO

File exists: Add to end of file Re-use file

2. Press **Enter** and continue with the process of establishing the call. Enable displays the Telecom screen with the end of the file inside. Continue with the session as normal.

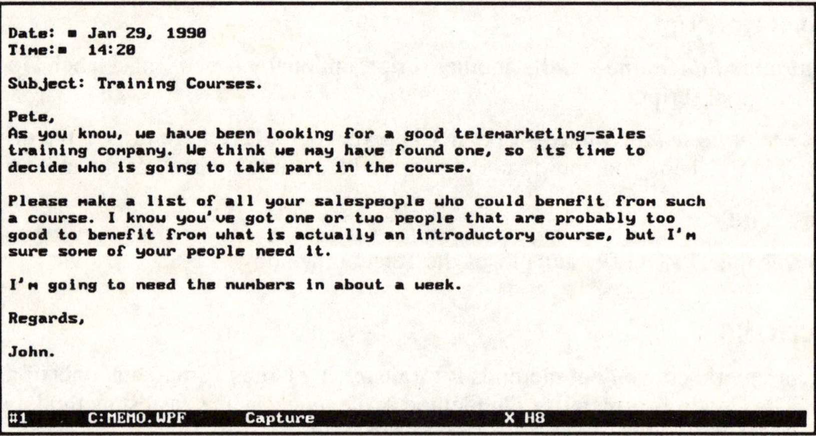
Date: ▪ Jan 29, 1990
Time:▪ 14:20

Subject: Training Courses.

Pete,
As you know, we have been looking for a good telemarketing-sales training company. We think we may have found one, so its time to decide who is going to take part in the course.

Please make a list of all your salespeople who could benefit from such a course. I know you've got one or two people that are probably too good to benefit from what is actually an introductory course, but I'm sure some of your people need it.

I'm going to need the numbers in about a week.

Regards,

John.

#1 C:MEMO.WPF Capture X H8

3. When you are ready to transmit the information press **Up Arrow** to move into the word processing screen and set a block on the text you wish to send. (Put the cursor in the beginning and press **F7**, then put the cursor at the end and press **F7**.)

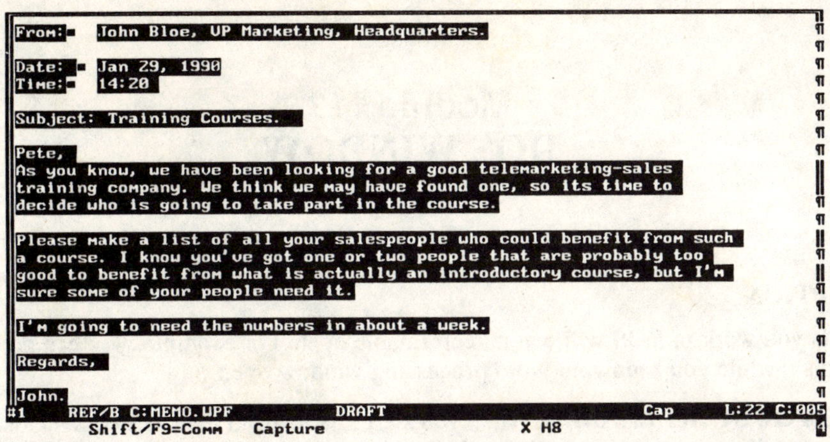

4. Press **Shift-F9** to go back to the Telecom screen. Press **F8** and Enable transmits the data.
5. After you have finished your session press **F10**, type **DYN**, and press **Enter** to terminate the session without saving data.
6. Turn to Module 106 to continue the learning sequence.

Module 113
DOS WINDOW

DESCRIPTION

Enable lets you work in DOS while you keep Enable open. For example, you can go to DOS to format a disk, while you keep your word processing window open.

BEFORE YOU START ENABLE When you start Enable from the DOS commands, you must use a memory-allocation parameter. This tells Enable how much of the computer's RAM (Random Access Memory) to use for Enable, memory-resident programs (such as Sidekick or some spelling and thesaurus programs), buffers, virtual disk drives, and so on, and how much to save for the DOS window.

For example, you have 640K RAM. Typing "enable 576" and pressing Enter opens Enable and leaves 64K for the DOS window. The amount you should leave for the DOS window depends on what you want to do with it. If all you want to do is look at directories and use other simple DOS commands 40K is probably enough. But if you want to run programs you must leave enough room for them to operate.

OPENING A DOS WINDOW At the Main Menu type MD (MCM;DOS). Enable displays the DOS prompt. Press F10 to see the Top Line Menu.

```
 Windows  Quit
Open, close, and switch windows
The IBM Personal Computer DOS
Version 3.00 (C)Copyright IBM Corp 1981, 1982, 1983, 1984

C:\ENABLE>
```

Type Q to close the window, or W to see the window options.

```
 Windows  Quit
1. Open a window
2. Go to another window
3. Go to the next window         rp 1981, 1982, 1983, 1984
4. Display window status lines
5. Close current window
```

You can open another window, go to the next window, display the Window Status screen, or close the DOS window (the same as selecting Quit).

NATIVE & NON-NATIVE MODES In Native mode all keystrokes are considered DOS keystrokes. In Non-Native mode Enable monitors all your keystrokes looking for ones that perform Enable commands. When you first enter the DOS window you are in Non-Native mode, so Enable is automatically monitoring your keystrokes. Turn Native mode on and off by pressing Alt-Backspace. (You can exit from the window while in Native mode by typing "exit" and pressing Enter.)

These are the Non-Native keystrokes that perform commands:

Alt-Up Arrow	Displays the next window up.
Alt-Down Arrow	Displays the next window down.
Alt-5 (Num Keypad)	Lets you change the size and position of the DOS window.
Alt-Home	Displays the Main Menu.

CAUTION

Do not issue an Enable start-up command or run CHKDSK or CHKDSK/F from the DOS window.

CHANGE THE WINDOW SIZE AND POSITION You can change the size of the DOS window and move it in the same way you would a word processing window. Press Alt-5 (the 5 on the numeric keypad) and Enable puts a border around the screen, as shown in the following illustration.

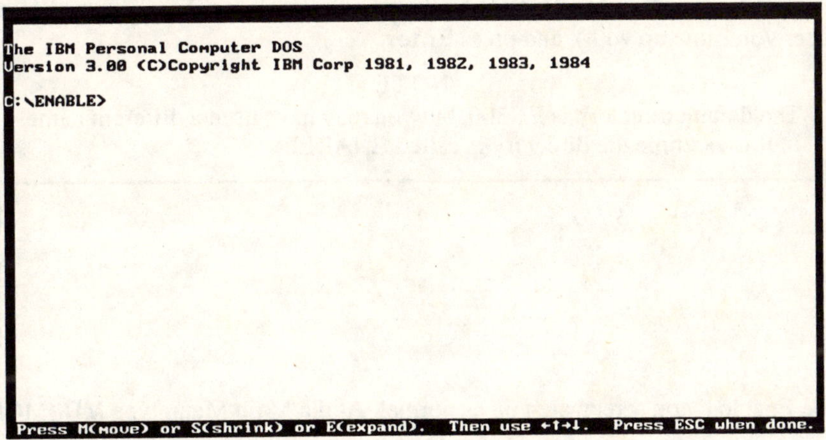

Type M (Move), S (Shrink), or E (Expand) and then press the arrow keys (or press R to shrink or expand in all directions). When you have finished, press Esc.

(If you are using a color monitor you may not be able to change the DOS window size unless you have added the line DEVICE=C:*pathname*\ANSITSG.SYS to your CONFIG.SYS file. ANSITSG.SYS is a file from the Enable disks, and should have been copied onto your hard disk drive when you installed Enable.)

COPY TO AND FROM THE DOS WINDOW You can copy data from a DOS window to a word processing or DBMS window, and vice versa. To copy from the DOS window to the other window use the usual method (for example, in word processing press F10 and type C1CBO (Copy;Copy;Change Options;Block;Other Window) and select the window). When Enable displays the DOS window you can use the PgUp, PgDn, Home, and End keys to move around the window. Set a block using F7, and press Alt-F5.

To copy from the other window to the DOS window, press Alt-F5 in the DOS window. Enable displays the Interwindow Copy Options screen. Select the other window, set the block, and press Enter. (Of course, copying to the DOS window probably won't be much use to you.)

APPLICATIONS

Using the DOS window lets you perform DOS commands without leaving Enable. For example, suppose you need to build several new directories. Instead of closing Enable, building the directories, and logging back on, you can use the DOS window. You may also want to format disks, print a directory tree, print a DOS file, and so on.

TYPICAL OPERATION

In this activity you open Enable, log on, and open the DOS window.

1. Find out how much RAM memory your computer has. Subtract 64 from that figure. For example, you have 512K RAM; subtract 64 to give you 448.
2. At the DOS prompt, and in the Enable directory you have set up, type **enable 448** (or the number you came up with), and press **Enter**.

NOTE

The default directory is EN300, but you may have used a different name. In this example the directory is called ENABLE.

3. At the Enable logon screen sign on as normal. At the Main Menu type **MD** (MCM;DOS).
4. Enable displays the DOS window. Press **F10** and type **Q** to exit the window.
5. Turn to Module 114 to continue the learning sequence.

Module 114
FILES

DESCRIPTION

Enable has a number of commands that help you manage your files. These range from simple commands that list the files a directory contains, to those that set file attributes or let you view the contents of a file without actually opening it.

WHAT IS A FILE? As you know by now, Enable stores your data in files. Whether that information is a word processing document, a spreadsheet, a database, or any other kind of data, it is stored in a file that shares some characteristics with other files.

All files have a *filename*, which is from 1 to 8 characters, and usually have 3-character extensions. The name is chosen by you. It can be letters, numbers, underscores, or (except in the case of DBMS files) special characters (& $ # @ % ! ' ( ) – { } ^ ~). The extension is usually chosen by Enable and indicates the file-type.

All filenames also have a *disk-drive identifier* and a *directory path*, although you do not always see these and do not always need to enter them. (You only need to enter them if you want to retrieve a file from, or store a file in, a disk or directory other than the default data directory.) A directory name may be up to 8 characters, and the entire directory path may be up to 64 characters, including backslashes (you can nest directories within directories). You can use DOS commands to build directories, or use Enable's Utility Menu commands.

For example, C:\ENABLE\FILENAME.WPF indicates a file on disk C, in the directory named ENABLE, with the name FILENAME, and the extension .WPF (indicating it is a word processing file). Notice that the disk drive, directory, and filename are separated with backslashes (\), while the filename and extension are separated with a period.

Path Aliases Enable assigns aliases to pathnames that are more than one level deep. For example, you have a directory named BOOK in a directory named ENABLE. The path is C:ENABLE\BOOK\. Enable assigns this an alias, a type of shorthand. The first alias is +001, the second is +002, and so on, in the order that the directories are created. You can type an alias in place of a directory path.

Extensions File *extensions* indicate the type of file. You can make up your own extensions (but don't use the $ sign), in which case you must include the extension when you tell Enable to use or retrieve a file. Otherwise Enable assigns each file an extension.

The following table shows the file extensions that Enable recognizes.

System Files

.$PR	Profiles
.BAT	Batch files
.COM	Executable DOS files
.EXE	Executable DOS files

.MC	Named MCM menu
.MCM	System-wide macros
.MNU	Named system-wide menus (the default MCM menu is MCM.MNU)
.TSG	Enable programs

Word Processing Files

.DOC	Multimate and PeachText
.MNU	Menu (the default is WP.MNU)
.WP	Named menus
.WP@	Automatic document-save files
.WPF	Document
.WPI	Index
.WPM	Macros
.WPP	Print (temporary print files, deleted after printing)
.WPT	Table of Contents
.WTA	Table of Authority

Spreadsheet Files

.ASC	ASCII files
.CAL	SuperCalc spreadsheets
.DIF	DIF format spreadsheets
.MNU	Menu (the default is SS.MNU)
.SM	Named menus
.SSF	Spreadsheets
.SSM	Macros
.SSP	Print (temporary print files, deleted after printing)
.WK1	Lotus 1-2-3 release 2 or Symphony spreadsheets
.WKS	Lotus 1-2-3 release 1A spreadsheets

DBMS (Database) Files

.$BF	Database definition
.$IF	Input forms
.$RF	Report forms
.@@@	Backup files
.ASC	ASCII files
.CTF	Copy transfer forms
.DAT	Condor3 databases
.DB	Named menus
.DBF	Database
.DBM	DBMS macros
.DBT	Memo files
.DEF	Database definitions used as databases
.DTA	PC-File III database
.ERR	Error sets
.MNU	Menu (the default menu is DB.MNU)
.MTF	Merge transfer forms
.NDX	Index
.SS	Select sets
.SSn	Internal record processing

.UTF	Update transfer forms
WINDOWn.m	Window import files

Graphics Files

.FNT	Graphics fonts
.GO*n*	Graphics file associated with a word processing document
.GRF	DBMS settings
.GRM	Macros
.GRP	Print or Plot files (PRINTPLOT.GRP, temporary files)
.GRS	Current graph settings (SETTING*n*.GRS, temporary files)
.PLT	Plot file

Telecommunications Files

.$TP	Setups
.MNU	Menu (the default is TP.MNU)
.TP	Named telecommunications menus
.TPF	Capture-to-disk files and files received by File Transfer
.TPK	Keyboard Mapping Tables
.TPM	Macros
.TPT	Transmit/Receive Mapping Tables
.TPU	Unattended Transfer Forms
.WPF	Word processing files; Capture-to-memory and edit versions of Mapping Tables and Transfer Forms

FILE FUNCTIONS There are several menus and directories that let you carry out file-management procedures. The "top level" is the Directory of Files. The following flow diagram shows you how to get to the other levels.

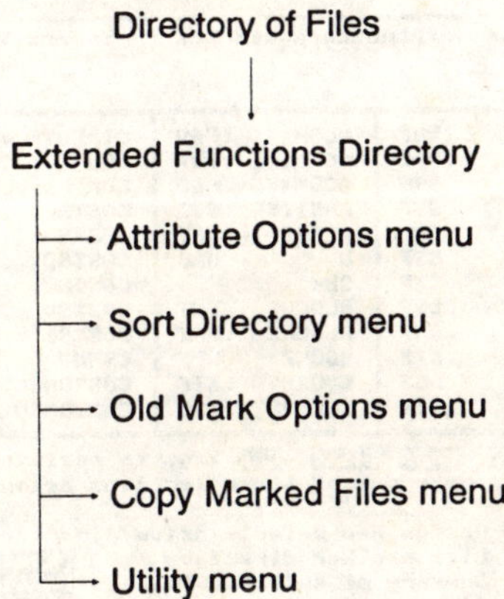

THE DIRECTORY OF FILES This directory lists the files in each directory, and provides file-management functions.

Displaying the Directory You can display the directory from the Main Menu by typing MF (MCM;Files) and typing the character corresponding to the types of files you want to see (Word Processing, Spreadsheet, Telecom, DBMS, or All).

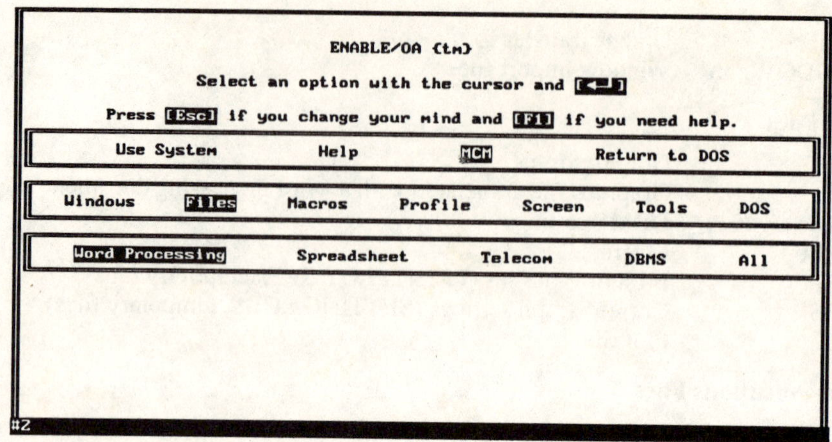

You can also view the directory when you are revising a file. Type ? and press Enter at the "Enter name" prompt. Enable displays only files relating to the type of file you want to revise.

To select the directory while inside a word processing file press F10 and type M22 (MCM;Files; File Directory); in a spreadsheet press F10 and type MFW (MCM;Files;Spreadsheet-Files) or MFP (MCM;Files;Print-Files); in the DBMS Interact screen type 82 (MCM;Files). Enable displays only files relating to the type of file you are working in (only word processing files if you are in a word processing document).

NOTE

Earlier versions of Enable/OA called Worksheet-Files Spreadsheet-Files.

The following screen shows the directory of files.

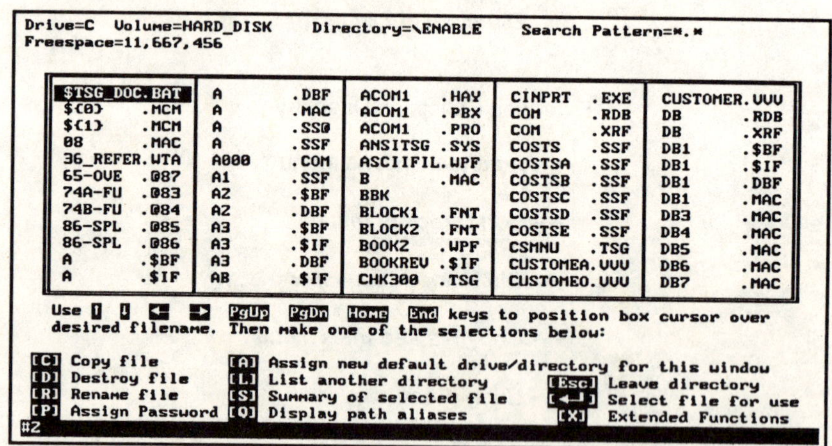

The top of the screen displays the default disk drive; the disk volume name; that file's directory (or the path alias), the Search pattern (indicating which files are displayed—*.* means all files, *.WP* means word processing, etc.); and *Freespace*, the amount of unused space on the disk.

NOTE

Files currently in use, except spreadsheet and word processing files, are indicated by an asterisk next to the name. Enable displays a warning if you attempt to open them.

Directory of Files Functions If you reached the directory by typing a ? at an "Enter name" prompt, select the file you want to use by highlighting it and pressing Enter. Or use one of the file-management functions by highlighting the file and typing a letter from the following list. Use the arrow keys, PgUp and PgDn to select the file.

NOTE

You cannot copy, destroy, rename, or assign a password to .TSG files (Enable system files).

A - Assign disk or directory Displays files from another disk or directory, and changes the default drive for the current window (that is, if you return to the Directory of Files later Enable displays files from the specified disk and directory). Enable prompts for the disk, and then the directory.

C - Copy file Makes a copy of the file. Enable prompts for the disk, then the directory, then the filename. (Floppy users can replace the system disk with the new data disk.)

D - Destroy file Permanently removes the file. Enable prompts you to confirm (type Y and press Enter). You cannot destroy files in use, or read-only files (discussed later in this module).

L - List another directory Displays files from another disk or directory, but does not change the default (see A, in this table). Enable prompts for the disk, directory, and search pattern. Enter a filename, or DOS wild cards * and ? and extension type (*.WPF, for example).

P - Assign password Assigns a password to a file. (Enable will prompt you for the password each time you try to open the file.) You can only assign passwords to files in EnableOA format. You can also assign a password to PRINTQ.TSG, the print queue file. If a file already has a password Enable prompts for the old one before it prompts for the new one. If you press Enter when Enable prompts for the new password the password is removed.

Q - Display path aliases Blanks out the list of files and displays the various aliases and pathnames Enable has created. Press any key to continue.

R - Rename file Renames the file or lets you move it to another directory. Enable prompts for the directory name and then the filename.

S - Summary of selected file Displays, at the top of the screen, the filename, date and time it was last saved, and its size.

X - Extended functions Displays the Extended Functions Directory.

Esc - Leave directory Returns you to the Main Menu.

THE EXTENDED FUNCTIONS DIRECTORY Type X at the Directory of Files to see the following screen.

```
86-SPL  .085     8/03/89     6:43:48          3 Files      4,087 bytes marked
 <DIR>  ..                    [.D.S..]    74B-FU  .084      3,312  [A.....]
 <DIR>  BOOK                  [.D....]    86-SPL  .085      2,551  [A.....]
 <DIR>  BOOK1                 [.D....]    86-SPL  .086      2,551  [A.....]
 <DIR>  BOOK2                 [.D....]    A       .$BF      1,024  [A.....]
 <DIR>  BOOK3                 [.D....]    A       .$IF      1,024  [A.....]
 <DIR>  BOOK4                 [.D....]    A       .DBF      1,536       20 R
 <DIR>  BOOK5                 [.D....]    A       .MAC        512  [A.....]
$TSG_DOC.BAT           42     [A.....]    A       .SS0      3,072  [A.....]
$(0)     .MCM          512    [A.....]    A       .SSF      3,072  [A.....]
$(1)     .MCM          512    [A.....]    A000    .COM      2,041  [A.....]
08       .MAC        1,024    [A.....]    A1      .SSF      3,072  [A.....]
36_REFER.WTA           733    [A.....]    A2      .$BF      1,024  [A.....]
65-OVE   .087        2,172    [A.....]    A2      .DBF      1,536       20 R
74A-FU   .083       20,674    [A.....]    A3      .$BF      1,536  [A.....]

Point to file using ARROWS, PGUP, PGDN, HOME, END keys, then select function.
 [F7] Mark/Unmark file      [A] Attribute options        [Esc] Leave directory
[sF7] Mark file range       [L] List new path/pattern    [<-┘] Select file for use
[aF7] Unmark all files      [S] Sort directory            [C] Copy marked files
  [-] Reverse all marks     [T] TextScan marked files     [D] Destroy marked files
  [F] Find next mark        [V] View file/directory       [R] Rename marked files
  [W] Wildcard marking      [O] Old Mark options          [X] Utility Menu
#2 C:\ENABLE\*.*                           201 Files    5,113,179 bytes used
```

Enable displays <DIR> at the top of the list of files in the Extended Functions Directory (see the previous screen). Below this, Enable displays the names of any subdirectories in the directory you are presently viewing, each name preceded by <DIR>. For example, in the previous screen you can see that the directory named Enable has several subdirectories: Book, Book1, and so on. Placing the arrow to the left of one of the subdirectory names and pressing Enter displays the files in that directory. Placing the arrow to the left of the top <DIR> and pressing Enter makes Enable move up DOS' "directory tree." In this case selecting <DIR> displays the *root* directory (the "top" directory, the one at the bottom of the directory tree), because, as you can see from the status line, the directory named Enable is a subdirectory of the root directory.

TIP: Although you can use List another directory or List path/pattern to move to other directories, using the <DIR> is the quickest and easiest way to move between directories.

Select a file by moving the arrow in the border at the left of each column. The top of the column displays the name of the selected file, and the date and time it was last saved. If you have marked files it also displays the number and size of those files.

This directory provides more information about each file in the list. It shows the name and extension, the file size (in bytes), and an attribute code, displayed in brackets ([ ]). The codes are as follows:

Code	*Name & Description*
A	Archive—Indicates that the file has not been archived with the DOS BACKUP command. Using BACKUP automatically removes A.
D	Directory—A directory, not a file.
V	Volume label—A DOS disk volume label, not a file.
S	System file—Indicates a DOS system file.
H	Hidden file—A DOS hidden file, not shown by the DOS DIR command.
R	Read-only—A read-only file. Read-only files can only be viewed using the View option in the directory; you cannot open a read-only file.
*nnn*R	Database records—Database files are followed by the number of records and the letter R, unless you set another attribute at the Attribute Options Menu.

The codes A, H, R, and S can also be set or removed at the Attribute Options Menu. You can replace these codes with the Old Marks in braces ({ })—see the Old Marks Options Menu, later in this module.

In addition, the status line displays the window number, current path and search pattern, the number of files in the directory, and the total size (in bytes) of all the files.

The following list shows the available file-management functions.

- (hyphen) - Reverse marks All marked files are unmarked, and unmarked files are marked. If no files have been marked Enable marks all of the files.

A - Attribute options Displays the Attribute Options Menu.

C - Copy marked files Displays the Copy Marked Files Menu.

D - Destroy marked files Permanently removes all the marked files. Enable asks you to confirm. Type Y and press Enter; then type D. You cannot delete open, .TSG, or read-only files.

F - Find next mark Moves the arrow to the next marked file.

F7 - Mark/Unmark files Marks (highlights) the selected file, or unmarks it.

Alt-F7 - Unmark all files Unmarks all marked files.

Shift-F7 - Mark file range Marks (highlights) a range of files. Select the first file, press Shift-F7, select the last file, and press Shift-F7 again.

L - List new path/pattern Displays a different directory. Enable has three options: a new directory and wildcard (search) pattern, a new directory only, and a new search pattern only. This then works like L (List another directory) in the Directory of Files.

O - Old marks options Displays the Old Marks Menu.

R - Rename marked files Lets you change the filename and/or move the file to another directory. Enable prompts for the directory and then for the "new name or wildcard pattern." Enter the new name, or, if you are moving all the files to another directory, type *.* to keep the same names. If you want to change all the extensions to .ASC, for example, type *.ASC to keep the names the same. The renamed files are displayed followed by "R" until you press any key.

S - Sort directory Displays the Sort Directory Menu.

T - TextScan marked files Searches marked files for a text string up to 50 characters long. Enable unmarks files that do not contain the string, and puts "T" next to the file size. It puts * next to the ones that do contain the text. Press Esc to interrupt the textscan, and C to continue or Q to quit.

V - View file/directory Displays the contents of the selected file or directory. Enable displays the file-type for Enable word processing files: 0 to 17 is Enable 2.0 or earlier, 19 is Enable 3.0. If you placed a comment on the first line of a macro Enable displays the comment. It also displays the first line of a word processing Document Title. You can use cursor movement keys to move through the file.

W - Wildcard marking Enable prompts for the files to mark. Enter a name, with wild cards if you want. Use * to replace multiple characters, or ? to replace single characters. For example, *.WPF marks all .WPF files. BOOK??.WPF marks all .WPF files that have 6-character names beginning with book.

X - Utility menu Displays the Utility Menu.

Esc - Leave directory Returns to the Directory of Files. You can also set section 9 of your profile to make Enable prompt you to confirm before exiting—type Q to confirm.

The Attribute Options Menu The Attribute Options Menu is displayed by typing A at the Extended Functions Directory. The available attributes are Archived (backed up using DOS BACKUP), Hidden File (a DOS hidden file), Read-only (you can only view the file using the directory View function, you cannot open the file), and System file (a DOS system file). The following list shows the available options (only options not explained in the previous lists are included).

M - Mark by attributes Enable displays a menu of attributes (A=archived with DOS BACKUP, H=Hidden File, R=Read-only file, and S=System file). Type the letters representing the attributes you want and press Enter. Enable marks all the files with those attributes.

R - Reset file-attributes First mark the file. Then type R and Enable displays the list of attributes. Type the letters representing the attributes you want to remove, and press Enter.

S - Set file-attributes Works like Reset, except it sets the attributes.

T - Toggle Old Marks/Attributes Replaces the attributes (displayed next to the filename in brackets - [ ]) with the Old Marks (displayed in braces—{ }). See the Old Marks Menu later.

Esc- Exit to Directory Menu Displays the Extended Functions Directory.

The Sort Directory Menu Type S at the Extended Functions Directory to see this menu. It lets you sort the listed files into a different order. Enable begins by displaying the files in alphabetical filename order. Use one of the following options to change that order.

+ - *Forward order* Ascending order (0-9, A-Z). Press + and type one of the letters.

– - *Reverse order* Descending order (9-0, Z-A). Press + and type one of the letters.

D - Date/Time Sorts by the date and time of the last file-save.

E - Extension Sorts by extension, putting files into extension groups.

N - Filename Sorts by filename.

S - File size Sorts by file size.

U - Unsorted Lists the files in the order they actually appear on the disk.

Esc - Exit Returns to the Extended Functions Directory without sorting the files.

The Old Marks Options Menu Old marks are codes Enable uses to show the result of the operations you use while you are in the files directories. They are not very old marks, actually, because Enable removes them as soon as you leave the current directory; when you return the fields are blank. The codes are displayed in braces ({ }). These are the codes:

a	archive bit reset at the Attribute Options Menu or the Copy Marked File Menu
c	copied
m	marked
r	renamed by copy at the Copy Marked Files Menu
s	skipped by copy during a copy procedure at the Copy Marked Files Menu
t	text not found during a TextScan
*	text found during a TextScan

When you first enter the Extended Functions Menu these codes are not displayed. Type O at the Extended Functions Menu to see the Old Marks Menu, and then type T to replace the attributes (displayed next to the filename in brackets — [ ]) with the Old Marks (displayed in braces { }). See the Typical Operation for an example screen.

The following list shows the available options (only options not explained in the previous lists are included).

NOTE

You must be displaying the Old Marks before you can use these options. Type T to toggle between displaying the attributes and the Old Marks.

A - Remove all Old Marks Removes all the codes from within the braces.

M - Mark selected files Type the codes you want and press Enter. Enable marks all the files with those Old Marks.

R - Remove selected Marks Type R and Enable displays the list of marks. Type the character you want to remove from the braces, and press Enter to remove them from the selected file.

The Copy Marked Files Menu Display the Copy Marked Files Menu by typing C at the Extended Functions Directory. Enable displays the following screen.

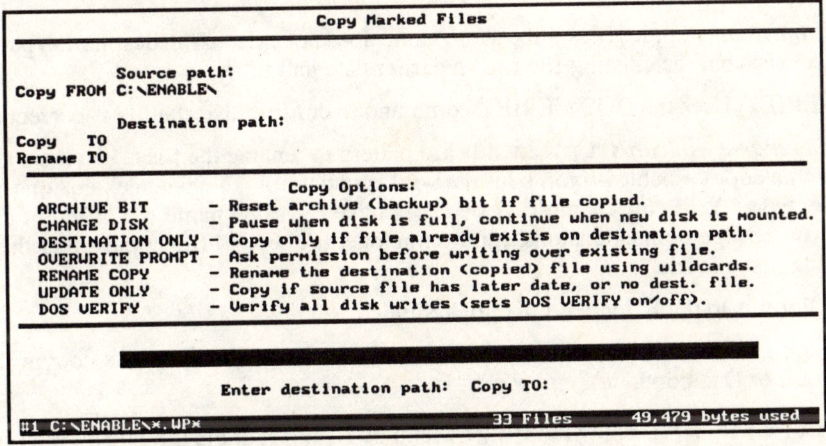

```
Copy Marked Files

Source path:
Copy FROM C:\ENABLE\

Destination path:
Copy    TO
Rename TO

Copy Options:
ARCHIVE BIT        - Reset archive (backup) bit if file copied.
CHANGE DISK        - Pause when disk is full, continue when new disk is mounted.
DESTINATION ONLY - Copy only if file already exists on destination path.
OVERWRITE PROMPT - Ask permission before writing over existing file.
RENAME COPY        - Rename the destination (copied) file using wildcards.
UPDATE ONLY        - Copy if source file has later date, or no dest. file.
DOS VERIFY         - Verify all disk writes (sets DOS VERIFY on/off).

Enter destination path:   Copy TO:
#1 C:\ENABLE\*.WP*                       33 Files      49,479 bytes used
```

Enter the destination path. (You must enter the path even if you are copying a file into the same directory.) Press Enter and Enable displays the following screen.

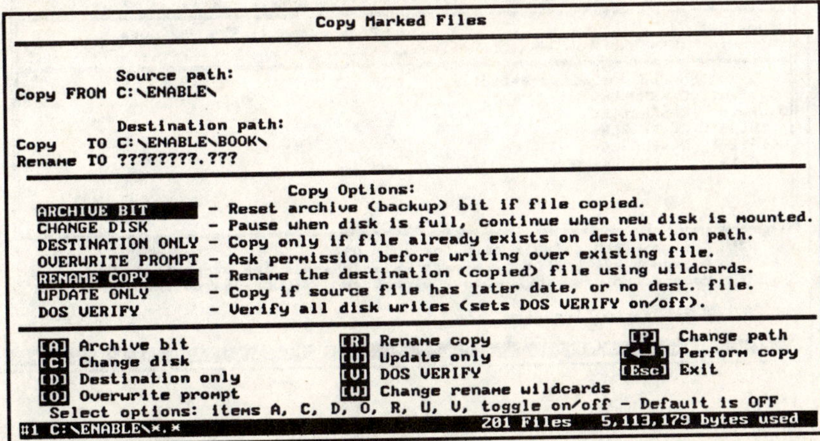

```
Copy Marked Files

Source path:
Copy FROM C:\ENABLE\

Destination path:
Copy    TO C:\ENABLE\BOOK\
Rename TO ????????.???

Copy Options:
ARCHIVE BIT        - Reset archive (backup) bit if file copied.
CHANGE DISK        - Pause when disk is full, continue when new disk is mounted.
DESTINATION ONLY - Copy only if file already exists on destination path.
OVERWRITE PROMPT - Ask permission before writing over existing file.
RENAME COPY        - Rename the destination (copied) file using wildcards.
UPDATE ONLY        - Copy if source file has later date, or no dest. file.
DOS VERIFY         - Verify all disk writes (sets DOS VERIFY on/off).

[A] Archive bit            [R] Rename copy              [P] Change path
[C] Change disk            [U] Update only              [←┘] Perform copy
[D] Destination only       [V] DOS VERIFY               [Esc] Exit
[O] Overwrite prompt       [W] Change rename wildcards
 Select options: items A, C, D, O, R, U, V, toggle on/off - Default is OFF
#1 C:\ENABLE\*.*                        201 Files   5,113,179 bytes used
```

The following list describes the available options. Type the character, and Enable highlights the description line in the center of the screen.

A - Archive bit Removes the A from the attributes indicator (in brackets — [ ]). Puts a in the Old Marks braces. Indicates a backup has been made.

C - Change disk If copying to a floppy disk, it tells you when the disk is full and lets you put another one in. If Enable comes to a file that will not fit on the remaining space it skips that file and copies the next file that is small enough to fit. The skipped file remains marked, is given the Old Mark of s, and is copied to the next disk you insert.

D - Destination only Only copies files that already exist in the destination directory. The existing file is written over (depending on your response to the Overwrite prompt, if any).

O - Overwrite prompt If a file of the same name exists in the destination directory Enable prompts to ask if it should copy over it, skip that file, or stop the copy operation.

P - Change path Prompts you for a new destination path.

R - Rename copy Renames the copied files. You must also use the Change Rename Wildcards option.

U - Update only Only copies files if the same name does not exist in the destination path, or if the name exists but the existing file has an earlier date and time.

V - DOS VERIFY Uses the DOS VERIFY command to confirm that the file is correctly copied.

W - Change rename wildcards Uses a wild card pattern to rename the files. You must also type R (Rename copy). Enable prompts for the wild card pattern. To change extensions but not the name, type *.WPF, for example. If two files have the same name but different extensions, and you change both extensions to the same one, the second file copies over the first one, leaving just one file.

Esc - Exit Returns to the Extended Functions Menu.

When you are ready to copy the files, press Enter. Press Esc to interrupt the copying (and then press Q to quit or C to continue).

THE UTILITY MENU Display the Utility Menu by typing X at the Extended Functions Menu.

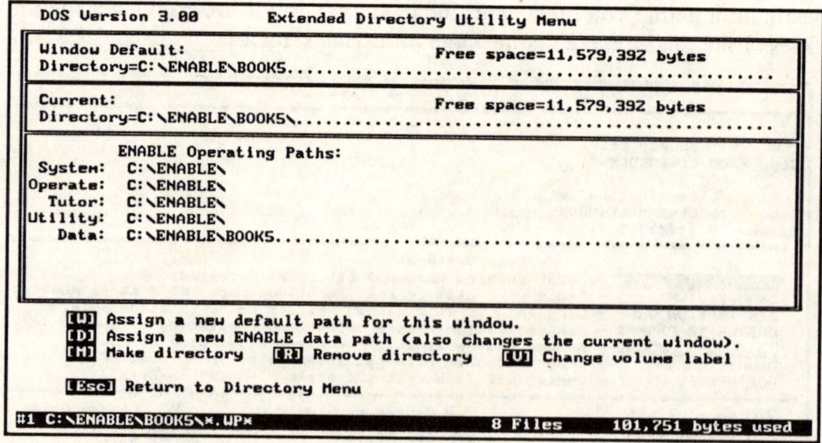

The following list describes the Utility Menu options.

W - Assign default path Prompts for the new default path for the window. Changes the default path for the window you are in, not for any other windows.

D - Assign data path Prompts for the new data directory. This does not affect open windows, but next time you create a file it is placed in this directory, and the next time you open a directory it displays files from this path.

M - Make directory Creates a new directory (DOS MKDIR command). Type the full path name (for example, \ENABLE\BOOK\SECTION2) and press Enter.

R - Remove directory Deletes a directory. Type the full name and press Enter.

V - Change volume label Changes the disk volume label. Enable displays a blank box. Type the name in the box and press Enter. The name is displayed above the box, and the box is cleared. Press Esc.

Esc - Exit Returns to Extended Functions Directory.

APPLICATIONS

These file functions make life a lot easier. You can use them to copy and move files between directories and even disks; delete old files; assign passwords to files; search for particular files; search marked files for specific lines of text, and so on. When you have been working with Enable for a while you will discover how much time and effort these features can save.

TYPICAL OPERATION

In this activity you open the Directory of Files from the Main Menu and carry out various procedures.

1. At the Main Menu type **MFA** (MCM;Files;All). Enable displays the Directory of Files. Experiment with PgUp, PgDn, and the arrow keys to see how you can select files.

2. Select any file and type **S**. Enable displays the file's name, size, and date and time of the last save above the list of files.

3. Type **X** to see the Extended Functions Directory. Type **S** to see the Sort Menu.

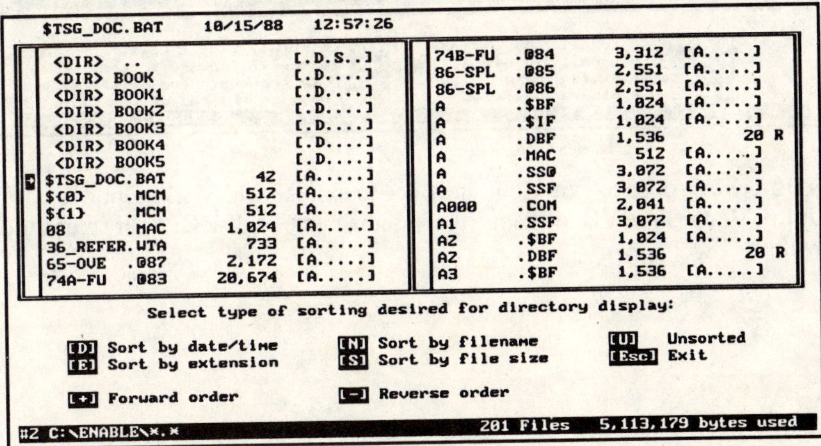

4. Type **–E** to sort the files in reverse order, by extension. Enable displays the Extended Functions Diagnostics Menu options, and lists the files in the new order.
5. Type **O** to view the Old Marks Options Menu and **T** to display the Old Marks braces as shown in the next screen.

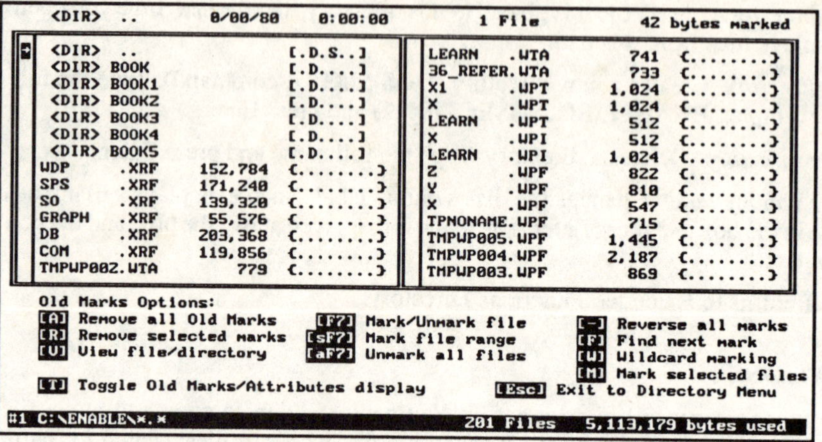

6. Select any file with a .WPF extension, and type **V**. Enable displays the file. Your screen looks something like this:

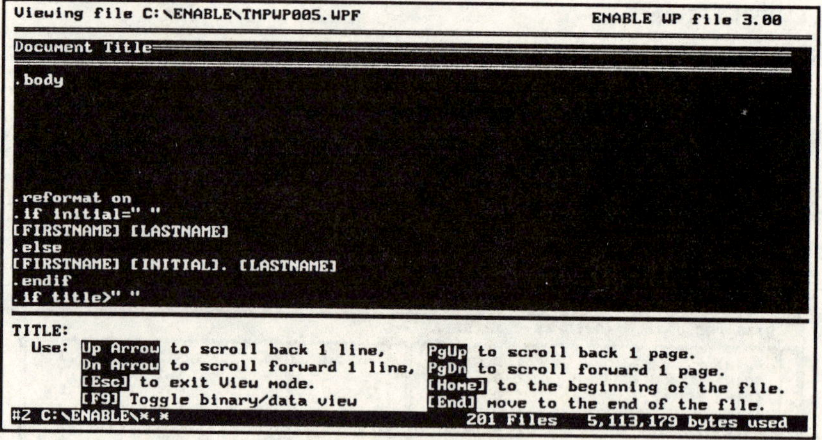

7. Press **Esc** twice (once to exit View, and once to exit the Old Marks Options). Type **X** to see the Utility Menu. Type **VC** to change the volume name of disk **C**. Your screen looks like the following:

```
DOS Version 3.00        Extended Directory Utility Menu
Window Default:                           Free space=11,544,576 bytes
Directory=C:\ENABLE\...................................................
Current:                                  Free space=11,544,576 bytes
Directory=C:\ENABLE\...................................................
         ENABLE Operating Paths:
 System:  C:\ENABLE\
Operate:  C:\ENABLE\
  Tutor:  C:\ENABLE\
Utility:  C:\ENABLE\
   Data:  C:\ENABLE\...................................................

                  Create/Change/Delete a volume label:
         HARDDISK    = current volume label
                     Press [Esc] to exit without changing current volume label.
           Enter the new volume label, and press [←┘]
         Press [←┘] when blank to DELETE the current volume label
    Periods and wildcard characters will be converted to underscore characters
#2 C:\ENABLE\*.*                                201 Files    5,113,179 bytes used
```

8. If you want to change the volume name, type the new name, press **Enter**, and press **Esc**. Otherwise just press **Esc**.
9. Press **Esc** three times to return to the Main Menu.
10. Turn to Module 115 to continue the learning sequence.

Module 115
MACROS

DESCRIPTION

Macros automate common Enable tasks. You build the macros to suit the way you use Enable—if you carry out certain tasks over and over again, build a macro and then just press three keys to automatically complete those tasks.

Macros are stored in files named \${*n*}.*mm*M, where *n* is the name you assigned to the macro, and *mm* indicates the type of macro (WP = word processing, DB = DBMS, GR = graphics, TP = telecommunications, SS = spreadsheet, MC = MCM, that is, system-wide). You can only use macros that are in the data directory—if you build a macro and then change to another data directory, you can't use that macro.

However, if you build a spreadsheet macro and assign the macro to a cell or range, the macro is stored with the spreadsheet, not in another file, so the macro is always available for that spreadsheet (although there are limits to what these types of macros can do).

There are three ways to create macros: the Alt-F9 method; using the MCM/Macros option on the Main Menu; and putting macros in spreadsheet ranges or cells.

CREATING MACROS WITH ALT-F9 With this method you actually build the macro by doing it, effectively showing Enable what you want it to do. For example, you want to go to the Utility Menu from word processing and change the default data directory. To begin building the macro, open a word processing file, press Alt-F9 and press \ (Backslash). Then type the macro name.

Macro Names A macro name is one key—it can be any key except Backslash, Minus sign, Equal sign, End, PgUp, PgDn, or the arrow keys. You can name a macro with a combination of Shift, Ctrl, or Alt with a function key. For example, you could name a macro Ctrl-F5. (There are two exceptions—you cannot use Alt-F9 or Ctrl-F2.) You cannot combine any other keys—Shift-7 is normally &, but as far as macros go, Enable regards it as 7.

Recording the Macro When you have named the macro Enable displays MAC in the status line. Begin the procedure you want to automate. In the example mentioned earlier (going to the Utility Menu and changing the default data directory), press F10 and type M22XXD. This procedure normally displays the Top Line Menu, selects Files, Directory, displays the Utility Directory, and displays the default data directory prompt. Enable records all these keystrokes. When you have finished press Alt-F9 and press End.

Special Commands There are two special commands you can enter while recording the macro. If you want Enable to stop at some point and wait—press Ctrl-I. When you use the macro Enable stops at that point, waits for you to input some information, and continues when you press Enter.

You can also make Enable wait for a keystroke rather than Enter. Press Ctrl-_ (underscore) while you are recording the macro. When you use the macro Enable waits at that point until you press any key, and then continues. You could use this to pause while you read some information or view a graph, and then continue when you press a key.

Recording Macros Without Executing In the procedure just described Enable actually carries out the procedure as you press the keys. If you want to build a macro without actually executing the procedure, press Alt-F9 and press = (Equal sign). Enter the macro and press Alt-F9 and End to finish.

Using the Macro To use the macro, press Alt-F9 and press the macro key (the macro's name). Enable displays "mac" in the status line during the procedure. You can cancel the macro by pressing Ctrl-Break.

NOTE

A macro can only be used in the same application in which it was created, and the macro file must be in the same data directory.

BUILDING MACROS WITH MCM/MACROS This procedure lets you write a macro "script" in a word processing file. At the Main Menu type MMC (MCM;Macros;Create), and Enable displays five options—Word Processing, Spreadsheet, Telecom, DBMS, and MCM. Select one of these options. Enable prompts for the key to associate with the macro (that is, the macro name). Type the key to and Enable displays a blank word processing screen, with Automatic Reformat turned off.

You can include comment lines by typing two semicolons (;;) and following them with the comment (up to one line). If you want a comment longer than one line put semicolons on each line. You might want to begin the macro with a comment describing what the macro does. Then enter the commands and keystrokes using the following macro codes:

To Enter...	*Type this code...*
F1	{F1}
F2	{F2}
F3	{F3}
F4	{F4}
F5	{F5}
F6	{F6}
F7	{F7}
F8	{F8}
F9	{F9}
F10	{F10}
Esc	{Esc}
Tab	{Tab}
Home	{Hom}
Up Arrow	{Up}
Left Arrow	{Left}
Right Arrow	{Right}
Down Arrow	{Down}
PgUp	{PgUp}
PgDn	{PgDn}
End	{End}
Ins	{Ins}
Del	{Del}
Backspace	{BS}
Enter	~
Ctrl-Enter	{LF}

To Enter...	*Type this code...*
{	{{}
}	{}}
~	{~}
Alt-*x*	{&*x*} (for example, {&F4})
Ctrl-*x*	{^*x*} (for example, {^Home})
Shift-*x*	{!*x*} (for example, {!F7})
Alt-Up Arrow	{PrevW}
Alt-Down Arrow	{NextW}
Alt-End	{CloseW}
Alt-Home	{OpenW}

Errors:

If error found, perform commands	{If Error}*commands*
If no error, perform commands	{If Error}*commands*
Terminate If-commands	{Endif}

Menu:

Display menu	{Do Menu}*name~*
Make named menu the default	{Menu}*name~*
Perform named Macro	{Do Macro}*name~*
Repeat	{*n*x} (*n* is the number of times to repeat—for example, {10x}{~} means press Enter ten times.)
Sound Tone	{Beep}

Status line:

Display message in status line	{Send}(S)*message~*
Remove message	{Send}(R)
Timed Pause	{*n*x}{Pause} (*n* is the number of seconds)

Video Display:

Freeze (Doesn't display changes on the screen while macro is running)	{Voff}
Restore	{Von}

NOTE

Don't include {Von} during a graph-building procedure or change a word processing file from draft to final form while the screen is frozen. Also, putting {Von} as the very last command in a macro can cause problems. Put it just before the end of the macro, or follow it by ~, {Up}, or {PgUp}.

Wait for input	{?}
Wait for input *x*	{^F9}*x* (where *x* is a key)
Wait for keystroke	{Wait}

Window:

Go to named window	{GotoW}*name~*
Name the current window	{Wname}*name~*

Enter the text and commands in the sequence you want to perform them. If you want to access a menu command, type {F10} and then type exactly what you would type to use it yourself. For example, type {F10}LD1 to create a table of authorities entry. In some circumstances you have to select commands or options by moving the highlight to the option and pressing Enter. For example, to turn off a special character set you could type {F10}L{{6x}{Down}~{Up}~ to select the Top Line Menu, type L, press Down Arrow six times, press Enter, press Up Arrow, and press Enter.

Do not leave any spaces that you do not intend Enable to actually type. The following screen shows an example of a simple macro.

```
;;This macro begins telecommunications while I am working in a word processing¶
;;file                                                                          ¶
{OpenW}UTCUENABLE~DATA{^F9}~                                                    ¶
;;This displays the Main Menu; types UTCU (Use System/Telecom/Communicate/      ¶
;;Use Setup; types Enable and presses Enter at the Setup name prompt; types     ¶
;;DATA at the filename prompt; and waits for me to press Enter. If I want I     ¶
;;can complete the name of the capture-to-memory file before I press Enter --   ¶
;;for example, I could type 12, making the name DATA12.

#2          C:${T}.WPM          DRAFT                                  L00008C00
```

Save the Macro When you have finished the macro, save the file in the same way you would any word processing document. You can rename it if you want, but if you do you will be unable to use the macro using the Alt-F9 procedure—you can only use it from a user-defined menu (see Module 116) or from a macro file by using the {Do Macro} command.

If Enable finds an error it will not save the file until you correct the error. Enable highlights the first error it sees, but there may be more.

Using the Macro The macro script is used in the same way you use the Alt-F9 macros. Type Alt-F9 and then press the key (the macro name). The macro must be in the data directory you are using at that moment. You can cancel the macro by pressing Ctrl-Break.

Revising the Macro If you need to modify the macro, type MMR (MCM;Macros;Revise) at the Main Menu. Enable asks you which type of macro. Select the type and then press the macro key (the macro name). Enable displays the file. You can also type MML (MCM;Macros;List) at the Main Menu to see a list of the macros in the data directory. Select the macro and press Enter. (If you renamed the macro with a non-standard name, you will not see it.)

Enable may have changed the macro file's format a bit, as you can see in the following screen, but its basic commands and comments remain the same.

```
;;This macro begins telecommunications while I am working in a word process
;;ing
;;file
{OpenW}
UTCUENABLE~
DATA{^F9}
~
;;This displays the Main Menu; types UTCU (Use System/Telecom/Communicate/
;;Use Setup; types Enable and presses Enter at the Setup name prompt; types
;;
;;DATA at the filename prompt; and waits for me to press Enter. If I want I
;;
;;can complete the name of the capture-to-memory file before I press Enter
;; --
;;for example, I could type 12, making the name DATA12.

#2          C:${T}.WPM          DRAFT                    L00001C001
```

Make your changes and save them as before.

CAUTION

If Enable finds an error and you do not correct it and then save the file, Enable deletes both the original and revised versions of the file.

SPREADSHEET MACROS Spreadsheets have additional macros that are actually stored with the spreadsheets, in a cell or range. This not only means they are always available to that spreadsheet (they can't end up in different directories), but they are compatible with Lotus 1-2-3. There is a limitation with this type of macro though—it only works while the spreadsheet is in the active window, so if you build a macro that calls another window the macro stops until you return to the spreadsheet.

Building the Spreadsheet Macro Enter the macro commands in a column of cells (Enable executes the command in the top cell first, and then works its way down the column). Then name the column—press F10 and type WRNC (Worksheet;Range;Name;Create), and type \ (backslash) and a one-character name. When Enable prompts for the range enter the entire column of commands.

Using the Spreadsheet Macro To use the macro press Shift-F9 and type the one-character range name.

Additional Spreadsheet Macro Commands If the following commands are the first items in a cell, precede them with an alignment character (<, >, or ^) so that Enable does not mistake the slash as the Top Line Menu key.

If-Then decision	/XI(*condition*)~*action*
Go to cell x for more macro commands	/XG*cell~*
Execute a subroutine at cell x	/XC*cell~*
Return from subroutine	/XR
Display message and wait for label entry	/XL*message~cell~*
Display message and wait for number	/XN*message~cell~*
Pause and process user-defined menu	/XM*cell~*
Quit macro	/XQ
Evaluate an Expression	/XE*expression~cell~*

NOTE

Any macro command immediately after /XM, /XL, or /XN is treated as an escape code. If you don't want the command treated as an escape code put it in the next cell down. (Enable 2.0 macros must be revised before you use them.)

Wherever a cell address is requested you can substitute a range name.

Macro Libraries You can build library-files, with the extension .LIB, to store spreadsheet macros. The library has rows of macros, usually with a label to the left of each macro.

Enter @MACRO(*#Filename,"Display cell, Execute cell"*) into a cell in the spreadsheet in which you want to use the macro. Enable asks if you want to activate links with the other spreadsheet now—select Files to activate the link. Enable executes the macro in the *Execute cell* and displays the label from the *Display cell* in the macro cell (if there is no display cell, enter the execute cell twice).

Startup Macros You can make Enable automatically use a macro when you open a file by naming the range \0. You can also execute that macro by pressing Shift-F9 and typing 0.

APPLICATIONS

The uses for macros are numerous. Simple uses include building "glossaries" of boiler-plate text; when you want to enter a commonly used piece of text, just call the macro. You can also use it to build a file—for example, suppose each month you have to build a spreadsheet showing all your department's expenses. You could build a macro that opens the file, fills in the titles and headers, and moves to each cell in turn, waiting for your input and moving to the next cell when you press Enter.

You could even build a simple desktop presentation system, automatically drawing graphs in sequence. Or build tutorials that your employees can use to learn the way you want them to use Enable. You can also use macros to speed up your telecommunications sessions, making them more efficient and cheaper.

TYPICAL OPERATION

In this activity you create a word processing document, create a macro that contains your address, and then use the macro.

1. Create a word processing document.
2. Press **Alt-F9**, \ (Backslash), and type **A**. Notice that MAC is displayed in the status line. Enable will record any keystrokes you make now.
3. Press **Alt-F6** to insert a ruler. Type **L**. Press and hold the **Spacebar** until the cursor has moved to column 40. Type **T** and press **Enter**.
4. Press **Tab** and type the first line of your address.
5. Press **Enter**, press **Tab**, and type the second line of your address. Continue like this, typing your complete address, and end by pressing **Enter**.

6. Press **F10**, type **L2**, and press **Enter** to insert a default ruler. Your screen looks something like this.

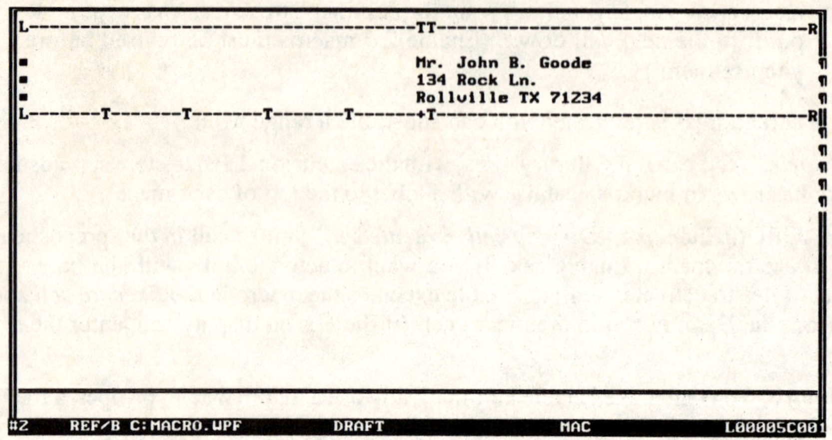

7. Press **Enter** to accept the ruler. Then press **Alt-F9** and **End**. MAC disappears from the status line, and the macro recording has finished.
8. Move the cursor down a few lines, or even to another file in the same directory if you wish. Press **Alt-F9** and type **A**, and Enable enters your address.
9. Turn to Module 116 to continue the learning sequence.

Module 116
MENU GENERATION

DESCRIPTION

Enable has its own extensive menu system, but if you don't like the way the menus work, or if you want to build specialized menus for particular applications, you can build your own.

You can create menus for any application except Graphics, and menus can be used in a particular application or in several applications.

NOTE

> Before you can build menus you must understand how to use macros. See Module 115.

BUILDING MENUS Close all the windows. (You can open more windows later, if you wish, by pressing F10 and typing WM11.) At the Main Menu type MTMC (MCM;Tools;Menus;Create). Enable prompts for a filename.

Menu Names The type of name you enter depends on what you want to do with the menu.

If you want to use the menu from anywhere in Enable by pressing Ctrl-F10 and typing one character; type a one-character filename and press Enter. Enable adds the .MNU extension.

If you want to use the menu in a specific application by pressing Ctrl-F10 and typing one character; type the one-character name and one of the following extensions: .WP (word processing), .SM (spreadsheet), .MC (MCM), .DB (DBMS), and .TP (telecom). Press Enter.

If you want to use the menu in a specific application by pressing Shift-F10 (you don't need to type a character); type WP, SS, DB, TP, or MCM and press Enter—Enable adds the .MNU extension. This is called the default menu, and you can only have five of these, one for each application.

If you want to use a non-standard name you can do so, but such menus can only be used by calling them from a macro file or another menu.

Sizing the Menu Enable now displays two screens of instructions. Press Enter twice to get past them. The next screen is a word processing screen with the Modify-Size border around it. You are going to build a menu "window," the window that Enable displays over the window you are working in when you call the menu. Press S (Shrink), E (Expand), or M (Move) and then press an arrow key to change the size or move the window (or press R to shrink or expand in all directions at once). When you have the menu the size and location you want, press Esc.

Entering the Menu Options Now type the options just as you want to see them in the menu. An example is shown in the following screen.

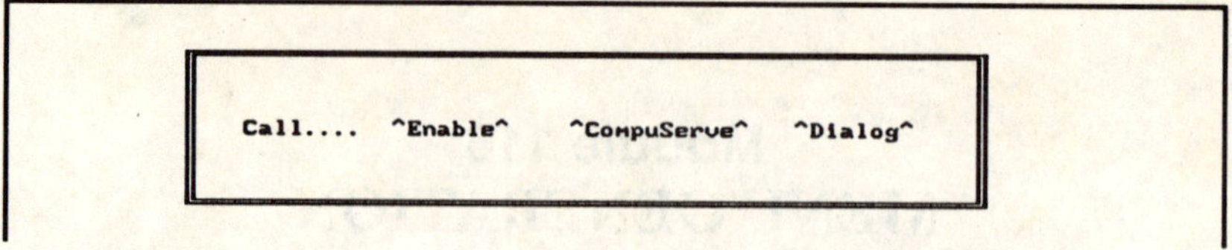

There are two types of menu options: *select-only* and *data-entry*. Select-only options can be selected by moving the cursor to them and pressing Enter or by pressing a key (you specify which key during this procedure). Data-entry options have a space into which the user types data—this data is stored in memory as MNU:*Fieldname*, where *Fieldname* is the name you give the option in the next step. This data is used later on by a macro built into the menu or called from the menu, or can even be used in Dot Command (Procedural Language) reports. The options shown in the previous screen are select-only (they are enclosed by carets). Separate select-only options by at least one space. If you want to use a data-entry option you don't need to use carets; Enable inserts a data-entry field after the option name, so make sure that you leave enough space for the data to the right of the option name.

Entering Option Definitions In the next step you tell Enable what to do with each option. Place the cursor on the space in front of the select-only caret, or to the left of the area the data will be entered (in the case of data-entry options), and press Shift-F9. Enable displays the following screen. Enter a fieldname (it doesn't have to be the same name as the option on the menu). This name is used to call the menu option from macros and other menus.

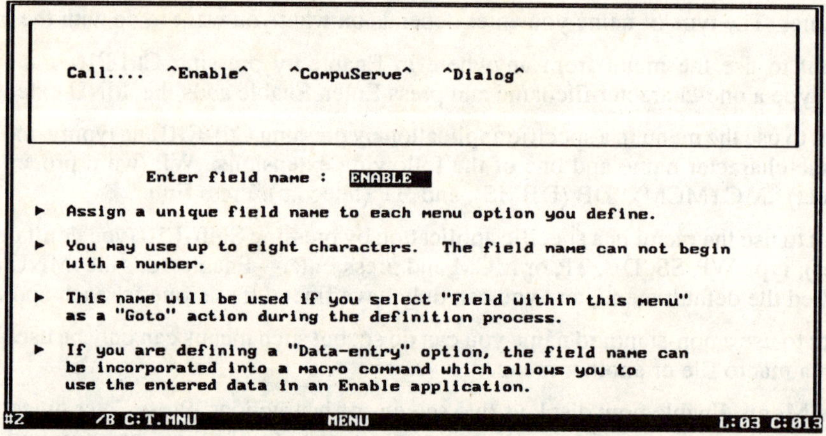

Press Enter to see the first screen of prompts.

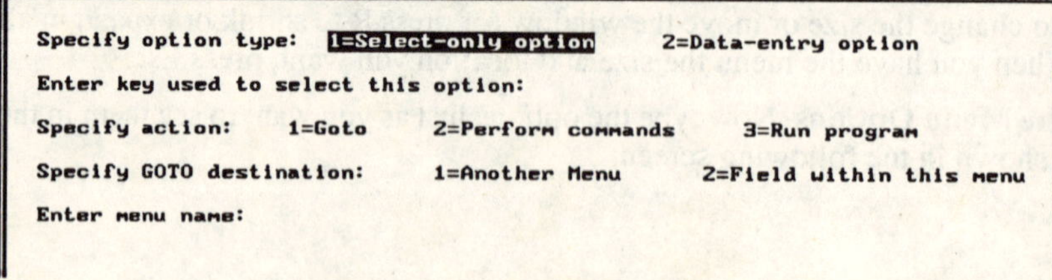

The prompts that follow vary greatly, depending on the "route" you take. The following flow diagram shows which answers lead to which prompts, and the explanations of each prompt follow the diagram. Refer to the diagram as you read the text.

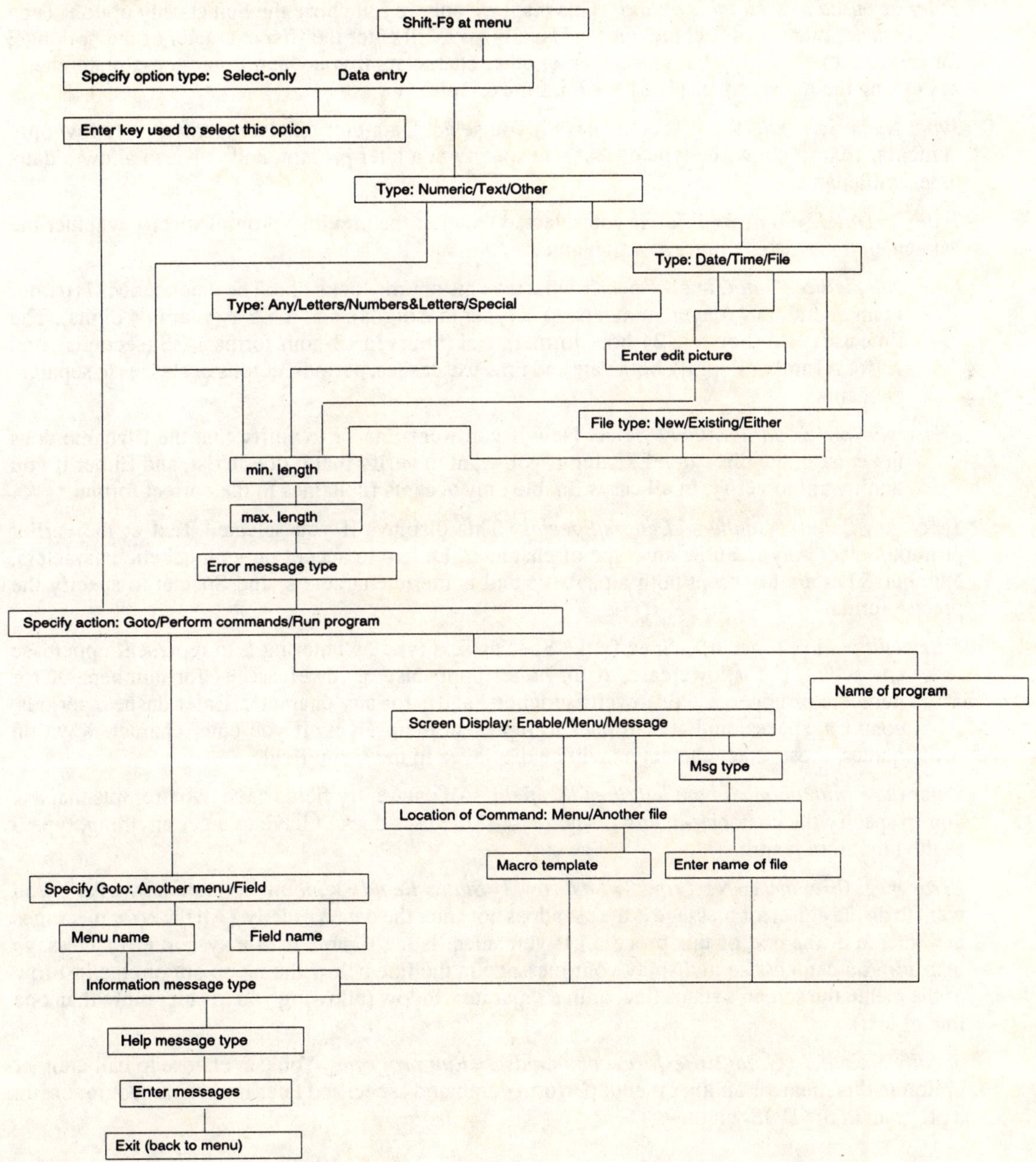

Specify option type: 1=Select-only/2=Data-entry Select the option type. Select-only options initiate some kind of action, while data-entry options let you type in data that is stored by MCM and used in the macro you build or specify later in this procedure.

Enter key used to select this option This displays only if you chose the Select-only option. Type the character that will select the option. Usually you will enter the first character of the option (E for Enable, for example), but you can enter other characters if you want. Enter non-alphanumeric keys using the macro codes ({F5} for F5, for example).

Type: Numeric/Text/Other This displays if you select Data-entry. Select Numeric to allow only numbers, Text to allow the type of text you specify at a later prompt, and Other to allow a date, time, or filename.

Type: 1=Date/2=Time/3=File If you selected Other at the previous prompt specify whether the data entered is a date, a time, or a filename.

Enter edit picture (Date/Time) Specify what the date or time looks like. The date uses MM (month in numbers), DD (day in numbers), YY (year in 2 digits), and YYYY (year in 4 digits). The time uses HM (hours in 24-hour format), HH (hours in 12-hour format), SS (seconds), and X (for A [am] or P [pm]), both date and time use dashes, periods, colons or slashes to separate elements.

File type:New/Existing/Either Select New if you want Enable to verify that the filename does not exist in the directory, Existing if you want to verify that it does exist, and Either if you don't want to verify. In all cases Enable only accepts filenames in the correct format.

Type: Any/Letters/Numbers&Letters/Special This displays if you selected Text at the earlier prompt. Select Any to allow any type of character, Letters to accept only alphabetic characters, Numbers&Letters to accept both alphabetic and numeric characters, and Special to specify the precise format.

Enter edit picture (Special) Specify the Special Text type by entering L to represent uppercase characters, U for lowercase, A for either uppercase or lowercase, N for numbers, X for numbers or uppercase or lowercase letters, and ? for any character. Enter dashes, periods, commas, spaces, and apostrophes to represent themselves. If you enter characters within quotes, those exact characters will be displayed in the menu field.

Enter the minimum/maximum length of this field All data-entry fields have two prompts that ask you to specify the character-length of the field. If the user doesn't have to enter anything, type 0 as the minimum length.

Error msg: 0=None/1=Next row/2=Last row/3=Status line/4=Window Enable now asks if you want to display an error message if the user does not enter the data correctly. (All the error messages are entered at the end of this process.) If you select None Enable uses a system error message instead. You can choose to display your message in the line below the menu option, the last row of the menu, the screen's status line, or in a separate window (allowing you to enter more than one line of text).

Specify action: 1=Goto/2=Perform commands/3=Run program You can choose to call another option in this menu or another menu; perform commands specified later in this procedure; or run a program in the DOS window.

Enter name of program or batch file Enter the disk, directory, filename, and extension (.BAT, .COM, or .EXE) of the program you want to run. In order to use this option you must open Enable using the memory allocation command so that Enable can open a DOS Window. See Module 113 for information about the DOS Window.

Specify GOTO destination: 1=Another menu/2=Field in this menu You can go to another menu, or another field in the same menu.

Enter menu name If you select Another menu Enable prompts for the name of that menu. Include the extension. You can use menus with non-standard names if you want. Enable will display the new menu when the user selects this option. If you want the options in the first menu to remain displayed, add the names to the second menu.

Enter name of existing field or one you will define If you select Field Enable prompts for the fieldname (the name you entered after pressing Shift-F9 at the earlier field). For example, the user could enter data at a field and then automatically move to another option on the menu.

Screen Display: 1=Standard Enable/2=Menu/3=Message This prompt appears if you select Perform commands at the Specify action prompt. This tells Enable what to do with the screen while it is performing commands: remove the menu and display the various Enable screens as the the commands are performed (although you can include {Voff} in the macro you enter later to stop the screens from changing—see the module on macros, Module 115); leave the menu on the screen until Enable has finished the commands (Enable automatically uses {Voff} before beginning); or display a message until Enable has finished the commands (again, Enable uses {Voff}).

NOTE

{Voff} turns off video-display refresh so that you don't see the screen change during the commands. {Von} turns the display back on at the end of the commands, but sometimes Enable does not turn it on properly. You may want to add a {Von} near the end of a macro to ensure the display is turned back on properly. However, {Von} commands at the end of a macro can cause partial screen display. To avoid this, either put the {Von} earlier in the macro, or follow it by another keystroke such as Enter (~) {Up}, or {PgUp}.

Msg type: 1=Next row/2=Last row/3=Status line/4=Window If you selected Message at the previous prompt, Enable lets you select where the message will be displayed: in the row below the menu option, the last row of the menu, the status line, or a separate window. (All the error messages are entered at the end of this process.)

Location of command: 1=Within menu/2=Another file Select Within-menu if you want to enter the macro in this menu procedure, or Another-file if the macro is saved elsewhere.

Macro Template If you select Within-menu Enable displays a template, as shown in the following screen.

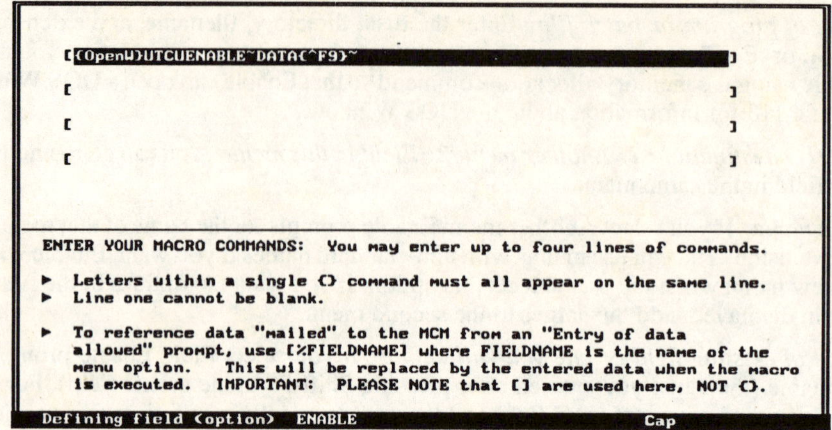

Enter your macro here. You can enter up to four lines of 100 characters each. Do not split commands in braces between lines.

To use the data you input at this or another field, type "[*%Fieldname*]" (replace *Fieldname* with the name of the option that you entered after pressing Shift-F9—this could be another data-entry option in this menu). For example, you might build a menu that prompts for a company name; the macro could then open a Database Interact screen, open the EDIT command screen, open a database, and enter CNAME= at the Index prompt followed by the company name you entered at the menu.

Enter name of file containing macro If the macro is in another file Enable prompts for the name of the file. The file may be in a standard format ($\{x\}$.*yz*M, where *x* is the one-character name and *yz* is WP, SS, GR, DB, TP, or MC); however you can also use non-standard macro names.

Info msg: 0=None/1=Next row/2=Last row/3=Status line/4=Window Enable now asks if you want to display a message, explaining what the option does, when the user puts the cursor on the option. You can choose to display your message in the line below the menu option, the last row of the menu, the screen's status line, or in a separate window (allowing you to enter more than one line of text).

Help msg: 0=None/1=Next row/2=Last row/3=Status line/4=Window Enable now asks if you want to display a message if the user presses F1 while the cursor is on this menu option.

Entering messages After you complete the last prompt Enable returns you to the menu, if you have not requested any messages. If you have requested error, info, or help messages Enable asks you to define them now. If you selected the Window-message options Enable displays a screen modify-size box so that you can build a special window to hold the message; otherwise Enable displays a message entry space, as shown in the following screen. Enter the message and press Shift-F9 to display the entry space for the next message or return to the menu.

```
Call....  ^Enable^   CompServe^   ^Dialog^

INFORMATION MESSAGE DISPLAYED WHEN CURSORS RESTS ON OPTION

                    <Next Row>
Only one line of text will be displayed when you use the menu,
regardless of the number of lines you enter here.

After you have entered (or revised) the one line of text, then
press SHIFT/F9 to save the text and continue.

  Calls up the Compuserve Setup

#2      /B C:T.MNU          MENU                       L:01 C:030
```

MENU COLORS If you have a color monitor you can specify the color of the background, characters, and cursor. At the menu press F10 and type FC (Form Design Options;Color), and Enable displays the Colors Menu.

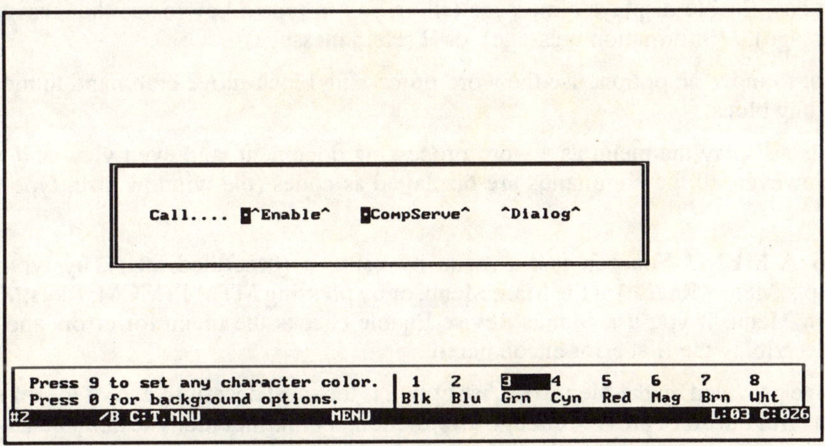

(You can also turn this menu on and off by pressing Shift-F1.)

To specify the color of the characters, type 9 and then the number corresponding to the color. You can then type the characters, or use the word processing text segment commands to apply the color to existing text: Ctrl-C to apply it to a character, Ctrl-W for a word, Ctrl-L for a line, Ctrl-S for a sentence, or Ctrl-P for a paragraph.

To specify the color of the background type 0 and Enable displays the Background Options Menu. Type the number corresponding to the background you want to change (the window and character backgrounds, all the character backgrounds, only the window, or specific character backgrounds) and Enable displays another list of colors; type the number of the color you want. The color immediately changes unless you selected specific-character background, in which case you apply the color with the text segment commands. You can also type 5 at the Background options to change the color intensity.

Applying Color to the Cursor To define the color of the cursor when it is placed on this option apply a background color to the caret (^) immediately before the Select-only option. Select the color, place the cursor on the caret, and press Ctrl-C.

Applying Color to Messages You can apply color to the messages. When Enable displays the message entry space at the end of the option definition procedure, turn on the Color Menu, select a color, and type the text. Or, use the steps already described to apply the colors to existing text.

Removing and Changing Colors To remove colors, press Alt-N and then use the text segment commands to "apply" the removal to the text. To change a color, remove the previous one before trying to apply the new one.

SAVING THE MENU When you have finished building your menu press F10 and type FS (Form Design Options;Save) and press Enter to save the menu with the same name. Then press F10 and type FQQ to close the document.

REVISING A MENU You can revise a menu while you are still displaying the file, or return to the file later by closing all the windows and typing MTMR (MCM;Tools;Menus;Revise). To change your responses to the prompts, place the cursor on the block in front of the option and press Shift-F9; Enable displays the prompts again. To view the messages without going through the prompt sequence, place the cursor on the block and look at the status line—for each type of message the option has, Enable displays a message telling you to type a key to see the message. Type E (Error message), I (Information message), or H (Help message).

If you want to move an option, use the word processing block-move command to move the text and preceding block.

You can also display the menu as a word processing document, and even view and modify the macros. However, all the commands are displayed as codes (the window size, type identifiers, etc.).

TESTING A MENU You can test a menu by using it (described later), by typing MTMR (MCM;Tools;Menus;Revise) at the Main Menu, or by pressing MTMT (MCM;Tools;Menus;Test) at the Main Menu. If you use Menus/Revise Enable checks the menu for errors and displays a message describing the first error encountered.

The message provided by the Menus/Revise option is the most descriptive, so if the other methods indicate an error but don't provide enough information, try this method. The document is displayed as a word processing document with arrows pointing to the error. Correct the error, delete the lines with the arrows, and save the file.

USING THE MENUS To use a default menu (xx.MNU) press Shift-F10 and Enable displays the menu. To use a single-character-name menu, press Shift-F10 and Enable prompts for the name. Type the character and Enable displays the menu. Menus with an extension of .MNU can be used in any application. Those with any other extension can only be called from the correct application.

If two menus have the same name (for example, T.MNU and T.WP) and you are in the appropriate application (in this case word processing), Enable uses the menu designed specifically for that application, not the .MNU menu.

Once you have called a menu, use it like a usual Enable menu, pressing arrow keys to move around and pressing Enter or typing a character to select an option.

PROCEDURAL LANGUAGE COMMANDS Information entered into menus can be used in procedural language commands. Refer to MNU:*fieldname* in the command. For example, if the fieldname is COST, the data entered at COST is stored in MNU:COST.

APPLICATIONS

These special menus are extensions of macros. The difference is that you can call a list of macros by typing one character—you don't have to remember the names of each macro, just select them straight from the menu. You can also enter information to be used by the macro. You can use these menus to customize Enable for your specific applications, or to let you call up other programs while you are working in Enable. For example, you might want to use a grammar-checking program in the DOS window while you remain in Enable.

TYPICAL OPERATION

In this activity you use the address-macro you built in Module 115 in a menu. That macro should be in the same data directory as the one you are currently using.

1. At the Main Menu type **MTMC**. When Enable prompts for a name type **A.WP** and press **Enter**.
2. Press **Enter** twice and Enable displays the modify-window-size screen. Type **S** and use the arrow keys to shrink the window until it looks about the same as the screen shown below. Press **Esc**.
3. Type **^Enter Address^**, **Date**, and **Ref #** in the positions shown on the next screen.
4. Move the cursor to the space before the first caret and press **Shift-F9**. Enable displays the following screen. Type **ADDR** and press **Enter**.

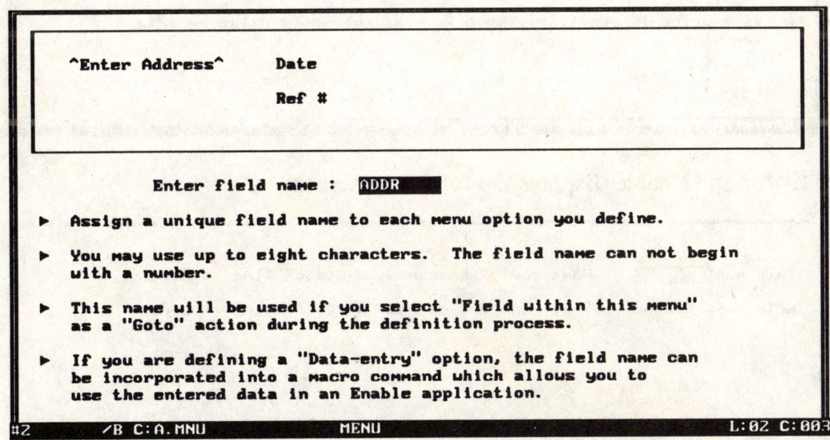

5. Type **1** to choose "Select-only option," type **E** as the key to be used to select the option, and press **Enter**. Then type **2322** to select the following choices: 2=Perform commands, 3=Message, 2=Last row, 2=Another file. Your screen looks like the following:

```
Specify option type:   1=Select-only option        2=Data-entry option

Enter key used to select this option:  E

Specify action:     1=Goto       2=Perform commands      3=Run program

Screen Display:    1=Standard Enable     2=Menu     3=Message

Msg type:   1=Next row  2=Last row  3=Status line   4=Window

Location of commands:   1=Within Menu            2=Another file

▶  Select this option if the macro commands you wish to execute are
   contained in a macro file on disk.

Revising field (option)  ADDR
```

6. On the next page type **${a}.wpm** at the filename prompt. This is the name of the macro file built in Module 115.

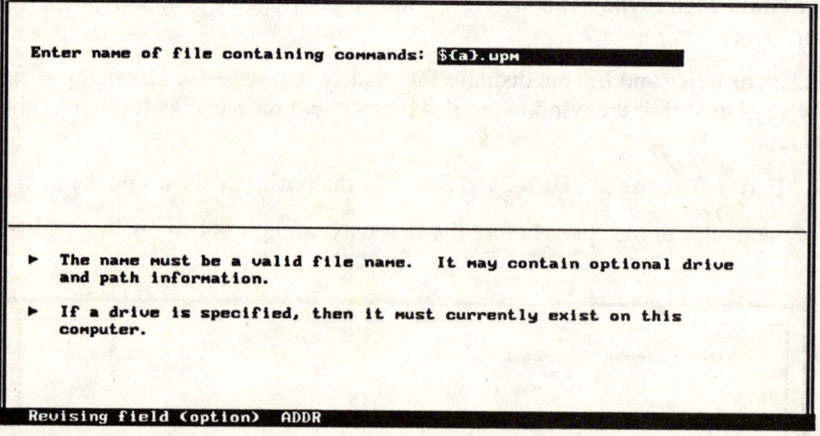

7. Press **Enter** and Enable displays the following screen.

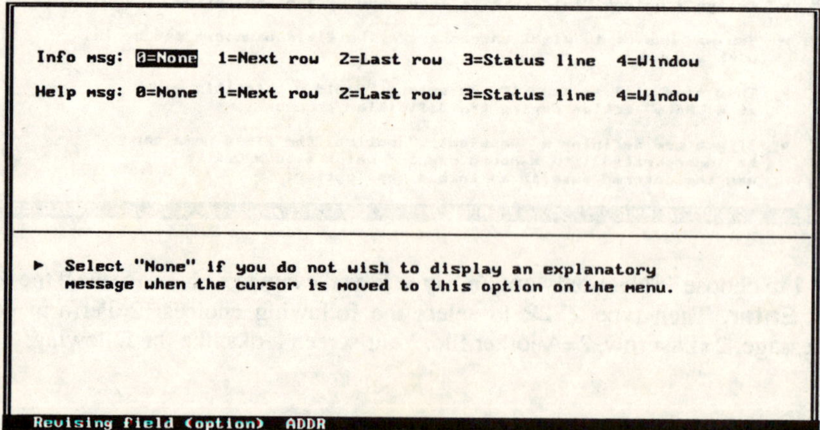

8. Press **Enter** twice and Enable prompts for the message displayed when the macro begins. Type **Typing address into letter...**

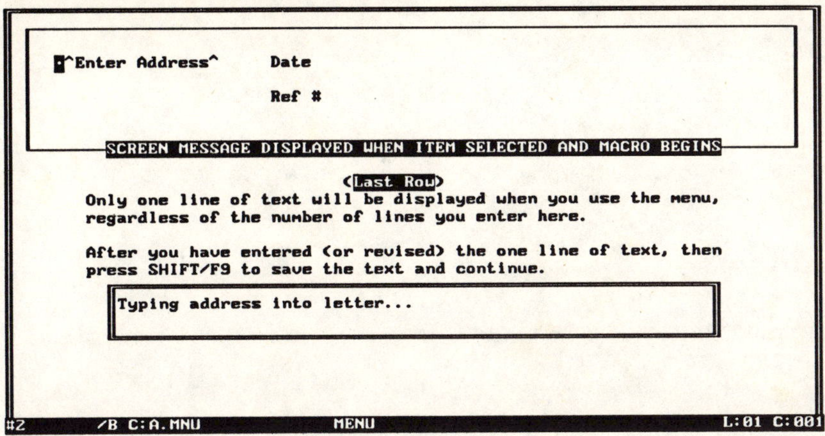

9. Press **Shift-F9** to save the message and then press **F10** and type **FSS** to save the file. Press **F10** and type **FQQ** to close the file.
10. Create a word processing document. Press **Enter** to accept the default ruler. Press **Ctrl-F10** and Enable prompts you for the menu's name. Type **A** and the menu is displayed (A is the name you gave the file in step 1).
11. Type **E** and Enable displays the message in the last line.

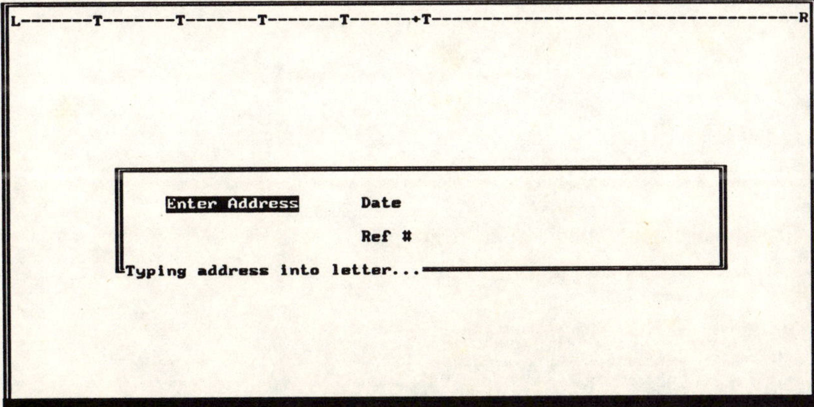

12. Enable enters your address for you. Press **F10** and type **QY** to close the file without saving.

NOTE

You could also define the other options in the menu as data-entry, and build macros to use the entries to type the date and a reference number into your letter.

This completes the learning sequence.

Appendix A
TERMS AND DEFINITIONS

Term	*Definition*
@function	A built-in formula, allowing you to use complicated spreadsheet formulas without building them yourself. (See Module 74.)
Address	The location of a spreadsheet cell, identified by the column and row intersection; for example, G5. Often used to reference a cell in a formula.
Alt (Alternate Key)	The Alt key is used in combination with other keys to execute commands, bypassing system menus. Alt is held down while the associated key is pressed.
Anchor Cell	The spreadsheet cell from which a range is pointed out (the first cell, where you type a period to begin pointing out the address).
Argument	Data acted upon by an @function, usually enclosed in parentheses.
ASCII	Abbreviation for the American Standard Code for Information Interchange. It uses decimal and hexadecimal numbers to represent characters.
Asynchronous Transmission	A communications mode where a start and stop bit are inserted between every 8-bit word. Most PC communications (including Enable's) are asynchronous.
Automatic Date	A word processing function that automatically inserts the current date in a document.
Automatic Reformat	A word processing feature that automatically adjusts text to maintain margins when characters are inserted or deleted.
Back up	To make a copy of a file on another disk as a security measure in case the original is damaged or destroyed.
Bar Graph	A graph representing data with vertical bars.
Baud Rate	Unit of measurement of the speed of data transmission (the number of signaling elements per second). This is not always the same as bits per second.
Bit	A binary digit—the smallest unit of information in a computer. Bits are 1 or 0, and are grouped in bytes (8 bits) to represent characters.
Block	A highlighted rectangle of text, spreadsheet cells, or database records that can be copied, moved, deleted, or saved.
Border Area	The area at the top and left of a spreadsheet that identifies the rows and columns.
Bulletin Board	A computerized method for users to receive and leave messages.
Cell	A rectangular box at the intersection of a spreadsheet row and column, where information is entered.
Cell Address, Absolute	A spreadsheet cell address that refers to a specific cell and does not change when the formula containing the address is moved or copied. Uses the format A1.

Term	*Definition*
Cell Address, Mixed	A spreadsheet cell address where one element (the row or column) is absolute and the other is relative. See Cell Address, Absolute, and Cell Address, Relative.
Cell Address, Relative	A spreadsheet cell address contained in a formula that refers to a cell by its position relative to the cell containing the formula. The address changes if you move or copy the formula. Uses the format A1. For example, if a formula containing A1 is moved two cells to the right, A1 becomes C1.
Cell Indicator	A code appearing in the spreadsheet's information display area that indicates the cell's format.
Character	A letter, number, punctuation, or special symbol.
Circular Reference	See Reference, Circular. A spreadsheet formula that refers to formulas that in turn refer back to the first formula.
Column	A vertical line of cells in a spreadsheet, labeled with a letter in the border area.
Column Width	The width, in characters, of a spreadsheet column.
Command	Any function performed through a series of keystrokes or by selecting from a menu.
Comment	(1) Lines of text in a word processing document that do not print out. (2) Text in dot command, macro, mapping table, or modem table scripts (preceded by ;;), that is not regarded as a command.
Communications (COMM) Port	The port used by a computer to transmit data to a modem, serial printer, or plotter.
Concatenation	The combining of two spreadsheet or database text strings.
Copy	To duplicate text, data, spreadsheet cells, or graphics in another file or within the same file.
Ctrl (Control key)	The Ctrl key is used in combination with other keys to execute commands, bypassing system menus. Ctrl is held down while the associated key is pressed.
Cubic Range	A spreadsheet range that spans two or more levels in a 3D spreadsheet. See Range.
Cursor	A symbol on the screen that indicates the position of the next typed character.
Data Group	Spreadsheet cells or database fields used to draw a graph.
Database	A collection of information grouped into logical units called *records*.
Database Definition	The description of a database that tells Enable how to group the data and what to do with it.
Database Description	An optional database "title" that describes the purpose of the database.
DBMS	Database Management System, the Enable application that builds and uses databases.
DBMS Command Chart	See Interact Screen.
Default	A standard setting that tells Enable what to do if the user does not make a selection.
Delete	To remove a character in word processing, or cell contents in a spreadsheet. The meaning in the database application is significantly different—deleted records are not actually removed, they are simply labeled as deleted. They can later be restored or destroyed.

Term	Definition
Destroy	To permanently remove deleted records from a database, or a file from the file directory.
Directory of Files	A list of files on a disk. Provides file-management features such as copy, delete, sort, etc.
Disk Drive	A piece of hardware that stores computer data on a disk.
DOS	Disk Operating System. The program used to give your computer basic commands. It is the foundation that Enable sits upon.
Dot Commands	Programming-type commands used in the DBMS application. The commands are always preceded with a period, thus "dot" command. (See also Procedural Language.)
Draft Form	The word processing editing mode. (See also Final Form.)
Duplex	A data transmission mode in which the computers both use the same lines to transmit data to each other. Full Duplex allows the computers to transmit simultaneously; in Half Duplex the computers take turns.
Edit	To change text or data.
Edit Mode	The mode, accessed by pressing F4, in which you can edit spreadsheet cells.
Embedded Commands	Word processing commands that cause the printer to perform special functions such as printing the date or including another file.
Error Messages	Messages displayed on the screen that indicate incorrect conditions.
Expert Commands	Keystroke sequences that let you bypass menus to execute commands more efficiently and quickly.
Exploded Pie Chart	A pie chart with one or more wedges separated from the main body of the chart.
Extended Functions Directory	A directory of files, reached from the Directory of Files, that provides more advanced file-management commands.
Extension	See File Extension.
False	A logical state, the opposite of True. The system may perform a spreadsheet or database function based on whether a specified condition is true or false.
Field	The smallest unit of data in a database. Records consist of one or more fields of data.
File	A collection of data stored together with a specified name.
File Extension	The part of a filename following a period, up to 3 characters. Indicates the type of file. FILENAME.WPF indicates a word processing document. In some cases the extension is optional.
File Summary Screen	A screen that displays information about the word processing file currently displayed in the window.
Final Form	A word processing display mode in which the document appears as it will when printed. (Also See Draft Form.)
Find	A word processing and DBMS command that searches for specified text or data.
Footer	Information repeated at the bottom of each printed page in a word processing, spreadsheet, or DBMS document.

Term	Definition
Format	(1) DOS procedure that prepares disks for use. (2) Word processing arrangement of text using the Layout commands. (3) The way a file is stored, which defines which programs can use the file (Enable format, WordStar format, etc.) (4) The way that numbers are displayed in a spreadsheet or graphic.
Formula	A spreadsheet instruction that determines the cell contents.
Function Keys	The keys labeled F1 to F10 (or F12). Used to carry out certain commands.
Hardware	The physical components of a computer system (the disk drives, monitor, computer boards, etc.)
Header	Text that is automatically repeated at the top of each page in a word processing, spreadsheet, or database document.
Hidden Column	A spreadsheet column with a width of 0. You cannot see the contents of the column until you use a command to reset the column width.
High-Low-Close Graph	A special type of XY graph typically used to present stock prices.
Index	(1) An alphabetical listing of terms in a word processing document. (2) An alphanumeric listing of values in particular fields in a database.
Information Display Area	The area at the top of a spreadsheet that contains menus, mode labels, and cell addresses and contents.
Input Form	An on-screen form used in DBMS to enter data into a database.
Interact Screen	A list of DBMS commands also called the DBMS Command Chart. Serves as the DBMS "Main Menu."
Justification	The alignment of text to produce a straight margin.
Label	A text entry in a spreadsheet cell intended for display only, not for use in commands.
Landscape and Portrait Modes	The way text, data, or graphs are printed on the paper—lengthwise (landscape), or sideways (portrait).
Layout Options	Word processing options used to define the layout of the text.
Legends	Data group labels in a graph.
Line Graph	A graph in which each data group is plotted as a series of points joined by a line.
Logical Operators	Words in spreadsheet formulas and DBMS commands used to express conditions. Also called Boolean operators, they are AND, OR, and NOT.
Macro	A series of keystrokes stored in a macro file that allow you to perform a series of commands by pressing three keys. Also called keyboard mapping in telecommunications.
Mail Merge	A feature that generates form letters, documents, and labels using a special document and a database of names and addresses.
Main Menu	The menu displayed after the Sign-On screen or when you open a window.
Mapping	A procedure using Transmit/Receive Tables to filter telecommunications data before it is transmitted or after it is received.
Marked Records	DBMS records highlighted in DISPLAY or BROWSE modes. They can be manipulated as a group.
Marked Text	Sections of text highlighted in a word processing document. Unlike a block, marked text does not have to be contiguous.
Master Control Module (MCM)	The module that controls the integration of the individual Enable applications. Controls windows, file-management, menu generation, profiles, and macros.

Term	*Definition*
Mathematical Operator	A symbol, such as = or *, that represents a mathematical procedure.
Menu	A list of options. Enable has various different types of menus: the Main Menu (displayed when you first enter Enable); the Top Line Menu (displayed when you press F10 in applications); user-generated menus (displayed when you press Shift-F10 or Ctrl-F10 and a code); and the DBMS Interact screen (displayed when you type UDI at the Main Menu).
Mode Indicator	The block in the top right of a spreadsheet that indicates the current operation.
Modem	The device that converts a computer's digital information into the analog signal that can be transmitted on phone lines.
Modem Tables	"Scripts" that let you use modems that Enable does not normally support, or modify the way a modem operates.
Monitor	The video display connected to your computer. You may also see the terms VDT, CRT, terminal, console, display, screen, and video.
Numeric Tabs	Tabs used to align columns of numbers in word processing.
Outline Format	An automatic procedure for adding section headings to word processing documents.
Page Form	Format options for printing documents.
Paper Clip	A way to mark a word processing page so you can refer to it later.
Paragraph Markers	The ¶ character displayed on the right margin, indicating the end of a paragraph.
Parity	Error checking method during data transmission.
Pie Chart	A graph in which the values are represented by wedges in a circle.
Plotter	A device used to draw graphs. Generally gives better resolution than a graphics printer and may be able to plot with colors.
Pointer	The block in a spreadsheet that indicates the cell you are working in.
Pointing	Highlighting a rectangular group of spreadsheet cells (a range) so that you can use them in a command.
Print Density	The number of dots per inch used when printing a graph. The higher the density the better the resolution.
Print Form	The format used for printing documents.
Procedural Language	A series of dot commands used to produce database reports.
Profile	A set of instructions telling Enable how to operate in each application. Each user can personalize his or her own profile.
Protection	A feature that protects spreadsheet cells from being changed.
Protocol	A set of specifications used to establish the telecommunications connection between two computers.
Quit	An option that closes a file without saving changes.
RAM	Random Access Memory. The computer's memory that provides temporary storage of data.
Range	A rectangular group of spreadsheet cells which are treated as a group in certain commands.
Range Marker	The cell in a range diagonally opposite the Anchor Cell.
Record	A set of related fields of data in a database.
Reference, Circular	See Circular Reference.
Report Form	The DBMS form used to design the format of a printed report.

Term	Definition
Restore	The feature that retrieves archived or backed-up database records and files.
Row	A horizontal line of cells in a spreadsheet, labeled with a number in the Border Area.
Ruler	The word processing feature that defines the page margins, tabs, and centering point.
Save	The command used to store data in a file on a disk.
Scrolling	Moving to areas of a file or document that are not currently displayed on the screen.
Select Set	A subset of database records created using FIND or SORT.
Setup	A file containing instructions that tell Enable how to establish a telecommunications link with another computer.
Sign-On Screen	The first screen Enable displays when you start the program.
Sort	Arranging database records in alphanumeric order, or arranging lines or paragraphs in a word processing document.
Special Character Set	Characters that are not on the typical keyboard.
Split Window	A spreadsheet window split into two parts so you can view different sections of the spreadsheet at the same time.
Spreadsheet	An electronic version of an accounting spreadsheet, that allows you to enter complex formulas and automatically makes calculations for you.
Stacked Bar Graph	A bar graph with data groups displayed as shaded or colored bars stacked on top of each other.
Start Bit	A bit used in asynchronous communications to indicate the beginning of a character.
Start-Up	Starting the Enable program.
Status Line	A line at the bottom of each window providing information about current operations, the cursor position, the file, and so on.
Stop Bit	A bit used in asynchronous telecommunications to indicate the end of a character.
String	Text entered into a spreadsheet cell.
Synchronous Transmission	A communications mode that does not use start and stop bits. The data is sent at regular intervals and the sender and receiver are synchronized with each other. More efficient than asynchronous transmission.
System Status Screen	A screen that lists information about open windows.
Table of Authorities	A list of references and their page numbers, built automatically in word processing.
Table of Contents	A list of topics and their page numbers, built automatically in word processing.
Tabs	Alignment settings for columns and indentations in word processing. Indicated on the ruler.
Telecommunications	A procedure using telephone networks to transmit data.
Text Attributes	Special text formats, such as boldface, underlined, and superscript.
Text Segment Commands	Commands used to apply text attributes to segments of text.
Three Dimensional (3D) Spreadsheet	A spreadsheet with up to 32 pages or *levels*, allowing large amounts of data to be managed more easily. The user can view one, two, or three levels at once.

Term	*Definition*
Toggles	Commands that alternately turn options on and off.
Top Line Menu	A menu displayed at the top of the screen indicating available options. Displayed by pressing F10.
True	A logical state, the opposite of False. The system may perform a spreadsheet or database function based on whether a specified condition is true or false.
Turnaround Character	A special character used in telecommunications to indicate that the other computer may now transmit data.
Unattended File Transfer	Transmitting files automatically when the user is not present. Achieved using an Unattended File Transfer script to give Enable commands.
Undelete	A command that removes a database record's "deleted" label.
User-Defined Shorthand	A word processing feature that allows you to type a few characters to represent a much longer string of characters.
Where Clause	A set of conditions in a database command that selects the records to be operated on.
Wild Card	A character used to replace one or more characters when searching for text in word processing (FIND), using Where Clauses and Index Search Statements in DBMS, or searching for files in the directories.
Window	A screen "page" that contains an open file. Enable can use up to eight windows at once. You can move from window to window, and by reducing the sizes you can display several at the same time.
Worksheet	Another common term for a spreadsheet.
X-Axis	The horizontal line at the bottom of a graph.
Xon/Xoff Protocol	A telecommunications protocol used to send stop and go signals so that data is only transmitted when the receiving computer is ready.
XY Graph	A graph in which values are plotted according to both the X- and Y-axis values, unlike a standard Line Graph in which the values are plotted along against the Y-axis in the order they appear in the data group.
Y-Axis	The vertical line at the side of a graph.

Appendix B
PROFILES

INTRODUCTION

User profiles let you customize Enable, modifying hundreds of features to work the way your hardware or applications dictate. Profiles are sets of instructions that tell Enable how to operate. You can have several different profiles; one for each user, for example. Profiles are stored in a file called PROFILE.$PR (or PROF$*xx*.$PR, where *xx* is your network ID).

Enable comes with several profiles: DEFAULT, COLOR, TUTORL, and TUTOR. When you log on to Enable you can bypass the profile prompts by pressing End—Enable automatically uses the profile called DEFAULT in that case.

You can change the DEFAULT profile to suit you, rename DEFAULT and create a new profile called DEFAULT, or create a profile with a different name and type that name when you logon.

MODIFYING A PROFILE

Close all windows before opening profiles. At the Main Menu type MP (MCM;Profiles). Enable displays an instruction screen. Press Enter and Enable displays the following screen.

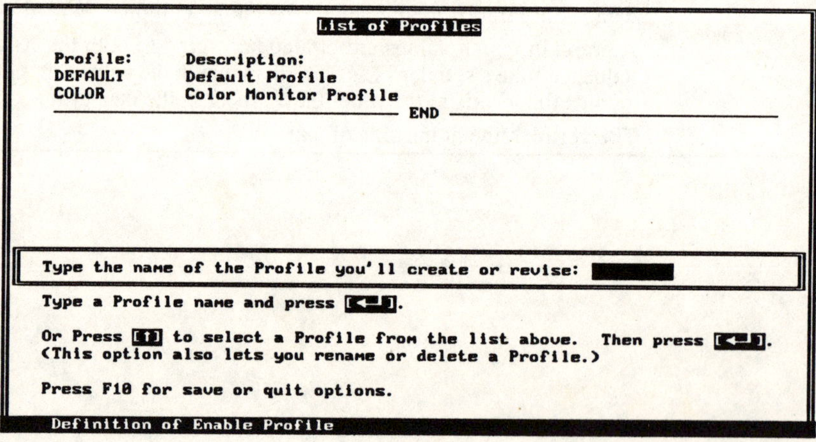

Press Up Arrow to move the cursor into the list of profiles; select a profile and press Enter. Or, type the name of a new or existing profile and press Enter. Enable displays the next screen, listing the different categories of information.

```
                         Categories

Profile description:  Default Profile

1. HARDWARE           Printer and plotter options
2. PAGE FORM          Page size, top and bottom margins
3. SPECIAL TEXT       Screen display of bold, italics, etc.
4. WORD PROCESSING    Word Processing options, including Print Form
5. TELECOMMUNICATIONS Quick-connect and Terminal emulation options
6. DATABASE           Database options
7. SPREADSHEET        Spreadsheet options
8. GRAPHICS           Graphics options
9. SYSTEM             Special system-wide options

► Use the highlighted space to type in a description of the Profile.

► Press [Esc] to return to previous menu.

► Press [↓] to select a category.

  Revising DEFAULT Profile     Esc=Exit Menu     F10=Exit Profile
```

CHANGING INFORMATION IN A CATEGORY

Move through the screens by typing the first character of each choice, or by moving the cursor to the choice and pressing Down Arrow or Enter. Placing the cursor on a choice and then saving the profile is not sufficient—you must press Enter or Down Arrow before saving. The following text lists and explains the items in each category.

1. HARDWARE

Do you want to change the printer options? Select No to go straight to the plotter options.

Current printer: The name of your printer. Press F7 to select from a list of printers "installed" when you used Enable's installation procedure. If you do not select a printer you may still be able to do simple printing.

Should printer connection be verified? Tells Enable to check the printer's connection before beginning printing, and display an error message if there are problems.

Type of printer interface: Select Parallel or Serial.

Which parallel port are you using? Select LPT1, LPT2, or LPT3.

Which serial port are you using? Select COMM1 or COMM2.

Baud rate:—Select a baud rate from 110 to 9600.

Select one of the options listed below: Select the correct protocol, or select option 4 to specify your own protocol.

Do you wish to change the plotter options? Select No to bypass the plotter options.

Enter plotter code: Select from a list of 10 plotters, displayed at the bottom of the page.

Type of plotter interface: Select Parallel or Serial.

Plotter output should be directed to: Select COMM1, COMM2, or File if you selected a serial plotter-port. You can redirect the output to a different location just before plotting.

Baud rate:—Select a baud rate from 110 to 9600.

Select one of the options listed below: Select the correct protocol, or select option 4 to specify your own protocol.

Does your hardware use Xon/Xoff protocol? Check your printer's documentation.

2. PAGE FORM

The prompts in this section are the same as those found in the Page Form accessed from the Top Line Menu. For example, in word processing, press F10, type P, and press PgDn twice. See Module 35, Print, in the Word Processing section of this book.

3. SPECIAL TEXT

Enable displays the following screen.

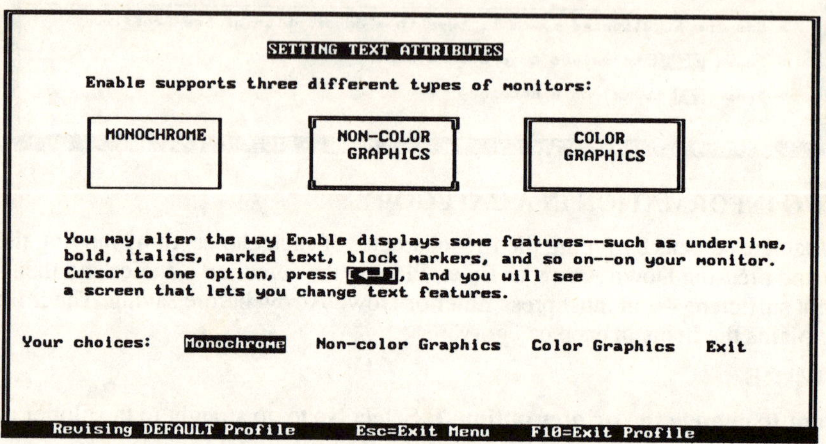

Your choices: Monochrome/Non-color Graphics/Color Graphics Select your monitor type.

Monochrome Enable displays the following screen if you select Monochrome.

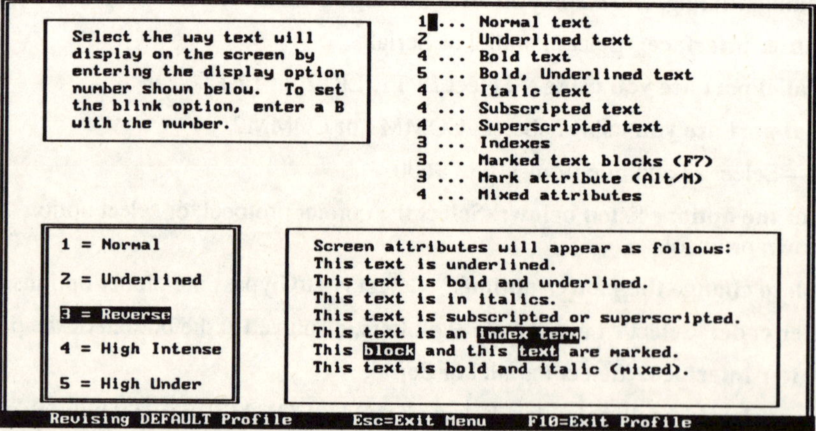

For each type of text listed in the top right of the screen select one of the options in the bottom left. The box in the bottom right shows you what your selections look like. Type B, for example, if you want the text to blink.

Non-color Graphics If you select Non-color Graphics Enable displays the following screen.

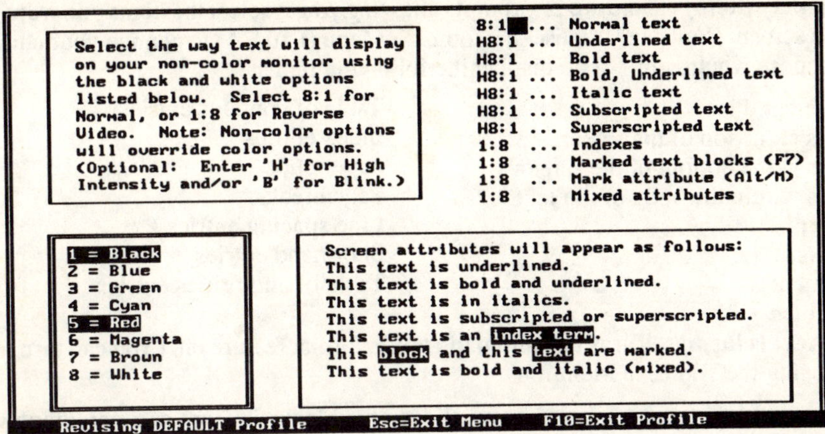

For each type of text listed in the top right of the screen select one of the options in the bottom left. Use only 1 and 8 (black and white). 8:1 is normal, and 1:8 is reverse video. The box in the bottom right shows you what your selections look like. Type B if you want the text to blink, or H if you want to use High Intensity.

Color Graphics If you select Color Graphics you see the following screen. You can select any of the colors. The first number is the character color; the second number (entered if you want to highlight the text) is the highlight color. You can also use B and H, as in the other screens.

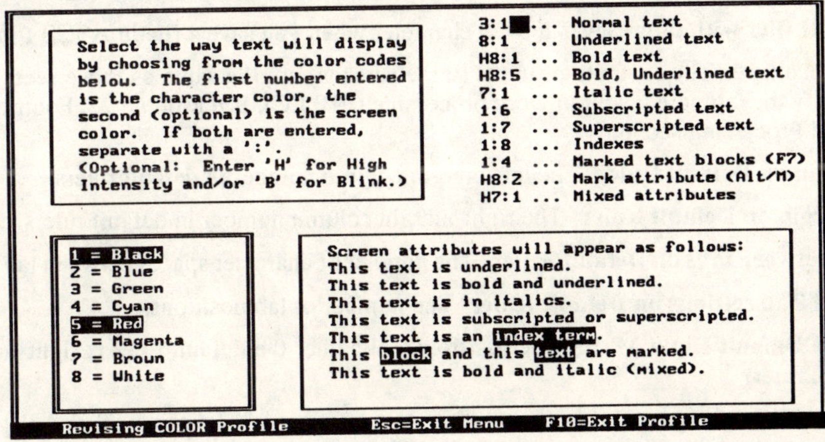

4. WORD PROCESSING

Yes No...Display (item) There are 15 prompts allowing you to select the items you want to display on the screen. (You can later use the Top Line Menu (F10 EA) to change your choices.) You can choose whether or not do display the following items:

Document titles	Table of contents entries
Rulers at the top of the screen	Index entries
Rulers at the bottom of the screen	Paper clips
Rulers within the body of the text	Page breaks
Headers	Line spacing entries
Footers	Shorthand entries
Comments	Table of authorities entries
Footnotes	

Automatic text reformat Turns the automatic text reformat feature on. (You can turn it off or on later using the Top Line Menu.)

Leading blanks retained during reformat Keeps the blanks in front of a paragraph when you reformat it.

Document title prompt in new document Displays the Document Title entry space when you create a new document.

Do you wish to be prompted to verify text deletion? If you delete text using the Top Line Menu Enable asks you to confirm by typing Y.

Backup existing files when saving When you save a file Enable saves the previous version in a .WP@ file.

Display tab characters in document Displays a block each time you press Tab.

Save ASCII files with tabs Saves the tab character when you save a file in ASCII format.

Footnote prompts The footnote prompts (three screens) are the same as those seen when you modify the footnote layout in word processing (F10 LC). See Module 23, Footnotes, in the Word Processing section.

Left Margin on Default Ruler The left-margin column number in default rulers.

Right Margin on Default Ruler The right-margin column number in default rulers.

Distance between tabs on Default Ruler The number of character spaces between tab positions.

Number of Tab settings on Default Ruler The number of tab positions.

Should the Default Right Margin be justified? Whether the default ruler is right-justified (R in the ruler).

Should the F2/Right position to space after last character? Pressing F2 and Right Arrow moves the cursor to the space after the last character on the line if you select Yes, or the last character if you select No.

Number of keystrokes between automatic document saves: Enter 0 if you do not want to use automatic document save. Otherwise, enter the number of keystrokes. Enable saves the work in a file named TMPWP00*n*.WPF, where *n* is the window number.

Number of copies: (and subsequent prompts) This page of prompts is from the first page of the Print Form (F10 P). See Module 35, Print.

Table of Contents prompts These 7 or 8 prompts are from the Modify Table of Contents options (F10 L94). See Module 44, Table of Contents.

Select Master Dictionary: You can select the standard, legal, or medical dictionaries for use in the Spell Check.

Enter user dictionary path: Tells Enable where the Spell Check user dictionary is filed (the pathname).

5. TELECOMMUNICATIONS

Baud rate: Specify the default baud rate for transmissions.

Select one of the options described below: Select the default transmission protocol.

Select type of Duplex: Choose the default duplex, Half or Full.

Which of your computer's COMM ports are you using? Select COMM1, COMM2, or Z404.

Key to stop script: Select Esc or Alt-E. Early revisions of EnableOA do not include this option. Using the chosen key while an unattended-transfer script is running aborts the script.

Terminal Emulation? Select No emulation, VT-100, VT52, or AT&T4410.

Transmission type? Select Polled or Interrupt. Interrupt-driven format can cause data loss, so Polled is the standard. (Received data is always Interrupt-driven.)

Modem table choice: Select ACOM or BCOM. This allows you to have two sets of modem tables, ACOM*n*.TPX and BCOM*n*.TPX, where *n* is the COMM number.

Filtered disk capture: You can use the same filtering, mapping, and 8th-bit stripping used by Capture-to-memory for Capture-to-disk, or you can save "raw" data on the disk.

Prompt for Quick-connect background capture file: You can tell Enable not to display the filename prompt when you begin a Quick-Connect session (the file is used for Capture-to-memory).

6. DATABASE

Database Creation Format? You can select EnableOA (the default) or Enable 2.0 formats. If you select EnableOA, the created file: is compatible with dBASE III, but not dBASE II; has as many records as your disk can store; and must be indexed if you want to use it on an earlier version of Enable (which will only be able to use the first 65,536 records).

If you select Enable 2.0 format, the file: is compatible with dBASE II, but not dBASE III; is fully compatible with EnableOA; and can only have 65,536 records.

Pass thru? Select Yes if you want to allow data looked-up in one database to be modified and the change "passed thru" to the database the information came from.

Numeric fields in ADD/EDIT should be: Select Left or Right justified. (If you select Right, the text is still left justified in Display.)

Number of transactions between flushing files to disk... The number of records added or modified before Enable automatically saves the records. Enter 0 or blank to disable the option.

Stop on all database errors? If you select yes you must press Enter to continue after even minor errors.

DISPLAY records option: Select Full Page if you want Enable to collect together all the records before displaying them, or Immediate to add the records to the displays as Enable retrieves them (this causes the screen to flicker).

REPORT print option: Select Spool Report to place the report in a disk file which is then sent to the printer or system queue (see section 9, System of this appendix). Select Print Immediately to send the file to the printer right away. Enable puts you in a different window. If the printer is not available the report is not printed. You cannot use .INPUT commands with Print Immediately. This option conserves disk space.

7. SPREADSHEET

Protect all cells in spreadsheet? Select Yes, and when you turn Global Protection on all the cells are protected.

Convert Lotus 1-2-3 macros? Select Yes to convert macros from imported Lotus 1-2-3 files to Enable command sequences.

Display zero values in cells? Select No to leave empty cells blank, and Yes to display 0.

Do you wish to indicate pointer location on borders? Select Yes if you want Enable to indicate, on the row and column borders, where the pointer is.

Recalculation options: Select 1 to recalculate the entire file, including data from linked databases, when you press F5. Select 2 to recalculate only changed entries, circular references, @NOW, @TODAY, and @RAND.

8. GRAPHICS

Function keys are arranged: Select Vertically or Horizontally. This information is used by the Perspective II graphics program, not by Enable.

9. SYSTEM

What action should occur when Backspace is pressed? Select 1 (blank the character above the cursor), 2 (move the cursor to the left without deleting anything), 3 (blank the character to the left), or 4 (delete the character to the left).

What effect should shift key have when in Caps Lock? Select 1 (letters remain in uppercase) or 2 (letters are lowercase).

What effect should Enter have in Insert mode? Select 1 (put a paragraph marker at the end of the line) or 2 (split the line, like Ctrl-Enter).

Do you want to use the system print queue? Select Yes to place documents in the system queue. (Press Alt-F2 to put them at the back of the queue, or Shift-F2 to put them at the beginning.)

Use Q(uit) to exit the extended directory screen? Select Yes to stop Esc from exiting the Extended Directory Screen.

USING A COLOR MONITOR

Enable actually comes with two default profiles—one for color monitors, and one for monochrome. The color-monitor profile has the SPECIAL TEXT features already set up for a color screen. If you have a color monitor change the DEFAULT profile's name (to DEFAULT2, for example), and then change COLOR to DEFAULT. (This allows you to press End when you logon to Enable to automatically select the color-monitor profile.)

To rename a profile, highlight it, type R, type the new name, and press Enter.

SAVING PROFILES

When you want to save your changes press F10 and type S (Save). To exit the profiles press F10 and type Q. The changes you have made are not used by Enable until you log on to Enable the next time.

Appendix C
DATABASE KEYBOARD

DATABASE FUNCTION KEYS

Key	*Description*
F1	Display Help messages
F4	Edit field in DISPLAY
F5	Save and advance to next record in ADD, EDIT, and VERIFY
F6	Save and go to the previous record in ADD, EDIT, and VERIFY
F7	Mark block of records in DISPLAY (press at beginning and end of block)
F8	Copy information between ADD and EDIT in input forms
F8	Display masked entry in VERIFY
F9	Expert Commands
F10	Top Line Menu
Alt-F2	Print from Page Form
Alt-F3	Delete response to prompt at command screen, or blank text field in input form
Alt-F6	Ignore record entry in ADD, EDIT, and VERIFY
Alt-F7	Clear marked records
Alt-F9 \ *x*	Start recording macro named *x*
Alt-F9 End	Stop recording macro
Alt-F9 *x*	Execute macro named *x*
Alt/F10	Save form
Ctrl-F1	Hypertext Help
Ctrl-F2	Cancel printing
Ctrl-F5	Switch to ADD mode from EDIT
Ctrl-F10 *x*	Display user-defined menu with a single-character name, *x*
Shift-F1	Switch to QUERY mode from ADD, EDIT, or VERIFY
Shift-F5	Specify new Index clause in ADD, EDIT, or VERIFY
Shift-F6	Specify new Where clause in ADD, EDIT, or VERIFY
Shift-F9	Execute macro in ADD or EDIT
Shift-F9	Position field ("Put it Here!") in input or report forms
Shift-F9	Validate accuracy of form and complete the transfer in COPY, MERGE, and UPDATE
Shift-F10	Display default user-defined menu

DATABASE CURSOR MOVEMENT KEYS

Description	*Key Sequence*
Command Screens	
Bypass prompts	End
Move to next prompt	Tab
Into field-names box	PgDn
Display Screen	
Top	Ctrl-Home
Bottom	Ctrl-End
Left one screen	Shift-Tab
Right one screen	Tab
Next page	PgDn
Previous page	PgUp
Automatic Scroll	
Forward by record	Alt-F9 Down Arrow
Forward by page	Alt-F9 PgDn
Automatic Scroll (Cont.)	
Backward by record	Alt-F9 Up Arrow
Backward by page	Alt-F9 PgUp
Right	Alt-F9 Right Arrow
Left	Alt-F9 Left Arrow
Stop scrolling	Ctrl-Break
Input Forms	
To first field on page	Home
To last field on page	End
Next field	Tab, Enter, or Down Arrow
Previous field	Shift-Tab
End of previous field	Up Arrow
Next page	PgDn
Previous page	PgUp

DATABASE EXPERT COMMANDS

Command	*Key Sequence*
Autolock	
Toggle to invoke LAN .autolock on subsequent database reads in same window	F9 A
Buffer	
Change database buffer to:	
512 bytes	F9 B 1
1024 bytes (1K)	F9 B 2
2048 bytes (2K)	F9 B 4
4096 bytes (4K)	F9 B 8
8192 bytes (8K)	F9 B A
16384 bytes (16K)	F9 B B
Change 30-buffer limit to maximum possible with available memory	F9 B M
Return to 30-buffer limit	F9 B D
Show current size of limit	F9 B ?
Call Command Screens	
Add	F9 C A
Archive	F9 C 3
Backup	F9 C 4
Browse	F9 C B
Copy	F9 C C
Delete	F9 C 1
Destroy	F9 C 6
Display	F9 C D
Edit	F9 C E
Export	F9 C 0
Find	F9 C F
Graph	F9 C G
Index	F9 C I
Merge	F9 C M
Rename	F9 C 7
Replace	F9 C R
Report	F9 C 9
Restore	F9 C 5

DATABASE EXPERT COMMANDS (CONT.)

Command	*Key Sequence*
Call Command Screens (Cont.)	
Sort	F9 C S
Undelete	F9 C 2
Update	F9 C U
Verify	F9 C V
Display	
Directory of files	F9 D
Display of sys:record and deleted fields: Disabled	F9 F D
Enabled	F9 F E

NOTE

Use this to disable the sys:record and deleted fields in the command screen FIELDS prompt.

Command	*Key Sequence*
Display of Index prompt at end of editing session:	
Disabled	F9 I D
Enabled	F9 I E
Error Stop	
Reverses the "Stop on all database errors" setting in user profile	F9 E
Turn off error stop and .autolock	F9 R
Marking Records in DISPLAY or BROWSE	
Marking	Alt-M
Remove marking	Alt-N
Multitasking	
Begin Multitasking	Alt-Tab
Quit	
End the Database session	F9 C Q
Records	
Move to next	Alt-PgDn
Move to previous	Alt-PgUp
Save	
Save data on disk ("flush" buffers to disk)	F9 U
	F9 C Q
Window Commands	
Open	F9 W O or Alt-Home
Close	F9 W C or Alt-End
Go to window *n*	F9 W *n* G
Go to next	F9 W A or Alt-Up Arrow
Go to previous	F9 W B or Alt-Down Arrow
Return to previous size	F9 W P
Modify shape or location	F9 W L
Zoom to full size	F9 W Z
Window Summary Screen	F9 W ?
Index Prompt at End of EDIT for Select Set	
Disable	F9 I D
Enable	F9 I E

During input- or report-form design, word processing commands are also available.

Appendix D
GRAPHICS KEYBOARD

GRAPHICS FUNCTION KEYS

Key	*Description*	*Key*	*Description*
F1	Display Help messages	Alt-F9 End	Stop recording macros
F9	Expert commands	Alt-F9 *x*	Use macro named *x*
Alt-F9 \ *x*	Record system macro named *x*	Ctrl-F2	Cancel printing and plotting

GRAPHICS EXPERT COMMANDS

Command	*Key Sequence*	*Command*	*Key Sequence*
Window Commands		Go to next	F9 W A or Alt-Up Arrow
Open	F9 W O or Alt-Home	Go to previous	F9 W B or Alt-Down Arrow
Close	F9 W C or Alt-End	Return to previous size	F9 W P
Go to window *n*	F9 W *n* G		

Appendix E
SPREADSHEET KEYBOARD

SPREADSHEET FUNCTION KEYS

Key	*Description*	*Key*	*Description*
F1	Display Help messages	Alt-F9 \ *x*	Record system macro named *x*
F2	Go to... (see Pointer Movement commands)	Alt-F9 End	Stop recording system macros
F3	Insert row at pointer	Alt-F9 *x*	Use system macro named *x*
F4	Edit mode	Alt-F10	Save file
F5	Recalculation	Ctrl-F1	Hypertext Help
F6	Move to other side of split window or to next level when two or three levels of a 3D spreadsheets are displayed	Ctrl-F2	Cancel printing
F7	Make relative cell reference while pointing to cell	Ctrl-F10 *x*	Display user-defined menu with single-character name, *x*
F8	Copy cell contents	Ctrl-PgDn	Move to next level in a 3D spreadsheet
F9	Expert commands	Ctrl-PgUp	Move to previous level in a 3D spreadsheet
F10	Top Line Menu	Ctrl-Home	Go to level A, cell A1 in a 3D spreadsheet
Alt-F1	Display Function-key chart	Ctrl-End	Go to the last level and the last data-cell in a 3D spreadsheet
Alt-F2	Print file	Shift-F7	Display spreadsheet and graph simultaneously (On/Off)
Alt-F3	Delete the row at pointer	Shift-F9 *x*	Activate spreadsheet macro named *x*
Alt-F4	Center contents of cell	Shift-F10	Display user-defined menu (default)
Alt-F5	Copy between windows		
Alt-F6	Skip protected cells		
Alt-F7	Display Graphics Selection Menu		
Alt-F8	Move cell contents		

SPREADSHEET POINTER MOVEMENT

Movement	*Key Sequence*
Move Pointer	
Up one cell	Up Arrow
Down one cell	Down Arrow or Ctrl-Enter
Left one cell	Left Arrow
Right one cell	Right Arrow
Up one page	PgUp
Down one page	PgDn
Right one screen	Tab
Left one screen	Shift-Tab
Move Pointer to...	
Cell A1 (or 1st cell after titles)	Home
Intersection of highest row/ column	End Home
Move Pointer to... (Cont.)	
Cell *row/column*	F2 *row/column*
First cell in range	F2 *range name*
First non-blank cell in row	F2 Left Arrow
Last non-blank cell in row	F2 Right Arrow
Move Pointer From...	
Blank cell to next non-blank in direction of arrow	End Arrow
Non-blank cell to last non- blank cell in direction of arrow	End Arrow

SPREADSHEET EXPERT COMMANDS

Movement	*Key Sequence*
Cell Alignment	
Center	F9 Ins + or F9 Del +
Left	Ctrl-[
Right	Ctrl-]
Delete	
Delete row	F9 Del L
Erase range	F9 Del B
Undo deletion	F9 U
Display	
Directory of files	F9 D
List of formulas	F9 L F
List of range names	F9 L N
Highlight Cells	
After "anchoring" cell when defining a range, highlights all used cells.	End Home
Insert	
Insert row	F9 Ins L
Multitasking	
Begin Multitasking	Alt-Tab
Save	
Display save options	F9 S Z
Display save filename	Alt-F10
Save and close spreadsheet	F9 S Home
Save and close Enable	F9 S End
Save, close, and create another	F9 S C
Save, close, and revise another	F9 S R
Save and continue	F9 S E
Save with a new name	F9 S N
Save in DIF format	F9 S D
Save a range	F9 S B

SPREADSHEET EXPERT COMMANDS (CONT.)

Movement	*Key Sequence*	*Movement*	*Key Sequence*
Scroll (Auto)		**Window Commands**	
Forward by row	Alt-F9 Down Arrow	Open	F9 W O or Alt-Home
Forward by page	Alt-F9 PgDn	Close	F9 W C or Alt-End
Backward by row	Alt-F9 Up Arrow	Go to window *n*	F9 W *n* G
Backward by page	Alt-F9 PgUp	Go to next	F9 W A or Alt-Up Arrow
Right by cell	Alt-F9 Right Arrow	Go to previous	F9 W B or Alt-Down Arrow
Left by cell	Alt-F9 Left Arrow	Return to previous size	F9 W P
Stop scrolling	Ctrl-Break	Modify shape or location	F9 W L
Split Window		Zoom to full size	F9 W Z
Clear	F9 W X	Window Summary Screen	F9 W ?
Split horizontally	F9 W H		
Split vertically	F9 W V		
Synchronize scrolling	F9 W S		
Unsynchronize scrolling	F9 W U		

Appendix F
TELECOMMUNICATIONS KEYBOARD

TELECOMMUNICATIONS FUNCTION KEYS

Key	*Description*	*Key*	*Description*
F1	Display Help messages	Alt-F9 \ *x*	Record macro named *x*
F7	Turn Capture-to-memory On/Off	Alt-F9 End	Stop recording macro
		Alt-F9 *x*	Use macro named *x*
F8	Transmit marked data in word processing screen	Ctrl-F1	Hypertext Help
F9	Expert Commands	Ctrl-F10 *x*	Display user-defined menu with single-character name, *x*
F10	Top Line Menu	Shift-F2	Start/Stop printing incoming data
Alt-F7	Turn Capture-to-memory Off		
Alt-F8	Transmit marked data in word processing screen without copying to Telecom screen	Shift-F9	Switch to Telecom screen from word processing screen
		Shift-F10	Display default user-defined menu

TELECOMMUNICATIONS EXPERT COMMANDS

Command	*Key Sequence*
Bypass	
Bypass Quick-Connection Form prompts	End
Capture	
To disk - open a file	F9 T Home
To disk - On/Off	F9 T F7
To disk - close file	F9 T End
To memory - On/Off	F9 T C
Clear Xoff	
Clear Xoff if you don't receive Xon after receiving Xoff	F9 T X
Convert 8th Bit	
Convert 8th bit of incoming data to 0	F9 T 8
Disconnect	
Disconnect (End Session)	F9 T D or Alt-End
Filter Mapping	
Receive Mapping On/Off	F9 T 1
Transmit Mapping On/Off	F9 T 2
Multitasking	
Begin Multitasking	Alt-Tab

TELECOMMUNICATIONS EXPERT COMMANDS (CONT.)

Command	*Key Sequence*
Print	
Turn printing On/Off	F9 T P
Setup Parameters:	
Ignore special characters	F9 T O 7
Process all characters but 240-255	F9 T O 9
Replace special characters with ~	F9 T O 8
Convert line feeds to carriage returns	F9 T O 1
Ignore all line feeds	F9 T O 2
Ignore line feeds with carriage-returns	F9 T O 0
Convert tabs to one space	F9 T O 4
Don't modify tabs	F9 T O 6
Ignore tabs	F9 T O 3
Move to next column	F9 T O 5
Switch to Word Processing Mode	
Normally	Up Arrow
During Terminal Emulation	PgUp

NOTE

In the word processing screen all the usual word processing keyboard commands are available.

Command	*Key Sequence*
Terminal Emulation	
Display options	F9 T E
Transmit	
Break signal	Ctrl-B
Xon	Ctrl-Q
Xoff	Ctrl-S
Window Commands	
Open	F9 W O or Alt-Home
Close (Disconnect)	F9 W C or Alt-End
Go to window *n*	F9 W *n* G
Go to next	F9 W A or Alt-Up Arrow
Go to previous	F9 W B or Alt-Down Arrow
Return to previous size	F9 W P
Modify shape or location	F9 W L
Zoom to full size	F9 W Z
Window Summary Screen	F9 W ?

Appendix G
WORD PROCESSING KEYBOARD

WORD PROCESSING FUNCTION KEYS

Key	*Description*	*Key*	*Description*
F1	Display Help messages	Alt-F6	Insert previous ruler above cursor
F2	Cursor control (see Cursor Movement commands)	Alt-F7	Clear block
F3	Insert line below cursor	Alt-F8	Move block
F4	Delete word	Alt-F9 \ *x*	Record system macro named *x*
F5	Repeat Find command		
F6	Repeat Find and Replace command	Alt-F9 End	Stop recording macros
		Alt-F9 *x*	Use macro named *x*
F7	Set block (press at start and end)	Alt-F10	Save file
		Ctrl-F1	Hypertext Help
F8	Copy block within window	Ctrl-F2	Cancel printing
F9	Expert commands	Ctrl-F10 *x*	Display user-defined menu with single-character name, *x*
F10	Top Line Menu		
Alt-F1	Display function-key chart		
Alt-F2	Print file	Shift-F7	Set column as block (press at both ends)
Alt-F3	Delete line		
Alt-F4	Center line	Shift-F10 *x*	Display user-defined menu (default) named *x*
Alt-F5	Copy block between windows		

WORD PROCESSING CURSOR MOVEMENT KEYS

Movement	*Key Sequence*	*Movement*	*Key Sequence*
Move cursor to...		**Column**	
Attribute		Column *x*	F2 *n* Spacebar
Next	F2 A		
Previous	F2 Up Arrow A	**Comment**	
		Next	F2 N C
Block		Previous	F2 Up Arrow N C
Beginning of the block	F2 Up Arrow B		
End of the block	F2 B	**File**	
		End of file	Ctrl-End
		Beginning of file	Ctrl-Home

WORD PROCESSING CURSOR MOVEMENT KEYS (CONT.)

Movement	*Key Sequence*
Footer (draft mode)	
Next	F2 F
Previous	F2 Up Arrow F
Footnote (draft mode)	
Next	F2 N F
Previous	F2 Up Arrow N F
Header (draft mode)	
Next	F2 H
Previous	F2 Up Arrow H
Index (draft mode)	
Next	F2 I
Previous	F2 Up Arrow I
Line	
First character on line	F2 Left Arrow
Last character on line	F2 Right Arrow
Margin to Margin	F2 Tab
Page	
Beginning	F2 Home
End	F2 End
n **pages down**	F2 ***n*** PgDn
n **pages up**	F2 ***n*** PgUp
Next Break	F2 PgDn
Previous Break	F2 PgUp
Paper clip	
Next	F2 M C
Paper clip ***n***	F2 ***n*** M C
Previous	F2 Up Arrow M C
Paragraph	
Beginning	F2 Up Arrow P
End	F2 P
Repeat	
Repeat the last F2 command	F2 F2
Ruler	
Next	F2 R
Previous	F2 Up Arrow R
Sentence	
Beginning	F2 Up Arrow S
End	F2 S
Screen	
Down one screen	Ctrl-PgDn
Down one-half screen	PgDn
Up one screen	Ctrl-PgUp
Up one-half screen	PgUp
Bottom left of screen	End
Top left of screen	Home
Scroll (Auto)	
Forward by line	Alt-F9 Down Arrow
Backward by line	Alt-F9 Up Arrow
Forward by page	Alt-F9 PgDn
Backward by page	Alt-F9 PgUp
Right	Alt-F9 Right Arrow
Left	Alt-F9 Left Arrow
Stop Scrolling	Ctrl-Break
Tab	
Next tab	Tab
Previous tab	Shift-Tab
Table of Authorities (TOA)	
Next TOA entry	F2 M A
Previous TOA entry	F2 Up Arrow M A
Table of Contents	
Next entry	F2 T
Previous entry	F2 Up Arrow T
Word	
To left	Ctrl-Left Arrow
To right	Crtl-Right Arrow

WORD PROCESSING EXPERT COMMANDS

Command	*Key Sequence*
Alignment	
Block left	F9 B L
Block right	F9 B R
Line left	Ctrl-[
Line right	Ctrl-]
Hanging indent	Alt-H
Block	
Begin column-block function	F9 . (period) F7
Cancel column-block function	Esc
Calculate	
Calculate formula to left of cursor	F9 +
Center	
Block	F9 B +
Line	F9 Ins + or Alt-F4
Change Case	
Change to uppercase	Alt-F
Change to lowercase	Alt-K
Compile	
Index	F9 C I
Shorthand	F9 C S
Table of Authorities	F9 C A
Table of Contents	F9 C T
Copy	
Block	F9 B C
Delete	
Character at cursor	Del
Character left of cursor	Backspace
(The function of Backspace can be changed in your user profile)	
Block	F9 Del B
Delete (Cont.)	
File, from cursor to end	F9 Del Ctrl-End
File, from cursor to start	F9 Del Ctrl-Home
Line, entire	F9 Del L
Line, from cursor to end	F9 Del Down Arrow
Line, from cursor to beginning	Ctrl-Backspace
Marked text	F9 Del M T
Page, from cursor to last break	F9 Del PgUp
Page, from cursor to next break	F9 Del PgDn
Page breaks, system	F9 Del M P
Paper clips, all	F9 Del M C
Paragraph, from cursor to end	F9 Del P
Paragraph marker	F9 Del Enter
Screen, from cursor to bottom	F9 Del End
Screen, from cursor to top	F9 Del Home
Sentence, from cursor to end	F9 Del S
Spaces to left of cursor	F9 Del Backspace
Spaces to right of cursor	F9 Del Spacebar
Spaces both sides of cursor	F9 Del Del
Word to left of cursor	F9 Del Left Arrow
Word to right of cursor	F9 Del Right Arrow
Undo (restore last deleted text)	F9 U
Undo last deleted line, at cursor	Esc
Display	
Directory of Files	F9 D
Comments	F9 O N C
Document Title	F9 O N T
Footers	F9 O F
Footnotes	F9 O N F

WORD PROCESSING EXPERT COMMANDS (CONT.)

Command	*Key Sequence*
Display (Cont.)	
Headers	F9 O H
Index entry space	F9 O I
Line spacing marker	F9 O S
Page breaks	F9 O M P
Paper clips	F9 O M C
Ruler at bottom of screen	F9 O R B
Ruler at top of screen	F9 O R T
Rulers within text	F9 O R W
Rulers, remove all	F9 O R O
Shorthand entry space	F9 O N S
Table of Authorities entry	F9 O A T
Table of Contents	F9 O T
Draft/Final	
Toggle between Draft and Final	F9 O D
Find	
Find	F9 F T
Find and Mark	F9 F M
Find and Replace	F9 F R
Repeat Find	F9 F A
Repeat Find and Replace	F9 F N
Hanging Indent	
Create Hanging Indent	Alt-H
Hard Spaces and Hyphens	
Hard hyphen	Alt- - (hyphen)
Hard space	Alt-=
Index	
Use text as index entry	Alt-X
Compile	F9 C I
Insert	
Block (copy)	F9 Ins B
Comment entry space	F9 Ins N C

Command	*Key Sequence*
Insert (Cont.)	
Document Title	F9 Ins N T
File (Enable prompts for name)	F9 Ins D
Footer entry space	F9 Ins F
Footnote entry space	F9 Ins N F
Header entry space	F9 Ins H
Index entry space	F9 Ins I
Line	F9 Ins L
Page break	F9 Ins M P
Paper clip *n*	F9 Ins *n* M C
Ruler (previous)	F9 Ins R or Alt-F6
Shorthand entry space	F9 Ins N S
Table of Authorities entry space	F9 Ins A
Table of Contents entry space	F9 Ins T
Line Spacing	
Set line spacing to *n*	F9 Ins *n* S
Margins	
Release	Ctrl-M
Set left margin at cursor	Alt-L
Set right margin at cursor	Alt-R
Set justified right margin at cursor	Alt-J
Move	
Block	F9 B M
Multitasking	
Begin Multitasking	Alt-Tab
Paragraph	
End paragraph at end of line	Enter
(The function of Enter can be adjusted in your user profile.)	
End paragraph at cursor	Ctrl-Enter

WORD PROCESSING EXPERT COMMANDS (CONT.)

Command	*Key Sequence*
Reformat	
Automatic, On/Off	F9 O A R
Reformat Paragraph	F9 O A P
Retain blanks in reformat	F9 O A B
Repeat	
Last F9 command	F9 F9
Save	
Display save prompts	F9 S Z
ASCII format:	
Block	F9 S A B
Marked text	F9 S A M
File and continue	F9 S A D
File with new name and continue	F9 S A N
Enable format:	
Block	F9 S B
File and close	F9 S Home
File, close, and open another	F9 S C
File, close, and revise another	F9 S R
File, close, and close Enable	F9 S End
File and continue	F9 S E
File with new name	F9 S N
Marked text	F9 S M
Save macro (in MACRO CREATE)	F9 S =
Shorthand	
Compile	F9 C S
Sort	
Display Sort options	F9 E S
Special Character Sets	
Box drawing	F9 O C B
Foreign char, set 1	F9 O C F
Special Character Sets (Cont.)	
Foreign char, set 2	F9 O C T
Greek characters	F9 O C G
Miscellaneous characters	F9 O C S
Turn off any set	F9 O C O
Spell	
Display Spell Check options	F9 E C
Table of Authorities	
Compile	F9 C A
Table of Contents	
Compile	F9 C T
Tabs	
Turn display on/off	F9 O M T
Set Tab at cursor	Alt-T
Clear Tab at cursor	Alt-E
Clear all Tabs	Alt-A
Transpose	
2 char to left of cursor	Ctrl-T
Window Commands	
Open	F9 W O or Alt-Home
Close	F9 W C or Alt-End
Go to window *n*	F9 W *n* G
Go to next	F9 W A or Alt-Up Arrow
Go to previous	F9 W B or Alt-Down Arrow
Return to prev. size	F9 W P
Modify shape or location	F9 W L
Zoom to full size	F9 W Z
Window Summary Screen	F9 W ?

WORD PROCESSING SPECIAL TEXT ATTRIBUTES

Attribute	*Key Sequence*	*Attribute*	*Key Sequence*
Display attribute in status line	Alt-S	Index entry	Alt-X
Boldface	Alt-B	Marked	Alt-M
Change to uppercase	Alt-F	Normal	Alt-N
Change to lowercase	Alt-K	Proportional	Alt-P
Compressed	Alt-C	Quality	Alt-Q
Double-strike	Alt-D	Subscript	Alt-V
Elite	Alt-E	Superscript	Alt-A
Italic	Alt-I	Underlined	Alt-U
		Wide	Alt-W

TEXT SEGMENT COMMANDS

Command	*Key Sequence*	*Command*	*Key Sequence*
(Use to Apply Special Text Attributes)		Sentence	Ctrl-S
Block	Ctrl-B	Page	Ctrl-G
Character	Ctrl-C	Paragraph	
Word	Ctrl-W	Ctrl-P	
Line	Ctrl-L		

Appendix H
ADVANCED TELECOMMUNICATIONS FEATURES

TERMINAL EMULATION

Enable has VT-100, VT-52, and AT&T4410 terminal emulation. Select the terminal in the setup or in the Telecom Top Line Menu by pressing F10 and typing OE (Other;Emulation). The Top Line Menu also lets you turn emulation on and off during a session, and swap between different modes without leaving the Telecom screen.

WORD PROCESSING SCREEN To move into the word processing screen during terminal emulation press PgUp, not Up Arrow.

CAPTURE DATA Capture-to-disk is the only reliable data capture method during terminal emulation.

VT-100 & VT-52 Enable does not support the VT alternative character sets or double-width and double-height characters. The numeric keypad has two modes; Cursor and Host. Num Lock switches between modes.

Cursor Mode; Num Lock light off The numeric keypad works as normal, except that PgUp moves you into the word processing screen.

Host Mode; Num Lock light on, NUM in the Status Line The keypad is in Numeric mode when Enable receives ESC= from the host (applications such as spreadsheets) or Alternate Keypad mode when it receives ESC (text editors). When in Numeric mode you can still use the cursor keys by pressing and holding Shift while you press the keys.

In Alternate Keypad mode the keys operate according to the following table (the first four function keys on the PC are also affected):

PC Keys	*Emulate these VT keys*
F1	PF1 (GOLD)
F2	PF2
F3	PF3
F4	PF$
0 to 9	0 to 9
–	–
*	,
.	.
+	Enter

To emulate the VT Delete key press Del (in Cursor mode) or Ctrl-Backspace (in Host or Cursor mode).

Display Attributes in VT Emulation You can modify the Special Text section of your profile to determine how attributes are displayed.

To Display these VT attributes	*Select these Enable attributes*	*Mono*	*Graphics & Color Graphics*
Normal	Normal	1	8:1
Bold	Bold	4	H8:1
Bold & Underlined	Bold & Underlined	5	H8:3
Underscore	Underlined	2	H3:1
Blink	Superscript	B1	B8:1
Negative (reverse)	Mark attribute (Alt-M)	3	1:8
Combination of atts.	Mixed attributes	B3	B1:8

The last column in the table is a suggestion only. You can use any color.

Supported Features The following features are supported by emulation.

- High Speeds (to 9600 baud)
- Snap-shot; press PgUp and Enable displays the word processing screen and sends Xoff to the host. Press Shift-F9 to return to the Telecom screen and send Xon to tell the host to send the next snap-shot.
- Scrolling Regions
- Terminal Setup Form; press Alt-S to see this form. Lets you select Autowrap, New Line, and 80 or 132 columns. (Use Ctrl-Right Arrow, -Left Arrow, -], and -[to move across the columns.
- Recognizes Host's Tab Sets

TRANSMIT/RECEIVE MAPPING TABLES

These features let you send special characters, and filter incoming data to remove or replace certain characters. The setup lets you ignore characters not on the keyboard, substitute ~ for characters not on the keyboard, ignore characters with ASCII codes from 240 to 255, or use a Transmit/Receive Mapping Table.

NOTE

The mapping tables filter data saved during both Capture-to-memory and Capture-to-disk. However, you can change your user profile to save "raw" data during Capture-to-disk.

CREATE A TABLE At the Main Menu type MTTTC (MCM;Tools;Telecom;Transmit/Receive Map;Create). Enter the filename (Enable adds .WPF). The procedure works much like building an Unattended Transfer Form (see Module 112, Transmit Data). Begin with TELECOMMUNICATIONS DIVISION. VER=1. The other headings are optional. Enable assumes (regardless of the headings) that the first line of characters should be ignored, those in the second line should be replaced, and that non-dot-command text after these lines are options. (A line of characters may wrap onto the next line, but do not split macro equivalents or ASCII codes between two lines. End the list by pressing Enter.)

Begin a list of characters in column one. Specify characters by keyboard symbol (in double or single quotation marks, but do not use left-single), ASCII decimal code, macro equivelent, or word processing special character. The Mapping Table is case sensitive; telling Enable to ignore Z still lets z through. When Ignoring, separate with commas. When replacing, follow with = and the replacement character, and separate pairs with commas. You can also indicate a range to ignore (234..237 or "A".."F").

The Options section lets you convert text to uppercase or lowercase. Simply type Uppercase or Lowercase. End the table with .END

The table looks like this:

```
.TELECOMMUNICATIONS DIVISION. VER=1
.IGNORE CHARACTERS SECTION.
{Esc},127,"$"
.REPLACE CHARACTERS SECTION.
{^C}=13
.OPTION SECTION.
Lowercase
.END
```

SAVING THE TABLE Save this in the same manner that you save an Unattended Transfer Form. Press F10, type C (Create Table), type filename, and press Enter. Enable adds .TPT. If you want to save the word processing file for editing later you must also use the word processing Save command.

USING THE TABLE To use the table for received data build a setup and select "Use Filter/mapping table" at the "Enter receive filter option" prompt (screen 7). Enable prompts for the table name. (Enter the .TPT filename.) If you want to use the table for transmitted data, select Yes at the "Will you use a transmit filter/mapping table?" prompt (screen 8) and enter the filename.

When you make your connection Enable automatically filters and maps the characters. These options can be turned off using the expert commands for changing specifications online.

Restrictions Enable will not map characters during Enable, Xmodem, and Kermit file transfers, or while capturing-to-disk.

When Xon/Xoff is on Enable filters or maps the data before seeing if it is an Xon/Xoff character.

Special handling of incoming linefeeds and tabs is done after filtering.

Special handling of outgoing linefeeds is done before mapping.

ASCII characters with codes 240 to 255 are used internally. Enable automatically ignores these incoming characters. You cannot replace them.

KEYBOARD MAPPING TABLES

Keyboard Mapping is a form of macro, associating a series of operations with just one key.

CREATING A TABLE At the Main Menu type MTTKC (MCM;Tools;Telecom;Keyboard Mapping;Create). Enter a name. Enable adds .WPF. The procedure is similar to building a Transmit/Receive Mapping Table. See the following page for an example. The first two lines are mandatory.

List the macro codes of the keys you want to define, followed by = and the key's definition. Enter one definition per line. You can map all valid keys (see Module 115, Macros). Enter text you want to transmit in double or single quotation marks (don't use left-single). Indicate Enter using a tilde (~).

```
TELECOMMUNICATIONS DIVISION. VER=1
.KEYBOARD MAPPING SECTION.
{F2}="Go Business"~
{!F3}=D~1~{F10}FRX
.END
```

In this example pressing F2 transmits "Go Business" and pressing Shift-F3 transmits "D" followed by a carriage return, "1" followed by a carriage return, presses F10, and types FRX (Files;Receive;Xmodem).

SAVING THE TABLE Save this in the same manner that you save an Unattended Transfer Form. Press F10, type C (Create Table), type filename, and press Enter. Enable adds .TPK. If you want to save the word processing file for editing later you must also use the word processing Save command.

USING THE TABLE To use the table for received data build a setup and select Yes at the "Will you use a keyboard mapping table" prompt (screen 8). Enable prompts for the table name. (Enter the .TPK filename.)

You can also use the table if you haven't defined it in the setup or if you used Quick-Connect. At the Telecom screen press F10 and type OM (Other;Map). Enable lets you specify a mapping table and turn it on and off.

MODEM TABLES

A modem table lets you use a modem that Enable does not usually support, or change how a supported modem operates. Enable has several sample modem table files, in your data directory or data disk. You may have some or all of these:

ACOM1.HAY	For Hayes-compatible modems
ACOM1.PRO	For Prometheus modems
ACOM1.PBX	For systems using a PBX
ACOM1.300	For 300 baud modems
ACOM1.AVK	For AVATEX 1200 modems
ACOM1.MIC	For systems using a Micom Data Switch
ACOM1.RVK	For Racal Vadic V AZIZ modems

You can view and edit these tables in word processing (select ASCII). If you want to use them you must change their names according to the rules laid out next. The following screen shows the first part of ACOM1.HAY.

```
L-------T-------T-------T-------T--+----T----------------------------R--------
.TELECOMMUNICATIONS DIVISION
;;
;;   HAYES 1200 and 2400 modem table
;;    (and any Hayes compatible modem)
;;
.SECTION PORTTEST
.SETDELAY 0,","
.TEST "~"
.STOP
;;
;;
.SECTION INITIALIZE
.LOOP 1,10
.SEND "ATQV1E0~"
.WAIT4 1,"OK~",INIT0L
.GOTO INIT1
.LABEL INIT0L
.ENDL 1
.GOTO QUIT
;;
.LABEL INIT1
.DELAY .1
#Z        /B C:ACOM1.HAY          DRAFT                              L00001C001
```

The commands follow the same general rules applying to mapping tables and transfer forms.

Save the form in ASCII format with the extension .TPX. The name you should use depends on what you have set for the Modem table in your user profile, ACOM or BCOM. If you set ACOM and are using COMM1, name the file ACOM1.TPX. If you set BCOM and are using COMM2 call it BCOM2.TPX. If you are using a modem table in a network you can add your user ID to the name (ACOM1*id*.TPX). If you don't want to use a modem table all the time name it something else and rename it just before you use it. When you make a call Enable automatically searches for a modem table—if it finds the table it uses the table and displays External in the status line. If it cannot find one it uses its default tables and displays Internal in the status line. Disconnect in the normal way. (Enable searches for disconnect information in your modem table and uses that.)

COMMANDS

.ALTERNATE—Ends the current connection attempt and tells Enable to try the alternate setup defined in the setup you are using.

.BEEP—Your computer beeps, drawing your attention to something.

.DELAY *number*—Pauses the specified number of seconds. Can use tenths (1.1).

.DIAL *"prefix","suffix"*—Tells Enable to dial the number in your setup. You must include the prefix "ATDT" and the suffix "~" with Hayes-compatible auto-dial modems. Enable inserts the number between the two. Use the prefix ATDP for pulse.

.DROPDTR—Tells Enable to drop the connection by turning off DTR.

.END—Optional; tells Enable it has reached the end of the table. Otherwise Enable assumes the last command in the file is the end.

.EXIT—Tells Enable to stop executing the rest of the commands and return to the Main Menu.

.GOTO—See the Unattended Transfer Form commands in Module 112.

.LABEL *name*

.SECTION *name*—These two commands are interchangeable. See .LABEL in the Unattended Transfer Form commands in Module 112.

.LOCAL "*string*"—Displays a message on your screen and the TPLOG file. The message is not transmitted.

.REDIAL—Performs initialization and dialing again if connection not completed. Same as typing R for redial.

.SEND "*string*"—Transmits a string of characters, such as commands.

.STOP—Tells Enable it has finished commands in a particular section.

.TEST "*character*"—Tests the COMM port by transmitting the character. You can type the quotes without the character to test without transmitting.

.WAIT4 seconds,"*string*",labelname—The same as the Unattended Transfer Form commands in Module 112.

Appendix I
PRINT QUEUE

INTRODUCTION

Enable has a print queue file called PRINTQ.TSG. This file is only used if you have selected Yes at the "Do you want to use system print queue?" prompt in Section 9 of your user profile.

If your profile does use the print queue, each time you send a document to a printer that is in use or offline Enable enters the document's name in the print queue. When the printer is available Enable prints the document in the print queue and erases its name from the queue.

ADDING DOCUMENTS TO THE PRINT QUEUE

You can add a document to the print queue by displaying the document and pressing Alt-F2 to add it to the end of the queue, or Shift-F2 to add it to the beginning of the queue (you cannot use Shift-F2 with DBMS reports). You can also send documents to the print queue by typing UWP (Use;Word Processing;Print) at the Main Menu—type the name and press Enter.

EDITING THE PRINTQ.TSG FILE

You can open the PRINTQ.TSG file as a word processing file (use the .TSG extension when you enter the name). You can then use word processing features to add, copy, delete, or move filenames. The changes become effective when you save the file. You can also print the list of names in the file by pressing Alt-F2 while the file is displayed.

PRESSING CTRL-F2 (CANCEL)

If you press Ctrl-F2 Enable cancels the document currently printing, and stops the rest of the documents from printing. Pressing Alt-F2 adds a document to the queue and starts it running again; if you want to start again without adding a document, go to the Main Menu, type UWP (Use;Word Processing;Print), enter the path if necessary, type PRINTQ.TSG, and press Enter. You can cancel an entire print queue by turning off your printer, displaying PRINTQ.TSG in word processing, deleting the filenames, and saving the document.

Appendix J
START-UP PARAMETERS

The start-up parameters define how Enable runs once you have opened it. These parameters are used when you open Enable from the DOS prompt. (If you have a menu program you can build the commands into the menu, so that they are used automatically.)

When you open Enable you type the following at the DOS prompt:

```
>ENABLE (C:\Dirname,C:\Dirname,C;\Dirname,C:\Dirname,C:\Dirname)
```

NOTE

You may have built this command into a batch file, in which case you type the name of the batch file instead. The start-up parameters must be added to the batch file.

The command tells Enable in which directories to look for the System, Operate, Tutor, Utility, and Data files. If all these files are in the same directory you could type >ENABLE to start the system, but The Software Group does not recommend that you do this, as some procedures may not function correctly if you do. Instead you should type:

```
>ENABLE (,,,,C:\Dirname)
```

The start-up parameters give Enable extra information, and tell it to operate in a specific manner. These parameters are typed after the directory names; for example, type

```
>ENABLE (,,,,C:\DIRNAME) 500
```

and press Enter to assign 500K bytes of RAM to Enable.

The following table summarizes the commands:

Allocate memory	>ENABLE (,,,,C:\DIRNAME) *nnn*
Execute macro on start-up	>ENABLE (,,,,C:\DIRNAME) @*n*
Set video reaction speed	>ENABLE (,,,,C:\DIRNAME) V*n*
Do not load printer program	>ENABLE (,,,,C:\DIRNAME) N
Hold non-resident programs in memory	>ENABLE (,,,,C:\DIRNAME) M
Load Hypertext	>ENABLE (,,,,C:\DIRNAME)\H
Load Disk-EMS	>ENABLE (,,,,C:\DIRNAME),em

The following are only for Dual-Floppy-Disk systems:

Hold terminal emulation programs in memory	>ENABLE (,,,,C:\DIRNAME) R=(T1)
Hold file-transfer programs in memory	>ENABLE (,,,,C:\DIRNAME) R=(T2)
Hold graphics programs in memory	>ENABLE (,,,,C:\DIRNAME) R=(G)
Hold @functions in memory	>ENABLE (,,,,C:\DIRNAME) R=(F*n*,..)
Use internal modem on Data General/One	>ENABLE (,,,,C:\DIRNAME) C2
Use telecommunications on IBM Convertible	>ENABLE (,,,,C:\DIRNAME) C4
Initializes Leading Edge hardware	>ENABLE (,,,,C:\DIRNAME) A

ALLOCATE MEMORY—*nnn* Type the number of bytes of RAM you want to assign to Enable. This allows you to save part of the RAM to use the DOS window. From the total RAM (for example, 640K), subtract the amount you want to save for the DOS window (say, 40K). Type the result (600) after the Enable startup command.

EXECUTE STARTUP MACRO—@*n* Lets you automatically run startup macros, to retrieve specific files, for example.

SET VIDEO REACTION SPEED—V*n* The number *n* (from 1 to 9) depends on your hardware. Experiment until you find the fastest screen response without distortion.

DON'T LOAD PRINTER PROGRAM—N Doesn't load the printer program, giving you more RAM in systems with limited memory.

HOLD NON-RESIDENT PROGRAMS IN MEMORY—M Increases speed of some operations by holding some non-resident programs in RAM. Not recommended for systems with less than 448K.

LOAD HYPERTEXT—\H Loads the Hypertext Help-files.

LOAD DISK-EMS—,em Loads the Disk-EMS feature. Only used by hard-disk systems, this feature emulates EMS by paging data to disk. You can specify where to put the data by adding a path (",em=path" or ",em-path" if you are using a batch file with DOS variables.)

HOLD TERMINAL EMULATION PROGRAMS IN MEMORY—R=(T1) Loads the terminal emulation programs into memory, eliminating disk changes. Use only if you have 448K RAM or more.

HOLD FILE TRANSFER PROGRAMS IN MEMORY—R=(T2) Loads the telecommunications File Transfer programs into memory, eliminating disk changes. Use only if you have 448K RAM or more.

HOLD GRAPHICS PROGRAMS INTO MEMORY—R=(G) Loads the graphics program into memory, eliminating disk changes if you use the DBMS graphics. Use only if you have 448K RAM or more.

HOLD @FUNCTIONS IN MEMORY—R=(Fn,Fn,...) Loads the @ functions, specified by a two-digit code, into memory, eliminating disk changes. Use only if you have 448K RAM or more. The groups are as follows:

F03 (non-8087 processors) F19 (8087 processors)	@EXP, @EXP10, @LOG, @NLOG, @RAND, @STD, @VAR
F04 (non-8087 processor) F20 (8087 processors)	@ACOS, @ASIN, @ATAN, @ATAN2, @COS, @SIN, @SQRT, @TAN
F05	@FV, @PMT, @PV
F06	@BEG_MONTH, @DATE, @DATE$, @DAY, @END_MONTH, @JULIAN, @MONTH, @MONTH$, @TODAY, @WEEKDAY, @WEEKDAY$, @YEAR, @YEAR$

USE INTERNAL MODEM IN DATA GENERAL/ONE—C2 This tells Enable to access the COMM1 port as an internal modem.

USE TELECOMMUNICATIONS WITH IBM CONVERTIBLE—C4 Uses the IBM Convertible serial port for communications.

INITIALIZES LEADING EDGE HARDWARE—A Always use this if you have Leading Edge hardware.

Appendix K
3D SPREADSHEETS

INTRODUCTION

Later versions of Enable/OA have a feature called *3D spreadsheets.* This provides a sophisticated way to build large spreadsheets, by breaking spreadsheets into different *levels*, like pages in a book. Each level can use data from any other level. Unlike linked spreadsheets (described in Module 77), which are separate spreadsheets linked by special commands, a 3D spreadsheet is one spreadsheet with its data organized into a number of levels instead of spread out on one huge "sheet."

To build a 3D spreadsheet, simply create a normal spreadsheet and then press Ctrl-PgDn. Enable immediately displays another, blank, spreadsheet level, with "B:" in the top left corner of the border, as in the following screen:

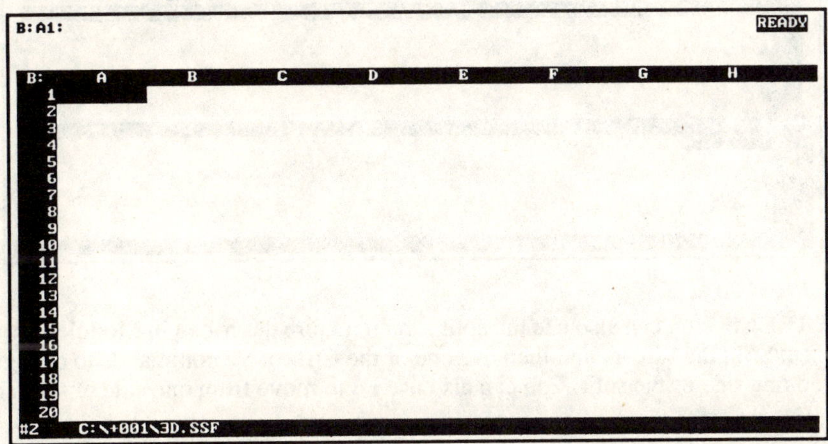

(You can also convert a spreadsheet to 3D by pressing Ctrl-PgUp. Enable displays level AF:, the 32nd level.) Notice also that the cell address in the top left corner has changed; Enable has added B: to each address. All the levels of a 3D spreadsheet have these level indicators, as you will see when you return to the first level. Enable adds A: to the top left corner of the border and to the cell addresses. You can build up to 32 levels—A: to AF:.

MOVING BETWEEN LEVELS

You can move between spreadsheet levels using these commands:

Ctrl-PgDn	Display the next level
Ctrl-PgUp	Display the previous level
Ctrl-Home	Display level A:, and put the pointer on cell A:A1

Ctrl-End	Display the last level, and put the pointer on the last cell containing data
F2 *n:xy*	Display level *n*, cell *xy*

VIEWING LEVELS

Enable lets you view levels in several different ways. Apart from the normal way, one level at time, you can see two or three levels at once, or hide levels.

VIEWING THREE LEVELS AT ONCE Press F10 and type MT3V (MCM;This Window; 3D;View) to see three levels. Enable displays the spreadsheet the pointer is in, plus the next two spreadsheets in sequence. You can move through the sequence using the Ctrl and F2 commands already described. The three-level view takes a little getting used to because it seems upside-down. If you are viewing levels A, B, and C, A is at the bottom and C is at the top. Press F6 to move the pointer between levels. The following screen shows a three-level view.

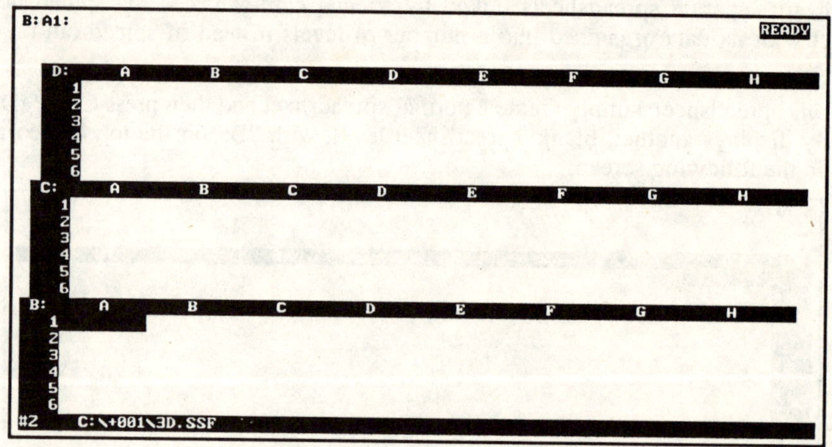

SPLIT SCREENS You can also use the split screen feature described in Module 86 to view two levels at once. Split the screen, and then use one of the Ctrl- or F2 commands to change the level displayed on one side of the split. You can also use F6 to move from one side of the screen to the other.

HIDING LEVELS You can hide spreadsheet levels by placing the pointer in the level you want to hide, pressing F10, and typing MT3H (MCM;This Window;3D;Hide this level). Once hidden, Enable will not display that level until you use the Redisplay Hidden level(s) command—press F10, type MT3R (MCM;This Window;3D;Redisplay Hidden level(s)). Then press Enter to redisplay all the hidden levels, or type a range that includes the level you want to reset. For example, type J:A1..J:A1 to reset level 1.

ENTERING FORMULAS

When you are entering a formula that refers to cells in the same level of the spreadsheet, enter them as normal; +A5*B7, for example. Enable converts the formula to the correct syntax; if you are in level D, Enable converts it to +D:A5*+D:B7. When you want to refer to a cell in another level, type the full cell address, including the level.

FUNCTIONS You can use 3D addresses in functions. Also, Enable has several functions used with 3D spreadsheets: @CURLEVEL, @INDEX3D, @LEVELS, @LLOOKUP, @LOOKUP3D, @THISLEVEL. For more information, see Module 74.

CUBIC RANGES You can build ranges that span levels. These multi-level ranges are called *cubic ranges.* For example, when you want to enter a range, type D:A1..F:A9. This specifies a range that will include all the cells from A1 to A9 in levels D, E, and F. You can also point out a cubic range. In the previous example you could type . (period) to anchor the range in cell D:A1, move the pointer to D:A9, press Ctrl-PgDn twice to move to level F, and press Enter. The following commands will not work with cubic ranges: Sort, Transpose, Move, and DBMS.

You can name cubic ranges in the same way you name ranges in ordinary, 2D spreadsheets. Pressing F2, typing the cubic-range name, and pressing Enter moves the pointer to the first cell in the first level of the cubic range. However, you can also create 1-level, relative ranges. Suppose you create a range called *here* that covers cells A:A1..A:A5. Later you are in level X. If you press F2, type !here, and press Enter, the pointer moves to the cell X:A1; it doesn't move to A:A1. This only works for normal, one-level ranges. If the range is a cubic range, the pointer moves to the first cell in the first level in that range.

ORDER OF OPERATION Enable uses this order of operation in 3D spreadsheets: down, right, and back. For example, Enable will work down a column, across a level, and then down to the next level.

TOP LINE MENU COMMANDS

The 3D spreadsheet has several Top Line Menu commands that do not appear in the Top Line Menu of a normal spreadsheet. Enable does not add these options to the Top Line Menus until you convert the spreadsheet to a 3D spreadsheet by pressing Ctrl-PgDn or Ctrl-PgUp.

You can use the Top Line Menu from any of the levels. Some commands act on all the levels, and others affect only the level the pointer is in. For example, setting the width of column A using Worksheet/Width changes the width of column A in all levels. The following commands affect all the levels:

- Audit/List
- Audit/Highlight
- Audit/Map
- Global/Format
- Global/Alignment
- Global/Width
- Global/Protection
- Global/Recalculation
- Worksheet/Erase
- Worksheet/Titles
- Worksheet/Width

WORKSHEET/INSERT AND WORKSHEET/DELETE The Insert and Delete commands have extra options in 3D spreadsheets. Enable allows you to insert or delete rows and columns, as in the normal spreadsheet, but it also lets you insert or delete levels. In addition, when you insert or delete a row or column, Enable will ask you if you want to do so in all levels or just the level the pointer is in.

COPYING DATA

Although copying data is almost the same in a 3D spreadsheet as in a 2D spreadsheet, there are a few differences.

COPYING BETWEEN LEVELS As already described, you can point out cubic ranges; ranges that span two or more levels. You can use this feature when you are copying data from one level to another, and can even build a template and copy it to several levels at the same time. For example, suppose you have a 12-level 3D spreadsheet that you use for businesss expenses, one level for each month. You could build a template for January with all the necessary row and column headings—let's suppose it covers the range A1 to K30. Then press F10, type WC (Worksheet;Copy) and type or point out the range A1..K30. Press Ctrl-PgDn to move the pointer to level B, move the pointer to B:A1, and type . (period) to anchor the TO:range. Then press Ctrl-PgDn ten times and press Enter. Enable copies the range from level A: to the next 11 levels.

You can use this to copy ordinary, two-dimensional ranges, or to copy cubic ranges.

Stacks Stacks are ranges of single cells that spread across several levels. A:B7..J:B7 is a stack. When you copy a stack, specify a single cell as the TO:range, unless you want multiple copies. For example, copying a stack to A:C10..A:C12 produces three new stacks.

Slices A slice is a single row or column in several layers. A:B7..J:B12 is a slice. Specifying a single cell as the TO:range copies the slice once. Specifying a multi-cell TO:range copies the slice more than once.

COPYING DATA FROM OTHER SPREADSHEETS The technique described in Module 89 for opening another spreadsheet works differently in 3D spreadsheets. Pressing F10 and typing MFS (MCM:Files;Spreadsheet-Files) displays a directory of spreadsheet files. If you select a filename, press Enter, and type Y (Yes), one of two things happens:

The Current Spreadsheet is a 2D Spreadsheet If the current spreadsheet is a 2D spreadsheet, the current spreadsheet is closed and the selected spreadsheet is opened.

The Current Spreadsheet is a 3D Spreadsheet If the current spreadsheet is a 3D spreadsheet, the data from the selected spreadsheet is copied into the current spreadsheet. If the selected spreadsheet is a 2D spreadsheet, the entire spreadsheet is copied into the 3D spreadsheet, filling the level the pointer is in. If the selected spreadsheet is a 3D spreadsheet, the first level, level A:, is copied onto the the level the pointer is in. In either case, the previous data in that level is lost.

TIP: This is a convenient way to build 3D spreadsheets by combining 2D spreadsheets. Create a spreadsheet and then go from level to level importing the 2D spreadsheets, one per level. Then you can add formulas linking cells in different levels.

COPYING TO A WORD PROCESSING FILE Copy data to a word processing file using the method described in Module 46. Enable separates the data by level, beginning with the data from the first level.

COPYING TO A DATABASE Copying data from a spreadsheet to a database is described in Module 57, Import Data. If you are importing from a closed file (that is, not using the Interwindow Copy option), you can import data from several levels, as long as they are prepared correctly. Level A: must be prepared as described in Module 57 (fields in columns, beginning in column A, and the first three rows are field definitions). Enable reads the data from level A: and then goes to the first row of level B: looking for more data.

If you are using the Interwindow Copy option in the Copy command screen, copying data from an open window, you cannot use cubic ranges, but you can point out several 2D ranges, in different levels. When you select Window, Enable displays the Window Summary screen. Select the spreadsheet file. Enable prompts for the data definition range. Type or point out the data definition range and press Enter. Enable then prompts for the data range. Type or point out the range of data cells in level A: and press Enter. Then type another range, or go to another level (using the Ctrl- or F2 commands) and point out another range. Press Enter again if you want to select yet another range. Continue until you have selected all the ranges, and then press Alt-F5 after selecting the last range. (Or, if you pressed Enter after the last range, press Esc.) Enable continues with the Copy command. See Module 57 for more details.

PRINTING 3D SPREADSHEETS

You can print a 3D spreadsheet in much the same way that you print a 2D spreadsheet. You can print the entire spreadsheet or specify a range to print, but in either case Enable prints data from each level on a separate page.

MACROS

When using macros in 3D spreadsheets, remember to take into account the changes in the Top Line Menu. The 3D Top Line Menu is not the same as the one in 2D spreadsheets, so your macros may act differently if you don't allow for the differences.

SAVING 3D SPREADSHEETS

Pressing Alt-F10 and pressing Enter, or pressing F10 and typing SA (Save;Accept Options) saves the entire spreadsheet, in Enable's 3D format. You can also change the options to save a range in 3D format, to save a range in 2D format, or to save in another spreadsheet format (Lotus 1-2-3). Enable only saves other formats as 2D spreadsheets. When Enable saves a 3D spreadsheet in a 2-dimensional spreadsheet it changes the references to the other levels by removing the level indicator; Z:B27 becomes B27.

If you choose to save a normal, non-cubic range, Enable asks if you want to "Relocate saved range to the top level?" If you say No, Enable saves the spreadsheet in 3D format, but only the data in the specified level remains, and that level remains where it was in the level hierarchy. If you say Yes, Enable saves the range in a normal, 2-dimensional spreadsheet.

If you are not saving the entire file, remember that if you don't change the filename Enable will place the saved ranges in the original file, and you will lose all the data you have saved previously.

Appendix L
ASCII CHARACTER CHART

ASCII Value	*Character*	*ASCII Value*	*Character*	*ASCII Value*	*Character*	*ASCII Value*	*Character*
000	(null)	030	(cursor up)	060	<	090	Z
001	☺	031	(cursor down)	061	=	091	[
002	☻	032	(space)	062	>	092	\
003	♥	033	!	063	?	093	]
004	♦	034	"	064	@	094	^
005	♣	035	#	065	A	095	—
006	♠	036	$	066	B	096	‘
007	(beep)	037	%	067	C	097	a
008	◘	038	&	068	D	098	b
009	(tab)	039	'	069	E	099	c
010	(line feed)	040	(	070	F	100	d
011	(home)	041	)	071	G	101	e
012	(form feed)	042	*	072	H	102	f
013	(carriage ret)	043	+	073	I	103	g
014	♫	044	,	074	J	104	h
015	☼	045	-	075	K	105	i
016	►	046	.	076	L	106	j
017	◄	047	/	077	M	107	k
018	↕	048	0	078	N	108	l
019	‼	049	1	079	O	109	m
020	¶	050	2	080	P	110	n
021	§	051	3	081	Q	111	o
022	▬	052	4	082	R	112	p
023	↨	053	5	083	S	113	q
024	↑	054	6	084	T	114	r
025	↓	055	7	085	U	115	s
026	→	056	8	086	V	116	t
027	←	057	9	087	W	117	u
028	(cursor right)	058	:	088	X	118	v
029	(cursor left)	059	;	089	Y	119	w

ASCII Value	*Character*	*ASCII Value*	*Character*	*ASCII Value*	*Character*	*ASCII Value*	*Character*
120	x	154	Ü	188	╝	222	▐
121	y	155	¢	189	╜	223	▀
122	z	156	£	190	╛	224	α
123	{	157	¥	191	┐	225	β
124	¦	158	Pt	192	└	226	Γ
125	}	159	ƒ	193	┴	227	π
126	~	160	á	194	┬	228	Σ
127	⌂	161	í	195	├	229	σ
128	Ç	162	ó	196	─	230	µ
129	ü	163	ú	197	┼	231	τ
130	é	164	ñ	198	╞	232	Φ
131	â	165	Ñ	199	╟	233	Θ
132	ä	166	ª	200	╚	234	Ω
133	à	167	º	201	╔	235	δ
134	å	168	¿	202	╩	236	∞
135	ç	169	⌐	203	╦	237	Ø
136	ê	170	¬	204	╠	238	ε
137	ë	171	½	205	═	239	∩
138	è	172	¼	206	╬	240	≡
139	ï	173	¡	207	╧	241	±
140	î	174	«	208	╨	242	≥
141	ì	175	»	209	╤	243	≤
142	Ä	176	░	210	╥	244	⌠
143	Å	177	▒	211	╙	245	⌡
144	É	178	▓	212	╘	246	÷
145	æ	179	│	213	╒	247	≈
146	Æ	180	┤	214	╓	248	°
147	ô	181	╡	215	╫	249	•
148	ö	182	╢	216	╪	250	·
149	ò	183	╖	217	┘	251	√
150	û	184	╕	218	┌	252	^{n}
151	ù	185	╣	219	█	253	^{2}
152	ÿ	186	║	220	▄	254	■
153	Ö	187	╗	221	▌	255	(blank 'F')

Appendix M
EXERCISES

1. About This Book
   a. What are the sections of this book?
   b. What does each module of the book describe?
2. EnableOA Overview
   a. What are the EnableOA applications?
   b. What is the function of the Main Menu?
   c. How many windows can you open?
   d. How do you use multitasking?
3. Opening and Closing Enable
   a. How do you open Enable from the DOS prompt?
   b. How do you bypass the Sign-On screen?
4. A Sample Session with Enable Word Processing
   a. How do you create a word processing document?
   b. What does Tab do?
   c. How do you select Spell Check?
   d. How do you print the letter?
   e. How do you save a file?
5. A Sample Session with Enable DBMS
   a. What is the procedure for displaying the Interact screen?
   b. How do you exit the Edit screen?
   c. How do you edit entries in DISPLAY?
   e. What is the procedure for displaying a report?
6. A Sample Session with Enable Spreadsheet
   a. What does \= do when entered into a cell?
   b. What is the pointer?
   c. How do you move the pointer to cell A1?
   d. What does @SUM(d5..d19) do?
   e. How can you print the spreadsheet?
7. A Sample Session with Enable Graphics
   a. How do you enter graphics mode from the spreadsheet?
   b. What is an exploding pie chart?
   c. How do you move back up the menu "tree?"
   d. How do you save the spreadsheet and graph settings?

8. A Sample Session with Enable Telecommunications
   a. What is a baud rate?
   b. How do you get to the Quick Connection Form?
   c. How do you select options in the Quick Connection Form?
   d. What does pressing F10, typing DYY, and pressing Enter do?

9. Word Processing Overview
   a. What are some of the major features of Enable's word processing?
   b. Which Top Line Menu option lets you use a thesaurus?
   c. Where in the word processing screen can you see the window number?
   d. What does REF in the status line mean?

10. Align Text
    a. How do you insert a default ruler?
    b. What does xxxxx on the ruler mean?
    c. How can you change margin settings without displaying the ruler?
    d. How do you center a line of text?
    e. What is the purpose of %TAB?

11. Blocking/Marking Text
    a. How do you mark text?
    b. What does Alt-F7 do?
    c. What does Ctrl-L do?
    d. How can you move a block to the left of the screen?

12. Calculator
    a. Give some examples of mathematical operators.
    b. How do you perform a calculation?
    c. How do you sum the numbers in a column?
    d. If there is a $ sign in the calculation, what will happen?

13. Columns (Multiple)
    a. How do you build a column-setting ruler?
    b. What happens when you press F9 and type OD? What do you see?
    c. Name an application for this feature.
    d. How do you end columnar format?

14. Comment Lines/Paper Clips
    a. How do you insert comment lines? Paper clips?
    b. How do you search for a paper clip?
    c. What happens if you press F10 and type EA4?
    d. Why would you want to use these features?

15. Cursor Control
    a. How do you move one character left or right? One line up or down?
    b. How do you move to the previous tab position?
    c. What will pressing F2 and typing H do? What if you type NC instead?
    d. How do you stop scrolling momentarily?
    e. How do you move to the top of the file?

16. Date Insertion, Automatic
    a. How do you make Enable insert the date?
    b. What happens when you change to Final mode?

   c. Where does Enable get the date from?
   d. How many date formats are there, and where do you define them?

17. Delete Text
   a. If you press Ctrl-Backspace, what happens?
   b. How do you display the Delete Options Menu?
   c. How can you delete one word?
   d. What does pressing Esc do?

18. Document Mode (Draft/Final)
   a. Will Enable display paper clips in Final mode?
   b. What two methods are there for changing between modes?
   c. Why would you want to use Draft mode?
   d. What does the status line display in Draft mode? And Final mode?

19. Edit Text
   a. How do you insert text?
   b. How do you insert blank lines?
   c. What happens if you press Ctrl-T?
   d. How do you convert an entire paragraph to uppercase?
   e. How do you insert a paragraph marker?

20. Embedded Print Commands
   a. What does %ALT do?
   b. Which command will print another file with the current one?
   c. Where do you place embedded commands?
   d. Which command is the exception to the rule?

21. File Summary/File Directory
   a. How do you display the File Summary?
   b. What information does the File Summary contain?
   c. How can you check the number of words in a file?
   d. What are some of the things you can do in the File Directory?

22. Find/Replace/Mark Text
   a. What does pressing F10 and typing F2 do?
   b. How do you search from the cursor position?
   c. If you are replacing text, how do you make Enable stop so you can verify?
   d. What is Find and Mark?
   e. Name a few uses for these features.

23. Footnotes
   a. What is the difference between reference numbers and footnote symbols?
   b. How do you insert a footnote?
   c. Where do you define the footnote symbol style?
   d. What is a footnote continuation message?
   e. How do you reset the footnote symbol sequence?

24. Hard Spaces
   a. What does a hard space do?
   b. How do you enter a hard space?
   c. Name a use for hard spaces.

25. Headers and Footers
    a. How do you insert headers and footers?
    b. If you enter a ruler in a header, what does that ruler affect?
    c. How can you enter page numbers in this format: Page *9*?
    d. How do you alternate odd and even pages?
    e. How do you delete a header or footer?

26. Hyphenation
    a. When is the best time to use automatic hyphenation?
    b. What is a soft hyphen?
    c. What does Z in the ruler do? What does z do?
    d. How does hyphen-duplication occur?

27. Importing Non-Enable Documents
    a. Name four word processing formats Enable can use.
    b. How do you import a Samna file?
    c. Why would you want to use this feature?

28. Indexing
    a. What is the index text-attribute command?
    b. How do you insert an index marker?
    c. How do you compile the index?
    d. How many subheadings can be added to an index marker?

29. Line Spacing
    a. What does the %LINES 3 command do?
    b. How do you use the Top Line Menu to set the line spacing?
    c. Which method measures in lines per inch, and which in lines?
    d. What does the line spacing setting in Page Form do?

30. Mail Merge
    a. How do you get to the Mail Merge screen?
    b. What are the three major steps in building a mail-merge document?
    c. How do you check database field names?
    d. Suggest some applications for Mail Merge.

31. Move or Copy Text
    a. How do you copy an entire file?
    b. How do you move a block of text within the document?
    c. How do you move a block of text between windows?
    d. What is the shortcut to copy from another window?

32. Open a Document
    a. What do you type at the Main Menu to open a document?
    b. What happens if you type ? at the filename prompt and press Enter?
    c. How do select a file from the list?
    d. What happens if you press Enter as soon as you see the default ruler?

33. Outlines
    a. Explain what Enable's outline feature is.
    b. What is the significant limitation of Enable's outline feature?
    c. What do you type to place the section number?
    d. What happens when you change to Final mode?

34. Page Break
    a. How do you insert a page break?
    b. What is a conditional page break, and how do use it?
    c. How do you delete page breaks?
    d. When would you want a conditional page break?
35. Print
    a. What do you type if you want to print from the Main Menu?
    b. What does Shift-F2 do?
    c. How do you select a specific page to print?
    d. How do you save the new print specifications?
36. Quit (Exit a File)
    a. How do you use the Top Line Menu to quit?
    b. What does Alt-End do?
    c. What must you remember before using quit?
37. References Table (Table of Authorities)
    a. What is a Table of Authorities used for?
    b. How do you insert an entry space?
    c. What does /S mean?
    d. What happens when you compile the table?
38. Reformatting
    a. When do you use Automatic Reformatting?
    b. How do you resume hanging indents?
    c. What does Retain Blanks do?
    d. What happens if you press F10 and type ED?
39. Save Document
    a. When should you save your document?
    b. What key do you type with Alt as a shortcut?
    c. What do you do if you want to save the block, not the entire file?
    d. What happens if you use a new filename?
40. Shorthand
    a. What does this feature do?
    b. How do you define the abbreviations?
    c. How do you compile the abbreviations?
41. Sort Lines or Paragraphs
    a. How do you sort on a paragraph?
    b. Why must you have a paragraph marker before the first paragraph?
    c. If you are sorting numerically and have 22 numbers, how do you type the first 9?
    d. Why would you want to sort paragraphs?
42. Special Characters
    a. What are the four character sets?
    b. How do you select the box-drawing set?
    c. How do you create an Em-dash?
    d. Which expert command turns off the special characters?

43. Spell Check and Thesaurus
    a. How do you select the Spell Check?
    b. What is the difference between "Add - as entered" and "Add - Lowercase?"
    c. Where is the user dictionary filed?
    d. How do you look up a word in the thesaurus?
    e. How do you select a synonym in the thesaurus?
44. Table of Contents
    a. How do you omit page numbers?
    b. What does U typed in the entry space mean?
    c. How do you copy the Table of Contents entries into the text?
    d. How and when do you compile the table?
    e. How do you print the table with the document?
45. Text Attributes
    a. How do you display the Attribute Help screen?
    b. What does Alt-V do?
    c. What is the difference between the status-line and the diamond attributes?
    d. How do you apply an attribute to a word? A line?
    e. How do you delete attributes?
46. Windows
    a. How many windows can you open?
    b. How do you go to another window using the Top Line Menu?
    c. What does Alt-Home do?
    d. How do you zoom to full screen size?
47. Database Overview
    a. What is the difference between a field and a record?
    b. How many records can Enable have?
    c. What is a .$BF file?
    d. What is the Interact screen?
48. Add Records (ADD)
    a. How do you get to the Add screen from the Main Menu?
    b. What does F5 do in the Add screen?
    c. How do you enter data into a Memo field?
    d. How do leave the Add screen?
49. Backups (BACKUP, ARCHIVE, RESTORE)
    a. What is the difference between BACKUP and ARCHIVE?
    b. What are the two file options in ARCHIVE?
    c. How do you make a backup if you have a floppy-disk system?
    d. How do you Restore data from an archive?
50. Create a Database (Database Definition)
    a. How do you open the Database Definition screen?
    b. What happens if you don't enter a default input form name?
    c. How do you do a Quick field definition?
    d. What is an edit picture?
    e. How do you print your database definition?

51. Delete Data (DELETE, UNDELETE, DESTROY)
    a. Explain the difference between Delete and Destroy.
    b. How do you delete marked records?
    c. How do you use Undelete?
    d. Why would you want to delete records without destroying them?
52. Dot Commands (Procedural Language) - Reports
    a. What is a dot command?
    b. What is the basic format of the dot command report?
    c. What happens if you type ;; in the first two columns?
    d. What goes in the introduction section?
    e. What goes in the break section?
53. Dot Commands - Input-Form Macros
    a. What is an input form macro?
    b. What is a postfield macro?
    c. What does .IF NAME=JONES mean?
    d. What does the .UPDATEKEY command do?
54. Dot Commands - Where and Fields Prompts
    a. What does .DEFINE COSTN=COST*2 do?
    b. How do you use .DEFINE to build lengthy where clauses?
    c. What is .OPEN used for?
55. Edit (EDIT, VERIFY, REPLACE, RENAME)
    a. How do you edit in DISPLAY?
    b. What does VERIFY do?
    c. How do you use REPLACE?
    d. How do you rename a database?
56. Export Data to an ASCII File (EXPORT)
    a. What is comma-separated format?
    b. How wide is the final document?
    c. Why would you want an ASCII database file?
57. Import Data (UPDATE, COPY, MERGE)
    a. How do you import data from a word processing file?
    b. What does Update do?
    c. What does Merge do?
    d. How can you use read-only data in other screens?
    e. Suggest some applications for these commands.
58. Index a Field (INDEX)
    a. What does the INDEX command do?
    b. How many indexes can a database have?
    c. If you select No at "Allow Duplicates," what happens if you have duplicates in the index?
59. Input-Form Design
    a. What is an input form?
    b. How can you use Enable's standard input form?
    c. How do you "Put it Here!"?

   d. How could you add the system record number to the input form?
   e. What is the Another Database prompt for?

60. Interact and Command Screens
   a. What are these screens used for?
   b. How do you select items on the Interact screen?
   c. What happens if you press End in the command screens?
   d. What does the Index prompt do?
   e. What does the Where prompt do?

61. Modify a Database
   a. How do you select a field name?
   b. How do you add a field? Delete a field?
   c. What is in the $B@ file?
   d. How do you make existing records compatible?

62. Report Design and Generation (REPORT)
   a. Why would you use SORT before using REPORT?
   b. What is a columnar report?
   c. What are the four report-output options?
   d. What is a Put it Here! report?
   e. How can you use read-only data in reports?

63. Select Sets (FIND, SORT) and Error Sets
   a. What is a select set?
   b. What happens to the database when you change data in a select set?
   c. What does FIND do?
   d. What does the Index field in FIND do?

64. View and Mark Records (DISPLAY, BROWSE)
   a. What is the difference between DISPLAY and BROWSE?
   b. How do you mark records?
   c. What does Alt-M do?
   d. Suggest a reason for marking records.

65. Spreadsheet Overview
   a. What does a spreadsheet do?
   b. What is the Mode Indicator?
   c. Name the two ways to select the Top Line Menu.
   d. What is a cell address?
   e. How many rows does the spreadsheet have?

66. Align Data
   a. How do you align all the spreadsheet's values on the left?
   b. What is range alignment?
   c. Which type of alignment takes precedence over all others?
   d. What does the cell indicator show, and how?

67. Audit (List, Highlight, Map)
   a. What three List options are there?
   b. How do you highlight dependent cells?
   c. What is # in a Map?
   d. Why would you want to use Map?

68. Column Width
    a. How do you make a column disappear?
    b. How do adjust a single column?
    c. What can you do with a hidden column?
    d. How can you build an asterisk border using this feature?

69. Copy and Move
    a. What three commands does this module describe, and what do they do?
    b. What happens if the copy-to range is protected?
    c. What is a relative-address formula?
    d. What happens to a formula when you move the data the formula references?

70. Data-Fill
    a. How do you modify a range using Data-Fill?
    b. What happens to existing data if you use Initialize?
    c. When does Enable finish filling the cells?

71. Enter and Edit Data
    a. What are values, formulas, and labels?
    b. How does Enable know you are entering a formula?
    c. How long can a label be?
    d. How do you apply attributes to a label?

72. Erase
    a. How do you erase a cell?
    b. How do you erase a range?
    c. What does pressing F10 and typing WE do?
    d. Why would you erase a worksheet?

73. Format Cells
    a. Name the ten types of format?
    b. How do you format the entire spreadsheet?
    c. How do you format one cell?
    d. What is +/– format?
    e. What does the cell indicator (F,4) mean?

74. Functions
    a. What does a function do?
    b. What does @AVG do?
    c. How would you sum a column?
    d. What happens if you enter @PI in a cell?

75. Import (Combine, DBMS, Other Spreadsheets, and ASCII files)
    a. What happens when you combine spreadsheets?
    b. What are the three combine options?
    c. How could you enter word processing data into a spreadsheet?
    d. What does the DBMS command do?

76. Insert or Delete Rows and Columns
    a. How do you insert a row?
    b. How do you delete a column?
    c. What happens if the row or column has protected cells?

77. Linking Spreadsheets?
    a. What does the @LINK function do?
    b. How can you view the Link Options screen?
    c. What do you do if the supporting spreadsheet is modified?
    d. Why do you need to link spreadsheets?

78. Open Spreadsheet and Move Pointer
    a. How do you create a new spreadsheet?
    b. What does pressing F2 and typing g5 do?
    c. How can you skip protected cells?
    d. What happens when you press Scroll Lock followed by an arrow key?

79. Print
    a. How do you "quick-print?"
    b. What are the two Execute options?
    c. How do set the print range?
    d. What happens if you select List-Formulas?
    e. What is a printer-control code file?

80. Protect Cells
    a. What effect does the user profile have on this feature?
    b. What does pressing F10 and typing WGPA do?
    c. What are the cell indicator codes related to this feature?
    d. Why protect cells?

81. Quit
    a. How do you exit a spreadsheet?
    b. What should you remember to do before quitting?

82. Range Selection
    a. Describe the three ways to define ranges.
    b. How do you view a list of range names?
    c. How can you use a range name in a formula?
    d. How small can a range be?

83. Recalculate
    a. What user profile prompt affects this feature?
    b. What is manual recalculation?
    c. How do you make Enable recalculate?
    d. What is a circular reference?

84. Save
    a. Name three spreadsheet formats.
    b. How do you save the spreadsheet in Enable format?
    c. What does Alt-F10 do?
    d. What is the .WKS extension?

85. Sort Ranges
    a. How do you select the sort-range?
    b. What are the primary and secondary keys?
    c. Why sort ranges?
    d. How do you view the options before sorting?

86. Split the Screen
    a. How do you synchronize scrolling?
    b. How do you jump from one side to the other?
    c. What happens to the right/lower screen's characteristics when you unsplit the screen?
    d. How do you split the screen vertically?

87. Titles
    a. What does a "frozen" title do?
    b. How do you clear frozen titles?
    c. Why would you want to freeze titles?

88. Transpose Rows and Columns
    a. How do you transpose a row?
    b. How are formulas adjusted?
    c. How can you move data into an overlapping position?
    d. What happens if the new position contains protected cells?

89. Windows and Files
    a. How do you modify the window's size?
    b. What does Alt-Home do?
    c. How do you view a list of print-files?
    d. Name two ways to go to another window.

90. Graphics Overview
    a. What are the ten different graphs?
    b. What is a graph settings file?
    c. Where does Enable store graph settings?
    d. What other files can you import into word processing?

91. Axes
    a. What is 1=X-axis data?
    b. What are the X- and Y-axis formats?
    c. If you are building a pie chart, what other selection must you make?
    d. The x-axis data must be numeric in what kind of graph?

92. Data Groups
    a. What is a data group?
    b. How do you define a spreadsheet data group?
    c. What significance does the data group order have?
    d. How do you remove a data group?

93. Display (and Copy to Word Processing)
    a. Which mode should you use if you want to copy the graph?
    b. How do you change the size of the graph?
    c. How do you copy the graph into word processing?
    d. What does Shift-F7 do in the spreadsheet?

94. Draw and Print
    a. How do you get the highest quality printout?
    b. What is a .PLT file?
    c. When should you select a wide pen?
    d. How big is a "portrait" graph?

95. Graph Format
    a. What is the Scale option?
    b. What is Ign-pts?
    c. How can you change the size of the y-axis labels?
    d. What does the Grid option do to a pie chart?

96. Graph Type
    a. Name the types of vertical bar graph.
    b. What options can you define for the pie chart?
    c. Explain the difference between a line graph and an XY-graph.
    d. What is an HLC graph used for?

97. Headings
    a. How do you reach the headings menu options?
    b. How can you use ASCII special characters?
    c. What is the Main-sub?
    d. How do you select Roman2 for the Main Title?

98. Import Graphics
    a. Name two other graphics that can be imported.
    b. How do you import into word processing?
    c. What is a .GOn file?
    d. How can you find lost .GOn files?

99. Menus
    a. How do you select menu options?
    b. What does the X-axis-format/Y-axis-format/...Legend data menu do?
    c. How do you reach the menu where you select the graph type?
    d. What do you type to reach the menu where you select the grid?

100. Save
    a. How do you save database graph settings?
    b. How do you save spreadsheet graph settings?
    c. What is the difference between saving settings and saving a graph in a word processing file?

101. Select Graphics Mode
    a. How do you select graphics from the spreadsheet?
    b. How do you copy graph settings?
    c. How many graph settings can you create?
    d. What is a .GRF file?

102. Telecommunications Overview
    a. What is a modem?
    b. Why do you build setups?
    c. What does Unattended File Transfer do?
    d. What can Keyboard Mapping do for you?
    e. How do you filter incoming characters?

103. Calling Using Quick-Connect
    a. Why use Quick-Connect instead of a setup?
    b. How do you select COMM2?

c. What do you do if you want to capture data in a word processing file?
d. How do you use an auto-dial modem?

104. Calling Using Setup
   a. How do you select the setup?
   b. What indications of the steps taken does Enable give?
   c. How do you tell Enable to redial if the line is busy?
   d. How and when do you transmit the log-on messages in the setup?

105. Capture Data
   a. Name the two types of capture.
   b. How do you turn on Capture-to-memory?
   c. Why use Capture-to-disk?
   d. In what format is Capture-to-disk data saved?

106. Changing Specifications Online
   a. What are the Cost options?
   b. How do you add a line feed to transmitted lines?
   c. What does F9 TO1 do?
   d. How do you ignore tabs?

107. Disconnect and End Session
   a. What is the difference between Disconnect and Hang-up?
   b. What type of captured data is Enable referring to when it asks if you want to save it?
   c. What happens if you say you want to save data? What do you do?

108. Interacting Online
   a. How do you get into the Word Processing screen?
   b. What do the Tele Top-Line options do?
   c. How can you tell if Xon/Xoff is turned on?
   d. How do you tell Enable to send a Break signal?
   e. How do you get from the Word Processing screen back to the Telecom screen?

109. Print
   a. How do you turn on printing?
   b. What is the status line indicator for printing?
   c. How do you print data captured to memory?

110. Receiving Calls
   a. How do you receive calls using setups?
   b. Using Quick-Connect and an auto-dial modem, how do you dial the call?
   c. How do you turn off Answer mode?

111. Setup
   a. What is the purpose of a setup?
   b. How to you create a setup?
   c. How can you avoid character "echo?"
   d. What does Xon/Xoff do?
   e. How can you tell Enable to use an alternative setup?

112. Transmit Data
   a. How do you select Capture-to-memory data for transmission?
   b. What does Alt-F8 do?

   c. How do you select a file for transmission?
   d. How do you select Enable protocol?

113. DOS Window
   a. How do you use the memory allocation parameter?
   b. How do you open the DOS window?
   c. What are non-native keystrokes?
   d. Think of three ways you could use the DOS window.

114. Files
   a. What is an .ASC file?
   b. How can you display the Directory of Files?
   c. What is the Sort function for?
   d. How do you mark files?
   e. What are Old Marks?

115. Macros
   a. How do you create a macro with Alt-F9?
   b. How do you use a macro?
   c. What is the macro code for Backspace?
   d. How do you use macro scripts?

116. Menu Generation
   a. Where could you use menu X.MNU? What about menu WP.MNU?
   b. How do you make Enable use a DOS program from the menu?
   c. Where are the macros used by menus?
   d. What does Shift-F1 do?
   e. How do you apply background color to the entire window?

Index

Other Illustrated Books From Wordware

Spreadsheet

Lotus 1-2-3 Release 2.2
JOHN MUELLER
Designed for first-time and experienced users, this book includes all features and functions of Lotus 1-2-3. Learn to create, edit, and print useful worksheets and graphs simply by following the detailed instructions and illustrated examples. For additional help turn to the complete macro reference, the sample macro listings, and the graphical representation of Lotus's menu trees. This book is ideal as a comprehensive learning and reference tool!
1-55622-166-5 • **$21.95**
softbound • 320 pages

Lotus 1-2-3 Release 3
JOHN MUELLER
A complete, in-depth reference with dozens of practical examples. This book provedes coverage for the many new features of the long-awaited Release 3 from Lotus Development Corporation. Learn how to create spreadsheets that are three-dimensional. Specific, practical examples show you how to organize worksheets, consolidate templates, and create formulas within a worksheet using Lotus' new capabilities.
1-55622-160-6 • **$21.95**
softbound • 320 pages

Microsoft Excel 2.10 For IBM PC's and compatibles
PAUL SCHLIEVE and JON YOUNG
All the skills, techniques, and tips required to operate this popular spreadsheet program are contained in this comprehensive guide. Step-by-step procedures and hands-on activities build the experience needed to link worksheets, create timesaving macros, and use Excel's charting capabilities. Fully illustrated throughout, this book is an indispensable reference for Excel users at any stage.
1-55622-109-6 • **$21.95**
softbound • 384 pages

Operating Systems

Microsoft Windows 2.0
ROBERT E. WHITSITT II and LANA K. BRYAN
This comprehensive reference/tutorial includes all the features of Windows up to version 2.0. Learn to work with several applications simultaneously and shift among them easily and quickly. Complete and clear descriptions of the Program Information File (PIF) Editor, Print Spooler, and Clipboard features are included. Depend on this valuable guide to master the fundamentals as well as the subtle details of this popular operating system.
1-55622-069-3 • **$19.95**
softbound • 304 pages

MS/PC-DOS 4.0 Sixth Edition
RUSSELL A. STULTZ
This complete, timesaving reference contains all the significant updates to the world's most popular operating system. The novice-to-expert DOS user is led keystroke-by-keystroke through a sequence of exercises designed to provide hands-on experience. Use the new text-based DOSSHELL to initiate powerful DOS utilities. Each command is detailed in brief, easy-to-understand modules which make this book an indispensable reference.
1-55622-111-8 • **$21.95**
softbound • 272 pages

Word Processing

Microsoft Word 5.0

JOHN MUELLER and WALLY WANG

Everything you need to know to use Microsoft Word 5.0 is included in this comprehensive guide. Working examples use, modify, and create Word stylesheets and provide working models that are easily adapted to your personal needs. Top-quality documents are easily achieved by following the step-by-step approach of this book. Ready access to commands and functions make this an in-depth reference tool. It covers versions 4.0 through 5.0.

1-55622-021-9 • **$21.95**
softbound • 288 pages

WordPerfect 5.01

JORDAN GOLD

In this perinnial top seller you'll find the latest features and graphic import capabilities of the most recent version of WordPerfect. Learn to expedite formulas and equations with the new Equation Editor. Pull-down menus have been added to this version as well as more extensive PostScript printer support, a new Tables feature, and much more. Hands-on exercises demonstrate how to use the new codes that have been added to the Macro Editor. Follow the step-by-step instructions in this book to become proficient at WordPerfect.

1-55622-174-6 • **$23.95**
softbound • 450 pages

WordStar Professional Release 5

RUSSELL A. and DIANNE STULTZ

Master a host of WordStar Release 5 features including advanced page preview, footnotes/endnotes, windowing, TelMerge, ListMerge, and many more. Practical hands-on activities demonstrate the new user interface and the pull-down menus used to initiate the latest functions. This step-by-step learning guide is also a complete reference to the advanced document features available in WordStar 5.0.

1-55622-074-X • **$21.95**
softbound • 304 pages

Database Management

dBASE III Plus

RUSSELL A. STULTZ

This complete guide to dBASE III Plus commands and functions provides a step-by-step tutorial for beginners and a quick reference for the familiar dBASE user. Easy-to-understand examples illustrate new commands, correct syntax, and file structures. Enter, manipulate, and retrieve large volumes of data and develop customized application programs. Create a filing system, then write procedures to store, retrieve, edit, and display on-screen menus and user-help information.

0-915381-92-3 • **$19.95**
softbound • 384 pages

dBASE IV

RUSSELL A. STULTZ

Grasp the power and flexibility of dBASE IV commands, functions, system memory variables, and SQL commands as you work through the hands-on examples contained in this clearly written book. Fully operational, annotated programs help you create and use menu bars, pop-ups, windows, macros, user-defined functions, and more. Practical development activities probe the Control Center, and WYSIWYG report, label, query, view and application generators. Explore the latest programming techniques of this top-selling database management program. Ideal for learning and teaching, this book is an in-depth reference for the dBASE IV developer.

1-55622-116-9 • **$21.95**
softbound • 512 pages

FoxBASE+ 2.1

BOB GRANILLO

This illustrated tutorial will guide the novice step-by-step through the FoxBASE+ software. Create professional looking windows and light-bar menus, and learn to use data structures such as one- and two-dimensional arrays. Streamline record retrieval and reloading by using the GATHER and SCATTER commands. Programming tips and easy-to-understand examples make this book an excellent reference for the intermediate and advanced user and will add speed and flexibility to your applications.

1-55622-168-1 • **$23.95**
softbound • 352 pages

Business Professional Books From Wordware

The Business Side of Writing

RUSSELL A. STULTZ

If you regard writing as a business rather than an art, this book can provide the reference information you need for a successful career in writing or publications management. These guidelines help organize and refine your approach to project planning, cost estimating, project research, financial control, development, and production. Mr. Stultz addresses the tools, techniques, methodologies, and processes to plan, manage, and automate publications development and production with emphasis on the bottom line.

1-55622-157-6 • **$15.95**
hardbound • 224 pages • 6 x 9

Hawks Do, Buzzards Don't
The Complete Job-Finding Guide

GEORGE MCINTOSH

This handbook for the individual seeking a career change incorporates the proven design and techniques of a professional outplacement program. It leads the reader through a step-by-step process of self evaluation and career assessment, effective written and verbal communications, a proactive self-marketing plan, and an opportunity for long-term control of one's career. Those who read the book feel good about themselves as their sense of self-worth and confidence is restored.

1-55622-171-1 • **$18.95**
softbound • 288 pages • 6 x 9

Occupying the Summit
The Guide to Successful Retirement Planning

ROBERT W. SHAFFER

With retirement now encompassing as much as 25 percent of our lifespan, this book offers sound advice for making that time the best phase of life. Practical guidance and hands-on worksheets help evaluate current status, determine goals, and develop a positive retirement strategy. Regardless of income and age level, this book provides the essential principles and foresight necessary to successfully anticipate and prepare for a financially independent, healthy, and fulfilling retirement.

1-55622-102-9 • **$15.95**
softbound • 304 pages • 6 x 9

Innovation, Inc.
Unlocking Creativity in the Workplace

GROSSMAN, RODGERS, and MOORE

Unlock your hidden potential to reach a new plane of creative thinking. Seek new avenues of problem solving by elevating your ability to conceive ideas. Techniques and exercises in this book expand your creativity. The authors take you on a journey designed to spark confidence by reorganizing your thinking processes and patterns. Learn to use innovative thinking to inspire fresh ideas and formulate imaginative concepts.

1-55622-054-5 • **$14.95**
softbound • 256 pages • 6 x 9

Business Emotions
A New Business Concept

RICHARD M. CONTINO

Revolutionize your thinking, conditioning, and approach. Learn why emotions are a controlling factor in every success and failure situation. This practical book will guide you through the maze of hidden psychological issues in a simple and straightforward manner. Achieve predictable, positive, and immediate results. The author introduces unique concepts in and practical techniques for emotional awareness, self-analysis, and effective business functioning.

1-55622-058-8 • **$14.95**
softbound • 184 pages • 6 x 9

Steps to Strategic Management
A Guide for Entrepreneurs

DR. RICK MOLZ

This book will help the entrepreneur uncover opportunities for a more successful business. A fictitious person, business, and product illustrate how this system works. Nine key steps to strategic management are developed and followed by real-world business applications. This system is used worldwide by sophisticated organizations of all types and sizes. The case example approach and readable style make this strategic method easy to understand and apply.

1-55622-050-2 • **$13.95**
softbound • 184 pages • 6 x 9